Annual Index

to

POPULAR MUSIC RECORD REVIEWS 1977

1977

by
Dean Tudor
and
Linda Biesenthal

The Scarecrow Press, Inc.
Metuchen, N.J. & London
1979

Library of Congress Catalog Card No. 73-8909

ISBN 0-8108-1217-7

TABLE OF CONTENTS

INTRODUCTION

We continue to believe that the modern library has a major responsibility in preserving the American and international musical tradition in popular music. We likewise believe that popular recorded music should be widely available in all types of libraries. This reference work, then, is to aid in the selection of records for these collections.

This book is primarily an <u>index</u> to record <u>reviews</u>. It can be used to find particular reviews and/or be used as a record selection tool based on the evaluations given by the reviews themselves. We have not listed certain data because of a lack of space and time. This year's index offers citations to 5697 individual records; in the 1976 volume, 5586 were cited. The total number of reviews indexed for 1977 increased to 12,708 from last year's 12,346. We hope to offer a comprehensive index to popular recorded music by continually reevaluating our sources and the popular music media.

The responsibilities for the general preparation, editorial work, and comments have been shared by the co-compilers.

Dean Tudor
Linda Biesenthal

December 17, 1978

EXPLANATION OF THE FORMAT

This index to record reviews has 11 sections arranged according to musical form: rock; mood--pop; country; old time music and bluegrass; folk; jazz; blues; soul, reggae and salsa; popular religious; show and humor; and "anthologies and concerts." Within each section the arrangement is alphabetical by artist. Each record is numbered for easy reference and for retrieval by use of the Artist Index.

The discographic information is displayed as follows:

Number. ARTIST [surname inverted]. Album Title. Label and Serial Number (number of discs per set). Reel-to-Reel Tape Serial Number. Four Track Cartridge Serial Number. Eight Track Cassette Serial Number. (Country of Origin [if not U.S.]). (Reissued Release).

The review information is displayed as follows:

Periodical abbreviation. Month or number of issue numerically expressed as "month-day" or "month/month." Page citation. Number of words in review [rounded to nearest 25]. Reviewer's evaluation.

"Anthologies and concerts" are entered in the last section under their common name or titles.

Notes

Evaluation: A scale of 0 to 5 has been used to rate the opinions of each record reviewer. This is a simple numerical translation. This should indicate to the user the general evaluation of any single review or group of reviews. Bear in mind the importance of the specialist magazines. "0" means a completely poor production. (In some cases the reviewer so thoroughly rejected an album that

the compilers of this Index could have assigned a -5 to several reviews.) "2½" is either a review that is non-critical and descriptive,
or a review where the pros and cons of a release appear to balance
out. And "5" is a superb recording--an ultimate release. There
were very few of these awarded. These numerical evaluation trans-
lations were based on both the compilers' experiences and the terms
of reference under which the reviewer works. By the latter is
meant the non-musical concern of the reviewer. For instance, the
music may be worthwhile, but a particular album may be down-
graded in the eyes of reviewers for any number of reasons: poor
pressing, poor recording qualities, derivative stylings, excessive
duplication among previous reissues, poor packaging, lack of liner
notes, and so forth--all non-musical. It is important to bear in
mind that only the reviews are numerically translated, not the record nor the music itself. In certain cases, the compilers have
strongly disagreed with the reviewer, but that has not affected their
numerical evaluation of the review itself. No review of less than
25 words is included here.

Tapes: Tape numbers for Reel-to-Reel, Cartridges, and
Cassettes were given only where known or available to Schwann or
Harrison. The absence of a tape number does not mean that a tape
is not available for a particular release since often record companies issue the tape versions somewhat later than the discs. The
compilers have not listed tape information for foreign records, nor
for quadraphonic sound as this latter is still in flux. Note that
most tapes bear the same serial number as the phonodisc.

Country of Origin: This is not given when there is also an
American release; the comparable initial foreign release is not given
as the disc will be available in the United States. The exception
has been made for deleted domestic offerings or reissued material.
"(E)" stands for a release from the British Isles; all other countries
have their names spelled out. Prices in foreign currency are not
given for foreign releases because of the changeable international
monetary situation and differences in tax and excise applicability
(both domestic and foreign) for libraries.

Show Music: Immediately following the entry by title, the user is informed of the composer, the lyricist, and the arranger, where such information is known. After the basic discographical information but before the review citations, the source of the performance is given (e.g., Original Film Soundtrack, or Original London Cast).

More Than One Artist: The compilers have not analyzed each record to pull out the major artists. Apart from the evaluative nature of such an effort (calling for judgment) the sheer numbers cannot be coped with. However, two aspects were noted:

ARTIST and ARTIST: This means that the two perform together on the release, and have been given equal billing by the record company.

ARTIST/ARTIST: This means that there are two artists who are not performing together. Usually, one side is devoted to one artist, and the flip side is devoted to the other.

Both of these secondary artist entries have been indexed in the Artist Index (along with prominent performers from the Show category).

Abbreviation List

ARG	American Record Guide	CRE	Creem
AU	Audio	CS	Country Style
BGU	Bluegrass Unlimited	CZM	Crazy Music
BM	Black Music	DB	Down Beat
BS	Black Stars	EDS	English Dance and Song
BSR	Blue Sky Review	EUR	Eurock
BU	Blues Unlimited	FOL	Folkscene
CAC	Cassettes and Cartridges	FR	Folk Review
CAD	Cadence	GP	Guitar Player
CC	Canadian Composer	GR/GRA	Gramophone
CFS	Come for to Sing	HBS	Hot Buttered Soul
CIR	Circus	HF	High Fidelity
CK	Contemporary Keyboard	JEMF	John Edwards Memorial
CM	Country Music		Foundation Quarterly
CMP	Country Music People	JF	Jazz Forum
CMR	Country Music Review	JJ	Jazz Journal International
CO	Coda	JM	Jazz Magazine
CR	Consumer Reports	JR	Jazz Report
CRA	Crawdaddy	LB	Living Blues

MG	Music Gig	RR	Records and Recording
MH	Modern Hi-Fi and Music	RRE	Record Review
MJ	Music Journal	RS	Rolling Stone
MM	Melody Maker	RSP	Record Special
MN	Muleskinner News	RT	Ragtimes
MR	Mississippi Rag	SC	Soul Cargo
NK	New Komotion	SMG	SMG
OLR	Ontario Library Review	SN	Swinging Newsletter
OTM	Old Time Music	SO	Sing Out
PIC	Pickin'	SOU	Sound
PMS	Popular Music and Society	SR	Stereo Review
PRM	Phonograph Record Maga- zine	ST	Storyville
		TM	Traditional Music
RA	Ragtimer	TP	Trouser Press
RC	Rocking Chair	VV	Village Voice
RFJ	Radio Free Jazz	WHO	Who Put the Bomp
RM	Record Month	ZZ	Zigzag
RO	Rock		

THE PERIODICALS INDEXED

The totals of reviews refer to popular music records only. The addresses are mainly for placing subscriptions; in many cases, the Editorial Offices are located elsewhere. In all, 12,708 reviews were indexed from 71 magazines. Prices quoted are in American dollars, and are the prices for overseas subscriptions in the case of British publications. Most of these magazines have articles concerning popular music. If this is the case, then they are indexed in our companion index: Popular Music Periodicals Index, 1973+ (Scarecrow Press, 1974+). The magazines added for this year are:

Blue Sky Review	Record Special
Come For to Sing	Rocking Chair
Eurock	SMG
Folkscene	Soul Cargo
Hot Buttered Soul	Swinging Newsletter
Music Gig	Trouser Press
New Kommotion	Village Voice
Rag Times	Zigzag

Dropped for a variety of reasons (cessations, mergers, slowness in arrival, change of policy, etc.) are: Country Rambler, Ethnomusicology, Footnote, Listening Post, Talking Blues.

AMERICAN RECORD GUIDE. [new series] 1976- monthly $7.50 p. a.
  One Windsor Place, Mellville, N.Y. 11746
  For almost 40 years, ARG was a leading journal of music criticism (mainly classical). After its suspension in 1973, it returned in November of 1976. Popular music relates to folk and jazz.
  No. of 1977 reviews: 8

AUDIO. 1917- monthly $10 p.a.
  North American Pub. Co., 134 N. 13th St., Phila., Pa. 19107
  Contains articles on audio equipment. Record reviews tend to emphasize sound dynamics. Lengthy reviews of jazz records.
  No. of 1977 reviews: 292

BLACK MUSIC. 1974- monthly $18 p.a.
  IPC Business Press (sales and distribution) Ltd.; Subscription Dept., Oakfield House, Perrymount Road, Haywards Heath,

Sussex RH16 3DH, England
A glossy but expertly edited magazine concerned with blues,
  rhythm 'n' blues, soul, gospel, reggae, disco and jazz.   Good
  reviews of records, and various current awareness services.
  A major cut above black fanzines.
No. of 1977 reviews: 377

BLACK STARS.   1974-   monthly $10 p. a.
Johnson Pub. Co., 820 S. Michigan Ave., Chicago, Ill.   60605
Incorporating Tan Magazine, this glossy features soul music.
No. of 1977 reviews: 51

BLUE SKY REVIEW.   1975-   irregular $4 for 6 issues
1605 Jones Street, San Francisco, Cal.   94109
A small magazine mainly concerned with blues and western music.
No. of 1977 reviews: 5

BLUEGRASS UNLIMITED.   1966-   monthly $7 p. a.
Broad Run, Va.   22014
Popular approach to the growing field of bluegrass.   Excellent
  articles on current scene and expert reviews.   Oldest of blue-
  grass specialty magazines.
No. of 1977 reviews: 284

BLUES UNLIMITED.   1963-   irregular $10 p. a.
8 Brandram Road, Lewisham, London SE13 5EA, England.
The leading blues magazine, with exceptional photographs and
  good record reviews.   Music covered includes: Cajun, old
  timey, and gospel, plus rhythm 'n' blues.
No. of 1977 reviews: 124

CADENCE.   1976-   monthly $8 p. a.
Rt. 1, Box 345, Redwood, N. Y.   13679
An exceptionally well-developed jazz and blues magazine, pocket-
  sized, with superb coverage of virtually every jazz record released in North America, Japan, France, Sweden, etc.   In-
  depth interviews also cover artists' relations with the industry.
No. of 1977 reviews: 985

CANADIAN COMPOSER/COMPOSITEUR CANADIEN.   1967-   10
  nos. /yr $2. 50 p. a.
Suite 904, 40 St-Clair Ave. W., Toronto M4V 1M2, Canada
The organ of the Composers, Authors and Publishers Association
  of Canada (CAPAC), an agency similar to BMI and ASCAP.
  Articles and record reviews deal with Canadian classical and
  popular artists and composers.
No. of 1977 reviews: 87

CASSETTES AND CARTRIDGES.   1973-Oct. 1977.   Ceased.
No. of 1977 reviews: 349

CIRCUS.   1969-   bi-weekly $14 p. a.

747 Third Avenue, New York, N. Y.   10017
A rock fan magazine with many photos and biographies of current
   stars. Intended for a younger audience. Reviews are sur-
   prisingly critical for a "puff" mag.
No. of 1977 reviews: 285

CODA.   1958-   bi-monthly $12 for 10 issues
P. O. Box 87, Postal Station J, Toronto, Ont. M4J 4X8, Canada
World coverage. Leads the field of jazz magazines with in-depth
   articles and thorough jazz and blues record reviews.
No. of 1977 reviews: 200

COME FOR TO SING.   1975-   quarterly $4 p. a.
Old Town School of Folk Music, 909 W. Armitage St., Chicago,
   Ill.   60614
A well put together folio-sized magazine concerning the Chicago
   folk music scene. Record reviews, articles, opinions, songs
   and music.
No. of 1977 reviews: 51

CONSUMER REPORTS.   monthly $11 p. a.
P. O. Box 1000, Orangeburg, N. Y.   10962
Began to review a few popular music records in 1975.
No. of 1977 reviews: 4

CONTEMPORARY KEYBOARD.   1975-   monthly $12 p. a.
P. O. Box 907, Saratoga, Cal.   95070
A spinoff from Guitar Player, emphasizing all aspects of key-
   boards (piano, organ, electronic music synthesizer, etc.).
   Record reviews, book reviews, equipment reviews, articles
   on personalities, music, instructions, tips.
No. of 1977 reviews: 159

COUNTRY MUSIC.   1972-   monthly $8. 95 p. a. ; $14. 95/2yrs
475 Park Avenue South, New York, N. Y.   10016
This glossy magazine for C & W fans has popular articles and
   non-critical record reviews.
No. of 1977 reviews: 144

COUNTRY MUSIC PEOPLE.   1970-   monthly $4 p. a.
Powerscroft Rd., Footscray, Sidcup, Kent, England
British C & W fan magazine with an emphasis on the country
   music scene in England. Some historical articles.
No. of 1977 reviews: 236

COUNTRY MUSIC REVIEW.   monthly $9 p. a.
19 Westbourne Rd., London N7 8AN England
British C & W music magazine with excellent articles on performers and current country scene. Good evaluative reviews.
No. of 1977 reviews: 263

COUNTRY STYLE.   1976-   monthly $12 p. a.
11058 W. Addison St., Franklin Park, Ill.   60131

Tabloid newspaper style, reminiscent of early Rolling Stone magazine. Short pithy articles on the current stars, as well as
some coverage of country music history.
No. of 1977 reviews: 80

CRAWDADDY. 1966-   monthly $7.95 p.a.; $14/2yrs; $19/3yrs
72 Fifth Ave., New York, N.Y.   10011
American rock music and youth culture brought together in this
pioneer magazine. Like Rolling Stone this is not just about
rock.
No. of 1977 reviews: 296

CRAZY MUSIC; the journal of the Australian Blues Society.   1974-
quarterly $2 Australian
P.O. Box 1029, Canberra City, ACT 2601, Australia
Well-written blues magazine, devoted to the local Australian
scene as well as interesting recordings from the Oceania area.
No. of 1977 reviews: 56

CREEM. 1969-   monthly $10 p.a.
187 S. Woodward, Birmingham, Mich.   48011
Calls itself "America's only rock 'n' roll magazine." A hip
counterculture mag with a format much like Crawdaddy. Probably the most entertaining record reviews in the business.
No. of 1977 reviews: 240

DOWN BEAT. 1934-   biweekly (21 nos./yr) $11 p.a.; $18/2yrs
Maher Publications, Inc., 222 W. Adams St., Chicago, Ill. 60606
Contains jazz news, interviews, transcriptions of improvised jazz
solos.
No. of 1977 reviews: 373

ENGLISH DANCE AND SONG.   1936-   quarterly $4 p.a.
English Folk Dance and Song Society, Cecil Sharp House, 2 Re-
gents Park Rd., London NW1 7AY, England
Covers dance, song, folklore and crafts, with thoughtful, though
brief, record and book reviews. Includes subscription to
Folk Music Journal (an annual).
No. of 1977 reviews: 34

EUROCK. 1975-   quarterly $4 p.a.
3158 Burnside, Portland, Oregon 97214
An excellent fanzine, devoted exclusively to European rock music
of the classical-electronic school.
No. of 1977 reviews: 28

FOLK REVIEW. 1971-   monthly $8 p.a.
Austin House, Hospital St., Nantwich, Cheshire, England
Monthly journal of British folksingers with profiles, articles, and
reviews. Positive proof of the booming British folk scene.
No. of 1977 reviews: 222

FOLKSCENE. 1973-   monthly $7 p.a.; $12 for 2 years

P. O. Box 64545, Los Angeles, Cal. 90064
A West Coast folk music magazine, pocket sized, and full of
   articles detailing current singer-songwriters.
No. of 1977 reviews: 150

GRAMOPHONE. 1923-   monthly $16.50 p. a.
   General Gramophone Publications, Ltd. , 177-179 Kenton Rd. ,
      Harrow, Middlesex, HA3 OHA, England
   Solid journal on record collecting and audio equipment. Attempts
      to be comprehensive in coverage in all fields of music.
   No. of 1977 reviews: 428

GUITAR PLAYER. 1967-   monthly $12 p. a.
   Box 615, Saratoga, Cal. 95070
   The magazine for material on guitars, guitar playing, and guitar
      players. Record reviews are oriented toward guitars. Col-
      umns of instructions, tips, and equipment reviews.
   No. of 1977 reviews: 184

HIGH FIDELITY. 1951-   monthly $7.95 p. a.
   1 Sound Ave. , Marion, Ohio 43302
   Articles on audio equipment. Record reviews are chiefly classical.
   No. of 1977 reviews: 254

HOT BUTTERED SOUL. 1968-1977
   A soul and r'n'b magazine now continued by Soul Cargo (q. v.);
      ceased publication with No. 52.
   No. of 1977 reviews: 72

JAZZ FORUM. 1967-   bimonthly $12 p. a.
   Grand Central Station, P. O. Box 2805, New York, N. Y. 10017
   Printed in Poland but distributed through Austria, this magazine
      speaks for the International Jazz Federation (formerly, Euro-
      pean Jazz Federation) with articles, concert reports, and rec-
      ord reviews of mainly modern jazz (and European jazzmen).
   No. of 1977 reviews: 127

JAZZ JOURNAL INTERNATIONAL 1948-   monthly $14 p. a.
   7 Carnaby St. , London WIV 1PG, England
   Excellent detailed articles, with thorough descriptive and disco-
      graphic information for all reviews and articles. Now owned
      by Billboard.
   No. of 1977 reviews: 309

JAZZ MAGAZINE. 1976-   quarterly $10 p. a.
   30 Makamah Beach Road, Northport, New York 11768
   An attractive package emphasizing good layout and graphics,
      printed on quality paper. Articles concentrate on living and
      modern performers; record reviews.
   No. of 1977 reviews: 97

JAZZ REPORT. 1958-   irregular 6 nos. /$3
   Box 476, Ventura, Cal. 93001

"The record collector's magazine" (subtitle), this is an informal
mimeographed publication with record reviews and book reviews concentrating on the "trad" period.
No. of 1977 reviews: 64

JOHN EDWARDS MEMORIAL FOUNDATION QUARTERLY
    [J. E. M. F. Q.] 1963-   quarterly $10 p. a.
Folklore and Mythology Center, University of California at Los
    Angeles, Los Angeles, Cal. 90024
A scholarly journal-type presentation of articles dealing with
    American folklore and old time music plus country music in
    particular. Sections deal with discographies, commercial
    graphics, histories of songs. Record reviews and in-depth
    reviews of books.
No. of 1977 reviews: 32

LIVING BLUES. 1970-   bimonthly $6 p. a.
    2615 N. Wilton Ave., Chicago, Ill. 60614
Good American coverage of modern blues through news and ar-
    ticles. Record and book reviews tend to be slim.
No. of 1977 reviews: 84

MELODY MAKER. weekly $39 p. a.
    IPC Business Press (Sales & Distribution) Oakfield House, Per-
    rymount Rd., Haywards Heath, Sussex RH16 3DH, England
This is probably the best of the five British weeklies devoted to
    popular music. It devotes a great deal of space to non-rock
    items, such as jazz, folk, blues, soul, reggae, country, and
    so forth, both in its reviews and in its articles. There is
    also much material here on audio equipment and problems.
No. of 1977 reviews: 1187

MISSISSIPPI RAG; the voice of traditional jazz and ragtime. 1974-
    monthly $5 p. a.
    P. O. Box 19068, Minneapolis, Minn. 55419
Tabloid format on newsprint. Good, in-depth reviews. Histor-
    ical articles; excellent coverage of concerts and festivals (with
    photos).
No. of 1977 reviews: 54

MODERN HI-FI AND MUSIC. 1973-   quarterly $10 p. a.
    699 Madison Ave., New York, N. Y. 10021
Articles on stereo equipment. Record reviews are popular and
    evaluative.
No. of 1977 reviews: 71

MULESKINNER NEWS. 1970-1977
    Box 7A, Ruffin, N. C. 27326
Articles on bluegrass performers, playing bluegrass instruments,
    schedules of festivals and performances. Good reviews of
    bluegrass and old time music. In 1978, became Music Country.
No. of 1977 reviews: 28

MUSIC GIG. 1974-   monthly $7.97 p.a.
  415 Lexington Ave., New York, N.Y. 10017
  Tabloid format in the same vein as Rolling Stone, but covering
    only popular music. Reviews are quite crisp and to the point.
  No. of 1977 reviews: 393

MUSIC JOURNAL. 1943-   monthly (exc June & Aug) $11 p.a.
  370 Lexington Ave., New York, N.Y. 10017
  A general interest magazine for music educators, covering clas-
    sical and popular music. Most reviews are for mood-pop or
    jazz items (the latter by Stanley Dance).
  No. of 1977 reviews: 103

NEW KOMMOTION. 1974-   quarterly £3 p.a.
  3 Bowrons Ave., Wembley, Middlesex HAO 4QS, England
  Probably England's best oldies magazine, concentrating on current
    output of reissued long-playing discs, advising on future reis-
    sue programs. A good read.
  No. of 1977 reviews: 181

OLD TIME MUSIC. 1971-   quarterly $4 p.a.
  33 Brunswick Gardens, London W8 4AW, England
  American country old time music. Transcriptions and disco-
    graphic essays. Record reviews of old time string band mu-
    sic.
  No. of 1977 reviews: 82

ONTARIO LIBRARY REVIEW. 1916-   quarterly $3/3yrs
  Ontario Provincial Library Service, 14th Floor, Mowat Block,
    Queen's Park, Toronto M7A 1B9, Canada
  Includes a regular record review column, concerned with "Cana-
    dian Content." No music book reviews.
  No. of 1977 reviews: 95

PHONOGRAPH RECORD MAGAZINE. 1969-   monthly $6 p.a.
  6922 Sunset Blvd., Hollywood, California 90028
  Once supported by United Artists, this tabloid concentrates on
    recordings with a touch of humor (e.g. "Blindfold tests" sa-
    tires). Good coverage of soul and jazz.
  No. of 1977 reviews: 60

PICKIN'. 1974-   monthly $9 p.a.
  134 N. 13th Street, Philadelphia, Pa. 19107
  This handsome magazine is devoted to bluegrass and old-time mu-
    sic. Good historical articles, interviews and excellent materi-
    al on stringed instruments. Many technical articles and mu-
    sical tablatures.
  No. of 1977 reviews: 236

POPULAR MUSIC AND SOCIETY. 1971-   quarterly $6 p.a.;
    $15/3yrs
  318 South Grove Street, Bowling Green, Ohio 43402
  An interdisciplinary journal "concerned with music in the broad-

est sense of the term" (editorial policy).   Scholarly articles,
books are reviewed.   Record reviews usually not signed.   Very
slow publication.
No. of 1977 reviews: 21

RADIO FREE JAZZ.   1974-   monthly $12 p. a.
  6737 Annapolis Road, P. O. Box 2417, Landover Hills, Maryland
  20784
  Mainly intended for jazz radio programmers, this tabloid has
  good coverage of current records plus assorted articles of
  varying quality.   The jazz news is quite excellent, as are the
  playlists.
  No. of 1977 reviews: 81

RAG TIMES.   1968-   bimonthly $4 by membership only
  Maple Leaf Club, 5560 West 62d St. , Los Angeles, Cal.   90056
  Articles, news, book and record reviews, for the ragtime fans.
  Good coverage, complements the Ragtimer.
  No. of 1977 reviews: 15

RAGTIMER.   1962-   bimonthly $8 by mbrship only
  Ragtime Society, Inc. , P. O. Box 520, Station A, Weston, M9N
  3N3, Canada
  Articles, news, book and record reviews.   Reproduction of sheet
  music.   Loose-leaf format.   Record reviews tend to go outside ragtime music per se.
  No. of 1977 reviews: 29

RECORD MONTH.   1975-   monthly $12 p. a.
  216 Carlton Street, Toronto M5A 2L1, Canada
  While there is a distinct emphasis here on Canadian music, this
  periodical is valuable for its "international" outlook from a
  Canadian perspective.
  No. of 1977 reviews: 15

RECORD REVIEW.   1976-   bimonthly $6 p. a.
  P. O. Box 91878, Los Angeles, California   90009
  "In-depth articles blending review, interview, biography, and dis-
  cussion of a cross-section of the latest record releases"--all
  put in perspective with an artist's or group's previous recordings.   Unlike most record review media, much space is given
  to individual track analyses.
  No. of 1977 reviews: 185

RECORD SPECIAL.   1977-   bimonthly $6 p. a.
  P. O. Box 675, La Habra, Cal.   96031
  Developed out of an information sheet from Southern Record Sale.
  Tries to be exhaustive in reissues in the fields of: blues, old
  time music, jazz, bluegrass, gospel, rockabilly, folk, British
  folk, etc.
  No. of 1977 reviews: 277

RECORDS AND RECORDING.   1957-   monthly $14. 90 p. a.

Hanson Books, Artillery Mansions, 75 Victoria St., London SW1,
England
Record news and reviews, chiefly classical. Popular music
stress strong "rock" and "jazz" and "blues" reviews.
No. of 1977 reviews: 357

ROCK. 1976-   bimonthly $12 p. a.
257 Park Avenue South, New York, New York 10010
A typical rock magazine, with articles and pictures and record
reviews. Printed in Time-size format, with newspaper stock.
No. of 1977 reviews: 42

ROCKING CHAIR; the review newsletter for librarians and popular
music fans who buy records. 1977-   monthly $6. 95 p. a.
Cupola Productions, Box 27, Philadelphia, Pa. 19105
No. of 1977 reviews: 308

ROLLING STONE. 1968-   biweekly $20 p. a.
Straight Arrow Publishers, 625 Third St., San Francisco, Cal.
94107
America's strongest youth culture magazine, now moving away
from just music to a description of a life style in general.
Very opinionated book and record reviews.
No. of 1977 reviews: 477

SMG; for record collectors. 1973-   bimonthly $5 p. a.
23 Holmwood Road, Rainworth, Mansfield, Notts. NG 21OHS, England
"An oldies-orientated fanzine--Any artists or types of music which
have definite collector appeal are grist for our mill, and our
approach is fax'n'info-based rather than the subjective critical
essay style"--Editorial, Jan. 1977.
No. of 1977 reviews: 95

SING OUT. 1950-   bimonthly $7. 50 p. a.
270 Lafayette St., N. Y., N. Y. 10012
News on the folk, blues, and bluegrass scene, plus book and
record reviews. Very slow publication.
No. of 1977 reviews: 50

SOUL CARGO. 1977-   4 issues a year $7 p. a.
67 Albert Terrace, Wolstanton, Newcastle, Stafts., England
"The magazine for facts & info soul fans"--editorial, issue 1.
An oldies-centered magazine, carrying on from Hot Buttered
Soul.
No. of 1977 reviews: 21

SOUND. 1970-   10 nos. /yr $5 p. a.
62 Shaftesbury Ave., Toronto M4T 1A4, Canada
Articles on audio equipment and the Canadian music scene.
No. of 1977 reviews: 160

STEREO REVIEW. 1958-   monthly $7. 98 p. a.

P. O. Box 2771, Boulder, Colo. 80302
Audio equipment news, articles on performers and composers.
Heavier emphasis on popular music than High Fidelity.
No. of 1977 reviews: 645

STORYVILLE. 1965-   bimonthly $5 p. a.
66 Fairview Dr. , Chigwell, Essex, England IG7 6HS
This magazine tends to concentrate on "trad" or "classic" jazz,
blues, and subsequent re-interpretations or revivals. Articles
are devoted to exploring minor figures or minor facts about
major performers in this genre, as well as copious discographies of the period. A good research-oriented magazine.

SWINGING NEWSLETTER. 1977- $15 p. a.
c/o Jazz Forum Publications/Distribution, Grand Central Station,
    P. O. Box 2805, New York, N. Y. 10017
News from the International Jazz Federation, with record reviews.
No. of 1977 reviews: 6

TRADITIONAL MUSIC. 1975-   3 x year £1. 20
90 St. Julian's Farm Road, London SE27 ORS, England
Examines all aspects of folk music in Great Britain, especially
    with long in-depth articles on the older countryside singers.
    Many songs and texts; first-rate long record reviews.
No. of 1977 reviews: 20

TROUSER PRESS; America's only British rock magazine. 1974-
    bimonthly $6 p. a.
Box 822, 147 W. 42d St. , New York, New York 10036
An American-produced magazine concentrating exclusively on
    British rock music. The opposite of Zigzag.
No. of 1977 reviews: 150

VILLAGE VOICE. 1951-   weekly $18 p. a.
80 University Place, New York, New York 10003
In addition to investigative reporting and features about New York
    City, the Voice has a first-rate pop music section.
No. of 1977 reviews: 222

WHO PUT THE BOMP. 1974-   quarterly [but irregular] $8 for
    eight issues
P. O. Box 7112, Burbank, Cal. 91510
The leading "oldies" magazine, the only one on glossy paper and
    with color photographs. Good articles on rock 'n' roll re-
    vivals and on the early rock period of the 1960s.
No. of 1977 reviews: 7

ZIGZAG. 1970-   monthly $12 p. a.
19 Kennet Street, Reading, Berks. , England
During 1977, this magazine, which used to specialize in American
    rock music from a British viewpoint, turned to punk rock. One
    of the most respected of the underground rock magazines.
No. of 1977 reviews: 70

ROCK

Rock music developed from Britain with the English "beat" and "blues" groups. These bands re-exported to America the styles and songs created by black American music, primarily the gospel-infused rhythm'n'blues. But rock had other roots too. It borrowed its form and feeling from the blues, the call and response riffs plus the driving repetitious rhythms from r'n'b, improvisation from jazz, melismatic singing from gospel, and social consciousness from folk music. By so doing, rock music became almost parasitic, absorbing and transmuting all aspects of popular music (with deleterious results) as well as the main influences in these other forms of music. This synthesis is augmented by its pragmatic but diverse nature, for rock music tends to re-emphasize styles of music in reinforcement patterns. Whatever works is usually good, and stylists tend to stay in one mode of performing with little variation or exploration. The audience works in a similar but fickle fashion, and there is a common expression: "You are as big as your last record." For this reason, many performers do not switch styles.

Rock music is essentially studio-oriented. The recording studio and electronics are its primary instruments, unlike the vocals in the blues, the instruments of jazz, or the microphones of the pop singer. Songs were created and written in the studio; there they are also mixed and edited from 32 tracks down to two or four, and the music electronically altered for dynamics, textures, volume, echo, and so forth. Technology gave rock musicians new instruments such as the electric piano, the electronic synthesizer, the devices of fuzz tone, reverberation, and wah-wah. The amplifier enabled the speaker systems (and hence the musician) to possess raw, swinging power. Tapes and albums gave the musician time to lay out all his ideas, enough room for suites, operas, extended songs, variations, experimentation with unstructured music, etc.

Rock music also advanced 1950s rock and roll. During that decade, smart operators uncovered post-war black music and recast the mold to fit young, urbane white singers. The beat was still there, but the voice was silky instead of rough, the accompanying rhythms were simple instead of complex, and the lyrics were changed to prevent misunderstandings in words out of context. But the British blues bands, by side-stepping rock and roll and emulating the source of rock and roll, dramatically reversed the sequence. And, as is common in every popular music field, once the traditional elements or the borrowed songs run out, then the performers

21

have to create their own materials.   Given the existing technology
and format, several streams opened up.   The established 32-bar
song with a bridge was the first to give way to such innovations
borrowed from jazz as changing time signatures and shifting meters,
and from r'n'b came blunt lyrics and screaming vocals.   In time
this led to the performer creating all of his own material.   This
was a true singer-performer-songwriter, for the groups now play
their own instruments and sing their own songs.   Many of the finer
soloists and groups even had complete control over their product,
down through the editing, album design, and liner notes.   Their instrumental prowess expanded so that both guitar licks (configurations
within a chord) and guitar runs (configurations bridging notes between chords in a progression), as borrowed from jazz and country
music, could easily be performed.   They borrowed the mobile electric bass from soul music to pin down the rhythm, thus freeing the
drummer from merely keeping the beat.   While the 1950s rock and
roll scene projected an alienation against parental control of teen-
agers, and defined the society of the rock and roll admirer, it took
rock music to crystallize and fuse this feeling of frustration into an
ideology and a youth culture of peer control.   This, of course, relates to the post-World War II baby boom, for in the era of rock
and roll the large young audience was growing up from 10 to 15
years of age; with rock in 1964, they were at least eight years
older (18-23) and now in a position to solidify any fragmented alienation.

But rock music is fragmented when it comes to fans that
support the music.   Not only are there different formats, but also
there are diversified themes that might not appeal to all persons interested in rock music.   Some of the handles given to these formats
include country-rock, jazz-rock, blues-rock, folk-rock (and a subgenre, good-time-rock), punk-rock (or pop-rock), soft-rock (usually
equated with modern rock and roll), acid-rock, and hard-rock (better known now as "heavy metal music").

Blues-rock came first.   The blues revival in the United
States was a culmination of the urban folk music and urban blues
craze, the developing British rock music based on black music, and
accented by the proliferation of skiffle or jug bands in England.
Rock musicians in England further extended the country blues-folk-
jug band idiom into Chicago blues.   They tried to approximate the
unintentional distortion of electric blues recordings (unintentional,
because the Chicago blues men used old equipment that was falling
apart and malfunctioning).   They experimented with fuzz-tone and
sustained notes.   The leaders were Jimmy Page, Eric Clapton, and
Jeff Beck (all ex-Yardbirds), plus Jimi Hendrix from the United
States, who both traveled to England for his success and picked up
an English bassist and drummer.   He was profoundly influenced by
Clapton.   Vocalists, however, simply did not exist.   For some reason, none was ever found that was better than mediocre.   The two
vocal leaders--Robert Plant of Led Zeppelin, and Rod Stewart--had
to spend a decade in developing.   On the other hand, American
groups such as Electric Flag, Paul Butterfield's Blue Band, and the

Blues Project had several good vocalists. But their recordings
were strictly in the Chicago mold, changing only with added ampli-
fication--and cleaning up the distortion. Unfortunately, this made
the blues as interpreted seem monotonous and lacking in excitement.

Blues-rock was most of the "British invasion" of the mid-
sixties when rock and roll was given a big shot in the arm by amplification. After the Beatles came several similar pop groups, followed by a whole alphabet of British musicians working in the blues
mode. American imitators of British imitators of Chicago blues
quickly followed, and by the end of the 1960s, folk-rock, acid-rock
and blues-rock co-existed in neat categories. But then folk-rock
transmuted into troubador music, and blues-rock adopted some of
the technical devices of the fading acid-rock. The results of this
latter subgenre was heavy metal music.

Acid Rock, also known as psychedelic rock, had several intents. One was to reproduce the distorted hearing of an individual
under the influence of LSD or other hallucinogens. Another was to
recreate for a drugless individual the illusion of psychedelia through
the music and an on-stage visual light show. A third was to create
music while under the influence of drugs. Unfortunately, this third
intent does not work, as drugs severely restrict one's technical abil-
ities (as was the case with John Fahey). All of this should not be
construed as to condone the use of drugs, but merely to reproduce
or recreate its musical effects. Acid rock was originally for those
not on drugs, but not all acid rock was suitable for those who took
drugs and went on trips. Psychedelic rock was intended for listening, and not for dancing. This abrupt shift in a form of music that
previously had rhythmic capabilities to produce happiness dramatically changed the whole concept of rock music. To reproduce disturbed music, the musicians needed electronic technology for advanced amplification and weird sounds.

The music was developed mainly in San Francisco in 1965
by the Jefferson Airplane and the Grateful Dead; however, the style
was developed earlier by the Beatles, who showed the paths through
structural complexities, rhythmic intricacies, and other experimentation. They composed "Norwegian Wood" and "Day in the Life, " employing Indian raga music styles and the sitar (this Oriental association followed drugs around, even if the hallucinogen was marijuana).
Some of the music even reflected social themes found in folk music,
especially the stream of consciousness ideas of Bob Dylan. Progression in acid rock embraces sustained and languid melodies, complex instrumentation, variety and imaginative stylings, and imagery
in lyrics. The musical phrases came in lurches of surging power,
a sort of tripping and uncertain movement. As with art, acid rock
dealt with tone, coloration, texture, and density. Most live concerts,
which went on for hours (such as those of the Grateful Dead), added
improvisation for spontaneous effects. On record, the long timings
of each track allow for some development of the many themes, and
the variations on a chord. The one drawback to the intellectual
music of acid rock (but one of its attractions to the folk element) is

that "finesse replaces visceral excitement. " It is "head" music that needs no surging energy nor buoyancy as was happening in regular rock music of the time.   The period of acid rock extended to 1970, and included such material as Van Dyke Parks' Song Cycle, the Beach Boys' "Good Vibrations, " the Rolling Stones' "Paint It Black, " and the Byrds "Eight Miles High. "   Since 1970, acid rock returned infrequently because of the expense of touring light shows and the limited scope of experimentation.

Heavy metal music seemed to take the worst offerings of acid-rock and blues-rock.   The music played by groups here demanded an extraordinary volume, distortion and mechanical riffing. Keyboards and electric basses were added to the music of lead guitarists and some rather pedestrian drummers.   Much of the music deliberately disregarded the dancing and rhythmic aspects, sticking with the propensity of acid-rock towards "non-swing" music (e.g. Led Zeppelin's "Dazed and Confused").   Much of the singing and the lyrics were subordinated to the instrumental sound, which preferred "chaos over coherence. "   Thus, within a relatively easy blues progression there appears to be a jackhammer approach for solos rather than a developed set of thematic variations.   This was called "blitzkrieg obbligatos, " and a typical example can be found by Eric Clapton on Cream's "Spoonful. "   The basic elements of this music were very monotonous, but to be successful heavy metal relied on imaginative performers to project a unique sound, and thereby become "stylists" through technical tricks.   When innovations ceased to exist (or when they were never there), then the lack of imagination quickly forced the band to become an exponent of punk rock.

This term described the "trash with flash. "   Everything was thrown at an audience except good music.   Punk rock was mainly done by those who wanted to play the blues--an easy medium--but couldn't.   They evolved a style which didn't require virtuosity.   The guitar solo was dropped, as the guitarist was deficient, in favor of the insistent riff being played by all instruments at once.   The lyrical quality changed to reflect weird violence, madness, drugs, disease and pestilence.   Not only are some of these groups dull, but they are also short on ideas.   They all begin to sound alike, and were appreciated by an audience which largely couldn't keep pace with musical development.   Their few redeeming values lie in the stageshow of themes, lights, and stories, such as contributed by Alice Cooper, David Bowie, and Lou Reed.   These are enjoyable in themselves, but fall flat on discs which transmit only the aural passages.   Older groups from the past included MC5, Iggy Pop and the Stooges, Blue Cheer, Iron Butterfly, Velvet Underground, and Grand Funk Railroad.   Influences back and forth across the Atlantic follow the route of, for example, the Chicago blues to British blues to Grand Funk Railroad to Black Sabbath to the Blue Oyster Cult, with each emulating the sound of the immediate predecessor.

Experimentation has not always been successful, but in the rock music world it did help to pave the way for derivative and pop groups.   As rock music is pragmatic, then whatever sells must be good, and the whole industry begins emulation. Most rock experiments are done by reasonably proficient groups who can convince recording companies that their work should be made available to the masses who so rarely buy this type of music anyway. Much of it is contrived and self-conscious; most of it is simple, derived in turn from the classics or from jazz. Some strength does come from underground or counter-culture fans (usually a loyal cult), but usually they go through the mainstream of records unnoticed until some other musician tries his hand with a simple modification and succeeds. Their sources are mainly acid-rock and the new electronic instrumentation. Heavy metal groups did contribute "theater rock, " where the music is presented as a whole conception of light, sound, story and performance. But they are a failure on disc because the albums are very incomplete, containing aural information only. Jim Morrison of the Doors started it all with his long, improvised live concert renditions of his ten-minute album songs. The latest extension of the show tunes has been such groups as Queen, Kiss, and the New York Dolls.

Country-folk-rock is the fusion of material and traditions derived from the folk-music idiom with the instrumentation and beat of rock. It is an amorphous combination of blues, rock and roll, country music, popular music and protest songs. Its greatest impact was in the mid-1960s when protest songs merged with rock rhythms, and this type of music found a new audience. Its next manifestation was as country-rock, which meant going through the folk process from traditional sources to written materials. Country-rock was favored by those who could sing; folk-rock was left to those who couldn't sing, but simply growled in the time-honored folk tradition. The last permutation after country-rock became the troubador or singer-songwriter, who was essentially first a folk-type and then a rock musician. At this level the merger was not as complete because the folk-derived lyrics dominated.

The singer-song writer developed out of the folk and country tradition. Now called troubadors (and troubettes for some), they bring personal visions through their unique place and role in popular music. A popular song is a 50-50 relationship between the words and the music. The words were not meant to be read as poetry. In the troubador's song, the records can stand alone as poetry, or be poetry put to music. This is a crucial distinction, and it marks a dramatic shift in popular music history. Some of the strongest troubadors have been displaced poets (Richard Farina, Bob Dylan, Leonard Cohen, Paul Simon, Tim Hardin).

To understand the troubador phenomenon one must first understand the conditions of the late 1950s and 1960s folk revival. The folk purists either preferred "authentic" singers from the past (forgetting that these singers themselves were interpreters) or memorizations of every phrase and nuance lifted off Library of Congress or old-time music commercial recordings. Audiences recognized both as "roots, " with the memorizers standing in for the originals. A clear fossilization of performing styles emerged. At the same

time, Alan Lomax's philosophy of "to be folk, you live folk" found
acceptance with other singers and audiences. The dichotomy of
"purism" vs. "life experiences" split the folk music world. The
pattern (which, incidentally, was established during the 1920s with
old-time music) was to listen to early records and to do imitations,
with some singers eventually adapting the material creatively to de-
velop their own musical styles. Such a process was common to
blues, jazz, rock, etc. But it took Bob Dylan to put it all together. He made it possible for the acceptance of folk-singers to
emerge from their fossilized self-made traps to be "living experience" singers with original words, music, styles and variations.

The existence of the troubador actually began with the folk
revival of the Depression. In this earlier period, the stress was
on anonymity. But in the 1960s, with alienation from society and
singing protest songs of persuasion, the stress became focussed.
The lyrical ballads of troubadors look back to older British forms
in themes:

1. Life and Nature, which stresses that all natural phenomena are
    interdependent and sympathetic. This "pathetic fallacy" resulted
    in landscape and scenery songs, plus idyllic viewpoints. Three
    specific manifestations here include:
    (a) the erotic songs of similes and images, concentrating on
        sexual euphemisms such as germination or fruitfulness.
    (b) the ritualistic manner of life form cycles, concentrating on
        dances, ceremonies, and "good times" generally,
    (c) metaphorically extending the pleasures of love between part-
        ners to that of the whole natural environment (and vice
        versa), quite often as an echo of reinforcement.

2. Pure Love, dealing with stories of success, non-success, and
    bitter frustrations, quite often presented in the first person.

3. Psycho-analytic Autobiographies, in which a selection of self-
    conscious expressions and subconscious ideas are presented in
    the manner of the bluesman "to talk it out. "

4. Commentaries, presenting some criticism but offering few or
    no solutions. Most songs here are rhetorical in nature, indi-
    cating the condition and merely describing it. As most people
    have jobs and/or the basic necessities of life, then it is mainly
    the imperfections of society that are pointed out rather than the
    root evils. Alienation and outrage makes this an individual dis-
    content rather than the anonymous cohesion found in the 1930s.
    Three specific types here include:
    (a) a social commentary on the manner of urban life, in which
        the singer tries to define social reality,
    (b) a political commentary,
    (c) a labor commentary about jobs, industries, capitalism,
        working conditions, etc.

Troubadors can promote many superficialities. In attempting to jump on the band wagon, many have produced puzzling responses. One critic called them the "quack minstrels of a non-existent America." Something does appear to be out of sequence when the children of well-to-do parents start singing about "hard times" that they have never experienced. Other material falls into a too-common pattern: there is slight biographical material, meaning that the singers remain closed to their private lives; the Dylan "stream of consciousness" has been overdone by lesser mortals; much material concerns drugs, lost love, or country music influences; and the general pattern of many songs has been characterized as being "landscapes" or scenery songs.

By analyzing rock lyrics, these can be grouped together into eight distinct themes (in no particular order):

1. Summertime Paeans--Odes to the good life of celebration and surfing. These can also be instrumentals, and because of their good-time nature and relation to soft-rock, most love ballads fall within this category.

2. Dance Music--This is happy music, with no social commentary. Throughout the last 25 years it had limited popularity, but it was unpretentious and honest, stressing the dance rhythms. In 1976 it resurged as "disco" music.

3. Sexual Themes--Either implied or explicit, sexual adventures also included sadism, masochism, and perversions. Originally, this was the derivation of the term "rock and roll," as physical emulation of sexual intercourse. Sexuality was the one dominant theme of 1950s r'n'b.

4. Rebellion--Either non-violent (the self-consciousness of growing up and the loss of innocence, coupled with the need for group or peer unity) or violent (the protest against the establishment of law, police, complacency, war efforts in Viet Nam). This music was best handled in the form of a satire or of a parable. If it was too explicit, then, as with early sexual songs, the record was banned from the airwaves.

5. Civil Rights--Social causes espoused by whites in the 1960s, and then by blacks in the 1970s. Strange as it may seem, white rock music in the 1970s has been silent on the matter of civil rights.

6. Social Concerns--Problems, but few solutions, are discussed in rock music. Material here concerns pride, interracial relationships, slums, ghettos, "messages," "lessons," and "advice."

7. Drugs--Either implied or explicit, along with psychedelic trips, acid music, similes and metaphorical expressions.

8. Lifestyles--The world of the rock super star, usually a male

macho world, concerning his musical roots and life on the
road.

Nearly every magazine has an article now and then on rock
music or a rock personality. Generally magazines with adequate reviews and occasional articles include High Fidelity and Stereo Review. Specific periodicals geared to the rock fan come and go depending upon finances. The ones that have remained include Circus,
Creem, and Melody Maker. Crawdaddy and Rolling Stone are less
than half music, and have been since 1972.

Specific periodicals examine one aspect of rock music. Contemporary Keyboard and Guitar Player provide guidance and instruc-
tion for performing on those respective instruments. Popular Music
and Society will examine sociological impact, while Down Beat will
investigate jazz-rock.

According to the reviews for 1977, the following appear to
be the best ROCK records:

ATLANTA Rhythm Section. A Rock and Roll Alternative.
    Polydor PD1-6080
BEACH Boys. Love You. Reprise MSK 2258
BLUE Oyster Cult. Spectres. Columbia PC 35019
BOWIE, David. Heroes. RCA AFL1-2522
BOWIE, David. Low. RCA CPL1-2030
CHAPLIN, Blondie. Asylum 7E-1095
CHEAP Trick. In Color. Epic PE 34884
COODER, Ry. Showtime. Warner Brothers BS 3059
COSTELLO, Elvis. My Aim is True. Columbia JC 35037
DAMNED. Stiff Records SEEZ 1 (E)
EDMUNDS, Dave. Get It! Swan Song 8418
FLEETWOOD Mac. Rumours. Warner Brothers BSK 3010
FOREIGNER. Atlantic SD 18215
GABRIEL, Peter. Atco SD 36-147
HARRIS, Emmy Lou. Luxury Liner. Warner Brothers BS
    2998
HASLAN, Annie. Annie in Wonderland. Sire 6046
HEART. Little Queen. Portrait PR 34799
HILLAGE, Steve. L. Atlantic SD 18205
JOY. Fantasy F 9538
McLEAN, Don. Solo. United Artists UALA 652-H2 (2 discs)
MORRISON, Van. Period of Transition. Warner Brothers
    BS 2987
PARKER, Graham, and the Rumor. Heat Treatment. Mer-
    cury SRM1-1117
PINK Floyd. Animals. Columbia JC 34474
RONSTADT, Linda. Simple Dreams. Asylum 6E-104
RUMOUR. Max. Mercury SRM1-1174
STEELY Dan. Aja. ABC 1006
SUPERTRAMP. Even in the Quietest Moments. A & M SP
    4634
TELEVISION. Marque Moon. Elektra 7E-1098

TOWNSHEND, Peter and Ronnie Lane. Rough Mix.   MCA 2295
WAITS, Tom.   Foreign Affairs.   Asylum 7E-1117
YOUNG, Neil.   American Stars 'n' Bars.   Reprise MSK 2261

1 AC/DC.   High Voltage.   Atco SD 36-142
       AU   March p87.   150w.   3
       TP   Dec. 1976/Jan. 1977 p31-2.   250w.   4

2 AC/DC.   Let There Be Rock.   Atco SD 36-151
       CIR Oct. 13 p75-6.   100w.   3
       MG   Oct. p59.   75w.   3

3 ACE.   No Strings.   Anchor AN 2020
       AU   Sept. p89.   150w.   2
       MM   Jan. 22 p22.   300w $2\frac{1}{2}$
       RS   Apr. 7 p76.   150w. $1\frac{1}{2}$

4 AIRBORNE.   Songs for a City.   Ocean 1 (Canada)
       CC   Dec. p34.   50w.   3

5 AKKERMAN, Jan and Kaz Lux.   Eli.   Atlantic SO18270
       GP   June p137.   225w. $3\frac{1}{2}$
       MG   Feb. p53.   200w. $2\frac{1}{2}$

6 ALBERTO Y LOST TRIOS PARANOIAS.   Italians from Outer
   Space.   Transatlantic TRA 349
       TP   Nov. p42.   225w.   4

7 ALICE Cooper.   Alice Cooper Show: Live Las Vegas.   Warner
   Bros. K3138.   Cart. M83138.   Cass. M53138
       MM   Jan. 7 p17.   300w. $\frac{1}{2}$

8 ALICE Cooper.   Lace & Whiskey.   Warner Bros. BSK-3027.
   Cass. M5-3027.   Tape M8-3027
       CIR July 21 p58-9.   575w.   1
       CRA July p68.   125w.   2
       GR   July p237.   25w. $1\frac{1}{2}$
       HF   July p149.   150w.   3
       MG   July p51.   200w.   2
       RS   July 14 p67.   450w. $2\frac{1}{2}$
       SR   Oct. p90.   225w.   3
       VV   Oct. 3 p65.   50w. $2\frac{1}{2}$

9 ALKATRAZ.   Doing a Moonlight.   UA UAS 30001 (E)
       MM   Feb. 12 p26.   50w.   1
       TP   Apr. -May p31.   125w.   3

10 ALLMAN, Gregg.   Playin' Up a Storm.   Capricorn CPO181.
   Tape M80181
       CIR Aug. 4 p57.   400w.   3

CK   Aug.   p49.   25w.   4
CRA   Aug.   p82.   600w.   3
GR   Oct.   p715.   50w. $2\frac{1}{2}$
HF   Aug.   p110-11   575w. $4\frac{1}{2}$
MG   Aug.   p59.   100w. $3\frac{1}{2}$
MM   July 16   p26.   350w.   1
RRE   May-June   p26-7.   425w. $2\frac{1}{2}$

11   ALLMAN Brothers Band.   Wipe the Windows, Check the Oil,
Dollar Gas.   Capricorn 2CX0177 (2 discs)
AU   Feb.   p76.   50w. $2\frac{1}{2}$
CAC   March   p453.   200w.   3
CIR   Feb. 14   p12.   650w.   3
GP   Feb.   p113.   150w.   4
GR   Feb.   p1332.   100w.   1
HF   Feb.   p144.   50w.   4
RO   May   p14.   500w. $3\frac{1}{2}$
RS   March 10   p67-8.   350w. $2\frac{1}{2}$
SMG   May   p21.   125w.   4
SR   April   p88.   187w.   4

12   ALPHA Band.   Arista AL 4102
CIR   Feb. 14   p12-13.   225w.   3
CIR   Feb. 14   p13.   200w.   1
CMR   May   p31.   100w.   3
CRA   Jan.   p77.   125w.   5
GR   April   p1617.   50w.   4
MG   Feb.   p54.   150w.   3
MM   Feb. 26   p30.   100w.   4
RR   May   p86.   150w. $3\frac{1}{2}$
SR   April   p88.   75w.   2

13   ALPHA Band.   Spark in the Dark.   Arista AB 4145
MG   Dec.   p56.   50w.   1
RS   Nov. 3   p110.   525w.   2

14   AMAZING Blondel.   Live in Tokyo.   DJM DJF 20503 (E)
MM   July 16   p27.   50w.   1

15   AMAZING Rhythm Aces.   Toucan Do It Too.   ABC ABCL
5219
CM   July   p52.   300w.   4
CMR   June   p17.   225w.   3
MM   June 11   p19.   250w. $4\frac{1}{2}$
RS   June 2   p78.   225w.   2

16   AMBROSIA.   Somewhere I've Never Travelled.   Twentieth Century T 510
RS   March 24   p72.   750w. $3\frac{1}{2}$

17   AMERICA.   Harbor.   Warner Bros. BSK 3017.   Cart. M83017.
Cass. M53017
RRE   May-June   p21, 62.   600w.   3

RS   April 21   p72.   300w.   1
SR   July   p92.   75w.   2$\frac{1}{2}$

18   AMERICAN Tears.   Powerhouse.   Columbia PC 34676
CRA   Aug.   p80-1.   750w.   3

19   AMESBURY, Bill.   Can You Feel It.   Capitol ST 11528
OLR   March   p53-4.   25w.   3$\frac{1}{2}$

20   ANACOSTIA.   MCA 2269
MG   Aug.   p61.   100w.   1$\frac{1}{2}$
OLR   Dec.   p290-1.   25w.   2$\frac{1}{2}$

21   ANIMALS and Sonny Boy Williamson.   Newcastle-on-Tyne, Dec.
1963.   Charly CR 30 0016 (E)
CAC   July   p130.   150w.   3$\frac{1}{2}$
MM   April 16   p23.   50w.   2
SMG   May   p20.   100w.   4

22   APRIL Wine.   Live at the El Mocambo.   London PS 699
SOU   Sept.   p60.   400w.   2

23   APRIL Wine.   The Whole World's Goin' Crazy.   Decca London
PS 675
CAC   Jan.   p377.   300w.   2
HF   Jan.   p142.   200w.   4

24   ARDLEY, Neil.   Kaleidoscope of Rainbows.   Gull GULP 1018
(E)
RR   Jan.   p85.   300w.   4

25   ARIZONA.   RCA LPL 1 5123
HF   Jan.   p144.   100w.   4

26   ARTFUL Dodger.   Babes on Broadway.   Columbia PC 34846
CIR   Dec.   22   p68.   300w.   3$\frac{1}{2}$
MG   Dec.   p55.   50w.   2$\frac{1}{2}$

27   ARTMAN, Gilbert.   Urban Sax.   Cobra
EUR   V2/#1   p31-2.   200w.   3$\frac{1}{2}$

28   ASHRA.   New Age of Earth.   Virgin V2080 (E)
MM   June 25   p20.   200w.   3

29   ATLANTA Rhythm Section.   A Rock and Roll Alternative.   Poly-
dor PD1 6080
CRA   March   p80.   2001.   4
CS   April 21   p18.   100w.   3
DB   March 10   p26.   300w.   5
GR   July   p237.   75w.   3
MG   April   p51.   75w.   4
MM   May 14   p31.   250w.   4$\frac{1}{2}$
RS   March 24   p65-6.   550w.   4

30 AUGER, Brian. Happiness Heartaches. Warner Bros., BS
    2981
        CAD March p45-6. 75w. $2\frac{1}{2}$
        DB Sept. 8 p34. 350w. $1\frac{1}{2}$

31 AUT'CHOSE. Le Cauchemai Amércain. CBS 90379 (Canada)
        CC March p33. 50w. 3

32 AUTOMATIC Fine Tuning. Charisma CAS 1122
        RS March 10 p71. 50w. $2\frac{1}{2}$

33 AVERAGE White Band. Person to Person. Atlantic K60127
        BM March p50-1. 425w. 4
        CAC April p9. 150w. $2\frac{1}{2}$
        HF April p137. 450w. 3
        GR March p1467. 125w. $4\frac{1}{2}$
        MG April p14. 125w. 2
        MM Feb. 5 p23. 325w. $3\frac{1}{2}$
        RR March p96. 200w. 3

34 AVERAGE White Band and Ben E. King. Benny and Us. At-
    lantic SD 19105. Tape TP-19105
        AU Dec. p115. 200w. 3
        HF Oct. p144. 300w. $2\frac{1}{2}$
        MG Oct. p61. 75w. $1\frac{1}{2}$
        MM Aug. 20 p15. 250w. $3\frac{1}{2}$
        RC Oct. p11. 150w. 4
        RS Sept. 22 p70, 72. 150w. 3
        SR Nov. p86. 125w. 4
        VV Sept. 12 p54. 450w. 3

35 AXELROD, David. Strange Ladies. MCA 2283.
        RRE Nov.-Dec. p41. 150w. $3\frac{1}{2}$

36 AXTON, Hoyt. Snowblind Friend. MCA MCA-2263. Cass.
    C-2263. Cart. T-2263
        CM Aug. p52. 400w. 3
        CMP Sept. p39. 175w. 4
        CRA July p74. 200w. $1\frac{1}{2}$
        CS May 19 p19. 200w. 4
        GR Oct. p715. 50w. $3\frac{1}{2}$

37 AYERS, Kevin. Yes, We Have No Mananas. ABC 1021
        CIR Sept. 15 p68. 350w. 3
        RRE Jan.-Feb. p24. 150w. $3\frac{1}{2}$
        VV May 23 p59. 250w. $3\frac{1}{2}$

38 AZTEC Two-Step. Two's Company. RCA APL1-1497. APS1-
    1497
        SR Feb. p86. 200w. 4

39 B. T. Express. Energy to Burn. Columbia PC 34178
        CAC Feb. p415. 50w. 3

40 BABYS. Chrysalis CHR 1129
    CIR   April 28 p14.   150w. $2\frac{1}{2}$
    CRA   March p74.   325w. $3\frac{1}{2}$
    MM   Feb. 26 p30.   500w.   3
    PRM   Feb. p34-5.   600w. $3\frac{1}{2}$
    SR   June p94.   150w.   4

41 BABYS. Broken Heart. Chrysalis CHR 1150
    MG   Dec. p56.   50w. $\frac{1}{2}$
    RC   March p6.   75w. $1\frac{1}{2}$

42 BACHMAN-Turner Overdrive. Freeways. Mercury SRM 1-3700
    CAC   July p130.   225w.   4
    CIR   June 9 p54.   175w.   2
    MG   May p51.   125w. $3\frac{1}{2}$

43 BACHMAN-Turner Overdrive. Live in Japan. Mercury SRM 1-3703
    SOU   Oct. p66.   250w.   4

44 BAD Company. Burnin' Sky. Swan Song SS 8500. Cart. TP-8500. Cass. CS8500
    CIR   June 23 p60.   900w.   2
    GR   May p1757-8.   50w.   1
    MG   May p49.   1000w. $3\frac{1}{2}$
    MM   Feb. 19 p25.   500w.   3
    RRE   May/June p10-2.   1300w. $2\frac{1}{2}$
    RS   May 19 475w.   3
    SR   July p92.   125w.   2

45 BAKER, Ginger. Eleven Sides of Baker. Mountain TOPC 5005 (E)
    CAC   May p49.   350w.   2
    CIR   Aug. 4 p60.   200w.   1
    GR   June p110.   75w.   3

46 BAND. Best of the Band. Capitol ST 3927 (Reissue)
    CMR   Jan. p29.   100w.   4
    MM   Jan. 22 p46.   100w.   3
    RS   Jan. 13 p48.   50w. $2\frac{1}{2}$
    SMG   Jan. p26.   100w.   4

47 BAND. Islands. Capitol EST 11602
    AU   June p116.   100w.   1
    CIR   May 12 p12-3.   1000w. $4\frac{1}{2}$
    CMR   July p19.   175w.   3
    GP   June p136.   100w.   3
    HF   May p113.   900w.   5
    MM   April 9 p23.   500w.   3
    OLR   Dec. p291.   50w.   4
    PRM   April p35.   550w. $4\frac{1}{2}$
    RRE   May-June p25.   600w. $4\frac{1}{2}$

    RS   May 19   800w. $2\frac{1}{2}$
    SR   June p94.   125w.   0
    ZZ   May p36.   550w. $3\frac{1}{2}$

48 BARCLAY James Harvest.   Best of.   EMI Harvest TC 2013 (E)
    (Reissue)
        CAC April p9.   225w. $2\frac{1}{2}$

49 BARCLAY James Harvest.   Octoberon.   MCA-2234.   Cart.
    MCAT-2234
        AU   May p88.   150w.   1
        CAC Jan. p376.   100w.   4
        SR   June p94.   75w.   2

50 BAREFOOT Jerry.   Barefootin'.   Monument MG 7610
        MM   Oct. 27 p22.   200w. $4\frac{1}{2}$

51 BATT, Mike.   Schizophrenia.   Epic EPC 82001 (E)
        MM   Aug. 20 p14.   250w.   3
        TP   Dec. p40.   250w.   2

52 BATTIATO, Franco.   Melle le Gladiator.   Bla (Italy)
        EUR V2/#2 p25.   75w.   3

53 BATTIATO, Franco.   Za, Cafe-Table-Musik.   Dischi (Italy)
        EUR V2/#2 p25.   75w.   4

54 BAUMANN, Peter.   Romance '76.   Virgin V2069 (E)
        MM   May 14 p30.   200w.   4
        RS   Aug. 25 p55.   50w. $2\frac{1}{2}$

55 BAY City Rollers.   It's a Game.   Arista AL 7004.   Tape 8301-
    700
        CIR Oct. 13 p75-6.   200w.   2
        CRA Oct. p64.   500w.   1
        MM   Sept. 3 p46.   300w.   3
        SR   Nov. p86, 87.   150w.   2

56 BEACH Boys.   The Beach Boys Love You.   Reprise MSK 2258.
    8tr: M82258.   C: M52258
        AU   July p90.   150w.   1
        CIR June 9 p52-3.   700w.   4
        CRA May p64.   800w. $2\frac{1}{2}$
        GR   June p110.   50w. $1\frac{1}{2}$
        HF   May p114.   350w.   4
        MG   June p52.   200w.   3
        MM   March 19 p27.   650w. $3\frac{1}{2}$
        PRM April p36.   500w.   3
        RR   June p93.   100w.   3
        RS   May 5 p73.   800w. $3\frac{1}{2}$
        SR   July p92-3.   300w.   3
        VV   May 9 p57.   550w. $4\frac{1}{2}$
        ZZ   May p38.   150w. $4\frac{1}{2}$

57   BEACH Boys.   Live in London '69.   Capitol ST-11584
       CIR   March 17   p17-8.   400w.   3
       SOU   March   p38.   500w.   1
       SR   April   p88-9.   200w.   2

58   BEACH Boys.   Stack of Tracks.   EMI Capitol EST 24009 (E)
     (Reissue)
       CAC   May   p9.   150w.   2
       GR   April   p1617.   25w. $2\frac{1}{2}$
       MM   Feb. 5   p23.   50w. $2\frac{1}{2}$

59   BEATLES.   At the Hollywood Bowl.   Capitol SMAS 11638.
     Cart. 8XW-11638.   Cass. 4XW-11638
       CIR   July 21   p59-60.   400w.   2
       CIR   July 21   p60.   300w.   3
       CIR   July 21   p61.   150w. $3\frac{1}{2}$
       CIR   July 21   p61.   200w. $3\frac{1}{2}$
       CIR   July 21   p61.   300w.   3
       CRA   Aug.   p62.   300w.   3
       GR   Aug.   p353.   225w.   4
       HF   Aug.   p111.   400w.   4
       MG   July   p51.   200w. $4\frac{1}{2}$
       RC   July   p14.   100w.   5
       RRE   May-June   p7-8, 10-11.   1600w. $4\frac{1}{2}$
       SMG   Sept.   p25.   125w.   5
       SOU   July   p42.   250w.   3
       SR   Aug.   p88.   375w.   4
       VV   June 13   p36.   125w.   4

60   BEATLES.   The Beatles' Tapes.   Polydor 2683 068
       TP   Dec. 1976/Jan. 1977   p34.   375w.   4

61   BEATLES.   Live! at the Star-Club in Hamburg, Germany, 1962.
     Atlantic LS2-7001 (2 discs)   Tape CS2-7001.   Cart. TP2-7001
       CRA   Aug.   p62.   300w.   3
       GR   Aug.   p353.   200w. $3\frac{1}{2}$
       HF   Aug.   p111.   400w.   3
       RC   July   p14.   100w.   4
       SMG   Sept.   p25.   125w.   5
       SOU   June   p43.   500w.   3
       SR   Aug.   p88.   37w. $2\frac{1}{2}$
       VV   June 13   p36.   150w. $4\frac{1}{2}$

62   BEAU Dommage.   Une Autre Jour Arrive en Ville.   Capitol ST
     70 048
       CC   May   p35.   50w. $2\frac{1}{2}$
       OLR   Dec.   p294.   25w.   3

63   BE-BOP Deluxe.   Live! In the Air Age.   Harvest SKB 11666.
     Cart. 8xtt 11666.   Cass. 4XTT 11666
       MG   Oct.   p55.   150w.   3
       RR   Sept.   p93.   100w. $3\frac{1}{2}$
       RRE   Nov.-Dec.   p19.   700w. $2\frac{1}{2}$

RS Oct. 6 p85. 550w. 3
SR Dec. 200w. 2½
TP Sept. p33-4. 300w. 2

64 BE-BOP Deluxe. Modern Music. Harvest ST-11575
CAC Jan. p477. 150w. 2
CIR March 17 p19. 175w. 3½
GP March p112. 175w. 4
RRE Jan. -Feb. p23. 125w. 3½

65 BECK, Bogert and Appice. Live in Japan. Epic ECPJ-4 (2 discs) (Japan)
AU Feb. p79. 200w. 3
RSP Nov. -Dec. p27. 50w. 4

66 BECK, Jeff with the Jan Hammer Group. Live. Epic PE 34433. Tape PEA-34433. Cass. PET-34433
CIR June 23 p67. 200w. 1½
DB June 16 p31. 325w. 3
GP Sept. p118. 175w. 4
RR July p96. 25w. 3
RRE March-April p24-6. 1200w. 4½
RS June 16 p58, 60. 400w. 1½
SR Sept. p94. 150w. 2
TP April/May p28. 500w. 5

67 BEDFORD, David. Instructions for Angels. Virgin V2090 (E)
MM Oct. 8 p32. 325w. 3½

68 BEDFORD, David. The Odyssey. Virgin V2070
SOU Feb. p40. 600w. 1
TP Dec./Jan. p33-4. 375w. 3

69 BEE GEES. Children of the World. ROS RS-1-3003. Cart. 8T1-3003. Cass. CT1-3003
CAC Jan. p477. 100w. 4
GR Jan. p1197. 50w. 3½
MG Feb. p55. 125w. 2½
RR Jan. p84. 100w. 4½
SR Jan. p86. 100w. 2

70 BEE Gees. Gold. RSO RS-1-3006 (Reissue)
CRE March p63. 50w. 3½
RS Jan. 13 p47. 25w. 2½

71 BEE GEES. Here at Last ... Live. RSO RS-2-3901
MM Aug 13. p20. 250w. 4½
RR Sept. p93. 100w. 3½
SR Sept. p94, 52. 125w. 5

72 BENNETT, Brian. Rock Dreams. DJM DJF 20499 (E)
NK Spring p39. 50w. 2½

73 BERRY, Mike. Rock's in My Head.   Sire SASD 7524
        CIR   March 31 p21.   300w. $2\frac{1}{2}$
        CRA   April p106.   75w. $1\frac{1}{2}$
        MG   April p51.   125w. $4\frac{1}{2}$
        RS   Jan. 27 p70.   125w. $3\frac{1}{2}$
        TP   Feb. /Mar. p29-30.   750w.   4

74 BETTS, Dickey. Dickey Betts & Great Southern.   Arista AL
    4123
        AU   Sept. p91.   150w.   3
        CIR   Aug. 4 p58.   350w.   3
        GP   June p136.   125w.   3
        GR   July p234.   50w.   3
        MG   June p52.   125w.   1
        MM   April 30 p30.   200w.   2
        RRE   May-June p26-7.   425w.   3
        RS   June 16 p64, 66.   400w.   2
        SR   Sept. p94.   150w.   3

75 BETWEEN. Contemplation. Wergo
        EUR   V2/#2 p22.   175w.   4

76 BIG John's Rock 'n' Roll Circus.   On the Road.   DJM DJF
    20511 (E)
        MM   Aug. 6 p17.   50w.   2

77 BIG Wha-Koo.   ABC AB-971
        CMR   June p11.   150w.   3
        MG   May p51.   125w. $4\frac{1}{2}$

78 BILLION Dollar Babies. Battle Axe.   Polydor PD 1-6100.
    Cass. CT 1-6100.   Cart. 8T 1-6100
        CIR   Sept. 29 p59-60.   300w. $2\frac{1}{2}$
        CRA   July p68.   125w. $2\frac{1}{2}$
        HF   July p149.   150w.   3
        MM   Aug. 13 p20.   250w. $1\frac{1}{2}$
        RS   July 14 p67.   450w.   3
        SR   Oct. p90-1.   200w. $3\frac{1}{2}$

79 BIRTH Control. Backdoor Possibilities.   Brain 60-019 (W.
    Germany)
        RS   March 10 p69.   100w.   2

80 BISHOP, Elvin. Hometown Boy Makes Good.   Capricorn CP
    0176 M80176
        CAC   April p9-10.   200w. $2\frac{1}{2}$
        CRA   Jan. p78.   200w. $2\frac{1}{2}$
        CRE   March p59.   300w. $2\frac{1}{2}$
        MG   Feb. p54.   125w.   2
        MM   Jan. 29 p25.   250w.   3
        RS   Feb. 10 p103.   400w.   3
        SR   March p94.   50w.   0

81 BISHOP, Elvin. Raisin' Hell: Elvin Bishop Live! Capricorn
    2CP0185 (2 discs); Tape L80185; Cass. L50185
        CIR Nov. 10 p60. 125w.   2
        GP   Dec. p153. 25w. $3\frac{1}{2}$
        MM   Oct. 8 p29. 200w. $3\frac{1}{2}$
        RS   Nov. 3 p104. 350w.   3
        SR   Dec. 175w.   3

82 BLACK Oak Arkansas. Ten-Year Overnight Success.   MCA
    2224
        CAC April p8. 125w. $2\frac{1}{2}$
        CIR Jan. 31 p13-4. 300w.   1
        MM   March 19 p30. 150w. $1\frac{1}{2}$

83 BLACK Sabbath. Technical Ecstasy.   Warner Bros. BS 2969
        AU   March p88. 200w.   2
        GP   March p113. 100w.   4
        SR   Feb. p87. 100w.   2

84 BLACKFOOT Sue. Strangers.   Import IMP 1007
        TP   Nov. p40. 125w.   4

85 BLOCK, Rory. I'm in Love.   Blue Goose 2022
        RS   April 7 p75. 550w.   3

86 BLOCK, Rory. Intoxication.   Chrysalis (E)
        MM   Jan. 7 p16. 50w.   3

87 BLONDIE.   Private Stock PS 2023
        CIR June 23 p62. 300w. $2\frac{1}{2}$
        CRA March p74. 300w.   2
        MG   April p51. 125w. $3\frac{1}{2}$
        MM   April 9 p22. 350w.   3
        PRM Feb. p35. 350w.   3
        RC   April p4. 250w.   4
        RS   April 7 p69. 450w. $2\frac{1}{2}$
        TP   Feb./March p30. 375w.   4
        ZZ   May p39. 125w. $2\frac{1}{2}$

88 BLOOMFIELD, Mike. Analine.   Takoma B 1059
        GP   Dec. p153. 75w. $3\frac{1}{2}$
        SR   Dec. 450w.   4

89 BLOOMFIELD, Mike. If You Love These Blues, Play 'em As
    You Please.   Guitar Player Records 3002
        FOL Aug. p26-7. 350w. $1\frac{1}{2}$
        RRE Jan.-Feb. p24. 225w.   4
        RS   March 10 p68. 300w. $3\frac{1}{2}$

90 BLUE. Another Night Time Flight.   Rocket MCA PIG 2290
        CRA Oct. p78. 275w. $3\frac{1}{2}$
        GR   Oct. p715. 25w.   3
        MM   Sept. 17 p212. 300w.   2

91   BLUE Oyster Cult. Spectres. Columbia 35019
      MM Nov. 5 p20. 650w. 4
      RC Dec. p13-4. 250w. 4
      RS Dec. 29 p66, 68. 1000w. $3\frac{1}{2}$

92   BLUNSTONE, Colin. Planes. Epic EPC 81592 (E)
      CAC Aug. p165. 250w. 3
      TP June/July p38. 200w. $1\frac{1}{2}$

93   BOLIN, Tommy. Private Eyes. Columbia 34329
      GP Feb. p113. 25w. 3

94   BOND, Graham, Organization. The Beginning of Jazz Rock.
      Charly CR 300017 (E) (Reissue)
      NK Summer p38. 50w. 4

95   BONOFF, Karla. Columbia PC 34672. Tape PCA 34672.
      Cass. PCT 34672
      AU Dec. p116. 150w. 3
      CIR Dec. 8 p77. 450w. 2
      CRA Oct. p78. 250w. 4
      FOL Dec. p24-5. 300w. 5
      HF Nov. 475w. $3\frac{1}{2}$
      MG Nov. p52. 25w. $3\frac{1}{2}$
      RC Nov. p11. 150w. 4
      RS Oct. 20 p90. 325w. $2\frac{1}{2}$
      VV Oct. 3 p65. 50w. $3\frac{1}{2}$

96   BOOMTOWN Rats. Mercury SRM 1-1188
      GR Nov. p920. 75w. 2
      MM Aug. 27 p21. 450w. 5
      RS Dec. 1 p82. 375w. $2\frac{1}{2}$
      VV Nov. 28 p66. 50w. 4

97   BOSTON. Epic PE 34188
      CAC April p10. 200w. 4
      RO May p19. 650w. 3

98   BOWIE, Davie. Heroes. RCA APL 2522
      MM Oct. 1 p23. 900w. 4
      RC Dec. p5. 150w. 4
      RR Dec. p85-6. 125w. $4\frac{1}{2}$
      VV Dec. 19 p79. 400w. $3\frac{1}{2}$
      ZZ Oct. p32. 500w. $3\frac{1}{2}$

99   BOWIE, David. Low. RCA CPL 1-2030
      CAC March p452. 250w. $1\frac{1}{2}$
      CIR March 17 p14. 1050w. 3
      CIR March 31 p15. 400w. $3\frac{1}{2}$
      CRA April p97. 650w. $3\frac{1}{2}$
      DB May 19 350w. p17. 5
      GR April p1617. 200w. 3
      HF April p138. 250w. 3

MG   May   p51.   150w.   4½
MM   Jan.   22 p23.   550w.   3
PRM   Feb.   p34.   350w.   4
RC   April   p2.   250w.   3
RR   April   p87.   75w.   2
RS   April 21   575w.   p64.   2½
RSP   March-April p61.   300w.   2
SR   May   p83.   150w.   3
ZZ   Feb.   p30.   950w.   4

100   BOWIE, David.   Starting Point.   London LC50007 (Reissue)
      AU   Dec.   p115.   75w.   1
      TP   Oct.   p42.   125w.   2

101   BOWN, Andy.   Come Back Romance, All Is Forgiven.   Capitol
      ST 11672
      RS   Sept.   22 p77.   350w.   3
      TP   Sept.   p35.   100w.   0

102   BOXER.   Absolutely.   Epic PE 34812
      GR   Sept.   p522.   50w.   2½
      MM   July 16   p22.   300w.   0
      TP   Nov.   p38.   225w.   2

103   The BOYS.   NEMS NEL 6001 (E)
      MM   Sept. 10   p23.   325w.   3½
      TP   Dec.   p38.   250w.   1½

104   BRAMLETT, Bonnie.   Lady's Choice.   Capricorn CPO169
      GR   Jan.   p1197.   50w.   3½

105   BRAND X.   Livestock.   Arista 9824
      MM   Dec. 3   p28.   425w.   4

106   BRAND X.   Moroccan Roll.   Passport (dist. by ABC)
      98022
      CK   Aug.   p48.   150w.   3½
      MG   July   p53.   125w.   3
      MM   April 30   p20.   500w.   5
      RS   July 14   p69-70.   400w.   2½

107   BRAND X.   Unorthodox Behaviour.   Passport PPSO 98019
      CRA   March   p73.   50w.   3

108   BRANSCOMBE, Alan.   The Day I Met the Blues.   EMI EMC
      3197 (E)
      MM   Oct. 29   p28.   375w.   2½

109   BRECKER Brothers.   Don't Stop the Music.   Arista AL 4122
      DB   Oct. 6   p33.   250w.   3
      MM   Sept. 3   p22.   125w.   2
      RS   June 16   p58-60.   400w.   1½

110   BRIGHTON, Ian.   Marsh Gas.   Bead 3 (E)
          MM   Nov. 5 p32.   350w. $3\frac{1}{2}$

111   BROMBERG, Dave.   How Late'll You Play 'til. Fantasy
       79009 (2 discs)
          AU   Jan. p76.   250w.   5
          CMR   June p14.   300w.   4
          GR   May p1758.   50w.   2
          MM   Feb. 26 p29.   500w.   4
          SR   Feb. p87.   150w.   4
          ZZ   Jan.   450w. $3\frac{1}{2}$

112   BROOKS, Elkie.   Two Days Away.   A&M SP-4631
          CAC   Aug. p165.   200w. $3\frac{1}{2}$
          GR   Aug. p354.   100w.   3
          MG   Oct. p59.   75w. $1\frac{1}{2}$
          MM   June 4 p20.   450w.   4
          RR   Aug. p84.   25w.   2
          SR   Oct. p91.   225w. $4\frac{1}{2}$

113   BROWN, Peter and Piblokto.   My Last Band.   Harvest SASM
       2017 (E)
          MM   Sept. 3 p17.   100w.   3

114   BROWNE, Jackson.   The Pretender.   Asylum 7E-1079 ET8-
       1079
          AU   Feb. p74.   200w. $3\frac{1}{2}$
          AU   March p78.   400w.   1
          CIR   Jan. 31 p10-1.   850w. $3\frac{1}{2}$
          CRA   Jan. p68-9.   1100w.   3
          MG   Jan.   625w. $3\frac{1}{2}$
          RC   June p2.   350w. $4\frac{1}{2}$
          RO   May p11.   800w. $3\frac{1}{2}$
          RR   Jan. p84.   150w.   2
          RS   Jan. 27 p62, 64-5.   1750w.   3
          SR   March p91-2.   700w.   4

115   BROWNSVILLE Station.   Private Stock PS 2026
          MG   July p51.   150w. $4\frac{1}{2}$

116   BRUCE, Jack.   How's Tricks.   RSO 239180 (E)
          CIR   Aug. 4 p60.   200w. $1\frac{1}{2}$
          GR   June p110.   75w.   3
          MM   May 14 p32.   450w.   4
          RR   July p96.   50w. $3\frac{1}{2}$
          RSP   May-June p21.   550w. $1\frac{1}{2}$
          VV   June 6 p47, 49.   425w.   4

117   BUCHANAN, Roy.   Loading Zone.   Atlantic SD 18219.   Tape
       TP 18219.   Cass. CS18219
          CIR   Sept. 29 p59.   250w.   3
          GP   Aug. p119.   150w.   4
          RSP   May-June p20.   375w. $3\frac{1}{2}$

SR' Oct. p86-7. 300w. 4

118 BUCKACRE. Morning Comes. MCA 2218
     CRA Jan. p79. 100w. 2½

119 BUCKEYE Politicians. Look at Me Now. Utopia BUU-1823
     BUSI-1823
     SR Jan. p86. 50w. 4

120 BUCKINGHAM, Lindsey and Stevie Nicks. Polydor 3177 240
     (Reissue)
     CAC April p10-1. 150w. 3
     MM Feb. 19 p26. 325w. 1

121 BUFFALO, Norton. Lovin' in the Valley of the Moon. Capi-
     tol ST 11625. Tape 8X 11625. Cass. 4X 11625
     AU Dec. p116. 200w. 3
     MG Oct. p59. 75w. 1½
     RS Sept. 8 p117. 500w. 3
     SR Dec. 200w. 3½

122 BUFFET, Jimmy. Changes in Latitudes, Changes in Attitudes.
     ABC AB-990
     CIR June 23 p65. 300w. 1
     CMP July p40. 150w. 4
     CRA May p80. 350w. 3½
     CS April 21 p18. 300w. 3½
     FOL Sept. p18-20. 1250w. 4½
     MM May 28 p23. 150w. 3½
     RC April p4. 100w. 1½
     RR Sept. p93. 50w. 2½
     RS April 7 p80. 200w. 2
     RSP May-June p60, 62. 700w. 4
     SR June p94. 125w. 3

123 BURGESS, Sonny. Legendary Sun Performer. Charly CR 30
     136 (E) (Reissue)
     NK Autumn p50. 150w. 4

124 BURLESQUE. Acupuncture. Arista ARTY 151 (E)
     MM Feb. 12 p26. 400w. 4

125 CAFE Jacques. Round the Back. Columbia JC 35294
     MM Nov. 12 p20. 325w. 3½

126 CAIN, Jonathon, Band. Windy City Breakdown. Bearsville
     BR 6969
     CRA Aug. p76. 300w. 3

127 CALE, John. Guts. Island ILPS 9459. Cart. Y 81-9459.
     Cass. 2C19459
     HF Aug. p111-12. 225w. 3½
     MG June p52. 200w. 3½

SR   Aug.   p81-2.   700w.   5

128   CALIFORNIA, Randy.   Future Games.   (no label cited)
VV   April 4 p51.   200w. $2\frac{1}{2}$

129   CALVERT, Robert.   Capt Lockhead and the Starfighters.   Import LMP 1011 (E)
TP   Oct.   p41-2.   300w.   2

130   CAMEL.   Rain Dances.   Decca (E)
MM   Nov. 12 p29.   350w. $3\frac{1}{2}$

131   CAMEO.   Cardiac Arrest.   Casablanca CAL 2015
BM   Oct.   p48.   125w.   4
MM   Oct. 22 p18.   125w. $3\frac{1}{2}$
SC   No. 1 p16.   75w. $1\frac{1}{2}$

132   CAMPI, Roy.   Born to Rock.   Rollin' Rock LP011
NK   Autumn p45.   100w. $3\frac{1}{2}$
RC   Nov. p8-9.   200w. $2\frac{1}{2}$
WHO Nov. p40-1.   325w.   4

133   CAMPI, Roy.   Rockabilly Rocket.   Rollin' Rock LP 013
RC   Oct.   p3.   150w. $2\frac{1}{2}$
RSP 1:3 p33.   250w.   2

134   CAN.   Flow Motion.   Harvest 1C 062-31837 (Germany)
CAC   March p453.   100w.   3
EUR   No. 7/8 p38-9.   325w.   2
MM   Jan. 8 p18.   250w.   2
RS   March 10 p69, 71.   100w.   2
TP   Dec. -Jan. p27.   175w.   2

135   CAN.   Opener.   United Artists SLS 50400 (E) (Reissue)
CAC   Feb.   p414.   125w.   3
MM   Jan. 8 p18.   250w. $3\frac{1}{2}$

136   CAN.   Saw Delight.   Virgin V2079 (E)
MM   March 19 p28.   400w. $4\frac{1}{2}$
RS   Aug. 11 p55.   50w. $2\frac{1}{2}$
TP   June/July p39.   125w. $2\frac{1}{2}$

137   CAPTAIN Beyond.   Dawn Explosion.   Warner Bros. BS 3047
GP   Oct.   p129.   150w.   4
RS   Aug. 25 p60.   300w. $1\frac{1}{2}$

138   CARAVAN.   Better by Far.   Arista SPARTY 1008 (E)
MM   Oct. 8 p30.   375w.   4
RR   Nov.   p114.   100w. $2\frac{1}{2}$
TP   Dec.   p38.   225w. $2\frac{1}{2}$

139   CARAVAN.   The Canterbury Tales.   Decca DKL-R 8/1-2 (2 discs) (E)

    CAC Feb. p414. 300w. 2
    GR Feb. p1335. 25w. $3\frac{1}{2}$
    TP April-May p31. 500w. 4

140 CARMEN, Eric. Boats Against the Current. Arista AB 4214.
     Cart. 83014214. Cass. 5301 4214
     AU Dec. p114. 150w. 1
     CIR Nov. 10 p57-8. 425w. 4
     HF Nov. 275w. $2\frac{1}{2}$
     MG Nov. p52. 50w. 2
     RC Oct. p8. 50w. $1\frac{1}{2}$
     RS Sept. 22 p70. 500w. 1
     SR Dec. 175w. $1\frac{1}{2}$
     TP Nov. p40. 250w. 0
     VV Sept. 19 p66. 400w. 2

141 CARTER, Valerie. Just a Stone's Throw Away. Columbia PC
     34155
     CIR April 14 p18-9. 550w. $4\frac{1}{2}$
     CRA May p81. 400w. 3
     GR Aug. p354. 100w. 4
     PRM April p35. 275w. $2\frac{1}{2}$
     RS March 24 p62. 400w. 4
     RS April 7 p83. 50w. $3\frac{1}{2}$
     SR June p95. 75w. 3

142 CATE Brothers. Band. Asylum 7E-1116
     MM Oct. 29 p25. 200w. $4\frac{1}{2}$

143 CATE Bros. In One Eye and Out the Other. Asylum 7E-
     1080 ET 8-1080
     BM Jan. p52. 150w. 3
     CIR Feb. 28 p16. 275w. $4\frac{1}{2}$
     HF Feb. p144. 50w. 3
     MG Jan. 200w. $2\frac{1}{2}$
     SR March p94. 100w. 2

144 CERRONE. Love in C Minor. Cotillion 9913
     MM April 2 p22. 50w. 1

145 CERRONE. Paradise. Cotillion 9917
     MM Sept. 17 p21. 175w. $1\frac{1}{2}$

146 CHAMPS. Best of. London ZGH 141 (E) (Reissue)
     NK Summer p37. 50w. 4
     SMG Sept. p25. 75w. $3\frac{1}{2}$

147 CHAMPS. Everybody's Rock In. Challenge CHS 2500 (E)
     (Reissue)
     RSP March-April p31. 300w. $2\frac{1}{2}$

148 CHAMPS. Go Champs Go. London LPX 459 (E) (Reissue)
     NK Winter p37. 75w. 4

149   CHAMPS. Rare Items, 1958-1962. Decca LPX 498 (Reissue)
       NK Autumn p42. 50w. 4

150   CHAPIN, Harry. Dance Band of the Titanic. Elektra 9E-301
       (2 discs)
          MM Sept. 24 p28. 300w. 3
          RC Oct. p6-7. 250w. 4½
          SOU Nov. p56. 300w. 4

151   CHAPIN, Harry. On the Road to Kingdom Come. Elektra
       7E-1082 ET8-1082
          SR Feb. p87. 150w. 2

152   CHAPIN, Tom. Life Is Like That. Fantasy F-9520
          SR April p89. 100w. 5

153   CHAPLIN, Blondie. Asylum 7E-1095
          CIR May 26 p58. 175w. 4
          MM Sept. 3 p18. 175w. 2½
          PRM April p35. 250w. 4½
          VV Aug. 22 p55, 57. 400w. 4
          VV Oct. 3 p65. 100w. 3½

154   CHARLIE. No Second Chance. Janus JXS 7032. Cass. H5-
       7032. Cart. H8-7032
          CAC April p11. 250w. 2½
          HF Aug. p112. 350w. 4
          MM April 2 p20. 175w. 2½
          RC Aug. p11. 75w. 2½

155   CHATER, Kerry. Part Time Love. Warner BS 3008
          OLR Dec. p291. 25w. 1½

156   CHEAP Trick. Epic PE-34400. Cart. PEA-34400
          AU Oct. p175. 250w. 3½
          CIR May 12 p15. 100w. 2
          RS May 5 p61. 375w. 4
          SR Sept. p75. 225w. 2

157   CHEAP Trick. In Color. Epic PE 34884
          AU Dec. p114. 250w. 4½
          CIR Dec. 8 p74. 250w. 3½
          CIR Dec. 8 p74. 325w. 3
          DB Dec. 15 p19. 350w. 3
          HF Nov. 50w. 3½
          MG Nov. p49. 600w. 4
          MG Nov. p52. 25w. 4
          MM Sept. 17 p21. 450w. 4
          RS Sept. 22 p61, 63. 950w. 3½
          TP Oct. p39. 300w. 3½
          VV Nov. 28 p66. 50w. 3½
          WHO Nov. p42. 1000w. 3

158   CHICAGO.   IX--Their Greatest Hits.   Columbia PC 33900
      (Reissue)
         SMG Jan. p26. 300w. 4

159   CHICAGO.   X.   Columbia PC 34200
         RSP Jan. -Feb. p23. 150w. $2\frac{1}{2}$

160   CHICAGO.   XI.   Columbia JC 34860
         RC Oct. p4. 125w. 3
         RS Nov. 3 p93-4. 1400w. $3\frac{1}{2}$
         RSP Nov. -Dec. p22. 450w. $2\frac{1}{2}$
         SOU Dec. p56. 300w. 4

161   CHILLIWACK.   Dreams, Dreams, Dreams.   Mushroom MRS
      5006
         RS March 24 p71. 300w. $3\frac{1}{2}$

162   CHINA.   Rocket PIG 2292
         MG Nov. p51. 25w. $2\frac{1}{2}$
         MM Dec. 21 p15. 50w. 2
         SOU Nov. p56. 150w. 2

163   CHRISTMAS, Keith.   Stories Form the Human Zoo.   Manti-
      core (E)
         MM Jan. 22 p23. 250w. $3\frac{1}{2}$

164   CHRONICLE.   Like a Message from the Stars.   All Ears CH
      11477
         TP Nov. p42. 150w. 2

165   CITY Boy.   Dinner at the Ritz.   Mercury SRM1 1121
         CAC June p90. 225w. $1\frac{1}{2}$
         CRA May p71. 175w. 4
         MM March 26 p21. 250w. 4
         RS April 7 p83. 100w. $2\frac{1}{2}$

166   CITY Boy.   Young Men Gone West.   Mercury SRM-1-1182
         MM Oct. 8 p29. 325w. 4
         RC Nov. p16. 75w. 3
         TP Nov. p38. 250w. 4

167   CLAPTON, Eric.   No Reason to Cry.   RSO RS-103004.   Cart.
      T1-3004
         AU Sept. p91. 200w. 4
         GR Jan. p1197. 50w. $1\frac{1}{2}$
         SR Feb. p88. 150w. 4

168   CLAPTON, Eric.   Slowhand.   RSO RS 1 3030
         RC Dec. p7. 150w. $4\frac{1}{2}$
         RS Dec. 29 p68-9. 600w. $3\frac{1}{2}$

169   CLARK, Gene.   Roadmaster'.   A&M 27 897 ET
         RS March 10 p71. 50w. $2\frac{1}{2}$

170 CLARK, Gene. Two Sides to Every Story. RSO 2394176
      CAC   June   p92, 94.   200w.   3
      CMR   June   p17.   150w.   3
      MM   March 26   p19.   800w. $4\frac{1}{2}$
      RS   May 18   p65.   225w.   1
      ZZ   March   p24.   650w. $3\frac{1}{2}$

171 CLASH.   Epic 82000 (E)
      CRA   Sept.   p70.   150w.   3
      MM   April 16   p21.   550w.   3
      RR   July   p95-6.   75w.   3
      TP   Sept.   p37.   200w.   4
      ZZ   May   p39.   150w. $1\frac{1}{2}$

172 CLIMAX Blues Band.   Gold Plated.   Sire - SASD 7523.   Cart.
    8147-7523H.   Cass. 5147-7523H
      CAC   Jan.   p376.   100w.   3
      GR   Jan.   p1197.   25w. $3\frac{1}{2}$
      SR   Aug.   p87.   100w. $3\frac{1}{2}$

173 CLOVER.   Unavailable.   Mercury SRM 11169
      CAC   June   p94.   250w. $2\frac{1}{2}$
      CRA   Oct.   p78.   300w.   3
      MM   Jan. 7   p17.   200w. $3\frac{1}{2}$
      RS   Sept. 8   p117-8.   250w. $2\frac{1}{2}$
      VV   Oct. 3   p65.   50w.   1
      ZZ   April   p46-7.   500w.   3

174 CLOVERDALE, David.   Whitesnake.   EMI Purple (E)
      CAC   Aug.   p162.   300w. $3\frac{1}{2}$
      MM   June 11   p19.   175w. $3\frac{1}{2}$

175 CLUSTER and Eno.   Sky (E)
      EUR   V2/#2   p23.   175w.   4

176 COCHRAN, Jackie.   Rockabilly Legend.   Rollin' Rock 010 (Re-
    issue)
      RC   May   p9.   250w.   3
      SMG   Sept.   p26.   125w.   4

177 COCKER, Joe.   Live in L A.   Cube HIFLY23 (E) Cart.
    KFLY23
      CAC   Feb.   p416.   100w.   3
      GR   April   p1617.   50w.   3
      MM   Jan. 22   p23.   250w. $3\frac{1}{2}$

178 COFFEY, D.   Back Home.   Westbound 300.
      MM   July 16   p27.   50w.   2

179 COHEN, Leonard.   Death of a Ladies Man.   Warner BS 3125
      MM   Nov. 12   p20.   550w.   0
      RS   Feb. 9   p93, 95.   1250w. $3\frac{1}{2}$

180   COLLINS Kids. Town Hall Party.   CCL 1141 (E)
      NK   Spring p40. 50w. 3

181   COLOSSEUM II.   Electric Savage.   MCA 2294
      MM   July 16 p21. 350w. 4

182   COMMANDER Cody. Rock 'n' Roll Again.   Arista AL 4125
      RS   Sept. 8 p116. 400w. 2

183   COMMANDER Cody and His Lost Planet Airmen.   We've Got
      a Live One Here.   (2LP set) Warner Brothers K 66043
      CMR   June p16. 200w. 3

184   COODER, Ry.   Chicken Skin Music.   Reprise MS 2254
      CMP   April p58. 125w. 4
      FOL   June p19-20. 550w. 5
      FR   Jan. p26. 200w. 4
      GP   Feb. p113. 50w. 4
      MM   Jan. 15 p17. 250w. $3\frac{1}{2}$
      SR   Jan. p84. 200w. 4

185   COODER, Ry.   Show Time.   Warner BS 3059.   Cart M8 3059.
      Cass. M5 3059
      CIR   Oct. 27 p67-8. 300w. 2
      CIR   Dec. 22 p66-7. 600w. 4
      GR   Nov. p920. 75w. $2\frac{1}{2}$
      HF   Sept. p137. 150w. $3\frac{1}{2}$
      MG   Nov. p51. 25w. 2
      MM   Aug. 13 p20. 450w. $4\frac{1}{2}$
      RC   Oct. p13-4. 200w. 4
      RR   Oct. p88. 50w. 4
      RS   Aug. 11 p63, 65. 350w. 3
      SR   Dec. 250w. 4

186   COOLIDGE, Rita. Anytime... Anywhere.   A&M SP-4616.
      Cart. 8T-4616.   Cass. CS-4616
      CAC   June p94. 200w. $2\frac{1}{2}$
      CMP   July p37. 175w. 4
      SR   Sept. p95-6. 100w. 2

187   CORNWELL, Charlotte, Julie Covington, and Rula Lenska.
      Rock Follies.   Polydor 2302 054 (E)
      GR   May p1757. 50w. 1

188   COSTELLO, Elvis.   My Aim Is True.   Columbia JC 35037.
      Cart. JCT 35037.   Cass. JCA 35037
      HF   Dec. p138. 800w. $4\frac{1}{2}$
      MG   Dec. p55. 125w. 4
      MM   July 23 p17. 400w. 5
      RC   Nov. p2. 100w. $4\frac{1}{2}$
      RS   Dec. 1 p69-70, 73. 1000w. 4
      TP   Oct. p42-3. 300w. 5
      VV   Nov. 28 p66. 50w. 4

ZZ Aug. p34. 350w. 4

189 COUGAR, Johnny. Chestnut Street Incident. MCA 225
CRA Jan. p71. 125w. 1

190 COYNE, Kevin. In Living Black and White. Virgin PZ
34757
MM Feb. 19 p25. 450w. 3
RR April p87. 50w. 3
TP Sept. p35. 150w. 3
VV Oct. 3 p65. 50w. 4

191 CRACK of Dawn. Columbia ES 90336 (Canada)
OLR March p54. 25w. 3

192 CRACK the Sky. Lifesong LS 6000
ZZ June p38-40. 350w. $2\frac{1}{2}$

193 CRACK the Sky. Animal Notes. Lifesong LS6005
CRA March p78. 150w. 3
CRE March p63. 50w. $1\frac{1}{2}$
MM May 21 p22. 250w. 3
ZZ June p38-40. 350w. $3\frac{1}{2}$

194 CRACK the Sky. Live! Lifesong Records [no serial number]
GP Aug. p120. 50w. 3

195 CRACKIN'. Makings of a Dream. Warner BS 2989
HF April p148. 50w. 3

196 CRAIG, Eela. One Niter. Vertigo 6360 635 (West Germany)
CK Dec. p73. 50w. $2\frac{1}{2}$
TP Feb./March p26. 75w. $2\frac{1}{2}$

197 CRAWFORD, Randy. Every Thing Must Change. Warner BS
2970
VV Sept. 5 p60. 300w. 4

198 CRAWLER. Epic PE 34900
AU Dec. p116. 100w. 1
GR Sept. p522. 100w. 5
MG Dec. p56. 50w. 1
MM July 2 p22. 200w. $3\frac{1}{2}$
RC Nov. p14. 50w. 3
RS Oct. 20 p92. 325w. $3\frac{1}{2}$
TP Nov. p39. 150w. 2

199 CRAZY Cavan and the Rhythm Rockers. Crazy Rhythm. Rockhouse 7510 (E)
RSP 1:3 p31. 100w. $1\frac{1}{2}$

200 CRAZY Cavan and the Rhythm Rockers. Our Own Way of
Rockin. Charly CRL 5001 (E)

MM   May 28 p24.   250w.   5
RSP V1/#3 p31.   125w.   3

201 CREACH, Papa John.   The Cat and the Fiddle.   DJM 11 (E)
     MM   Nov. 5 p19.   275w.   2½

202-3 CREAM.   Disreali Gears.   RSO 3010 (Reissue)
     RSP March/April p11-2.   100w.   2½

204 CREAM.   Fresh Cream.   RSO 3009 (Reissue)
     RSP March/April p11.   200w.   2

205 CREAM.   Goodbye.   RSO 3013 (Reissue)
     RSP March/April p12.   150w.   3

206 CREAM.   Live.   RSO 3014 (Reissue)
     RSP March/April p12.   75w.   2½

207 CREAM.   Live, Vol. 2.   RSO 3015 (Reissue)
     RSP March/April p12.   350w.   3½

208 CREAM.   Wheels of Fire.   RSO 3802 (2 discs) (Reissue)
     RSP March/April p12.   150w.   3

209 CROCE, Jim.   The Faces.   Lifesong Elsdp 900 (E) (Reissue)
     MM   Aug. 6 p16.   50w.   3½

210 CROCE, Jim.   Photographs & Memories.   Lifesong ELSLP
     5000 (E)
     CMR Jan. p30.   100w.   4
     MM   Jan. 29 p25.   25w.   3½

211 CROSBY, Stills & Nash.   CSN.   Atlantic SD 19104.   Cart.
     TP 19104.   Cass. CS 19104
     CIR Sept. 8 p59.   600w.   2½
     CRA Sept. p82.   775w.   2
     CS   Nov. p19.   225w.   3½
     MM   June 25 p22.   400w.   3½
     RC   July p10.   250w.   5
     RR   Aug. p83.   150w.   1½
     SR   Sept. p108.   725.   1
     VV   July 4 p45.   500w.   3
     ZZ   July p34.   750w.   2

212 CROSBY, David, Graham Nash.   Live.   ABC AA 1042
     MM   Nov. 19 p27.   375w.   1½
     RS   Feb. 9 p96.   325w.   3

213 CUMMINGS, Burton.   Burton Cummings.   Portrait PR 34261.
     Cass. PC 34241
     AU   Feb. p75.   600w.   2½
     CIR Jan. 17 p16-7.   400w.   2
     HF   Feb. p144.   50w.   1

OLR June p14. 25w. 3½
RM Jan. p7. 600w. 5
SR Feb. p92. 100w. 2

214 CUMMINGS, Burton. My Own Way to Rock. Portrait PR
34698. Cass. PRA-34698
AU Oct. p173. 200w. 3
CIR Oct. 13 p76-7. 200w. 2½
HF Sept. p131. 200w. 3½
MG Sept. p52. 75w. 3
RC Nov. p11. 50w. 2½
SOU Oct. p61. 200w. 4
SR Nov. p88. 350w. 5
VV Aug. 1 p51. 50w. 2½

215 CUTLER, Ivor. Jammy Smears. Virgin V2065 (E)
MM Feb. 19 p22. 100w. 4
RR Jan. p85. 25w. 3

216 DALTREY, Roger. One of the Boys. MCA 2271. Cass.
MCAC-2271. Tape MCAT-2271
CAC July p130-1. 125w. 2½
CIR Sept. 29 p58. 375w. 2
CRA Aug. p74. 300w. 4
GR July p234. 75w. 3½
MM May 21 p26. 450w. 4
RR Aug. p84. 50w. 3½
RS Aug. 11 p63. 375w. 3
SOU Sept. p63. 350w. 2
SR Oct. p91. 250w. 4
TP Sept. p33. 400w. 3

217 DAMNED. Stiff SEEZ 1 (E)
CRA Sept. p70. 150w. 3
MM Feb. 19 p24. 600w. 3½
RR May p86. 300w. 3½
RS Oct. 6 p103. 100w. 1½
ZZ March 900w. 2½

218 DANIELS, Charlie. High Lonesome. Epic 34377
CS Feb. 10 p16. 350w. 4
CM April p53. 300w. 4
CMP March p38. 100w. 2
CMR June p10. 300w. 3
DB March 24 400w. 3½
GP May p128. 75w. 3
MG April p55. 150w. 3
MM Feb. 26 p26. 300w. 1
RO May p16. 375w. 4

219 DANIELS, Charlie. Nightrider. Kama Sutra KSLP 7009
(Reissue)
CMR June p17. 150w. 3

220 DANKO, Rick. Arista AL 4141
     VV Dec. 19 p77-80. 250w. 2

221 DANNY and the Juniors. Rock 'n' Roll Is Here to Stay.
     Singular 569
     RSP March-April p29. 300w. 3

222 DAVIS, Hank. I'm Hank David. Reditu LP115 (Netherlands)
     NK Winter p33. 50w. 3

223 DEAD Boys. Young, Loud and Snotty. Sire SR 6038
     CIR Dec. 8 p75-6. 475w. 3½
     HF Nov. 250w. 3
     MG Dec. p55. 50w. 3
     MM Dec. 21 50w. 0
     RS Nov. 17 p96. 450w. 3½

224 DEAF School. Don't Stop the World. Warner BS K56364 (E)
     MM March 19 p30. 600w. 2½

225 DEAF School. Second Honeymoon. Warner Bros. K 56280 (E)
     CRA July p80. 325w. 2½
     CIR July 7 p49. 650w. 3½
     TP Dec. 1976/Jan. 1977 p33. 300w. 4

226 DEARDOFF and Joseph. Arista AL 4092
     CIR March 17 p19-20. 25w. 0
     HF April p148. 50w. 3

227 DEEP Purple. Made in Europe. Warner PR 2995
     AU March p89. 150w. 3
     CIR Feb. 28 p13-14. 350w. 2½
     RS Jan. 27 p70. 150w. 1½

228 DEEP Purple. Powerhouse. Purple (E)
     MM Dec. 21. p15. 50w. 0

229 DEEP Purple. Shades of. Harvest SHSM 2016 (Reissue)
     CAC June p94. 250w. 2½
     MM June 11 p19. 175w. 3½
     RR June p93. 75w. 2

230 DEES, Stephen. Hip Shot. RCA APL1-2186
     CIR Sept. 8 p60. 250w. 3

231 DEJA Vu. Get It Up for Me. Capitol ST 11604
     OLR Dec. p291. 50w. 2½

232 DEJA Vu. A Story for Everyone. Capitol ST 11527
     OLR March p54. 25w. 2

233 DELANEY, Bramlett. Class Reunion. Prodigal.
     ZZ June p40. 175w. 2

234 DERRINGER, Rick.   Sweet Evil.   Blue Sky DZ-34470
        CIR   May 26   p57.   250w.   2
        MM   April 2   p19.   200w.   1½

235 DETECTIVE.   Swan Song SSK 59405 (E)
        MM   Sept. 10   p20.   50w.   1½
        RR   Sept.   p93.   25w.   2½
        RSP   May-June   p18.   800w.   2½

236 DEVILLE, Mink.   Capitol ST 11631.   Cart. 8XT 11631.   Cass.
     4XT 11631
        SR   Aug.   p87, 90.   225w.   3

237 DICTATORS.   Manifest Destiny.   Asylum 7E-1109.   Cass.
     TC5-1109.   Cart. ET8-1109
        CRA   Aug.   p74.   500w.   4
        MG   July   p51.   125w.   3
        MM   Oct. 1   p24.   400w.   5
        SOU   Nov.   p55.   250w.   3
        SR   Oct.   p94.   400w.   5
        TP   June/July   p33.   500w.   5
        ZZ   Aug.   p33.   400w.   3

238 The DINGOES.   Five Times the Sun.   A&M SP 4636
        MG   Oct.   p60.   50w.   2½
        RS   Sept. 22   p77.   325w.   3
        TP   Oct.   p41.   300w.   ½

239 DIONNE, Vincent and Michel-Georges Brégent.   Deux.   Capitol
     ST 70-052 (Canada)
        CC   Dec.   p35.   50w.   3

240 DIRTY Angels.   Kiss Tomorrow Goodbye.   Private Stock PS
     2020 8305-2020H
        MG   Feb.   p54.   100w.   3½
        SR   March   p95.   50w.   0
        TP   April/May   p30.   200w.   5

241 DIRTY Tricks.   Hit and Run.   Polydor PD1-6104
        MM   Jan. 7   p76.   225w.   2

242 DIRTY Tricks.   Night Man.   Polydor PD-1-6082
        TP   Dec. 1976/Jan. 1977   p32.   350w.   4

243 DR Buzzard's Original Savannah Band.   RCA APL1-1504
        MG   Feb.   p55.   125w.   5

244 DR Feelgood.   Be Seeing You.   United Artists UAS 30123 (E)
        MM   Sept. 17   p20.   450w.   3½
        TP   Dec.   p37.   250w.   2½

245 DR Feelgood.   Sneakin' Suspicion.   Columbia PC 34806
        AU   Dec.   p118.   150w.   2

> CRA   Sept.   p68.   400w.   2½
> MM   May 14   p28.   550w.   4½
> TP   Sept.   p34.   250w.   2½

246   DR Feelgood.   Stupidity.   UA UAS 29990 (E)
> RS   March 10   p71.   25w.   2½
> TP   Feb./March   p31-2.   350w.   4

247   DR Hook and the Medicine Show.   Sylvia's Mother.   Columbia
PC 31458
> CAC   Aug.   p167.   250w.   2½

248   DOCTORS of Madness.   Figments of Emancipation.   Polydor
2383 403 (E)
> TP   Feb./March   p32.   300w.   0

249   DODD, Cal.   New Horizons.   Rising Records RILP 102
(Canada)
> OLR   June   p140.   25w.   1½

250   DONOVAN.   Arista AB 4143.   Cart. 8301 4143.   Cass. 5301
4143
> CIR   Nov. 10   p59-60.   225w.   1½
> HF   Nov.   50w.   2
> MG   Dec.   p56.   50w.   1
> RC   Oct.   p13   200w.   2½
> SR   Dec.   150w.   2

251   DOOBIE Brothers.   Best of.   Warner BS 2978 (Reissue)
> GR   Jan.   p1197.   50w.   2½
> RS   Jan. 13   p48.   100w.   3½

252   DOOBIE Brothers.   Livin' on the Fault Line.   Warner BSK
3045.   Cart. M8 3045.   Cass. M5 3048
> CIR   Dec. 8   p73.   450w.   3½
> GR   Oct.   p715.   50w.   3
> HF   Nov.   275w.   3
> MG   Nov.   p51-52.   50w.   3
> MM   Sept. 10.   p26.   175w.   4
> RC   Nov.   p3.   75w.   4½
> RR   Nov.   p115.   25w.   3½
> RS   Nov. 3   p101.   350w.   2

253   DOOBIE Brothers.   Toulouse Street.   Stereotype WSTQ
2634QF
> AU   Jan.   p91.   400w.   3

254   DOORS.   Best of.   Elektra EQ 5035 (Reissue)
> GR   Jan.   p1194.   50w.   3

255   DOWNLINERS Sect.   The Sect.   Charly CR 30122 (Reissue)
(E)
> MM   April 16   p21.   200w.   2

255a DRAKE, Nick. Bryter Layter. Antilles AN7028
      SR Dec. 200w. $3\frac{1}{2}$

256   DRAKE, Nick. Five Leaves Left. Antilles AN (Reissue)
      CIR Jan. 31 p15-16. 325w. $3\frac{1}{2}$

257   DRISCOLL, Julie and Brian Auger. London 19964-67. Charly
      (E) (Reissue)
      MM March 19 p30. 250w. $3\frac{1}{2}$

258   DRURY, Ian. New Boots and Panties. Stiff SEEZ 4 (E)
      MM Oct. 1 p26. 650w. $4\frac{1}{2}$
      TP Dec. p37. 250w. 3

259   DUFFARD, Pascal. Dien et Fou. CBS (France)
      EUR V2/#1 p35. 300w. 4

260   DYLAN. Desire. Columbia PC-33893
      RM Jan. p8. 600w. 5

261   DYLAN. Hard Rain. Columbia PC 34349
      GR Jan. p1197. 50w. 2
      RC June p7. 200w. 4

262   DYNAMITE, Kid. Kid Dynamite. Cream CR-1003. Cart.
      8316-1003H
      SR March p104. 100w. 2

263   The EAGLES. Hotel California. Asylum 7E-1084
      AU March p82. 600w. 3
      CAC March p453-4. 100w. $2\frac{1}{2}$
      CIR March 17 p15. 450w. 1
      CM June p49. 350w. 5
      CMP April p58. 100w. 2
      CMR June p10. 150w. 3
      CRA March p68-70. 1150w. $2\frac{1}{2}$
      CRE March p60. 525w. 1
      GR March p1467. 75w. 3
      MG April p49. 750w. 4
      PRM Feb. p16. 425w. 4
      RC May p7. 150w. 3
      RO May p10. 650w. $4\frac{1}{2}$
      RR Feb. p93. 75w. $3\frac{1}{2}$
      RS Feb. 24 p62. 300w. 3
      SR April p87. 225w. 5
      ZZ Jan. 700w. 3

264   EARTHQUAKE. Levelled. Beserkley BS 0054
      CIR Sept. 15 p69. 250w. $2\frac{1}{2}$
      MM Dec. 21 p14. 200w. $2\frac{1}{2}$
      TP Sept. p36. 125w. 2

265   EASY Street. Under the Glass. Polydor 2383 444 (E)

CAC Feb. p417. 200w. $3\frac{1}{2}$
RR Sept. p93. 25w. $2\frac{1}{2}$

266 EDDIE and the Hot Rods. Life on the Line. Island ILPS
9509
VV Nov. 28 p66. 50w. 3

267 EDDIE and the Hot Rods. Teenage Depression. Island
ILPS9457. Cart. Y81-9457. Cass. ZC1-9457
CRA April p112. 50w. 1
MG June p52. 200w. $3\frac{1}{2}$
RC Oct. p7. 200w. 2
RS May 5 500w. $3\frac{1}{2}$
SR Sept. p97. 275w. 4
TP April/May p30. 525w. 0

268 EDDY, Duane. Tokyo Hits. Reprise 24027 (France) (Reissue)
NK Autumn p42. 75w. 4

269 EDGE, Graeme. Paradise Ballroom. London TXS 121
CIR Oct. 27 p68-9. 100w. 0

270 EDMUNDS, Dave. Get It. Swansong SS 8418. Cart. TP-
8418. Cass. CS-8418
AU Sept. p91. 100w. 4
CIR Sept. 15 p67. 250w. $4\frac{1}{2}$
GR June p110. 150w. $3\frac{1}{2}$
HF Aug. p112, 113. 400w. 4
MG July p51. 150w. $3\frac{1}{2}$
MM April 2 p19. 600w. $3\frac{1}{2}$
NK Spring p39. 100w. 4
RC Oct. p14. 175w. $3\frac{1}{2}$
SMG Sept. p26. 325w. $4\frac{1}{2}$
SR Aug. p90. 325w. $4\frac{1}{2}$

271 EDWARDS, John. Life, Love and Living. Cotillon SD 9909
MG May p55. 100w. 3
RS Feb. 10 p103. 225w. 3

272 EDWARDS, Jonathan. Sailboat. Warner Bros. BS 3020.
Cart. M83020. Cass. M53020
SR July p94. 150w. 5

273 EGAN, Walter. Fundamental Roll. Columbia PC-34679.
Cart. PCA-34679. Cass. PCT-34679
AU July p90. 200w. 3
CIR June 9 p54-5. 450w. $3\frac{1}{2}$
GR July p237. 25w. 3
MG June p52. 150w. $4\frac{1}{2}$
MM June 11 p19. 175w. 2
RS May 5 325w. 3
SR Sept. p97. 100w. 2

274   EGG Cream.   Egg Cream.   Pyramid PY-9008
      SR Nov. p88, 94. 150w. 5

275   801. Live. Island ILPS 9444
      DB Oct. 20. p26. 300w. 4
      RSP March-April p62. 300w. 3
      TP Feb./March p32. 450w. 4

276   ELECTRIC Light Orchestra. The Light Shines On.   EMI
      SHSM 2015 (E) (Reissue)
      CAC July p131. 125w. 3

277   ELECTRIC Light Orchestra. A New World Record.   United
      Artists UA-LA679-G UA-EA679
      CIR Jan. 17 p14-5. 400w. 3
      CIR Jan. 17 p25, 27. 800w. $2\frac{1}{2}$
      CRA Jan. p79. 175w. $3\frac{1}{2}$
      GR Feb. p1335. 25w. 3
      HF Feb. p144. 50w. 4
      RM Jan. p10. 600w. 5
      RSP Jan.-Feb. p13-5. 1575w. 4
      SR Feb. p83. 300w. 4

278   ELECTRIC Light Orchestra. Out of the Blue.   Jet UAR 100
      (2 discs) (E)
      MM Nov. 5 p26. 400w. 4

279   ELLIMAN, Yvonne. Love Me. RSO RS-1-3018 8 8T-1-3018
      c CT-1-3018
      RS June 2 p78. 175w. $2\frac{1}{2}$
      SR June p96. 75w. 2

280   EMBRYO. Bad Heads and Bad Cats.   April (West Germany)
      EUR V2/#1 p28. 300w. $4\frac{1}{2}$
      MM Feb. 12 p26. 175w. $3\frac{1}{2}$

281   EMBRYO. Live. April (West Germany)
      MM Feb. 12 p26. 175w. $3\frac{1}{2}$

282   EMERSON, Lake & Palmer. Works, Volume 1.   Atlantic SD
      2-7000 (2 discs) Cart. TP-2-7000.   Cass. CS 2-7000
      CIR July 7 p37. 750w. 1
      CRA Sept. p66. 600w. $2\frac{1}{2}$
      DB Oct. 6 p28-9. 400w. $2\frac{1}{2}$
      GR June p110. 100w. $2\frac{1}{2}$
      HF July p149. 250w. 4
      MG June p49. 550w. $3\frac{1}{2}$
      MM March 5 p26. 800w. $3\frac{1}{2}$
      RC Aug. p5. 200w. 3
      RS June 2 625w. 3
      RSP May-June p16-9. 2000w. $2\frac{1}{2}$
      SOU July p42. 250w. 3
      SR July p116. 575w. $2\frac{1}{2}$

VV   July 11   p47.   600w.   3

283   EMPEROR.   Private Stock PS 2029
       RC   Oct.   p4.   200w.   2½

284   ENGLAND.   Garden Shed.   Arista ARTY 153 (E)
       RS   Aug.   25   p55.   50w.   3

285   ENGLAND Dan and John Ford Coley.   I Hear Music.   A and M
       SP4613.   Cart.   4613
       SR   March   p95.   100w.   2

286   The ENID.   In the Region of the Summer Stars.   BUK 52001
       MM   Sept.   3   p46.   200w.   3½
       SR   April   p89.   125w.   3

287   ETHOS.   Open Up.   Capitol, ST-11616
       CK   Aug.   p49.   25w.   4

288   EVERLY Brothers.   The New Album.   Warner K56415 (E)
       NK   Autumn   p43.   250w.   4
       RR   Dec.   p86.   50w.   2½

289   FACES.   Best of.   Riva (E) RVLD 3 (2 LP Set)
       MM   May 28   p26.   225w.   3½

290   FACES.   Snakes and Ladders.   Warner BS 2897 (Reissue)
       AU   March   p89.   150w.   2
       CIR   Feb.   28   p14.   300w.   3
       CIR   Apr.   28   p17.   150w.   3½
       RS   Jan.   13   p48.   100w.   4

291   FALCONER, Roderick.   New Nation.   United Artists UA-LA
       615G
       AU   Jan.   p76.   200w.   3
       RM   Jan.   p5.   650w.   5

292   FALCONER, Roderick.   Victory in Rock City.   United Artists
       LA 777G
       AU   Dec.   p115.   75w.   2
       MM   Oct.   1   p23.   50w.   1
       RC   Oct.   p4.   100w.   2
       RS   Oct.   6   p94.   400w.   2½

293   FERGUSON, Jay.   Thunder Island.   Asylum 7E 1115
       MG   Dec.   p55.   50w.   2½

294   FERRIER, Al and Warren Storm.   Boppin' Tonight.   Flyright
       LP525 (E) (Reissue)
       CZM   June   p30.   25w.   2½
       NK   Summer   p40.   50w.   4

295   FERRY, Bryan.   In Your Mind.   Atlantic SD 18216.   Cart.

TP-18216.   Cass. CS-18216
   CIR   May 26   p54-5.   750w. $4\frac{1}{2}$
   MG   June   p52.   200w.   5
   MM   Feb. 18   p22.   500w.   5
   RC   May   p1.   200w. $4\frac{1}{2}$
   RR   May   p87.   50w.   2
   RS   June 2   500w. $3\frac{1}{2}$
   SR   Aug.   p90, 92.   200w. $3\frac{1}{2}$
   VV   June 20   p51.   400w. $3\frac{1}{2}$
   VV   Aug. 1   p51.   50w. $3\frac{1}{2}$

296 FERRY, Bryan.   Let's Stick Together.   Atlantic SD 18187.
     Cart. TP 18187
      SR   Jan.   p87.   100w.   3
      TP   Dec. 1976/Jan. 1977 p31.   550w.   5

297 FIRE Ballet.   Too, too....   Passport PPSD-98016   Cart.
     8167-98016
      SR   Feb.   p92.   100w.   0

298 FIREFALL.   Atlantic SD 18174
      AU   Jan.   p82.   200w.   3
      CS   Dec.   p28.   150w.   4

299 FIREFALL.   Luna Sea.   Atlantic SD 19101
      AU   Dec.   p116.   200w.   3
      CIR   Nov. 10   p58.   350w. $2\frac{1}{2}$
      CRA   Oct.   p68.   325w.   3
      MM   Oct. 8   p29.   225w.   0
      RS   Sept. 22   p64, 67.   700w. $1\frac{1}{2}$
      VV   Oct. 3   p65.   50w.   2

300 FLAME.   Queen of the Neighbourhood.   RCA APL1-2160.
     Cart. APS1-2160.   Cass. APK1-2160
      MM   Aug. 6   p16.   50w.   3
      SR   July   p94-5.   250w.   3

301 FLAMIN' Groovies.   Still Shakin'.   Buddah BDS 5683
      CIR   May 12   p15-6.   300w. $3\frac{1}{2}$
      CRA   July   p78.   125w.   3
      SR   June   p96, 100.   175w.   3

302 FLAMIN' Groovies.   Teenage Head.   Kama Sutra KSMD 101
     (2 discs)
      SMG   May   p21.   100w.   4

303 FLEETWOOD Mac.   The History of.   CBS 88227 (E) (Reissue)
     (2 discs)
      CAC   May   p51.   200w.   3
      MM   April 16   p23.   250w.   4
      RR   June   p94.   50w.   3

304 FLEETWOOD Mac.   Rumours.   Warner Bros. BSK 3010

AU   July p93.   250w.   4
CIR   April 14 p15-6.   1150w.   3
CRA   April p95.   900w.   4
GR   May p1757.   50w.   2
HF   April p39.   250w. $4\frac{1}{2}$
MG   April p49.   500w. $3\frac{1}{2}$
MM   Feb. 19 p26.   325w. $1\frac{1}{2}$
PMR   April p34.   500w. $3\frac{1}{2}$
RC   April p8.   450w.   5
RO   July p76.   800w. $3\frac{1}{2}$
RR   April p87.   150w.   3
RS   April 21 750w.   4
RSP   May-June p14-5, 62.   550w.   4
SR   June p100.   175w.   0

305   FLINT, Bernie.   I Don't Want to Put a Hold On You.   EMI
      EMC 3184 (E)
         MM   July 16 p27.   50w.   2

306   FLUDD.   '71-'77 from Attic.   Attic LAT 1027 (Canada)   (Re-
      issue)
         CC   Nov.   p37.   100w.   3
         SOU   Oct.   p61.   200w.   4

307   FOCUS.   Ship of Memories.   ABC SA 7531 (Reissue)
         GP   Oct.   p129.   150w.   3

308   FOGELBERG, Dan.   Nether Lands.   Epic PE 34185
         AU   Oct.   p172.   250w.   4
         CAC   Aug.   p162.   300w.   3
         CIR   Dec. 8 p75.   275w.   3
         CRA   Sept.   p80-1.   275w.   3
         GP   Sept.   p119.   50w. $3\frac{1}{2}$
         MM   July 16 p26.   250w. $3\frac{1}{2}$
         RC   July p13.   200w.   2
         SR   Nov.   p94.   275w.   5

309   FOGHAT.   Live.   Bearsville K6971
         MM   Oct. 8 p29.   50w.   3

310   FOGHAT.   Night Shift.   Bearsville BR 6962
         MG   Feb.   p54.   125w.   3
         MM   Feb. 12 p25.   50w. $2\frac{1}{2}$
         RS   Feb. 10 p105.   275w.   4
         SR   April p90.   75w. $2\frac{1}{2}$

311   FOOL'S Gold.   Mr Lucky.   Columbia PC 34878
         CRA   Oct.   p70.   200w. $2\frac{1}{2}$
         MM   Dec. 21 p14.   50w.   3

312   FOREIGNER.   Atlantic SD 18215.   Cart. TP-18125.   Cass.
      CS-18125
         CIR   June 23 p60.   850w.   4

HF   July p152. 700w. 4
MM   June 4 p23. 300w. $3\frac{1}{2}$
RC   Oct. p14. 50w. $1\frac{1}{2}$
RS   June 2. 400w. $3\frac{1}{2}$
SOU June p41. 500w. 5
SR   Sept. p97-8. 225w. 2
TP   June/July p33-4. 300w. $4\frac{1}{2}$
VV   June 27 p73. 350w. $1\frac{1}{2}$

313   FOSTER, Bruce. After the Snow.   Millennium MNLP 8000
      CRA Aug. p76. 300w. 3
      RS   Sept. 8 p118. 175w. $1\frac{1}{2}$
      SR   Nov. p94, 100. 150w. 5

314   FOSTER Brothers. On the Line.   Rocket ROLL 10 (E)
      MM   Dec. 21 p15. 50w. 2

315   FOX. Blue Hotel. GTO GTLP 020 (E)
      MM   June 4. p28. 450w. $2\frac{1}{2}$

316   FRAMPTON, Peter. I'm in You. A&M SO 4704. Cass. CS-
      4704. Cart. 8T-4704
      AU   Sept. p86. 150w. 5
      CAC Aug. p166. 200w. $1\frac{1}{2}$
      CIR Sept. 8 p58-9. 1225w. $2\frac{1}{2}$
      CRA Sept. p68. 700w. 2
      GR   Aug. p354. 150w. $1\frac{1}{2}$
      HF   Sept. p137-8. 400w. $1\frac{1}{2}$
      MG   Aug. p59. 125w. 2
      MM   June 11 p19. 475w. $3\frac{1}{2}$
      RC   July p2-3. 350w. 5
      RSP May-June p12-4. 700w. $1\frac{1}{2}$
      SR   Oct. p96. 275w. $3\frac{1}{2}$
      VV   Aug. 1 p51. 50w. $2\frac{1}{2}$

317   FRANKS, Michael. Sleeping Gypsy. Warner Bros. BS3004.
      Cart. M83004. Cass. M53004
      RC   Aug. p7. 150w. 3
      SR   July p95. 200w. 5

318   FREDERICK, Jeffrey and the Clamtones. Spiders and Moon-
      light. Rounder
      VV   Nov. 28 p66. 50w. $3\frac{1}{2}$

319   FREE. Free and Easy, Rough and Ready. Island ILPS 9453
      (Reissue)
      GR   March p1467. 50w. 3

320   FRESH. Get Fresh. MCA MCF 2797 (E)
      MM   July 16 p27. 50w. 4
      RR   Sept. p93. 25w. $2\frac{1}{2}$

321   FRIEDMAN, Dean. Lifesong LS 6008

RC May p4. 150w. 4½
SR June p100, 102. 75w. 2

322 FRIEDMAN, Kinky. Lasso From El Paso. Epic EPC 81640
     CMR June p12. 150w. 3
     HF Feb. p144. 50w. 1
     MG Feb. p56. 125w. 0
     RS Feb. 24 p68. 275w. 1½
     SR March p96. 200w. 3

323 FRINGE Benefit. Capricorn CP 0183
     MG Aug. p59. 125w. 3

324 FROESE, Edgar. Macula Transfer. Brain 60 008 (West
     Germany)
     EUR No. 7/8 p40-1. 350w. 4
     RS March 10 p69. 100w. 2½

325 FUNGUS. Negrom (Netherlands)
     MM May 14 p32. 50w. 2

326 FURY, Bill. Story of. Decca DPA 3033/4 (E) (2 discs) (Re-
     issue)
     CAC May p51. 125w. 3
     NK Spring p42. 150w. 3½
     SMG May p20. 225w. 5

327 G Band. Paris Match. CBS (E)
     MM Jan. 8 p18. 50w. 2½

328 GABRIEL, Peter. Peter Gabriel. Atco SD 36-147. Cart.
     TP36-147. Cass. CS 36-147
     AU July p96. 600w. 4
     CAC June p90. 300w. 1½
     CIR April 28 p15-6. 500w. 3
     GR July p237. 25w. 3½
     HF June p120. 600w. 4
     MG June p49-51. 1600w. 3½
     MG June p52. 150w. 1½
     MM Feb. 26. p25. 800w. 3
     RC Oct. p6. 150w. 4
     RS May 5 575w. 3½
     SR Aug. p92, 93. 225w. 2½
     VV May 2 p59. 350w. 3½

329 GALDSTON & Thom. American Gypsies. Warner Bros. BS
     3037
     SR Sept. p98. 125w. 2

330 GALLAGHER, Rory. The Best Years. Polydor 2438 414
     (E) (Reissue)
     CAC Jan. p376. 200w. 3

331 GALLAGHER, Rory. Calling Card. Chrysalis CHR 1124
    CIR Jan. 17 p17. 175w. $3\frac{1}{2}$
    CRE March p62. 600w. 4
    GP Jan. p97. 100w. $4\frac{1}{2}$
    MG Jan. 75w. 3
    RC May p8. 150w. $3\frac{1}{2}$
    RSP Jan. -Feb. p23. 100w. $3\frac{1}{2}$

332 GALLAGHER, Rory. Live. Polydor 2384 079 (E)
    CAC June p85. 150w. 3
    MM May 14 p33. 25w. $4\frac{1}{2}$

333 GALLAGHER & Lyle. Love on the Airwaves. A & M SP-
4620. Cart. 8T-4620
    CAC April p12. 300w. 4
    MM Jan. 1 p14. 650w. 4
    RR March p96. 50w. 3
    RS April 21 275w. 4
    SR June p102. 75w. 2

334 GASOLIN'. Sadan. CBS 88207 (Holland)
    TP Feb. /March p26. 150w. 0

335 GEILS. Monkey Island. Atlantic SD 19103. Cart. TP-19103.
Cass. CS-19103
    CIR Nov. 10 p59. 350w. $2\frac{1}{2}$
    GR Nov. p920. 75w. $3\frac{1}{2}$
    HF Oct. p146. 425w. 5
    MG Sept. p51. 100w. $2\frac{1}{2}$
    MM Oct. 8 p35. 350w. 3
    RR Nov. p115. 25w. 3
    SR Oct. p96. 250w. 3

336 GENESIS. In the Beginning. London LC 5006 (Reissue) (E)
    TP Oct. p42. 125w. $2\frac{1}{2}$

337 GENESIS. Seconds Out. Charisma GE 2001 (E)
    MM Oct. 15 p23. 350w. 5

338 GENESIS. Spot the Pigeon. Charisma GEN 001 (E)
    RS Aug. 25 p55. 50w. $2\frac{1}{2}$

339 GENESIS. Trick of the Tail. Atco SD 36-129
    AU Jan. p80. 300w. $4\frac{1}{2}$
    RM Jan. p11-2. 1000w. 5

340 GENESIS. Wind & Wuthering. Atco SD 36-144. Cart. TP
36-144
    AU July p96. 600w. 4
    CIR June 23 p61-2. 675w. 2
    CK April p48. 275w. 3
    CRA March p73. 500w. 2

341   GENTLE Giant.   Playing the Fool.   Capitol SKBB-11592
        CK   April   p48.   229w.   3
        CRA   May   p79.   250w.   3
        GP   July   p129.   225w.   5
        GR   May   p1758.   75w. $2\frac{1}{2}$
        RC   Oct.   p6.   100w.   4

342   GERRY and the Pacemakers.   Best.   EMI NUT 10 (E) (Reis-
      sue)
        NK   Autumn   p46.   25w. $3\frac{1}{2}$

343   GIBB, Andy.   Flowing Rivers.   RSO RS-1-3019.   Cart. 8T-
      1-3019
        SR   Nov.   p102.   150w.   3

344   GIBBONS, Steve.   Caught in the Act.   MCA 2305
        RS   Dec. 29   p71, 73.   375w.   2

345   GIBBONS, Steve.   Rollin' On.   MCA-2243.   Cart. MCAT-2243
        CAC   April   p8.   250w. $3\frac{1}{2}$
        CIR   April 14   p17-8.   350w.   3
        GR   May   p1757.   25w. $2\frac{1}{2}$
        MM   Feb. 12   p26.   400w. $3\frac{1}{2}$
        RS   May 19   375w. $3\frac{1}{2}$
        SR   Aug.   p93.   150w. $2\frac{1}{2}$

346   GILDER, Nick.   You Know Who You Are.   Chrysalis CHR
      447
        RC   Oct.   p7.   50w.   2
        WHO   Nov.   p40-1.   150w.   4

347   GILLIAN, Ian.   Clear Air Turbulence.   Island ILPS 9500
        GR   July   p237.   25w. $2\frac{1}{2}$
        MM   April 30   p29.   250w. $3\frac{1}{2}$

348   GILLIAN, Ian.   Golden Earring Live.   Polydor 2625034 (2
      discs)
        RR   Dec.   p86.   75w.   1

349   GLASS, Philip.   North Star.   Virgin PZ 34669
        AU   Aug.   p84.   250w.   4
        CRA   July   p72.   200w.   3
        DB   May 19   200w.   3
        MG   Aug.   p63.   150w. $2\frac{1}{2}$
        MM   May 14   p27.   300w.   4
        RS   June 2   p78.   275w. $3\frac{1}{2}$
        VV   March 21   p59.   125w.   3

350   GLITTER Band.   Makes You Blind.   Arista 4109
        TP   Feb./March   p30-1.   425w.   4

351   GODDO.   Fatcat/Polydor 2424901 (Canada)
        CC   June   p30.   50w.   3

SOU   May   p59.   500w. $4\frac{1}{2}$

352   GOLDEN Earring.   Contraband.   Polydor 2310 491 (E)
      CAC   June   p90.   100w.   3

353   GONG.   Shamal.   Virgin V2046
      SOU   Feb.   p43.   400w.   1

354   GOODHAND-TAIT, Philip.   Oceans Away.   Chrysalis CHR 1113
      CK   Jan.   p51.   25w. $4\frac{1}{2}$

355   GOODHAND-TAIT, Philip.   Teaching an Old Dog New Tricks.
      Chrysalis CHR 1146
      RC   Oct.   p11-2.   100w. $3\frac{1}{2}$

356   GOODMAN, Steve.   Say It in Private.   Asylum 7E-1118.   Cart.
      ET8 1118.   Cass. TC5 1118
      HF   Dec.   p139.   100w. $2\frac{1}{2}$
      MM   Dec. 3   p20.   300w.   0

357   GORDON, Robert and Link Wray.   Private Stock PS 2030
      CRA   Aug.   p78, 80.   300w. $3\frac{1}{2}$
      MG   Aug.   p59.   125w.   4
      MM   Aug. 27   p22.   300w.   4
      NK   Autumn   p45.   100w. $4\frac{1}{2}$
      RC   Dec.   p15.   100w.   3
      RS   Aug. 25   p58-9.   400w.   3
      SOU   Dec.   p55.   250w.   3
      TP   Oct.   p40-1.   350w. $3\frac{1}{2}$
      VV   Aug. 29   p74.   400w.   3
      WHO   Nov.   p40-7.   325w.   3
      ZZ   Oct.   p32-3.   200w.   4

358   GORDON, Rosso.   Legendary Sun Performer.   Charly CR
      30133 (E)
      NK   Autumn   p50.   100w. $4\frac{1}{2}$

359   GOTTSCHING, Manuel.   New Age of Earth.   Isadora ISA
      9003
      EUR   No. 7/8   p42.   275w.   3

360   GRATEFUL Dead.   Terrapin Station.   Arista AL 7001.   Cart.
      8301-700
      AU   Nov.   p114.   700w.   5
      CIR   Oct. 27   p66-7.   300w.   3
      HF   Nov.   450w.   3
      MG   Oct.   p59.   75w.   2
      RC   Oct.   p5.   125w.   4
      RR   Oct.   p89.   100w. $3\frac{1}{2}$
      RS   Oct. 6   p85-6.   400w.   3
      SR   Nov.   p102.   350w.   3
      VV   Sept. 5   p59.   500w.   4

361   GRATEFUL Dead.   Wake of the Flood/From the Mars Hotel.
      Grateful Dead Records 104 (2 discs)
          MM   March 19   p28.   300w.   3

362   GRATEFUL Dead.   What a Long, Strange Trip It's Been.
      Warner 2W3091 (2 discs)
          RC   Dec.   p9.   100w.   5

363   GREAVES, John, Peter Blegvad, Lisa Herman.   Kew Rhone.
      Virgin V2082 (E)
          MM   July 23   p18.   325w.   4

364   GREENFIELD.   Sanctuary.   Casino CA 1004 (Canada)
          OLR   March   p54.   25w.   2

365   GREG and Paul.   A Year at the Top.   Casablanca NBLP
      7068.   Cart. NBLP8 7068.   Cass. NBLP5 7068
          HF   Nov.   75w. $2\frac{1}{2}$

366   GRIN, Featuring Nils Lofgren.   Best of.   Epic PE 34247 (Re-
      issue)
          RS   Jan. 13   p48, 51.   100w.   4

367   GRINDERSWITCH.   Pullin' Together.   Capricorn CP 0173
          MM   Feb. 26   p25.   200w.   3

368   GROSS, Henry.   Release.   Lifesong LS 6002
          AU   Aug.   p88.   150w.   0

369   GROSS, Henry.   Show Me to the Stage.   Lifesong LS6010
          RS   May 5   p69.   250w.   2
          SR   June   p102, 104.   125w.   3

370   GRYPHON.   Treason.   Harvest SHSP 4063 (E)
          CAC   Aug.   p162.   300w.   2
          GR   July   p234.   75w.   3
          MM   June 25   p21.   200w. $2\frac{1}{2}$
          RR   Sept.   p93.   100w.   3

371   GUESS Who.   The Way They Were.   RCA APL1 1778 (Reissue)
          OLR   June   p140.   25w.   3

372   GUTHRIE, Arlo.   Amigo.   Reprise MS 2239.   Cart. 2239
          AU   Feb.   p78.   100w.   1
          FR   June   p29.   100w.   2
          HF   Jan.   p143.   250w.   3
          RS   Jan. 27   p65.   300w. $3\frac{1}{2}$
          SR   Jan.   p88.   100w.   4

373   HAAZZ & Co.   Unlawful Noise.   KGB 7076 (E)
          MM   Nov. 19   p34.   75w.   0

374   HACKETT, Steve.   Voyage of the Acolyte.   Chrysalis CHR

1112
>   AU Jan. p80. 300w. 4

375 HAGAR, Sammy. Capitol ST 11599
>   RC June p8-9. 250w. $3\frac{1}{2}$
>   RSP March-April p28. 400w. $3\frac{1}{2}$

376 HALEY, Bill and the Comets. Rock Around the Clock. MCA
>   CDL 8017 (E) (Reissue)
>   CAC March p454. 125w. 2
>   NK Summer p40. 25w. 4

377 HALL, Daryl and John Oates. Beauty on a Back Street. RCA
>   AFL 1-2300. Cart. AFK 1-2300. Cass. AFS 1-2300
>   CIR Nov. 24 p73. 600w. 2
>   HF Dec. 8 p135. 450w. $2\frac{1}{2}$
>   MG Dec. p56. 75w. 2
>   MM Oct. 8 p35. 350w. 3
>   RC Nov. p3. 100w. $2\frac{1}{2}$
>   RS Oct. 20 p87. 550w. 4

378 HALL, Daryl and John Oates. Bigger Than Both of Us. RCA
>   APL 1-1467. Cart. APS1-1467.
>   AU Jan. p77. 300w. $2\frac{1}{2}$
>   SR Jan. p88. 50w. 3

379 HALL, Daryl and John Oates. No Goodbyes. Atlantic 19137
>   (Reissue)
>   MM May 14 p33. 50w. 3

380 HALL, Daryl and John Oates. Past Times Behind. Chelsea
>   547
>   CAC June p95. 150w. 2

381 HAMEL, Peter Michael. Nada. Wergo.
>   EUR V2/#2 p72. 175w. 4

382 HAMILTON, Dirk. Alias i. ABC AB 976
>   CIR April 14 p16-7. 250w. $2\frac{1}{2}$
>   RS June 2 400w. $3\frac{1}{2}$
>   RSP Nov.-Dec. p29. 325w. 3

383 HAMMILL, Peter. Over. Charisma CAS 1125 (E)
>   MM May 14 p31. 50w. 0
>   TP June/July p38-9. 275w. 3

384 HAMMILL, Peter. The Quiet Zone/The Pleasure Zone.
>   Charisma CAS 1131 (E)
>   RR Nov. p114-5. 50w. $2\frac{1}{2}$

385 HARLEY, Steve. Face to Face. EMI EMSP 320 (E) (2 discs)
>   RR Oct. p88. 100w. 3
>   TP Sept. p33. 375w. 2

386   HARLEY, Steve and Cockney Rebel.   Love's a Prima Donna.
      Capitol ST-11596
          CIR   Jan. 31   p16.   200w.   0
          SOU   April   p55.   400w.   4
          TP   Feb./March   p29.   350w.   0

387   HARPER, Roy.   One of Those Days in England (Bullinaming-
      vase).   Chrysalis CHR 1138
          AU   June   p114.   250w. $4\frac{1}{2}$
          CAC   Aug.   p163.   300w.   3
          MM   Feb. 12   p25.   650w. $3\frac{1}{2}$
          RR   May   p86.   175w. $3\frac{1}{2}$
          SR   Oct.   p98.   225w. $4\frac{1}{2}$
          TP   June/July   p33.   300w.   3

388   HARPER, Roy.   The Sophisticated Beggar.   Polydor BBX
      502 (Reissue) (E)
          CAC   July   p131.   125w.   3

389   HARRIS, Emmylou.   Luxury Liner.   Warner Brothers BS
      2998
          CIR   March 17   p16.   425w. $4\frac{1}{2}$
          CM   May   p61.   200w.   1
          CMP   March   p43.   150w.   4
          CMR   April   p33.   575w.   5
          CS   March 24   p16.   450w. $4\frac{1}{2}$
          CRA   April   p115.   650w.   4
          GR   March   p1467.   150w. $4\frac{1}{2}$
          HF   March   p139.   450w.   4
          MM   Jan. 15   p17.   600w.   5
          NK   Spring   p42.   100w.   4
          RS   March 24   p60, 62.   600w.   3
          RSP   March-April   p54-6.   1500w.   4
          SR   May   p86, 80.   250w.   5
          VV   Feb. 28   p47, 51.   300w. $3\frac{1}{2}$
          ZZ   Feb.   475w.   5

390   HARRISON, Don.   Not Far From Here.   Mercury SRM 1-1185
          MG   Dec.   p56.   50w.   2
          RS   Nov. 3   p104, 108.   475w.   2

391   HARRISON, Don.   Red Hot.   Atlantic SD18208.   Cart. TP-
      18208.   Cass. CS-18208
          CIR   March 31   p18-9.   400w.   3
          CRA   March   p81.   200w.   4
          RS   March 10   p73.   250w.   3
          SR   July   p95.   200w. $2\frac{1}{2}$

392   HARRISON, George.   The Best of George Harrison.   Capitol
      ST 11578.   Cass. 8XT-11578 (Reissue)
          AU   Feb.   p75.   50w.   4
          CIR   Feb. 14   p17.   200w.   4
          RR   Feb.   p93.   200w. $2\frac{1}{2}$

      RS   Jan. 13   p48.   50w. $3\frac{1}{2}$
      SR   March   p96.   250w.   2

393   HARRISON, George.   Thirty Three and 1/3.   Dark Horse DH
      3005
      AU   April   p85.   150w.   2
      CAC   March   p454.   150w. $2\frac{1}{2}$
      CIR   Feb. 14.   p17, 20.   800w. $2\frac{1}{2}$
      CIR   March 31   p12-3.   300w.   3
      CRA   March   p65-6.   425w. $3\frac{1}{2}$
      CRE   March   p60-1.   700w. $1\frac{1}{2}$
      GR   Feb.   p1332.   125w.   3
      HF   March.   p140.   200w.   2
      MG   Feb.   p54.   200w. $1\frac{1}{2}$
      RS   Jan. 13   p52.   250w. $2\frac{1}{2}$
      SR   March   p96.   250w.   3

394   HATTLER, Hellmut.   Bassball.   Harvest (West Germany)
      EUR   V2/#2   p24-5.   200w.   4

395   HAVENS, Richie.   The End of the Beginning.   AatdM SP-
      4598
      AU   March   p90.   150w.   2
      BM   Jan.   p45.   100w.   3
      MM   Jan. 15.   p17.   150w.   3
      SR   Jan.   p92.   100w.   4

396   HAVENS, Richie.   Mirage.   A&M SP 4641.   Cart. 8T 4641.
      Cass. CS 4641
      HF   Dec.   p139.   75w. $3\frac{1}{2}$
      RC   Nov.   p8.   100w.   3

397   HAWKINS, Dale.   Chess ACRR 703 (Reissue)
      NK   Spring   p37.   125w.   5
      RSP   1:3   p32.   225w.   3
      SMG   Sept.   p25.   100w.   4

398   HAWKWIND.   Astounding Sounds, Amazing Music.   Charisma
      CDS 4004
      TP   Dec. 1976/Jan. 1977   p34.   375w.   3

398a HAWKWIND.   Quark, Strangeness and Charm.   Charisma CDS
      4008 (E)
      GR   Sept.   p522.   50w. $2\frac{1}{2}$
      MM   June 25   p21.   500w.   3
      TP   Oct.   p44.   350w. $3\frac{1}{2}$

399   HAZEL, Eddie.   Games, Dames and Guitar Thangs.   Warner
      BS 3058.   Cart. M8 3058.   Cass. M5 3058
      HF   Nov.   50w. $2\frac{1}{2}$
      MG   Dec.   p62.   100w.   2

400   HEAD East.   Gettin' Lucky.   A&M SP4624

RSP   May-June   p61.   300w.   3

401   HEART.   Dreamboat Annie.   Arista ARTY 139 (E)
        RM   Jan.   p14.   400w.   5
        RR   Jan.   p84.   100w. $3\frac{1}{2}$

402   HEART.   Little Queen.   Portrait PR-34799.   Cart. PRA-
      34699.   Cass.   PRT-34799
        CIR   Sept. 15   p67-8.   350w.   3
        CRA   Aug.   p68.   150w.   2
        HF   Aug.   p114.   300w. $3\frac{1}{2}$
        MG   Aug.   p59.   100w. $1\frac{1}{2}$
        MM   June 4   p24.   550w. $4\frac{1}{2}$
        OLR   Dec.   p291.   50w. $4\frac{1}{2}$
        RC   Oct.   p5.   50w. $2\frac{1}{2}$
        SOU   July   p40.   300w.   4
        SR   Sept.   p98.   125w.   4
        VV   June 13   p49, 51.   200w. $2\frac{1}{2}$

403   HEART.   Magazine.   Mushroom MRS5008
        MM   Sept. 17   p20.   300w.   1
        RC   Nov.   p10-1.   150w. $4\frac{1}{2}$

404   HEARTBREAKERS.   L. A. M. F.   Track 2409 218 (E)
        MM   Oct. 15   p24.   400w.   2
        ZZ   Oct.   p33-4.   300w. $4\frac{1}{2}$

405   HEARTSFIELD.   Collector's Item.   Columbia PC-34456
        GP   Aug.   p120.   50w.   3

406   HEAVY Metal Kids.   Kitsch.   RAK SRAK 523 (E)
        MM   May 28   p20.   175w.   1

407   HELL, Richard.   Ork 81976
        AU   Nov.   p119.   150w. $2\frac{1}{2}$

408   HELL, Richard and the Voidoids.   Blank Generation.   Sire
      SR 6037
        CIR   Nov. 24   p74, 76.   450w.   3
        MG   Nov.   p51.   25w. $4\frac{1}{2}$
        MM   Oct. 8   p30.   550w.   3
        RS   Oct. 20   p90.   500w. $2\frac{1}{2}$
        VV   Sept. 26   p62.   300w. $3\frac{1}{2}$
        ZZ   Oct.   p33.   200w. $3\frac{1}{2}$

409   HELM, Levon.   And the RCO All-Stars.   ABC 1017
        VV   Dec. 19   p79-80.   250w.   2

410   HENDERSON, Michael.   Goin' Places.   Buddah BDS 5693.
      Cart. BDT 5693.   Cass. BDC 5693
        HF   Nov.   50w.   2

411   HENDRIX, Jimi.   Voice in the Wind.   DJM (Reissue) (E)

CAC   Jan.   p378.   250w. $3\frac{1}{2}$

412   HIGGS, Joe.   Life of Contradiction.   Grounation GROL 508
CRA   April   p100-1.   400w. $4\frac{1}{2}$

413   HILL, Dan.   Hold On.   Twentieth Century T526
CRA   May   p79-80.   250w. $2\frac{1}{2}$

414   HILL, Dan.   Longer Fuse.   GRT 9230 1073
CC   Oct.   p34.   100w.   3
SOU   Oct.   p70.   350w.   5

415   HILL, Joe Scott.   The Rockin' Rebel.   Redita 113 (Nether-
lands) (Reissue)
NK   Winter   p34.   75w.   4
RSP   March-April   p31-2.   150w.   3

416   HILLAGE, Steve.   L.   Atlantic SD 18205
CK   April   p49.   25w.   4
CRA   March   p74-5.   600w. $3\frac{1}{2}$
GP   May   p128.   100w.   4
RS   March 24   p66.   450w.   3
SOU   May   p60.   100w.   1
SR   April   p90.   112w.   4
TP   Feb. -March   p29.   350w.   5

417   HILLAGE, Steve.   Motivation Radio.   Atlantic SD 19144
MG   Dec.   p52.   250w. $3\frac{1}{2}$
MM   Oct. 8   p26.   500w. $3\frac{1}{2}$
RR   Nov.   p115.   75w. $3\frac{1}{2}$

418   HILLMAN, Chris.   Clear Sailin'.   Asylum 7E-1104
CRA   Oct.   p68.   325w.   3
GR   Oct.   p715.   50w. $2\frac{1}{2}$
MM   Sept. 10   p24.   225w.   2

419   HOELDERLIN.   Rare Birds.   Spiegelei
EUR   V2/#2   p26.   250w.   4

420   HOLLIES.   Clarke, Hicks, Sylvester, Calvert, Elliott.   Epic
PE 34714
CRA   Aug.   p81.   300w.   3
HF   Aug.   p114.   250w. $2\frac{1}{2}$

421   HOLLIES.   Hollies Live.   Columbia PES 90401 (Canada)
SR   April   p98.   275w.   5
TP   Feb./March   p31.   350w.   5

422   HOLLIES.   Live Hits.   Polydor 2383 428 (E)
SMG   May   p22.   125w.   4

423   HOLLIES.   Russian Roulette.   Polydor 2383 421 (E)
MM   Jan. 22   p46.   75w.   3

RS   May 19 275w. $3\frac{1}{2}$
SR   April p98. 275w.   1
TP   Feb. -March p31. 350w.   5

424   HOLLY, Buddy.   MCA Coral 8034 (Reissue) (E)
        CRA   April p106.   25w. $4\frac{1}{2}$

425   HOLLY, Buddy.   Legend.   MCA Coral CDMSP 802 (2 discs)
        (Reissue)
        CRA   April p106.   75w.   4

426   HOLLY, Buddy.   Live.   Cricket C00-1000 (E)
        NK   Autumn p48.   100w.   4
        RSP   1:3 p30.   500w.   3
        SMG   Sept. p25.   350w.   2

427   HOLLY, Buddy.   The Nashville Sessions.   MCA Coral CDMSP
        802 (Reissue)
        CRA   April p106.   25w. $3\frac{1}{2}$

428   HOLLY, Buddy and Bob Montgomery.   Western and Boys.
        MCA Coral CDLM 855 (Reissue)
        MM   Dec. 21 p14.   150w. $2\frac{1}{2}$

429   HOLLY, Buddy and the Crickets.   The Chirping Crickets.
        MCA Coral CDLM 8035 (Reissue)
        CRA   April p106.   25w. $3\frac{1}{2}$

430   HOMETOWN Band.   Flying.   A&M SP 4605 (Canada)
        MM   April 2 p22.   300w.   4
        OLR   June p141.   50w.   3

431   HOODOO Rhythm Devils.   Safe in Their Homes.   Fantasy F-
        9522.   Cart. 8160-9522(H).   Cass. 5160-9522(H)
        CRA   July p80.   100w. $3\frac{1}{2}$
        RC   Aug. p2.   200w.   3
        SR   Sept. p102.   175w. $3\frac{1}{2}$

432   HOT Tuna.   Hoppkorv.   Grunt BLF1-1920
        AU   Feb. p76.   100w. $2\frac{1}{2}$
        GP   Jan. p97.   50w. $2\frac{1}{2}$
        SR   March p102.   100w.   3

433   HUNTER, Ian.   Overnight Angels.   Columbia PC 34721.   Cart.
        PCT 34721.   Cass. PCA 34721
        AU   Aug. p87.   200w.   4
        HF   Sept. p145.   50w.   2
        MM   May 21 p26.   450w.   0
        TP   Sept. p34-5.   225w. $2\frac{1}{2}$

434   HUNTER, Steve.   Swept Away.   Atco SD 36-148
        CIR   June 23 p65-6.   300w.   1
        GP   Sept. p118.   125w. $3\frac{1}{2}$

435   HUNTERS.   Teen Scene.   Fontana 9290 203 (E) (Reissue)
      NK   Winter   p37.   50w. $3\frac{1}{2}$
      SMG   May   p22.   150w.   3

436   HYDRA.   Rock the World.   Polydor PD-1-6096
      GP   July   p129.   50w.   3

436a IAN, Janis.   Miracle Row.   Columbia PC 34440
      AU   May   p89.   200w. $4\frac{1}{2}$
      CAC   Aug.   p167.   225w. $2\frac{1}{2}$
      CIR   June 9   p55-6.   150w.   4
      HF   April   p144.   200w.   2
      MM   May 14   p30.   250w. $2\frac{1}{2}$
      RR   June   p93.   50w. $2\frac{1}{2}$
      SR   June   p100.   550w.   4

437   IGGY Pop.   The Idiot.   RCA APL1-2275
      CIR   May 12   p13-4.   400w.   3
      MG   May   p51.   150w.   4
      RC   May   p6.   200w. $3\frac{1}{2}$
      RS   May 5   250w.   3
      SR   June   p110, 112.   400w.   0
      ZZ   April   p45-6.   800w. $4\frac{1}{2}$

438   IGGY Pop.   Lust for Life.   RCA AFL 1-2488
      CIR   Dec.   22   p68.   200w.   0
      HF   Nov.   275w.   3
      MG   Nov.   p49.   325w.   4
      MM   Aug.   27   p19.   500w.   2
      RC   Dec.   p10.   100w. $3\frac{1}{2}$
      RR   Dec.   p85-6.   125w.   3
      TP   Nov.   p36, 37.   300w.   4
      VV   Oct.   3   p65.   175w. $4\frac{1}{2}$
      ZZ   Sept.   p32.   450w.   4

439   IGGY and the Stooges.   Metallic K.O.   Skydog SGIS 008
      VV   Nov.   28   p66.   50w. $2\frac{1}{2}$
      ZZ   Jan.   500w. $3\frac{1}{2}$

440   IGGY and the Stooges.   Raw Power.   Columbia 31464
      MM   June 4   p20.   300w.   3

441   ILLUSION.   Out of the Mist.   Island ILPS 9489 (E)
      CRA   Sept.   p78, 80.   325w.   3
      TP   June/July   p38.   300w.   3

442   ISIS.   Breaking Through.   United Artists, UA-LA706-G
      CK   May   p49.   50w. $2\frac{1}{2}$

443   JACK the Lad.   Jackpot.   UA UAS 29999 (E)
      CAC   Jan.   p378.   125w.   3
      TP   Feb./March   p33.   150w.   4

444 JACKSON Hawke. Columbia PES 90417 (Canada)
     CC Nov. p34. 100w. 3
     SOU Nov. p58. 300w. $4\frac{1}{2}$

445 JACKSON Hawke. Forever. Columbia 90375 (Canada)
     CC Jan. p32. 50w. 3
     OLR June p141. 25w. 3

446 JACKSON, Wanda. Rockin' with. Capitol CAPS 1007
     CMP Oct. p40. 200w. 4
     MM Aug. 6 p17. 50w. $2\frac{1}{2}$
     NK Summer p38. 100w. 5

447 The JAM. In the City. Polydor PD 1-6110
     AU Dec. 100w. 1
     CIR Nov. 10 p60. 250w. $3\frac{1}{2}$
     CRA Sept. p70. 150w. $2\frac{1}{2}$
     GR July p237. 50w. $3\frac{1}{2}$
     MG Oct. p59. 50w. $3\frac{1}{2}$
     MM May 28 p23. 550w. $3\frac{1}{2}$
     RR Aug. p83. 100w. $2\frac{1}{2}$
     RS Oct. 6 p89. 300w. $2\frac{1}{2}$
     TP Sept. p39. 185w. 2
     VV Aug. 29 p73. 400w. $3\frac{1}{2}$
     ZZ June p36, 38. 600w. $3\frac{1}{2}$

448 The JAM. This Is the Modern World. Polydor 2383 475 (E)
     MM Nov. 12 p25. 525w. $3\frac{1}{2}$

449 JAMES Gang. Jesse Come Home. Atco SD 36-141
     AU March p87. 150w. 2

450 JAMESON, Nick. Already Free. Bearsville BR 6972
     MM Oct. 8 p29. 50w. 3
     RS Dec. 1 p79-80. 200w. $3\frac{1}{2}$

451 JANE. Live Recording. Brain 80.001-2 (West Germany)
     RS March 10 p71. 100w. 2
     TP Feb./March p26. 150w. 4

452 JARRE, Jean Michel. Oxygene. Polydor, PD-1-6112
     CK Nov. p64. 350w. 4
     MM Sept. 3 p22. 450w. 3
     SOU Nov. p55. 200w. 4

453 JEFFERSON Starship. Flight Log. Grunt CYL2-1255 (2 discs)
     CAC May p49. 450w. 5
     CIR May 12 p17-8. 475w. $3\frac{1}{2}$
     GR April p1617. 100w. 2
     MM Feb. 5 p23. 525w. $3\frac{1}{2}$
     RO July p72-3. 550w. $2\frac{1}{2}$
     SR Sept. p104, 52. 50w. not rated

454 JEFFREYS, Garland. Ghost Writer.   A&M SP4629
      CIR May 12 p13. 350w. 5
      CRA May p68, 70. 400w. 4
      DB Sept. 8 p32-3. 450w. 5
      HF June p120. 250w. 4
      MM June 4 p28. 400w. 4
      RR July p96. 50w. 4
      RS April 21 400w. 4
      VV March 21 p55. 400w. 5

455 JELLY. A True Story. Asylum 7E-1096
      RS May 19 300w. 3

456 JETHRO Tull. Songs from the Wind.   Chrysalis CHR 1132
      AU May p88. 350w. 5
      CIR June 9 p53. 500w. 4
      MM Jan. 29 p24. 550w. $2\frac{1}{2}$
      RC April p9. 200w. $4\frac{1}{2}$
      RR April p87. 150w. $2\frac{1}{2}$
      RRE May-June p23, 62. 700w. $2\frac{1}{2}$
      SR Aug. p94. 225w. 2

457 JIGSAW. Pieces of Magic. Splash CDLP 1003 (E)
      MM Nov. 12 p26. 3

458 JOEL, Billy. The Stranger. Columbia JC 34987.   Cart.
JCT 34987.   Cass. JCA 34987
      CIR Dec. 22 p68-9. 350w. $1\frac{1}{2}$
      HF Dec. p135-6. 475w. 4
      RC Oct. p5. 100w. $2\frac{1}{2}$
      RS Dec. 29 p71. 325w. 3

459 JOHN, Elton. Blue Moves. MCA Rocket 2-11004.   Cart.
MCAT 2-11004
      AU March p86. 250w. 1
      CIR Jan. 17 p51, 53. 900w. $2\frac{1}{2}$
      CIR March 31 p20. 250w. 1
      CK Jan. p50. 100w. 5
      CRA Jan. p82. 850w. 2
      SOU Jan. p41. 100w. 5
      SR Feb. p96. 150w. 2

460 JOHNSON, General. Arista AL 4082
      CRA March p78. 200w. 3
      MG Feb. p55. 125w. 2
      RS Feb. 24 p62, 65. 300w. 3

461 JOHNSTON, Bruce. Going Public. Columbia PC-34459.
Cass. PCT-34459. Cart. PCA-34459
      CIR Dec. 8 p76-7. 250w. $1\frac{1}{2}$
      CRA Aug. p77. 225w. $2\frac{1}{2}$
      MM Sept. 3 p18. 175w. 0
      RS Aug. 11 p69. 350w. 1

SR Oct. p100. 175w. $4\frac{1}{2}$

462 JOURNEY. Next. Columbia PC 34311
    MM Feb. 19 p24. 225w. $3\frac{1}{2}$

463 JUDAS Priest. Sin After Sin. Columbia PC 34787
    CIR Oct. 13 p77. 200w. $3\frac{1}{2}$
    MG Oct. p60. 50w. $1\frac{1}{2}$

464 KALAPANA. II. Abbatoir KALP 004
    RC Dec. p7. 100w. $3\frac{1}{2}$

465 KALEIDOSCOPE. When Scopes Collide. Island Records ILPA
    9462 (Reissue)
    AU April p86. 150w. $3\frac{1}{2}$
    FOL July p23-4. 775w. $3\frac{1}{2}$
    MM April 23 p22. 125w. 0
    RR May p86. 50w. 3
    RS June 2 p80. 300w. 2

466 KANSAS. Leftoverture. Kirshner PZ 34224
    GP March p113. 25w. $2\frac{1}{2}$
    RC April p2. 100w. 3
    RS Jan. 27 p70. 100w. 3

467 KAWASAKI, Ryo. Juice. RCA, APL1-1855
    CK Jan. p51. 25w. 4
    HF Jan. p145. 200w. 3

468 KENSON, Johnny. New Sound in Rock and Roll. Dial LP 001
    (Netherlands)
    NK Winter p34. 75w. $3\frac{1}{2}$

469 KIHN, Greg. Again. Beserkley PZ 34779
    AU Oct. p174. 150w. 3
    CIR Dec. 8 p77. 275w. 3
    MG Aug. p59. 100w. $1\frac{1}{2}$
    SR Nov. p106. 200w. 4
    TP Sept. p6. 125w. 2
    ZZ Nov. p32-3. 300w. 3

470 KING, Carole. Simple Things. Capitol SMAS 11667
    CIR Oct. 13 p75. 225w. 2
    CK Dec. p73. 25w. $2\frac{1}{2}$
    CRA Oct. p63. 400w. 1
    GR Oct. p715. 50w. $3\frac{1}{2}$
    MG Oct. p59. 75w. 2
    RC Oct. p11. 50w. $3\frac{1}{2}$
    RS Sept. 8 p113-4. 550w. $1\frac{1}{2}$
    SOU Sept. p60. 250w. 5
    VV Oct. 3 p65. 25w. $1\frac{1}{2}$

471 KING Harry. Divided We Stand. EMI 3188

MM Sept. 17 p21. 300w. $3\frac{1}{2}$
TP Nov. p41. 150w. 0

472 KINGFISH. Live and Kickin'. Jet LA 732-6
MM July 16 p22. 250w. $3\frac{1}{2}$

473 KINKS. Pye File FILD 001 (E) (Reissue)
NK Autumn p46. 25w. $3\frac{1}{2}$

474 KINKS. Sleepwalker. Arista AL 4106
AU June p116. 150w. 3
CIR April 28 p12-3. 100w. $4\frac{1}{2}$
CRA May p67-8. 1300w. 3
HF May p115. 400w. 4
MG April p51. 200w. 2
MM Feb. 26 p24. 900w. 4
RS April 7 p83. 50w. 4
RS April 21 375w. $3\frac{1}{2}$
SOU May p56. 300w. 5
SR May p86. 100w. 3
VV March 7 p45. 400w. $3\frac{1}{2}$
ZZ March 675w. $1\frac{1}{2}$

475 KISS. Alive. Casablanca CALD5001-1/2 (2 LP set)
MM June 4 p20. 25w. 2

476 KISS. Alive II. Casablanca 7076 (2 discs)
MM Dec. 21 p15. 50w. 2

477 KISS. Destroyer. Casablanca 7027
MM June 4 p20. 25w. 2

478 KISS. Dressed to Kill. Casablanca CAL 2008
CAC July p134. 50w. 0

479 KISS. Love Gun. Casablanca CHR 1131
CIR Sept. 8 p57-8. 700w. $2\frac{1}{2}$
CRA Oct. p64. 500w. 3
HF Oct. p148. 250w. $3\frac{1}{2}$
MG Sept. p52. 100w. $3\frac{1}{2}$
MM Sept. 10 p23. 200w. $1\frac{1}{2}$
RC July p12. 300w. $3\frac{1}{2}$
RS Aug. 25 p53-4. 425w. $2\frac{1}{2}$
SR Nov. p106, 108. 400w. 4

480 KISS. Rock and Roll Over. Casablanca NDLP 7037
AU March p82. 600w. 4
CAC June p90-1. 250w. 3
CIR Feb. 14 p10-1. 1250w. 1
CIR Feb. 28 p13. 350w. $2\frac{1}{2}$
MG Jan. 400w. 3
RO May p18. 675w. 2

481   KLAATU.   Capitol ST 11542
          GR   July   p234.   50w. $2\frac{1}{2}$
          RO   July   p71, 97.   1900w. $3\frac{1}{2}$
          SMG   Sept.   p26.   100w.   3

482   KLAATU.   Hope.   Capitol ST-11633
          CC   Nov.   p34.   100w.   3
          HF   Dec.   p139.   75w. $2\frac{1}{2}$
          SOU   Oct.   p64.   500w.   5
          TP   Nov.   p40.   125w.   4

483   KNIGHTON, Reggie.   Columbia PC 34685
          AU   Sept.   p87.   200w.   3
          CRA   Oct.   p78.   200w.   3
          RSP   Nov.-Dec.   p29.   300w.   3

484   KOOPER, Al.   Act Like Nothing's Wrong.   United Artists,
      UA-LA702-G
          CK   March   p57.   25w.   3
          CRA   Jan.   p70.   850w.   4
          SR   March   p104.   200w.   3

485   KORNER, Alexis.   Get Off My Cloud.   Columbia PC 33427
          CRA   June   p71.   400w.   4

486   KRAAN.   Wiederhorn.   Harvest (West Germany)
          EUR   V2/#2   p24.   175w.   4

487   KRAFTWERK.   Trans-Europe Express.   Capitol SW 11603
          AU   Aug.   p84.   250w.   4
          CIR   Aug. 4   p60-1.   350w. $1\frac{1}{2}$
          VV   May 23   p59.   325w. $2\frac{1}{2}$

488   KRAMER, Billy J.   Best of.   EMI NUT 9 (E) (Reissue)
          MM   Sept. 10   p20.   50w. $2\frac{1}{2}$
          NK   Autumn   p46.   25w. $3\frac{1}{2}$
          RR   Oct.   p88.   25w. $2\frac{1}{2}$

489   KRAZY Kat.   China Seas.   Mountain TOPC 5004 (E)
          MM   Jan. 29   p23.   200w.   1
          TP   June/July   p39.   125w.   2

490   KURSAAL Flyers.   Five Live Kursaals.   CBS 82253 (E)
          RR   Dec.   p86.   25w. $1\frac{1}{2}$

491   KURSAAL Flyers.   Golden Mile.   CBS 81622 (E)
          TP   Feb./March   p32-3.   450w.   5

492   L. A. Express.   Shadow Play.   Caribou PZ 34355.   Cart.
      PZA 34355
          MM   March 5   p24.   225w.   3
          SR   March   p104.   300w.   2

493   LA Dusseldorf.   Nova 622550 AO
      EUR   No. 7/8 p43.   275w.   4

494   LAINE, Denny.   Holly Days.   Capitol ST-11588.   Cass.   4XT-
      11588.   Cart.   8XT-11588
      CIR   March 31 p21.   300w.   3
      CRA   April p106.   75w.   3½
      RR   Aug.   p83-4.   75w.   2
      RS   June 16 p63.   800w.   2
      SR   Oct.   p104.   375w.   2½
      TP   Feb. /March p29-30.   750w.   3

495   LAING, Corky.   Makin' It on the Street.   Elektra 7ES-1097
      OLR   Dec.   p291.   50w.   1½

496   LAKE.   Columbia PC34763
      MM   July 16 p27.   50w.   2½
      RS   Sept. 22 p78.   250w.   2

497   LANCASTER, Jack/Robin Lumley.   Marscape.   RSO 2394 170
      CAC   Jan.   p376.   300w.   3½
      RS   March 10.   p71.   50w.   3
      TP   Feb. /March p33.   250w.   2½

498   LASO.   MCA MCF 2804 (E)
      MM   Aug. 13 p20.   50w.   0

499   LASRY, Teddy.   E=MC2.   RCA
      EUR   V2/#1 p34.   250w.   4

500   LAVENDER Hill Mob.   Lavender Hill Mob.   United Artists
      UA-LA719-G.   Cart.   EA719-H
      CC   March p32.   50w.   3
      MM   June 4 p20.   50w.   1
      SR   July p96.   100w.   2
      VV   March 14 p81, 83.   3

501   LAW.   Breakin' It.   MCA 2240
      SOU   April p51.   400w.   3

502   LEADON, Bernie and Michael Georgiades.   Natural Progres-
      sions.   Asylum 7E 1107
      CIR   Dec. 8 p74.   100w.   0
      CRA   Oct.   p68.   325w.   3½
      CS   Dec.   p29.   100w.   3
      MG   Oct.   p59.   75w.   2½
      MM   Sept. 3 p18.   200w.   0
      RC   Nov.   p4-5.   75w.   1
      RS   Oct. 6 p86.   175w.   ½

503   LED Zeppelin.   Presence.   Swan Song SS 8416
      AU   Jan.   p81.   350w.   4

504   LED Zeppelin.   The Song Remains the Same.   Swan Song
      SS2-201
          AU   Feb.   p78.   400w.   4
          CIR Jan.   17 p13.   650w. $3\frac{1}{2}$
          CRA Jan.   p73.   350w.   3
          GP   Feb.   p113.   25w.   2
          GR   Jan.   p1197.   50w. $3\frac{1}{2}$
          RSP Jan. -Feb.   p16-9.   1600w. $1\frac{1}{2}$
          SR   Feb.   p96.   150w.   2

505   LIGHTFOOT, Gordon.   Summer Dream.   Reprise MS 2246
          CS   Jan.   p16.   150w. $4\frac{1}{2}$
          OLR Sept.   p224.   25w.   4

506   LINDENBERG, Udo.   No Panic.   Decca KTXC R116 (E)
          CAC April   p14.   200w.   3

507   LINDENBERG, Udo & Das Panik Orchester.   Sister King Kong.
      Telefunken 622609 AS (West Germany)
          TP   Feb./March   p26.   250w.   5

508   LITTLE Feat.   Time Loves a Hero.   Warner Bros. BS 3015
          AU   Aug.   p87.   250w.   4
          CIR June 23.   p55-7.   1300w. $3\frac{1}{2}$
          CRA July   p82.   750w.   2
          GP   July   p129.   175w.   4
          GR   July   p234.   150w.   5
          HF   July   p150.   600w.   4
          MG   July   p51.   125w.   2
          MM   May 7   p21.   500w. $4\frac{1}{2}$
          RR   July   p96.   100w.   4
          SR   Oct.   p104.   200w. $2\frac{1}{2}$
          VV   May 16   p55.   100w. $1\frac{1}{2}$

509   LITTLE River Band.   Diamantia Cocktail.   Harvest SW 11645
          MG   Sept.   p52.   75w. $2\frac{1}{2}$
          MM   Oct. 8   p29.   200w. $2\frac{1}{2}$
          RC   Nov.   p13.   300w. $2\frac{1}{2}$
          RS   Aug. 25   p57.   250w. $1\frac{1}{2}$

510   LODGE, John.   Natural Avenue.   London PS 683.   Cart.
      8-683.   Cass. 5-683
          CAC April   p 14.   200w.   0
          CIR Oct. 27   p68-9.   100w.   0
          RS   June 16   p66.   150w.   1
          SR   Sept.   p104.   75w.   4

511   LOFGREN, Nils.   I Came to Dance.   A&M SP-4628.   Cart.
      T-4628.   Cass. CS-4628
          AU   June   p118.   100w.   2
          CAC May   p50.   300w.   4
          CIR June 9   p53-4.   450w. $3\frac{1}{2}$
          GR   May   p1757.   50w.   4

HF   June p122.   250w.   2
MM   March 5 p31.   400w.   4
RS   May 5 400w.   3
SR   July p93.   400w.   5

512   LOFGREN, Nils.   Night after Night.   A&M 8439
MM   Oct. 15 p25.   450w. $4\frac{1}{2}$
RS   Dec. 1 p77, 78.   500w.   2
RSP   Nov. -Dec.   p21.   250w. $3\frac{1}{2}$

513   LOGGINS, Kenny.   Celebrate Me Home.   Columbia PC-34655.
Cass. PCT-34655.   Cart. PCA-34655
CRA   July p74.   275w. $2\frac{1}{2}$
CS   Nov. p18.   250w. $3\frac{1}{2}$
MM   Aug. 6 p17.   50w.   0
RS   June 16 p66, 69.   350w.   2
SR   Oct. p106.   175w.   3

514   LOGGINS, Kenny and Jim Messina.   The Best of Friends.
Columbia PC 34388 (Reissue)
RS   Jan. 13 p47.   25w. $2\frac{1}{2}$
SMG   May p23.   125w.   1

515   LONE Star.   Columbia PC 34475
AU   Oct. p175.   250w. $2\frac{1}{2}$
CRA   May p76-7.   300w. $2\frac{1}{2}$
SR   June p104.   50w.   4
TP   Dec./Jan.   p33.   250w.   0

516   LONE Star.   Firing on All Six.   Columbia PC 34937
RR   Nov. p115.   50w.   2

517   The LOST Gonzo Band.   Thrills.   MCA MCA-2232.   Cart.
MCAT 2232
CRA   Jan. p77.   125w. $1\frac{1}{2}$
SR   Feb. p97.   150w.   3

518   LOVIN' Spoonful.   Golden Hour (E) (Reissue)
CAC   June p95.   200w.   4

519   LOW, Andy Fairweather.   Be Bop 'n' Holla.   A&M SP-4602
MM   Jan. 1 p14.   200w.   2
RR   Jan. p84.   150w. $3\frac{1}{2}$
SR   July p97.   150w.   5

520   LYALL, William.   Solo Casting.   EMI EMA 780 (E)
CAC   Jan. p388.   225w. $3\frac{1}{2}$
MM   Jan. 8 p18.   50w. $1\frac{1}{2}$
RS   Aug. 25 p55.   75w. $2\frac{1}{2}$

521   LYNX.   Missing Lynx.   Quality SV 1933 (Canada)
OLR   June p141.   50w.   4

522   LYNYRD Skynyrd. One More From the Road.   MCA MCA2-6001
      GP   Feb. p113. 50w. 3
      GR   Jan. p1197. 50w. 2½
      RO   May   p17. 400w. 2
      SR   Jan. p92. 50w. 3

523   LYNYRD Skynyrd. Street Survivors.   MCA 3029
      MM   Oct. 29 p23. 200w. 4

524   MC 5.   Back in the USA.   Atlantic K50346 (Reissue)
      GR   May   p1758. 75w. 4
      MM   April 2 p22. 200w. 3
      RR   May   p86. 25w. 3

524a MC 5.   Kick Out the Jams.   Elektra K 42027 (E)
      GR   Aug. p354. 50w. 1½
      MM   June 4 p20. 300w. 3½

525   McCARTNEY, Paul. Wings Over America.   Capitol SWCO-
      11593.   8X3C11593 (3 discs)
      RSP March-April p16-9. 1950w. 4½
      SOU Feb. p42. 300w. 4½
      SR   March p101. 600w. 4

526   McDONALD, Country Joe. Best of.   Golden Hour GH 865
      (E) (Reissue)
      CAC June p108. 50w. 3
      CMP July p38. 200w. 3

527   McDONALD, Country Joe. Goodbye Blues.   Fantasy 9525
      MM   June 4 p28. 150w. 2

528   McGARRIGLE, Kate and Anna McGarrigle.   Warner BS 3862
      AU   July p92. 175w. 4

528a McGARRIGLE, Kate and Anna McGarrigle.   Dancer with Bruised
      Knees.   Warner BS 3014
      AU   July p92. 175w. 4
      CC   April p36. 75w. 3
      CRA May   p72. 600w. 4½
      FR   June p33. 300w. 4
      GR   April p1617. 200w. 3½
      MM   Jan. 29 p27. 525w. 4½
      RC   Aug. p7. 250w. 4½
      RS   May 5 1050w. 3½
      SR   June p106. 650w. 5
      VV   March 28 p49, 8a. 350w. 4½
      ZZ   Feb. 400w. 3

529   McGUINN, Roger. Thunderbyrd. Columbia PC-34656.   Cart.
      PCA-34656.   Cass. PCT-34656
      AU   June p116. 150w. 2
      CIR June 23 p66-7. 400w. 2

          MM   May 14 p32.   650w.   3½
          RS   April 21 325w.   3½
          SR   July p97, 99.   225w.   2½
          ZZ   May p36-7.   775w.   2½

530-1 McGUINNESS, Flint. Lo and Behold. DJM (E)
          CAC Jan. p380.   250w.   2

532   McLAUCHLAN, Murray. Boulevard.   Island ILTN 9423
          CRA May p79.   300w.   3
          HF   March p140.   300w.   4
          MG   Feb. p54.   125w.   2½
          OLR March p54.   25w.   5
          RS   Feb. 10 p105.   375w.   4
          SR   March p108.   150w.   3

533   McLAUCHLAN, Murray. Hard Rock Town.   Island ILTN 9466
          AU   Dec. p118.   350w.   4½
          CC   Oct. p34.   100w.   3
          SOU Oct. p59.   300w.   5

534   McLEAN, Don.   Prime Time.   EMI ARI. 4149 (E)
          MM   Jan. 7 p16.   325w.   1½

535   McLEAN, Don.   Solo.   United Artists LA 652
          AU   Feb. p78.   100w.   3
          FOL Feb. p13-5.   900w.   5
          GP   Feb. p113.   50w.   4½
          SR   June p87.   200w.   5

536   MAGMA. Inedits. Tapioca
          EUR V2/#1 p30.   200w.   4

537   MAGMA. Udu Wudu. Tomato 6001
          MG   Oct. p60.   75w.   3

538   MAHOGANY Rush. IV. Columbia KC 34190
          MM   Jan. 15 p34.   125w.   1½
          OLR March p54.   25w.   3

539   MAHOGANY Rush. World Anthem. Columbia PC 34677
          CIR Sept. 29 p60-1.   150w.   2
          MM   July 16 p22.   250w.   4
          RR   Nov. p115.   50w.   3½

540   MALLARD. In a Different Climate.   Virgin V 2077
          MM   April 9 p27.   200w.   3½
          RR   July p96.   75w.   5
          VV   Oct. 3 p65.   75w.   3

541   MAMA'S Pride. Uptown and Lowdown.   Atlantic SO36-146
          MM   April 16 p23.   50w.   2½

542 MANCHESTER, Melissa. Help Is On the Way. Arista AL
     4095. Cart. 8301-4095H
          HF   Feb. p144. 50w. 2
          RS   Feb. 10 p103. 375w. 2
          SR   March p104, 105. 75w. 3

543 MANCHESTER, Melissa. Singin'. Arista 4136. Cart. 8301-
     4136(H)
          HF   Oct. p152. 150w. 2
          MG   Sept. p51. 125w. 1
          RS   Sept. 22 p72. 300w. $1\frac{1}{2}$
          SR   Nov. p108. 150w. 2

544 MANDRILL. We Are One. Arista AB 4144. Cart. AT8 4144.
     Cass. ATC 4144
          HF   Dec. p136. 325w. $3\frac{1}{2}$

545 MANN, Carl. Sunnyvale 4330 906
          CRA Oct. p66-7. 50w. $2\frac{1}{2}$

546 MANN, Carl. Legendary Sun Performer. Charly CR 30-140
     (E)
          NK   Autumn p50. 50w. $3\frac{1}{2}$

547 MANN, Manfred. Best. EMI NUT7 (E) (Reissue)
          NK   Autumn p46. 25w. $3\frac{1}{2}$
          MM   Sept. 10 p24. 200w. 3
          RR   Oct. p88. 375w. $3\frac{1}{2}$

548 MANN, Manfred. 1971-73. Vertigo (E) (Reissue)
          MM   Aug. 13 p20. 200w. 3

549 MANN, Manfred. The Roaring Silence. Warner Bros. BS
     2965. Cart. M82965
          SR   March p104. 300w. 2

550 MARTIN, Ricci. Beached. Epic PE 34834
          MG   Nov. p52. 25w. $2\frac{1}{2}$

551 MARTINEZ, Hirth. Big Bright Street. Warner BS 3065
          MG   Nov. p51. 25w. $2\frac{1}{2}$
          RS   Oct. 20 p92. 250w. $2\frac{1}{2}$
          VV   Oct. 3 p65. 50w. 3

552 MARTYN, John. So Far So Good. Island ILPS-9484. Cart.
     Y81-9484
          RR   May p86-7. 50w. $2\frac{1}{2}$
          SR   Nov. p108. 250w. 4

553 MASON, Dave. Certified Live. Columbia PG 34174. Cart.
     PGA 34174
          MM   Jan. 8 p18. 50w. $3\frac{1}{2}$
          RR   March p96. 200w. $3\frac{1}{2}$

SR March p108. 150w. 4

554 MASON, Dave. Let It Flow. Columbia PC-34680. Tape
PCT-34680. Cass. PCA-34680
GP Aug. p120. 50w. $2\frac{1}{2}$
MG July p51. 75w. 3
MM July 2 p21. 225w. $2\frac{1}{2}$
RC June 16 p69, 71. 400w. 2
SR Sept. p106. 250w. 4
ZZ June p36. 600w. 2

555 MASON, Harvey. Earth Mover. Arista 4096 (E)
MM Feb. 19 p25. 125w. $2\frac{1}{2}$

556 MATCHBOX. Riders in the Sky. Rockhouse 7612
NK Spring p42. 100w. 3

557 MATRIX IX. RCA ALP1-2452
CR Dec. p73. 50w. $2\frac{1}{2}$

558 MATTHEWS, Ian. Hit and Run. Columbia PC-34671. Cart.
PCA-34671. Cass. PCT-34671
CIR May 26 p57. 175w. $2\frac{1}{2}$
RS June 2 p91. 200w. $2\frac{1}{2}$
SR Aug. p98. 175w. $2\frac{1}{2}$
ZZ May p38. 200w. 3

559 MAYALL, John. Lots of People. ABC AB-992
SR May p88. 75w. 2

560 MAYALL, John. Primal Solos. London LC50003 (Reissue)
TP April/May p29-30. 850w. 3

561 MEAT Loaf. Bat Out of Hell. Epic PE 34974
RS Dec. 29 p77. 300w. $2\frac{1}{2}$

562 MECO. Music Inspired by Star Wars and Other Galactic Funk.
Millenium MNLP 8001. Tape MNL8 8001. Cass. MNL5-8001
MG Dec. p59. 75w. 2
SR Dec. 175w. $2\frac{1}{2}$

563 MEDICINE Head. Two Man Band. Barn 2314 102 (E)
CAC Feb. p418-9. 250w. 2
MM Jan. 22 p23. 50w. $1\frac{1}{2}$

564 MELANIE. Golden Hour of. Golden Hour GH861 (E) (Reissue)
CAC April p14. 225w. 3
GR April p1608. 50w. $2\frac{1}{2}$
MM March 19 p31. 50w. 3

565 MELANIE. Photograph. Atlantic SD 18190. Cart. TP
18190. Cass. CS 18190
HF Feb. p144. 50w. 3

       RS   Jan. 13 p55.   325w.   3
       SR   March p95.   175w.   4

566   METRO.   Transatlantic TRAG 340 (E)
       CAC   May p52.   300w. $4\frac{1}{2}$
       MM   May 14 p33.   50w. $1\frac{1}{2}$
       RR   May p87.   50w. $3\frac{1}{2}$
       TP   June/July p39.   125w.   3

567   MIDDLETON, Tom.   One Night Lovers.   Columbia ES 90326
       OLR   March p54.   25w. $2\frac{1}{2}$

568   MIDLER, Bette.   Broken Blossom.   Atlantic SD 19151
       RS   Feb. 9 p99.   500w.   2

569   MIDLER, Bette.   Live at Last.   Atlantic SD 2-9000 (2 discs)
       CIR   Aug. 4 p58.   200w.   3
       MG   July p51.   125w.   1
       MM   July 16 p27.   50w.   1
       SR   June p77.   760w.   3
       VV   June 20 p51.   300w.   5

570   MILK 'n' Cookies.   Island ILPS 9320
       TP   April/May p31.   375w.   4

571   MILLER, Bruce.   Rude Awakening.   A&M SP 9018 (Canada)
       OLR   March p55.   25w. $3\frac{1}{2}$

572   MILLER, Frankie.   Full House.   Chrysalis CHR 1128
       AU   July p91.   300w.   4
       CIR   Oct. 13 p76.   150w. $3\frac{1}{2}$
       CRA   July p8.   225w.   3
       GR   June p110.   75w.   4
       RR   July p95.   50w.   3
       RS   June 2 325w.   3
       VV   July 4 p69.   100w. $3\frac{1}{2}$

573   MILLER, Steve.   Book of Dreams.   Capitol SO-11630
       AU   Nov. p117.   250w.   3
       CIR   Sept. 15 p66-7.   850w. $1\frac{1}{2}$
       CRA   Aug. p76.   300w. $3\frac{1}{2}$
       GR   Aug. p354.   50w. $2\frac{1}{2}$
       HF   Sept. p145.   50w. $1\frac{1}{2}$
       MG   Aug. p57.   100w.   4
       MM   May 21 p22.   500w.   3
       RS   July 14 p60, 62.   1200w. $3\frac{1}{2}$
       RSP   May-June p16-7.   650w.   2
       SMG   Sept. p26.   75w.   4
       SOU   July p40.   350w.   2
       SR   Oct. p106.   200w. $3\frac{1}{2}$

574   MINK Deville.   Capitol ST 11631
       CIR   Aug. 4 p58-9.   400w. $2\frac{1}{2}$

CRA Aug. p78. 400w. $3\frac{1}{2}$
GR Sept. p522. 125w. 3
MM June 4 p23. 300w. 0
RC Aug. p16. 150w. 3
RS July 14 p70. 400w. 3
RSP Nov. -Dec. p29. 200w. $3\frac{1}{2}$
VV May 23 p55. 250w. 4

575 MR Big. Photographic Smile. Arista 4083
AU April p86. 300w. 2
CAC July p31. 100w. 2
CRA May p71. 175w. 4
HF April p148. 50w. 3
MM April 16 p23. 350w. 3

576 MITCHELL, Joni. Don Juan's Reckless Daughter. Asylum
BB101 (2 discs)
VV Dec. 19 p79. 750w. 3

577 MITCHELL, Joni. Hejira. Asylum 7E-1087 ET8-1087
AU March p84. 400w. 4
CRE March p59. 550w. $3\frac{1}{2}$
GR Feb. p1332. 100w. $4\frac{1}{2}$
HF March p138. 600w. 4
MG Feb. p53. 375w. 2
OLR Sept. p224. 25w. $2\frac{1}{2}$
RO May p12. 900w. $3\frac{1}{2}$
RR Feb. p93. 75w. 5
RS Feb. 10 p99, 100. 1525w. $3\frac{1}{2}$
SR March p106. 800w. 3

578 MONEY, Eddie. Columbia PC 34909
MM Oct. 22 p18. 250w. 5

579 MONICK, Suzie. Melting Pots. Adelphi AD 4107
AU Feb. p87. 200w. 4
RSP vol. 1 no. 3 p20. 100w. $2\frac{1}{2}$
SR March p108. 200w. 4

580 MONIES. Double A. GTO (E)
MM Dec. 3 p24. 300w. 2

581 MOODY Blues. Caught Live + 5. London 2PS 690/1 (2 discs)
Cart. 2PS8-690/1. Cass. 2PS5-690/1
CIR Oct. 27 p68-9. 100w. 2
RSP May-June p24. 550w. 5
SMG Sept. p25. 125w. 3
SR Sept. p106, 110. 225w. $2\frac{1}{2}$

582 MOON. Turning the Tides. Epic EPC 82084 (E)
MM June 11 p19. 200w. $3\frac{1}{2}$
RR Nov. p115. 25w. $3\frac{1}{2}$

583   MOORE, Stevie.   Phonography.   Vital VS 0001
      TP Dec. p36. 150w. 3

584   MORAZ, Patrick.   Out in the Sun.   Import IMP 1014
      CK Dec. p72. 100w. 3
      TP Nov. p39, 40. 175w. 5

585   MORRIS, Christopher.   MCA 2282
      MG Sept. p52. 75w. 3
      RS Oct. 6 p96. 300w. 2

586   MORRISON, Van.   A Period of Transition.   Warner Bros. BS
      2987.   Cass. M52987.   Cart. M82987
      AU Aug. p86. 150w. 4
      CIR Aug. 4 p57-8. 500w. $2\frac{1}{2}$
      DB Sept. 8 p36, 38. 400w. 4
      GR July p234. 50w. 4
      MM April 23 p22. 750w. 2
      RC June p6. 300w. $4\frac{1}{2}$
      RS May 19 300w. 2
      RSP May-June p15, 24. 700w. 3
      SR Oct. p106, 115. 275w. 3

587   MORSE Code.   Procreation.   Capitol SKAO 70046 (Canada)
      OLR Dec. p293-4. 25w. 2

588   MORTIFEE, Ann.   Baptism.   Capitol ST 6437 (Canada)
      OLR March p55. 25w. $3\frac{1}{2}$
      RM Jan. p15. 200w. 5

589   MOTORHEAD.   Chiswick WIK 2 (E)
      TP Dec. p39. 250w. $2\frac{1}{2}$

590   MOTORS. 1.   Virgin V 2089
      MM Sept. 10 p23. 325w. $3\frac{1}{2}$
      RR Nov. p115. 75w. $3\frac{1}{2}$

591   MOTT the Hoople.   Greatest Hits.   Columbia PC 34368 (Re-
      issue)
      CIR Feb. 14 p11. 750w. $2\frac{1}{2}$
      RS Jan. 13 p48. 100w. 2

592   MOXY.   Ridin' High.   Mercury 1-1161
      MM Sept. 3 p22. 25w. $3\frac{1}{2}$

593   MUD.   Greatest Hits   RAK SRKA6755 (E) (Reissue)
      RC Nov. p6. 125w. $4\frac{1}{2}$

594   MUD.   It's Better Than Working.   Private Stock (E)
      CAC Feb. p419. 125w. 1

595   MUD.   Mudpack.   Private Stock PVLP 1022 (E)
      RC Nov. p6. 125w. $2\frac{1}{2}$

596   MULDAUR, Geoff.   Motion.   Reprise MS 2255
      CIR   Jan. 17 p17.   300w.   0
      MG   Jan.   p47.   175w. $2\frac{1}{2}$
      SR   Feb.   p100.   150w.   4

597   MULDAUR, Maria.   Sweet Harmony.   Stereotype RST 2205C
      AU   Jan.   p91.   400w.   3

598   MURPHY, Elliott.   Just a Story from America.   Columbia
      PC-34653.   Cart.   PCA-34653.   Cass.   PCT-34653
      CIR   May 26 p55.   500w.   1
      CIR   May 26 p55.   500w.   3
      CRA   May p68, 70.   400w. $2\frac{1}{2}$
      HF   June p122.   250w.   2
      MG   May p51.   125w.   2
      MM   June 4 p28.   375w.   3
      RS   May 19 p47.   425w. $4\frac{1}{2}$
      SR   Aug.   p98, 100.   375w.   2

599   NASTY Pop.   Mistaken I.D.   Polydor 2302 056 (E)
      RS   Aug. 25 p55.   50w. $2\frac{1}{2}$
      TP   June/July p35-6.   225w. $1\frac{1}{2}$

600   NAZARETH.   Expect No Mercury.   A&M SP4666
      MM   Dec. 3 p24.   300w.   4

601   NAZARETH.   Play 'n' the Game.   A&M 4610
      CIR   April 14 p18.   400w.   1
      CRA   Jan. p74.   400w.   3
      MM   Jan. 1 p15.   450w. $4\frac{1}{2}$
      RRE   March-April p60.   300w.   3
      RS   March 24 p74.   200w. $1\frac{1}{2}$

602   NEKTAR.   Magic Is a Child.   Polydor PD-1-6115
      CR   Dec. p73.   50w. $2\frac{1}{2}$

603   NELSON, Rick.   Intakes.   Epic PE 34420
      RS   Nov. 17 p97.   400w. $1\frac{1}{2}$

604   NELSON, Rick.   Singles Album, 1963-76.   MCA Coral CDL
      8063 (E) (Reissue)
      NK   Autumn p48.   25w.   4

605   NEW Central Connection Unlimited.   NCCU Super Trick.
      United Artists LA729-G
      MM   Oct. 15 p23.   200w. $2\frac{1}{2}$

606   NEW Commander Cody Band.   Rock 'n' Roll Again.   Arista
      4125
      CIR   Dec. 8 p77.   250w. $2\frac{1}{2}$
      MG   Oct. p59.   25w.   0
      MM   Aug. 27 p21.   250w. $3\frac{1}{2}$
      RR   Dec. p86.   50w. $1\frac{1}{2}$

607   NEW Legion Rock Spectacular. Wild Ones. Spectacular SPLP
      7777
        WHO Nov. p40-1. 325w. 4

608   NEW Riders of the Purple Sage. Best of.   Columbia PC
      34367 (Reissue)
        CMP March p37. 150w. 3
        MM Jan. 22 p46. 50w. $2\frac{1}{2}$
        RR April p87. 50w. 3

609   NEW Riders of the Purple Sage. Who Are These Guys? MCA
      MCF 2793
        CMR July p20. 100w. 3
        RR June p93. 25w. 3
        SR May p91. 75w. 4

610   NEWMAN, Randy. Little Criminals. Warner BSK 3079.
      Cart. M8 3079. Cass. M5 3079
        HF Dec. p134-5. 600w. $3\frac{1}{2}$
        MG Dec. p55. 100w. 4
        MM Oct. 22 p18. 400w. $3\frac{1}{2}$
        RRE Nov.-Dec. p20. 450w. $3\frac{1}{2}$
        RS Dec. 1 p69-70, 73. 1000w. 1

611   NILSSON, Harry. Early Tymes. Musicar MUS 2505. Cart.
      MCR 8T-2505. Cass. MCR CA 2505
        RC July p4. 300w. 2
        SR Nov. p105. 300w. 2

612   NILSSON, Harry. Knnillssonn. RCA APL1-2276. Tape
      AFK1-2276. Cass. AFS1-2276
        GR Nov. p919. 25w. 2
        HF Oct. p158. 300w. 3
        MG Oct. p59. 75w. $1\frac{1}{2}$
        MM Sept. 3 p21. 300w. $\frac{1}{2}$
        RS Sept. 22 p63. 375w. $2\frac{1}{2}$
        SOU Oct. p62. 300w. $4\frac{1}{2}$
        SR Nov. p105. 300w. 4

613   NITTY Gritty Dirt Band. Dirt, Silver and Gold.   United
      Artists LA670L31 (3 discs)
        CRA March p77. 500w. $2\frac{1}{2}$
        MG April p55. 125w. $2\frac{1}{2}$
        MM March 5 p24. 350w. $3\frac{1}{2}$
        ZZ Feb. p46. 850w. 4

614   NOVA. Wirgs of Love. Arista 4150
        MM Oct. 1 p48. 50w. 2
        RR Nov. p114. 150w. 4

615   NUGENT, Ted. Cat Scratch Fever. Epic JE 34700
        CIR Sept. 8 p59-60. 600w. $2\frac{1}{2}$
        GP Dec. p153. 100w. 3

GR   Sept.   p522.   100w.   3
MG   Aug.   p59.   125w.   3½
MM   Jan.   18 p21.   300w.   4
RC   Oct.   p5.   50w.   2

616   NUGENT, Ted.   Free-For-All.   Epic PE 34121
CIR   Feb.   28 p10-1.   1000w.   3
GP   March p112.   175w.   4
GR   Jan.   p1197.   50w.   3
HF   Jan.   p144.   250w.   3

617   NUTZ.   Hart Nutz.   A&M 4623
MM   April 2 p20.   200w.   3

618   NYRO, Laura.   Season of the Lights.   Columbia PC 34786
FOL   Dec.   p13, 21.   1000w.   2½
MM   Sept.   3 p46.   250w.   3
RR   Nov.   p115.   50w.   3
RS   Aug.   11 p69.   325w.   2½
VV   April 4 p49, 51.   275w.   3

619   O Band.   The Knife.   United Artists UAG 30077 (E)
MM   Aug.   27 p21.   200w.   2
TP   Dec.   p39.   200w.   2

620   ODYSSEY.   RCA APL1-2204
MG   Dec.   p62.   125w.   2½

621   OFFENBACH.   A&M SP 9027 (Canada)
CC   June p30.   50w.   3

622   OFFENBACH.   Never Too Tender.   A&M SP 9025 (Canada)
CC   Feb.   p32.   50w.   3
MM   April 2 p22.   300w.   3½
OLR   June p141.   25w.   2

623   O'KEEFE, Danny.   American Roulette.   Warner BS 3050
CRA   Oct.   p78.   250w.   3½

624   OMAHA Sheriff.   Come Hell or Waters High.   RCA APL1-
2022
AU   Nov.   p119.   200w.   3
MM   July 16 p27.   50w.   3

625   ORBISON, Roy.   Sunnyvale 9330 904 (Reissue)
CRA   Oct.   p66-7.   50w.   3

626   ORBISON, Roy.   Regeneration.   Monument MG 7600
CRA   April p105.   450w.   2
MM   March 19 p30.   250w.   3
SOU   March p37.   300w.   2

627   OTWAY, John and Wild Willy Barrett.   Polydor 2383 453 (E)

MM   May 28 p28.   550w.   4
TP   Nov. p41, 42.   250w.   2½

628   OUTLAWS. Hurry Sundown.   Arista 4135
        CIR   Aug. 18 425w.   3½
        CMR   Sept. p17.   125w.   2
        GR   Aug. p354.   100w.   3½
        MM   June 18 p18.   250w.   3½
        RSP   May-June p23, 27.   450w.   3½

629   OUTLAWS. Lady in Waiting.   Arista AL 4070
        GP   Oct. p129.   150w.   4½

630   PFM. Jet Lag. Asylum 7E-1101
        CK   Nov. p65.   50w.   3
        MM   Aug. 27 p19.   300w.   2½
        RC   July p12.   200w.   3½
        RS   Aug. 25 p56.   200w.   3

631   PABLO Cruise. A Place in the Sun.   A&M SP 4625
      8 8T-4625
        MM   April 23 p21.   200w.   3½
        SR   June p109, 110.   175w.   3

632   PAGLIARO. Time Race. CBS PES 90408 (Canada)
        SOU   July p43.   200w.   4

633   PAICE-Ashton-Lord. Malice in Wonderland.   Warner Bros.
      BS 3038
        CAC   June p81.   300w.   3½
        CK   Aug. p49.   125w.   3½
        CRA   July p78.   225w.   2½
        RS   Aug. 25 p60.   300w.   4
        ZZ   April p47.   550w.   1½

634   PALMER, Robert. Some People Can Do What They Like.
      Island ILPS 9420
        AU   Jan. p79.   250w.   4
        CRA   Jan. p75.   325w.   3½
        GR   Feb. p1332, 1335.   50w.   3½
        SR   Feb. p100.   50w.   2

635   PARIS. Big Towne 2061.   Capitol ST 11650
        AU   Jan. p77.   300w.   2½
        ZZ   Jan.   500w.   4

636   PARKER, Graham. Heat Treatment.   Mercury SRM-1-117
        AU   March p89.   200w.   4
        CIR   Feb. 10 p11-2.   400w.   5
        DB   March 10 p24.   350w.   4
        GR   Feb. p1332.   75w.   4½
        RC   April p11.   200w.   4
        RR   Jan. p84.   150w.   4

637 PARKER, Graham. Stick to Me.   Mercury SRM-1-3706
  CIR Dec. 22 p66. 500w. $4\frac{1}{2}$
  MM Oct. 29 p24. 800w. 5
  RS Dec. 1 p73-4. 900w. $2\frac{1}{2}$
  RSP Nov.-Dec. p28. 200w. 3
  TP Dec. p34. 425w. 4
  VV Oct. 31 p59. 100w. 1
  VV Nov. 28 p66. 50w. 4

638 PARSONS, Alan. I Robot. Arista AL 7002
  CIR Sept. 29 p59. 250w. $2\frac{1}{2}$
  HF Oct. p158. 300w. 3
  MM July 23 p17. 250w. $4\frac{1}{2}$
  RC Oct. p10. 50w. 3
  RS Oct. 20 p83. 250w. 2
  SOU Oct. p66. 250w. 3
  SR Nov. p112. 225w. 0
  VV Aug. 29 p73. 500w. 4

639 PASSPORT. Iguacu. ATCO, SD 36-149
  CAD May p12. 50w. $2\frac{1}{2}$
  CK Aug. p49. 25w. 3
  MG June p53. 125w. 2

640 PEKKA. The Mathematician's Air Display. Virgin 2084
  MM Aug. 13 p20. 50w. $1\frac{1}{2}$

641 PERIGEO. Fata Morgana. RCA TPL1-1228
  RS Oct. 6 p96. 125w. $2\frac{1}{2}$

642 PERIGEO. The Valley of the Temples. RCA TPL1-1175
  CK March p56. 125w. 4

643 PERKINS, Carl. Sunnyvale 9330 903 (Reissue)
  CRA Oct. p66-7. 50w. $2\frac{1}{2}$

644 PERKINS, Carl. Long Tall Sally. CBS Embassy 31454 (E)
  (Reissue)
  CMP Aug. p40. 300w. 4
  NK Spring p40. 75w. 4

645 PERKINS, Carl. The Original. Charly 30-110 (Reissue)
  RSP Jan.-Feb. p36. 225w. 4

646 PETTY, Tom and the Heartbreakers. Shelter SRL 52006 (E)
  AU Feb. p76. 300w. 4
  CIR Jan. 31 p15. 150w. 2
  MG April p51. 125w. 5
  MM Feb. 26 p25. 375w. 3
  RC Oct. p2. 100w. $2\frac{1}{2}$
  RSP Nov.-Dec. p28. 200w. 3
  ZZ Feb. 700w. 4

647   PEZBAND. Passport PP 98021
       CRA   July p76.   200w.   2

648   PHILLIPS, Anthony. The Geese and the Ghost. Passport
       Records 98020
            AU   July p96.   600w.   3½
            GP   Aug. p120.   200w.   4

649   PHILLIPS, Glenn. Lost at Sea. Casablanca C 1519
            RR   May p87.   50w.   3

650   PHILLIPS, Glenn. Swim in the Wind. Virgin 2087 (E)
            MM   Nov. 19 p23.   250w.   3½

651   PHOENIX. Columbia PC 34476
            RS   March 10 p71.   25w.   2

652   PIERCE Arrow. Columbia PC 34805
            CIR   Sept. 8 p60.   100w.   2
            CRA   Oct. p70.   200w.   2½
            MG   Sept. p52.   75w.   1½
            RS   Aug. 11 p69.   475w.   3

653   PILOT. Morin Heights. EMI EMA 779 (E)
            RS   March 10 p71.   50w.   3

654   PINHAS, Richard. Rhizosphere. Cobra
            EUR   V2/#1 p31.   150w.   4

655   PINK Floyd. Animals. Columbia JC 34474. Cass. JCT-
       34474
            AU   May p86.   350w.   4
            AU   May p86.   450w.   4½
            CAC   April p8.   250w.   2½
            CIR   April 28 p13-4.   600w.   3
            CRA   April p104.   350w.   3
            DB   May 5 p24, 26.   325w.   1½
            GR   May p1757.   75w.   3½
            HF   May p118.   450w.   3
            MG   May p51.   125w.   3
            MM   Jan. 29 p22.   850w.   4
            RC   July p14-5.   350w.   5
            RO   July p74-5.   600w.   2
            RR   April p87.   200w.   3
            RS   March 24 p56, 57.   800w.   1½
            RSP   May-June p20.   800w.   1½
            SOU   April p55.   500w.   5
            SR   May p91, 93.   175w.   2
            TP   April/May p28.   325w.   4
            ZZ   March 900w.   4

656   PIPER. A&M SP-4615
            AU   Oct. p175.   250w.   3

CIR May 12 p14-5. 250w. 4
CRA May p76-7. 300w. $3\frac{1}{2}$
SR June p110. 150w. 3
TP June/July p34. 350w. $1\frac{1}{2}$

657 PIPER. Can't Wait. A&M SP 4654
SOU Dec. p56. 250w. 3
TP Dec. p36-7. 200w. $1\frac{1}{2}$

658 PIRATES. Out of Their Skulls. Warner Brothers BS 3155
GR Nov. p720. 50w. $3\frac{1}{2}$
MM Oct. 29 p23. 250w. $3\frac{1}{2}$
NK Autumn p45. 125w. $3\frac{1}{2}$
RR Dec. p86. 50w. 2

659 POCO. Indian Summer. ABC 989
CMR July p20. 300w. 3
MM May 14 p31. 250w. $4\frac{1}{2}$
RO Sept. p62. 200w. $3\frac{1}{2}$
ZZ June p40. 150w. 2

660 POCO. Rose of Cimarron. ABC ABCL 5166 (E)
CMR July p20. 25w. 3

661 POINT Blank. Arista AL 4087
HF Jan. p144. 100w. 4

662 POINT Blank. Second Season. Arista AL4137
RS Oct. 6 p102. 400w. 2

663 POPP, Marius. Panoramic Jazz-Rock. Elect record STM
EDE 02166 (Rumanian)
JF No. 49 p23. 50w. 3

664 POUSETTE-Dart Band. Amnesia. Capitol SW-11608. Cart.
8XW-11608. Cass. 4XW-11608
CAC Aug. p168. 300w. 2
SR Sept. p112. 125w. 2

665 PRATT, Andy. Shiver in the Night. Nemperor NE 443
AU Dec. p114. 150w. 1
CIR Nov. 10 p61. 350w. 2
HF Oct. p161. 200w. $2\frac{1}{2}$
MG Oct. p60. 50w. $2\frac{1}{2}$
MM Aug. 20 p14. 350w. $3\frac{1}{2}$
RR Nov. p114. 100w. $2\frac{1}{2}$
RS Sept. 22 p68, 70. 650w. $2\frac{1}{2}$
SR Dec. 550w. 4

666 The PRETTY THINGS. The Vintage Years. Sire SASH 3713-2
(Reissue)
CRE March p61. 350w. 4
RS Jan. 13 p51. 100w. 3

TP   Feb./March p31.   350w.   4

667   PRICE, Alan.   Shout Across the Street.   Polydor 2383 410
      AU   July p98.   300w.   4

668   PROCOL Harum.   Something Magic.   Chrysalis CHR-1130
      AU   July p76.   200w.   2
      CIR Sept. 15 p68-9.   300w.   3
      GR   May p1757 75w.   2
      MM   May 14 p33.   50w. $2\frac{1}{2}$
      RS   June 16 p71.   250w.   2
      RSP May-June p13.   600w. $3\frac{1}{2}$
      SOU May p59.   400w.   2
      SR   June p112.   125w.   0

669   PROKOP, Skip.   All Growed Up.   Quality SV 1948 (Canada)
      OLR Dec. p291.   25w.   4
      SOU June p40.   600w.   3

670   PROTHEROE, Brian.   I/You.   Chrysalis CHR 1108
      CK   Jan. p51.   25w.   4
      SR   Jan. p98.   100w.   3

671   PURE Prairie League.   Dance.   RCA AFL 1-1924
      CIR Feb. 14 p12.   175w.   1
      CMP Feb. p38.   100w.   3
      CMR Aug. p24.   100w.   1
      CS   Feb. 24 p27.   380w.   2

672   QUATEMAN, Bill.   Night After Night.   RCA APL1-2027.
      Cart. APS1-2027.   Cass. APK1-2027
      AU   May p90.   100w.   2
      CIR May 12 p19.   75w. $1\frac{1}{2}$
      MM   Aug. 6 p17.   50w. $1\frac{1}{2}$
      RS   Feb. 24 p66.   300w.   3
      SR   July p99.   250w. $2\frac{1}{2}$

673   QUEEN.   A Day at the Races.   Elektra 6E-1091
      AU   Sept. p88.   600w.   4
      CAC Feb. p414.   300w. $2\frac{1}{2}$
      CIR Feb. 28 p10.   550w. $2\frac{1}{2}$
      CRA March p82.   700w.   4
      CRE March p60.   550w. $\frac{1}{2}$
      GR   Feb. p1335.   25w. $2\frac{1}{2}$
      MG   April p51.   200w.   3
      RR   Feb. p93.   100w. $2\frac{1}{2}$
      RS   Feb. 24 p59, 61-2.   500w. $2\frac{1}{2}$
      RSP March-April p20-3.   1500w.   5
      SR   April p96.   300w.   4

674   The QUICK.   Mondo Deco.   Mercury SRM-1-1114
      RS   Feb. 24 p71.   200w. $1\frac{1}{2}$
      TP   Dec./Jan. p32.   300w.   3

675 RACING Cars. Downtown Tonight. Chrysalis CHR 1099
     AU Aug. p88. 150w. 4
     SR May p93. 150w. 4
     TP Feb./March p31. 500w. 2

676 RACING Cars. Weekend Rendezvous. Chrysalis CH-1149
     MM Sept. 10 p26. 375w. $3\frac{1}{2}$
     RC Dec. p16. 50w. 2
     RR Nov. p115. 25w. $3\frac{1}{2}$
     TP Nov. p37, 38. 175w. 5

677 RADIATORS from Space. TV Tube Heart. Chiswick WIK 4
     MM Oct. 22 p21. 550w. $3\frac{1}{2}$
     ZZ Nov. p33. 400w. $4\frac{1}{2}$

678 RAINBOW. On Stage. Oyster OY-2-1801
     CIR Oct. 13 p73. 250w. $1\frac{1}{2}$
     GP Nov. p137. 250w. 4
     MM Aug. 20 p18. 350w. 2
     RR Sept. p93. 100w. 3
     RS Aug. 25 p53-4. 175w. 2

679 RAITT, Bonnie. Sweet Forgiveness. Warner Bros. BS 2990.
     Cart. M82990. Cass. M52990
     AU July p89. 350w. 4
     CIR Aug. 18 400w. $3\frac{1}{2}$
     GP Nov. p137. 50w. $2\frac{1}{2}$
     GR July p234. 50w. $2\frac{1}{2}$
     HF June p127. 500w. 4
     MG June p49. 500w. 4
     MM May 7 p22. 350w. 2
     RC July p6. 300w. 2
     RS May 19 p69. 375w. $1\frac{1}{2}$
     SR Aug. p82-3. 325w. 5
     ZZ June p40. 125w. $3\frac{1}{2}$

680 RAM Jam. Epic PE 34885
     MG Dec. p56. 50w. $1\frac{1}{2}$
     MM Nov. 5 p19. 250w. $3\frac{1}{2}$
     RS Oct. 20 p94. 250w. 1

681 RAMONES. Leave Home. Sire SA 7528
     CRA April p110. 325w. 3
     RA April 7 p69-70. 300w. $2\frac{1}{2}$
     RR Aug. p83. 100w. $1\frac{1}{2}$
     RS April 7 p83. 50w. $3\frac{1}{2}$
     SR June p114. 400w. 3

682 RAMONES. Rocket to Russia. Sire SR 6042
     RS Dec. 29 p69-71. 400w. $3\frac{1}{2}$
     VV Nov. 28 p66. 50w. $4\frac{1}{2}$
     VV Dec. 12 p56. 425w. 2
     ZZ Dec. p40-1. 650w. $4\frac{1}{2}$

683   RANDALL, Elliott.   Elliott Randall's New York.   Kirschner
       PZ 34351
            ZZ   April p45.   550w. $3\frac{1}{2}$

684   RANKIN, Kenny.   The Kenny Rankin Album.   Little David 1013.
       Cart. TP-1013.   Cass. CS-1013
            CRA   May   p78-9.   300w.   2
            RS   May 5   p69.   225w.   3
            SR   July   p99-100.   150w.   4

685   RARE Earth.   Prodigal P6-10019
            RC   Oct.   p13.   50w. $2\frac{1}{2}$
            SC   No. 2   p17.   75w.   4

686   RED Shadow, The New Economics Rock and Roll Band.   Phys-
       ical 21-005
            SO   Jan./Feb.   p50.   150w. $2\frac{1}{2}$

687   REDDY, Teddy.   Spoonfed SP3301
            CIR   June 23   p67.   450w. $4\frac{1}{2}$
            PRM   Feb.   p35.   500w. $4\frac{1}{2}$

688   REED, Lou.   Rock and Roll Heart.   Arista AL 4100.   Cart.
       8301-4100
            CRA   Jan.   p71.   125w. $\frac{1}{2}$
            HF   Feb.   p148.   200w.   2
            RC   May   p10.   200w. $3\frac{1}{2}$
            RM   Jan.   p29.   550w. $1\frac{1}{2}$
            SR   Feb.   p100.   250w.   0

689   REED, Lou.   Walk on the Wild Side! Best of.   RCA APL1-
       2001 (Reissue)
            CAC   Aug.   p164.   250w.   4
            CRA   July   p64.   750w. $2\frac{1}{2}$

690   RENAISSANCE.   Novella.   Sire SA-7526
            CK   May   p49.   25w. $4\frac{1}{2}$
            SR   June   p112.   125w.   4

691   REX.   Columbia PC-34399
            MM   Feb. 26   p26.   250w.   3

692   RIOT Rockers.   Rockhouse 7702
            NK   Spring   p39.   75w. $3\frac{1}{2}$

693   RITENOUR, Lee.   Captain Fingers.   Epic PE 34426
            CAD   June   p21.   200w.   2
            DB   Dec. 15   p32.   250w. $2\frac{1}{2}$
            GP   Dec.   p152.   125w. $3\frac{1}{2}$
            HF   Sept.   p142.   75w.   1
            MG   July   p53.   100w. $3\frac{1}{2}$

694   RIVERA, Scarlet.   Warner Bros.   BS 3060

      CAD Aug. p26. 100w. 3
      CIR Aug. 18 225w. 1
      VV Aug. 1 p51. 50w. $1\frac{1}{2}$

695 ROCK-a-Teens. Woo-hoo. Roulette SR 25109 (Sweden) (Re-issue)
      NK Autumn p45. 25w. 4

696 RODEN, Jess. Blowin'. Island ILPS 9496
      AU Sept. p87. 100w. 3

697 RODEN, Jess. Play It Dirty... Play It Class. Island ILPS 9442
      GR Feb. p1335. 50w. 2
      RR March p96. 50w. $2\frac{1}{2}$
      TP April/May p31. 150w. 4

698 ROLLING Stones. Love You Live. Rolling Stone COC 2-9001 (2 discs) Cart. TP2-9001. Cass. CS 2-9001
      GR Nov. p920. 125w. $3\frac{1}{2}$
      HF Dec. p136, 140. 325w. $2\frac{1}{2}$
      MM Sept. 24 p27. 600w. 2
      RC Oct. p2. 250w. 5
      RS Nov. 17 p81, 85. 1450w. 4
      SOU Nov. p54. 200w. 2
      VV Oct. 31 p60. 100w. $1\frac{1}{2}$

699 RONSTADT, Linda. Different Drum. EMI Capitol ST 11269
      CAC July p132. 175w. 3
      GR July p234. 50w. $2\frac{1}{2}$

700 RONSTADT, Linda. Greatest Hits. Asylum 106 (Reissue)
      CIR July 7 p49. 250w. 3
      CM April p54. 425w. 4
      CMP March p38. 150w. 5
      CMR April p33-4. 150w. 4
      GR Feb. p1332. 100w. $4\frac{1}{2}$
      MM Feb. 5 p23. 100w. $3\frac{1}{2}$

701 RONSTADT, Linda. Hasten Down the Wind. Asylum 1072
      CMP Jan. p39. 150w. 2

702 RONSTADT, Linda. A Retrospective. Capitol SKBB 11629 (2 discs) (Reissue)
      CIR July 7 p49. 275w. $3\frac{1}{2}$
      CMP Aug. p37. 200w. 4
      CMR Sept. p16. 125w. 4
      GR Oct. p715. 75w. $2\frac{1}{2}$
      MM Aug. 20 p15. 350w. 1
      SOU Nov. p54. 250w. 4

703 RONSTADT, Linda. Simple Dreams. Asylum 6E-104. Cart. ET 8104. Cass. TC 5104

AU   Dec.   p115.   200w. $3\frac{1}{2}$
CIR   Oct.   27   p65-6.   500w.   3
CMP   Nov.   p39.   250w.   4
GR   Nov.   p920.   75w. $3\frac{1}{2}$
HF   Nov.   900w. $1\frac{1}{2}$
MG   Oct.   p55-6.   900w.   3
MM   Sept.   17   p18.   400w. $3\frac{1}{2}$
RC   Oct.   p3.   100w.   5
RR   Nov.   p115.   50w.   1
RS   Oct.   20   p79, 83.   950w.   3
RSP   Nov. -Dec.   p16-7.   450w.   4
SR   Dec.   575w. $3\frac{1}{2}$
VV   Nov.   7   p53.   600w. $3\frac{1}{2}$

704   ROTHER, Michael.   Flammende Herzen.   Sky 007 (West Germany)
EUR   V2/#2   p23.   175w.   3
RS   Aug.   25   p55.   100w.   3

705   ROUGH Trade.   Live.   Umbrella UMB DD 1 (Canada)
AU   May   p92.   600w. $2\frac{1}{2}$
AU   July   p93.   150w.   3
CC   March   p32.   50w.   3

706   RUMOUR.   Max.   Mercury SRM-1-1174.   Tape: MC-8-11174.
Cass.   MCR-4-1-1174
AU   Nov.   p116.   200w.   3
CIR   Sept.   29.   p58-9.   150w. $2\frac{1}{2}$
GR   Oct.   p715.   25w. $3\frac{1}{2}$
HF   Oct.   p150.   650w.   4
MG   Sept.   p52.   75w.   3
MM   July   23   p18.   500w.   3
RS   Aug.   25   p55-6.   400w. $3\frac{1}{2}$
SOU   Nov.   p59.   200w.   3
SR   Dec.   175w.   3
TP   Sept.   p34.   300w.   3

707   The RUNAWAYS.   Queens of Noise.   Mercury SRM 1-1126
CIR   March   17   p15-6.   450w. $3\frac{1}{2}$
GR   July   p237.   50w.   2
RR   June   p93.   25w.   1
SR   May   p94.   200w.   0

708   RUNDGREN, Todd.   Oops, Wrong Planet.   Bearsville BR6970
RR   Nov.   p115.   50w. $2\frac{1}{2}$

709   RUNDGREN, Todd.   Ra.   Bearsville BR 6965
AU   April   p84.   250w.   5

710   RUSH.   All the World's a Stage.   Mercury 2-7508 (2 discs)
CIR   Feb.   28   p12-3.   850w.   2

711   RUSH.   Caress of Steel.   Mercury 1-1046

MM Feb. 26 p30. 75w. $2\frac{1}{2}$

712 RUSH. A Farewell to Kings. Mercury SRM 1-1184
  CC Nov. p34. 100w. 3
  MM Nov. 5 p22. 250w. 4
  RC Oct. p2. 100w. 4
  VV Nov. 28 p66. 50w. 0

713 RUSSELL, Leon. Best of. Shelter 52004 (Reissue)
  MM Jan. 8 p18. 50w. 3

714 RUSSELL, Leon and Mary Russell. Make Love to the Music.
  Paradise PAK 3066
  CIR Dec. 8 p75. 275w. $2\frac{1}{2}$
  MG Sept. p51. 125w. 3
  SR Dec. 225w. 2

715 RUSSELL, Ray. Ready or Not. DJM DJF 20506 (E)
  GR Sept. p522. 25w. $1\frac{1}{2}$

716 SAINTS. I'm Stranded. Sire SR 6039
  CRA Sept. p70. 150w. $1\frac{1}{2}$
  MG Dec. p55. 25w. 1
  RC Oct. p13. 25w. 2
  RR Aug. p83. 25w. 1
  ZZ May p37. 200w. 3

717 SANTANA. Festival. Columbia PC 34423
  CAC March p452. 200w. $3\frac{1}{2}$
  CIR June 9 p56. 300w. 3
  CRA May p78. 300w. $2\frac{1}{2}$
  DB April 21 p23-4. 350w. 4
  GP May p129. 75w. 3
  HF April p146. 300w. 4
  PRM Feb. p41. 300w. $1\frac{1}{2}$
  RRE March/April p13-5. 1760w. 3
  SOU March p38. 500w. 5

718 SANTANA. Moonflower. Columbia C2-34914 (2 discs)
  MM Nov. 5 p25. 350w. 2
  RC Dec. p9. 100w. 4
  RS Dec. 29 p73-4. 400w. 2

719 SAVOY Brown. The Best of Savoy Brown. London LC 50000
  (Reissue)
  TP April/May p29-30. 850w. 4

720 SAYER, Leo. Endless Flight. Warner BS 2962
  CIR Feb. 28. p12. 350w. 4
  MG Feb. p54. 125w. 4
  RS Jan. 27 p65. 350w. $3\frac{1}{2}$
  SR March p114. 150w. 2

721   SAYER, Leo.   Thunder in My Heart.   Warner BS 3089.   Cart.
      M5 3089.   Cass. M8 3089
         CIR Dec. 22 p67.   200w.   0
         HF   Dec. p140.   350w. $2\frac{1}{2}$
         MM   Oct. 8 p32.   350w. $1\frac{1}{2}$
         RS   Dec. 1 p77.   550w. $3\frac{1}{2}$
         VV   Dec. 26 p58.   300w. $1\frac{1}{2}$

722   SCAGGS, Boz.   Down Two Then Left.   Columbia 34729
         MM   Dec. 21 p15.   250w. $1\frac{1}{2}$

723   SCHULZE, Klaus.   Mirage.   Island 9461
         EUR V2/#1 p29.   300w.   4
         MM   May 7 p22.   350w.   3

724   SCOTT, Jack.   Rocks.   Rock 'n' Roll 75-001 (Reissue)
         RSP Jan. -Feb. p35.   100w. $2\frac{1}{2}$

725   SEA Level.   Capricorn CP 0178
         CRA May p72.   300w.   3
         DB   April 21 p26, 30.   350w.   3
         GP   Aug. p120.   125w.   5
         HF   June p136.   200w.   2
         MG   May p51.   100w.   2
         MM   April 30 p30.   100w.   3
         RS   June 16 p64, 66.   400w. $3\frac{1}{2}$
         SR   July p100.   150w.   2

726   SEALS and Crofts.   Greatest Hits.   Stereotape WST2886A
      (Reissue)
         AU   Jan. p91.   400w.   3

727   SEALS and Crofts.   Sudan Village.   Warner Brothers BS 2976
         RR   March p96.   200w.   4
         RS   Feb. 24. p66.   175w. $2\frac{1}{2}$
         SR   April p99, 100.   150w.   2

728   SECRET Oyster.   Astarte.   CBS 81208 (Sweden)
         EUR No. 7/8 p37-8.   500w. $3\frac{1}{2}$

729   The SECTION.   Fork It Over.   Capitol ST 11656
         RS   Sept. 8 p114, 116.   175w. $2\frac{1}{2}$
         SR   Dec.   150w. $3\frac{1}{2}$

730   SEFFER, Yochk'o.   Delive/Neffesh Music.   Moshe-Naim
         EUR V2/#1 p30-1.   175w.   4

731   SEGER, Bob.   Live Bullet.   EMI Capitol TC2 STSP16 (2
      discs)
         CAC April p15.   200w. $4\frac{1}{2}$
         SMG Jan. p26.   125w.   2

732   SEGER, Bob.   Night Moves.   Capitol ST 11557

```
        CIR   Jan. 31   p11-2.   600w.   5
        MG    Jan.   150w.   3
        RC    Nov.   p13-4.   200w.   3½
        RS    Jan. 13   p51.   300w.   5
        SOU   March   p40.   500w.   2½
        SR    March   p114.   100w.   2
```

733 SELF, Ronnie.   Colde 2014 (Reissue)
        NK   Winter   p37.   50w.   4

733a SENSATIONAL Alex Harvey Band.   Big Hits and Close Shaves.
     Vertigo 6360147 (Reissue)
        RR   Aug.   p83.   50w.   3

734 SENSATIONAL Alex Harvey Band.   Stories.   Mountain TOPS
     112
        RRE   Jan. -Feb.   p24.   250w.   4

735 SEX Pistols.   The Boys.   Nems NEL 6001 (E)
        RR   Dec.   p85.   50w.   2½

736 SEX Pistols.   Ha! Ha! Ha!   Island ILPS 9511
        RR   Dec.   p85.   50w.   2

737 SEX Pistols.   Never Mind the Bullocks, Here's the....
     Warner Brothers BSK 3147
        VV   Nov. 28   p66.   100w.   4
        ZZ   Nov.   p32.   750w.   5

738 SFF.   Symphonic Pictures.   Brain 60.010 (West Germany)
        TP   Feb. /March   p26.   50w.   4

739-40 SHERBET.   Magazine Madonna.   MCA MCA-2304
        MG   Dec.   p56.   50w.   1
        TP   Nov.   p38, 39.   375w.   5

741 SHOES.   Black Vinyl Shoes.   Black Vinyl S-51477
        TP   Dec.   p35.   350w.   2½
        WHO   Nov.   p40.   75w.   4

742 SHOWADDYWADDY.   Arista 4114
        RC   June   p9-10.   200w.   3½
        TP   Feb. /March   p30-1.   425w.   3
        MM   Feb. 5   p23.   150w.   0

743 SIMON, Paul.   Greatest Hits.   Columbia PC 35032 (Reissue)
        RC   Dec.   p8.   100w.   5

744 SKYHOOKS.   Living in the Seventies.   Mercury SRM-1-1124.
     Cart. 81-1124.   Cass. 41-1124
        SR   July   p101.   200w.   2

745 SLADE.   Whatever Happened to....   Barn 2314103 (E)

RR   June p93.   75w. $2\frac{1}{2}$
TP   June/July p35.   300w.   2

746   SLAVE.   Cotillion 5200
       BM   July p49.   200w.   4
       HBS   June/Sept.   p23.   150w.   5
       MM   May 28   p29.   50w.   0

747   SLICK, Earl.   Razor Sharp.   Capitol ST-11570
       CIR   Jan. 17   p17.   200w.   2
       GP   Jan.   p97.   75w.   4

748   SLIK.   Arista 4115
       TP   Feb./March   p30-1.   425w.   3

749   SLOCHE.   Stadaconé.   RCA KLP1-0177
       OLR   Sept.   p226.   50w.   3

750   SMALL Faces.   Playmates.   Atlantic SD 19113
       CRA   Oct.   p76.   500w.   2
       GR   Oct.   p715.   100w.   3
       HF   Dec.   p140-1.   325w.   2
       MM   Oct. 15   p25.   250w.   2
       RRE   Nov.-Dec.   p26.   125w. $2\frac{1}{2}$
       RS   Oct. 6   p94.   300w.   1
       TP   Nov.   p37.   250w.   0

751   SMALL Faces.   Rock Roots: Singles Album.   Decca ROOTS5
       (E) (Reissue)
       MM   Sept. 10   p20.   50w.   4
       SMG   Sept.   p26.   250w.   5
       TP   Dec.   p40.   225w.   3

752   SMITH, Patti.   Horses.   Arista
       RM   Jan.   p13.   600w.   5

753   SMITH, Patti.   Radio Ethiopia.   Arista AL 4097.   Cart. 8301-
       4097H
       CRE   March p63.   100w. $2\frac{1}{2}$
       HF   Feb.   p148.   200w.   2
       MG   Jan.   800w. $3\frac{1}{2}$
       RC   April p5.   250w. $4\frac{1}{2}$
       RR   Feb.   p93.   125w.   2
       RS   Jan. 14   p51-2.   350w.   2
       SR   Feb.   p104.   700w.   3

754   SMITH, Warren.   Sun Story, Vol. 7.   Sonet Spotlight SPO
       132 (E) (Reissue)
       NK   Autumn   p40.   100w.   4

755   SMOKIE.   Bright Lights.   RSO 3029
       MM   Nov. 12   p29.   175w. $3\frac{1}{2}$

756 SMOKIE.   Greatest Hits.   EMI RAK 526
     CAC July p132.   150w.   3
     MM Nov. 12 p29.   175w. $3\frac{1}{2}$

757 SMOKIE.   Midnight Cafe.   RSO RS-1-3005
     RC June p9.   200w.   4

758 SNOW, Phoebe.   Shelter 52017
     RC June p5.   200w. $3\frac{1}{2}$

759 SNOW, Phoebe.   It Looks Like Snow.   Columbia PC 34387.
     Cass. PCA 34387
     CIR Jan. 31 p14.   300w.   3
     DB April 21 p27.   300w. $3\frac{1}{2}$
     MG Jan. 125w. $3\frac{1}{2}$
     MM Feb. 26 p26.   600w.   4
     RS Jan. 13 p55.   300w.   3
     SR Feb. p101.   200w.   4

760 SNOW, Phoebe.   Never Letting Go.   Columbia JC 34875.
     Cart. JCT-34875.   Cass. JCA-34875
     HF Dec. p139.   75w. $2\frac{1}{2}$
     MG Dec. p56.   50w.   2
     RS Dec. 1 p79.   325w.   2

761 SOCRATES.   Phos.   Cosmos PILPS 9013
     TP Dec. 1976/Jan. 1977 p27.   225w.   4

762 SOFT Machine.   At the Beginning.   Precision Charly CR
     30014 (E)
     CAC July p132.   125w.   3

763 SOFT Machine.   Triple Echo.   Harvest SGTW 800 (E) (3
     discs) (Reissue)
     RR Oct. p88-9.   150w. $2\frac{1}{2}$

764 SOUTHSIDE Johnny and the Asbury Jukes.   I Don't Want to
     Go Home.   Epic EPC 81515 (E)
     RR March p96.   50w.   2

765 SOUTHSIDE Johnny and the Asbury Jukes.   This Time It's for
     Real.   Epic PE 34668.   Cart. PEA-34668.   Cass. PET-34668
     CIR Sept. 8 p60-1.   1000w. $4\frac{1}{2}$
     CRA July p76.   575w.   2
     MG June p52.   200w.   4
     RC Oct. p2.   100w.   2
     RR June p93.   75w. $3\frac{1}{2}$
     RRE Nov.-Dec. p28-9.   275w. $3\frac{1}{2}$
     RS May 19 350w. $4\frac{1}{2}$
     SR July p94.   525w.   5

766 SPARKS.   Big Beat.   Columbia PC 34359.   Cass. PCA 34359
     CIR Feb. 28 p14.   250w. $1\frac{1}{2}$

MG   April p51. 125w. $2\frac{1}{2}$
RC   May   p1.   200w. $3\frac{1}{2}$
RM   Jan.   p29. 500w. 4
RS   March 10. p72. 350w. 3
SR   March p114. 150w. 2

767 SPARKS. Introducing. Columbia PC 34901
        CIR Dec. 22 p69. 200w. 0
        RS   Dec. 29 p65. 150w. 2
        TP   Dec. p35-6. 200w. $3\frac{1}{2}$

768 SPEDDING, Chris. Hurt. RAK SRAK 529 (E)
        GR   Nov. p920. 50w. $1\frac{1}{2}$
        MM   Oct. 1 p26. 250w. 1
        TP   Dec. p37-8. 250w. 2

769 SPHINX. Judas Escariot. Polydor 2393 166
        SOU Sept. p64. 350w. 3

770 SPIRIT. Future Games--A Magical Kahauna Dream.   Mercury
     SRM-1-1133
        ZZ   April p47-8. 600w. $3\frac{1}{2}$

771 SPLIT Enz. Dizrythmia. Chrysalis CHR 1145
        RC   Nov. p7. 300w. $3\frac{1}{2}$

772 SPLIT Enz. Mental Notes. Chrysalis CHR 1131
        CK   April p49. 100w. 3
        CRA April p111. 450w. 5
        HF   April p148. 50w. 3
        RS   April 7 p80, 82. 250w. $2\frac{1}{2}$
        SR   July p101. 150w. 2

773 STALLION. Casablanca 7040
        MM   June 4 p20. 25w. $2\frac{1}{2}$

774 STAMPEDERS. Hit the Road. MWC 709 (Canada)
        MM   Feb. 26 p30. 50w. 3
        OLR March p55. 25w. 4

775 STAMPEDERS. Platinum. MWC S 710 (Canada)
        CC   June p28. 50w. 3

776 STARCASTLE. Fountains of Light. Epic PE 34375
        CIR June 9 p58. 300w. 2
        RS   Feb. 24 p59, 61-2. 500w. 2

777 STARR, Ringo. Ringo's Rotogravure. Atlantic SD 18193.
     Cart. TP 18193
        AU   Feb. p75. 600w. $2\frac{1}{2}$
        CIR March 31 p12-3. 300w. 2
        CRA Jan. p78. 175w. 3
        GR   Jan. p1194, 1197. 50w. $3\frac{1}{2}$

RS   Nov. 17 p94.   375w.   2
SR   Feb. p102.   200w.   4

778 STARZ.   Capitol ST 11539
CIR   Jan. 31 p11.   600w.   5

779 STARZ.   Violation.   Capitol ST 11617
CIR   July 7   525w.   3

780 STATUS Quo.   Live.   Capitol SKBB 11623 (2 discs)
CAC   June p96.   100w.   2
GR   June p110.   50w.   1
MM   April 2 p22.   200w.   3

781 STEELY Dan.   Aja.   ABC A-1006
CIR   Dec. 8 p74.   450w. $2\frac{1}{2}$
DB   Dec. 1 p22, 23.   250w.   4
HF   Dec. p141-2.   425w.   5
MG   Dec. p52.   800w. $3\frac{1}{2}$
MG   Dec. p56.   50w. $2\frac{1}{2}$
MM   Sept. 17 p18.   700w. $3\frac{1}{2}$
RC   Oct. p2.   100w.   4
RR   Nov. p114.   325w. $4\frac{1}{2}$
RRE   Nov.-Dec. p25.   475w.   4
RS   Dec. 1 p74, 76.   1200w.   4

782 STEELY Dan.   The Royal Scam.   ABC ABCD 931
AU   Jan. p82.   200w.   4

783 STEVENS, Cat.   Izitso.   A&M SP-4702
AU   Nov. p119.   150w. $3\frac{1}{2}$
CIR   July 21 p60.   150w.   0
CK   Nov. p64.   75w.   5
CRA   July p63-4.   1400w. $1\frac{1}{2}$
GR   July p234.   50w.   3
HF   Sept. p145.   75w.   3
MM   June 4 p28.   200w. $3\frac{1}{2}$
RC   Oct. p3.   150w. $2\frac{1}{2}$
RR   July p96.   50w.   3
RRE   May-June p29, 62.   700w.   3
SR   Oct. p120.   175w. $2\frac{1}{2}$

784 STEVENS, John.   Chemistry.   Vinyl Vn 102 (E)
MM   Nov. 5 p31.   175w.   4

785 STEVENS, John.   Mazin' Ennit.   Phonogram 6360 141 (E)
MM   May 14 p27.   450w. $4\frac{1}{2}$

786 STEWART, Al.   Modern Times.   CBS 80477 (E)
CAC   Aug. p164.   250w.   2

787 STEWART, Al.   Year of the Cat.   Janus JXS-7022.   Cart.
8098-7022

CAC Feb. p414. 200w. $1\frac{1}{2}$
CIR March 31 p16-7. 400w. 3
MM Jan. 22 p22. 500w. 2
RRE Jan. -Feb. p23. 100w. $3\frac{1}{2}$
SR Feb. p103. 100w. 3

788 STEWART, John. Fire in the Wind. RSO 3027
MM Nov. 12 p26. 650w. $4\frac{1}{2}$

789 STEWART, Rod. Best of, Vol. 2. Mercury 7509
CIR April 28 p17. 150w. 3

790 STEWART, Rod. Foot Loose and Fancy Free. Warner Bros.
BSK 3092
MM Nov. 5 p25. 375w. $3\frac{1}{2}$
RRE Nov. -Dec. p18. 350w. 4
RS Dec. 29 p63-4. 900w. 2
VV Oct. 31 p59. 250w. $2\frac{1}{2}$
VV Nov. 28 p66. 50w. 3

791 STEWART, Rod. A Night on the Town. Warner Bros. BS
2938 M8 2938
SR Jan. p98. 225w. 3

792 STEWART, Rod. A Shot of Rhythm and Blues. Private Stock
PS 2021 (Reissue)
CIR April 28 p17. 150w. 2
RC April p100w. $1\frac{1}{2}$
RS Jan. 27 p68. 300w. 1

793 STILLS, Stephen. Best of. Atlantic K50327 (E) (Reissue)
GR March p1467. 50w. 3
MM Jan. 22 p46. 50w. $3\frac{1}{2}$

794 STILLS, Stephen and Neil Young. Long May You Run. Re-
prise MS 2253
GP Jan. p97. 50w. 4
HF Jan. p143. 100w. 3

795 STILLWATER. Capricorn CP 0186
CIR Nov. 10 p60. 125w. $3\frac{1}{2}$
MG Oct. p59. 75w. $3\frac{1}{2}$

796 STONE the Crows. Polydor 2482 279 (E) (Reissue)
CAC Feb. p415. 300w. 3

797 STOOGES. Elektra (E) (Reissue)
MM April 2 p22. 200w. $2\frac{1}{2}$

797a STOOGES. Fun House. Elektra (E) (Reissue)
MM April 2 p22. 200w. $2\frac{1}{2}$

798 STOOGES. Metallic K O. Skydog (France)

RRE   Nov. -Dec.   p26.   175w. $1\frac{1}{2}$

799   STRANGLERS.   IV Rattus Norvegicus.   A&M SP4648
  CIR   Oct. 27 p68.   300w. $2\frac{1}{2}$
  CRA   Sept.   p70.   150w.   4
  HF   Nov.   300w.   3
  MG   Oct.   p59.   50w.   2
  MM   April 23 p21.   450w.   0
  RC   Aug.   p8.   250w.   3
  RS   Sept. 22 p67-8.   800w.   4
  RS   Aug. 24 p55.   100w. $3\frac{1}{2}$
  ZZ   May p37-8.   500w.   3
  ZZ   June p41.   300w.   3

800   STRANGLERS.   No More Heroes.   A&M SP4659
  MM   Sept. 24 p28.   650w. $3\frac{1}{2}$
  RS   Dec. 29 p69.   550w.   2
  TP   Dec.   p34.   300w.   2

801   STRAPPS.   Secret Damage.   Harvest 11621 (E)
  TP   Sept.   p36.   200w.   0

802   STRAWBS.   Burning for You.   Oyster OY1-1604
  AU   Dec.   p115.   200w.   2
  HF   Oct.   p163, 166.   450w.   2
  MM   Sept. 3 p21.   150w. $2\frac{1}{2}$
  SR   Dec.   150w.   3
  TP   Sept.   p36.   125w.   0

803   STRAWBS.   Deep Cuts.   Oyster OY1-1603
  AU   March p90.   100w.   2
  CAC   June p381.   100w. $4\frac{1}{2}$
  RC   June p11.   250w.   2
  SR   Jan.   p98.   100w.   2

804   STREETWALKERS.   Vicious But Fair.   Mercury SRM1-1135
  CAC   June p91.   300w.   3
  CIR   June 23 p64.   300w. $4\frac{1}{2}$
  GR   April p1617.   100w. $3\frac{1}{2}$
  MG   July p51.   150w.   4
  MM   Jan. 29 p25.   500w.   1
  TP   April/May p30-1.   375w.   4

805   STUFF.   Warner Bros.   BS 2968
  CK   Jan.   p51.   25w.   4
  DB   Feb. 24 p28, 30.   300w. $4\frac{1}{2}$
  GP   March p112.   125w.   4
  MG   Jan.   125w. $2\frac{1}{2}$
  MM   Feb. 19 p22.   50w. $2\frac{1}{2}$
  RRE   Jan. -Feb.   p46.   100w.   3
  SR   Feb.   p103.   150w.   3

806   STUFF.   More Stuff.   Warner Brothers BS 3061

DB   Nov. 3   p22.   250w. $2\frac{1}{2}$
MG   Sept.   p52.   75w.   1
MG   Sept.   p53.   75w.   2
MG   Dec.   p59.   75w.   3

807   STYX.   Crystal Ball.   A&M SP 4604
MM   Jan. 29   p23.   250w.   2
RS   Jan. 13   p55.   200w.   3

808   STYX.   The Grand Illusion.   A&M SP 4637
MM   Sept. 3   p22.   25w.   2
RS   Nov. 3   p102.   300w.   2

809   SUPERCHARGE.   Horizontal Refreshments.   Virgin V2067 (E)
MM   March 19   p28.   500w. $3\frac{1}{2}$
RR   May   p87.   50w.   2

810   SUPERTRAMP.   Even in the Quietest Moments....   A&M SP-
4634
AU   Oct.   p175.   200w.   4
CAC   July   p134.   100w. $2\frac{1}{2}$
CIR   July 7   425w.   2
CK   Aug.   p49.   25w.   3
CRA   July   p65, 67.   650w. $1\frac{1}{2}$
GR   July   p237.   25w. $1\frac{1}{2}$
MG   Oct.   p59.   50w. $1\frac{1}{2}$
MM   April 30.   p27.   475w.   3
RC   July   p11.   250w. $4\frac{1}{2}$
RRE   May–June   p19.   800w. $2\frac{1}{2}$
SOU   May   p57.   600w.   5
VV   Nov. 28   p66.   50w.   2

811   SURFARIS.   Gone with the Wave.   MCA Coral CDL 8050 (E)
NK   Autumn   p42.   50w. $2\frac{1}{2}$

812   SUTHERLAND Brothers and Quiver.   Down to Earth.   Columbia JC 35293
MM   Sept. 17   p22.   400w. $3\frac{1}{2}$

813   SUTHERLAND Brothers and Quiver.   Slipstream.   Columbia
PC 34376
AU   Feb.   p74.   50w.   1

814   SWAMP Dogg.   Finally Caught Up with Myself.   Musico MUS
2504
RC   Aug.   p2.   300w.   3

815   SWAN, Billy.   Four.   Columbia 34473 (Reissue)
CIR   May 26   p58.   600w. $3\frac{1}{2}$
CMR   June   p13.   25w.   3
HF   April   p146.   200w.   4
MM   March 19   p31.   50w.   2
NK   Spring   p42.   50w.   3

RC May p11. 100w. $2\frac{1}{2}$
RS June 2 p78. 250w. $3\frac{1}{2}$
ZZ May p38-9. 150w. 2

816 SWEET. Off the Record. Capitol STAO 11636
    CIR Aug. 4 p61. 150w. 0
    CRA July p76. 200w. $1\frac{1}{2}$
    MM May 28 p28. 175w. 0

817 SWEET Blindness. Quality SV 1923 (Canada)
    OLR March p55. 50w. $4\frac{1}{2}$

818 SWEET Blindness. Energize. Quality 1943V (Canada)
    CC Sept. p32. 50w. 3

819 SYMPHONIC Slam. A&M SP 4619
    GP May p128. 100w. $3\frac{1}{2}$
    OLR Sept. p226. 50w. 2

820 T. REX. Dandy in the Underworld. EMI BLN 5005 (E)
    GR July p237. 50w. 3
    TP June/July p34-5. 400w. $2\frac{1}{2}$

821 TALKING Heads. Talking Heads '77. Sire SR 60336
    CIR Nov. 24 p74. 750w. $3\frac{1}{2}$
    HF Dec. p139. 75w. $3\frac{1}{2}$
    MG Dec. p55. 100w. $2\frac{1}{2}$
    MM Oct. 1 p24. 500w. 4
    RS Nov. 7 p98, 101. 550w. $4\frac{1}{2}$
    TP Nov. p38. 250w. 4
    VV Nov. 7 p53. 574w. 3
    ZZ Oct. p33. 200w. $3\frac{1}{2}$

822 TALLEY, James. Ain't It Something. Capitol ST-11695
    RS Oct. 20 p88, 90. 450w. 3
    VV Oct. 3 p61. 300w. 3
    VV Oct. 3 p65. 50w. 4

823 TALLEY, James. Blackjack Choir. Capitol ST-11605. Cart.
    8XT-11605. Cass. 4XT-11605
    CIR March 31 p14-5. 575w. $3\frac{1}{2}$
    CM June p53. 250w. 4
    CMP May p36. 150w. 4
    CMR June p12. 300w. 4
    CRA April p102. 200w. 3
    CS June 2 p16. 200w. $3\frac{1}{2}$
    MM April 23 p24. 550w. $3\frac{1}{2}$
    RC June p12. 250w. 3
    RS April 21 525w. 3
    SR May p94. 100w. 4

824 TANGERINE Dream. Encore. Virgin PZG 35014
    MM Nov. 19 p23. 500w. $4\frac{1}{2}$

825   TANGERINE Dream.   Sorcerer.   MCA 2277
      CRA Oct. p73. 125w. $1\frac{1}{2}$
      EUR V2/#1 p18. 300w. $2\frac{1}{2}$
      MM July 16 p23. 550w. 2

826   TANGERINE Dream.   Stratosfear.   Virgin PZ 34427
      AU Aug. p84. 250w. 2
      CIR June 23 p62. 550w. $2\frac{1}{2}$
      CRA July p72. 200w. $1\frac{1}{2}$
      EUR No. 7/8 p39-40. 400w. 4
      RS March 10 p69. 100w. 3
      SOU Jan. p43. 350w. 3

827   TAYLOR, Chip.   Somebody Shoot Out the Jukebox.   Columbia
      PC 34345.   Cart. CA 34345
      CM Feb. p52. 250w. 3
      RC June p6-7. 200w. 3
      RS Jan. p52-3. 200w. 2

828   TAYLOR, James.   Gorilla.   Stereotape WSTQ 2866 QF
      AU Jan. p91. 400w. 3

829   TAYLOR, James.   Greatest Hits.   Warner BS 2979 (Reissue)
      CAC March p456. 200w. 2
      MM Jan. 29 p25. 250w. 2
      RS Jan. 13 p48. 100w. 3

830   TAYLOR, James.   JT.   Columbia JC 34811.   Cass. JCT-
      34811.   Cart. 5CA-34811
      AU Nov. p117. 250w. 2
      CIR Sept. 29 p58. 250w. $3\frac{1}{2}$
      CRA Aug. p66. 400w. 3
      CS Dec. p28. 100w. 3
      HF Sept. p136-7. 800w. 3
      MG Sept. p51. 125w. $3\frac{1}{2}$
      RC Oct. p13. 150w. $2\frac{1}{2}$
      RS Aug. 11 p60, 63. 550w. $3\frac{1}{2}$
      SR Oct. p87-8. 550w. 5
      VV Aug. 1 p51. 50w. 3

831   TAYLOR, Vince.   MFP 2MO46-96857 (Belgium) (Reissue)
      SMG May p21. 150w. 3

832   TEAZE.   Force One FO 7001
      CC Jan. p32. 50w. 3

833   TELEVISION.   Marquee Moon.   Elektra 7E-1098
      AU May p90. 400w. 4
      CIR April 14 p14-5. 1000w. 3
      CRA April p107-9. 750w. 4
      GR July p237. 50w. $2\frac{1}{2}$
      MG April p49. 325w. 4
      MM April 9 p22. 350w. $3\frac{1}{2}$

RC   Dec.   p2.   100w.   3
RR   May   p86.   300w.   4½
RS   April 7   p70.   600w.   4
SR   May   p94.   75w.   0
VV   March 14   p81.   400w.   5

834   10 cc.   Deceptive Bends.   Mercury SRM-1-3702.   Cart. 81-
3702.   Cass.   41-3702
AU   Aug.   p86.   200w.   4
CRA   July   p65, 67.   650w.   3
MM   April 30   p29.   550w.   4
SR   Sept.   p88.   350w.   5

835   10 cc.   Live and Let Die.   Mercury SRM2-8600 (2 discs)
MM   Dec. 3   p27.   250w.   2

836   TEN Years After.   The Classic Performance of.   Columbia
PC 34366 (Reissue)
RS   Jan. 6   p48.   50w.   2

837   TEN Years After.   Greatest Hits.   London LC 5008 (E) (Reissue)
TP   Oct.   p42.   125w.   3

838   THEM.   The Story of Them, Featuring Van Morrison.   Lon-
don LC50001
CIR   May 26   p57-8.   300w.   2
TP   April/May   p29-30.   850w.   3

839   THIN Lizzy.   Bad Reputation.   Mercury SRM-1-1186
CIR   Nov. 24   p76-7.   350w.   2½
MG   Nov.   p51.   25w.   2
MM   Sept. 3   p17.   350w.   3½
RC   Nov.   p8.   75w.   3½
RS   Oct. 20   p83.   375w.   3½
TP   Nov.   p36.   350w.   0

840   THIN Lizzy.   Jailbreak.   Mercury SRM 1-1081
AU   Jan.   p82.   200w.   4

841   THIN Lizzy.   Johnny the Fox.   Mercury SRM1-1119
AU   Feb.   p74.   100w.   4
CIR   Feb. 28   p11-2.   300w.   2½
CRA   Jan.   p74.   400w.   3
GR   Jan.   p1197.   50w.   3½
MG   April   p51.   100w.   2½
RRE   Jan.-Feb.   p10-3.   1600w.   4
RS   Jan. 27   p67-8.   700w.   3
SOU   Feb.   p41.   500w.   2
SR   April   p100.   250w.   3
TP   Dec.-Jan.   p31.   250w.   5

842   THIN Lizzy.   Rocker (1971-1974).   London LC50004 (Reissue)

CIR   June 9   p56, 58.   200w.   2
TP   April/May   p29-30.   850w.   4

843   THOMAS, B. J.   MCA MCA2286.   Cass. MCAC 2286.   Cart.
MCAT 2286
HF   Nov.   50w.   2
SR   Dec.   500w.   4½

844   THOMAS, B. J.   From Texas to Tennessee.   DJM DJB
26079 (E) (Reissue)
CAC   Feb.   p419-20.   200w.   3
CMP   Jan.   p35.   100w.   1
NK   Winter   p37.   50w.   3

845   THOMPSON, Richard.   Live! (More or Less).   Island ISLA-
9421
CIR   Aug.   4   p61.   350w.   2½
RS   June   2   400w.   3
SR   June   p95.   250w.   5

846   THOROGOOD, George.   Rounder 3013
CAD   Dec.   p39-40.   150w.   2½

847   TIGER.   Goin' Down Laughin'.   EMI ST 11660
MG   Sept.   p51.   100w.   1
RSP   March-April   p62.   250w.   3½

848   TILLOTSON, Johnny.   Johnny Tillotson.   United Artists UA-
LA758-G.   Cart. UA-EA758-H
SR   Nov.   p114.   175w.   3

849   TIMEBOX.   The Original Moose on the Loose.   Cosmos CCLP
9016
TP   June/July   p34.   300w.   2½

850   TITUS, Libby.   Columbia PC34152.   Cass. PCT 34152.   Tape
PCA 34152
FOL   Dec.   p24.   250w.   3
HF   Nov.   75w.   3½
MG   Nov.   p52.   25w.   1
RS   Oct.   20   p92, 94.   475w.   2½
VV   Oct.   3   p65.   50w.   2

851   TOAN, Danny.   First Serve.   Atlantic Embryo SD535
MG   Dec.   p57.   100w.   2
RS   Nov.   3   p108.   175w.   3½

852   TOMITA, Isao.   Holst: The Planets.   RCA ARL 1-1919
DB   May 19   250w.   5
MM   June 4   p20.   375w.   3

853   TOMLINSON, Malcolm.   Coming Outta Nowhere.   A&M 4649
CC   Oct.   p35.   100w.   3

854 TOMORROW. Import IMP 1003 (E)
        TP Feb./March p31. 350w. 4

855 TOPAZ. Columbia AL 34934
        CIR Dec. 8 p75. 300w. $2\frac{1}{2}$
        RS Nov. 3 p110. 350w. 3

856 TORNADOS. Away From It All. Decca Box 622/3 (Belgium)
      (Reissue)
        CAC March p458. 200w. $1\frac{1}{2}$
        NK Spring p39. 50w. $3\frac{1}{2}$

857 TOUPIN, Robert. Capitol ST 70-049
        CC June p29. 50w. 3

858-9 TOWNSHEND, Peter and Ronnie Lane. Rough Mix. MCA
      2295
        CIR Dec. 22 p65-6. 500w. $3\frac{1}{2}$
        CRA Oct. p76. 500w. 4
        HF Dec. p140-1. 325w. 2
        MG Oct. p55-6. 600w. $3\frac{1}{2}$
        RC Nov. p15. 200w. $4\frac{1}{2}$
        RR Dec. p86. 100w. 3
        RS Oct. 6 p81-2. 1250w. $4\frac{1}{2}$
        TP Oct. p39. 575w. 5
        VV Oct. 3 p61-2. 600w. $3\frac{1}{2}$

860 TRAVERS, Pat. Makin' Magic. Polydor PD1-6103
        CAC June p91. 300w. 3
        CRA Oct. p69. 250w. $3\frac{1}{2}$
        MM April 2 p21. 300w. $3\frac{1}{2}$

861 TRAVERS, Pat. Pat Travers. Polydor PD-1-6079
        GP Jan. p97. 50w. 3

862 The TROGGS. The Vintage Years. Sire SASH 3714-2 (Re-
      issue)
        CRE March p61. 350w. $3\frac{1}{2}$
        RS Jan. 13 p51. 100w. 3
        TP Feb./March p31. 350w. 4

863 TROIANO, Domenic. Burnin' at the Stake. Capitol ST-11665
        MM Oct. 8 p32. 150w. 0
        RS Oct. 20 p94. 350w. $3\frac{1}{2}$
        SOU Oct. p66. 300w. 4

864 TROWER, Robin. In City Dreams. Chrysalis CHR 1148
        GP Dec. p153. 150w. 3
        MG Dec. p52. 250w. $3\frac{1}{2}$
        MM Oct. 8 p29. 500w. $4\frac{1}{2}$
        RC Oct. p16. 75w. 3
        RS Nov. 17 p90. 350w. $3\frac{1}{2}$
        RSP Nov.-Dec. p23. 450w. $3\frac{1}{2}$

865   TROWER, Robin.   Long Misty Days.   Chrysalis CHR-1107
       AU   Jan.   p78.   250w.   4
       AU   Jan.   p79.   100w. $3\frac{1}{2}$
       CIR   Jan.   17 p13-4.   450w.   3
       GR   Jan.   p1197   50w. $1\frac{1}{2}$
       HF   June   p142.   200w.   4
       SR   Feb.   p105.   150w.   2

866   The TUBES.   Now.   A&M SP4632
       AU   Sept.   p90.   200w.   1
       CIR   Aug.   18   425w.   3
       CRA   Sept.   p76-7.   1550w. $2\frac{1}{2}$
       MM   May 21   p25.   550w. $3\frac{1}{2}$
       RC   Dec.   p14.   300w.   3
       RR   Aug.   p83.   50w.   2
       RS   Aug.   11 p69.   275w.   2

867   TUCKER, Marshall, Band.   Carolina Dreams.   Capricorn
       CPK 0180.   Cart. M80180.   Cass. M50180
       CS   May 5 - p18.   200w. $3\frac{1}{2}$
       GR   July   p234.   50w. $1\frac{1}{2}$
       MM   April 30   p30.   100w. $3\frac{1}{2}$
       SR   July   p96-7.   150w.   5
       VV   March 7   p47.   275w.   3

868   TUCKER, Marshall, Band.   Long Hard Ride.   Capricorn
       2429 140
       CMR   Feb.   p30.   275w.   4

869   TURNING Point.   Creatures of the Night.   Gull GULP 1022
       (E)
       MM   Dec. 3   p32.   425w.   4

870   TWILLEY, Dwight, Band.   Twilley Don't Mind.   Arista AB
       4140.   Cass. 5301 4140.   Cart. 8301 4140
       CIR   Oct. 27   p68.   500w.   3
       CRA   Sept.   p65.   775w.   4
       HF   Nov.   p75.   650w. $3\frac{1}{2}$
       MG   Nov.   p51.   25w. $3\frac{1}{2}$
       MM   Nov. 5   p20.   450w.   3
       RS   Oct. 6   p86, 89.   400w.   3

871   ULTRAVOX.   Island ILPS 9449
       CRA   Sept.   p70.   150w.   2
       RR   May   p87.   25w. $2\frac{1}{2}$
       RSP   May-June   p62.   200w.   2
       TP   June/July   p36.   225w.   2

872   ULTRAVOX.   Ha! Ha! Ha!   Island (E)
       MM   Nov. 19   p28.   300w. $1\frac{1}{2}$

873   UNICORN.   One More Tomorrow.   Capitol ST11692
       HF   Dec.   p139.   100w.   1

874 UNIVERS Zero. Sabam 1313 (Belgium)
     MM Jan. 7 p16. 200w. 1

875 URIAH Heep. Firefly. Warner Brothers 3013
     CIR Aug. 4 p60. 200w. 0
     MM May 7 p21. 300w. 3½

876 UTOPIA. Oops! Wrong Planet. Bearsville BR 6970
     CIR Dec. 22 p67-8. 450w. 2
     CRA Oct. p70. 400w. 3
     RC Oct. p15. 100w. 3½
     RS Nov. 3 p101-2. 375w. 3½

877 UTOPIA. Ra. Bearsville BR6965. Cart. M8-6965. Cass.
     M5-6965
     CAC April p8-9. 200w. 4
     CIR April 14 p18. 500w. 2½
     CRA March p78. 300w. 2½
     MM Feb. 12 p26. 300w. 0
     RS April 7 p75-6. 350w. 3½
     SR Aug. p100. 150w. 0

878 VALDY. Hometown Band. A&M SP4592 (Canada)
     OLR March p56. 50w. 4½

879 VALLI, Frankie. Private Stock 2017
     CAC April p16. 125w. 3½
     MM May 14 p33. 50w. 2

880 VAN, Gary Paul and Dennis Lee Askew. Universe. PBR In-
     ternational 7002
     CK Nov. p65. 35w. 3

881 VAN Der Graaf Generator. The Quiet Zone/The Pleasure
     Dome. Charisma CAS 1131 (E)
     MM Sept. 24 p27. 300w. 3½
     TP Dec. p39. 250w. 3

882 VANELLI, Gino. Gist of the Gemini. A&M SP4596
     OLR Sept. p226. 25w. 1½

883 VANGELIS. Albedo 0.39. RCA AFL1-5136
     CAC Jan. p376. 300w. 3½

884 VANGELIS. Spiral. RCA AFL1-2627
     MM Dec. 21 p14. 200w. 1

885 VAN Zandt, Townes. Live at the Old Quarter, Houston, Tex-
     as. Tomato
     CIR Nov. 10 p58-9. 475w. 4
     VV Oct. 3 p61. 325w. 3½

886 VEHICULE. Skyline SKY10163-V

CC   Sept.   p34.   50w.   3

887 VENITA.   A Brighter Day.   D'Ardy Enterprises D76-01
     CAD   March   p28.   100w.   3

888 VIBRATORS.   Pure Mania.   Columbia JC 35038
     CRA   Sept.   p70.   150w.   2
     GR   Aug.   p354.   50w.   2
     MM   Sept. 10 p24.   200w.   0
     TP   Sept.   p39.   300w. $1\frac{1}{2}$
     WHO   Nov.   p40.   150w.   4

889 VIG, Tommy.   Somebody Loves Me.   Dobre 1005
     MJ   May   p31.   50w.   3

890 VINCENT, Gene.   Greatest.   Capitol CAPS 1001 (E) (Reissue)
     MM   April 16   p23.   50w. $2\frac{1}{2}$
     NK   Winter   p37.   125w.   4
     SMG   May   p21.   125w.   4

891 VINCENT, James.   Space Traveller.   Caribou PZ 34237
     GP   Feb.   p113.   125w.   3

892 VOLUNTEERS.   Arista 4103
     AU   Sept.   p89.   150w.   2
     CIR   April 28   p14-5.   150w.   0

893 WAITS, Tom.   Foreign Affairs.   Asylum 7E-1117
     RC   Dec.   p6.   250w. $4\frac{1}{2}$
     RS   Nov. 17   p94.   650w.   3

894 WAITS, Tom.   Nighthawks at the Diner.   Asylum 7E-2008 (2
     discs)
     RC   April   p4-5.   250w. $4\frac{1}{2}$

895 WAITS, Tom.   Small Change.   Asylum 7E-1078
     AU   March   p82.   150w. $4\frac{1}{2}$
     CK   Jan.   p51.   25w. $4\frac{1}{2}$
     DB   Feb. 24   p26-7.   400w.   4
     GR   July   p234.   100w. $2\frac{1}{2}$
     RR   July   p96.   50w. $3\frac{1}{2}$
     SR   Feb.   p105.   140w.   0

896 WAKEMAN, Rick.   Criminal Record.   A&M (E)
     MM   Nov. 5   p19.   400w.   4

897 WALDMAN, Wendy.   The Main Refrain.   Warner Bros. BS
     2974
     AU   March   p88.   100w.   4
     CIR   Jan. 17   p16.   700w.   2
     SR   Feb.   p105.   150w.   2

898 WALKER, Jerry Jeff.   A Man Must Carry On.   MCA 2-6003.

Cart. MCAT 2-6003 (2 discs)
  CMP Sept. p40. 325w. 5
  SR Nov. p114. 325w. 5
  VV Nov. 28 p66. 50w. $3\frac{1}{2}$

899 WALKER, Sammy. Warner BS 2961
  CIR Jan. 17 p15. 275w. $2\frac{1}{2}$
  RC April p10. 200w. $3\frac{1}{2}$

900 WALLENSTEIN. No More Love. RCA
  EUR V2/#1 p27. 250w. 4

901 WAMIL, Rick and Copperpenny. Fuses. Capitol ST 6410
(Canada)
  OLR March p56. 25w. $2\frac{1}{2}$

902 WATERMAN, Dennis. Waterman. DJM (E)
  MM Oct. 1 p48. 50w. 2

903 WAVEMAKER. New Atlantis. Polydor 2383 434
  SMG Sept. p26. 50w. 3

904 WAY, Bryan. Where Do You Go. Quality SU 1927 (Canada)
  OLR June p141. 50w. $2\frac{1}{2}$

905 WEBB, Jimmy. El Mirage. Atlantic SD 18218
  AU Nov. p115. 250w. 3
  CK Sept. p58. 75w. 3
  CRA Aug. p77. 225w. 4
  GR July p234. 50w. $3\frac{1}{2}$
  HF Sept. p145. 50w. $2\frac{1}{2}$
  RC Dec. p13. 100w. 2
  RS July 14 p67. 350w. $3\frac{1}{2}$
  SR Oct. p122. 250w. 3

906 WEISBERG, Tim. United Artists LA 773G
  MM Oct. 8 p29. 200w. $2\frac{1}{2}$
  SOU Oct. p62. 150w. 1

907 WEISBERG, Tim. Live at Last. A&M SP 4600
  DB Feb. 10 p21-2. 200w. $2\frac{1}{2}$

908 WELCH, Bob. French Kiss. Capitol ST-11663
  RS Nov. 3 p108-10. 325w. 2
  SOU Nov. p61. 400w. 4

909 WENZDAY. Loving You Baby. Skyline SKY 10160 (Canada)
  OLR March p56. 25w. 2

910 WENZDAY. Nearly Made It. Skyline SKY 10164 (Canada)
  OLR Dec. p291. 25w. 3

911 WET Willie. Left Coast Live. Capricorn 2429 151 (E)

GR Oct.   p715.   25w. $2\frac{1}{2}$

912 WHITE Horse.   Capitol ST-11687
RS Dec. 1 p80.   450w. 3
TP Nov. p39.   150w.   4

913 The WHITNEY Family.   Airways.   United Artists UALA 734G
HF Nov. 50w. 3

914 WHITTLE, Tommy.   Jigsaw.   Alama AJ 4501 (E) (Reissue)
MM Jan. 7 p18.   175w. $3\frac{1}{2}$

915 The WHO. Story of.   Polydor 2683069 (2 discs) (Reissue)
GR Jan. p1194.   100w. $2\frac{1}{2}$

916 WILD Cherry.   Electrified Funk.   Epic PE 34462
RS May 19 275w. 1

917 WILD Tchoupitoulas.   Island ILPS 9360
RC Dec. p15.   200w. $3\frac{1}{2}$

918 WILHELM.   United Artists /Zigzag UAZZI (E)
RS March 10 p71-2.   575w.   4

919 WILLIAMS, John.   Changes/The Height Below.   Cube TOOFA
12/1-2 (E) (2 discs) (Reissue)
GR Aug. p353.   50w. $3\frac{1}{2}$

920 WILSON, Dennis.   Pacific Ocean Blue.   Caribou PZ34354
CIR Dec. 8 p75.   325w.   4
HF Nov. 75w.   4
MG Dec. p55.   75w.   3
MM Sept. 3 p18.   175w.   2
RS Oct. 20 p86.   425w.   4

921 WILSON, Tony.   I Like Your Style.   Bearsville BR 6966
BM Jan. p45.   75w.   2
CIR May 26 p58.   100w. $3\frac{1}{2}$

922 WINCHESTER, Jesse.   Let the Rough Side Drag.   Bearsville
6964. Cart. M86964
AU March p90.   150w.   4
FOL May p26-7.   875w.   5
SR Jan. p99.   100w.   4

923 WINCHESTER, Jesse.   Nothing But a Breeze.   Bearsville BR
6968. Cart. M86968.   Cass. M56968
CIR July 7 p30.   100w. $2\frac{1}{2}$
MM July 16 p23.   200w.   0
RSP Nov.-Dec.   p26.   200w. $2\frac{1}{2}$
SR Sept. p118.   200w. $3\frac{1}{2}$
VV May 16 p55.   250w.   2

924   WINGS. Over America. Capitol SWCO-11593 (3 discs)
      CIR   March 31 p12-3.   300w. $3\frac{1}{2}$
      CRA   March p65-6.   425w. $3\frac{1}{2}$
      CRE   March p58.   950w.   4
      GR   March p1467.   75w.   3
      MG   Feb. p53.   625w. $3\frac{1}{2}$
      RR   Feb. p93.   200w. $1\frac{1}{2}$
      RS   Feb. 10 p103.   300w. $2\frac{1}{2}$

925   WINTER, Johnny. Nothin' But the Blues. Blue Sky PZ34813.
      Cart. PZA-34033.   Cass. PZT-34033
      AU   Nov.   p125.   150w.   4
      CRA   Oct.   p69.   250w.   3
      MM   Sept. 17 p21.   300w. $2\frac{1}{2}$
      RCA   Aug.   p13.   50w. $2\frac{1}{2}$
      RS   Aug. 25 p56.   325w. $3\frac{1}{2}$
      SR   Dec.   p84.   150w.   4

926   WINTER Brothers Band.   Atco SD36-145.   Cart. 8SD-36-145
      CM   Sept.   p51.   200w.   3

927   WINWOOD, Steve.   Steve Winwood.   Island ILPS-9494
      AU   Sept.   p86.   400w.   4
      CIR   Oct. 27 p69.   400w.   4
      CK   Nov.   p64, 65.   125w. $2\frac{1}{2}$
      CRA   Aug.   p69.   300w.   3
      GR   Sept.   p521.   125w. $3\frac{1}{2}$
      HF   Sept.   p140.   500w.   3
      MG   Sept.   p51.   75w.   2
      MM   July 2 p21.   300w. $3\frac{1}{2}$
      RC   Aug.   p13.   150w. $2\frac{1}{2}$
      RR   Sept.   p92.   200w.   3
      RS   Sept. 8 p114.   425w. $2\frac{1}{2}$
      SR   Nov.   p116, 118.   300w.   2
      VV   July 18 p47-8.   400w.   2
      VV   Aug. 1 p5.   125w. $1\frac{1}{2}$

928   WIRE.   Pink Flag.   Harvest SHSP4076
      ZZ   Dec.   p41-2.   350w.   3

929   WISHBONE Ash.   Classic Ash.   MCA MCF 2793 (E) (Reissue)
      MM   May 28 p27.   200w.   3
      RR   Aug.   p83.   50w.   3

930   WISHBONE Ash.   Front Page News.   MCA 2311
      MM   Oct. 15 p25.   200w. $3\frac{1}{2}$
      TP   Dec.   p36.   200w. $3\frac{1}{2}$

931   WISHBONE Ash.   New England.   Atlantic SD 18200.   Cart.
      TP 18200
      GR   Jan.   p1197.   25w.   3
      RS   March 24 p66.   200w.   3
      SR   April p102.   87w.   5

932 WOOD, Ron. Mahoney's Last Stand. Warner K50308 (E)
     GR Jan. p1197. 50w. 3

933 WOOD, Roy. Super Active Wizzo. Warner Brothers BS 3065
     RR Dec. p86. 50w. 1½

934 WOODS, Gay and Terry Woods. Renowned. Antilles 7029
     CAC Feb. p420. 200w. 3

935 WOODY Woodmansey's U-Boat. Bronze. BRON 501
     MM Sept. 10 p24. 125w. 3½
     TP Nov. p42. 200w. 0

936 WORKMAN, Nanette. Big Tree BT 89514
     OLR March p56. 25w. 1½

937 WRAY, Link. Rockin' and Hand Clappin'. Epic 53267 (E)
     (Reissue)
     RSP Jan.-Feb. p38. 200w. 2

938 WRIGHT, Gary. The Light of Smiles. Warner Bros. BS22951
     AU Aug. p12. 100w. 3
     CIR March 31 p17-8. 350w. 3½
     CK April p48. 100w. 3
     CRA April p111. 300w. 3
     SR June p115. 100w. 4

939 WRIGHT, Gary. Touch and Gone. Warner BSK 3137
     RS Feb. 9 p100. 400w. 1½

940 YAMASHTA, Stomu. Go Too. Arista AB 4138
     MG Nov. p52. 25w. 3
     VV Dec. 5 p61. 150w. 2

941 YARDBIRDS. Favorites. Epic E 34490 (Reissue)
     CIR Oct. 13 p74-5. 150w. 3

942 YARDBIRDS. Featuring Jeff Beck. Charly CR300-013 (E)
     SMG May p20. 100w. 4

943 YARDBIRDS. Greatest Hits. Epic PE 34491 (Reissue)
     CIR Oct. 13 p74-5. 150w. 3

944 YELLOW Dog. Virgin V2083 (E)
     MM June 4 p28. 450w. 3
     RR Sept. p93. 25w. 2½

945 YES. Going for the One. Atlantic SD 19106
     CIR Sept. 29 p57-8. 650w. 2½
     CK Oct. p65. 100w. 1½
     CRA Sept. p66. 600w. 2½
     MG Oct. p60. 50w. 3
     MM July 9 p22. 500w. 5

RS Sept. 8 p111, 113. 1000w. 3
SR Nov. p120. 225w. 5
VV Aug. 15 p52. 350w. $2\frac{1}{2}$

946 YOUNG, Jesse Colin. Love on the Wing. Warner Bros. BS
3033. Cart. M83033. Cass. M53033
MM April 23 p24. 300w. $1\frac{1}{2}$
SR Sept. p118. 200w. $4\frac{1}{2}$

947 YOUNG, Neil. American Stars and Bars. Reprise MSK 2261.
Cart. M8 2261. Cass. M5 2261
AU Nov. p117. 250w. 3
CIR Aug. 18 950w. $3\frac{1}{2}$
CMP Sept. p39. 250w. 3
CRA Aug. p66. 400w. 3
HF Sept. p144. 400w. 4
GR Aug. p354. 150w. $2\frac{1}{2}$
MG July p49. 300w. 5
MM June 18 p18. 850w. $4\frac{1}{2}$
RC July p2. 200w. 4
RS Aug. 11 p57-8. 825w. $3\frac{1}{2}$
SR Sept. p108. 725w. 3
VV Aug. 1 p51. 50w. $3\frac{1}{2}$

948 YOUNG, Neil. Decade. Reprise 3RS2257 (3 discs) (Reissue)
ZZ Dec. p42. 450w. 4

949 YOUNG, Neil. Zuma. Reprise M52242
OLR March p56. 50w. 3

950 YOUNG, Neil and Stephen Stills. Long May You Run. Reprise MS 2253
RO May p13. 750w. 4

951 ZAO. Typhareth. RCA
EUR V2/#2 p26-7. 200w. 4

952 ZNR. Barricade 3. RCA/Isadora
EUR V2/#1 p33. 300w. 3

953 Z Z Top. Tejas. London PS 680
CAC April p9. 200w. 2
CIR April 14 p17. 550w. 3
GR April p1617. 25w. 2
MG April p51. 200w. $3\frac{1}{2}$
RSP May-June p22, 62. 750w. 3
SMG May p22. 100w. $3\frac{1}{2}$
SR May p94. 75w. 4

954 ZAPPA, Frank. Zoot Allures. Warner Bros. BS 2970
CAC March p452. 200w. 3
CRE March p63. 450w. 3
DB May 19 200w. 5

GP   March p112-3.   150w.   5
MM   Feb. 26 p24.   500w. $2\frac{1}{2}$
RSP March-April p60.   400w.   4
SR   April p102.   125w.   2
ZZ   Jan.   575w. $3\frac{1}{2}$

955 ZEVON, Warren.   Asylum 7E 1060
AU   Jan.   p80.   300w. $3\frac{1}{2}$

[Numbers 956-1000 not used]

MOOD--POP

This section comprises what can largely be called derivative music. For mood, most of it is reinterpretive, second-generation sounds taken from the worlds of the other categories. The nasal twang of country has been dropped, the solo acoustic instrument of folk has been augmented by strings, the beat of rhythm & blues has been modified, the noise and distortion of rock has been softened, the swing of jazz is missing, and the harshness of the blues has been smoothed. All of this music has been given a characteristic full, lush sound, suitable for home stereo consoles or middle-of-the-road (M.O.R.) programming. Included here is dance music, lyrical music, plus other variants that do not jar the nerves, and is suitable for background music just one cut above the level of Muzak. Often this music has been called the Music of Middle America, or of the silent majority. It sells exceptionally well, notably through rackers and jobbers. Standards and ballads are its main repertoire, with borrowings from other fields (especially from the musical stage) for crooners and chanteuses. Usually the format is to create a specific sound for a specific entertainer (for example, Frank Sinatra, Tom Jones, Patti Page) and "bend" the selections chosen to that sound. Under this method, it is possible for each performer to record an album a month, relying on the set arrangements of the studio orchestra. Fortunately, this does not happen because the economics of the market will not sustain the glut. Still, it is not unheard of for an artist to release four or five records a year. The results in mood music is a mixed bag of Latin themes, light cocktail jazz, soft rock, and soft country and western.

This section also includes pop music that has been characterized as "bubble gum" or pre-teen variety that appeals mainly to the very young. Such music is based on derivative rock, and is characterized by Top 40 tunes, usually written by someone who is not the singer or performer. These lightweight selections bear common characteristics: they are short; they have sparse instrumentation; they have trite, redundant lyrics; and they leave no lasting impression. This is a singles market for 45 rpm releases, and consequently most albums have one or possible two hits, followed by nine or so selections to pad the album.

Both mood and pop share several things in common. They both tend to be regarded as background music and not taken seriously; they are listened to with regularity by the automobile driver and his captive passengers; they are listened to by the lonely housewife;

they can be soothing and incredibly beautiful if the melody and the
arrangements are considered equally in a lush sort of way; and they
are the bread-and-butter releases of the major record companies,
for these discs make money. Included here are a small minority
of BAND recordings: marching bands, military bands, pipers,
school bands, etc.

The reviewing media do not take this music seriously; they
have little to say about the music except disparaging comments.
The only magazines that give regular coverage are Audio and the
British publication Gramophone. The English market, judging from
the number of releases, appears to be larger than that in North
America, and draws on British, American and Continental sources.
Their reissues are more carefully planned, with the original mono-
phonic sound maintained, good liner notes, and packaging design.

According to the reviews in 1977, the following appear to be
the best records:

      CROSBY, Bing. Feels Good, Feels Right. London PS 679
      GALLANT, Patsy. Are You Ready for Love? Attic LAT
         1017 (Canada)
      JONES, Jack. The Full Life. RCA APL1-2067
      JONES, Jack. With One More Look at You. RCA APL1-2361
      LAINE, Cleo. Return to Carnegie. RCA APL1-2407
      McRAE, Carmen. At the Great American Music Hall. Blue
        Note BNLA 709-H2 (2 discs)
      MERRILL, Helen, and Teddy Wilson. Helen Sings, Teddy
        Swings. Catalyst CAT 7907
      OLIVOR, Jane. First Night. Columbia PC 34274
      REDBONE, Leon. Double Time. Warner Brothers BS 2871
      RICHMAN, Jonathan, and the Modern Lovers. Rock 'n'
        Roll with the Modern Lovers. Beserkely PZ 34800
      STREISAND, Barbra. Streisand Superman. Columbia JC
        34830

1001   ABBA. Arrival. Atlantic SD 18207.   Cart. TP-18207
        CAC Jan. p377. 125w. $3\frac{1}{2}$
        CRA March p78. 200w. 2
        GR Feb. p1332. 50w. 4
        RS April 7 p76. 400w. 2
        SR May p82. 112w. 5
        VV Feb. 28 p7. 300w. 3

1002   ABRAHAMSON, Ronney. Stowaway. True North TN 27
        OLR Dec. p293. 50w. 5

1003   ADAM, Cliff, Singers. Something Old, Something New.
    EMI One-up OU2167 (E)

GR   April   p1617.   25w. $2\frac{1}{2}$

1004   ALDRICH, Ronnie.   Focux On.   Decca (2 discs) (E) (Reissue)
       CAC   May   p54.   150w. $3\frac{1}{2}$

1005   ALDRICH, Ronnie.   Reflections.   Decca PFS4377 (E)
       CAC   Feb.   p415.   150w.   3
       GR   Feb.   p1332.   50w.   3

1006   ALDRICH, Ronnie.   With Love and Understanding.   Decca
       PFS4406 (E)
       GR   July   p234.   25w. $2\frac{1}{2}$

1007   ALESSI, Billy.   Alessi.   A&M SP-4608.   Cart. 8T-4608.
       Cass. CS4657
       CRA   Jan.   p80.   125w. $2\frac{1}{2}$
       MM   April 30   p30.   175w.   5
       RR   July   p96.   50w.   3
       SR   March   p94.   50w.   0

1008   ALESSI, Billy.   All for a Reason.   A&M 4657.   Cart. 8T-
       4657.   Cass. CS-4657
       MM   Dec. 21   p15.   50w. $1\frac{1}{2}$

1009   ALLARD, Michel.   Questerne GR 309 (France)
       CC   Oct.   p35.   100w.   3

1010   ALMEIDA, Laurindo.   Latin Guitar.   Dobre DR 1000
       GP   Feb.   p113.   100w.   4

1011   ALMEIDA, Laurindo.   Virtuous Guitar.   Crystal Clear Rec-
       ords CCS 8001
       CAD   May   p12.   75w.   4
       GP   May   p129.   50w. $2\frac{1}{2}$

1012   AMAR, Jacques.   Baccara BA 1701
       CC   April   p37.   50w.   3

1013   AMARO, Eugene.   Twilight Time.   United Artists UALA
       561G (Canada)
       OLR   June   p141.   25w.   2

1014   AMBROSE.   Decca DDV5003/4 (2 discs) (E) (Reissue)
       GR   Oct.   p715.   50w. $4\frac{1}{2}$
       RR   Dec.   p87.   50w.   3

1015   ANDREWS, Harvey.   Someday.   Transatlantic (E)
       CAC   Feb.   p415.   200w.   4

1016   ANKA, Paul.   Live.   RCA PL 42148 (E)
       MM   May 14   p31.   25w.   1

1017   ANKA, Paul.   The Music Man.   United Artists UA-LA 746-H

MM Sept. 3 p46. 50w. $2\frac{1}{2}$
SR Oct. p90. 200w. 5

1018   ANKA, Paul. The Painter. United Artists UA-La653-G
        UA-EA 653-H
        SR Feb. p86. 150w. 3

1019   ANTHONY, Julie. Hello In There. EMI 3132 (E)
        GR Jan. p1194. 50w. 3

1020   APHRODITE'S Child. 666. Vertigo 6641 581 (E) (2 discs)
        CAC June p91. 200w. $2\frac{1}{2}$

1021   ARBRE. Time and Again. DJM (E)
        CAC Jan. p377. 200w. 3

1022-3 AREL, Julie. Merci à Toi. Capitol ST 70045 (Canada)
        OLR Sept. p224. 25w. 5

1024   ASTAIRE, Fred. Live. Pye (E)
        CAC Jan. p380. 100w. 4

1025   ASTAIRE, Fred. Starring Fred Astaire. Columbia SG
        32472 (2 discs) (Reissue)
        AU March p94. 400w. 4

1026   AUSTIN, Sid. Soothing Soft Sax of. Charly (E)
        CAC Feb. p419. 50w. 3

1027   AZNAVOUR, Charles. Best of. RCA 90-071 (E) (Reissue)
        CAC Jan. p477. 100w. $3\frac{1}{2}$
        MM Jan. 1 p15. 50w. 0

1028   BACHARACH, Burt. Futures. A&M SP-4622. Cart. 8T-
        4622. Cass. CS-4622
        CAC May p50. 200w. 1
        GR May p1757. 100w. 1
        SR Aug. p92. 525w. $4\frac{1}{2}$

1029   BAKER, Robert. Organist. Sonor OR 10160 (Reel to Reel
        Tape)
        AU May p94. 150w. $3\frac{1}{2}$

1030   BALL, Kenny. Hello Dolly. Pye Golden Hour GH 636 (E)
        RR Dec. p86. 25w. $2\frac{1}{2}$

1031   BAND of the Duke of Edinburgh's Royal Regiment. Grosven-
        or GRS1056 (E)
        GR Sept. p521. 125w. 3

1032   BAND of the Royal Engineers (Aldershot). Marching. EMI
        Note NTS 117 (E)
        GR May p1750. 100w. 3

1033   BAND of the Royal Marines.   Marines on the March.   Decca
        SB 714 (E)
            GR   June   p109.   200w.   4

1034   BAND of the Royal Marines School of Music.   Crown Imperial.
        EMI Note NTS 123 (E)
            GR   June   p109.   175w. $3\frac{1}{2}$

1035   BAND of the Royal Marines School of Music.   Victory at
        Sea.   EMI Studio 2 TWOX1058 (E)
            GR   July   p226.   125w. $3\frac{1}{2}$

1036   BAND of the Third Battalion, the Queen's Regiment.   Jubi-
        lee.   Music Masters 05-4 (E)
            GR   Sept.   p521.   150w. $3\frac{1}{2}$

1037   BARNET, Charles.   The Complete, 1935-37.   RCA AMX2
        5526 (2 discs) (Reissue)
            CAD   May   p28.   50w.   2
            OB   Oct. 6   p35-7.   100w.   2
            MR   May   p7.   425w. $2\frac{1}{2}$

1038   BARNET, Charlie.   The Complete, 1944-49.   Golden Era
        15015
            CAD   Feb.   p42-3.   175w. $3\frac{1}{2}$

1039   BARNET, Charlie.   Fair and Warmer.   Golden ERA 15037
            CAD   Feb.   p42-3.   175w.   3

1040   BARRETTO, Ray.   Eye of the Beholder.   Atlantic 19140
            CAD   Nov.   p31.   75w.   3

1041   BARRETTO, Ray.   Tomorrow: Barretto Live.   Atlantic SD
        2-509.   Cart. TP2-509
            DB   April 21   p30.   350w. $3\frac{1}{2}$
            HF   Feb.   p142.   300w.   3
            SR   April   p88.   150w.   3

1042   BARRIE, Keath.   Reach Out.   United Artists UALA 673G
            CC   June   p32.   50w.   3

1043   BASSEY, Shirley.   Burn My Candle.   Philips SON 035 (E)
        (Reissue)
            GR   June   p110.   125w.   3

1044   BASSEY, Shirley.   Thoughts of Love.   United Artists UAS
        30011 (E)
            GR   Jan.   p1194.   100w. $3\frac{1}{2}$
            MM   Sept. 17   p20.   50w.   4

1045   BASSEY, Shirley.   20 Golden Film Hits.   EMI Note NTS
        112 (E)
            CAC   Feb.   p437.   50w.   3

GR   Jan.   p1194.   50w.   3

1046   BASSEY, Shirley.   You Take My Heart Away.   United Art-
       ists UALA751H
          RC   Nov.   p9.   125w.   3

1047   BELAFONTE, Harry.   Sings of Love.   RCA PL42176 (E)
          MM   May 14   p31.   50w.   3

1048   BELANGER, Marc.   Les Cordes en Liberté.   Kébec KD 931
       (Canada)
          CC   Nov.   p35.   100w.   3

1049   BEN, Jorge.   Tropical.   Island ILPS 9390.   Cart. Y81-9390.
       Cass. ZC1-9390
          PRM   April   p44.   375w. $2\frac{1}{2}$
          SR   July   p93.   125w.   4

1050   BENNETT, Tony.   Life Is Beautiful.   Improv 7112
          RC   May   p7.   150w. $4\frac{1}{2}$
          SR   Feb.   p86.   100w.   3

1051   BENNETT, Tony.   Sings Ten Rodgers and Hart Songs.
       Improv 7113
          RC   May   p7.   100w. $3\frac{1}{2}$

1052   BENNETT, Tony and Bill Evans.   Together Again.   Improv
       7117
          CAD   Oct.   p34.   50w.   4

1053   BESSES of the Barn Band.   English Brass.   Pye TB 3012
       (E)
          GR   Jan.   p1193.   200w. $3\frac{1}{2}$

1054   BILLO'S Caracas Boys.   Billo '77.   TH THS-2010
          SR   May   p82.   166w.   4

1055   BIM.   Raincheck on Misery.   Casino CA 1009 (Canada)
          OLR   June   p140.   25w.   3

1056   BLACK Dyke Mills Band.   Best of.   RCA PL25025 (E) (Re-
       issue)
          CAC   Sept.   p217-8.   150w.   4
          GR   July   p229.   150w.   4

1057   BLACK Dyke Mills Band.   Golden Hour of.   Pye GH 632 (E)
       (Reissue)
          GR   July   p229.   125w. $3\frac{1}{2}$

1058   BLACK Dyke Mills Band.   Lion and Eagle.   RCA PL 25089
       (E)
          GR   Oct.   p712.   150w. $3\frac{1}{2}$

1059   BLACK'S, Bill, Combo.   It's Honky Tonk Time.   Hi Records
       SHL 32104.   Cart. SHL8 32104
           CM   June p48.   250w.   2
           CMP Sept. p38.   150w.   3
           NK   Summer p38.   50w.   3

1060   BLAKE, Eubie.   Eubie Blake Song Hits with Eubie and His
       Girls.   Eubie Blake Music EBM 9
           RA   Jan. -Feb.   p5-7.   125w.   3½

1061   BLAKE, Eubie.   Proteges Live at the Theater De Lys.
       Eubie Blake Music EMB 8
           MJ   Jan. p28.   50w.   2½
           RA   Jan. -Feb.   p5-6.   75w.   3½

1062   BOHANNON, Hamilton.   Dance Your Ass Off.   Dakar 76917
           CAC Feb. p420.   50w.   1

1063   BOHANNON, Hamilton.   Phase II.   Mercury SRM 1-1159
           MG   Sept. p55.   100w.   2
           RS   Aug. 11 p69.   325w.   1

1064   BOLCOM, William and Joan Morris.   Vaudeville.   Nonesuch
       H 71330
           MR   June p10.   300w.   4

1065   BOSTON Pops Orchestra.   Simon and Garfunkel Songbook.
       Polydor 2482328
           GR   Nov. p919.   25w.   1½

1066   BOTICELLI Orchestra.   The Sound of Today.   London 44273
           GR   July p234.   25w.   3

1067   BOULAGE, Patti.   Handkerchief (E)
           MM   Feb. 5 p23.   50w.   1½

1068   BOWER, Laurie, Singers.   Back Home Again.   United
       Artists UALA 391G (Canada)
           OLR June p141-2.   75w.   2

1069   BOYLAN, Terence.   Asylum 7E 1091
           RC   Oct. p7.   50w.   2½

1070   BREAD.   Lost Without Your Love.   Elektra 7E-1094
           CAC April p10.   200w.   2½
           RS   April 21 175w.   4
           SR   May p83.   125w.   4

1071   BREGENT, Michel-Georges.   Et le Troisième Jour.   Capitol
       ST 70044 (Canada)
           CC   Feb. p33.   50w.   3

1072   BRETT, Paul.   Earth Birth.   RCA PL 25080 (E)

         MM   June 25 p22. 225w. 2
         RR   Sept. p93. 50w. 3

1073   BREWER, Teresa. Best of. RCA (Reissue)
         MM   Feb. 5 p23. 75w. 3

1074   BRISSON, Gaston. Kebec Disque KD 915 (Canada)
         CC   Feb. p30. 50w. 3

1075   BRITISH Caledonia Airways Pipe Band. Let's Go. DJM (E)
         MM   Jan. 22 p23. 50w. 1

1076   BRITISH Rock Orchestra. The Music of the Bay City Rollers.
         CAT (E)
         MM   Oct. 1 p48. 50w. 0

1077   BROTHERHOOD of Man. Images. Pye (E)
         MM   Nov. 12 p29. 50w. $2\frac{1}{2}$

1078   BROTHERHOOD of Man. Oh Boy. Pye NSPL 18517 (E)
         CAC June p92. 100w. $2\frac{1}{2}$

1079   BROTHERS. Sing Me. Bus Stop BUSLP8002 (E)
         GR   June p110. 50w. 3

1080   BROWN, Charity. Stay With Me. A&M SP 9022 (Canada)
         OLR Sept. p226. 25w. 3

1081   BROWN, Linda. Sing Along With Me. A&M SP 9012 (Canada)
         OLR June p142. 25w. $3\frac{1}{2}$

1082   BRUTUS. GRT 9230-1057 (Canada)
         CC   June p33. 50w. 3

1083   BRYAN, Dora. Sings Fivepenny Piece. EMI EMC 3170 (E)
         GR   April p1608. 75w. 2

1084   BRYANT, Allan. Space Guitars. CRI SD 366
         GP   Dec. p153. 75w. $2\frac{1}{2}$

1085   BYGRAVES, Max. Max-a-Million: Golden Hits of the 20s.
         Pye NSPL 18522 (E)
         GR   Nov. p919. 25w. 3

1086   BYGRAVES, Max. Max-a-Million: Golden Hits of the 30s.
         Pye NSPL 18526 (E)
         GR   Nov. p919. 25w. 3

1087   BYGRAVES, Max. Max-a-Million: Golden Greats of the 40s.
         Pye NSPL 18527 (E)
         GR   Nov. p919. 25w. 3

1088   BYRD, Jerry.   Steel Guitar Hawaiian Style.   Lehua Records
        SL 7023
            GP Aug. p119. 250w. 4

1089   CADO, Belle.   Anchor AN 2015
            HF April p148. 50w. $2\frac{1}{2}$
            MM Jan. 15 p17. 200w. $3\frac{1}{2}$

1090   CALDERA.   Capitol ST11571
            CAC April p8. 200w. 2
            HF Jan. p144. 150w. 3
            MM April 16 p23. 50w. 3

1091   CAMPBELL, Archie.   Elektra 7E-1075
            HF Feb. p145. 100w. 1
            MG Jan. 100w. $2\frac{1}{2}$

1092   CAMPBELL, Robert.   Living in the Shadow of a Downtown
        Movie Star.   Decca (E)
            MM Nov. 19 p24. 150w. $1\frac{1}{2}$

1093   CAMPO, Tony.   Garuda.   EMI EMC 3174 (E)
            RR Sept. p96. 25w. 1

1094   CAPTAIN & Tennille.   Come In From the Rain.   A&M SP-
        4700.   Cart. AAM-4700.   Cass. AAM-4700
            CAC June p92. 300w. $3\frac{1}{2}$
            CIR Sept. 29 p61. 500w. 0
            SR Aug. p86. 75w. 4

1095   CARD, Graeme.   Truly Fine ATF 010 (Canada)
            CC April p36. 75w. $2\frac{1}{2}$

1096   CARLTON Main Frickley Colliery Band.   Brass Band.   Gros-
        venor GRS 1043 (E)
            GR Jan. p1193. 150w. $3\frac{1}{2}$

1097   CARNES, Kim.   Sailing.   A&M SP-4606
            CRA May p78. 175w. 3
            HF April p139. 250w. 4
            MM April 16 p23. 50w. $1\frac{1}{2}$
            RS April 7 p78. 450w. 3
            SR May p83-4. 100w. 0

1098   CARPENTERS.   Live at the Palladium.   Decca DKL9/1-2
        (2 discs) (E)
            CAC March p453. 125w. $3\frac{1}{2}$
            GR Feb. p1332. 100w. $3\frac{1}{2}$

1099   CARPENTERS.   Passage.   A&M SP4703
            GR Dec. p1162. 150w. 3
            MM Oct. 15 p25. 350w. $1\frac{1}{2}$
            RR Dec. p86. 50w. 3

1100   CARROLL, Barbara. Barbara Carroll. Blue Note BN-LA
        645-G BN-EA645H
             SR Feb. p108. 100w. 0

1101   CARTWRIGHT, David. Masquerade. DJM DJF 20489 (E)
             MM Jan. 22 p46. 50w. 1

1102   CASSIDY, David. Gettin' It in the Street. RCA APL1-1852.
        Cart. APS1-1852. Cass. APK1-1852
             SR Sept. p94, 95. 125w. 3

1103   CENTRAL Band of the Canadian Forces. Les Français.
        London SW 99558 (Canada)
             OLR June p142. 50w. 4

1104   CENTRAL Band of the Czechoslovak Ministry of the Interior.
        Obránce Hranic. Panton 110571 (Czechoslovakia)
             GR Sept. p521. 125w. 3

1105   CENTRAL Band of the Royal Air Force. Wings. EMI
        Studio 2 TWOX-1059 (E)
             CAC Sept. p217. 200w. 4
             GR Sept. p518. 150w. $4\frac{1}{2}$

1106   CERVANTES, Frederico. Forever Real Concert Records
        FJC-1054
             CAD July p24. 200w. 4

1107   CERVANTES, Frederico. Heard Around the World, V. 1.
        Forever Jewell FJC 1020
             CAD March p28. 100w. 2

1108   CHACKSFIELD, Frank. Focus on. Decca KFOC 28057 (E)
        (2 discs) (Reissue)
             CAC April p11. 150w. $3\frac{1}{2}$
             GR March p1468. 100w. 3

1109   CHACKSFIELD, Frank. Vintage '52. London 44289
             GR Nov. p919. 50w. 3

1110   CHAMBERLAIN, Cathy. Rag 'n' Roll Revue. Warner BS
        3032
             CAD June p20. 100w. 3
             CIR June 23 p64-5. 200w. 1
             SR August p86. 125w. 2

1111-2 CHAQUITO. South of the Border. Philips (E)
             CAC Feb. p416. 50w. 4

1113   CHARBONNEAU, Christine. Quintessence. Polydor 2424
        139
             CC Sept. p35. 50w. 3

1114   CHER.   Cherished.   Warner BS 3046.   Cart. M83046.
        Cass. M53046
            CIR   Oct. 27 p69.   125w.   0
            HF   Nov.   275w. $2\frac{1}{2}$
            RS   Oct. 6 p90.   325w. $1\frac{1}{2}$

1115   CHER.   I'd Rather Believe in You.   Warner Bros. BS 2898
        M8 2898
            HF   Jan. p142.   150w.   4
            SR   Jan. p86.   30w.   0

1116   CHRISTIAN.   The First.   Polydor 2384-091 (E)
            MM   Feb. 12 p26.   50w. $2\frac{1}{2}$

1117   CHUNKY, Novi and Ernie.   Warner BS 3030
            RC   Oct. p7.   25w.   2
            RS   Aug. 24 p56.   250w. $2\frac{1}{2}$
            VV   Aug. 22 p57-8.   400w. $3\frac{1}{2}$

1118   CITY of Oxford Youth Band.   Brass Band Works.   Rediffu-
        sion Gold Star 15-56 (E)
            GR   Jan. p1193.   100w.   3

1119   CLAUDE, Renee.   L'Enamour le Desamour.   London LFS
        9019 (Canada)
            CC   Feb. p34.   50w.   3

1120   CLINCH, Paul.   Living Like a Rich Man.   Realistic RL 1000
        (Canada)
            CC   June p30.   50w.   3

1121   CLOONEY, Rosemary.   Greatest Hits.   CBS (E) (Reissue)
            CAC   Feb. p416.   100w.   3

1122   CLOONEY, Rosemary.   Nice to Be Around.   United Artists
        UAS 30008 (E)
            GR   July p233.   150w. $4\frac{1}{2}$
            MM   Sept. 17 p20.   125w. $3\frac{1}{2}$

1123   COGAN, Alma.   Collection.   EMI One-Up OU2168 (E) (Re-
        issue)
            GR   July p233.   25w. $3\frac{1}{2}$

1124   COHEN, Phyllis.   These Things I Would Do.   CBC (Canada)
            CC   Oct. p34.   100w.   3

1125   COLDSTREAM Guards Band.   Ballet in Ice.   RCA PL 25024
        (E)
            GR   April p1607.   100w. $3\frac{1}{2}$

1126   COLUMBO, Russ.   A Legendary Performer.   RCA CPL
        1-1756(e) (Reissue)
            SR   Jan. p90.   400w.   4

1127   COMDEN, Betty. A Party With.   Stet 52L 5177 (2 discs)
        SR Oct. p110. 425w. $4\frac{1}{2}$

1128   COMO, Perry. The Best of British Perry Como. RCA
        PS 12373 (E) (Reissue)
        MM Dec. 3 p20. 75w. 3

1129   COMO, Perry. A Legendary Performer. RCA CPLa-1752
        (Reissue)
        CAC Jan. p378. 150w. $3\frac{1}{2}$
        MM Dec. 3 p20. 75w. 3

1130   COMO, Perry. Sings Love Songs. RCA NL 42076 (E)
        CAC May p50. 150w. 4

1131   COMO, Perry. Swings. RCA (E)
        MM Jan. 1 p15. 100w. 3

1132   CONNIFF, Ray. If You Leave Me Now. CBS (E)
        MM Oct. 16 p23. 50w. 2

1133   COOK, Barbara. As of Today. Columbia PC-34493. Cart.
        PCA-34493. Cass. PCT-34493
        SR Aug. p83. 425w. 5

1134   CORY Band. American Express. Transatlantic XTRA 1169
        (E)
        GR May p1749-50. 100w. $3\frac{1}{2}$

1135   COTTON, Lloyd. Number II. Precision Twentieth Century
        ZCBT519 (E)
        CAC April p14. 50w. 2
        MM Feb. 26 p30. 50w. 1

1136   CROSBY, Bing. Beautiful Memories. United Artists UAS
        30116 (E)
        GR Dec. p1161. 75w. $3\frac{1}{2}$
        MM Nov. 12 p25. 200w. 3

1137   CROSBY, Bing. Bingo Viejo. London SH 8499 (E) Cart.
        KSACU8499
        GR April p1608. 125w. $2\frac{1}{2}$

1138   CROSBY, Bing. Feels Good, Feels Right. London PS 679
        CAC Feb. p416. 100w. $3\frac{1}{2}$
        GR Feb. p1332. 50w. 3
        SR May p84. 272w. 4

1139   CROSBY, Bing. A Legendary Performer. RCA CPL1-2086(e)
        (Reissue)
        CAC Aug. p165. 250w. $2\frac{1}{2}$
        RR June p95. 50w. $2\frac{1}{2}$
        SR July p93-4. 275w. 5

1140 CROSBY, Bing. On the Air. Aircheck 17 (Reissue)
      DB April 7 p31-3. 100w. 3

1141 CURTIS, Rick. Sings the Hits That Made John Denver. In-
      ternational Artists (E)
      CAC March p453. 50w. 2½

1142 CURTOLA, Bobby. Stickin' with Beautiful Things. RCA
      KPL 1-0165 (Canada)
      OLR Sept. p225. 50w. 3

1143 CZECHOSLOVAK Military Band. Marches. Supraphon 414
      1714 (Czechoslovakia)
      GR Sept. p578. 200w. 4½

1144 DACOSTA, Rita. Meets the Cedar Walton Trio. Finite
      1976-3
      CAD April p71. 96w. 2½

1145 DALTO, Jorge. Chevere. United Artists UA-LA 671-G
      CK May p48. 100w. 4½

1146 DAVIS, Sammy, Jr. At His Dynamic Greatest. MCA2-
      4109 (2 discs)
      DB Oct. 6 p35-7. 100w. 2½

1147 DAVIS, Sammy, Jr. It's a Musical World. Polydor [cas-
      sette] (E)
      CAC Jan. p378. 100w. 3

1148 DAVIS, Sammy, Jr. The Song and Dance Man. Twentieth
      Century BT426 (E)
      GR March p1468. 50w. 2

1149 DAVIS, William. Constructive Brass. Grosvenor GRS 1048
      (E)
      GR Jan. p1193. 100w. 3½

1150 DEAN, Roger. Cycles. Mosaic GCM 774 (E)
      RR Nov. p116. 75w. 3½

1151 DEARIE, Blossom. My New Celebrity Is Over. Daffodil
      BMD 103 (Reissue)
      SR April p89. 200w. 4

1152 DEARIE, Blossom. Sings, Vols. 1-3. BMD 101/3 (4 discs)
      CAD March p23, 26. 400w. 4

1153 DEE, Lenny. Organ Music. MCA 2301
      RC Nov. p8. 100w. 3

1154 DELGADO, Roberto. The Bouzouki King. Polydor 2371 702.
      Cart. 3150 702 (E)

GR   May   p1757.   25w. $2\frac{1}{2}$

1155   DELGADO, Roberto.   Fiesta for Dancing.   Polydor 2371 588
(E)
        CAC   Feb.   p416.   150w. $1\frac{1}{2}$

1156   DELGADO, Roberto.   South America in Super Stereo.   Polydor 2418 215 (E)
        GR   Nov.   p920.   25w. $1\frac{1}{2}$

1157   DENJEAN, Claude.   Moods.   Decca PFS 4390 (E)
        GR   Nov.   p920.   25w.   3

1158   DENVER, John.   Best of, Vol. 2.   RCA PL 42120.   Cart.
TPK 42120.   Cass. CPS 42120 (E) (Reissue)
        CAC   May   p51.   300w. $3\frac{1}{2}$
        CMP   May   p37.   150w.   4
        CMR   Aug.   p20.   100w. $3\frac{1}{2}$
        GR   April   p1608.   50w.   4

1159   DENVER, John.   Greatest Hits, Vol. 2.   RCA CPLI 1-2195.
Cart. CPSI 1-2195
        CM   Aug.   p46.   225w.   3
        RC   April   p11.   200w.   4

1160   DEODATO.   First Cuckoo.   MCA MCF 2728 (E)
        RR   Jan.   p63.   50w.   2

1161   DERRINGER, Glen.   The Handiwork of Glen Derringer.   Win
Mil Records 201
        CK   Nov.   p64.   100w. $4\frac{1}{2}$

1162   DESFORD Colliery Band.   Sounds of Brass.   Decca SB 328
        GR   July   p229.   125w.   4

1163   DIAMOND, Neil.   Beautiful Noise.   Columbia PC 33965
        RC   June   p7.   200w. $2\frac{1}{2}$

1164   DIAMOND, Neil.   Love at the Greek.   Columbia KC 2-34004.
CTX-34404
        CAC   Aug.   p166.   250w.   3
        MM   March 19 p31.   300w. $3\frac{1}{2}$
        SR   June   p96.   100w.   5

1165   DIEVAL, Jack.   All the Things You Are.   Peerless VEL
P1000 (E)
        MM   Aug. 27 p24.   175w.   3

1166   DISTEL, Sacha.   Love Is All.   Pye NSPL18504 (E)
        CAC   Feb.   p416.   100w.   3
        GR   Jan.   p1194.   50w.   3

1167   DORSEY, Jack.   Carpenters and King.   BBC REM 278 (E)

GR   Nov.   p919.   25w. $3\frac{1}{2}$

1168   DORSEY, Tommy.   Fanfare #1.   (Reissue)
       CAD   Jan.   p21, 22.   200w.   4

1169   DORSEY, Tommy.   At the Fat Man's.   Hep 9
       JJ   Feb.   p30.   250w.   4

1170   DORSEY, Tommy.   Complete, Vol. 1, 1935.   Bluebird
       AXM2-5521 (2 discs) (Reissue)
       MR   July   p9-10.   125w. $3\frac{1}{2}$

1171   DORSEY, Tommy.   Complete, Vol. 2, 1936.   RCA AXM2-
       5549 (2 discs) (Reissue)
       CAD   Aug.   p53.   250w.   3
       MR   July   p9-10.   125w. $3\frac{1}{2}$

1172   DOUGLAS, Carl.   Love, Peace and Happiness.   Pye (E)
       MM   May 14   p33.   50w.   1

1173   DREAM Express.   A Million in One, Two, Three.   EMI
       ECM 3193 (E)
       GR   Dec.   p1162.   25w.   3
       MM   Oct. 8   p29.   50w.   0

1174   DUBOIS, Claude.   Mellow Reggae.   Barclay 80271 (Canada)
       CC   Nov.   p35.   100w.   3

1175   DUFRESNE, Diane.   Maman Si Tu M'Voyais....   Barclay
       80270 (Canada)
       CC   June   p29.   50w.   3

1176   DUGUAY, Raôul.   L'Enrol.   Capitol SKAO 70042 (Canada)
       OLR   March   p56.   25w.   2

1177   DUNCAN, Lesley.   Everything Changes.   GM (E)
       MM   July 16   p27.   50w. $1\frac{1}{2}$

1178   DUNHAM, Sonny.   Hold Everything.   Golden Era 15044
       CAD   Feb.   p28-9.   100w.   4

1179   DUNN, Tom.   Melody Man.   United Artists UALA 658-G
       (Canada)
       OLR   Dec.   p293.   25w.   4

1180   DUTCHMAN, Michigan.   German Polka Favorites.   Jay JAY
       5070
       RC   April   p2.   50w. $2\frac{1}{2}$

1181   ECKSTINE, Billy.   Mr. B and the Band, the Savoy Sessions.
       SJL 2214 (2 discs) (Reissue)
       CAD   Feb.   p43.   150w.   3
       CO   Feb.   p22.   125w.   4

DB   March 10 p27.   300w.   4
MJ   Nov. p22. 100w. $2\frac{1}{2}$
RR   June p94. 50w. $3\frac{1}{2}$
SOU Jan. p49. 100w.   4

1182   ECKSTINE, Billy and Quincy Jones. At Basin Street East.
       Philips SON 028 (Reissue)
       RR   Feb. p94. 75w. $2\frac{1}{2}$

1183   EDWARDS, Bobby. Guitars, Guitars. Attic LAT 1004
       (Canada)
       OLR   June p142. 25w. $2\frac{1}{2}$

1184   EIKHARD, Shirley. Let Me Down Easy.   Attic LAT 1021
       (Canada)
       OLR   June p142. 50w.   3

1185   ESTELLE, Don. Lofty Sings. EMI (E)
       CAC   Feb. p417. 200w.   3

1186   ETRON Fou Leloublan. Batelages. Gratk-liel 2001 (France)
       MM   Jan. 7 p16. 200w.   4

1187   EVER Ready Band. Brass Band Music. Decca SB 329 (E)
       GR   Oct. p712. 150w.   3

1188   FABULOUS Poodles. Pye (E) NSPL 18530
       MM   Nov. 12 p26. 350w. $2\frac{1}{2}$

1189   FAITHFULL, Marianne. Dreamin' My Dreams. NEMS NEL
       6007
       CMP   Feb. p34. 200w.   4

1190   FAYE, Alice. On the Air. Totem 1011
       SR   Oct. p94. 275w.   3

1191   FAYE, Francis. Bad, Bad. Bethlehem BCP 6006 (Reissue)
       JR   V9/#3 unpaged. 25w.   3

1192   FELICIANO, José. Sweet Soul Music. Private Stock PS
       2022
       CAC   April p11-2. 250w.   2
       GR   May p1758. 25w. $2\frac{1}{2}$
       MM   May 7 p21. 200w. $3\frac{1}{2}$
       RC   Oct. p5. 250w. $3\frac{1}{2}$
       RS   Feb. 24 p65. 300w.   3
       SR   May p84, 86. 262w.   4

1193   FERRANTE & Teicher. Feelings. United Artists UA-LA
       662-G
       CK   Jan. p51. 25w.   4

1194   FIELDS, Gracie. The Amazing Gracie Fields. Monmouth-

Evergreen MES/7079 (Reissue)
SR Aug. p92. 175w. 5

1195 FIFTY Guitars. With Love From. Misicor 2506
RC Dec. p14-5. 100w. 3

1196 FIRMAN, Bert. 1925-1931. World Record Club SHB 30
(E) (2 discs) (Reissue)
ST. Feb. -March p115. 175w. 4

1197 FISET, Steve. Ange on Démon. London Deram XDEF 135
(Canada)
CC March p33. 50w. 3

1198 FITZGERALD, Ella. Ella. Verve 2352 170 (E) (Reissue)
MM March 5 p32. 200w. $4\frac{1}{2}$

1199 FITZGERALD, Ella. Memories. MCA Coral CB 20023
(Reissue)
JR V9/#4 unpaged. 50w. $2\frac{1}{2}$

1200 FITZGERALD, Ella and Joe Pass. Fitzgerald and Pass,
Again. Pablo 2310 772
CAC Jan. p390. 300w. $1\frac{1}{2}$
GR Feb. p1336. 125w. 4

1201 FONTAINE, Brigitte. Comme à la Radio. Saravah SH
10006 (France)
JF No. 46 p67, 69 75w. 5

1202 FORESTER, Louise. On Est Bien Mieux Chez-Vous. Gam-
ma GS 230 (Canada)
CC Feb. p33. 50w. 3
SR Jan. p87. 100w. 3

1203 FOUNTAIN, Pete. The Best of, Vol. 2. MCA 2-4095 (2
discs) (Reissue)
CAD Oct. p44. 550w. 4

1204 FOUR Seasons. Helicon. Warner Bros. BS 3016. Cart.
M83016. Cass. M53016
MM July 16 p27. 50w. $2\frac{1}{2}$
SR Oct. p96. 175w. $4\frac{1}{2}$
ZZ June p40. 150w. $3\frac{1}{2}$

1205 FOX, John, Singers. Fairest Isle. BBC REC 287 (E)
GR Dec. p1162. 50w. 3

1206 FRANCIS, Connie. 20 All-Time Greats. Polydor 2371290
(E) (Reissue)
GR Nov. p919. 50w. 3

1207 FRANCOIS, Claude. EMI EMC 3189 (E)

GR   Dec.   p1162.   25w.   3
GR   Dec.   p1162.   25w.   2½

1208   FRAPPER, Rodrigue.   Saccacomie.   Alonette AR 916 (Canada)
CC   Sept.   p33.   50w.   3

1209   FULL Circle.   Bean Records 101
CK   Nov.   p65.   25w.   3

1210   FUSION.   RCA KPL1-0178 (Canada)
OLR   Sept.   p224-5.   25w.   3

1211   GALLANT, Patsy.   Are You Ready for Love?   Attic LAT
1017 (Canada)
CC   Feb.   p32.   50w.   3
RC   Aug.   p10-1.   150w.   3

1212   GARY and Dave.   14 Greatest Hits.   Axe AXS 519 (Canada)
(Reissue)
CC   Sept.   p32.   50w.   3

1213   GELLER, Harold.   Mr. Melody.   Pye NSLPX 41053 (E)
GR   Feb.   p1332.   50w.   2½

1214   GERALDO Orchestra.   Hello Again.   Transatlantic TRA 332
GR   Jan.   p1194.   50w.   3

1215   GILBERTO, Astrud.   Once Upon a Summertime.   Verve
2352 172 (E)
CAC   March   p454.   150w.   3½

1216   GILLIES, Anne Lorne.   Open the Door Softly.   Philips 6308
276
GR   Jan.   p1194.   25w.   3

1217   GILSTRAP, James.   Love Talk.   Rox 102
CAC   March   p453.   50w.   2½

1218   GOLD, Andrew.   What's Wrong with This Picture?   Asylum
7E-1086
AU   April   p84.   350w.   3
CIR   May 26   p59-60.   750w.   4½
GR   Feb.   p1335.   50w.   2½
SR   May   p86.   200w.   3

1219   GOLD, E. Dee.   Please Let Me into Your Heart.   RCA
KPL1-0190 (Canada)
OLR   Sept.   p225-6.   25w.   4

1220   GOLDE, Frankie.   Atlantic SD 18196
RC   June   p8.   200w.   2
RS   Feb. 24   p69.   350w.   2½

1221 GOLDSBORO, Bobby. Epic EPC 82038
CMP Dec. p36. 200w. 3

1222 GOODMAN, Benny. 1935-1937. Sunbeam SB-149 (Reissue)
ST Feb.-March p115-6. 175w. 3

1223 GOODMAN, Benny. 1946. Jazz Society 508 (Reissue)
CO Dec. p23. 50w. 3

1224 GOODMAN, Benny. On the Air. Aircheck 16 (Reissue)
DB April 7 p31-3. 100w. 4

1225 GOODMAN, Benny. The War Years. Jazz Society AA 510
(Reissue)
JM Summer p63. 100w. 2½

1226 GOODMAN, Benny. With Small Groups, V. 1. Rarities 21
(Reissue)
JM 7:2 p65-6. 75w. 3

1227 GOODMAN, Benny. With Small Groups, V. 2. Rarities 30
(Reissue)
JM 1:2 p65-6. 75w. 3

1228 Le GRAND Cirque. Ordinaire. Capitol SKAO 70 041 (Canada)
OLR March p56. 25w. 3½

1229 GRANT, Earl. The Best of Earl Grant. MCA MCA1-4096
(2 discs) (Reissue)
CAD Oct. p25. 25w. 2½
CK Jan. p51. 125w. 5

1230 GREEN, Garland. Love Is What We Came For. RCA APL1-
2351
MM Sept. 24 p27. 50w. 3½

1231 GREEN, Jesse. Nice and Slow. EMI EMC 3164 (E)
CAC May p51. 125w. 3

1232 GREENSLADE, Arthur. Plays Abba's Greatest Hits. RCA
PL 13036 (E)
MM Aug. 6 p16. 50w. 2½

1233 GREGOR, Max. Happy Dancing. Polydor (E)
CAC Feb. p416. 25w. 2

1234 GRENADIER Guards Band. The Sounds of Pageantry. Decca
SB715 (E)
GR June p106, 109. 200w. 3½

1235 GRIFFITH, Bobby G. Love and Laughter. Badger Records
BALP 100 (Canada)

OLR   June   p142.   25w.   1

1236   GRIMETHORPE Colliery Band.   Band of the Year.   RCA
       PL 25046 (E)
              CAC   Sept.   p217.   100w.   3½
              GR   July   p226.   200w.   4

1237   GUS (Footwear) Band.   Kings of Brass.   EMI One-Up OU159
       (E) (Reissue)
              GR   Jan.   p1193.   100w.   4

1238   GUYS and Dolls.   Together.   Magnet MAG 5016 (E)
              GR   Dec.   p1162.   25w.   2½
              MM   Nov.   12   p29.   50w.   2

1239   HALCYON Dance Orchestra.   'My Blue Heaven,' All-Time
       Hits by Walter Donaldson.   Halcyon SHAL.10 (E)
              ST   June-July   p196-7.   350w.   4

1240   HALL, Adelaide.   That Wonderful.   Monmouth-Evergreen
       MES 7080
              CAD   May   p13.   75w.   4
              MJ   Sept.   p28.   100w.   4
              MR   June   p9.   425w.   3½

1241   HALL, Lani.   Sweet Bird.   A&M SP 4617
              MM   July 16   p27.   50w.   0
              SR   April   p89.   200w.   4

1242   HAMMOND Source Works Band.   Sounds of Brass.   Decca
       SB327 (E)
              GR   April   p1607.   100w.   3

1243   HANNA, Ken.   Jazz Dance Date.   Golden Era 15040
              CAD   Feb.   p28-9.   100w.   2

1244   HARDY, Haygood.   Maybe Tomorrow.   Attic LAT 1011 (Can-
       ada)
              MM   July 16   p27.   50w.   2
              OLR   Sept.   p226.   50w.   3

1245   HARMONIUM.   L'Heptade d'.   CBS PGF 90348 (Canada)
              CC   March   p34.   50w.   3

1246   HARRIS, Rolf.   Mirrored Images.   EMI TC EMC 3158 (E)
              CAC   April   p12.   200w.   3½

1247   HATCH, Tony.   Back Seat Drivin'.   Precision (no disc)
       Cart. Y8P 11057.   Cass. ZCP 11057 (E)
              CAC   Aug.   p167.   75w.   2½

1248   HATCHER, George.   Dry Run.   United Artists UAG 29997 (E)
              GR   Jan.   p1197.   50w.   3½

1249   HATCHER, George.   Have Band Will Travel.   United Artists
       EXP 100 (E)
          GR May p1758.   50w. $2\frac{1}{2}$

1250   HATCHER, George.   Talkin' Turkey.   United Artists (E)
          MM July 2 p21.   350w.   5

1251   HAYMES, Joe & His Orchestra.   1932-35.   RCA AXM2-5552
       (Reissue)
          CAD Aug. p52.   150w. $3\frac{1}{2}$
          MR July p9-10.   125w. $3\frac{1}{2}$

1252   HAYWARD, Justin.   Songwriter.   Deram DES 18073
          CAC April p12.   150w.   5
          MM Feb. 26 p26.   450w. $3\frac{1}{2}$
          RC June p9.   150w. $2\frac{1}{2}$
          RS May 5 250w. $2\frac{1}{2}$
          SOU May p57.   200w.   3

1253   HAZLEWOOD, Lee.   These Books Are Made for Walkin'.
       MGM 2354 036 (E) (Reissue)
          CAC Feb. p420.   25w.   2
          SMG Jan. p25.   325w.   4

1254   HEERESMUSIKKORPS 5 der Bunderwehr.   Royal Prussian
       Army Marches.   Telefunken AW 6 42031 (E)
          GR Sept. p521.   50w.   4

1255   HENDON Way.   Pye TB 3011 (E)
          GR Jan. p1193.   150w.   3

1256   HERDMAN, Priscilla.   The Water Lily.   Philco 1014
          RC Dec. p2.   208w. $3\frac{1}{2}$

1257   HERMAN, Keith.   Good News Day.   Midsong International (E)
          MM July 16 p22.   50w. $1\frac{1}{2}$

1258   HERSEY, Baird.   The Year of the Ear.   Bent BRS1
          MG Feb. p57.   100w. $3\frac{1}{2}$
          SR March p121.   150w.   5

1259   HEWITT, Winston.   Snap Shot.   Corner Store C 1003 (Can-
       ada)
          CC May p34.   50w.   3

1260   HEWSON, Paul.   Love Is.   Splash (E)
          MM April 16 p23.   50w.   0

1261   HIBBLER, Al.   Best.   MCA 2-4098 (2 discs) (Reissue)
          CAD Oct. p25.   25w. $2\frac{1}{2}$

1262   HILL, Vince.   Midnight Blue.   CBS (E)
          MM Jan. 1 p15.   50w.   1

1263   HIRT, Al.   So Good.   Audio Fidelity AFSD 6282
          CAD   April   p29-30.   108w.   3

1264   HOLIDAY, Billie and Ella Fitzgerald.   MCA 2-4099 (2 discs)
       (Reissue)
          JM   1:2   p56.   150w. $4\frac{1}{2}$

1265   HOPPER, Hugh.   Hopper Trinity Box.   Compendium FIDARO
       7
       MM   April 30   p26.   660w. $3\frac{1}{2}$

1266   HORNBY, Leslie.   Pleast Get My Name Right.   Mercury
       9102601 (E)
          RR   June   p93.   75w. $2\frac{1}{2}$

1267   HORNE, Lena.   A New Album.   RCA BXL 1-1799
          MM   Jan. 29   p28.   250w. $3\frac{1}{2}$

1268   HOWE, Catherine.   Silent Mother Nature.   RCA RS 1041
       (E)
          CAC   May   p52.   250w. $2\frac{1}{2}$

1269   HUMMINGBIRD.   Diamond Nights.   A&M SR 4661
          MM   Nov. 19   p23.   200w.   3
          SOU   Nov.   p55.   250w.   4

1270   HUMPERDINCK, Englebert.   After the Lovin'.   Epic PE
       34381 Pea-34381
          GR   Jan.   p110.   100w.   3
          SR   March   p102.   100w.   3

1271   HUMPERDINCK, Englebert.   Best of.   Decca DKL9/1-2 (E)
       (2 discs) (Reissue)
          GR   Feb.   p1332.   75w. $2\frac{1}{2}$

1272   HUMPERDINCK, Englebert.   Miracles.   Epic PE 34730.
       Cart. PET 34730.   Cass. PEA 34730
          SR   Dec.   75w. $1\frac{1}{2}$

1273   HUMPERDINCK, Englebert.   Very best of.   EMI EMC 3160
       (E) (Reissue)
          CAC   March   p454.   100w.   2

1274   HUNTER.   Penny Farthing (E)
          MM   May 14   p26.   350w.   4

1275   HYMAN, Dick.   Ferdinand "Jelly Roll" Morton: Some Rags,
       Some Stomps and a Little Blues.   Columbia M 32587
          RA   May-June   p6.   100w. $2\frac{1}{2}$

1275a HYMAN, Dick.   Keyboard Classics of the Nostalgia Years.
       Cadence CR 2001 (2 discs)
          RA   Sept./Oct.   p4-5.   200w. $4\frac{1}{2}$

1276   HYMAN, Dick.   Scott Joplin.   MCA 2098
       ARG   March   p47-8.   150w.   3
       CK   Jan.   p51.   25w.   3½
       CK   May   p49.   50w.   5
       SOU   March   p44.   100w.   4

1277   INGHAM, Keith.   The Music of Richard Rodgers.   World
       Records SH 236 (E) (Reissue)
       ST   Dec.   1976-Jan.   1977   p75-6.   550w.   4

1278   INSTANT Sunshine.   Funny Name for a Band.   EMI One-up
       OU 2187 (E)
       GR   Nov.   p920.   50w.   3
       MM   Jan.   7   p16.   50w.   3

1279   INTERCONTINENTAL Express.   London.   Compendium
       FIDARO 5 (E)
       MM   July 23   p22.   125w.   3

1280   ISAACS, Gregory.   Extra Classic.   Conflict (E)
       MM   Nov.   5   p20.   200w.   5

1281   JAGIELLO, Li'l Wally.   Happy Birthday, America.   Jay
       JAY 5148
       RC   April   p10-1.   200w.   3

1282   JAMES, Bob.   BJ3.   CTI CTI-6063.   Cart.   CT8603.   Cass.
       CTC6063
       SR   Aug.   p104.   225w.   2

1283   JAMES, Bob.   BJ4.   CTI 7074.   Cart.   CT8-7075.   Cass.
       CTC-7074
       CAD   June   p38.   50w.   4
       MM   Oct.   1   p28.   50w.   1½
       SR   Aug.   p104.   225w.   2

1284   JOHNSTONE, Malcolm.   Les Papillons.   KSK Recordings.
       GP   Aug.   p120.   50w.   3

1285   JONES, Gloria.   Vixen.   EMI EMC 3159 (E)
       MM   Feb.   12   p26.   50w.   2½

1286   JONES, Jack.   All to Yourself.   RCA TVL2 (E)
       CAC   July   p131.   225w.   4½
       GR   July   p233.   75w.   4
       MM   Sept.   17   p20.   50w.   5

1287   JONES, Jack.   The Full Life.   RCA APL1-2067
       CAC   May   p52.   150w.   4
       GR   April   p1608.   50w.   3
       SR   June   p104.   150w.   2

1288   JONES, Jack.   With One More Look at You.   RCA APL1-2361

GR Dec. p1162. 25w. 3
SR Nov. p98. 800w. 5

1289 JONES, Tom. Say You'll Stay Until Tomorrow. Epic PE-
34468. Cart. PEA-34468. Cass. PET-34468
GR July p233. 50w. 4
SR Sept. p104. 100w. 3

1290 JONES, Tom. Sings 24 Great Standards. Decca DKL7/1-2
(2 discs) (E)
CAC March p454-5. 150w. $2\frac{1}{2}$
GR Feb. p1332. 50w. 3

1291 JUSTER, Deane. Regarde en Moi. Kébec Disc (Canada)
CC April p37. 50w. 3

1292 KAEMPFERT, Bert. For the Road. Polydor (E)
CAC Jan. p380. 50w. $2\frac{1}{2}$

1293 KAEMPFERT, Bert. Safari Swings Again. Polydor 2310
494 (E)
GR May p1757. 75w. $3\frac{1}{2}$

1294 KAMAHL. Lovin' Kind. Philips 6357
GR Aug. p353. 50w. 2

1295 KATAKIS, Michael. A Simple Time. A&M SP 4635
MG Oct. p59. 50w. $1\frac{1}{2}$

1296 KERR, Anita. RCA APL 1 2298
RC Dec. p7-8. 100w. $4\frac{1}{2}$

1297 KING, Teddi. Lovers and Losers. Audiophile AP 117
SR May p86, 80. 350w. 5

1298 KING'S Singers. Swing. EMI EMC3157 (E)
CAC Feb. p417. 125w. $2\frac{1}{2}$

1299 KITTY and the Haywoods. Love Shock. Mercury SRM 1
1171
MG Oct. p63. 50w. 2

1300 KRAUS, Richard and the RCA Square Dance Orchestra. Let's
Square Dance. RCA DEM5-0080 (5 discs)
RC Nov. p11-2. 300w. $3\frac{1}{2}$

1301 KROG, Karin. Different Days, Different Ways. Philips
FOX 202 (Japan)
CAD May p19. 150w. $2\frac{1}{2}$

1302 KROG, Karin and Archie Shepp. Hi-Fly. Compendium
FIDARO 2 (E)
MM July 16 p28. 150w. 3

1303   KROG, Karin and Nils Lindberg.   The Malmo Sessions.
       Swedish RCA PL40014
          CAD   Aug.   p49.   175w.   4

1304   KYSER, Kay.   World of.   Columbia CG 33572 (2 discs)
       (Reissue)
          DB   Oct. 6 p35-7.   100w.   1
          JR   V9/#4 unpaged.   125w. $2\frac{1}{2}$
          RC   June p4-5.   300w. $3\frac{1}{2}$

1305   LAFLAMME, David.   White Bird.   Amherst AMH-1007
          SR   April p94.   125w.   4

1306   LAFRANCE, Claude.   Une Belle Soirée.   Kébec Disc KD
       918 (Canada)
          CC   Sept.   p35.   50w.   3

1307   LAINE, Cleo.   Feel the Warm.   EMI Note NTS 106 (Reissue)
          CAC   Feb.   p417-8.   200w. $3\frac{1}{2}$
          GR   Jan.   p1194.   50w. $3\frac{1}{2}$
          JJ   Jan.   p32.   300w.   3

1308   LAINE, Cleo.   Return to Carnegie.   RCA-APL1 2407.   Cart.
       APK1-2407.   Cass. APS1-2407
          GR   Dec.   p1161.   200w. $4\frac{1}{2}$
          SOU   Sept.   p62.   300w.   4
          SR   Dec.   475w. $4\frac{1}{2}$

1309   LAINE, Cleo and John Dankworth.   A Lover and His Lass.
       Esquire 301 (E) (Reissue)
          CO   Dec.   p22-3.   75w. $3\frac{1}{2}$
          GR   April p1618.   250w. $3\frac{1}{2}$
          MM   Jan. 15 p20.   750w.   4
          RR   Feb.   p94.   50w.   2

1310   LAINE, Cleo and John Williams.   Best Friends RCA RS
       1094 (Reissue)
          CAC   Feb.   p418.   200w.   3
          JJ   Jan.   p32.   300w.   3
          MM   Feb. 12 p27.   125w. $2\frac{1}{2}$
          SR   June p124.   200w.   4

1311   LAMOTHE, Pierre.   Une Autre Jour.   Filoson FIL 77102
       (Canada)
          CC   Dec.   p35.   50w.   3

1312   LANGFORD, Georges.   Bluenose.   Presqu'ille PE 7504
       (Canada)
          CC   March p34.   50w.   3

1313   LAPOINTE, Jean.   Face A/Face B.   Kébec Disc KD 930
       (Canada)
          CC   June p31.   50w.   3

1314   LARCANGE, Maurice.   Bal Musette.   Decca DPA 3039-40
        (2 discs) (E)
            GR Nov.   p920.   25w.   3

1315   LAST, James.   Christmas and....   Polydor 2371 405 (E)
            GR Dec.   p1161.   50w. $2\frac{1}{2}$

1316   LAST, James.   Classics Up to Date.   Polydor 2371 711 (E)
            GR July p234.   25w.   3

1317   LAST, James.   Happy Summer Nights.   Polydor 2371 658 (E)
            GR July p234.   25w.   3

1318   LAST, James.   Non-Stop Dancing 18.   Polydor 2371 723 (E)
            GR July p234.   25w.   3

1319   LAST, James.   Plays Robert Stolz.   Polydor 2371 768
            GR Nov.   p920.   25w.   3

1320   LAST, James.   Rock Me Gently.   Polydor (E)
            CAC Jan.   p378.   50w.   4

1321   LAWRENCE, Guy, and His Sizzling Syncopators.   Blue Goose
        2020
            AU   May p97.   400w. $3\frac{1}{2}$
            CAD Feb.   p29.   150w.   2
            MR   Feb.   p11.   300w.   3
            SR   June p92, 93.   500w.   5
            ST   May p157.   100w.   4

1322   LAWRENCE, Syd.   Band Beat.   BBC REB254 (E)
            CAC Feb.   p418.   50w.   3
            GR   Jan.   p1194.   25w.   3

1323   LEE, Peggy.   Live in London.   Mercury 1172
            GR   Nov.   p919.   75w. $3\frac{1}{2}$
            MM   Sept. 17 p20.   125w. $3\frac{1}{2}$

1324   LEE, Peggy.   Songs for My Man.   Capitol CAPS 1006 (E)
        (Reissue)
            GR   July p233.   125w.   4

1325   LEFEVRE, Raymond.   French Love Songs.   RCA Barclay
        80616.   Cart. B80616 (E)
            GR   April p1608.   50w. $2\frac{1}{2}$

1326   LEGRAND, Michel.   The Concert Legrand.   RCA RS 1087
        (E)
            MM   Jan. 1 p15.   75w.   0

1327   LEGRAND, Michel.   The Other Side of Midnight.   Twentieth
        Century T 542
            CRA Oct.   p73.   125w.   2

1328 LEGRAND, Michel. Special Magic of. MGM 2353 130 (E)
GR July p234. 25w. 3

1329 LEM. Machines. Wavefront Records
CK Dec. p72. 200w. $3\frac{1}{2}$

1329a LE Mesurier, John. What Is Going to Become of Us All.
Reprise K54080 (E)
GR March p1468. 100w. $2\frac{1}{2}$

1330 LEPAGE, Cyril. Marche LDM12704 (Canada)
CC Sept. p35. 50w. 3

1331 LEPAGE, Lawrence. Enfin. Disques Bleu DB 1002 (Canada)
CC Feb. p31. 50w. 3

1332 LEWIS, Dave. From Time to Time. Polydor 2383 420 (E)
MM Jan. 8 p18. 200w. 3

1333 LEYRAC, Monique. Chante Félix Leclerc. Polydor 2424
157 (Canada)
CC Sept. p33. 50w. 3

1334 LIBERACE. Piano Gems. American Variety International
AVL 6001
CK Jan. p51. 125w. $4\frac{1}{2}$

1335 LIFE Guards Band. A Souvenir of London. DJM 42062 (E)
GR July p226, 229. 150w. $3\frac{1}{2}$

1336 LIFESTYLE. MCA MCF 2809 (E)
MM Oct. 8 p29. 50w. 3

1337 LI'L Wally. In Miami Beach. Jay Jay 5097
RC June p10. 100w. $2\frac{1}{2}$

1338 LI'L Wally. There's More to a Wedding. Jay Jay 5119
RC Nov. p14-5. 50w. 3

1339 LI'L Wally and the Lucky Harmony Boys. 15 New Polka
Hits. Jay Jay 5149
RC Nov. p14. 50w. $2\frac{1}{2}$

1340 LINDH, Jason. Atlantic K50337 (E)
RS Aug. 25 p55. 75w. 2

1341 LISKA, David. Startin' All Over Again. Pharoah
RC April p1. 300w. $3\frac{1}{2}$

1342 LIVERPOOL Express. Tracks. Warner
MM Jan. 22 p46. 100w. 2

1343 LOBO. Come with Me. Power Exchange (E)

MM   Aug. 6 p16.   50w.   1

1344   LOCUST.   Playgue.   Annuit Coeptis AC 1004
       SR   May p86.   75w.   3

1345   LOMAX, Jackie.   Did You Ever Have That Feeling.   Capitol
       ST 11668
          MG   Oct.   p60.   75w.   2½
          RS   Nov. 3 p102, 104.   475w.   1½

1346   LOMAX, Jackie.   Livin' for Lovin'.   Capitol ST-11558.
       8XT-11558
          SR   Feb.   p96.   150w.   3

1347   LOS Indios Tabajaras.   Mellow Nostalgia.   RCA AP1-2082
          GP   Sept. p118.   125w.   4

1348   LOS Machacambos.   Machacambos Today.   Decca PFS 4409
       (E)
          GR   Nov. p920.   50w.   3

1349   LOSS, Joe.   Jitterbug and Jivewith.   EMI (E)
          CAC   Feb. p418.   50w.   3

1350   LOSS, Joe.   Swing Is the Thing.   Music for Pleasure (E)
          CAC   Feb. p418.   125w.   3

1351   LOVE, Geoffrey.   Big Band Dixieland.   Music for Pleasure
       (E)
          CAC   Feb. p418.   50w.   3

1352   LOVE, Geoffrey.   Magic Mandolins.   EMI (E)
          CAC   Feb. p418.   100w.   3

1353   LUMLEY, Robin.   Marscape.   RSO RS-1-3020
          CK   May p48.   100w.   4

1354   LYNN, Vera.   I'll Be Seeing You.   EMI (E) (Reissue)
          CAC   Jan. p380.   100w.   3

1355   McANALLY, Mac.   Ariola America ST 50019
          RC   Oct. p5.   150w.   4
          VV   Oct. 3 p65.   50w.   2½

1356   McDONOUGH, Dick and Carl Kress.   Guitar Genius in the
       1920's.   Jazz Archives JA-32
          CAD   April p41-2.   222w.   2½
          DB   April 7 p31-3.   100w.   3
          JM   Summer p61.   200w.   3

1357   MacGREGOR, Mary.   Torn Between Two Lovers.   Ariola
       America SMAS-50015.   Cart. 8XT-50015.   Cass. 4XT-
       50015

    CMR June p9. 150w. 3
    FOL May p25-6. 500w. $2\frac{1}{2}$
    GR Aug. p353. 75w. 3
    HF May p128. 600w. 3
    MM May 14 p32. 125w. 3
    SR June p104. 150w. 5

1358 MacKAY, Duncan. Score. EMI EMC 3168 (E)
    MM July 2 p21. 200w. $2\frac{1}{2}$
    RS Aug. 24 p55. 75w. 2

1359 MacLEAN, William. Pipe. Scottish Tradition Cassette
   Series TGMMC 501 (E)
    FR Sept. p29. 350w. 3

1360 McRAE, Carmen. As Time Goes By. Catalyst CAT-7904
    CO June p18-9. 375w. 3
    DB May 19 250w. 4

1361 McRAE, Carmen. At the Great American Music Hall. Blue
   Note BN-LA 709-H2 (2 discs) Cart. EA-709-1. Cass. CA-
   709-1
    CA Aug. p39. 300w. $4\frac{1}{2}$
    MJ Sept. p32. 25w. 2
    SR Aug. p106. 175w. 4

1362 McRAE, Carmen. The Finest: Bethlehem Years. Bethlehem BCP 6004 (Reissue)
    JR V9/#3 unpaged. 100w. $3\frac{1}{2}$

1363 McRAE, Carmen. The Greatest. MCA 2-4111 (2 discs)
   (Reissue)
    DB Oct. 6 p35-7. 100w. 4
    MJ Nov. p24. 75w. $2\frac{1}{2}$

1364 McRAE, Carmen. Here to Stay. MCA Coral CB 20018
   (Reissue)
    JR V9/#4 unpaged. 50w. $2\frac{1}{2}$

1365 McVAY, Ray. World of Latin Dancing. Philips (2 discs)
   (E)
    CAC Feb. p416. 50w. 2

1366 McWILLIAMS, David. EMI EMC 3169 (E)
    GR June p110. 50w. 3

1367 MADDOX, Johnny. Amoureuse. Redstone RSS 101
    JR V9/#3 unpaged. 200w. 5
    RT Sept. p4-5. 200w. 4

1368 MADORE, Michael. Le Komuso a Cordes. Barclay 80260
   (Canada)
    CC June p31. 50w. 3

1369   MAGGIE'S Blue Five.   Kenneth Records KS2038
        MR   Aug.   p16.   100w.   4

1370   MAJOR Surgery.   The First Cut.   Next NEXT 1
        MM   Dec.   3   p32.   200w.   1½

1371   MALECORNE.   Disque Hexagone 883004 (France)
        RSP   Jan. -Feb.   p18-9.   300w.   3

1372   MANCINI, Henry.   Mancini's Angels.   RCA APS1-2290
        GR   Nov.   p919.   25w.   3

1373   MANEIGE.   Ni Vent ... Ni Nouvelle.   Polydor 2424 143
        (Canada)
            CC   Sept.   p33.   50w.   3
            SOU   July   p42.   200w.   4

1374   MANGIONE, Chuck.   Feels So Good.   A&M SP 4658
            CAD   Dec.   p47-8.   50w.   1½

1375   MANGIONE, Chuck.   Jazz Brother.   Milestone M47042 (Re-
        issue)
            CAD   Oct.   p30-1.   275w.   0

1376   MANGIONE, Chuck.   Main Squeeze.   A&M Records SP 4612
            JJ   May   p49.   150w.   4½
            MM   March 5   p31.   200w.   2½
            RR   May   p88.   50w.   2½
            SR   April   p112.   37w.   0

1377   MANGIONE, Gap.   A&M SP-4621
            CK   April   p49.   25w.   3
            DB   June 16   p40.   175w.   ½

1378   MANHATTAN Transfer.   Coming Out.   Atlantic SD 18183.
        Cart. TP 18183
            GR   Jan.   p1194.   50w.   3½
            SR   Jan.   p92.   75w.   3

1379   MANILOW, Barry.   Barry Manilow Live.   Arista AL 8500
        (2 discs) Cart. 8301-8500.   Cass. 5301-8500
            HF   Sept.   p145.   75w.   1½
            RC   Oct.   p13.   75w.   3
            SR   Sept.   p104, 106.   350w.   5

1380   MANTOVANI.   American Encores.   London PS 915
            GR   Jan.   p1194.   25w.   3

1381   MANTOVANI.   More Golden Hits.   London PS 914
            CAC   Jan.   p381.   50w.   3½
            GR   Nov.   p919.   75w.   3

1382   MANUEL and Music of the Mountains.   Blue Tangos.   EMI

Note NTS 113 (E) Cart. 8X-NTS113.   Cass. TCNTS113 (E)
GR April p1608.   25w. $2\frac{1}{2}$

1383 MANUEL and Music of the Mountains. Masquerade. EMI (E)
CAC Feb. p418. 100w. $1\frac{1}{2}$

1384 MANZANERA, Phil. Listen Now.   Polydor Deluxe 2302 074
(E)
MM Oct. 29 p26.   550w. $4\frac{1}{2}$

1385 MARCH, Steve. Lucky.   United Artists UA-LA674-G
CK April p49. 100w. 4
SR May p86, 88. 175w. 4

1386 MARSHALL, Penny and Cindy Williams. Laverne and Shirley
Sing. Atlantic SD 18203
CIR Feb. 28 p14-5. 350w. 2
SR March p108. 50w. 0

1387 MARTELL, Lena. The Best of. Pye (E) (Reissue)
CAC Jan. p380. 100w. $1\frac{1}{2}$

1388 MARTELL, Lena. With a Very Special Love. Pye NSPL
18513 (E)
CAC May p52. 200w. $3\frac{1}{2}$

1389 MARTENS, Sido. Pisces. Negram (Netherlands)
MM Sept. 10 p23. 175w. 3

1390 MARTINO, Al. Sing My Love Songs. Capitol ST-11572.
Cart. 8XT-11572
CAC May p54. 25w. 3
SR June p104. 100w. 3

1391 MATERICK, Ray. Best Friend Overnight. Asylum 7 ESC-
10002 (Canada)
OLR March p54. 50w. 4

1392 MATHIS, Johnny. Greatest Hits, Vol. 4. CBS 86022 (E)
(Reissue)
CAC May p52. 150w. $3\frac{1}{2}$
MM Feb. 26 p30. 75w. 1
MM Sept. 17 p20. 50w. 3

1393 MATHIS, Johnny. I Write the Songs. CBS 81329 (E)
BM Sept. p46. 100w. 4

1394 MATHIS, Johnny. Mathis Is. Columbia PC 34441
GR June p110. 50w. 2
MM Sept. 17 p20. 50w. 3

1395 MELLY, George. At It Again. Reprise K 54084 (E)
JJ Jan. p32. 275w. 4

RR Feb. p94. 75w. 3

1396   MENDES, Sergio and the New Brasil '77.   Elektra 73-1102.
       Cart. ET8-1102.   Cass. TC5-1102
          GR July p234. 75w. $3\frac{1}{2}$
          MM Sept. 10 p20. 50w. 2
          SR Dec. 125w. 1

1397   MERCER, Johnny. Sings Mercer.   Capitol M-11637 (Reissue)
          RC Oct. p9. 200w. $3\frac{1}{2}$

1398   MERGER. Exiles in Babylon.   Sun-Star SUN 1001
          MM Nov. 19 p28. 350w. 4

1399   MERRILL, Helen. Autumn Love.   Catalyst 7912. (Reissue)
          CAD Nov. p34. 100w. $3\frac{1}{2}$

1400   MERRILL, Helen and John Lewis.   Mercury SRM-1-1150.
       Cart. MC-8-1-1150.   Cass. MCR-4-1-1150
          DB Nov. 3 p27-8. 450w. 5
          SR Aug. p106. 175w. 5

1401   MERRILL, Helen and Teddy Wilson.   Helen Sings, Teddy
       Swings.   Catalyst CAT 7907
          CAD June p45. 300w. $4\frac{1}{2}$
          DB May 19 250w. 4

1402-3 MERRILL, Robert and the Mormon Tabernacle Choir.   The
       White Cliffs of Dover.   CBS Classics 61791 (E)
          GR July p234. 75w. 3

1404   MICHEL, Jaques. Le Temps d'Aimer.   Polydor 2424-160
       (Canada)
          CC Nov. p35. 50w. 3

1405   MILES, John. Stranger in the City.   London PS 682
          CAC Feb. p419. 250w. $1\frac{1}{2}$
          GR March p1467. 100w. $3\frac{1}{2}$
          RO Sept. p62. 200w. $3\frac{1}{2}$
          RS June 2 425w. 3
          SR June p109. 50w. 3

1406   MILLER, Glenn. Carnegie Hall Concert.   RCA NL 42010
       (E) (Reissue)
          MM March 19 p32. 250w. 3
          RR June p94. 25w. $3\frac{1}{2}$

1407   MILLER, Glenn. The Complete, Vol. II, 1939.   RCA
       AXM2-5514 (2 discs) (Reissue)
          AU Aug. p91. 400w. 5

1408   MILLER, Glenn. His Uptown Hall Gang.   Esquire ESQ 302
       (E) (Reissue)

GR   April   p1618.   300w.   3½
MM   April 16   p25.   150w.   3½
RR   Feb.   p94.   125w.   2½

1409   MILLER, Glenn.   A Legendary Performer, Vol. 2.   RCA
APL1-2080
MM   Sept. 10   p20.   50w.   3
RR   Oct.   p90.   25w.   3

1410   MILLER, Glenn.   The Unforgettable.   RCA TVL1 (E) (Re-
issue)
MM   May 21   p28.   200w.   2½
RR   June   p94.   25w.   3

1411   MILLER, Glenn and Billy May.   Recorded Live in Concert.
Pye (E) (Reissue)
CAC   Jan.   p381.   100w.   2

1412   MINNELLI, Liza.   Tropical Nights.   CBS PC 34887
MM   Nov. 12   p26.   50w.   1

1413   MITCHELL, Guy.   American Legend.   CBC Embassy 31459
(Reissue)
CMR   Sept.   p7.   100w.   3½
MM   Nov. 12   p29.   50w.   1

1414   MITCHELL, Red.   Comme Je Suis.   Airedale LUL 508
(Canada)
CC   Oct.   p35.   100w.   3

1415   MONOPOLY, Tony.   I'll Have to Say I Love You in a Song.
EMI International INS 3006 (E)
GR   Nov.   p919.   25w.   3

1416   MONTGOMERY, Marian and Richard Rodney Bennett.   Surprise, Surprise.   Cube HIFLY24 (E)
GR   Dec.   p1161.   75w.   4

1417   MOORHOUSE, Alan.   The Band Plays On.   EMI 2176 (E)
GR   Nov.   p919-20.   25w.   3

1418   MORATH, Max.   Jonah Man.   Vanguard VSD 79378
JR   V9/#4   unpaged.   100w.   3½
RA   Nov./Dec.   p4.   150w.   2½

1419   MORRIS, Joan and William Bolcom.   Wild about Eubie; the
Music of Eubie Blake.   Columbia 34504
RA   May-June   p6-7.   150w.   4
SR   May   p82.   275w.   5

1420   MORTON, Ann J.   My Friends Call Me Annie.   Prairie Dust
PDLP-1661
SR   May   p90.   100w.   4

1421   MOST, Donny. Donny Most. United Artists UA-LA696-G
        SR March p112. 50w. 0

1422   MOUSKOURI, Nana. Love Goes On. Philips (E)
        CAC April p14. 125w. $3\frac{1}{2}$
        MM Jan. 1 p15. 50w. $1\frac{1}{2}$

1423   MOUSTAKI, Georges. More Moustaki. Polydor 2489 105
        (E)
        CAC Feb. p416. 50w. 3

1424   MULLER, Werner. Focus On. Decca (E)
        CAC Feb. p418. 50w. $2\frac{1}{2}$

1425   MULLER, Werner. Sentimental Journey. Decca PFS 4383
        GR Nov. p919. 25w. 3

1426   MUMPS. A Matter of Taste. MPS 68-169
        MM Dec. 3 p32. 150w. 1

1427   MUNICH Machine. Casablanca NBLP 7058
        MG Aug. p61. 75w.

1428   MURRAY, Anne. Keeping in Touch.   Capitol ST 11559
        CM Feb. p53. 200w. 4
        CMP Jan. p34. 150w. 4
        CMR March p29. 50w. 2
        OLR Sept. p226. 50w. $3\frac{1}{2}$
        SR Jan. p96. 150w. 3

1429   MURRAY, Bruce. Quality SV 1920 (Canada)
        OLR March p55. 75w. $1\frac{1}{2}$

1430   MUSCLE Shoals Horns. Born to Get Down.   Bang SHOT 001
        (E)
        MM April 2 p24. 250w. 3

1431   NEAR, Holly and Jeff Langley. You Can Know All I Am.
        Redwood 3600
        RC Dec. p3. 250w. $3\frac{1}{2}$

1432   NEW Excelsior Talking Machine. Decca SKL5266 (E)
        GR March p1468. 50w. $3\frac{1}{2}$

1433   NEWTON-JOHN, Olivia. Don't Stop Believin'. EMI EMC
        3162 (E)
        CM March p57. 375w. 4
        CMP Feb. p36. 175w. 3
        CMR March p28. 100w. 4
        GR Jan. p1194. 25w. 3
        MM Jan. 29 p25. 50w. 2
        SR Feb. p100. 100w. 3

1434   NEWTON-JOHN, Olivia.   Making a Good Thing Better.
       MCA-2280.   Cart. MCAT-2280
          CMP Sept. p40.   200w.   3
          CS   Dec.   p29.   100w.   0
          GR   Nov.   p919. 50w. $3\frac{1}{2}$
          HF   Sept. p144. 300w.   2
          MM   Sept. 10 p20. 50w.   2
          SR   Nov.   p110, 112. 275w.   5

1435   NIGRINI, Ron.   Rich Things.   Attic LAT 1010 (Canada)
          OLR March p55.   25w.   4

1436   NITE City.   20th Century Records T-528
          AU   July   p91.   300w.   4
          CK   Sept. p58.   75w. $3\frac{1}{2}$

1437   NUROCK, Kirk.   Adamo ADS 9504
          SR   May   p100, 101. 100w.   4

1438   O'CONNOR, Des.   After the Lovin'.   Pye NSPL18514 (E)
          CAC April p14.   125w.   3
          GR   March p1468. 50w. $3\frac{1}{2}$

1439   O'DAY, Alan.   Appetizers.   Pacific PC 4300
          CK   Dec.   p73.   25w.   3
          MM   Dec.   21 p15. 50w.   2
          RC   Dec.   p13.   50w. $3\frac{1}{2}$

1440   ODETTA.   It's Impossible.   Four Leaf Clover FLC 5007
       (Sweden)
          CAD Oct.   p26-7. 100w.   0

1441   OLIVOR, Jane.   Chasing Rainbows.   Columbia PC 34917
          VV   Oct.   17 p66. 100w. $1\frac{1}{2}$

1442   OLIVOR, Jane.   First Night.   Columbia PC 34274
          JR   V9/#4 unpaged. 50w. $2\frac{1}{2}$
          RC   Aug.   p12.   150w. $3\frac{1}{2}$

1443   OPUS 5.   Contre-courant.   Celebration CEL 1929 (Canada)
          OLR March p56-7. 25w.   2

1444   OSCAR.   Twilight Asylum.   DJM (E)
          MM   Jan.   1 p15. 75w.   1

1445   OSMOND, Donny and Marie.   New Season.   Polydor 6083
          MM   Feb.   12 p26. 50w.   0

1446   OSMOND, Marie.   This Is the Way I Feel.   Polydor PD
       1-6099
          SOU June   p42.   300w. $2\frac{1}{2}$

1447   OSMONDS.   Brainstorm.   Polydor 6077

CAC Feb. p419. 125w. 1

1448   OSMONDS. Greatest Hits. Polydor 9005 (2 discs) (Reissue)
       MM Dec. 21 p15. 50w. 2

1449   PAHINUI, The Gabby, Hawaiian Band.   Warner Bros. BS 3023
       AU Dec. p137. 400w. 4
       SO March/April p52. 250w. 4½

1450   PARAMOR, Norrie. Silver Serenade.   BBC REB 272 (E)
       CAC Aug. p167. 125w. 2½
       GR July p235. 25w. 3

1451   PASADENA Roof Orchestra. Isn't It Romantic.   Transatlan-
       tic (E)
       CAC March p475. 50w. 3
       MM Feb. 12 p26. 150w. 3

1452   PATATO (Carlos Valdez). Ready for Freddy.   Latin Percus-
       sion Venturs LPV 419
       DB June 2 p28-9. 300w. 4

1453   PAULETTE, Laury. What Makes a Man.   Vanguard VSD
       79386
       RC Oct. p4. 125w. 3½

1454   PENNSYLVANIA Polka Cats. Stella 717
       RC Oct. p15. 50w. 2½

1455   PETER and Gordon. Best of.   EMI NUT8 (E) (Reissue)
       MM Aug. 20 p14. 125w. 2½
       NK Autumn p46. 25w. 3½
       RR Oct. p88. 25w. 2½

1456   PETERS and Lee. Invitation.   Philips 9109 217 (E)
       MM Jan. 1 p15. 50w. 3

1457   PHILIPSEK, Reynold. Bridge 9086
       GP July p129. 50w. 3

1458   PHILLIPS, Sid. Anthology, Vol. 1: Chicago and All That
       Jazz. Rediffusion Gold Star 15-58 (E) (Reissue)
       GR March p1471. 125w. 3½

1459   PHILLIPS, Sid. Best of.   One-up OU 2189 (Reissue)
       CO Dec. p87. 25w. 1½

1460   PHILLIPS, Sid. Hors d'Oeuvres.   Pye Golden HR GH (E)
       MM Feb. 12 p27. 125w. 3

1461   PIGNEGUY, John. Dreamsville.   BBC REC 275 (E)
       CAC Aug. p167. 225w. 4
       GR July p234. 50w. 3

1462   PITNEY, Gene.   Pitney '75.   Bronze BRON 314
        GR   Nov.   p919.   50w.   3

1463   PRESLEY, Elvis.   The Dorsey Shows.   Golden Archives 56-
        GA-100
            CM   April   p52.   425w.   4
            SMG   May   p22.   100w.   4

1464   PRESLEY, Elvis.   In Demand.   RCA PL 42003
            CAC   May   p54.   300w. $3\frac{1}{2}$
            MM   Jan.   29   p25.   450w.   3
            NK   Winter   p33.   50w. $2\frac{1}{2}$

1465   PRESLEY, Elvis.   Living You.   RCA LSP 1515
            NK   Autumn   p40.   25w. $2\frac{1}{2}$

1466   PRESLEY, Elvis.   Moody Blue.   RCA APL1-2428
            CM   Oct.   p51.   200w.   2
            CMP   Nov.   p36-7.   125w.   3
            CS   Aug.   25   p19.   150w.   3
            GR   Nov.   p919.   25w. $3\frac{1}{2}$
            HF   Oct.   p162.   125w.   1
            NK   Autumn   p40.   50w. $2\frac{1}{2}$
            SR   Nov.   p87.   400w.   2

1467   PRESLEY, Elvis.   The Sun Years.   Charly Sun 1001
            NK   Autumn   p40.   25w. $3\frac{1}{2}$

1468   PRESLEY, Elvis.   Welcome to My World.   RCA APL1-2274
            CM   July   p53.   300w.   2
            CMP   Pct.   p40.   225w.   3
            GR   Nov.   p919.   50w. $3\frac{1}{2}$
            MM   Sept.   3   p46.   50w. $3\frac{1}{2}$
            NK   Summer   p37.   50w.   3
            RSP   May-June   p58.   125w. $1\frac{1}{2}$

1469   PUSSYCAT.   First of All.   Sonet SNTF 725 (E)
            CAC   March   p455.   100w.   2
            MM   Jan.   8   p18.   50w. $1\frac{1}{2}$
            RC   Nov.   p15.   75w. $3\frac{1}{2}$

1470   RADIO Stars.   Songs for Swinging Lovers.   Chiswick (E)
            MM   Dec.   3   p23.   200w.   3

1471   RAY, Johnnie.   Greatest Hits, Vol. 1.   CBS CSP EN-13086
            CAC   Feb.   p419.   200w.   2

1472   READING, Wilma.   Pye NSPL 18508 (E)
            GR   Jan.   p1194.   25w.   3

1473   REDBONE, Leon.   Double Time.   Warner BS 2871
            AU   Oct.   p174.   250w. $4\frac{1}{2}$
            CAD   Feb.   p20.   150w. $3\frac{1}{2}$

CIR   March 31 p19.   350w. $3\frac{1}{2}$
CRA   April p112.   125w.   3
DB   June 2 p27.   300w.   3
FOL   July p26-7.   400w.   1
FR   April p30.   200w.   4
GP   May p129.   50w.   1
GR   March p1467.   75w.   3
MM   April 9 p22.   200w.   0
RC   July p8-9.   250w.   4
RS   March 10 p65, 66.   1175w. $2\frac{1}{2}$
RSP   1:3 p17.   225w.   3
SR   May p93.   125w.   3

1474   REDDY, Helen.   Ear Candy.   Capitol SO-11640.   Cass. 4XT-11640.   Cart. 8XO-11640
CRA   July p81.   175w.   2
GR   Nov.   p919.   75w. $3\frac{1}{2}$
HF   Sept.   p145.   50w. $1\frac{1}{2}$
MM   June 25 p22.   350w.   3
SR   Oct.   p118.   250w.   4

1475   REED, Les.   Focus on.   Decca FOS 25/26 (2 discs) (E) (Reissue)
CAC   April p15.   200w.   4
GR   March p1468.   25w.   3

1476   REGAN, Joan.   World of.   Decca SPA 472 (E)
GR   Feb.   p1332.   50w.   3

1477   REID, Clarence.   Alston 4404
RS   Feb. 10 p100.   25w.   2

1478   RHEAD Brothers.   Dedicate.   Harvest ST11669
RC   Oct.   p3.   100w. $3\frac{1}{2}$

1479   RICHARD, Cliff.   Every Face Tells a Story.   EMI EMC 3172 (E)
CAC   July p132.   225w. $3\frac{1}{2}$
GR   May p1757.   100w.   4
MM   March 5 p24.   550w.   3
NK   Spring p39.   75w.   3
RR   June p93.   50w. $2\frac{1}{2}$

1480   RICHARD, Cliff.   40 Golden Hits EMI EMTVS6 (E) (2 discs) (Reissue)
GR   Dec.   p1162.   75w. $3\frac{1}{2}$
MM   Oct. 15 p25.   250w.   3
NK   Autumn p48.   25w. $2\frac{1}{2}$
RR   Dec.   p86.   75w. $2\frac{1}{2}$

1481   RICHMAN, Jonathon and the Modern Lovers.   Beserkley 0048
RC   April p2-3.   300w. $4\frac{1}{2}$

1482   RICHMAN, Jonathon and the Modern Lovers.   Rock 'n' Roll
       with.   Beserkley PZ 34800
           CIR   Sept. 29 p59.   200w. $1\frac{1}{2}$
           MG   Sept. p52.   75w. $1\frac{1}{2}$
           MM   July 2 p23.   750w. $1\frac{1}{2}$
           RC   Nov. p5.   125w.   4
           RS   Aug. 25 p55.   550w.   1
           SR   Dec. p90.   225w.   1
           VV   July 25 p51.   550w.   5
           ZZ   Aug. p33.   425w. $3\frac{1}{2}$

1483   RILEY, Billy Lee.   Legendary Sun Performer.   Charly CR
       30-131 (E) (Reissue)
           NK   Autumn p45.   75w.   4

1484   RILEY, Howard.   Intertwine.   Mosaic GCM 771 (E)
           MM   Sept. 3 p24.   225w.   3
           RR   Nov. p116.   50w.   3

1485   ROBERTS, Bruce.   Elektra 7E 1119
           RS   Dec. 29 p64-5.   900w.   3

1486   ROCK Follies.   '77.   Polydor 2302 072 (E)
           MM   May 28 p27.   850w.   3

1487   ROGERS, Brian.   Plays the Melodies of Gallagher & Lyle &
       Fairweather-Low.   A&M (E)
           MM   Oct. 1 p23.   50w.   3

1488   ROLLER.   Goblin.   Attic LAT 1031 (Canada)
           RC   Nov. p9-10.   50w.   4

1489   ROSSI, Walter.   Aquarius AQR 514 (Canada)
           SOU   May p58.   450w.   4

1490   ROUGH Diamond.   Island ILPS 9490
           GR   July p237.   25w. $1\frac{1}{2}$
           MM   May 14 p31.   450w. $3\frac{1}{2}$

1491   ROUSSOS, Demis.   The D. R. Magic.   Mercury SRM1-1162
           GR   Aug. p353.   50w.   2

1492   ROYAL Hawaiian Girls Glee Club.   Hawaiian Hula Music.
       Waikiki ST 336
           RC   May p10.   100w. $3\frac{1}{2}$

1493   ROZA, Lita and Dennis Lotis.   Ted Heath Years.   Decca
       SPA 497 (E)
           GR   June p110.   125w. $3\frac{1}{2}$

1494   RUBETTES.   Best of.   State ETAT 8 (E) (Reissue)
           SMG   Jan. p27.   100w.   3

1495   RUBETTES. Sign of the Times. Polydor (E)
       CAC   Feb.   p419.   50w.   2

1496   RUBINOOS. Beserkley BZ 0051
       CIR   Aug. 18 p49.   300w. $2\frac{1}{2}$
       CRA   Sept.   p78.   200w.   4
       RC   Oct.   p6.   25w. $2\frac{1}{2}$
       TP   Sept.   p35-6.   175w.   3
       ZZ   Aug.   p33-4.   400w.   3

1497   RYAN'S Fancy. Brand New Songs.   RCA KXL1-0202 (Canada)
       CC   May p34.   50w.   3
       OLR   Dec.   p293.   50w.   3

1498   SAD Café. Fanx Ta'ra.   RCA PL 25101
       MM   Oct. 8 p35.   20w. $4\frac{1}{2}$
       RR   Dec.   p86.   50w.   2

1499   SAGER, Carole Bayer. Elektra 7E1100
       RC   Aug.   p12.   150w.   3
       RR   Aug.   p84.   25w.   2
       RS   June 16 p69.   350w.   3
       VV   May 30 p65.   375w.   5

1500   SAILOR. The Third Step. Epic EPC 81637 (E)
       RRE   May-June p60.   250w. $3\frac{1}{2}$

1501   SANDPIPERS. Overdue. Satril (E) 4006
       MM   Feb. 26 p30.   50w. $1\frac{1}{2}$

1502   SCHAFFER, Janne. Katharsis. Columbia PC 34499
       GP   July p129.   125w.   4
       MG   July p53.   100w. $2\frac{1}{2}$

1503   SCHAUBROECK, Armand. I Came to Visit but Decided to
       Stay. Mirror III
       RC   Dec.   p3-4.   250w.   4

1504   SCHAUBROECK, Armand. A Lot of People Would Like to
       See A. S. Dead. Mirror 2 (3 discs)
       RC   Dec.   p3-4.   250w.   4

1505   SCHNEIDER, Helen. So Close. Windsong BHLI-2037. Cart.
       BHS1-2037. Cass. BHK1-2037
       CAC   Aug.   p168.   100w. $2\frac{1}{2}$
       RC   Nov.   p3.   50w. $2\frac{1}{2}$
       SR   July p98.   550w.   5

1506   SCOTS Guards Band. Salute to Pageantry.   EMI EMC 3179
       (E)
       GR   June p109.   225w. $3\frac{1}{2}$

1507   SCOTS Guards Band. Sousa Specials. Philips SON 036 (E)

GR May p1749. 50w. 4

1508 SCOTT, Ronnie. Great Scott. Esquire 303 (Reissue)
      RR Aug. p84. 50w. 3

1509 SEAL, Joseph. Plays. Pye PKL 5557 (E)
      GR April p1608, 1617. 25w. $2\frac{1}{2}$

1510 SEARCHERS. Pye File FILD 002 (E) (Reissue)
      NK Autumn p46. 25w. $3\frac{1}{2}$

1511 SECOMBE, Harry. Far Away Places. Philips 6308 286
      GR July p233-4. 3

1512 SEDAKA, Neil. And Songs. Polydor 2672-036 (E) (2 discs)
      NK Summer p38. 100w. 4

1513 SEDAKA, Neil. 50s and 60s. RCA AFL 1-2254 (Reissue)
      MM Sept. 10 p20. 50w. 2
      NK Summer p37. 25w. $3\frac{1}{2}$

1514 SEDAKA, Neil. Greatest Hits. Rocket Record PIG 2297
      (Reissue)
      RC Dec. p9-10. 150w. 4

1515 SEDAKA, Neil. A Song. Elektra 6E 102
      CRA Oct. p63. 400w. 1
      GR Dec. p1162. 50w. 3
      MG Aug. p59. 100w. 3
      NK Autumn p48. 25w. $3\frac{1}{2}$
      RC Oct. p14. 150w. $2\frac{1}{2}$
      RS July 14 p70. 350w. $2\frac{1}{2}$
      SR Oct. p118. 250w. 4
      VV June 20 p51, 54. 400w. 2

1516 SEDAKA, Neil. Sounds of. EMI MCA TCMCF2780. Cart.
      8X MCF 2780 (E)
      CAC April p15. 150w. 3
      GR April p1608. 75w. $2\frac{1}{2}$
      MM May 14 p53. 50w. $1\frac{1}{2}$

1517 SEEKERS. At the Talk of the Town. EMI (E) (Reissue)
      CAC Jan. p381. 200w. 3

1518 SEGUIN, Richard A. Rumeurs dans la Basse-Cour. Edi-
      tions Cinésources 10C10 (2 discs) (Canada)
      CC Nov. p36. 50w. 3

1519 SEGUIN. Festin d'Amour. CBS PFS 90385 (Canada)
      CC Feb. p31. 50w. 3

1520 SEVERINSON, Doc. Night Journey. Epic PE 34078

DB   April 21 p25.   150w. $2\frac{1}{2}$

1521   SHA NA NA.   Rock 'n' Roll Revival.   Pye Golden Hour 867
       MM   Nov. 12 p29.   50w. $3\frac{1}{2}$

1522   SHADOWS.   Rarities.   EMI NUT 2 (E) (Reissue)
       MM   Jan. 8 p18.   50w. $2\frac{1}{2}$
       NK   Winter p37.   50w. $3\frac{1}{2}$

1523   SHADOWS.   Shadoogie.   EMI C154-06129/30/31 (French)
       (Reissue)
       TP   Feb./March p33.   350w.   4

1524   SHADOWS.   Tasty.   EMI EMC 3195 (E)
       GR   Nov. p920.   25w.   3
       MM   Sept. 10 p26.   200w. $3\frac{1}{2}$
       NK   Autumn p48.   50w. $3\frac{1}{2}$

1525   SHADOWS.   Twenty Golden Hits.   EMI TC-EMTV3 (E) (Re-
       issue)
       CAC   April p15.   175w. $3\frac{1}{2}$
       GR   March p1468.   100w.   4
       MM   May 14 p33.   50w. $2\frac{1}{2}$
       RR   April p87.   50w. $1\frac{1}{2}$

1526   SHAW, Artie.   Best of.   RCA 11099 (E) (Reissue)
       MM   March 26 p22.   250w. $3\frac{1}{2}$
       RR   June p94.   25w.   3

1527   SHAW, Artie.   The Complete, Vol. 1.   Bluebird AXM2-5517
       (2 discs) (Reissue)
       AU   March p96.   800w.   3

1528   SHAW, Artie.   The Complete, Vol. 2:1939.   RCA AXM2-
       5533 (2 discs) (Reissue)
       CAD   May p28.   50w. $3\frac{1}{2}$
       CAD   Aug. p53.   175w.   3
       DB   Oct. 6 p35-7.   100w. $3\frac{1}{2}$

1529   SHAW, Artie.   Live, 1939, Vol. 3.   Jazz Guild 1005 (Re-
       issue)
       DB   Oct. 6 p35-7.   100w.   4

1530   SHAW, Artie.   Live, 1939, Vol. 4.   Jazz Guild 1007 (Re-
       issue)
       DB   Oct. 6 p35-7.   100w. $4\frac{1}{2}$

1531   SHAW, Artie.   Melody and Madness, Vols. 1 & 2.   Jazz
       Guild 1001/2 (2 discs)
       AU   March p94.   800w.   4

1532   SHAW, Artie.   Melody and Madness, Vols. 3 & 4.   Jazz
       Guild 1005/7 (2 discs)

          CAD   March   p38.   100w.   3

1533   SHELTON, Anne.   Decca DVL2 (E)
          GR   Oct.   p715.   50w.   4

1534   SHORTHOUSE, Bert and the Glenlomond Scottish Band.   Hag-
          manay Party.   DJM 26081 (E)
          MM   Jan. 22   p23.   50w.   2

1535   SILVER Convention.   Golden Girls.   RCA Midsong BKL1-2286
          MG   Sept.   p55.   100w.   3

1536   SILVER Convention.   Greatest Hits.   Magnet 6001 (E) (Re-
          issue)
          CAC   Aug.   p168.   100w. $2\frac{1}{2}$
          MM   June 4   p20.   50w.   3

1537   SILVER Convention.   Madhouse.   RCA Midsong BXL1-1824
          BM   Jan.   p47.   150w.   2
          MM   Jan. 22   p23.   50w. $1\frac{1}{2}$

1538   SIMON, Lucy.   Stolen Time.   RCA APL1-1745.   Cart. APS1-
          1745
          SR   Sept.   p112.   150w.   2

1539   SINATRA, Frank.   RCA NL 11586 (E) (Reissue)
          CAC   July   p142-3.   250w.   3
          MM   April 16   p25.   100w. $3\frac{1}{2}$
          RR   June   p94.   25w. $3\frac{1}{2}$

1540   SINATRA, Frank.   Portrait of....   Reprise K64039 (E) (Re-
          issue)
          GR   April   p1608.   400w. $3\frac{1}{2}$

1541   SINATRA, Frank.   Two Originals of.   Reprise (2 discs) (E)
          (Reissue)
          MM   Jan. 1   p15.   100w. $3\frac{1}{2}$

1542   SINATRA, Nancy.   Greatest Hits.   Private Stock 1018 (Re-
          issue)
          CAC   Aug.   p168.   175w. $3\frac{1}{2}$

1543   SINGANA, Margaret.   Where Is the Love.   Casablanca 7026
          VV   April 18   p70.   100w.   3

1544   SIRKEL and Co.   Charly (E)
          MM   April 16   p21.   175w. $1\frac{1}{2}$

1545   SISSLE, Noble and Eubie Blake.   Early Rare Recordings,
          Vol. 2.   Eubie Blake Music EBM 7 (Reissue)
          MJ   Jan.   p28.   50w.   3
          RA   Jan. -Feb.   p5-6.   125w.   5

1546   SOLOMON, Diane.   One Step at a Time.   EMI TC-EMC3163
       (E)
            CAC   April   p14.   50w.   1

1547   SOUL, David.   Playing to an Audience of One.   Private
       Stock 7001
            CIR   Nov.   10   p61.   25w.   0

1548   SOUL, David.   Private Stock PVLP 1012
            CAC   March   p455.   150w. $2\frac{1}{2}$
            CIR   Feb.   28   p14.   125w.   1
            GR   April   p1608.   50w. $2\frac{1}{2}$
            MM   Jan.   22   p23.   50w.   3
            RC   June   p5.   300w.   3

1549   SOUND 80.   A&M SP 9007 (Canada)
            OLR   June   p142.   25w. $3\frac{1}{2}$

1550   SOUND 80.   The Beginning.   A&M SP 9005
            OLR   June   p142.   25w.   4

1551   SOUTHERN Comfort.   Distilled.   EMI (E) (Reissue)
            CAC   Jan.   p381.   100w. $2\frac{1}{2}$

1552   SOXX, Bob B. and the Blue Jeans.   Phil Spector Interna-
       tional 2301 004 (E) (Reissue)
            SR   June   p118.   125w.   3

1553   SPACE.   Magic Fly.   United Artists LA 780-G
            MM   Sept.   17   p22.   250w. $2\frac{1}{2}$

1554   SPHEERIS, Jimmie.   Points of the Heart.   Epic PE 34276
            RS   Feb.   24   p68.   200w.   2

1555   STARLAND Vocal Band.   RCA Windsong BXL 1-1351
            CAC   Feb.   p419.   100w.   3

1556   STARLAND Vocal Band.   Rear View Mirror.   Windsong BHL
       1-2239.   Cass. BHK 1-2239.   Cart. BHS 1-2239
            HF   Aug.   p122.   250w. $3\frac{1}{2}$
            SR   Oct.   p91.   225w.   4

1557   STARR, Edwin.   Afternoon Sunshine.   GTO 019 (E)
            MM   Feb.   16   p30.   50w.   1

1558   STARR, Ruby.   Smokey Places.   Capitol ST 11643
            CIR   Nov.   24   p77.   200w. $2\frac{1}{2}$

1559   STEAMPACKET.   The First Supergroup.   Precision Charly
       30-00-20 (E)
            CAC   July   p132, 134.   200w. $3\frac{1}{2}$
            SMG   May   p20.   100w.   1

1560   STEELE, Tommy.   Focus on.   Decca KF28056 (2 discs) (E)
        (Reissue)
                CAC April p15.   250w.   3½
                GR March p1468.   25w.   3
                NK Spring p39.   50w.   3
                SMG May p21.   100w.   3

1561   STEVENS, Kelly/Carnival.   When You Wish upon a Star.
        AVL 6017
                MG Dec.   p59.   100w.   2½

1562   STEWART, Louis.   Out on His Own.   Livia LRLP1 (E)
                MM Sept. 24 p32.   175w.   3½

1563   STONE, Lew.   Decca DDV5005/6 (2 discs) (E) (Reissue)
                GR Oct.   p715.   125w.   4½
                MM Oct. 22 p28.   425w.   3½
                RR Dec.   p87.   50w.   3

1564   STOTT, Jack.   Rocks on.   Leroy 745 (Reissue)
                RSP Jan. -Feb.   p35.   100w.   2½

1565   STREISAND, Barbra.   Streisand Superman.   Columbia JC
        34830.   Cart. JCT 34830.   Cass. JCA 34830
                CIR Oct. 13 p74.   300w.   3
                GR Nov.   p919.   250w.   5
                HF Oct.   p166.   250w.   4½
                MG Sept.   p52.   50w.   3
                RC Oct.   p2-3.   250w.   4
                RR Oct.   p88.   125w.   2
                RS Aug. 11 p68.   400w.   3
                SR Oct.   p92.   700w.   4

1566   STRICKLIN, Al.   Brother Al Stricklin Now.   Texas Re-cord
        LP 1004
                AU Sept.   p95.   600w.   4
                CRA April p110.   75w.   3

1567   SULLIVAN, Maxine and Dick Hyman.   Shakespeare.   Mon-
        mouth-Evergreen 7038
                JF No. 48 p21.   75w.   4

1568   SULZMANN, Stan.   On Loan with Gratitude.   Mosaic GCM
        772
                MM Sept. 24 p32.   200w.   3

1569   SWEET Substitute.   Something Special.   Decca SKL5276 (E)
                GR Dec.   p1162.   50w.   2½

1570   SWINGLE II.   Rage and All That Jazz.   Columbia PC 34194
                JR V9/#3 unpaged.   200w.   0
                RA July-Aug.   p6-7.   125w.   3½

1571   SWINGLE II. Words and Music. CBS 81546 (E)
        RR Dec. p100. 50w. $2\frac{1}{2}$

1572   SYLVESTER, Victor. Back Seat Driving. Precision (E)
        CAC Aug. p167. 75w. $2\frac{1}{2}$

1573   TATE, Phil. Twenty-Five Silver Greats. BBC (E) (Reissue)
        CAC Aug. p170. 100w. $2\frac{1}{2}$

1574   TAYLOR, John and Norma Winstone. Azimuth. ECM 1-
        1099
            CAD Nov. p43-4. 250w. 2
            CK Dec. p73. 75w. 3
            MG Nov. p53. 251. $4\frac{1}{2}$
            MM Sept. 24 p32. 250w. 4
            RR Nov. p116. 50w. $3\frac{1}{2}$

1575   TEMPERANCE Seven. 21 Years on. DJM (E)
        CAC Jan. p381. 150w. $2\frac{1}{2}$

1576   TEW, Alan and Orchestra. Abba Songbook. CBS Embassy
        31550 (E)
            GR Nov. p919. 25w. $3\frac{1}{2}$

1577   TEW, Alan and Orchestra. Don't Cry for Me, Argentina.
        CBS (E)
            MM Aug. 6 p16. 50w. 2

1578   THIBEAULT, Fabienne. La Vie d'Astheure. Kébec-disc
        KD922 (Canada)
            CC June p29. 50w. 3

1579   THRILLINGTON, Percy "Thrills." EMI EMC 3173 (E)
        CAC July p134. 150w. $2\frac{1}{2}$
        GR July p234. 50w. $1\frac{1}{2}$

1580   TJADER, Cal. At Grace Cathedral. Fantasy 9521
        CAD April p36-7. 96w. $2\frac{1}{2}$
        DB Aug. 11 150w. $1\frac{1}{2}$

1581   TREMBLAY, Georges. Le Neuvième Silence. London LFS
        9017 (Canada)
            CC March p34. 50w. 3

1582   TWIGGY. Pleast Get My Name Right. Mercury SRM-1-
        1093
            CAC June p98. 150w. 2
            CIR June 23 p64. 125w. $2\frac{1}{2}$
            GR July p233. 125w. 3
            CS Jan. 27 p20. 250w. $3\frac{1}{2}$

1583   TYLER, Bonnie. Lost in France. RCA PL 25063 (France)
        RR June p93. 50w. 1

1584   TYLER, Bonnie.   The World Starts Tonight.   Chrysalis
       CHR1140
            CAC   Aug.   p170.   125w.   1½
            RC   Oct.   p6.   100w.   3

1585   TYSON, Sylvia.   Cool Wind from the North.   Capitol ST
       6441
            OLR   June   p142.   25w.   4
            SR   April   p100.   75w.   2

1586   TYSON, Sylvia.   Woman's World.
            FOL   May   p24-5.   700w.   2

1587   UNIT 4 + 2.   Remembering.   Decca REM 6 (E) (Reissue)
            CAC   May   p51.   50w.   3
            SMG   Sept.   p28.   25w.   2½

1588   USSR Defence Ministry Band.   Russian Marches.   HMV
       Melodiya CSD3782 (E)
            GR   Oct.   p712.   250w.   2½

1589   VALOIS et Jodoin.   La Vieille Ecole.   CBS FS 90323 (Can-
       ada)
            OLR   March   p57.   25w.   3

1590   VAN DYKE, Louis.   'Round Midnight.   Columbia M-34511
            SR   Aug.   p109.   175w.   2

1591   VAUGHAN, Frankie.   100 Golden Hits.   Ronco (E) (2 discs)
            MM   Jan. 7   p16.   50w.   3

1592   VAUGHAN, Sarah.   In Hi-Fi.   Columbia Encore EN13084
       (Reissue)
            CAD   June   p44.   200w.   3½

1593   VAUGHAN, Sarah.   Jazz Jamboree '75.   Polish Jazz Federa-
       tion [no #]
            CAD   March   p40-1.   125w.   4

1594   VAUGHAN, Sarah.   Recorded Live.   Emarcy Jazz Series
       EMS-2-412 (Reissue)
            CAD   Oct.   p52-3.   300w.   3

1595   VEREEN, Ben.   Ben Vereen.   Buddah BDS5680
            SR   Aug.   p100-1.   75w.   2

1596   VIGNEAULT, Gilles.   J'ai Planté un Chêne.   Le Nordet GVN
       1007 (Canada)
            CC   March   p33.   50w.   3

1597   VIGNEAULT, Gilles.   Tout le Monde Est Malheureux.   Solo
       SO 25503
            CC   Feb.   p33.   50w.   3

1598   VINTON, Bobby.   The Name Is Love.   ABC AB-981
       RC Oct. p10. 100w. $2\frac{1}{2}$

1599   VIRTUOSI Brass Band of Great Britain.   Brass Bands Works.
       Virtuosi VR 7608 (E)
       GR Jan. p1193. 150w. $3\frac{1}{2}$

1600   WAKELIN, Johnny.   African Man.   Pye (E)
       CAC July p132. 50w. $2\frac{1}{2}$
       MM May 14 p33. 50w. $1\frac{1}{2}$

1601   WALKER, Nancy.   Show Stoppers.   Stet 2002 (Reissue)
       SR July p107. 225w. $4\frac{1}{2}$

1602   WARD, Clifford T.   Waves.   Phillips (E)
       MM Jan. 1 p15. 200w. $3\frac{1}{2}$

1603   WASHINGTON, Dinah.   The Jazz Sides.   Mercury EMS-2-401
       (Reissue)
       DB April 21 p36. 150w. 4

1604   WASHINGTON, Dinah.   Sings Great Standards.   Vogue VJD
       522 (2 discs) (Reissue)
       MM March 5 p26. 250w. 3

1605   WASHINGTON, Dinah.   Very Best.   Philips Sonit 26 (E)
       HBS Jan. p17. 50w. 4
       RR Feb. p94. 150w. $2\frac{1}{2}$

1606   WEAVER, Dennis.   DJM DJF20504 (E)
       CMP May p39. 150w. 5
       CMR Sept. p6. 150w. $2\frac{1}{2}$

1607   WEAVER, Dennis.   McCloud Country.   DJM DJF 20479 (E)
       CMP Jan. p39-40. 200w. 3

1608   WEEDON, Burt.   Blue Echoes.   Polydor 2384 095 (E)
       CAC Aug. p170. 125w. 3
       MM Aug. 6 p16. 50w. $3\frac{1}{2}$
       NK Summer p38. 25w. 1

1609   WEEDON, Burt.   20 Super Guitar Greats.   EMI One-up 2167
       (E) (Reissue)
       NK Spring p42. 25w. $3\frac{1}{2}$

1610   WELSH Guards Band.   Friday Night Is Music Night.   Pre-
       cision BBC (E)
       CAC Sept. p217. 150w. $3\frac{1}{2}$

1611   WELSH Guards Band.   Royal Salute.   BBC REB274 (E)
       GR Sept. p521. 125w. $2\frac{1}{2}$

1612   WILEY, Lee.   On the Air.   Totem 1021

        CAD June p21.   75w.   2
        MR   June p10.   400w. $3\frac{1}{2}$
        SR   Aug. p109. 200w. 5

1613   WILLIAMS, Andy. Andy. Columbia 34299
        SR   Feb. p105. 150w. 4

1614   WILLIAMS, Paul. Classics. A&M SP 4701 (Reissue)
        GR   Dec. p1162. 50w. 3

1615   WILLIAMS, Roger. I Honestly Love You. MCA Stereotape
      MCAS 438-C
        AU   Jan. p91.   400w. 3
        RC   Oct. p4.   125w. $3\frac{1}{2}$

1616   WILSON, Nancy. I've Never Been to Me. Capitol ST-11659.
      Cart. 8XT-11659
        BM   Oct. p46. 250w. 3
        BS   Sept. p16. 200w. $3\frac{1}{2}$
        GR   Nov. p919. 25w. $2\frac{1}{2}$
        SR   Nov. p83, 84. 450w. 5

1617   WILSON, Nancy. This Mother's Daughter. Capitol EST
      11518
        BM   Jan. p52. 150w. 3
        GR   Jan. p1194. 25w. 3

1618   WINNICK, Maurice. Decca DVLI (E) (Reissue)
        GR   Oct. p715. 50w. 4
        MM   Oct. 22 p28. 50w. $3\frac{1}{2}$

1619   WYTE (Witkowski), Bernie. Barrels Full of Polkas. Stella
      SLP 966
        RC   Dec. p13. 50w. $3\frac{1}{2}$

1620   WYTE, Bernie. King of Polka Kings. Stella 49
        RC   Oct. p7. 100w. $3\frac{1}{2}$

COUNTRY

This section comprises material known to listeners and collectors variously as "C & W," the "Nashville Sound," or hillbilly music. The tie that binds this diverse field together and distinguishes it from "folk" is that it is commercial music played for a paying audience and recorded for the industry.

Bill Malone in his excellent study, Country Music, U.S.A. [Austin: University of Texas, 1968], offers the uninitiated a handy way to categorize this genre.

Before the 1920's: The Southern rural culture, existing outside of the mainstream of American life, had its own music, expressive of the culture and isolation. We put these into FOLK.

The 1920's: The emergence of individual country performers relying upon traditional music are recorded for the growing numbers owning "Victrolas" in rural America. Jimmy Rodgers and the Carter Family begin the "country music industry." We put these under OLD TIME MUSIC.

The 1930's: The emergence of individual stars, singing cowboys, advanced recording techniques, and the radio bring change but the songs still reflect the performer's origins.

The 1940's: World War II and the move to defense jobs and Southern military camps helps make country music nationally popular. This is the boom period of the industry.

The 1950's: Country music enters the urban market and loses many of its distinctive traits. Hank Williams spans the gulf between country and popular music but country-pop and the Nashville sound are replacing tradition.

The 1960's (and into the mid-1970's): Country-pop is counterbalanced by the urban folk revival and a renewed interest in traditional country music.

Country has immense popularity in the United States. This music, which is often accused of having no "class," is the daily sound heard by many million Americans. Hundreds of AM radio stations feature it and millions of albums are sold annually. It is the working man's music and the very lyrics tell us much about his concerns: patriotism, automation, unemployment, too rapid social change, unfaithful wives and husbands, alcohol, and the dreariness of the factory and trucking. It is important music for the popular record collection in a library since it has a direct appeal to that segment of the population that traditionally does not use the library much. According to the reviews, the following appear to be the best discs in 1977.

ALLEN, Rex, Jr. Rex. Warner Brothers BS 3054
ASLEEP at the Wheel. The Wheel. Capitol ST 11620
BANDY, Moe. I'm Sorry for You My Friend. Columbia KC 34443
COE, David Allen. Rides Again. Columbia KC 34310
COLTER, Jesse. Mirriam. Capitol ST 11583
ELY, Joe. MCA 2242
GIMBLE, Johnny. Texas Dance Party. Columbia KC 34284
HAGGARD, Merle. The Roots of My Raising. Capitol ST 11586
JAMES, Sonny. In Prison, In Person. Columbia KC 34708
JENNINGS, Waylon. Live. RCA APL1-1108
LYNN, Loretta. I Remember Patsy. MCA 2265
McCLINTON, Delbert. Love Rustler. ABC 991
NELSON, Willie. To Lefty from Willie. Columbia KC 34695
ROBBINS, Marty. Adios Amigo. Columbia PC 34448
STEWART, Gary. Your Place or Mine. RCA APL1-2199
TWITTY, Conway. Play, Guitar, Play. MCA 2262
WILLS, Bob. The Late Bob Wills' Original Texas Playboys Today. Capitol ST 11612

1621 ACUFF, Roy. Smokey Mountain Memories. DSM DJD 28034 (E) (2 discs) (Reissue)
        CMR June p7. 150w. 3
        NK Spring p39. 100w. 4

1622 ADAMS, Trevor. I Believe in Country Music. Tank BSS 124 (E)
        CMP May p33. 50w. 3

1623 ALLEN, Rex, Jr. Best of. Warner Bros. BS 3122 (Reissue)
        RRE Nov.-Dec. p31. 150w. 3

1624 ALLEN, Rex, Jr. Rex. Warner Bros. BS 3054. Cart. B8 3054
        CM Oct. p50. 200w. 4
        CMR Sept. p7. 200w. $3\frac{1}{2}$

1625 ALLEN, Rex, Jr. Ridin' High. Warner Brothers BS 2958
        CM Jan. p58. 375w. 2

       CMP   March p44.   125w.   4
       CMR   June p14.   200w.   3

1626   AMERICAN Flyer.   United Artists UAG 29991 (E) (Reissue)
       CMR   June p8.   100w.   3

1627   AMERICAN Flyer.   Spirit of a Woman.   United Artists UA-
      LA720-G
       MM   Aug. 27 p19.   300w.   1
       RS   Aug. 25 p60.   250w.   2
       SR   Nov. p86.   50w.   4

1628   ANDERSON, Bill.   Peanuts and Diamonds and Other Jewels.
      MCA 2222
       CM   Jan. p55.   325w.   1
       CMR   June p16.   200w.   3
       MM   May 14 p33.   50w.   3

1629   ANDERSON, Bill.   Scorpio.   MCA 2264
       CMR   Aug. p21.   200w. $2\frac{1}{2}$

1630   ANDERSON, Bill and Marylou Turner.   Billyboy and Marylou.
      MCA 2298
       RC   Nov. p5.   50w. $2\frac{1}{2}$

1631   ANDERSON, Lynn.   Wrap Your Love All Around Your Man.
      Columbia 34439
       CMP   Nov. p37.   125w.   3
       CMR   July p22.   150w.   3
       MM   Oct. 29 p23.   125w.   1

1632   ARNOLD, Eddy.   Eddy.   RCA APL 1-1817
       CMP   Feb. p39.   100w.   4
       CMR   April p37.   50w.   3
       MM   March 19 p31.   50w. $2\frac{1}{2}$

1633   ARNOLD, Eddy.   I Need You All the Time.   RCA APL 1-
      2277.   Cart. APS1 2277
       CM   Aug. p48.   300w.   1

1634   ASLEEP at the Wheel.   The Wheel.   Capitol ST-11620.
      Cart. 8XT-11620.   Cass. 4XT-11620
       CIR   Aug. 4 p61.   225w.   3
       CM   Aug. p48.   500w.   3
       CMP   May p34.   150w.   3
       CMR   July p20.   25w.   2
       DB   June 16 p39-40.   325w.   3
       GR   July p234.   75w.   3
       MM   May 14 p26.   375w.   4
       NK   Summer p38.   25w.   3
       OTM   Summer p35.   225w.   3
       RC   Aug. p5.   200w. $2\frac{1}{2}$
       RS   May 19 400w.   4

        SR   Aug.   p86.   125w.   4
        ZZ   May   p37.   225w.   3

1635   ASLEEP at the Wheel. Wheelin' and Dealin'.   Capitol ST
       11546. Cart. 8XT-11546. Cass. 4XT-11546
           CMP   Jan.   p35.   250w.   5
           CMR   Feb.   p30.   350w.   5
           NK   Winter p38.   50w. $3\frac{1}{2}$
           OTM Summer p35.   225w.   3
           SR   Jan.   p77.   100w.   4

1636   ATKIN, Peter. The Essential. RCA PL 25041 (E) (Reissue)
           RR   June   p94.   50w.   3

1637   ATKINS, Chet. The Best of. RCA APL1-1985. Cart.
       APS1-1985 (Reissue)
           CM   March p59.   250w.   3
           CMP   April p54.   150w.   3
           CMR   Aug.   p21.   100w. $3\frac{1}{2}$
           CS   March 24 p16.   250w. $3\frac{1}{2}$
           MG   Feb.   p56.   200w. $3\frac{1}{2}$
           MM   Nov. 12 p26.   75w. $3\frac{1}{2}$
           RC   May   p5.   150w.   3

1638   ATKINS, Chet. Me and My Guitar. RCA APL1 2405. Cart.
       APS1 2405. Cass. APK1 2405
           CM   Nov.   p36.   250w.   2
           GP   Dec.   p153.   100w.   4
           HF   Nov.   200w. $3\frac{1}{2}$
           MM   Jan. 7 p16.   50w.   3

1639   ATKINS, Chet. Picks on the Beatles. RCA NL 12002
           CMP   May   p35.   75w.   3
            CMR   June   p17.   200w.   3
           MM   April 16 p23.   50w. $1\frac{1}{2}$

1640   ATKINS, Chet and Les Paul. Chester 'N' Lester. RCA
       LSA 3290
           CAC   May   p50.   200w.   1
           CMP   Feb.   p39.   200w.   4
           CMR   May   p33.   75w.   3
           CRE   March p63.   25w.   3
           GR   April p1608.   25w. $3\frac{1}{2}$
           JJ   April p28.   150w. $3\frac{1}{2}$
           MM   Feb. 5 p23.   250w. $3\frac{1}{2}$

1641   AUTRY, Gene. Cowboy Hall of Fame. Republic IRDA R
       6012
           CMR   Jan.   p30.   75w.   2

1642   AUTRY, Gene. Favorites. Republic R 6013 (Reissue)
           RC   April p8.   50w.   3

1643   AUTRY, Gene. Live from Madison Square Garden. Republic
       IRDA R 6014 (Reissue)
           CMR Jan. p30. 75w. 2
           RC April p8. 50w. 3

1644   AUTRY, Gene. South of the Border. Republic 6011 (Reis-
       sue)
           RC April p8. 50w. 3

1645   AUTRY, Gene. Young Gene Autry, Vol. 3: Prairie Justice.
       Republic IRDA R 6012
           CMR Jan. p30. 75w. 4

1646   BAKER, Bobby. Birmingham Calverstone. Tank BSS 146
       (E)
           CMR March p27. 75w. 4

1647   BAKER, Carroll. RCA PL 10171
           CMP March p37. 150w. 3
           CMR April p37. 125w. 4

1648   BANDY, Moe. Best of, V. 1. Columbia 34715 (Reissue)
           CMR Sept. p16. 125w. $3\frac{1}{2}$
           RS Nov. 17 p87, 89, 91. 200w. 3

1649   BANDY, Moe. Cowboys Ain't Supposed to Cry. Columbia
       PC 34874. Cart. PCA 34874. Cass. PCT 34874
           CMP Nov. p37-8. 200w. 5
           HF Nov. 250w. $1\frac{1}{2}$
           MM Oct. 27 p23. 125w. 3

1650   BANDY, Moe. Here I Am Drunk Again. Columbia KC
       34285. Cass. CA 34285
           SR Feb. p86. 150w. 3

1651   BANDY, Moe. I'm Sorry for You My Friend. Columbia KC
       34443
           CM June p48. 300w. 4
           CMP May p35. 225w. 5
           CMR June p15. 200w. 3
           RS Nov. 17 p87, 89, 91. 200w. 3

1652   BARBARY Coast. Fistful of Roses. Tank BSS 184
           CMP Dec. p37. 150w. 4

1653   BARE, Bobby. Me and McDill. RCA APLI 2179
           CMR May p33. 100w. 4
           CS April 21 p18. 250w. 3

1654   BARE, Bobby. The Winner, and Other Losers. RCA APLI
       1786
           CMR May p33. 300w. 4

1655   BARLOW, Randy.   Arrival.   Mint Julep JULEP5 (E)
       CMP   Dec.   p38.   125w.   2

1656   BARRY, Joe.   ABC/Dot DO 2085
       CMP   Oct.   p40-1.   200w.   3

1657   BEGLEY, Philomena and Her Ramblin' Men.   Queen of the
       Silver Dollar.   Top Spin TSLP 86 (E)
       CMP   Feb.   p36.   100w.   4

1658   BELLAMY Brothers.   Plain and Fancy.   Warner Bros. BS
       6357
       CMP   Aug.   p36.   100w.   2
       CS   May 5   p18.   200w.   3

1659   BOONE, Pat.   Texas Woman.   Hitsville HVS 3003
       CMP   April   p54.   125w.   3
       CMR   July   p22.   300w.   3
       GR   June   p110.   100w. $3\frac{1}{2}$

1660   BRESH, Tom.   Kicked Back.   ABC Dot DO 2084.   Cart.
       8 2084
       CM   Nov.   p39.   200w.   3
       CMP   Sept.   p34.   225w.   3

1661   BRETT, Ann and Ray.   Somebody Loves You.   Sweet Folk
       and Country SFA 070 (Reissue)
       CMP   May   p35.   150w.   4
       CMR   June   p16.   150w.   3

1662   BROWN, Jim Ed and Helen Cornelius.   Born Believer.   RCA
       APL1 2399.   Cart. APS1-2399
       CM   Nov.   p37.   200w.   3

1663   BROWN, Jim Ed and Helen Cornelius.   I Don't Want to Have
       to Marry You.   RCA PL 12014 (Reissue)
       CMP   March   p38.   175w.   5
       CMR   May   p32.   100w.   3
       MG   Feb.   p56.   100w. $2\frac{1}{2}$
       MM   March 19   p31.   50w. $2\frac{1}{2}$

1664   BROWN, Joe.   Live.   Power Exchange PXLS 2002 (E)
       CMP   Sept.   p35.   300w.   3

1665   BURNETTE, Dorsey.   Things I Treasure.   Calliope CAL
       7006
       RRE   Nov.-Dec.   p31.   200w.   3

1666   BURNETTE, Hank C.   Don't Mess with My Ducktail.   Sonet
       SNTF 693 (E)
       CAC   March   p453.   200w.   3
       CMR   Feb.   p33.   75w.   5
       RSP   1:3   p31-2.   175w. $2\frac{1}{2}$

1667   CAMPBELL, Glen. Southern Nights.   Capitol SW-11601
         CM   May p58.   300w.   2
         CMP April p58.   125w.   3
         CMR June p12.   75w.   3
         GR   June p110.   50w. $3\frac{1}{2}$
         MM   May 14 p30.   175w. $3\frac{1}{2}$
         SR   June p95.   125w.   4

1668   CAMPBELL, Glen. Twenty Golden Greats.   Capitol EMTV 2
         (E) (Reissue)
         CAC Jan.   p378.   150w.   3
         CMP Jan.   p39.   75w.   4
         CMR Jan.   p30.   50w.   2
         GR   Jan.   p1194.   25w.   3

1669   CARROLL, Milton. Blue Skies.   Columbia KC 34114
         CMR May p32.   100w.   3

1670   CARTER, Wilf. Have a Nice Day.   RCA KXL1-0157 (Canada)
         OLR Sept.   p223.   50w.   4

1671   CARVER, Johnny. Best of.   ABD Dot DO 2083 (Reissue)
         CMP Aug.   p37-8.   100w.   3

1672   CASH, Johnny. Sunnyvale 9330901 (Reissue)
         CRA Oct.   p66-7.   50w. $2\frac{1}{2}$

1673   CASH, Johnny. The Johnny Cash Collection.   Pickwick PDA
         033 (E) (2 discs) (Reissue)
         CMR Sept.   p17.   100w.   3

1674   CASH, Johnny. The Last Gunfighter Ballad.   Columbia PC-
         34314.   Cass. CT-34314
         CAC Sept.   p220.   200w.   3
         CM   June p49.   300w.   3
         CMR May p31, 32.   350w.   3
         MM   March 19 p31.   50w.   2
         NK   Spring p42.   100w. $3\frac{1}{2}$
         SR   June p95.   175w.   4

1675   CASH, Johnny. The Original Johnny Cash.   Charly CR
         30113 (E) (Reissue)
         CMR Jan.   p31.   225w.   2

1676   CASH, Johnny. The Rambler.   Columbia KC 34833.   Cart.
         KCT 4 34833
         CM   Oct.   p54.   325w.   4
         CS   Aug. 25 p18.   150w.   3
         GR   Dec.   p1161-2.   75w.   3
         MM   Sept. 3 p21.   200w.   3
         NK   Autumn p43.   25w.   1

1677   CHALKER, Curly. Nashville Sundown.   Sonet SNTF 694 (E)

CMP Feb. p38. 150w. 3

1678 CHALMERS, Peter. The Lady and the Stranger. Old Road
      Music 33976 (Canada)
          CC June p28. 50w. 3

1679 CHAPMAN, Marshall. Me, I'm Feelin' Free. Epic KE
      34422
          CIR May 26 p56-7. 250w. $3\frac{1}{2}$
          CMR May p32. 100w. 3
          SR June p96. 150w. 3

1680 CHAVIN, Chinga. Country Porn. Country Porn Records
          CMR March p29. 125w. 4

1681 CHRISTENSON, Terry. The Ghosts of Forty Thieves. Corn-
      er Store C 1002 (Canada)
          OLR June p139. 25w. $2\frac{1}{2}$

1682 CLARK, Guy. Texas Cooking. RCA APL 1-1944
          CMP Feb. p36. 200w. 4
          CMR April p35. 200w. 5
          CS Dec. p29. 100w. 3
          RS June 13 p52-3. 200w. 2

1683 CLARK, Roy. My Music and Me. ABD DOT 2072
          CMP Aug. p36-7. 100w. 3
          GP Oct. p129. 75w. $3\frac{1}{2}$

1684 COE, Davie Allan. Rides Again. Columbia KC34310. Cart.
      CA34310. Cass. CT34310
          AU Sept. p90. 100w. 4
          CM June p52. 350w. 1
          CMR June p11. 250w. 4
          RC Nov. p13. 200w. $3\frac{1}{2}$
          SR Aug. p87. 175w. $3\frac{1}{2}$

1685 COE, David Allan. Tattoo. Columbia PC34870. Cart. PCT
      34870. Cass. PCA 34870
          HF Nov. 200w. $3\frac{1}{2}$
          MG Nov. p52. 50w. 3
          MM Sept. 3 p21. 200w. $3\frac{1}{2}$
          RS Nov. 17 p87, 89, 91. 200w. $2\frac{1}{2}$

1686 COE, David Allan. Texas Moon. Charly CRL 5005 (E)
          CMP Dec. p37. 150w. 4

1687 COLTER, Jessi. Diamond in the Rough. Capitol ST 11543
          HF Jan. p143. 150w. 2

1688 COLTER, Jessi. Miriam. Capitol ST 11583
          AU Nov. p118. 150w. $3\frac{1}{2}$
          CM Oct. p54. 150w. 4

        CMP   Dec.   p38.   150w.   5
        MM   Sept.   3   p21.   200w.   4
        SR   Dec.   125w. $2\frac{1}{2}$

1689   COOLEY, Spade.   Spade Cooley.   Club of Spade 00103
        CAD   July   p23.   100w.   2
        JEMF   Quarterly   no.   46   p103-4.   250w. $2\frac{1}{2}$

1690   COTTON, Gene.   Rain On.   ABC ABCL 2513
        CMP   April   p54.   100w.   2
        CMR   June   p15.   150w.   3

1691   COTTON Mill Boys.   Orange Blossom Special.   Hawk HALP
    158 (E)
        CMP   Feb.   p34.   150w.   4

1692   CRADDOCK, Billy.   The Country Sounds of.   Music for
    Pleasure MFP 50298 (E) (Reissue)
        CMP   Jan.   p38.   50w.   4

1693   CRADDOCK, Billy.   Live.   ABC DO 2082.   Cart. 8-2082
        CM   Nov.   p38.   225w.   4
        CMP   Sept.   p36.   225w.   3

1694   CRAMER, Floyd.   Chet, Floyd and Danny.   RCA APL 1-2311
        CK   Sept.   p58.   75w.   3

1695   CRAMER, Floyd.   Floyd Cramer and the Keyboard Kick
    Band.   RCA APL 1-2278
        CK   Aug.   p48-9.   100w.   4

1696   CRAWFORD, Jimmy.   A Ton of Steel.   Prize RRS 49805
        CMR   April   p21.   150w.   4

1697   CRISPIN, James.   This Is.   Tank BSS 134
        CMP   May   p33.   50w.   3

1698   CROCKETT, Howard.   From the Lonestar State.   CCL 1143
        NK   Summer   p40.   50w.   3

1699   CUNNINGHAM, Larry.   Remember Jim Reeves, Vol. 2.
    Release BRL 4068
        CMP   Feb.   p35.   100w.   2

1700   CUNNINGHAM, Larry and Margo Cunningham.   Yes, Mr.
    Peters.   Release XRL 5002
        CMP   Feb.   p35.   100w.   2

1701   CURLESS, Dick.   CB Special MB 313
        CMR   June   p9.   350w.   4

1702   DADI, Marcel.   Dadi's Pickin' Lights Up Nashville, Part
    Two.   Cezame CEZ-1019 (France)

GP Sept. p119. 200w. 5

1703 DADI, Marcel. Marcel Dadi and Friends Country Show.
Guitar World 4
PIC March p51. 200w. 5

1704 DAL Bello, Lisa. Look at Me. MCA 2249
CC Nov. p36. 75w. 3
SOU Dec. p55. 250w. 4

1705 DARLING, Gloria. Release BRL 4082 (E)
CMP Aug. p39. 150w. 5

1706 DARREN, Jenny. City Lights. DJM DJF-20497 (E)
MM March 19 p31. 50w. 0

1707 DAVE and Sugar. RCA APL1-1818
CMP Jan. p38. 225w. 4
RSP March-April p61-2. 250w. 3

1708 DAVIS, Jimmie and Buddy Jones. MCA VIM 4018 (Japan)
(Reissue)
JEMF Autumn p157-60. 200w. 5
OTM Summer p30-4. 500w. 4

1709 DAVIS, Mac. Thunder in the Afternoon. Columbia PC-
34313. Cart. PCA-34313. Cass. PCT-34313
CMP July p38. 125w. 2
CMR Aug. p21. 150w. 2
SR Aug. p87. 200w. 4

1710 DAVIS, Paul. Bang SHOT 002 (E)
CMP July p57. 125w. 3
CMR July p20. 150w. 3

1711 DAY, Jimmy. "All Those Years." Checkmate CMLF 1002
CMP Nov. p38-9. 150w. 5

1712 DENVER, Jennie and Slim Pickins. Live at the Spur and
Saddle Country Music Club. Westwood WRS 105 (E)
CMP March p43-4. 125w. 3
CMR March p27. 75w. 4

1713 DEREK, John and Country Fever. Country Music Trail,
Vol. 1. Maskerade FWS 3881 (E)
CMP Feb. p36. 200w. 5

1714 DEVINE, Sydney. Almost Persuaded. Philips 6308 291 (E)
MM Aug. 6 p17. 50w. 0

1714a DEVINE, Sydney. Devine Time. Philips 6308 283 (E)
CAC April p11. 125w. 3
CMP March p38. 150w. 3

1715   DEVINE, Sydney. This Song Is Just for You.   Sunset SLD
       501/2 (E) (2 discs)
           CMR   Jan.   p31.   50w.   5

1716   DICKSON, Barbara.   Morning Comes Quickly.   RSO RSO
       2394 188 (E)
           CMR   Sept.   p15.   100w.   1

1717   DINNER, Michael.   Tom Thumb the Dreamer.   Fantasy 9512
           CMR   March p29.   50w.   0
           FOL   July   p24-5. 750w. $2\frac{1}{2}$

1718   DONALDSON, James.   Justified.   Look LK LP-7
           CMP   May   p33.   100w.   5
           CMR   July   p18.   200w.   4

1719   DOONICAN, Val.   Some of My Best Friends Are Songs.
       Phillips 9286 783 (2 LP set)
           CAC   June   p94-5. 200w. 3
           CMR   July   p22.   150w. 3
           GR   Aug.   p353.   250w. 4
           MM   May 14 p31.   50w. $2\frac{1}{2}$

1720   DUDLEY, Dave.   Seventeen Seventy Six (1766).   United
       Artists UA LA 625
           CMR   Jan.   p28.   125w.   0

1721   DUNCAN, Johnny.   Columbia KC 34442
           CM   July   p54.   200w.   4
           CMR   June   p12.   150w.   3
           RC   Aug.   p4.   200w.   2

1722   DUSTY Chaps.   Honky Tonk Music.   Capitol ST 11614
           CS   May 19 p18.   125w. $3\frac{1}{2}$

1723-4 ELY, Joe.   MCA MCA-2242.   Cart. T-2242
           CIR   May 12 p16-7. 300w. $3\frac{1}{2}$
           CM   May   p59.   300w. 5
           CMP   Aug.   p36.   200w. 5
           HF   April p148.   50w.   2
           MM   Aug. 20 p17.   250w. $4\frac{1}{2}$
           RC   July   p5.   150w. 3
           RR   Nov.   p115.   50w.   4
           SR   May   p84.   112w. 3

1725   EMMONS, Buddy.   Sings Bob Wills.   Flying Fish 017
           AU   Feb.   p88.   450w. 5
           CMP   May   p38.   150w. 5
           CMR   Sept. p15.   100w. $2\frac{1}{2}$
           MM   Nov. 19 p23.   200w. $2\frac{1}{2}$
           OTM   Winter p28.   200w. $2\frac{1}{2}$

1726   EMMONS, Buddy.   Steel Guitar.   Sonet SNTF 708 (E)

    CMP Jan. p41. 125w. 5
    CMR Sept. p15. 100w. 3
    RSP March-April p61. 500w. $3\frac{1}{2}$

1727 EMMONS, Buddy and Buddy Spicher. Buddies. Sonet SNTF
    741 (E)
    CMP Nov. p38. 200w. 4

1728 ENGLEHART, Toulouse. Toullusions. Briar 4203
    RSP Jan.-Feb. p23. 100w. $3\frac{1}{2}$

1729 EVERLY, Don. Brother Juke Box. DJM DJF 20501 (E)
    CMP March p39. 125w. 3
    CMR June p9. 100w. 2
    MM April 2 p20. 250w. 4
    NK Spring p39. 100w. 4

1730 FAIRCHILD, Barbara. Free & Easy. Columbia PC 34868
    CMP Oct. p44. 300w. 5
    MM Oct. 29 p23. 125w. $3\frac{1}{2}$

1731 FAIRCHILD, Barbara. Mississippi. Columbia KC34307
    CMR Feb. p30. 100w. 0

1732 FAMILY Brown. I Am the Words, You Are the Music.
    RCA KXL1-0167 (Canada)
    OLR June p140. 50w. 2

1733 FARGO, Donna. The Best. ABC DO 2075 (Reissue)
    CM Aug. p50. 175w. 4
    CMP April p53. 150w. 5
    CMR July p22. 25w. 3
    MM April 30 p26. 25w. 3

1734 FARGO, Donna. Country Sounds of. Music for Pleasure
    MFP 50257 (E) (Reissue)
    CMP Jan. p38. 50w. 5

1735 FARGO, Donna. Fargo Country. Warner Bros. BS 2996.
    Cart. M82996. Cass. M52996
    CM Aug. p50. 175w. 3
    CMR July p22. 150w. 3
    SR Sept. p97. 125w. 2

1736 FARGO, Donna. On the Move. Warner BS 2926
    CMP March p40-1. 150w. 5

1737 FELTS, Narvel. Doin' What I Feel. ABD Dot DOSD 2065.
    Cart. DOSD-8-2065
    CM March p58. 300w. 2
    RC June p11. 200w. 3

1738 FELTS, Narvel. Reconsider Me. ABC DOSD 2025

NK   Winter p38.   25w.   3

1739   FELTS, Narvel.   The Touch of Felts.   ABC DOSD 2070.
       Cart. 8-DO-2070
              CM   July p53.   300w.   4
              CMP Aug. p38.   125w.   3
              CS   June 16 p16.   125w.   3

1740   FENDER, Freddy.   Best of.   ABC ABCL 5221 (E) (Reissue)
              CMR Aug. p20.   200w. $4\frac{1}{2}$
              NK   Summer p37.   50w. $3\frac{1}{2}$

1741   FENDER, Freddy.   If You Don't Love Me.   ABC Dot DO
       2090
              CMP Dec. p40.   150w.   3

1742   FENDER, Freddy.   If You're Ever in Texas.   ABC DOSD
       2061
              CIR Jan. 31 p16.   100w. $2\frac{1}{2}$
              CM   Feb. p52.   225w.   2
              CMP Jan. p35.   125w.   3
              CMR May p32.   50w.   3
              CS   Jan. p16.   200w.   3
              NK   Winter p33.   75w. $4\frac{1}{2}$

1743   FENDER, Freddy.   Since I Met You Baby.   GRT 8005 (Re-
       issue)
              NK   Winter p34.   75w.   4

1744   FORD, Gerry.   These Songs Are Just for You.   Emerald
       Gem GES 1164
              CAC Sept. p221.   50w.   3
              CMR June p12.   150w.   3

1745   FOUR Card Express.   Somewhere Between.   Tank BSS 154
       (E)
              CMR Jan. p31.   100w.   2

1746   FRIZZELL, Lefty.   ABC Collection.   ABC 30035.   Cart.
       ABC8T 30035 (Reissue)
              CM   Oct. p52.   200w.   4

1747   FROMHOLZ, Steven.   Frolicking in the Myth.   Capitol ST
       11611.   Cart. 8XT 11611
              CM   Sept. p52.   300w. $2\frac{1}{2}$
              MM   July 16 p23.   250w. $3\frac{1}{2}$

1748   FROMHOLZ, Steven.   A Rumor in My Own Time.   Capitol
       ST 11521
              CMR June p7.   100w.   3

1749   GATLIN, Larry.   Broken Lady.   Monument MNT 82004
              CMP May p37.   150w.   5

1750   GAYLE, Crystal.   We Must Believe in Magic.   United Artists
       UA-LA771.   Cart. UA-EA771
           MM Oct. 29 p23. 300w. 4
           SR Nov. p100. 200w. 5

1751   GIBSON, Bob.   Funky in the Country.   Living Legend Rec-
       ords (E)
           RSP March-April p20. 150w. $3\frac{1}{2}$

1752   GIBSON, Don.   Famous Country Musicmakers.   RCA PL
       42002 (E) (Reissue)
           CMP Sept. p34. 150w. 4
           CMR Sept. p16. 100w. $3\frac{1}{2}$

1753   GIBSON, Don.   Four Sides of.   DJM DJD 28029 (E) (2 discs)
       (Reissue)
           CMP March p44. 150w. 4
           NK Winter p37. 75w. 4

1754   GIBSON, Don.   I'm All Wrapped Up in You.   DJM DJF
       20502 (E)
           CMP April p52. 150w. 4
           ZZ May p39. 150w. 3

1755   GILLEY, Mickey.   First Class.   Playboy KZ-34776.   Cart.
       KZT-34776
           CM Oct. p50. 300w. 4

1756   GILLEY, Mickey.   Gilley's Smokin'.   Playboy PB 415
           CM March p58. 375w. 4
           CMR April p33. 50w. 3
           MG Jan. 150w. 4
           RC June p12. 200w. 3
           SR June p102. 150w. 0

1757   GIMBLE, Johnny.   Texas Dance Party.   Columbia KC
       34284
           CM Feb. p55. 450w. 4
           CMR June p14. 200w. 3
           CRA April p110. 75w. 3
           HF Feb. p145. 50w. 3
           MG Jan. 50w. $3\frac{1}{2}$
           RSP Jan.-Feb. p29. 350w. $2\frac{1}{2}$
           SR May p92. 250w. 5

1758   GLASER, Tompall.   The Wonder of It All.   ABC 1036
           RS Nov. 17 p87, 89, 91. 200w. $1\frac{1}{2}$

1759   GLASER, Tompall, and His Outlaw Band.   ABC ABCL 5211
           CMP March p39. 225w. 5
           CMR June p8. 150w. 3

1760   GLENN, John, and the Mainliners.   Back Again.   Mistry

MYLP 5002
    CMP May p33. 100w. 3

1761 GOLBEY, Brian. The Radio London Tapes. Waterfall
    TAD001
    CMP Dec. p38. 250w. 4

1762 GOOD Brothers. RCA KPL1-0168 (Canada)
    OLR June p140. 50w. $2\frac{1}{2}$

1763 GOODACRE, Tony. Thanks to the Hanks. Outlet SBOL 4024
    (E)
    CMP Jan. p39. 200w. 3
    CMR Jan. p31. 125w. 3

1764 GOODACRE, Tony. Written in Britain. Outlet SBOL 4027
    CMP Nov. p36. 250w. 4

1765 GOSDIN, Vern. Till the End. Elektra 7E-1112
    CM Nov. p39. 200w. 4

1766 GRAHAM, Mike. People Music. Mam MAME 3004
    CMP Dec. p40. 150w. 3

1767 GREEN, Lloyd. Ten Shades of Green. Checkmate CMLF
    1001
    CMP May p35. 150w. 3
    CMR June p13. 200w. 3
    MM May 14 p31. 50w. 2

1768 GREER, John. Country Requests. Homespun Records HRL
    123 (E)
    CMR March p27. 50w. 4

1769 GRIFF, Ray. The Last of the Winfield Amateurs. Capitol
    ST-11566
    RM Jan. p6. 900w. 5

1770 HAGGARD, Merle. My Farewell to Elvis. MCA 2314
    MM Dec. 21 p14. 150w. $3\frac{1}{2}$

1771 HAGGARD, Merle. My Love Affair with Trains. Capitol
    ST 11544
    CMP Feb. p36. 100w. 5

1772 HAGGARD, Merle. The Roots of My Raising. Capitol ST-
    11586
    CM April p52. 300w. 4
    CMP March p39-40. 150w. 4
    CMR May p33. 150w. 3
    CS April 21 p19. 150w. $2\frac{1}{2}$
    MG Feb. p56. 100w. $3\frac{1}{2}$
    MG April p55. 125w. 2

SR   April   p90.   175w.   4

1773   HAGGARD, Merle.   Songs I'll Always Sing.   Capitol SABB
      11531 (2 discs) Cart.   8XBB 11531
         CM   Sept.   p53.   300w.   3
         CMP   Aug.   p38.   125w.   4
         MM   Sept.   3   p17.   125w. $3\frac{1}{2}$

1774   HAGGARD, Merle.   A Working Man Can't Get Nowhere To-
      day.   Capitol ST-11693
         MM   Oct.   8   p32.   200w. $3\frac{1}{2}$

1775   HALL, Tom T.   About Love.   Mercury SRM-1-1139.   Cass.
      MCR-4-1149.   Cart.   M6-8-1-1139
         CM   Oct.   p53.   150w.   3
         CMR   Aug.   p21.   50w. $1\frac{1}{2}$
         CS   Jan.   2   p16.   200w.   4
         SR   Oct.   p98.   200w. $2\frac{1}{2}$

1776   HALL, Tom T.   The Magnificent Music Machine.   Mercury
      SRM-1-1111
         BGU   June   p36.   225w.   3
         CM   Jan.   p55.   250w.   4
         CMP   Jan.   p35.   200w.   5
         CS   Jan.   p16.   150w.   3

1777   HAMILTON, George, IV.   Back Home at the Opry.   RCA
      APL 1-0192
         CMP   Feb.   p34.   150w.   4
         CMR   March   p27.   300w.   5
         MM   Feb.   12   p26.   50w.   3

1778   HAMILTON, George, IV.   Country Songs of.   Music for
      Pleasure MFP 50295 (E) (Reissue)
         CMP   Jan.   p35.   75w.   3

1779   HAMILTON, George, IV.   Fine Lace and Homespun Cloth.
      Anchor ANCL 2022
         CMR   June   p15.   250w.   3
         CMP   April   p52.   300w.   5
         CS   June 16   p16.   200w.   4
         RC   Nov.   p12-3.   150w.   3

1780   HARGRAVE, Linda.   Just Like You.   Capitol ST 11564.
      Cart.   8ST 11564
         CM   Feb.   p53.   275w.   2

1781   HARRIS, Stewart.   Send Me a Rainbow.   Mercury SRM 1-1167
         CS   Dec.   p28.   100w.   2

1782   HART, Freddie.   The Pleasure's Been Mine.   Capitol ST
      11626
         CMP   Aug.   p37.   150w.   3

MM   Sept. 3   p22.   25w.   1

1783   HARVEST. Never Thirst Again.   Pure Joy PJ 103
       CS   May 19   p18.   250w.   3

1784   HAWKES, Chip. Chip Hawkes' Nashville Album.   RCA PL
       15044
       CMR   June   p11.   250w.   4

1785   HEAD, Roy.   A Head of His Time.   ABC Dot DOSD 2066
       CS   Feb. 24   p27.   150w.   3
       MG   Feb.   p56.   75w. $3\frac{1}{2}$

1786   HENDERSON, Kelvin.   Black Magic Gun.   Checkmate CMLS
       1016
       CMP   Dec.   p36.   350w.   5

1787   HENLEY, Mark.   Riversong.   Sanskrit SR 0763
       CFS   Summer   p19.   150w.   4

1788   HIGH on the Hog.   Hogtied.   Sweet Folk and Country SPA
       062 (E)
       CMR   Jan.   p29.   75w.   3

1789   HILL, Don.   Country Scrapbook.   Peerless DT 012 (2 discs)
       (E)
       CMR   Sept.   p7.   125w.   0

1790   HOOPER, Danny.   Just a Part of Losing You.   MWS MWSL
       5 508
       CMP   April   p55.   100w.   2
       CMR   April   p33.   250w.   5

1791   HORTON, Johnny.   Rockin' Album.   Country Classics Li-
       brary CCL 1140 (Reissue)
       RSP   Jan. -Feb.   p35.   300w.   3

1792   HURREN, Bill.   Folks Like You.   BCMC (E)
       CMP   May   p33.   50w.   3

1793   HUSKY, Ferlin.   Country Sounds of.   Music for Pleasure
       MFP 50292 (E) (Reissue)
       CMP   Jan.   p38.   50w.   3

1794   INDIANS. We're Just Indians.   Hawk HALPX 154 (E)
       CMP   April   p53.   100w.   2

1795   JACKSON, Wanda.   I'll Still Love You.   DJM 20493 (E)
       CAC   Jan.   p390, 392.   3
       CMP   Jan.   p34.   100w.   4

1796   JAMES, Sonny.   In Prison, In Person.   Columbia KC-34708.
       Cart. CA-34708

CMP Aug. p38-9. 125w. 4
MM Sept. 17 p22. 250w. 3
NK Autumn p43. 50w. 3
RC Oct. p13. 100w. 4
SR Nov. p105-6. 275w. 4

1797 JAMES, Sonny. 200 Years of Country Music. Columbia
PC-34035
NK Winter p37. 25w. 4

1798 JAMES, Sonny. You're Free to Go. Columbia 34472
CMR June p14. 250w. 3

1799 JENNINGS, Waylon. Are You Ready for the Country. RCA
AFL1-1816
MM Jan. 22 p23. 75w. 1
NK Winter p38. 25w. 3
SMG Jan. p27. 275w. 4

1800 JENNINGS, Waylon. Live. RCA APL1-1108
CIR May 17 p18. 175w. $4\frac{1}{2}$
CIR March 17 p18. 175w. $4\frac{1}{2}$
CM April p53. 450w. 5
CMP March. p37. 175w. 5
CMR April p37. 175w. 5
CS Feb. 24 p27. 450w. $4\frac{1}{2}$
MG April p55. 100w. 3
MM Feb. 12 p26. 50w. 3
RC June p12. 150w. 3

1801 JENNINGS, Waylon. Ol' Waylon. RCA APL1-2317. Cart.
APS1-2317. Cass. APK1-2317
CAC Sept. p220. 150w. $3\frac{1}{2}$
CM Sept. p55. 300w. 3
CMR Aug. p20. 800w. $4\frac{1}{2}$
HF Aug. p118. 250w. $3\frac{1}{2}$
MM July 9 p23. 500w. 2
SR Aug. p93, 94. 250w. $3\frac{1}{2}$

1802 JIM & Ginger. Ain't It Good to Have It All. ABC ABCD
938
AU Feb. p90. 50w. 2

1803 JONES, George. United Artists UXS 85 (2 discs) (Reissue)
CM March p63. 50w. 3

1804 JONES, George. All-Time Greatest Hits, Volume 1. Epic
KE-34692 (Reissue)
CM Sept. p51. 525w. 5
CMP Sept. p39. 250w. 5
HF Aug. p118-9. 250w. $3\frac{1}{2}$
MM Sept. 3 p17. 125w. 4
SR Sept. p116. 950w. $4\frac{1}{2}$

1805   JONES, George.   Alone Again.   Epic KE 34290
        CMP Jan. p34.   150w.   5
        CS Jan. p16.   75w.   3½

1806   JONES, George.   I Wanta Sing.   Epic PE 34717.   Cart.
        PZT 34717.   Cass. PEA 34717
        MG Nov. p51.   25w.   3½
        RS Nov. 17 p87, 89, 91.   200w.   2½
        SR Dec. 550w.   4

1807   JONES, George and Tammy Wynette.   Golden Ring.   Epic
        PE 34291
        CAC Feb. p433.   300w.   4½
        CMP Jan. p34.   100w.   3
        CMR June p10.   50w.   2

1808   JONES, Grandpa.   The Grandpa Jones Story.   CMH CMH
        9007
        BGU Jan. p23.   225w.   5

1809   JORDAN, Ted.   For the First Time.   Intermedia WRC 230
        (Reissue)
        CC Sept. p34.   50w.   3

1810   KARTMAN, Ronnie.   Honest Love.   Broadland BR 1951 (Can-
        ada)
        CC Sept. p32.   50w.   3

1811   KERSHAW, Doug.   Flip, Flop, and Fly.   Warner Bros. BS
        3025.   Cart. M83025.   Cass. M53025
        CMR Sept. p6.   200w.   1
        CS May 5 p18.   250w.   4½
        RC Aug. p13.   125w.   3
        SR Aug. p94, 98.   175w.   3

1812   KING, Don.   Dreams and Things.   Con Brio CBLP 052
        RC Oct. p11.   50w.   3½

1813   KRISTOFFERSON, Kris.   Songs of.   Columbia PZ 34687.
        Cass. PZA 34687
        CM Sept. p55.   250w.   4
        CMP July p38.   125w.   4

1814   KRISTOFFERSON, Kris.   Surreal Thing.   Columbia PZ-
        34254
        CMP Feb. p38.   100w.   3

1815   LABEEF, Sleepy.   Western Gold.   Sun 138
        SMG May p26.   75w.   2½

1816   LEACH, Curtis.   Indescribable.   Longhorn LP 003
        CMR May p32.   150w.   3

1817   LEE, Brenda. L. A. Sessions.   MCA MCF 2783 (E)
       CMP April p53. 125w. 2
       GR April p1608. 25w. 2½
       MM May 14 p33. 50w. 3

1818   LEE, Wilma, and Stoney Cooper.   Rounder Records 0066
       BGU Jan. p22. 250w. 2
       OTM Winter p25. 150w. 1
       PIC June p68. 225w. 5

1819   LEE, Wilma, and Stoney Cooper.   Satisfied.   DJM DJB 26085
       (E) (Reissue)
       CMP Jan. p40. 150w. 5
       CMR Feb. p30. 350w. 5
       OTM Winter p25. 150w. 2

1820   LEE, Wilma, and Stoney Cooper.   Sing the Carter Family's
       Greatest Hits.   Gusto-Starday SD 980
       RSP 1:3 p24-5. 200w. 3

1821   LEGG, Adrian. Requiem for a Friend.   Westwood WRS 125
       CMP Sept. p38. 250w. 4

1822   LEWIS, Jerry Lee. Sunnyvale 9330 905 (Reissue)
       CRA Oct. p66-7. 50w. 2½

1823   LEWIS, Jerry Lee. Country Class.   Mercury SRM-1-1109.
       Cart. MC-8-1-1109
       CM Jan. p58. 225w. 4
       CMP Jan. p35. 100w. 2
       HF Feb. p148. 200w. 4
       MG Jan. 175w. 4½
       NK Winter p37. 75w. 3

1824   LEWIS, Jerry Lee. Nuggets.   Charly CR 30121 (E) (Reissue)
       MM May 21 p22. 200w. 3
       NK Winter p34. 75w. 4
       ZZ June p40. 150w. 3½

1825   LEWIS, Jerry Lee. Nuggets, Vol. 2.   Charly CR 30-129
       (E) (Reissue)
       NK Autumn p50. 100w. 4

1826   LEWIS, Jerry Lee. The Original Jerry Lee Lewis.   Charly
       CR 30111
       CMR June p7, 8. 200w. 4
       RSP Jan. -Feb. p34. 200w. 3

1827   LOCKLIN, Hank. Golden Hits.   Ember CW 147 (E)
       CMR June p13. 200w. 3

1828   LUMAN, Bob. Alive and Well.   Epic 34445
       CMR June p15. 200w. 3

NK Summer p38. 50w. 3

1829   LUMAN, Bob.   Bob Luman Rocks.   DJM 22057 (E) (Reissue)
       CMP   March   p37.   150w.   3
       MM   Feb. 5   p23.   50w.   2½
       NK   Winter   p34.   125w.   2½

1830   LYNAM, Ray.   Country Favorites, Old and New.   Release
       BRL 4086 (E)
       CMP   Sept.   p34.   150w.   3

1831   LYNAM, Ray.   20 Shots of Country.   Release BRL 4069 (E)
       CMP   Feb.   p36.   100w.   3

1832   LYNCH and Lawson.   The First.   Jet UAS 30131
       CMP   Dec.   p36.   250w.   3
       MM   Jan. 7   p16.   50w.   2½

1833   LYNN, Loretta.   The Best.   MCA MCF 2787 (Reissue)
       CMP   April   p52.   150w.   5
       CMR   July   p20.   200w.   3
       MM   April 30   p26.   100w.   3½

1834   LYNN, Loretta.   I Remember Patsy.   MCA MCA-2265
       CM   Aug.   p52.   425w.   4
       CMP   Aug.   p37.   250w.   5
       GR   Nov.   p919.   25w.   3
       HF   July   p153.   200w.   4
       MM   Sept. 3   p17.   125w.   3
       SR   July   p106.   750w.   2½

1835   LYNN, Loretta.   Somebody Somewhere.   MCA MCA-2228.
       Cart. T-2228
       CMP   April   p52.   100w.   2
       CS   Jan.   p16.   100w.   3
       CS   June 16   p16.   125w.   3
       MM   April 30   p26.   100w.   3½
       SR   April   p83-4, 94.   400w.   5

1836   LYNN, Loretta.   This Is.   Music for Pleasure MFP 50329
       (E) (Reissue)
       CMP   Sept.   p39-40.   150w.   3

1837   McCALL, C. W.   Rubberduck.   Polydor PD 1-6094
       CMR   June   p11.   100w.   3

1838   McCALL, Jim.   Pickin' and Singin'.   Vetco 3010
       CMR   Aug.   p21.   150w.   3½

1839   McCLAIN, Charly.   Here's.   Epic KE 34447
       CMR   June   p12.   300w.   4

1840   McCLINTON, Delbert.   Genuine Cowhide.   ABC ABCD 959

CS   Jan.   27   p20.   200w.   4

1841   McCLINTON, Delbert.   Love Rustler.   ABC 991.   Cart.
       022AB 991
           CM   May   p61.   250w.   4
           CS   April 21   p19.   250w.   4
           HF   April   p145.   200w. $4\frac{1}{2}$
           NK   Spring   p42.   75w. $3\frac{1}{2}$
           RS   May 19   350w. $3\frac{1}{2}$

1842   McCORISON, Dan.   MCA MCF 2276 (E)
           CMP   Sept.   p38.   350w.   5
           NK   Autumn   p43.   25w. $2\frac{1}{2}$

1843   McCOY, Charlie.   Play It Again, Charlie.   Monument MC6630
           SR   May   p88, 90.   175w.   5

1844   McDANIEL, Mel.   Gentle to Your Senses.   Capitol ST 11694.
       Cart. 8XT11694
           HF   Dec.   p136.   225w.   4

1845   McDERMOTT, Chuck.   Follow the Music.   Back Door BDF
       7477
           MM   Oct. 29   p26.   100w. $2\frac{1}{2}$
           RS   Nov. 17   p87, 89, 91.   200w.   2

1846   McGELL, Hugo.   Truckin' Country.   GW GW 101 (E)
           CMP   Jan.   p34.   125w.   4

1847   McGHEE, Parker.   Big Tree K 50349
           CMP   July   p37-8.   225w.   4

1848   MACK, Lonnie.   Home at Last.   Capitol ST 11619
           CM   July   p55.   300w.   4
           CMR   July   p21.   150w.   3
           CRA   July   p74.   200w.   2
           SR   Dec.   175w.   3

1849   MacLELLAN, Gene.   If It's Alright with You.   EMI ST
       11535 (Canada)
           OLR   Sept.   p223.   50w.   4
           SOU   June   p44.   500w.   2

1850   MADDOX, Rose.   Reckless Love and Bold Adventure.   Tako-
       ma Records D-1055
           BGU   May   p39.   250w.   4
           FOL   June   p21.   475w.   3
           PIC   Oct.   p58.   125w. $2\frac{1}{2}$
           RSP   March-April   p26.   100w.   3

1851   MADDOX, Rose.   Sing a Little Song of Heartache.   Pickwick
       6163 (Reissue)
           FOL   June   p21.   50w. $2\frac{1}{2}$

1852   MAGGARD, Cledus.   Two More Sides.   Mercury SRM-1-1112.
        Cart. MCR4-1-1112
            CM Feb. p54.   375w.   2

1853   MAHAN, Larry.   King of the Rodeo.   Warner Brothers BS
        2959
            CM Jan. p56.   475w.   2
            CMR April p35.   150w.   4

1854   MANDRELL, Barbara.   Lovers, Friends and Strangers.
        ABC Dot 2076
            CMP Sept. p39-40.   200w.   3
            CS Aug. 25 p18.   50w.   3

1855   MANDRELL, Barbara.   Midnight Angel.   ABC Dot DOSD
        2067
            CM May p60.   200w.   3
            CMP Feb. p34.   200w.   5

1856   MANIFOLD, Keith.   Inheritance.   DJM 22061
            CMP March p44.   175w.   3
            CMR June p15.   150w.   3

1857   MAXINE, Brian.   I'm Your Man.   DJM 22077 (E)
            CMP Oct. p44.   200w.   5
            MM Oct. 1 p28.   50w.   1½

1858   The MAYFIELDS.   Green Fields Re-visited.   DorLayle 101
            BGU May p43.   50w.   3
            PIC July p68-9.   275w.   3
            RSP April-May p24.   175w.   1½

1859   MEAL Ticket.   Code of the Road.   EMI ONS 3008 (E)
            MM July 23 p17.   225w.   2½

1860   MEAL Ticket.   Three Times a Day.   EMI International INS
        3010 (E)
            CMP Nov. p39.   300w.   5

1861   MEMPHIS Horns.   Get Up and Dance.   RCA APL 1-2198
            MM Nov. 5 p22.   50w.   3

1862   The MERCEY Brothers.   Homemade.   RCA KPL 1-0188
        (Canada)
            CMP March p37.   125w.   2
            CMR April p36.   250w.   5
            OLR Sept. p223.   25w.   2½

1863   MIKI and Griff.   Rockin' Alone.   Golden Hour GH 631 (E)
        Cart. ZCGH631
            CMP May p39.   125w.   3
            GR April p1608.   25w.   2½

1864   MIKI and Griff. This Is.   Pye PKL 5547 (E)
        GR Jan. p1194.   25w.   3

1865   MILLER, Jody. Here's.   Epic 34446
        CMP May p34.   200w.   4
        CMR June p17.   200w.   3

1866   MILLER, Roger. Off the Wall.   Windsong BHL-1-2337.
        Cart. BHK-1-2337.   Cass. BHF-1-2337
        CM Nov. p40.   200w. $2\frac{1}{2}$
        HF Oct. p156, 158.   400w.   5

1867   MILLER, Roger. Spotlight on.   Philips 6619 029 (E) (2
        discs) (Reissue)
        CMP Sept. p34-5.   400w.   4
        CMR Sept. p7.   125w. $3\frac{1}{2}$
        NK Autumn p43.   50w.   4

1868   MILSAP, Ronnie. It Was Almost Like a Song.   RCA APL1-
        2439
        CK Dec. p73.   25w.   2
        CMP Nov. p37.   200w.   5

1869   MILSAP, Ronnie. Live.   RCA APL1-2043
        CM March p58.   250w.   3
        CMP March p40.   125w.   3
        CMR June p16.   150w.   3
        HF Feb. p145.   100w.   3
        MG Feb. p56.   200w. $3\frac{1}{2}$
        MM Feb. 12 p25.   50w.   3
        RC June p6.   150w.   3

1870   MONTANA, Patsy, and Judy Rose. Mum and Me.   Look
        LK/LP 6039
        CMP Feb. p35.   150w.   3

1871   MOUNTAIN Line. Awayday.   Westwood WRS 109
        CMP July p38.   100w.   3

1872   MOUNTAIN Line. Dim Lights: Thick Smoke.   Red Rag
        RRR 011 (E)
        CMP Oct. p40.   200w.   3

1873   MURPHY, Michael. Flowing Free Forever.   Epic PE 34220
        CMP April p58.   125w.   3
        MG Feb. p56.   150w. $2\frac{1}{2}$
        MM Feb. 26 p25.   300w.   3

1874   NASHVILLE Bar Association. Chimer NBA 1011
        GP Dec. p152.   400w. $3\frac{1}{2}$

1875   NELSON, Jim. The Country Music of.   Mint Julep 2
        CMR Sept. p6-7.   50w.   0

1876   NELSON, Willie.   Before His Time.   RCA APL1-2210.
        Cart. APS1-2210
            CM Oct. p50. 200w. 4
            CS June 2 · p16. 250w. 2

1877   NELSON, Willie   Live.   RCA LSA 3277
            CMP Jan. p34. 150w. 3

1878   NELSON, Willie.   The Longhorn Jamboree.   Plantation PLP
        24 (Reissue)
            BSR No. 7 unpaged. 250w. 2½
            MM May 14 p33. 50w. 1½
            NK Spring p40. 50w. 2½

1879   NELSON, Willie.   To Lefty from Willie.   Columbia KC
        34695. Cart. CA-34695
            CMR Sept. p17. 300w. 3½
            CS Aug. 25 p19. 150w. 4½
            HF Sept. p141, 144. 300w. 3½
            RC Oct. p5. 100w. 5
            SR Nov. p110. 275w. 3

1880   NELSON, Willie.   The Troublemaker.   Columbia KC 34112.
        Cart. CA 34112
            CAC Jan. p392. 300w. 3
            CMP Feb. p36. 125w. 3
            CMR Aug. p23. 100w. 1½
            RS Jan. 13 p52-3. 200w. 3
            SR Feb. p88. 175w. 4

1881   NESMITH, Michael.   From a Radio Engine to the Photon
        Wing. Pacific Arts/Island ILPA 9486
            FOL May p2-3. 250w. 2½
            FOL Aug. p15, 22. 1050w. 4½
            MG June p52. 200w. 3½
            RRE May-June p59. 100w. 2½
            SOU Oct. p68. 150w. 4
            SR Oct. p115, 118. 250w. 3½
            ZZ April p46. 425w. 4

1882   NESMITH, Mike.   Pretty Much Your Standard Ranch Stash.
        Island ILPS 9440 (Reissue)
            CMP May p36. 150w. 5
            CMR June p11. 250w. 4

1883   NEW England Conservatory Country.   Fiddle Band.   Colum-
        bia M 33981
            JR V9/#3 unpaged. 200w. 3

1884   NEWBURY, Mickey.   Rusty Tracks.   ABC AH-44002
            CM June p50. 325w. 3
            CMP May p39. 150w. 5
            CMR July p23. 250w. 3

CS   May 5 p18.   150w.   3
RC   Aug. p2-3.   300w.   2
SR   May p91.   100w.   4

1885   NEWMAN, Jimmy C.   Progressive C. C.   Charly CRL 5006
(E)
CMP   Dec. p37.   250w.   5
MM   Dec. 3 p28.   100w. $3\frac{1}{2}$
NK   Autumn p43.   50w.   4

1886   NIELSEN, Chris.   Lady from Virginia.   MWS MWSL 5 509
CMR   April p33.   50w.   0

1887   NOAK, Eddie.   Look LK/LP 6041
CMP   Feb.   p37.   200w.   4

1888   O'KANE, Gerry.   Boot BOS 7167 (Canada)
CC   Feb.   p30.   50w.   3

1889   OVERSTREET, Tommy.   Vintage '77.   ABC DO 2071
CM   July p55.   200w.   2
CMR   July p20.   150w.   3
CS   June 2 p16.   100w.   3

1890   OWENS, Buck.   Buck 'Em.   Warner BS 2952
CMP   April p53.   300w.   5
CMP   July p40.   50w.   5
MM   June 25 p20.   300w. $1\frac{1}{2}$
NK   Summer p40.   25w. $2\frac{1}{2}$

1891   OXFORD, Vernon.   I Just Want to Be a Country Singer.
RCA LSA 3281 (E)
CMP   Feb.   p36.   75w.   3
CS   Feb. 10 p16.   250w. $3\frac{1}{2}$

1892   PACHECO, Tom.   The Outsider.   RCA APL1-1887
CIR   Jan. 31 p16.   350w.   4
HF   Feb.   p144.   50w.   3
RS   April 7 p76, 78.   250w.   3

1893   PARTON, Dolly.   All I Can Do.   RCA APL1-1665.   Cart.
APS1-1665
CAC   Feb.   p433.   200w. $4\frac{1}{2}$
CIR   Jan. 17 p15-6.   300w.   4
SR   Jan.   p96.   100w.   3

1894   PARTON, Dolly.   And Friends at the Goldband.   Goldband
MG   April p55.   150w. $2\frac{1}{2}$

1895   PARTON, Dolly.   Here You Come Again.   RCA APL1-2544
MM   Dec. 3 p23.   850w.   5

1896   PARTON, Dolly.   New Harvest... First Gathering.   RCA

APL 1-2188
    CIR   May 26   p57.   175w.   2
    CM   July p54.   400w.   3
    CMR   July p18.   500w.   4
    CRA   July p78.   350w.   2
    CS   June 2 p17.   200w.   3
    MM   April 9 p24.   750w. $2\frac{1}{2}$
    RC   July p5.   250w.   3
    RSP   May-June p56-8.   1650w. $3\frac{1}{2}$

1897   PARTON, Dolly.   Story.   CBS Embassy 31582 (Reissue)
        CMP   Oct.   p40.   250w.   5

1898   PARTON, Stella.   Country Sweet.   Elektra 1111
        CMP   Oct.   p41.   250w.   5
        MM   Dec. 3 p28.   100w. $1\frac{1}{2}$

1899   PARTON, Stella.   I Want to Hold You in My Dreams Tonight.
    Mint Julep 9 (E) (Reissue)
        CMP   Feb.   p34.   150w.   4
        CMR   June p17.   200w.   3
        MM   Feb. 12 p25.   50w.   1

1900   PAYCHECK, John Austin.   11 Months and 29 Days.   Epic
    KE 33943
        CMR   June p10.   100w.   3

1901   PAYCHECK, Johnny.   Slide Off Your Satin Sheets.   Epic
    PE 34693
        CMR   Sept.   p17.   125w.   3

1902   PAYNE, Roy.   Outlaw Heroes.   RCA XKL1-0163
        OLR   June p140.   25w.   3

1903   PEARSON, Johnny.   If You Leave Me Now.   Penny Farthing
    557 (E)
        MM   Oct. 1 p23.   50w.   1

1904   PETERSON, Coleen.   Beginning to Feel Like Home.   Capitol
    ST 11567
        OLR   Sept.   p223-4.   50w. $3\frac{1}{2}$

1905   PINE Island.   No Curb Service Anymore.   Green Mountain
    GMS 1052
        AU   Oct.   p177.   300w.   2

1906   PLACE, Mary Kay.   Tonite at the Capri Lounge; Loretta
    Haggers.   Columbia PC 34353.   Cart. CA 34353
        CIR   Jan. 17 p16.   325w. $2\frac{1}{2}$
        CIR   Jan. 31 p13.   150w.   2
        CM   Feb.   p52.   325w.   3
        HF   Feb.   p145.   100w.   3
        SR   Feb.   p100.   300w.   4

1907   POWELL, Patsy. Thank You for Loving Me. Country Mu-
       sic Recordings CHFR073
           CMP   July   p37.   125w.   3

1908   POZO Seco Singers with Don Williams. Best of. CBS Em-
       bassy EMB 31455 (E)
           CMP   Aug.   p36.   125w.   4
           CMR   Sept. p7.   100w.   3
           CMR   Sept. p16.   50w.   1
           MM   Aug. 6 p17.   50w.   2

1909   PRICE, Ray. Hank 'n' Me. ABC/Dot DOSD-2062. Cart.
       8310-2062
           CM   Feb.   p56.   425w.   1
           CS   May 19   p18.   200w.   3
           HF   Feb.   p145. 100w.   3
           MG   Jan.   100w. $3\frac{1}{2}$

1910   PRICE, Ray, and the Cherokee Cowboys. Reunited. ABC/
       Dot DO-2073
           CM   July   p54.   200w.   2
           CS   Jan. 2 p17.   100w. $2\frac{1}{2}$

1911   PRIDE, Charley. Best of, Vol. 3.   RCA APL 1-2023
           CAC   Jan.   p392.   125w.   3
           CMP   Feb.   p38.   75w.   4
           CMP   Nov.   p36.   125w.   4
           MM   Sept. 10 p20. 50w. $3\frac{1}{2}$

1912   PRIDE, Charley. She's Just an Old Love Turned Memory.
       RCA APL1-2261. Cart. APK1-2261. Cass. APS1-2261
           CMR   July   p22.   300w.   4
           GR   Aug.   p352. 50w.   3
           SR   Dec.   p76.   125w.   2

1913   PRIDE, Charley. Sunday Morning with Charley Pride. RCA
       APLI-1359. Cart. RCA APSI-1359
           CM   Sept.   p56.   75w.   3

1914   PROPHET, Ronnie. RCA PL 10164
           CMP   March p41.   125w.   2
           CMR   May   p33.   25w.   2
           MM   March 19 p31. 50w.   2

1915   RABBITT, Eddie. Elektra 7E 1105
           CMR   Sept. p15.   100w.   2

1916   RABBITT, Eddie. Rocky Mountain Memories. Elektra
       K52037
           CMP   May   p37.   200w.   4

1917   RAINWATER, Marvin. Some Old, Some New, Especially for
       You. Westwood WRS 101

CMP Feb. p35. 150w. 2

1918 RANDALL, Alan. World of. Decca SPA 492 (E) (Reissue)
      GR April p1608. 25w. $2\frac{1}{2}$

1919 RANKARNA, with Matt Radberg. Six Guys, Twelve Songs.
      Polydor (Sweden)
      MM Jan. 29 p25. 25w. 0

1920 REED, Jerry. Both Barrels. RCA APL1-1861
      CMR Sept. p7. 125w. 3

1921 REED, Jerry. East Bound and Down. RCA APL1-2516
      RRE Nov. -Dec. p30. 275w. 3

1922 REED, Jerry. Rides Again. RCA APLI-2346. Cart. APSI-
      2346
      SR Nov. p112, 114. 125w. 5

1923 REEVES, Del. 10th Anniversary. United Artists UALA687G.
      Cart. UALA687H
      CM April p52. 300w. 4

1924 REEVES, Del and Billie Joe Spears. By Request. United
      Artists UA LA 649-G
      CMR May p34. 150w. 3

1925 REEVES, Jim. I Love You Because. RCA APL 1-1224
      CMP March p43. 100w. 3
      CMR May p32. 50w. 3
      GR April p1608. 50w. $2\frac{1}{2}$
      MM March 19 p30. 50w. $1\frac{1}{2}$

1926 REEVES, Jim. It's Nothing to Me. RCA APL 1-2309 (Re-
      issue)
      CMP Aug. p36. 100w. 3
      GR Nov. p919. 75w. 3

1927 REEVES, Jim. A Legendary Performer. RCA RS 1078 (E)
      (Reissue)
      CAC Jan. p392. 150w. 2
      CMP Feb. p36. 100w. 4
      CMR March p28. 225w. 5

1928 RICH, Charlie. Take Me. Epic KE 34444. Cart. EA 34444
      CAC Sept. p221. 175w. $2\frac{1}{2}$
      CMR July p21. 300w. 3
      CRA Oct. p66-7. 50w. $2\frac{1}{2}$
      MM March 19 p30. 50w. $2\frac{1}{2}$
      NK Summer p38. 50w. $2\frac{1}{2}$
      SR July p100. 150w. 4

1929 RILEY, Jeannie C. Harper Valley PTA. Plantation 1

(Reissue)
    CAC Jan. p392. 125w. 3

1930   ROBBINS, Hargus. Country Instrumentalist of the Year.
        Elektra 7E 1110
        CK Oct. p65. 100w. 3

1931   ROBBINS, Marty. Adios Amigo.   Columbia 34448
        CAC Sept. p221. 150w. $2\frac{1}{2}$
        CM Aug. p48. 300w. 4
        CMP May p34. 150w. 3
        CMR May p33. 75w. 3
        MM March 19 p30. 250w. $3\frac{1}{2}$

1932   ROBBINS, Marty. Border Town Affair. Embassy EMB
        31391 (E) (Reissue)
        CAC Jan. p392 100w. 2
        CMP Feb. p38. 100w. 3
        CMR April p33. 25w. 3

1933   ROBBINS, Marty. Don't Let Me Touch You. Columbia KC
        35040
        MM Dec. 21 p15. 50w. 1

1934   ROBBINS, Marty. El Paso City. Columbia KC 34303.
        Cass. CA 34303
        CM Jan. p57-8. 400w. 3
        SMG Jan. p26. 125w. 1
        SR Jan. p98. 75w. 2

1935   RODGERS, Jimmie. Country Music Hall of Fame. RCA
        LPM 2531 (Reissue)
        CM March p56. 25w. 3

1936   RODRIGUEZ, Johnny. Reflecting. Mercury SRM 1-1110
        CM Feb. p54. 425w. 3
        CMP Feb. p34. 125w. 2
        CMR June p10. 150w. 3

1937   ROGERS, Kenny. United Artists UAS 30046
        CMP May p37. 150w. 4
        CMR July p21. 1500w. 4
        HF March p147. 200w. 4

1938   ROGERS, Kenny. Daytime Friends. United Artists LA
        754-G (E)
        MM Oct. 8 p29. 50w. 3

1939   ROY, Lee. RCA KXL1-0162 (Canada)
        OLR Sept. p224. 50w. $2\frac{1}{2}$

1940   RYAN, Charlie. Hot Rod. King 751
        NK Winter p37. 50w. 4

1941   SAMUELSONS.   The Swedish Way.   Impact R3253
       CMP Dec.   p38.   150w.   3

1942   SANDERS, Harlan.   Off and Running.   Epic KE 34305
       CS Jan.   p16.   100w.   3

1943   SAWYER, Ray.   Capitol ST 11591
       CAC Aug.   p168.   100w. $2\frac{1}{2}$
       CMP April p55.   150w.   2
       CMR June p16.   200w.   3
       HF April p148.   50w.   2

1944   SAYERS, Pete.   Watermelon Summer.   Xtra XTRA 1168 (Re-
       issue)
       CMP March p27.   150w.   5
       CMR May p31.   175w.   3

1945   SCOTT, Dewitt.   Keepin' It Country (Almost).   Midland MD
       10004
       CMR April p21.   125w.   4

1946   SCRUGGS, Earl.   Family Portrait.   Columbia 34346
       CMR Feb.   p33.   175w.   3
       CRA March p77.   100w. $3\frac{1}{2}$
       CS Feb. 10 p16.   250w. $3\frac{1}{2}$

1947   SCRUGGS, Earl.   Live from Austin City Limits.   Columbia
       PC 34464.   Cart.   PCA 34464
       CM Aug.   p46.   300w.   3

1948   SCRUGGS, Earl.   Strike Anywhere.   Columbia PC 34878.
       Cass.   PCT 34878.   Cass.   PCA 34878
       HF Nov.   75w. $3\frac{1}{2}$

1949   SEALS, Troy.   Columbia KC 34271
       CMR May p32.   125w.   3
       RS Jan. 13 p52-3.   200w. $2\frac{1}{2}$

1950   SHEPARD, Jean.   The Good Shepard.   United Artists 30044
       (E)
       CMP May p34.   200w.   5

1951   SHEPPARD, T. G.   Nashville Hitmaker.   Hitsville HVS 3002
       CMP April p55.   150w.   5
       NK Spring p39.   50w.   1

1952   SIOUX.   Anchor ANCL 2019
       CMR April p37.   100w.   2
       MM Jan. 22 p46.   50w.   2

1953   SMITH, Cal.   I Just Came Home to Count Memories.   MCA
       MCA-2266.   Cart.   MCA-T-2266
       CM Aug.   p50.   350w.   4

RC Oct. p6. 150w. $3\frac{1}{2}$

1954 SMITH, Carl. This Lady Loving Me. ABC AH 44005
    CMR Sept. p15. 125w. $3\frac{1}{2}$

1955 SMITH, Carl. A Way with Words. DJM DJF 20587 (E) (Re-
    issue)
    CMP May p39. 150w. 5
    MM May 14 p31. 50w. 1
    NK Spring p39. 50w. 3

1956 SMITH, Connie. Famous Country Music Makers. RCA PL
    42000 (E) (2 discs) (Reissue)
    CMP May p38. 200w. 5
    CMR July p23. 350w. 4

1957 SMITH, Connie. I Don't Wanna Talk It Over Anymore. Co-
    lumbia KC 34270
    CMR June p16. 200w. 3

1958 SMITH, Mack Allen. The Delta Sound. Redneck RLP500
    CMP May p37. 125w. 4
    CMR March p28. 175w. 5
    NK Spring p37. 250w. $4\frac{1}{2}$

1959 SMITH, Margo. Songbird. Warner Brothers BS 2955
    CMP April p53. 200w. 5

1960 SNOW, Hank. #104--Still Moving On. RCA APL1-2400.
    Cass. APS1-2400
    CM Oct. p51. 500w. 5
    RC Oct. p5. 50w. 4

1961 SONS of the Pioneers. MCA VIM 4099 (Japan) (Reissue)
    JEMF Autumn p157-60. 200w. 5
    OTM Summer p30-4. 500w. 4

1962 SONS of the Pioneers. Western Country. Granite 1007
    CS Jan. p16. 100w. 3
    RC April p6. 150w. 4

1963 SOVINE, Red. Teddy Bear. Starday SD 968X
    CMP Feb. p38. 150w. 3
    CMR April p33. 75w. 4
    CMR Aug. p21. 200w. 3

1964 SPEARS, Billy Jo. Everytime I Sing a Love Song. United
    Artists UAS 30109 (E)
    GR Nov. p919. 25w. 3
    MM Sept. 10 p20. 50w. 3

1965 SPEARS, Billy Jo. If You Want Me. United Artists LA
    748-G

MM   April 30 p20.   100w.   3

1966   SPEARS, Billy Jo.   I'm Not Easy.   United Artists LA 684G
       CS   Jan. 27 p20.   100w.   3
       RC   May p3.   200w.   3

1967   STAMPLEY, Joe.   All These Things.   ABD/Dot DOSD 2058
       CS   Feb. 10 p16.   150w. $3\frac{1}{2}$

1968   STAMPLEY, Joe.   Saturday Nite Dance.   Epic KE 34732
       RS   Nov. 17 p87, 89, 91.   200w. $3\frac{1}{2}$

1969   STAMPLEY, Joe.   Ten Songs About Her.   Epic 34356
       CM   Jan. p58.   250w.   4
       CMR   June p10.   200w.   3
       CS   Feb. 10 p16.   150w. $3\frac{1}{2}$

1970   STATLER Brothers.   The Country America Loves.   Mercury
       SRM 1-1125
       CM   June p53.   250w.   1
       CMR   June p10.   75w.   2
       RC   July p13.   200w.   4
       RRE   May-June p59.   75w.   3
       SR   July p101.   2

1971   STEAD, Joe.   Obscenities.   Sweet Folk and Country SFA
       1000 (E)
       FR   July p35.   250w.   2

1972   STEAGALL, Red.   Texas Red.   ABC Dot DOSD 2068
       CM   March p57.   200w.   1
       CMR   March p30.   150w.   5
       MG   Feb. p56.   125w. $1\frac{1}{2}$

1973   STEVENS, Ray.   Feel the Music.   Warner Brothers BS
       2997.   Cart. M8-2997
       CM   May p59.   300w.   3

1974   STEVENS, Ray.   For the Record.   Warner Brothers BS
       2914
       CM   Sept. p58.   75w.   2

1975   STEVENS, Stu.   Command Performance.   Major Oak MO5
       (E)
       CMR   Jan. p31.   425w.   4

1976   STEVENS, Suzanne.   Love Is the Only Game in Town.   Capi-
       tol ST 6439 (Canada)
       OLR   March p55.   25w.   3

1977   STEWART, Gary.   Your Place or Mine.   RCA APL1-2199.
       Cart. APS1-2199.   Cass. APK1-2199
       CM   Sept. p50.   350w.   4

CMP   July   p38.   200w.   5
CRA   July   p74.   200w.   3
CS   May 19 p18.   250w.   4
HF   Aug.   p122.   250w.   4½
RS   June 16 p71.   350w.   1½
SR   Sept.   p115.   150w.   4

1978   STEWART, Wynn. After the Storm. Playboy PB416. Cart.
        PBT 416
        CM   March   p59.   225w.   4
        HF   Feb.   p145.   100w.   4
        MG   Jan.   125w.   4½

1979   STONE Mt. Boys. Songs of the Pioneers. Old Homestead
        OHRC 90032
        PIC   July   p64.   125w.   2

1980   STRINGBAND. Thanks to the Following. Nick 4 (Canada)
        CC   March   p34.   50w.   3

1981   SULLIVAN, John. Mint Julep JULEP4
        CMP   Dec.   p38.   125w.   4

1982   TAYLOR, Allan. The American Album. Rockburgh CREST
        28 (Reissue)
        CMP   Nov.   p37.   200w.   3
        FR   Sept.   p34.   150w.   3
        MM   Sept. 3 p44.   175w.   3½

1983   TENNESSEE Stud. Making Music for Money. Tank BSS 166
        (E)
        CMR   March   p27.   125w.   0

1984   38 Special. A&M SP4638
        CRA   July   p78-9. 200w.   2
        CS   June 2 p17.   150w.   1½
        VV   Aug. 1 p51.   50w.   2

1985   THOMPSON, Hank. Back in the Swing of Things. ABC/
        Dot DOSD 2060
        AU   Feb.   p89.   400w.   3

1986   THOMPSON, Hank. Country Sounds of. Music for Pleasure
        MFP50301 (E) (Reissue)
        CMP   Jan.   p38-9. 100w.   4

1987   THOMPSON, Hank. The Thompson Touch. ABC/Dot DO-
        2069. Cart. DO8T-2069
        CM   Aug.   p46.   250w.   2
        CMP   July   p40.   50w.   5
        CMR   Aug.   p22.   400w.   3
        MM   May 14 p26.   375w.   4½
        NK   Autumn p42.   25w.   2½

1988   THOMPSON, Sue.   Story.   DJM DJD28024 (E) (2 discs) (Re-
        issue)
            NK   Winter p34.   75w.   3½

1989   TILLIS, Mel.   Heart Healer.   MCA MCA-2252.   Cart. T-
        2252.   Cass. C-2252
            SR   Aug.   p100.   100w.   3

1990   TILLMAN, Floyd.   Best.   Columbia KC 34334
            AU   Nov.   p133.   500w.   3½
            CM   Feb.   p54.   350w.   5
            CMR June p10.   200w.   4
            HF   Feb.   p145.   100w.   4
            MG   Jan.   100w.   3½
            RS   Jan. 13 p52-3.   200w.   3½
            SR   May   p92.   250w.   4

1991   TRAVIS, Dave.   Knight of the Road.   Stoof MU 7426
            CMP May   p35.   300w.   5

1992   TRAVIS, Merle.   Merle Travis' Guitar.   Capitol SM-650
        (Reissue)
            CM   March p61.   50w.   4

1993   TRENT, Buck.   Bionic Banjo.   ABC-Dot DOSO 2058
            CMR March p29.   100w.   4
            FOL May   p8.   25w.   2

1994   TRENT, Buck.   Oh Yeah! ABC/Dot 2077
            CMP Oct.   p44.   150w.   3

1995   TUBB, Ernest.   Story.   MCA MCA2-4040 (2 discs) (Reissue)
            CMR March p28,   350w.   5

1996   TUBB, Ernest and Loretta Lynn.   Story.   MCA 2-4000 (2
        LP set) (Reissue)
            CMR July   p23.   300w.   3

1997   TUCKER, Tanya.   Here's Some Love.   MCA 2213
            CM   Jan.   p55.   300w.   3
            CMR April p35.   100w.   4
            SR   Jan.   p99.   100w.   4

1998   TUCKER, Tanya.   Ridin' Rainbows.   MCA MCA-2253.   Cart.
        MCAT-2253
            CMP April p57.   150w.   3
            MM   June 11 p19.   175w.   1½
            SR   June   p115.   75w.   0

1999   TUCKER, Tanya.   You Are So Beautiful.   Columbia PC
        34733 PCT 34733 PCA 34733
            CMP Nov.   p37.   125w.   5
            HF   Nov.   50w.   3½

2000   TWITTY, Conway. Best of, Vol. 2. MCA 2235. Cart.
        MCAT 2235 (Reissue)
            CM   March p57. 300w. 3
            GR   Aug. p353. 50w. 3

2001   TWITTY, Conway. I Can't See without You. MCA DL75335
            NK   Summer p38. 25w. 1

2002   TWITTY, Conway. I've Already Loved You in My Mind.
        MCA MCA 2293
            CM   Nov. p36-7. 200w. 3

2003   TWITTY, Conway. Play, Guitar, Play. MCA 2262
            CMP   May p38. 150w. 4
            CS   May 5 p19. 200w. $4\frac{1}{2}$
            GR   Aug. p353. 50w. 3
            MM   July 16 p27. 50w. $3\frac{1}{2}$
            NK   Summer p38. 50w. 3

2004   TWITTY, Conway and Loretta Lynn. Dynamic Duo. MCA
        MCA 2278
            CMR   Sept. p15. 125w. $2\frac{1}{2}$

2005   VIPERS Skiffle Group. Skiffle Hits. One-Up OU 2148 (E)
        (Reissue)
            CAC   Feb. p437. 200w. 3
            CMR   Jan. p29. 200w. 3

2006   WADE, Al. Al Wade Sings. Sunshine Me SM3 (E)
            CMR   March p27. 50w. 0

2007   WAGONER, Dale. Kentucky Style Steel. Midland MD 10005
            CMR   April p19-20. 250w. 5

2008   WAKELEY, Jimmy. Presents Merle Travis. Shasta 523
        (Reissue)
            RSP   March-April p18. 175w. $3\frac{1}{2}$

2009   WAKELEY, Jimmy. The Way They Were Back Then. Shasta
        LP517. Cart. 8T-517
            CM   Jan. p56-7. 475w. 3

2010   WATSON, Gene. Because You Believed in Me. Capitol ST
        11529
            CMR   Jan. p28. 75w. 2

2011   WATSON, Gene. Paper Rosie. Capitol E-ST 11597
            CM   June p52. 300w. 3
            CMP   April p57. 150w. 5
            CMR   June p15. 200w. 3
            CS   May 5 p18. 125w. 3

2012   WEATHERLY, Jim. AB AB 982

CS   March 24 p16.   150w.   3

2013   WEIR, Rusty.   Black Hat Saloon.   Columbia PC 34319
       MG   Jan.   50w. $\frac{1}{2}$
       RS   Jan.   p52-3.   200w. $2\frac{1}{2}$

2014   WELLS, Tracy.   Country Sunshine.   Homespun Records HRL
       124 (E)
       CMR   March   p27.   50w.   4

2015   WEST, Dottie.   When It's Just You and Me.   United Artists
       UA-LA740-G.   Cart.   UA-EA740-H
       SR   Nov.   p116.   150w.   3

2016   WHELAN, Cliff.   Welcome to My World.   Sweet Folk and
       Country SFA 061 (E)
       CMR   June   p16.   150w.   3

2017   WHITE, Bob.   Collectors' Series.   Front Hall FHR 011
       CFS   Summer   p19.   125w.   4
       FR   Aug.   p32.   150w.   3
       RC   Aug.   p61.   150w.   3

2018   WHITMAN, Slim.   Home on the Range.   United Artists UATV
       30102
       CMP   Oct.   p40.   200w.   3
       MM   Oct.   8 p29.   50w. $1\frac{1}{2}$

2019   WHITMAN, Slim.   Red River Valley.   United Artists UAS
       29993 (E)
       CMP   March   p37.   150w.   1

2020   WIGGINS, Roy.   Memory Time.   Power Pak PO 226
       CMR   April   p19.   200w.   5

2021   WILKINS, Little David.   King of All the Taverns.   MCA
       MCA-2215.   Cart.   MCAT-2215
       CM   Jan.   p55.   575w.   2
       CS   Jan.   p16.   100w.   3

2022   WILLIAMS, Diana.   Capitol ST 11587
       CMR   June   p7.   75w.   3
       SR   April   p100.   166w.   2

2023   WILLIAMS, Doc.   Best.   GW 102 (Reissue)
       CMP   March   p44.   150w.   5
       CMR   March   p30.   150w.   4

2024   WILLIAMS, Don.   Country Boy.   ABC DO-2088
       MM   Oct.   16 p24.   350w.   3
       NK   Autumn   p43.   25w.   3
       RS   Nov.   3 p108.   300w.   2

2025   WILLIAMS, Don. Visions. ABC/Dot DO-2064
          CM   May p58.   300w.   2
          CMR April p29-30.   600w.   5
          GR   April p1608.   25w. $2\frac{1}{2}$
          MM   Feb. 19 p25.   350w. $2\frac{1}{2}$

2026   WILLIAMS, Hank. The Essential. MGM 2354004 (Reissue)
          CAC Jan. p392.   150w.   3
          CMP Jan. p35.   50w.   3

2027   WILLIAMS, Hank. Live at the Grand Ole Opry. MGM
       1-5019 (Reissue)
          CAC Jan. p392.   150w.   3
          CM   March p62.   50w.   4
          CS   Jan. 27 p20.   350w. $3\frac{1}{2}$

2028   WILLIAMS, Hank, Jr. One Night Stands. Warner Bros.
       BS 2988.   Cart. M82988.   Cass. M52988
          CIR Nov. 10 p60-1.   175w.   4
          CM   July p52.   300w.   3
          CRA July p74.   200w.   3
          SR   Sept. p115, 118.   150w.   4

2029   WILLIAMS, Leona. A Woman Walked Away. DJM DJM
       22060 (E)
          CMP March p40.   150w.   5

2030   WILLIAMS, Texas T. 14 All-Time Country Hits. Homespun
       HRL115
          CMP May p33.   50w.   3

2031   WILLIAMS, Tim. Writin' This Song. Maple Haze MH 7637
       (Canada)
          CC   March p34.   50w.   3

2032   WILLS, Bob. In Concert. Capitol SKBB 11550 (2 discs)
          SR   May p92.   250w.   4

2033   WILLS, Bob. The Late Bob Wills' Original Texas Playboys
       Today.   Capitol ST 11612
          AU   Sept. p95.   600w.   4
          CM   Aug. p47.   250w.   4

2034   WILLS, Bob. Remembering...the Greatest Hits of Bob Wills.
       Columbia KC 34108 (Reissue)
          CMR Jan. p28.   125w.   5

2035   WILLS, Bob. The Tiffany Transcriptions. Tishomingo
       TSHO-BEO1
          CM   Jan. p54.   375w.   5
          OTM Summer p35.   300w.   4

2035a WILLS, Bob. Today. Capitol ST 11612 (American Issue)

        CMR   July p20. 250w. 3
        OTM   Summer p29. 250w. 3

2036   WILSON, Larry Jon. Loose Change.   Monument MG7615
        MM   Oct. 22 p22. 200w. 4

2037   WILSON, Steve, Jr. My Kinda Country.   Arny's Shack ASO10
        CMR   June p12. 200w. 3

2038   WINSTON, Mark. A Word Before You Go.   Dara MPA 019
(E)
        CMR   Aug. p23. 150w. 3

2039   WISE, Chubby. Grassy Fiddle.   Stoneway 157
        PIC   Jan. p53. 120w. $2\frac{1}{2}$

2040   WISE, Chubby. Sweet Milk and Peaches.   Stoneway STY-
164
        BGU   Sept. p23. 75w. 3
        PIC   Dec. p60. 125w. 1

2041   WISEMAN, Mac. Story. CMH 9001 (2 discs) (Reissue)
        AU   Sept. p98. 450w. 4

2042   WOODETTES. Just One Rose Will Do.   Glory Land 117
        PIC   Dec. p55. 150w. $1\frac{1}{2}$
        RC   Oct. p3. 75w. $2\frac{1}{2}$

2043   WYNETTE, Tammy. Let's Get Together.   Epic KE-34694
Cart. EA-34694
        CMP   July p40. 225w. 5
        CS   Aug. 25 150w. 2
        SR   Nov. p118, 120. 300w. 3

2044   WYNETTE, Tammy. No Charge.   Embassy EMB 31386 (E)
(Reissue)
        CMP   Feb. p36. 150w. 5

2045   WYNETTE, Tammy. You and Me.   Epic PE 34289
        CAC   Feb. p433. 150w. 4
        CMP   Jan. p41. 125w. 4

2046   YONCO, Frank. Drinking the Beer and Singing a Country
Song. Sweet Folk and Country SFA071 (E)
        CMP   April p57. 100w. 3

2047   YOUNG, Faron. The Best, Vol. 2.   Mercury SRM 1-1130
(Reissue)
        CMP   April p55. 125w. 4
        CMR   June p11. 150w. 3
        MM   Feb. 19 p22. 50w. $3\frac{1}{2}$

2048   YOUNG, Steve. Renegade Picker.   RCA PL 11759 (E)

(Reissue)
    CMP Feb. p35. 250w. 5
    CMR June p11. 200w. 3
    MM Jan. 1 p15. 300w. 4
    ZZ March 250w. $3\frac{1}{2}$

2049 YOUNG, Steve. Seven Bridges Road. Sonet SNTF 705 (E)
    CMP Jan. p40. 150w. 4
    CMR Jan. p30. 300w. 5
    ZZ March p17. 250w. $3\frac{1}{2}$

OLD TIME MUSIC and BLUEGRASS

The significant movement in this field is not the decay of the Nashville Sound, but the re-emergence of older styles that are rapidly capturing a new audience. These older styles center upon "bluegrass" and the old time Southern string band.

Old time music is pre-bluegrass, commercial folk music and comes from the Southern mountains. It usually features fiddles, banjos and guitars. The term "bluegrass" does not refer to a geographic area but comes from the name of Bill Monroe's string band, the Blue Grass Boys. Bluegrass music is recognizable and distinctive; it features a high-pitched, strident style of two- three- or four-part harmony and five instruments--fiddle, guitar, mandolin, string bass, and five-string banjo. Bluegrass has been around for three decades but has never been an overwhelming commercial success.

Today the primitive, non-commercial sound of bluegrass music is stirring up a revival of interest in the more traditional roots of country music. There is something about this hard-driving sound that has captured the imagination not only of rural people but urban youngsters. The growth of summer-time bluegrass festivals has been phenomenal and to attend one is to have an almost déjà vu feeling of Woodstock. Even more significant is the growth of record companies recording and releasing this style of music.

According to the reviews, the best of 1977 were:

ARKANSAS Sheiks. Whiskey Before Breakfast. Bay 204
AULDRIDGE, Mike. Flying Fish FFO29
BAKER, Kenny. Plays Bill Monroe. County 761
BLAKE, Norman. Live at McCabe's. Takoma D 1052
BLAKE, Norman and Red Rector. County 755
BLUE Sky Boys. County 752
CLIFTON, Bill and Red Rector. Are You from Dixie? Bear
    Family 15013 (West Germany)
GRISMAN, David. The Rounder Album. Rounder 0069
HUNTER, Tommy. Deep in Tradition. June Appal 007
MELFORD, Michael. Mandolin Fantasy. Flying Fish 023
RED Clay Ramblers. Twisted Laurel. Flying Fish 030
REED, Ola Belle. My Epitaph. Folkways FA 2493
RENO, Don and Bill Harrell. Dear Old Dixie. CMH 6201
SELDOM Scene. New Album. Rebel 1561

2050   ABRAMS, Bob and Steve Mote.   Private Release 30024
        CFS   Summer   p20.   125w.   2
        OTM   Spring   p28-9.   200w. $2\frac{1}{2}$

2051   The ACME Bluegrass Co.   99 44/100% Pure Instrumental.
        Old Homestead 90071
        BGU   Feb.   p29.   50w. $3\frac{1}{2}$
        PIC   May   p66.   150w.   4

2052   The ACME Country Band.   Bluegrass Machine.   Westwood
        Recordings WRS 114 (E)
        BGU   July   p32.   275w.   4
        CMR   June   p13.   300w.   4

2053   ALEXANDER Brothers.   One Way Up Above.   Pine Tree
        536
        PIC   Feb.   p55.   75w. $2\frac{1}{2}$

2054   The ARKANSAS Sheiks.   Whiskey Before Breakfast.   Bay 204
        BGU   Jan.   p29.   75w. $4\frac{1}{2}$
        FOL   June   p24-5.   375w. $4\frac{1}{2}$
        OTM   Spring   p28.   300w. $2\frac{1}{2}$
        PIC   June   p66.   225w.   4

2055   ARWEN Mountain.   Five of a Kind.   Chelsea House 2003
        BGU   Sept.   p22.   50w.   3
        PIC   Dec.   p56.   125w.   3
        SO   July/Aug.   p49-50.   200w.   3

2056   AULDRIDGE, Mike.   Flying Fish FF 029
        BGU   May   p34.   300w.   3
        CS   Feb. 24   p27.   350w.   3
        GP   March   p112.   200w.   4
        PIC   Sept.   p60.   150w. $4\frac{1}{2}$
        RC   Oct.   p12.   150w.   5
        RSP   March-April   p19.   450w. $4\frac{1}{2}$

2057   B. G. Express.   Outlet Recordings STLP-1007
        BGU   Sept.   p22.   50w.   2
        PIC   Dec.   p58-9.   125w. $1\frac{1}{2}$

2058   BAKER, Duck.   There's Something for Everybody in America.
        Kicking Mule 124
        PIC   July   p65.   125w.   3

2059   BAKER, Kenny.   Plays Bill Monroe.   County 761
        BGU   April   p19.   200w. $4\frac{1}{2}$
        MN   8:3   p16-7.   400w. $3\frac{1}{2}$
        OTM   Spring   p26.   550w. $2\frac{1}{2}$
        PIC   Aug.   p58.   275w. $4\frac{1}{2}$
        RSP   Jan.-Feb.   p25.   125w.   3

2060   BARBEE, Eddie.   The Eddie Barbee Tapes.   Pine Breeze

PBK 903
   HF   July   p148.   250w.   4

2061   BARENBERG, Russ.   Bluegrass Guitar: Country Cooking.
   Music Minus One 185
      PIC   Jan.   p52.   100w.   3

2062   BARRIER Boys & the Ozark Mountain Boys.   Pickin' and
   Singin'.   Old Homestead OHCS 108 (Reissue)
      BGU   Oct.   p24.   350w.   2

2063   BEASLEY, Larry.   On Banjo.   Alpha Records 07511-29
      BGU   March   p26.   125w. $3\frac{1}{2}$

2064   BELLE, Ola.   Reed My Epitaph.   Folkways FA 2493
      RSP   1:3   p18.   225w. $2\frac{1}{2}$

2065   BERESFORD Creek.   Beresford Creek I.   Live Oak LOR-
   1001
      BGU   Oct.   p26.   75w.   3

2066   BERLINE, Byron, Sam Bush and Mark O'Connor.   In Concert.   Mark O'Connor Productions 2
      PIC   Dec.   p55.   250w. $1\frac{1}{2}$

2067   BLAKE, Norman.   HDS 701
      CMR   Sept.   p15.   125w. $3\frac{1}{2}$
      OTM   Winter   p28.   200w.   3

2068   BLAKE, Norman.   Live at McCabe's.   Takoma D-1052
      AU   Aug.   p81.   300w.   3
      BGU   May   p40.   250w.   4
      GP   May   p128.   100w.   4
      PIC   Sept.   p60.   150w.   5
      RSP   March-April   p24.   50w. $4\frac{1}{2}$
      SR   June   p116.   100w.   3

2069   BLAKE, Norman.   Old and New.   Flying Fish 010
      CMR   May   p33.   1
      SR   Jan.   p100.   150w.   4

2070   BLAKE, Norman.   Whisky Before Breakfast.   Rounder 0063
      CMP   Nov.   p38.   150w.   3

2071   BLAKE, Norman and Red Rector.   County 755
      BGU   Jan.   p22.   150w.   5
      CMR   March   p30.   350w.   5
      FOL   Sept.   p11-2.   100w. $3\frac{1}{2}$
      PIC   June   p66.   225w.   4

2072   BLAYLOCK, Bill.   A Gentleman and His Banjo.   Atteiram
   API-L-1539
      BGU   Jan.   p26.   100w.   5

2073   BLUE Denim. Vol. 2. Old Homestead 90061
        BGU May p37. 150w. 4

2074   BLUE Sky Boys. County Records 752
        PIC March p50. 125w. 5
        BGU April p20, 21. 275w. 4

2075   BLUE Sky Boys. Bluebird AXM2-5525 (2 discs) (Reissue)
        BGU April p20, 21. 275w. 4
        CM March p56. 50w. 3

2076   BLUE Sky Boys. Rounder 0052
        BGU April p20, 21. 275w. 4
        CMP Sept. p38. 400w. 5
        PIC June p71. 325w. 4
        RSP Jan. -Feb. p25. 150w. 3½

2077   BLUE Sky Boys. Presenting the Blue Sky Boys. JEMF 104
        (Reissue)
        BGU July p34. 150w. 4
        PIC Aug. p58. 275w. 4½

2078   BLUEGRASS Blackjacks. Blackjack's Country. Pine Tree
        Records, PTSLP-502
        BGU Feb. p29. 75w. 4

2079   BLUEGRASS Blend. Blendin' Grass. Cascade BGB 101
        BGU July p32. 125w. 4

2080   BLUEGRASS Blossoms. A Slice of Bluegrass. Zytglogge-
        Verlag 210 (Switzerland)
        CMR Aug. p22. 450w. 3

2081   The BLUEGRASS Experience. Live at the Pier. Round-
        hole Records 6564
        BGU Jan. p30. 75w. 3
        PIC May p63. 100w. 2½

2082   BLUEGRASS Five. Bluegrass from the Missouri Hills. Pro-
        fessional Artist 7633-97
        BGU June p37. 75w. 2½

2083   BLUEGRASS Kats. Kattin' Around. Playhouse 256
        BGU June p40. 100w. 3
        PIC Jan. p52-3. 300w. 3

2084   BLUEGRASS Kinfolks. Big Country Bluegrass (no serial no.)
        BGU Nov. p29. 100w. 2½

2085   BLUEGRASS Long Distance. Long Distance Bluegrass. Ce-
        zame CEZ 1033 (France)
        BGU Sept. p16. 125w. 0

2086   BLUEGRASS Saturday Night.   Kentucky Bound.   River City
        Records PD 02175
            BGU   May   p43.   50w. $2\frac{1}{2}$
            PIC   Oct.   p59-60.   200w.   3

2087   BLUEGRASS Special.   Mountains, Mines and Memories.   King
        Bluegrass 554
            PIC   Feb.   p52.   225w.   3

2088   BLUEGRASS Symphony.   The Road.   Studio 1 Records SLP
        035
            BGU   March   p27.   100w.   3

2089   BLUEGRASS Travelers.   Raisin' Cain.   Mag Records RSE-
        447
            BGU   April   p24.   75w.   2

2090   BOGGY Bottom String Band.   American Banjo.   Tennessee
        Dulcimer Works.
            PIC   March   p50.   200w.   2

2091   BOND, Johnny.   Rides Again.   Shasta LP 516
            CMR   June   p7.   250w.   4

2092   The BONHAM Brothers.   Two Generations.   Kiamachi KMB
        106
            BGU   Aug.   p33.   150w.   0

2093   BOOT Hill.   Steel Rail.   Ateiram APIL-1548
            BGU   Nov.   p26.   200w.   3
            PIC   Nov.   p54.   100w. $2\frac{1}{2}$

2094   BOTTLE Hill.   Light Our Way Along the Highway.   Biograph
        RC6009
            BGU   Feb.   p24.   75w.   4
            MN   V7/#1   p17.   400w. $3\frac{1}{2}$
            PIC   Feb.   p54.   75w.   3

2095   BOYD, Bill.   Bill Boyd's Cowboy Ramblers.   RCA Bluebird
        AXM2-5503 (2 discs) (Reissue)
            JEMF   no. 46   p103.   100w.   5

2096   The BOYS From Indiana.   One More Bluegrass Show.   King
        Bluegrass KB 545
            BGU   Jan.   p28.   150w.   5

2097   BRANDENBURGER, Kirk.   Fiddlin' Around.   Professional
        Artist 7733145
            BGU   Nov.   p26.   125w.   3

2098   BREAKFAST Special.   Rounder 3012
            BGU   Sept.   p21.   200w.   0
            PIC   Aug.   p61-2.   250w.   4

2099   BROCK, Dan & Jenny Brock.   High Flying.   Lemco 770323
       BGU   Sept.   p19.   200w.   3

2100   BROCKETT, Jaime.   North Mountain Velvet.   Adelphi AD-
       1028
       AU   Oct.   p173.   250w.   4
       BGU   Oct.   p24, 25.   300w.   0

2101   BROTHER Oswald and Charlie Collins.   Oz and Charlie.
       Rounder 0060
       PIC   Feb.   p52.   250w.   3

2102   The BROTHERS 'n Bluegrass.   BNB 0041
       BGU   July   p35.   75w.   4

2103   BROWN, Abe.   Banjo Revolution.   CEA - LP1001
       PIC   May   p61.   200w.   3

2104   BROWN, Hylo.   CCL 1124 (West Germany) (Reissue)
       RSP   Jan. -Feb.   p30.   250w.   3

2105   BROWN, Milton.   Taking Off.   String 804 (E) (Reissue)
       CMP   Oct.   p41.   250w.   5
       FR   Dec.   p27.   100w.   4
       MM   Sept. 3   p46.   50w.   4

2106   BROWN, Milton/Clayton McMichen.   MCA VIM 4014 (Japan)
       JEMF   Autumn   p157-60.   200w.   5
       OTM   Summer   p30-4.   500w.   4

2107   BRUCE and Dad.   Mandolin and Guitar Instrumentals (private
       pressing).   Frank L. Carter 702 Yorkhaven Rd. Cincinnati,
       Ohio 45240
       BGU   Jan.   p30.   75w. $2\frac{1}{2}$

2108   BRUNER, Cliff/Rice Brothers Gang.   MCA VIM 4016 (Japan)
       (Reissue)
       JEMF   Autumn   p157-60.   200w.   5
       OTM   Summer   p30-4.   500w.   4

2109   BRYSON, Wally and the Blaylock Brothers.   Just Jamming.
       Davis 33026
       PIC   March   p53.   75w.   5

2110   BURKE, John.   Touring That City.   Artist's Records 750115
       BGU   June   p41.   50w. $2\frac{1}{2}$
       PIC   June   p68.   100w.   4

2111   BURNS, Jethro.   Flying Fish FFO42
       CAD   Nov.   p31, 32.   25w.   5
       RC   Nov.   p11.   100w.   4

2112   BUSH, Sam and Alan Munde.   Together Again for the First

Time.   Ridge Runner RRR 0007
BGU   Sept.   p20.   200w.   3

2113   CALLAHAN Brothers.   Old Homestead OHM 90031 (Reissue)
BGU   Nov.   p28.   300w. $2\frac{1}{2}$

2114   CANTRELL, Kenny and the Green Valley Boys.   Home
Sweet Home Revisited.   SPBGMA 7601
PIC   Jan.   p55.   160w.   2

2115   CARAWAN, Guy.   Green Rocky Road.   June Appal 021
CFS   Summer   p22-3.   150w.   4
FR   June   p25.   300w.   2
OTM   Spring   p29.   100w.   2
PIC   Oct.   p57.   250w. $3\frac{1}{2}$
RSP   1:3   p22.   125w. $2\frac{1}{2}$
SO   March-April   p51.   100w. $4\frac{1}{2}$

2116   CAROLINA Tar Heels.   Can't You Remember?   Bear Family
15507 (West Germany) (Reissue)
CMR   June   p9.   350w.   4

2117   CARPENTER, French.   Elzic's Farewell.   Kanawha 301 (Reissue)
FOL   May   p4.   150w.   4

2118   The CARROLL County Ramblers.   Adelphi AD-2006
BGU   Sept.   p18.   200w.   4
CFS   Autumn   p27.   100w.   4

2119   CARTER, Bruce and Frank Carter.   Homespun Bluegrass.
(no label) 6081 N5
PIC   Oct.   p59.   100w. $2\frac{1}{2}$

2120   CARTER Family.   MCA VIM 4012 (Japan)
JEMF   Autumn   p157-60.   200w.   5
OTM   Summer   p30-4.   500w.   4

2121   CARTER Family.   Country's First Family.   Columbia KC
34266
CMR   Jan.   p31.   200w.   3

2122   CARTER Family.   On Border Radio.   JEMF 101 (Reissue)
CM   March   p56.   50w.   3

2123   The CENTRAL Park Sheiks.   Honeysuckle Rose.   Flying
Fish 026
BSR   No. 7   unpaged.   200w.   3
CRA   April   p110.   75w.   5
CS   April 7   p19.   300w. $4\frac{1}{2}$
GP   June   p136.   75w. $3\frac{1}{2}$
OTM   Winter   p28.   50w.   3
PIC   Sept.   p62.   200w.   2

SO   May/June p47, 49.   225w.   4½
SR   June p95, 96.   75w.   2

2124   CHANDLER, Dillard.   The End of an Old Song.   Folkways
       FA 2418
          OTM   Spring p23.   250w.   3½

2125   CITY Limits Bluegrass Band.   Live at the Oxford Hotel.
       Biscuit City 1309
          BGU   May p44.   75w.   3

2126   CLEMENTS, Vasser.   The Bluegrass Session.   Flying Fish
       FF038
          CAD   Nov. p31.   75w.   2½
          RC   Dec. p8.   150w.   4½

2127   CLIFTON, Bill.   Clifton & Company.   County 765
          BGU   Oct. p24.   150w.   4
          PIC   Dec. p55-6.   250w.   3½

2128   CLIFTON, Bill.   Come by the Hills.   County 751
          AU   Oct. p180.   400w.   4

2129   CLIFTON, Bill and Red Rector.   Another Happy Day.   Coun-
       ty 758
          BGU   Oct. p24.   150w.   4
          MN   V8/#2 p16.   500w.   2½
          PIC   July p69.   225w.   4½

2130   CLIFTON, Bill and Red Rector.   Are You from Dixie.   Bear
       Family 15013
          BGU   July p33.   125w.   5
          CMP   Nov. p36.   125w.   4
          CMR   March p28.   325w.   5
          PIC   Aug. p60.   200w.   3

2131   CLINE, Curly Ray.   Bread and Water.   Rebel SLP 1566
          BGU   Dec. p19.   200w.   2½

2132   COBB, Ray.   Traditional Songs of Bluegrass.   Old Home-
       stead OHS 90057
          OTM   Winter p27.   100w.   2

2133   COLLINS, G. F.   Bluegrass Pickin.   Heritage VII
          MN   V8/#1 p17.   125w.   3

2134   COLLINS, Randall and Jerry Moore.   Georgia Fiddler.   At-
       teiram 1536
          PIC   March p55.   150w.   4

2135   The CONNER Brothers.   County 763
          BGU   August p31.   200w.   4
          RSP   1:3 p24.   75w.   2

2136   CORNBREAD.   Sum of Us Records D2010
       PIC   June   p75.   100w.   4

2137   CORPORATE Square.   Atteiram Record Co.   API-L-1533
       BGU   Feb.   p30.   75w.   3

2138   The COUNTRY Coalition.   Potato Pickers.   White Cloud 5022
       PIC   Aug.   p75-6.   150w.   2

2139   COUNTRY Cookin' with the Fiction Brothers.   Flying Fish
       019
       MN   V7/#1   p16.   200w.   1½

2140   COUNTRY Express.   Hadley 1227 (Australia)
       PIC   March   p53.   350w.   5

2141   COUNTRY Gazette.   Out to Lunch.   Flying Fish FFO27
       BGU   May   p40, 41.   200w.   2
       RC   May   p9.   150w.   3
       SR   May   p84.   150w.   4

2142   COUNTRY Gazette.   What a Way to Make a Living.   Ridge
       Runner 0008
       BGU   Aug.   p30.   225w.   4
       CMP   Sept.   p36.   250w.   4
       CMR   Sept.   p17.   200w.   3½
       MM   Nov.   5 p19.   200w.   2
       RSP   1:3   p21.   500w.   3½

2143   The COUNTRY Gentlemen.   Joe's Last Train.   Rebel SLP-
       1559
       BGU   May   p34.   200w.   3
       CS   May   19 p19.   200w.   3
       PIC   Aug.   p59.   225w.   2½

2144   COUNTRY Ham.   Old Time Mountain Music.   Vetco LP 510
       BGU   Aug.   p32.   100w.   4
       PIC   Aug.   p77.   250w.   5

2145   COUNTRY Ramblers.   Heartbreakers.   Music Club 11002
       (Switzerland)
       BGU   March   p26.   125w.   3

2146   CRARY, Dan.   Lady's Fancy.   Rounder 0099
       GP   Dec.   p152.   75w.   3
       PIC   Aug.   p64-5.   375w.   3

2147   CRAWFORD, Roy.   Alabama Fiddling--Roy Crawford Style.
       Davis Unlimited Records DU 33027
       BGU   March   p24.   175w.   5
       PIC   Aug.   p77.   225w.   0
       RSP   1:3   p24-5.   300w.   2½

2148   CROSSROADS. Bluegrass Memories.   CMH-6211
        BGU   April p19. 100w. 3
        OTM   Spring p27, 30. 150w. 1

2149   CROUCH, Dub and Norman Ford.   Footprints in the Snow.
        King Bluegrass Records KB-548
        BGU   Feb. p25. 125w. 4
        MN   V8/#1 p17. 200w. 2½

2150-1 CROW, Alvin. High Riding. Polydor PD 1-6102.   Cart.
        8T-1-PD1-6102
        CM   Sept. p50. 325w. 4
        RC   Oct. p10. 125w. 3½
        VV   Nov. 28 p66. 50w. 3

2152   CROW, Alvin and the Pleasant Valley Boys.   Long Neck NR
        6751
        AU   Oct. p181. 600w. 4
        CRA   April p110. 75w. 3

2153   CROWE, J. D. Starday SLP 489
        RSP   1:3 p17-8. 300w. 2½

2154   CUSTER'S Grass Band. Northwind [no serial number]
        BGU   Nov. p27. 200w. 3

2155   DALHART, Vernon. Old Time Songs.   Davis Unlimited DU-
        33030 (Reissue)
        BGU   Aug. p34. 175w. 4
        OTM   Winter p23. 250w. 3
        PIC   July p68. 200w. 4½
        RSP   March-April p23. 400w. 4½

2156   DAN, Curly, Wilma Ann and the Danville Mountain Boys.
        New Bluegrass Songs. Old Homestead 90053
        OTM   Winter p26. 50w. 3
        PIC   June p70. 150w. 4

2157   DAVIS, Gary. Finger Picking Good. G. D. Productions
        467576
        BGU   July p36. 75w. 4

2158   DAVIS, Hubert and the Season Travelers.   It's Bluegrass
        Time Again. Stoneway Records STY-1611
        BGU   Jan. p24. 175w. 4

2159   DAWKER Mountain Valley Boys.   Bound to Ride. Deck Hill
        6042-14
        PIC   May p64. 175w. 2

2160   DELMORE Brothers. MCA VIM 4017 (Japan) (Reissue)
        JEMF   Autumn p157-60. 200w. 5
        OTM   Summer p30-4. 500w. 4

2161   DELMORE Brothers.   Best of the Delmore Brothers.   Star-
        day SLP 962
            CMR   April   p35.   100w.   4

2162   DENNY, Clyde and Marie Denny.   Monticello.   Country Star
        11
            BGU   Nov.   p29.   100w. $2\frac{1}{2}$

2163   DICKENS, Hazel and Alice Gerrard.   Rounder Records 0054
            BGU   May   p36.   400w.   3
            OTM   Winter   p30.   475w.   3
            RSP   Jan.-Feb.   p24.   50w.   1
            RSP   May-June   p59.   100w. $2\frac{1}{2}$
            SO   May/June   p49-50.   700w. $4\frac{1}{2}$

2164   DILLARD-Hartford-Dillard.   Glitter Grass from the Nash-
        wood Hollyville Strings.   Flying Fish 036
            BGU   Oct.   p23.   275w.   3
            CFS   Autumn   p27.   125w. $2\frac{1}{2}$
            CMP   Aug.   p39.   200w.   5
            CMR   Sept.   p6.   525w. $4\frac{1}{2}$
            MM   July 23   p18.   300w. $3\frac{1}{2}$
            RC   Dec.   p11.   100w. $2\frac{1}{2}$
            RSP   1:3   p27.   600w.   3

2165   DILLARDS.   Versus the Incredible LA Time Machine.   Sonet
        SNTF 743 (E)
            CMP   Dec.   p40.   275w.   5
            RC   Dec.   p15.   100w. $2\frac{1}{2}$

2166   DIXIE Bluegrass Boys.   Grass Along the River.   Lucy Opry
        LO-76-01
            PIC   Sept.   p61.   100w.   2

2167   DIXIE Bluegrass Boys.   Something New.   Kim-Pat 7607
            BGU   July   p36.   50w.   2

2168   DIXIE Bluegrass Boys.   Sweetest Gift.   Kim-Pat 7608
            BGU   July   p36.   50w.   2

2169   DIXIE Dregs.   Freefall.   Capricorn CP 0189
            CK   Oct.   p64.   75w.   3
            MM   Nov.   12   p29.   50w. $\frac{1}{2}$

2170   DIXIE Gentlemen, with Tut Taylor.   Blues and Bluegrass.
        Old Homestead OHS 90024
            CMR   June   p9.   100w.   3

2171   DOUGLAS, Wilson.   The Right Hand Fork of Rush's Creek.
        Rounder 0047
            FOL   May   p9.   200w.   3
            RSP   Jan.-Feb.   p29.   250w.   2
            SO   May/June   p47.   150w. $3\frac{1}{2}$

2172   DREADFUL Snakes. Harvey's Records 010
        PIC Oct. p57-8. 225w. 2

2173   DRY Branch Fire Squad. Live at the Crying Cowboy Con-
        cert Saloon. RT 513
        BGU Dec. p19. 100w. 2½

2174   EANES, Jim. A Statesman of Bluegrass Music. Jessup
        Bluegrass Records MB 152
        BGU July p34. 175w. 2

2175   EAST Virginia. Sings of Witches and Whippoorwills. Lark
        2274
        BGU Oct. p22. 375w. 5

2176   EASTWOOD, Wiley with Luther Greer. Star City Swing.
        Outlet 1009 (Reissue)
        BGU Dec. p22. 100w. 1½

2177   EDMONDS, Norman. Train on the Island. Davis Unlimited
        33002 (Reissue)
        OTM Spring p24. 400w. 2½
        PIC March p54. 125w. 4

2178   ELLIOT, Albert and the Blue Ridge Partners. Mag RSR-258
        BGU March p26. 125w. 3

2179   ENLOE, Lyman. Rugged Road. SPBGMA 7602
        PIC Feb. p54. 150w. 4

2180   ETCETERA STRING BAND. The Harvest Hop. Moon 200
        PIC Aug. p65. 175w. 2

2181   EXTENDED Play Boys. Belt 002
        RSP Jan.-Feb. p31. 75w. 2½

2182   FAIRCHILD, Raymond. King of the Five String Banjo.
        Rural Rhythm 263
        PIC March p52. 90w. 0
        PIC May p68. 500w. 3

2183   FALLS City Ramblers. Early Indiana Days. Palm Tree 101
        BGU Sept. p18. 200w. 3

2184   FARR Brothers. South in My Soul. Cattle Records, LP 1
        (West Germany) (Reissue)
        JEMF No. 46 p104. 150w. 4

2185   The FAST Flying Vestibule. Union Station. Rolling Donut
        RD-1000
        BGU May p42. 150w. 3

2186   FAULKNER, Nolan. The Legendary Kentucky Mandolin of

Nolan Faulkner. Old Homestead 90064
    BGU   Jan. p25.   140w.   4
    OTM   Winter p26. $2\frac{1}{2}$
    PIC   July p66.   175w.   2

2187   FENNIG'S All Stars.   Saturday Night in the Provinces.
       Front Hall FHR-05
            FOL   May p8.   100w.   1
            RC   Nov.   p10.   225w.   4
            SO   March/April p50, 51.   250w.   5

2188   FERGUSON, Dave.   Somewhere Over the Rainbow.   Ridge
       Runner 0003
            CMP   March p41, 43.   150w.   5
            CMR   April p35.   175w.   5
            PIC   Feb.   p54.   125w.   5

2189   FLATT, Lester.   Flying Fish 015
            PIC   Dec.   p58.   150w. $3\frac{1}{2}$

2190   FLATT, Lester.   Lester Raymond Flatt.   Sonet SNTF 717
            CMP   Sept.   p39.   275w.   5

2191   FLATT, Lester.   Heaven's Bluegrass Band.   CMH 6207
            BGU   July p34.   100w.   4
            OTM   Winter p27.   100w.   2
            PIC   June p72.   225w. $4\frac{1}{2}$
            RSP   Jan.-Feb.   p27.   100w. $1\frac{1}{2}$

2192   FLATT, Lester.   Rollin'.   Power Pak PO 293 (E)
            CMR   Aug.   p22.   200w. $3\frac{1}{2}$

2193   FLATT, Lester and Earl Scruggs.   The Golden Era.   Round-
       er/Columbia P-13826
            BGU   Aug.   p31.   175w.   5
            RSP   1:3 p28.   125w. $3\frac{1}{2}$

2194   FLATT, Lester and Earl Scruggs.   The Golden Years.
       County/Columbia P-13810
            BGU   Aug.   p31.   175w.   5
            PIC   Aug.   p77.   250w.   5
            RSP   1:3 p28.   125w. $3\frac{1}{2}$

2195   FLATT, Lester and Earl Scruggs.   Live at Carnegie Hall.
       Columbia CS 8845 (Reissue)
            CM   March p56.   25w.   3

2196   The FLOYD County Boys.   Hard Times in the County.
       Sonyatone ST-1003
            BGU   Aug.   p34.   175w.   3
            RSP   1:3 p23.   125w. $3\frac{1}{2}$

2197   The FOX Brothers.   Starr Records SLP 1146

BGU   July   p36.   50w.   2

2198   FRAZIER, Moss.   All Fiddler.   Davis Unlimited 33023
       PIC   April   p69.   175w.   3

2199   FRIENDS of Bluegrass.   The Leaves Are Slowly Falling.
       Countryside Records CS 2002
       BGU   June   p40.   50w.   2
       PIC   Aug.   p70.   175w.   3

2200   FROG and the Greenhorns.   My Tennessee Girl.   Starr 1080
       PIC   Aug.   p72.   175w.   3

2201   FRONT Porch String Band.   Smilin' at You.   Front Porch
       Records FPK-909
       BGU   Aug.   p35.   100w.   3
       PIC   Nov.   p53.   225w. $2\frac{1}{2}$

2202   GARDNER, Frances and Olen Gardner.   Heritage 602
       BGU   May   p43.   50w. $2\frac{1}{2}$

2203   The GILLIAN Brothers.   Fiddlin' and Pickin'.   1976-001
       PIC   June   p74-5.   200w. $2\frac{1}{2}$
       RSP   March-April   p24.   50w.   3

2204   GOINS Brothers.   Take This Hammer.   Rebel 1568
       BGU   Dec.   p20.   150w. $2\frac{1}{2}$

2205   GOLD Rush.   The Deep South.   Goodhope GH 1002
       BGU   July   p35.   150w.   4

2206   The GOOD Old Boys.   Pistol Packin' Mama.   United Artists/
       Round UAS29951
       OTM   Summer   p38.   300w.   5

2207   The GORDONS.   Southern Illinois Bluegrass.   [no label]
       PIC   Feb.   p52.   75w.   2

2208   GRANT, Bill and Delia Bell.   Fourteen Memories.   Kiamichi
       KMB 104
       BGU   Feb.   p25.   125w.   4
       CMR   March   p20-30.   350w.   5

2209   GRAVES, Josh with Bobby Smith and the Boys from Shiloh.
       Vetco 3025
       PIC   Jan.   p55.   300w.   5

2210   GRAVES, Josh, Bobby Smith and the Boys from Shiloh.
       Sweet Sunny South.   CMH-6209
       BGU   April   p23.   150w.   3
       OTM   Spring   p26-7.   200w. $2\frac{1}{2}$
       PIC   Oct.   p56.   100w.   3
       RSP   Jan.-Feb.   p28.   300w.   2

2211   GRAYSON and Whittier.   Goin' Down Lee Highway, 1927-29.
       Davis Unlimited 33033 (Reissue)
           BGU   Dec.   p21.   150w.   3
           PIC   Nov.   p55.   150w.   3
           RSP   1:3   p18-9.   500w.   3½

2212   GREGORY, W. L. & Clyde Davenport (with Gary Gregory).
       Homemade Stuff.   Davis Unlimited DU-33028
           BGU   May   p40.   200w.   4
           OTM   Spring   p24-5.   250w.   2½
           PIC   July   p67.   175w.   4

2213   GRIFFIN, Chuck & Pauline/Williams, Johnny & Nettie.   Cas-
       cade Country-Something Different.   Voyager VRLP 318-S
           BGU   Aug.   p35.   150w.   4

2214   GRIFFITH, Big Jim.   The Dixie Cowboy.   Sonyatone Records
       ST-1002
           BGU   March   p26.   75w.   4
           FOL   Aug.   p4.   125w.   4
           OTM   Spring   p28.   300w.   2
           RSP   Jan.-Feb.   p24.   50w.   2½

2215   GRISMAN, David.   Kaleidoscope.   Flying Fish 05
           CAD   July   p30.   250w.   4½
           CFS   Summer   p21.   100w.   4
           GP   June   p136.   150w.   4
           PIC   Aug.   p59-60.   200w.   2
           RC   Oct.   p3.   250w.   3
           RSP   1:3   p22.   300w.   3½
           VV   Aug.   29   p73-4.   500w.   1½

2216   GRISMAN, David.   The Rounder Album.   Rounder Records
       0069
           BGU   Jan.   p28.   274w.   5
           GP   March   p113.   25w.   4
           MN   V1/#1   p17.   400w.   5
           OTM   Winter   p29.   450w.   3½
           PIC   March   p52.   150w.   4

2217   GRITZBACH, George.   Had Your Gritz Today?   Kicking
       Mule 126
           AU   June   p123.   350w.   4
           BGU   Oct.   p26.   75w.   3
           GP   May   p128-9.   100w.   3½
           SO   Jan./Feb.   p49.   75w.   3½

2218   GROSSMAN Brothers.   Golden Skies.   Dixie Licks 0001
           BGU   May   p43.   50w.   2½

2219   GUNNING, Sarah Ogan.   The Silver Dagger.   Rounder 0051
           OTM   Spring   p23.   150w.   3½

2220   HAND, Cal. The Wylie Butler. Takoma Records C-1056
       BGU   June p40, 41. 100w. $2\frac{1}{2}$
       CAD   July p22. 100w. 3
       GP   May p128. 75w. 3
       RSP   March-April p24. 50w. 2

2221   The HANKEY Mountain Express. Close Enough for Blue-
       grass!! Major MLP 2148
       BGU   Jan. p23. 100w. $4\frac{1}{2}$

2222   HARDIMAN, Charles. On the Well Beaten Path to Bluegrass.
       Hillside [No label number]
       BGU   May p37. 100w. $3\frac{1}{2}$

2223   HARTFORD, John. Mark Twang. Flying Fish 020
       AU   Feb. p90. 150w. 3
       BGU   March p26. 75w. $2\frac{1}{2}$
       CMR   Jan. p29. 300w. 4
       OTM   Winter p28. 50w. $3\frac{1}{2}$

2224   HARTFORD, John. Nobody Knows What You Do. Flying
       Fish 028
       BGU   March p26. 100w. $3\frac{1}{2}$
       CM   April p54. 375w. 4
       CMR   June p14. 350w. 4
       CS   Jan. 27 p20. 250w. 1
       MM   June 4 p24. 300w. 4
       OTM   Winter p28. 50w. 2
       PIC   June p70-1. 150w. 3
       RC   Aug. p14. 150w. $3\frac{1}{2}$
       RSP   Jan.-Feb. p23. 100w. 1
       SR   March p102. 350w. 4

2225   The HEIGHTS of Grass. Introducing the Heights of Grass.
       Cascade 006
       BGU   Jan. p23. 120w. 4
       PIC   May p60-1. 75w. $2\frac{1}{2}$

2226   HENLEY, Jimmy. One for the Record. TIG 7612
       PIC   March p51-2. 200w. 4

2227   HILL, Dudley. From a Northern Family. Voyager 317S
       AU   Oct. p178. 400w. 4
       PIC   Sept. p62. 200w. 4

2228   HILL, Wade. Lonesome Old Song. Old Homestead Records
       OHS 90074
       BGU   June p39. 100w. 2

2229   HOBBS Sisters & Bob Goff, Jr. Wanted! Royal Records
       [no serial no.]
       BGU   July p36. 100w. 3

2230   HODGES, Ernie. North Carolina Fiddling. Davis Unlimited
       Records DU 33031
              BGU March p25.   125w.   3½
              PIC Sept. p59.   200w.   3

2231   HOMESTEAD Act. Elmo & Patsy.   Kim Pat 7558
              PIC March p52.   90w.   0

2232   HOMESTEAD Act. Playing Possum.   Kim-Pat 7443
              PIC Jan. p56.   225w.   0

2233   HUCKABEE, Dan. Why Is This Man Smiling?   Ridge Runner
       RRR0004
              GP   Sept. p119. 50w.   3
              MN   8:3 p17. 200w.   3
              PIC Oct. p56.   150w.   3

2234   HUGHEY, Ron. Country Fiddlin' Ozark Style.   American
       Heritage AH491-511
              RSP March-April p25.   200w.   2½

2235   HUNTER, Thomas Hal (Tommy). Deep in Tradition.   June
       Appal 007
              BGU March p23.   100w.   4
              PIC July p67.   200w.   4½
              RSP March-April p25.   150w.   3½

2236   INDIAN Creek Delta Boys. Davis Unlimited DU-33029
              BGU May p36.   50w.   3
              OTM Spring p28.   250w.   2½
              PIC July p68-9.   275w.   4
              SO   May/June p47.   150w.   4

2237   JARRELL, Tommy. Joke on the Puppy.   Mountain 310
              PIC Aug. p72.   325w.   4

2238   JARRELL, Tommy. Sail Away Ladies.   County 756
              BGU April p23.   200w.   3
              FOL May p5.   325w.   5
              PIC June p72.   225w.   5
              RSP Jan.-Feb. p30-1.   250w.   3
              SO   July/Aug. p50.   125w.   4

2239   JARRELL, Tommy and Fred Cockerham. Music from Round
       Peak. Heritage 10
              PIC Aug. p76-7.   250w.   4½

2240   JENKINS, Snuffy and Pappy Sherill. Crazy Water Barn
       Dance. Rounder Record 0059
              BGU Jan. p29.   75w.   4
              PIC March p51.   125w.   4

2241   JERNIGAN, Doug. Roadside Rag. Flying Fish Records

FF 024
    BGU Feb. p27. 300w. 5
    CAD Jan. p17. 100w. 4
    CRA March p68. 75w. 3
    CM May p58. 200w. 4
    OTM Winter p28. 150w. 2
    RSP Jan.-Feb. p21. 200w. 2

2242 JIM and Jesse. Volume One. CBS AP 19 (Japan)
    RSP Jan.-Feb. p26. 150w. $4\frac{1}{2}$

2243 JIM & Jesse. Jim and Jesse Show. DJM 22067 (E)
    MM Aug. 6 p17. 50w. 3

2244 JIM and Jesse. Songs about Our Country. Old Dominion
    498-08
    PIC Feb. p50. 200w. $2\frac{1}{2}$

2245 JIM & Jessie & the Virginia Boys. Superior Sounds of
    Bluegrass. Old Dominion OD 498-05
    CMR Jan. p30. 250w. 5

2246 JOHNSON, Earl and His Clodhoppers. Red Hot Breakdown.
    Country 543 (Reissue)
    JEMF No. 45 p48. 250w. $4\frac{1}{2}$
    RSP Jan.-Feb. p26. 200w. $3\frac{1}{2}$

2247 JONES, Al and Frank Necessary and the Spruce Mtn. Boys.
    Rounder 0050
    PIC Feb. p56. 60w. 5

2248 JONES, Bill. Bluegrass Favorites. SPBGMA 773-03
    BGU Nov. p27. 100w. 3

2249 JONES, Ramona. Back Porch Fiddlin', Vol. 1. Happy Val-
    ley Records
    PIC Jan. p54. 300w. 4

2250 JONES Brothers and the Log Cabin Boys. Hard Bluegrass
    Music at Its Best. Playhouse 257
    PIC Jan. p56. 200w. 4

2251 KEITH, Bill. Something Auld, Something Newgrass, Some-
    thing Borrowed, Something Bluegrass. Rounder RB-1
    FOL Sept. p13, 16, 17. 400w. $2\frac{1}{2}$
    MN V7/#7 p17. 450w. 5
    PIC May p60. 150w. 5

2252 KENTUCKY Colonels. 1965-1966. Rounder 0070
    FOL July p7. 250w. $3\frac{1}{2}$
    JEMF No. 45 p47-8. 150w. $3\frac{1}{2}$
    OTM Spring p27. 250w. 3
    RSP Jan.-Feb. p31. 350w. $3\frac{1}{2}$

2253   KENTUCKY Colonels.   Appalachian Swing.   United Artists
        UAS 29514 (Reissue)
            FOL   July   p6.   250w.   5

2254   KENTUCKY Colonels.   Living in the Past.   Briar BT 7202
        (Reissue)
            FOL   May   p9.   4½
            FOL   July   p6-7.   250w.   4
            JEMF   No. 45   p47-8.   150w.   3½

2255   KENTUCKY Gentlemen.   Kentucky Heritage.   King Bluegrass
        KB 560
            BGU   June   p40.   100w.   2½
            RSP   March-April   p23.   50w.   3

2256   KESSINGER, Clark.   Memorial Album.   Kanawha 327 (Re-
        issue)
            RSP   Jan.-Feb.   p27.   250w.   3½

2257   KINFOLK.   Bluegrass Is Kinfolk.   Kim-Pat KP7601
            BGU   Sept.   p20.   200w.   3

2258   KING, Clinton and the Virginia Mountaineers.   Blue Ridge
        Bluegrass.   Revonah RS 917
            BGU   Jan.   p24.   115w.   3
            PIC   June   p68.   225w.   4

2259   KNOPF, Bill.   On Banjo.   America Heritage 401-524
            BGU   July   p35.   150w.   3
            PIC   Sept.   p62-3.   75w.   5
            RSP   March-April   p21.   125w.   3½

2260   LAMB, Grant.   Tunes from Home.   Voyager 312
            BGU   Jan.   p30.   75w.   3

2261   LAMBERT, Curley.   Bluegrass Evergreen.   Old Homestead
        OHS 90072
            BGU   Dec.   p20.   300w.   3½

2262   LAMBERT, L. W. and the Blue River Boys.   Anvil 373
            PIC   Aug.   p73-4.   250w.   3

2263   LAMBERT, L. W. & the Blue River Boys.   The Old, Old
        Man.   Anvil Records RSR-376
            BGU   June   p38.   150w.   3

2264   LAMBETH, David and the High Lonesome Ramblers.   Blue
        Ridge Mountain Music.   King Bluegrass 556
            PIC   April   p64.   150w.   2½

2265   LANDERS, Jake.   Single.   Old Homestead OHS 90073
            PIC   Nov.   p55-6.   225w.   3

2266   LAST Straw String Band.   Jack Rabbit 001
         FOL   Aug.   p5.   50w.   2½
         PIC   Sept.   p58.   275w.   3½
         RSP   1:3   p23.   125w.   3½

2267   LAUR, Katie.   Cookin' with Katie.   Vetco 3028
         BGU   Sept.   p22.   75w.   2
         PIC   Aug.   p58-9.   250w.   3½

2268   LAUREL Mountain Grass.   Vokes 501
         BGU   May   p44.   75w.   3
         PIC   Feb.   p50.   50w.   2½

2269   LE Page, Denis.   Larger than Life.   Boot BBG 6001
         BGU   Nov.   p28.   150w.   2½

2270   LILLY, Mike & Wendy Miller.   Hot 'n Grassy.   Old Home-
         stead 90068
         BGU   Oct.   p25.   250w.   3

2271   LOST and Found.   First Time Around.   Outlet STLP 1002
         RSP   March-April   p24.   25w.   2½

2272   The LOST and Found.   The Second Time Around.   Outlet
         1006
         PIC   April   p67.   100w.   3

2273   LOST Kentuckians.   Body and Soul.   Lemco 053
         BGU   Jan.   p29.   150w.   2½
         PIC   Aug.   p75.   225w.   3½

2274   LUNDY, Emmett W.   Fiddle Tunes from Grayson County.
         String STR802
         CMP   Aug.   p39.   150w.   5
         OTM   Summer   p36.   650w.   5

2275   LUNDY, Ted and Bob Paisley and the Southern Mountain Boys.
         Slipping Away.   Rounder 0055
         PIC   Feb.   p51.   125w.   2½

2276   LUNSFORD, Bascom Lamar.   Music from South Turkey
         Creek.   Rounder 0065
         SO   May/June   p47.   225w.   2½

2277-8   McCLENDON, Jimb and Neal Jordan.   Hard Drivin' Blue-
         grass.   Janlynn Records JL 7157
         BGU   Jan.   p30.   50w.   3½

2279   McCOURY, Del and the Dixie Pals.   Collection Special.
         Grassound 102
         MN   V8/#2   p17.   300w.   4

2280   McCUMBERS Brothers.   Hillbilly Hobo.   Old Homestead

90065
   BGU Jan. p27. 150w. 4
   OTM Winter p27. 50w. $2\frac{1}{2}$
   PIC Aug. p74. 175w. 0

2281 McLAIN Family Band. Country Life CLR 7
   PIC Oct. p56-7. 200w. 3

2282 McLAIN Family Band. On the Road. Country Life Records
CLR-6
   BGU May p38. 100w. $3\frac{1}{2}$
   MN V8/#2 p16. 350w. 3
   PIC March p50. 150w. $4\frac{1}{2}$

2283 McMICHEN, Clayton. The Traditional Years. Davis Unlimited 33032 (Reissue)
   RSP 1:3 p19. 450w. 4

2284 McNEELY, Larry. Live at McCabes. Takoma D 1060
   RC Dec. p9. 200w. 4

2285 McNEELY, Larry. Rhapsody for Banjo. Flying Fish 025
   BGU April p24. 50w. 2
   CAD March p40. 125w. $2\frac{1}{2}$
   CFS Summer p22. 125w. 4
   GP Sept. p119. 50w. 5
   OTM Winter p27. 150w. 3
   PIC July p69. 100w. $4\frac{1}{2}$
   RSP March-April p62. 250w. 3
   SR June p109. 150w. 4

2286 MACON, Dave. First Row, Second Left. Bear Family
15518 (West Germany)
   CMR July p20. 250w. 3

2287 MACON, Dave. Fun in Life. Bear Family 15519 (West
Germany)
   CMR July p20. 150w. 3

2288 MACON, Dave. The Gayest Old Dude in Town. Folk Variety FU 12503 (West Germany)
   CMR July p20. 25w. 3

2289 McPEAK Brothers. County 764
   BGU Nov. p26. 200w. 3

2290 MADDOX Brothers and Rose. 1946-1951, Vol. 1/2. Ar-
hoolie 5016/17 (2 discs) (Reissue)
   BGU Dec. p21. 200w. $3\frac{1}{2}$
   CFS Summer p20-1. 150w. 3
   RSP 1:3 p29. 500w. $3\frac{1}{2}$

2291 MAPHIS, Joe. Grass 'n' Jazz. CMH 6215

BGU   Nov.   p29.   75w.   2

2292   MARTIN, Benny.   Tennessee Jubilee.   Sonet SNTF 703 (E)
          CMP   Jan.   p41.   150w.   5
          CMR   Jan.   p29.   350w.   5

2293   MELFORD, Michael.   Mandolin Fantasy.   Flying Fish 023
          BGU   July   p30.   250w.   4
          CAD   Jan.   p17.   125w. $3\frac{1}{2}$
          CMR   June   p7.   300w.   4
          CRA   March   p67-8.   75w.   4
          OTM   Spring   p27.   150w.   1
          RSP   March-April   p19.   125w. $2\frac{1}{2}$
          SR   April   p94, 96.   150w.   4

2294   MIDDLE Spunk Creek Boys.   Major 2002
          BGU   April   p24.   50w.   2

2295   MILLER, Wendy and Mike Lilly.   Country Grass.   Old
       Homestead OHS 90049
          MN   V8/#1   p17.   150w.   2

2296   MONROE, Bill.   Volumes 1, 2.   CBS 20 AP11/12 (2 discs)
       (Japan)
          RSP   Jan. -Feb.   p24.   350w.   3

2297   MONROE, Bill.   High, Lonesome Sound.   MCA 110 (Reissue)
          CM   March   p56.   50w. $2\frac{1}{2}$

2298   MONROE, Bill.   Sings Bluegrass, Body & Soul.   MCA 2251
          CM   July   p53.   300w.   5
          CMR   July   p21.   300w.   3
          PIC   Sept.   p58.   300w. $3\frac{1}{2}$
          RSP   March-April   p20-21.   400w. $1\frac{1}{2}$

2299   MONROE, James.   James Monroe Sings Songs of Memory
       Lane of His Uncle Charlie Monroe.   Atteiram API-L-1532
          BGU   Feb.   p28.   150w.   5

2300   MOODY, Clyde.   A Country Tribute to Fred Rose.   Old
       Homestead OHS 90059
          BGU   Jan.   p22.   275w.   4
          OTM   Winter   p26.   50w.   2

2301   MOORE, Charlie.   The Original Rebel Soldier.   Wango 114
          MN   8:3   p17.   200w. $4\frac{1}{2}$

2302   The MOORE Brothers.   Writing a Song to You.   King Blue-
       grass Records KB 549
          BGU   Feb.   p28.   50w.   2
          PIC   May   p64.   150w.   4

2303   MORGAN Brothers.   Northern Lights.   Blue Ridge Pro-

ductions 101
    BGU Jan.   p30.   75w. $3\frac{1}{2}$
    PIC July p62. 125w. $4\frac{1}{2}$

2304   MORRIS, Leon. International Bluegrass. Jessup Michigan
Bluegrass MB 113
    CMR March p30. 200w. 5

2305   The MUDDY Bottom Boys. Slaughter on the Highway.
Grassroots GR-002
    BGU March p25. 225w. 5
    PIC Sept. p60. 200w. 2

2306   MURPHY, Dudley and Deanie. At Home. Caneycreek CCLP-
0015
    PIC June p74. 75w. 4

2307   MUSGRAVE, David, Paul Buskirk, Shot Jackson. Dobro,
Shobro, Steel. Stoneway STY 144 (Reissue)
    CMR Aug. p21. 150w. 3

2308   NECESSARY, Frank. Songs of the Pioneers. Old Homestead 90032
    BGU April p24. 50w. $2\frac{1}{2}$

2309   NEW City Grass. All about You. Wildfire
    BGU Nov. p26. 100w. $1\frac{1}{2}$

2310   NEW Grass Revival. Fly through the Country. Flying Fish
016
    CMR April p35. 150w. 4

2311   NEW Grass Revival. When the Storm Is Over. Flying Fish
032
    BGU Aug. p33. 175w. 5
    CFS Summer p21. 125w. 5
    OTM Summer p38. 375w. 4
    PIC Aug. p68. 225w. 4
    RC Aug. p9. 200w. 3

2312   NEW South. Rounder 0044
    CMP Oct. p42. 300w. 5

2313   NORTH Country Grass. Kentucky's Callin'. Old Homestead
90062
    PIC Feb. p50. 125w. 4

2314   NORTHERN Lights. Revonah 923
    PIC Nov. p52. 275w. 5

2315   OAK Ridge Boys. Y'all Come Back Saloon. ABC/Dot DP
2093
    CMP Dec. p40. 225w. 5

2316 O'CONNOR, Mark. Pickin' in the Wind. Rounder 0068
 CMP Oct. p42. 250w. 5
 OTM Winter p29. 350w. 4

2317 OLD Kentucky String Band. Twilight Is Stealing. Old Home-
 stead 90008
 BGU Feb. p24. 150w. 5
 PIC July p62. 200w. $2\frac{1}{2}$
 RSP March-April p17-8. 250w. 3

2318 O'ROARK, Mike and the Freeborn Men. Somewhere in Be-
 tween. King-Bluegrass 547
 BGU Jan. p25. 215w. 4
 PIC Feb. p51-2. 100w. $2\frac{1}{2}$

2319 OSBORNE Brothers. From Rocky Top to Muddy Bottom.
 CMH 9008 (2 discs)
 RSP Nov. -Dec. p31. 200w. 3

2320 The OSBORNE Brothers. Number 1. CMH 6206. Cart.
 CMH-8-6206
 BGU March p24. 175w. 5
 CM April p58. 350w. 3
 MN V8/#2 p16. 500w. $3\frac{1}{2}$
 OTM Winter p27. 100w. $1\frac{1}{2}$
 PIC Aug. p64. 200w. 3
 RSP Jan. -Feb. p22. 250w. 4

2321 The OUTDOOR Plumbing Co. The Outdoor Plumbing Company. Rebel SLP-1560
 BGU Aug. p34. 150w. 4

2322 OZARK Mountain Daredevils. Men from Earth. A&M SP-
 4601. Cart. 8-4601
 CMR Jan. p30. 100w. 0
 SR Jan. p96. 75w. 2

2323 PANCERZEWSKI, Joe. The Fiddling Engineer. Voyager
 VRLP 3155
 RSP 1:3 p25-6. 125w. 3

2324 PERKINS, J. T. Fiddle Favorites-Perkins Style. Davis
 Unlimited 33017
 PIC Feb. p55. 50w. 3

2325 PERKINS, J. T. Just Fine Fiddling. Davis Unlimited DU
 33007
 BGU March p22. 100w. 4

2326 PERRY, Bill. Bluegrass Jam. King Bluegrass KB 551
 BGU Jan. p29. 50w. 2

2327 PERRY County Music Makers. Going Back to Tennessee.

Davis Unlimited DU 33024
    CFS   Autumn   p25-6.   200w.   4
    OTM   Spring   p25.   450w.   4

2328   PHILLIPS, Stacey.   All Old Friends.   Revonah 930
    MN   V7/#1   p16.   400w. $3\frac{1}{2}$
    PIC   June   p72.   175w. $2\frac{1}{2}$

2329   PIERCE, Otis.   Every Bush and Tree.   Bay 102
    OTM   Spring   p25.   100w.   2

2330   PIKE, Fred and Sam Tidwell.   The Last Log Drive.   Revonah RS 922
    MN   V8/#1   p17.   200w. $2\frac{1}{2}$

2331   The PINEY Pickers.   The Piney Pickers Play Bluegrass. Kim-Pat KPL-7612
    BGU   Sept.   p22.   50w.   0

2332   The PINEY Ridge Boys.   Flat Land Bluegrass.   King Bluegrass 553
    BGU   Feb.   p24.   100w.   4

2333   PLANK Road Stringband.   Carryon Records-This is it
    BGU   Aug.   p36.   150w.   3

2334   POOLE, Charlie.   Volume 4.   County 540
    MN   V8/#1   p16.   300w.   3
    OTM   Winter   p23.   250w. $4\frac{1}{2}$

2335   POOR Richard's Almanac.   Ridge Runner RR 0022 (Reissue)
    OTM   Winter   p30.   200w.   3

2336   POTTER, Dale.   Unique Fiddle Style of.   Stoneway 166
    BGU   Dec.   p22.   125w.   2

2337   POWERS, Ted & Hubert Powers.   Powers Town Music.   MAG RSR-295
    BGU   Sept.   p22.   75w.   4

2338   POWERS, Ted & Hubert Powers.   Two Generations of Old Time Fiddling.   MAG (no no.)
    BGU   Sept.   p22.   75w.   4

2339   RFD Boys.   RFD No. 3.   Pretzel Bell   738
    BGU   April   p22.   150w.   3
    PIC   July   p67.   50w.   2

2340   RED Clay Ramblers.   Stolen Love.   Flying Fish FF 009
    MN   V8/#2   p17.   300w. $3\frac{1}{2}$

2341   The RED Clay Ramblers.   Twisted Laurel.   Flying Fish 030
    BGU   July   p34.   125w.   4

CMP Sept. p40. 200w. 3
CMR May p34. 350w. 4
FOL Aug. p5. 125w. 4
PIC Aug. p66. 500w. $4\frac{1}{2}$
RC May p6. 250w. $4\frac{1}{2}$
RSP Jan.-Feb. p26-7. 400w. $2\frac{1}{2}$
SO May/June p49-50. 700w. $4\frac{1}{2}$
SR June p116. 125w. 4

2342 RED, White, and Bluegrass Band. Red White & Bluegrass
'76. Playhouse 258
PIC Jan. p53-4. 110w. 2

2343 REED, Blind Alfred. How Can a Poor Man Stand Such
Times and Live. Rounder 1001 (Reissue)
CAD Nov. p16. 25w. $4\frac{1}{2}$

2344 REED, Ola Belle. My Epitaph-A Documentary in Song and
Lyric. Folkways Records FA 2493
BGU July p31. 540w. 4
CFS Summer p22. 125w. 4
FOL Dec. p25, 27. 400w. 4
FR June p35. 200w. 4
PIC Sept. p58-9. 150w. $4\frac{1}{2}$
SO March/April p50. 350w. $4\frac{1}{2}$
SMG May p26. 75w. 3

2344a RENO, Don & Bill Harrell. Dear Old Dixie. CMH-6201
BGU Aug. p33. 150w. 5
MN 8:3 p16. 300w. 4
OTM Winter p27. 100w. $2\frac{1}{2}$
PIC March p54. 100w. 4

2345 RENO, Don and Bill Harrell. The Don Reno Story. CMH
9003 (2 discs)
PIC Aug. p62. 200w. $4\frac{1}{2}$

2346 RICE, Tony. Rounder 0085
BGU Oct. p22. 350w. 4
CFS Autumn p26. 125w. 5
FOL Sept. p12-3. 400w. 4
RSP 1:3 p26. 350w. $3\frac{1}{2}$

2347 RICE, Tony. California Autumn. Rebel SLP 1549
FOL May p8. 50w. $4\frac{1}{2}$

2348 RILEY, Bartow. Panhandle Texas Fiddling. Kanawha 315
RSP Jan.-Feb. p21. 125w. $2\frac{1}{2}$

2349 ROBERTSON, Eck. Sonyatone STR 201R
FOL May p4-5. 200w. $3\frac{1}{2}$
OTM Winter p23, 25. 250w. 3
RSP Jan.-Feb. p32. 250w. 3

2350   ROBINS, Butch.   Forty Years Late.   Rounder 0086
        BGU   July   p30.   540w.   4
        FOL   Sept.   p12.   125w.   3
        PIC   Oct.   p58.   250w.   3
        RSP   1:3   p20.   175w.   3

2351   ROCKY Mountain Boys.   Burning Bluegrass.   MAG RSE-293
        BGU   Sept.   p23.   50w.   3

2352   The ROSSLYN Mountain Boys.   Adelphi AD 2010
        CMR   July   p21.   150w.   3
        RC   Aug.   p15.   300w.   2

2353   ROUSTABOUTS.   Rolling on the River.   Davis Sound RSE-
        528
        BGU   Sept.   p23.   75w. $2\frac{1}{2}$

2354   RUTLAND, Georgia Slim.   Raw Fiddle.   Kanawha 325
        RSP   Jan.-Feb.   p21.   150w. $3\frac{1}{2}$

2355   RYAN, Buck.   Draggin' the Bow.   Rebel 1552
        BGU   April   p18.   50w. $2\frac{1}{2}$
        PIC   Jan.   p55.   150w.   0

2356   ST. Pierre, Simon.   Fiddler from Maine.   Revonah RS 926
        PIC   Dec.   p54.   150w. $3\frac{1}{2}$

2357   ST. Pierre, Simon.   The Woods of Maine.   Revonah RS920
        PIC   June   p66.   175w.   5
        RSP   March-April   p26.   75w. $3\frac{1}{2}$

2358   SALLY Mountain Show.   Joshua.   Professional Artists
        753388
        PIC   Feb.   p54-5.   250w.   0

2359   SAUCEMAN, Carl & the Green Valley Boys.   Rich-R-Tone
        LP-8104
        BGU   June   p36.   175w. $3\frac{1}{2}$
        PIC   Aug.   p70.   275w.   2

2360   SAUCEMAN Brothers.   The Early Days of Bluegrass, Vol. 7.
        Rounder 1019 (Reissue)
        BGU   June   p36.   200w.   4

2361   SAWTOOTH Mountain Boys.   Home Comfort 001
        BGU   Jan.   p27.   225w.   5
        PIC   June   p71.   25w.   2

2362   SCHWARZ, Tracy and Eloise Schwarz.   Home Among the
        Hills.   Bear Family FV 12007
        CMR   May   p32.   100w.   4

2363   SCOTT, Carl and Ronnie Massey.   Mountain Guitars.   Outlet

1004
    PIC   Sept.   p60-1.   200w. $4\frac{1}{2}$
    RSP   March-April   p20.   50w. $3\frac{1}{2}$

2364   SECOND Generation.   State of Mind.   CMH Records CMH-
    6208
    BGU   Feb.   p27.   300w.   4
    PIC   July   p66.   250w.   2

2365   SECOND Generation.   We Call It Grass.   Rebel SLP 1546
    FOL   May   p8.   100w.   2

2366   SELDOM Scene.   Live at the Cellar Door.   Rebel SLP
    1547/48 (2 discs)
    AU   Feb.   p87.   400w. $3\frac{1}{2}$

2367   SELDOM Scene.   The New Seldom Scene Album.   Rebel 1561
    BGU   June   p37.   200w. $4\frac{1}{2}$
    CS   March 24   p16.   2250w. $3\frac{1}{2}$
    MN   8:3   p16.   350w.   4
    RSP   March-April   p18.   175w.   4

2368   SHELTON, Allen.   Shelton Special.   Rounder 0088
    BGU   July   p31.   540w.   4
    RSP   1:3   p20.   350w.   5

2369   SHELTON, Eddie.   Expedition.   STN 00101
    BGU   June   p38, 39.   150w.   3
    PIC   Oct.   p58.   50w.   1

2370   SHELTON Brothers and Carlisle Brothers.   MCA VIM 4011
    (Japan)
    JEMF   Autumn   p157-60.   200w.   5
    OTM   Summer   p30-4.   500w.   4

2371   SHENANDOAH Cutups.   Bluegrass Spring.   Revonah 921
    BGU   Jan.   p27.   140w.   5
    MN   V8/#1   p16.   200w.   3

2372   SHENANDOAH Cutups.   A Tribute to the Louvin Brothers.
    Revonah 919
    PIC   Jan.   p52.   75w.   4

2373   SHUBB, Wilson and Shubb.   Live.   Pacifica 001
    BGU   March   p27.   125w.   4
    PIC   Aug.   p68-9.   250w.   4

2374   SHUPING, Garland and Wild Country.   Old Homestead 90069
    PIC   April   p69.   50w.   4

2375   SKAGGS, Ricky.   That's It!   Rebel SLP 1550
    FOL   May   p7.   125w. $4\frac{1}{2}$

2376   SKINNER, Jimmie.   Sings Bluegrass, Vol. 2, with Josh
       Graves.   Vetco 3027
          BGU   July   p30.   126w.   2
          PIC   Sept.   p59.   200w.   2

2377   SMALLWOOD, Bob.   Rebel Soldier, Your Memory Will Never
       Die.   Old Homestead Records, 90030
          PIC   April   p66.   300w.   3

2378   SMITH, Glen and the Mountain State Pickers.   Fiddler.   Blue-
       tick Records BTR-101
          BGU   March   p26.   50w.   0
          PIC   April   p68.   175w.   3

2379   SMITH Brothers Bluegrass Orchestra.   Oldgrass, Newgrass,
       Bluegrass.   CMH 6203
          PIC   June   p68-9.   150w. $3\frac{1}{2}$

2380   SMITH Brothers Dirt Band.   Once over Easy.   Ham & Eggs
       (no no.)
          BGU   Jan.   p29.   100w.   3
          PIC   May   p66.   125w.   3

2381   SOUTHERN Express.   North and South.   Mountain 307
          MN   V7/#1   p16.   200w.   3

2382   The SOUTHERN Sounds of Grass.   For the First Time.
       Golden Circle Records GCR 001
          BGU   Jan.   p29.   175w.   3

2383   SPARKS, Larry.   Sings Hank Williams.   County 759
          BGU   Nov.   p28.   200w. $3\frac{1}{2}$

2384   SPENCER, Tom.   Songs: Silly and Sentimental.   Davis Un-
       limited DU 33034
          BGU   Dec.   p22.   75w.   2
          OTM   Spring   p25.   100w.   3

2385   SPICHER, Buddy.   American Sampler.   Flying Fish 021
          BGU   March   p27.   50w.   4
          CAD   Jan.   p32.   300w. $3\frac{1}{2}$
          CFS   Summer   p23.   100w.   4
          CRA   March   p67-8.   75w. $3\frac{1}{2}$
          OTM   Winter   p28.   150w. $1\frac{1}{2}$
          PIC   Aug.   p61.   175w.   2
          RSP   Jan. -Feb.   p24-5.   300w. $2\frac{1}{2}$

2386   SPICHER, Buddy and Buddy Emmons.   Buddies.   Flying
       Fish 041
          MM   Sept. 3   p21.   200w.   5
          RS   Nov. 3   p110.   175w. $3\frac{1}{2}$

2387   SPRUNG, Roger and the Progressive Bluegrassers.   Blue-

grass Gold, Vol. I.   Showcase S-4
PIC Sept. p61. 75w. 2

2388 STANLEY, Ralph. Old Home Place.   Rebel 1562
BGU   July p33. 200w. $2\frac{1}{2}$
MN   V8/#1 p16. 300w. $2\frac{1}{2}$
RSP   March-April p26. 125w. 4

2389 STAR Spangled Washboard Band.   A Collector's Item.   Flying Fish 031
BGU   Aug. p36. 75w. 0
CAD   June p22. 75w. 2
FS   Nov. p26-7. 375w. $4\frac{1}{2}$

2390 STECHER, Jody. Going Up on the Mountain. Bay Records 210
BGU   Oct. p26. 75w. 2
FS   Nov. p25. 600w. 3
RSP   1:3 p27. 450w. 5

2391 STONEMANS. Cuttin' the Grass.   CMH 6210
BGU   April p23. 75w. $2\frac{1}{2}$
OTM   Spring p27, 30. 150w. 1
PIC   Aug. p68. 200w. 2
RSP   Jan.-Feb. p30. 250w. 1

2392 STONEY Creek. The Stoney Creek Family Reunion Album.
Lemco 061
BGU   Feb. p29. 75w. 3

2393 STONEY Point. Back in the Hills.   Rosewood SP8H1002
RSP   March-April p26. 100w. $3\frac{1}{2}$

2394 STOWE, Ferrell. Stowe on the Dobro.   SPBGMA 7733-04
BGU   Oct. p22. 200w. 4
PIC   Dec. p61. 125w. 3

2395 The SUGARLOAF Ramblers. Daybreak in Dixie.   Galaxie III Productions
PIC   Jan. p54. 150w. 0

2396 SULLIVAN Family. The Prettiest Flowers Will Be Blooming.
Atteiram API-L-1518
MN   8:3 p16. 150w. 4

2397 SUNDELL, Jon. The Eagle and the Sparrow.   June Appal
JA 008
FR   Aug. p32. 500w. $2\frac{1}{2}$
OTM   Spring p29-30. 100w. 2

2398 The SUNDOWN Valley Boys. Smokin' Bluegrass.   Pine Tree 535
PIC   Feb. p57. 50w. 4

2399   SUNNYSIDERS. Instrumental Side of the.   Jessup MB 153
        BGU Nov.   p28.   50w.   3

2400   TAINAKA, Robert.   Old Time Music.   Old Homestead 90056
        PIC Feb.   p55.   50w.   2

2401   TALL Timber Bluegrass.   The Best of Bluegrass.   Eagle
        EB-TT-BG-500
        BGU Feb.   p29.   75w. $3\frac{1}{2}$

2402   TANAKA, Robert.   Old Time Music.   Old Homestead OHS
        90056
        BGU Jan.   p30.   75w. $3\frac{1}{2}$

2403   TANNER, Gid.   A Cow Likker Still in Georgia.   VRLP 303
        CM March p56.   50w. $2\frac{1}{2}$

2404   TAYLOR, Earl & the Stoney Mt. Boys.   Body and Soul.
        Vetco 3026
        BGU May   p41.   200w.   3
        PIC Aug.   p72.   175w. $4\frac{1}{2}$

2405   The TENNESSEE Rail Splitters.   Fiddlin' Sound of the Old
        Man from the Mountain.   Staff BP3286
        OTM Summer p37.   250w.   3

2406   THEOBALD, Mike & the Bluegrass Country.   Caught with
        the Grass.   Bluegrass Seed Record Co. (no no.)
        BGU Jan.   p30.   50w.   2
        PIC May   p68.   75w.   2

2407   THOMAS, Buddy.   Kitty Puss.   Rounder 0032
        FOL May   p5.   150w. $4\frac{1}{2}$

2408   TOTTLE, Jack.   Back Road Mandolin.   Rounder 0067
        BGU April p22, 23.   150w.   3
        MN V7/#1 p16.   300w.   3
        PIC April p64.   225w. $4\frac{1}{2}$

2409   TOWNSHEND, Graham.   The Fiddle.   Rounder 7002
        CMP Oct.   p41.   150w.   2
        FOL June p5.   75w. $4\frac{1}{2}$
        RSP Jan.-Feb. p24.   300w.   4

2410   TRAPEZOID.   Skyline 107
        PIC Aug.   p74.   275w.   4

2411   TRISCHKA, Tony.   Heartlands.   Rounder 0062
        MN V7/#1 p17.   350w.   3

2412   TUCKER, George.   Rounder Records 0064
        BGU March p26.   100w.   3

2413   The TUNSTALL Trio. On the Sunny Banks. CMC 6082N5
       BGU Sept. p16. 150w. 4

2414   UPTOWN Bluegrass. Hand Picked. King Bluegrass 552
       BGU Feb. p26. 100w. 3
       PIC March p55. 50w. 5

2415   UPTOWN Bluegrass. Uptown Bluegrass III. Mistletoe Rec-
       ords MR101
       BGU Sept. p17. 125w. 0

2416   VAL, Joe and the New England Bluegrass Boys. Rounder
       0025
       MN V7/#1 p17. 150w. 3

2417   VAL, Joe & the New England Bluegrass Boys. Not a Word
       from Home. Rounder 0082
       BGU Sept. p17. 175w. 4
       PIC Nov. p54. 225w. 3$\frac{1}{2}$

2418   VARNEY, Lowell. Instrumental Sounds of the Banjo Pickin'
       Boy. From West Virginia. Jessup MB 150
       BGU Oct. p23. 150w. 3
       PIC Aug. p71. 150w. 3$\frac{1}{2}$

2419   The VOICES of Bluegrass. Vol. 2. Revonah 918
       BGU May p42. 200w. 3
       PIC May p69. 150w. 4

2420   WARREN County String Ticklers. Live at Waterhole 1.
       Warren County Records WCR102
       BGU Nov. p28. 50w. 1$\frac{1}{2}$

2421   WATSON, Doc. Two Days in November. Poppy PPLA-210
       CM March p56. 100w. 2$\frac{1}{2}$

2422   WATSON, Doc. Watson Family Tradition. Topic 12TS336
       (E) (Reissue)
       FR Sept. p35. 300w. 5

2423   WATSON, Doc; Clint Howard; and Fred Price. Old Time
       Concert. Vanguard VSD 107/8 (2 discs)
       RSP Nov.-Dec. p31. 200w. 2$\frac{1}{2}$

2424   WATSON, Doc & Merle Watson. Lonesome Road. Artist
       UA-LA 725-G
       CM Nov. p39. 200w. 2
       CS Dec. p29. 200w. 4$\frac{1}{2}$
       GP Oct. p129. 150w. 4
       RC Oct. p11. 50w. 4$\frac{1}{2}$
       SR Oct. p120. 122. 250w. 4$\frac{1}{2}$

2425   WERNICK, Peter. Bluegrass Banjo. Music Minus One 180

PIC   April   p66.   275w.   3

2426   WHALEN, Steve.   Fiddlin' Steve Whalen.   Old Homestead
       90058
       PIC   Jan.   p53.   125w.   5

2427   WHEAT Straw.   The Wheat Goes On.   Old Homestead 90063
       BGU   Jan.   p27.   100w.   3
       PIC   May   p68.   75w.   2½

2428   WHITE, Buck & the Down Home Folks.   Live at the Picking
       Parlor.   County 760
       BGU   May   p41.   200w.   2
       PIC   Nov.   p52.   250w.   3½

2429   WHITE, Buck and the Down Home Folks.   That Down Home
       Feeling.   Ridge Runner RRR 0006
       BGU   Dec.   p21.   200w.   3
       PIC   Nov.   p52.   250w.   4

2430   WHITE, Clarence and Roland White.   Rounder 0070
       PIC   April   p66-7.   300w.   4

2431   WHITE, Roland.   I Wasn't Born to Rock 'n Roll.   Ridge
       Runner RRR0005
       BGU   April   p16.   250w.   4
       FOL   July   p7, 15.   225w.   5
       OTM   Summer   p38.   325w.   3
       PIC   Aug.   p62.   250w.   0
       RSP   March-April   p22.   250w.   4

2432   WHITE Brothers.   Rounder Records 0073
       AU   Oct.   p179.   200w.   4½
       BGU   May   p35.   200w.   3
       FOL   July   p7.   150w.   4½
       RSP   March-April   p17.   225w.   4

2433   WILLIAMS, Robin.   Journey's Edge.   Flying Fish Records
       FOL   June   p17-8, 26.   1, 800w.   5

2434   WILLIAMS, Robin and Linda Williams.   Robin and Linda
       Williams.   Flashlight 3003
       PIC   Aug.   p76.   350w.   3½

2435   WILLIAMSON, George and Mary Williamson.   Appalachian
       Echoes.   Homestead 80006
       PIC   Jan.   p52.   150w.   4

2436   WILLIAMSON, George and Mary Williamson.   Appalachian
       Echoes.   Old Homestead OHS 80006
       BGU   March   p22.   100w.   4

2437   WINE, Melvin.   Cold Frosty Morning.   Poplar LP 1

        BGU   Feb.   p29.   75w.   3
        OTM   Summer p36-7.   425w. $2\frac{1}{2}$
        PIC   Aug.   p75.   300w.   4

2438   WISEMAN, Mac. ABC Collection. ABC AC30033 (E) (Re-issue)
        CMR   Sept.   p16.   225w. $3\frac{1}{2}$

2439   WISEMAN, Mac. Country Music Memories. CMH-6202
        BGU   June p39.   150w.   4
        OTM   Spring p26-7.   200w. $2\frac{1}{2}$
        PIC   Sept.   p61.   125w.   2

2440   WISEMAN, Mac and Shenandoah Cutups. New Traditions, Vol. 2. Vetco LP509
        BGU   Dec.   p29.   175w.   3
        MN   V8/#2 p16.   350w. $4\frac{1}{2}$
        PIC   Dec.   p54.   150w. $3\frac{1}{2}$

2441   WOOTEN, Art. A Living Legend. Homestead 104
        PIC   Oct.   p56.   225w. $3\frac{1}{2}$

2442   YARBROUGH, Rual. Just Me. Old Homestead 90066
        BGU   Feb.   p28.   175w.   4
        PIC   Aug.   p62.   200w. $3\frac{1}{2}$

FOLK and ETHNIC

It is difficult to arrive at a definition satisfactory to performers, reviewers, and listeners that explicitly defines the broad spectrum of recordings indexed under FOLK. Even the experts find themselves in basic disagreement. For example, Grove's Dictionary of Music and Musicians [vol. 3, New York: St. Martin's, 1954; p182] describes this genre as "any music which has entered into the heritage of the people, but can be assigned to no composer, school, or as a rule, even period. In general, it may be defined as a type of music which has been submitted for many generations to the process of oral transmission."

In contrast to Grove's learned point of view, Pete Seeger, dean of American folksingers, points out [in The Incompleat Folksinger, New York: Simon & Schuster, 1972; p5] that "folk music" was a term invented by 19th-century scholars and today covers such a multitude of kinds of music as to be almost meaningless. For Seeger, it is homemade music played mainly by ear and arising out of older traditions, but with a meaning for today. In fact, he even rejects the term "folksinger," preferring the more awkward appellation "professional singer of amateur music."

The final word on the subject may come from the great Big Bill Broonzy who is credited with the statement, "Folk music just got to be sung by peoples; ain't never heard no horse singing."

Attempting to categorize the records reviewed in 1977 and indexed in this volume has caused some difficulty. The user of this index will find, along with the many familiar names with long connections in performing traditional music, many other names unfamiliar to folk followers. Possibly one reason for the confusion that seems to have hold of what was once a well-defined musical genre may be the transitional nature of the current folk scene. Popular acceptance of folk music is at a near record low. The world of popular music, caught up in the rock explosion that began with Elvis Presley and the Beatles, has passed folk music by. The folk revival of the early 1960's is now a part of the historical parade of popular musical tastes and the genre has been relegated to the few still surviving "coffee houses," the scattered folk festivals, and to re-releases of singers and instrumentalists who once commanded a much broader audience.

At least two major trends seem to offer a ray of light for

followers of the folk field.   The first is the emergence of the mod-
ern-day singer-songwriter who writes his/her own material.   Often
the singer-songwriter makes an attempt to find a base in the folk
tradition.   The sound of the acoustic guitar, though usually accom-
panied by electrical instruments, is once again being heard.   However, because of the tenuous relationship many of these artists have
to traditional music, they have been placed in the section of the book
reserved for ROCK.

Among the performers in this growing troubadour genre are
such as John Prine, Kris Kristofferson, Joni Mitchell, Randy Newman, Carly Simon, Murray McLauchlin, and Bruce Cockburn.   Listening to their often poetic and always intriguing music reveals that
their roots are not "arising from older traditions" but are deep, in
the popular concerns of the counter-culture.

A second trend may be more significant for the immediate
presence of folk music.   There was a period in the development of
modern popular music when every pop vocalist who carried an acoustic guitar was referred to as a "folksinger."   Today, when very little real folk music is currently reaching a mass audience, these
artists have been absorbed in the pop culture.   In England, however, the situation is somewhat different.   There are emerging several notable groups and individuals who have won both respect and
an audience for their highly personal arrangements of traditional
material.   They are deeply rooted in traditional music and draw
upon the past as well as on popular song styles to arrive at a medium that is both ancient and modern at the same time.   As well,
non-English roots in America (specifically Cajun and Chicano music)
promotes its brand of folk music, and it can be found here.

Finally, the distance between folk music and country (or
country and western) continues to grow.   As country and western
falls even further under the influence of rock the audience for an
older "Grand Old Opry" style becomes smaller.   At the same time
country-based music has begun to invade the rock and folk fields.
Listening habits, attendance at folk festivals, and new recordings
may indicate an awakening interest in a more rural and traditionally
based music.

According to the reviews, the best folk albums of 1977 are:

ALBION Dance Band.   The Prospect Before Us.   Harvest
     SHSP 4059 (England)
ANDERSON, Alistair.   Traditional Tunes.   Front Hall FHR 08
CHRISTL, Margaret and Ian Robb.   The Barley Grain for Me.
     Folk Legacy FSC 62
HERDMAN, Priscilla.   The Water Lily.   Philo 1014
HICKERSON, Joe.   Drive Dull Care Away.   Folk Legacy FSI
     58/59 (2 discs)
KAIRO, Peter.   Playing It Safe.   Physical Records PR 32-
     006

KOTTKE, Leo. Chrysalis CHR 1106
PALEY, Tom. Hard Luck Papa. Kicking Mule KM 201
VAN RONK, Dave. Sunday Street. Philo 1036

2443   ACKERMAN, Will. Turtle's Navel. Windham Hill C1001
        GP   May   p129.   50w.   3

2444   ADAM, Margie. Songwriter. Pleiades HB 2747
        SO   July/Aug.   p49.   100w.   3

2445   ADAMS, Derroll. Along the Way. Bestseller 4C 06223567
        (E)
        FR   April   p23.   100w.   3

2446   ADAMS, Derroll. Live. Sounds Superb 4M 048 23599 (E)
        FR   April   p23.   100w.   3

2447   ADAMS, Paul and Linda Adams. County Hirings. Sweet
        Folk and Country SFA 053
        FR   Feb.   p23.   250w.   2

2448   ALBA. Alba. Rubber Records RUB 021
        FR   July   p22.   100w.   3

2449   ALBION Country Band. Battle of the Field. Antilles An
        7027
        AU   Oct. 1   p181.   100w. $4\frac{1}{2}$
        RS   Jan. 27   p68.   150w.   3

2450   ALBION Dance Band. The Prospect Before Us. Harvest
        SHSP 4059
        FR   June   p19.   300w.   5
        MM   May 14   p26.   575w.   4
        RS   Aug. 25   p55.   50w. $2\frac{1}{2}$
        RSP   1:3   p14-5.   250w. $3\frac{1}{2}$

2451   ALBION Dance Band. Son of Morris On. Harvest SHSM
        2012 (E)
        RSP   1:3   p14-5.   250w. $3\frac{1}{2}$

2452   ALSOP, Peter. Asleep at the Helm. Flying Fish 034
        CFS   Summer   p22.   150w.   2
        FOL   July   p11-4.   1300w. $4\frac{1}{2}$
        RC   July   p14.   125w. $2\frac{1}{2}$

2453   ANDERSON, Alistair. Traditional Tunes. Front Hall FHR-
        08
        AU   Feb.   p89.   400w.   4
        FOL   July   p25-6.   500w. $4\frac{1}{2}$

FR   April   p23.   250w.   4
RC   Dec.   p11.   150w.   4
RSP   Jan.-Feb.   p16-7.   350w.   3
SO   May/June   p49.   175w.   4½

2454   ANDERSON, Eric.   The Best Songs.   Arista AL 4128
FS   Nov.   p15, 19.   800w.   3

2455   ANDREW, John and Lissa Anderson.   Louise--A Life Story.
Elsound EMLP 7604
FR   May   p20.   200w.   3

2456   AR Skloferien.   Folk Celtique.   Vogue VDM 30 194 (France)
RSP   Jan.-Feb.   p14.   200w.   3

2457   ARDOIN, Alphonse.   La Musique Creole.   Arhoolie 1070
OTM   Spring   p30.   200w.   2

2458   ARMSTRONG, Frankie.   Out of Love, Hope and Suffering.
Bay 206
FOL   March   p12-3.   550w.   5
FR   June   p26.   200w.   3
MM   Jan. 18   p42.   100w.   4

2459   ASHLAW, Ted.   Adirondack Woods Singer.   Philo 1022
RSP   1:3   p23-4.   350w.   3½

2460   ASPEY, Gary and Vera Aspey.   A Taste of Hotpot.   Topic
12TS299 (E)
FR   May   p20.   150w.   2

2461   ASPEY, Vera.   The Blackbird.   Topic 12TS356 (E)
MM   Nov. 19   p31.   250w.   4½

2462   ATTERSON, Alex.   Pushing the Business On.   Plant Life
PLR 005 (E)
FR   Oct.   p21.   500w.   4½
MM   Dec. 3   p31.   200w.   3½

2463   BACKHOUSE, Miriam.   Gypsy Without a Road.   Mother
Earth MUM 1203
FR   Sept.   p23.   350w.   4
MM   Sept. 3   p44.   200w.   2½

2464   BAEZ, Joan.   Blowin' Away.   Portrait 34697
MM   July 16   p23.   350w.   1
RC   July   p6-7.   300w.   4
RS   Aug. 25   p56.   350w.   2½
SOU   Sept.   p63.   300w.   5
SR   Nov.   p86.   200w.   4

2465   BAEZ, Joan.   Golden Hour SH863 (Reissue) (E)
CAC   June   p108.   100w.   3

2466   BAEZ, Joan.   Gulf Winds.   A&M SP-4603.   Cass.   8-4603
        AU   April p85.   150w.   2
        CAC March p474.   200w.   2½
        CIR Feb. 28 p14.   400w.   2
        HF   Feb.   p142.   250w.   3
        RS   Jan. 13 p51.   250w.   3
        SOU Jan.   p46.   300w.   2½
        SR   Feb.   p82.   450w.   4

2467   BAEZ, Joan.   The Lovesong Album.   Vanguard VSD 79/80
        (2 discs) (Reissue)
        FR   Jan.   p26.   100w.   3

2468   BAILES Brothers.   Old Homestead CS 103
        BGU Jan.   p26.   600w.   5
        PIC April p69-70.   325w.   3½

2469   BAILES Brothers.   Early Radio, Vol. 2.   Old Homestead
        OHCS 104
        BGU Dec.   p19.   125w.   2½
        PIC Nov.   p53-4.   225w.   2½

2470   BAILES Brothers.   I've Got My One Way Ticket.   Old Home-
        stead OHS 70009
        BGU Aug.   p35.   200w.   4

2471   BAILEY, Roy.   New Bell Wake.   Acorn CF 262 (E)
        RSP Jan. -Feb.   p14.   200w.   4½

2472   BAILEY, Roy and Leo Rosselson.   Love, Loneliness and
        Laundry.   Acorn CF 271 (E)
        FR   Aug.   p23.   200w.   5
        MM   May 14 p34.   400w.   4½

2473   BALFA Brothers.   J'ai Vu le Luop, le Renard et la Belette.
        Rounder 6007
        RSP 1:3 p39.   150w.   4

2474   BANJO Dan and the Mid-Nite Plowboys.   Snowfall.   Fretless
        109
        AU   Oct.   p127.   300w.   2½

2475   BATTLEFIELD Band.   Topic 12TS313 (E)
        FR   April p23.   100w.   3
        RSP 1:3 p16.   250w.   4

2476   BELLAMY, Peter.   Barrack Room Ballads of Rudyard Kip-
        ling.   Free Reed FRR 014 (E)
        FR   Sept.   p25.   50w.   4
        RSP March-April p16.   250w.   4½

2477   BELLAMY, Peter.   The Transports.   Free Reed FRR 021/2
        (E) (2 discs)

FR Nov. p25. 700w. 4

2478 BENNETT, Willie P. Hobo's Taunt. Woodshed WS 007
      SOU Dec. p54. 250w. 3

2479 BERESFORD Band. Yorkshire Dales Dance Night. Leader
      LEA 2069
      FR Dec. p26. 200w. 4

2480 BERKELEY, Roy and Tim Woodbridge. Innisfree/Green
      Linnet SIF 1007
      CFS Autumn p27. 75w. $3\frac{1}{2}$
      FR Oct. p23. 200w. 4

2481 BERMAN, Michael. Daughter of Darkness. Custom Cas-
      settes [no serial number] (E)
      FR Oct. p23. 100w. $2\frac{1}{2}$

2482 BIRCHILL, Bob. Will I Ever Get to Heaven. Willo' Wind
      Records WOW 1 (Canada)
      CC Nov. p36. 100w. 3

2483 BISHOP, Stephen. Carless. ABCD-954
      FOL Feb. p12-3. 625w. 5

2484 BOND, Peter. It's All Right for Some. Trailer. LER 2108
      (E)
      FR Oct. p23. 200w. 4
      MM Sept. 3 p44. 250w. 3

2485 BONFIELD-Dickson. Portage. Ahmek BD 101 (Canada)
      CC Feb. p30. 50w. 3

2486 BOOKBINDER, Roy. Ragtime Millionaire Featuring 'Fats'
      Kaplan. Blue Goose 2023
      CAD Nov. p41. 125w. 5

2487 BOTHY Band. Old Hag, You Have Killed Me. Polydor 2383
      417
      CAC Feb. p437. 150w. $3\frac{1}{2}$
      FR April p24. 200w. 3
      RSP Jan.-Feb. p18. 350w. $3\frac{1}{2}$

2488 BOTHY Band. Out of the Wind into the Sun. Polydor 2382
      456 (E)
      CAC Feb. p437. 150w. $3\frac{1}{2}$
      MM Dec. 3 p31. 300w. 4

2489 BOYS of the Lough. Good Friends, Good Music. Transat-
      lantic TRA 354 (E)
      MM Nov. 19 p31. 300w. $3\frac{1}{2}$

2490 The BOYS of the Lough. The Piper's Broken Finger.

Philo PH 1042
   AU   Sept.   p97.   200w.   4½
   CFS Autumn p26.   125w.   4
   EDS Summer p72.   150w.   2
   FR   May   p21.   200w.   5
   PIC Dec.   p54.   200w.   3½
   RSP March-April p11.   175w.   5
   SR   Nov.   p124.   200w.   5

2491   BRADSTREET, David.   A&M SP9026 (Canada)
   OLR   Dec.   p293.   50w.   3½

2492   BRADY, Paul & Andy Irvine.   Mulligan Records
   FOL   May   p3.   75w.   2½

2493   BRIMSTONE, Derek.   Shuffle River Farewell.   Rubber Records RUB 017 (E)
   FR   June   p19.   150w.   2½
   MM   April 23   p25.   125w.   2

2494   BULLY Wee.   Enchanted Lady.   Red Rag RR 007 (E)
   FR   June   p20.   100w.   2
   FR   April   p24.   200w.   4
   MM   Feb. 19   p28.   125w.   3½

2495   BURGESS, John.   The Art of the Highland Bagpipe, Vol. 1/2.
Topic 12TS291/326 (E) (2 discs)
   FR   May   p25.   150w.   4
   FR   Dec.   p27.   250w.   3

2496   BURKE, Kevin.   Sweeney's Dream-Fiddle Tunes from County
Sligo, Ireland.   Folkways FW-8876
   BGU   Aug.   p35.   100w.   5
   FOL   June   p5.   125w.   5
   FR   Oct.   p25.   250w.   2
   PIC   Aug.   p69.   325w.   3
   SO   July/Aug.   p50.   100w.   3

2497   BUTCHER, Eddie.   Once I Was a Daysman.   Free Reed FR
003 (E)
   FR   April   p25.   350w.   4
   MM   Feb. 19   p28.   150w.   3½

2498   BUTCHER, Eddie.   Shamrock, Rose and Thistle.   Leader
LEA 2070 (E)
   FR   April   p25.   350w.   4
   MM   Feb. 19   p28.   150w.   3½

2499   BUTLER, Edith.   SPPS PS 1909 (Canada)
   CC   Jan.   p33.   50w.   3

2500   CADDICK, Bill.   Sunny Memories.   Trailer LER 2097 (E)
   EDS   Winter   p114.   75w.   4

FR   March p20.   200w.   5
MM   Jan. 29 p27.   500w. $4\frac{1}{2}$

2501   CAMERON, John Allan.   Weddings, Wakes and Other Things.
Columbia GES 90343 (Canada) (2 discs)
       CFS Autumn p27.   150w.   4

2502   CAMERON Men.   Classic Scots Fiddle Recordings from the
Thirties.   Topic LP 12T 321 (E)
       EDS Winter p114.   150w.   3
       FR Dec. p29.   400w.   2

2503   CAMPBELL, Alex.   Big Daddy of Folk Music.   Antagon LP
3206 (E)
       FR March p20.   200w.   4

2504-5 CAMPBELL, Lorna.   Adam's Rib.   Cottage Records COT
701 (E)
       FR Feb. p23.   250w.   3

2506   CANNON, Sean.   The Roving Journey Man.   Cottage COT
411 (E)
       FR June p20.   200w.   4

2507   CARIGNAN, Jean.   Rend Homage à Joseph Allard.   Philo
FI 2012
       BGU May p43.   50w.   3
       CFS Summer p23.   125w.   5
       FOL June p6.   100w. $3\frac{1}{2}$
       SR March p114.   150w.   4

2508   CARLIN, Joanna.   Fancy That.   DJM DJF 20508 (E)
       FR Sept. p25.   200w.   4
       MM Aug. 6 p17.   50w. $3\frac{1}{2}$

2509   CARTER, Dorothy.   Troubadour.   Celeste
       RSP March-April p21.   100w.   2
       SO Jan./Feb. p48-9.   300w.   4

2510   CARTHY, Martin.   Topic 12TS 5340 (E) (Reissue)
       MM June 4 p58.   100w.   3

2511   CARTHY, Martin.   But Two Came By.   Topic 12TS343 (E)
(Reissue)
       MM June 4 p58.   100w.   3

2512   CARTHY, Martin.   Byker Hill.   Topic 12TS342 (E) (Reissue)
       MM June 4 p58.   100w. $2\frac{1}{2}$

2513   CARTHY, Martin.   Crown of Horn.   Topic 12TS300 (E)
       RS Jan. 27 p68.   75w.   3

2514   CARTHY, Martin.   Prince Heathen.   Topic 12TS344 (E)

(Reissue)
    MM   June 4   p58.   100w. $4\frac{1}{2}$

2515   CARTHY, Martin.   Landfall.   Topic 12TS345 (E) (Reissue)
    MM   June 4   p58.   100w. $2\frac{1}{2}$

2516   CARTHY, Martin.   Second Album.   Topic (E) (Reissue)
    MM   June 4   p58.   100w. $3\frac{1}{2}$

2517   CAZDEN, Joanna.   The Greatest Illusion.   Sister Sun Records
    FOL   Aug.   p23.   300w. $3\frac{1}{2}$
    SO   Jan./Feb.   p49-50.   100w. $2\frac{1}{2}$

2518   CAZDEN, Joanna.   Hatching.   Sister Sun 2
    SO   Jan./Feb.   p49-50.   100w.   3

2519   CAZDEN, Joanna.   Jade & Sarsaparilla.   Submaureen Records
    FOL   Aug.   p23.   150w. $4\frac{1}{2}$

2520   CELEBRATED Ratcliffe Stout Band.   Dan, Half-Dan and the Spacemen.   (no label)
    FR   June   p25.   200w.   3

2521   CENOTAPH Corner.   Ups and Downs.   Cottage COT 501
    FR   May   p21.   100w.   3

2522   CHAPMAN, Michael.   Lived Here 1968-1972.   Decca Cube GNAT 1 (E)
    CAC   May   p49.   125w.   3
    FR   June   p25.   150w.   3

2523   CHAPMAN, Michael.   The Man Who Hated Mornings.   Decca SKL 5290 (E)
    MM   Nov. 19   p24.   400w.   4

2524   CHIEFTAINS.   Bonaparte's Retreat.   Island ILPS 9432 (Reissue)
    FR   Feb.   p24.   450w.   3
    SR   May   p94.   125w.   4

2525   CHIEFTAINS.   Live.   Island ILPS 9501
    FR   Nov.   p27.   250w.   2
    MM   Aug. 6   p16.   400w. $2\frac{1}{2}$
    SR   Dec.   150w.   4

2526   CHRISTIAN, Meg.   I Know You Know.   Olivia LF 902
    SO   Jan./Feb.   p49.   225w.   4

2527   CHRISTL, Margaret and Ian Robb.   The Barley Grain for Me.   Folk Legacy FSC 62
    CFS   Autumn   p25.   150w.   5

      FR Dec. p29. 600w. 4
      RSP March-April p26. 75w. 4

2528 CINNAMOND, Robert. You Rambling Boys of Pleasure:
Traditional Stories and Ballads from Ulster. Topic 12T269
(E)
      TM No. 6 p4-5. 675w. 4

2529 CLANNAD. Dulaman. Gael Linn CEF 058
      MM May 14 p34. 125w. 4

2530 CLARKE, Eddie. Sailing into Walpole's Marsh. Innisfree/
Green Linnet 1004 (E)
      RSP V1/#3 p15. 225w. 3

2531 CLEVELAND, Sara. Philo 102
      CFS Summer p23. 125w. $3\frac{1}{2}$
      RSP 1:3 p28. 300w. 3

2532 COCKBURN, Bruce. Bruce Cockburn. True North 1 (Canada)
      FOL Aug. p16-7. 400w. 3

2533 COCKBURN, Bruce. High Winds White Sky. True North
TN 3 (Canada)
      FOL Aug. p17, 19. 125w. $3\frac{1}{2}$

2534 COCKBURN, Bruce. In the Falling Dark. Island ILTN9463
(Canada)
      AU June p114. 400w. $4\frac{1}{2}$
      CRA May p66. 300w. 3
      FOL May p2. 175w. 5
      FOL Aug. p20-1. 250w. $4\frac{1}{2}$
      GP Aug. p120. 50w. 4
      OLR Sept. p224. 25w. 4
      RS June 2 p80, 83. 350w. $3\frac{1}{2}$

2535 COCKBURN, Bruce. Joy Will Find a Way. True North TN
23 (Canada)
      FOL Aug. p20. 250w. 4

2536 COCKBURN, Bruce. Nightvision. True North TN 16 (Canada)
      FOL Aug. p20. 150w. $1\frac{1}{2}$

2537 COCKBURN, Bruce. Salt, Sun and Time. True North TN
16 (Canada)
      FOL Aug. p20. 200w. $2\frac{1}{2}$

2538 COCKBURN, Bruce. Sunwheel Dance. True North TNX 7
(Canada)
      FOL Aug. p19, 20. 300w. 4

2539 COE, Pete & Chris. Out of Season, Out of Rhyme. Trailer

LER 2098
    EDS Summer p73. 225w. 0
    FR Feb. p24. 150w. 4
    RSP 1:3 p16. 250w. $2\frac{1}{2}$

2540   COLEMAN, Michael. The Legacy of. Shanadine 33002 (E)
    FR Nov. p27. 250w. 3

2541   COLEMAN, Michael. Paddy Killoran's Back in Town. Shanadine 3303 (E)
    FR Nov. p27. 250w. 3

2542   COLLINS, Judy. Bread and Roses. Elektra 1076-Cart. -1076
    CAC Jan. p393. 125w. $1\frac{1}{2}$
    FR Feb. p25. 200w. 4

2543   COLLINS, Judy. So Early in the Spring; the First 15 Years.
    Elektra/Asylum 8E-6002 (2 discs) (Reissue)
    FR Dec. p31. 200w. 4
    GR Nov. p920. 50w. 3
    MM Sept. 3 p17. 500w. $3\frac{1}{2}$
    RC Dec. p5-6. 150w. $4\frac{1}{2}$
    RR Oct. p88. 175w. $2\frac{1}{2}$
    SR Dec. 750w. 4

2544   COLLINS, Kathleen. Shenachie 29002 (E)
    RSP Jan. -Feb. p17. 300w. 3

2545   COLLINS, Shirley. Amaranth. Harvest SHS 2008 (Reissue)
    EDS Spring p32. 75w. $4\frac{1}{2}$
    RS Jan. 27 p68. 200w. 3

2546   COLTMAN, Bob. Son of Child. Minstrel JD 205
    CFS Autumn p26. 150w. $3\frac{1}{2}$
    FR June p27. 350w. 1
    FS Nov. p21-2. 650w. $3\frac{1}{2}$
    RC Oct. p5-6. 300w. 4

2547   COONEY, Michael. A Singer of Old Songs. Front Hall 07
    RC Aug. p3-4. 200w. $3\frac{1}{2}$
    SO July/Aug. p49. 200w. $3\frac{1}{2}$

2548   COPPER, Bob. Sweet Rose in June. Topic 12TS 328 (E)
    FR Sept. p25. 250w. $3\frac{1}{2}$

2549   CORBETT, Ronnie and Ronnie Barker. The Two Ronnies.
    BBC REB 257 (E)
    GR Feb. p1335. 75w. $3\frac{1}{2}$

2550   CORRECTONE String Band. Black-Eyed Suzie. Swallowtail ST6
    CFS Summer p21. 100w. $1\frac{1}{2}$

2551 COSMOTHEKA. Wines and Spirits. Highway SHY 7001 (E)
FR Nov. p29. 100w. 3

2552 COSTELLO, Cecilia. Recording from the Sound Archives of
BBC. Leader LEE 4054 (E)
TM No. 6 p5-7. 1050w. 5

2553 COTTRELL, Jenes. Elzics Farewell. Kanawha 301
RSP Jan. -Feb. p22. 150w. 3

2554 CRONIN, Paddy. The Rakish Paddy. Fiddler 002
RSP March-April p15. 300w. 3

2555 CRONSHAW, Andrew. Earthed in a Cloud Valley. Trailer
LER 2104 (E)
FR Oct. p25. 150w. 4

2556 CUTLER, Adge. The Very Best of. EMI EMC 3191 (E)
FR Nov. p31. 50w. 2

2557 CUTTY, Gordon. A Grand Old Fashioned Dance. Free Reed
Records 006 (E)
FR Jan. p27. 300w. 4
SO May/June p49. 150w. 4

2558 DALGISH, Malcolm and Grey Larsen. Banish Misfortune.
June Appal JA 016
CFS Summer p21. 125w. 5

2559 DALY, Jackie and Seamus Creagh. Geal-Linn CEF 057
FR Aug. p23. 500w. 4

2560 DAVENPORT, Bob. Topic 12TS350 (E)
FR Dec. p31. 400w. 2

2561 DAVENPORT, Bob. Postcards Home. Topic 12TS318 (E)
FR June p27. 500w. 4
FS Nov. p20-1. 550w. 3
MM April 23 p50. 300w. 2

2562 DAWNWIND. Looking Back on the Future. Amron ARN 5003
(E)
FR Jan. p28. 100w. 3

2563 DAYHILLS. Mom's Favorite/Irish Music in America. Bis-
cuit City BC 1308
AU Sept. p96. 450w. 4
CFS Autumn p24. 150w. 4

2564 DECAMERON. Tomorrow's Pantomime. Transatlantic
[cartridge]
CAC Jan. p393. 225w. 2

2565   DENNY, Sandy.   Rendezvous.   Island ILPS 9433
       MM May 28 p24.   425w. $3\frac{1}{2}$

2566   DICKIE, James.   James F. Dickie's Delights: Scottish Fid-
       dling in the Style of Scott Skinner.   Topic 12T279 (E) (Reis-
       sue)
       EDS Spring p32.   125w. $2\frac{1}{2}$
       TM No. 6 p11-3.   500w. $3\frac{1}{2}$

2567   DOBSON, Bonnie.   Morning Dew.   Polydor 2383 400 (E)
       FR Jan. p28.   50w.   2

2568   DOCHERTY, Terry.   Teller of Tales.   Fellside FE 001 (E)
       FR Jan. p28.   100w.   1

2569   DONALD, Duck and and Kathy Fink.   Kissing is a Crime.
       Likeable 01
       PIC Aug. p70-1.   200w.   2

2570   DOUCET, Comey and Jimmy Thibodeaux.   Et Musique.   Swal-
       low LP 6024
       AU Nov. p134.   400w.   4

2571   DOUGHTY, Johnny.   Round Rye Bay for More Traditional
       Songs from the Sussex Coast.   Topic 12TS 324
       EDS Winter p114.   75w.   3
       FR July p22.   500w.   3

2572   DRANSFIELD, Barry.   The Fiddler's Dream.   Transatlantic
       TRA 322 (E)
       RSP Jan.-Feb. p17.   225w.   3

2573   DRANSFIELD, Robin and Barry.   Popular to Contrary Belief.
       Free Road FRR 018 (E)
       FR Dec. p33.   150w.   4
       MM Sept. 24 p31.   400w.   5

2574   DUNN & Rubini.   Diggin' It.   Prodigal 6-10013 (E)
       MM Jan. 1 p15.   50w.   1

2575   DYER-BENNETT, Richard.   The Essential.   Vanguard VSD
       95/96 (2 discs) (Reissue)
       AU Dec. p136.   400w.   4

2576   EBENEZER.   Tell It to Me.   Biograph RC 6007
       SO July/Aug. p49.   150w.   3

2577   ELLIOTT, Derek and Dorothy Elliott.   Yorkshire Relish.
       Traditional TSR 025 (E)
       RSP Jan.-Feb. p17.   250w. $3\frac{1}{2}$

2578   ELLIOTT, Ramblin' Jack.   Hard Travelin'.   Fantasy F
       24720 (2 discs) (Reissue)

AU   July   p89.   100w.   4½

2579   ENNIS, Seamus.   40 Years of Irish Piping.   Free Reed
       FRR 001/2 (E) (2 discs)
          FR   Jan.   p28.   300w.   3

2580   EVANS, Dave.   Take a Bite Out of Life.   Kicking Mule
       SNKF 122
          FR   April   p27.   300w.   4

2581   FAIRPORT Convention.   Island HELP 28 (E)
          RR   April   p87.   25w.   2

2582   FAIRPORT Convention.   The Bonny Bunch of Roses.   Ver-
       tigo 9102 125 (E)
          MM   Aug. 27   p22.   400w.   3
          TP   Oct.   p44.   350w.   3½

2583   FAIRPORT Convention.   Gottle o' Gear.   Island ILPS 9389
       (E)
          AU   Sept.   p99.   100w.   1
          RS   Feb. 24   p65.   200w.   1

2584   FAIRPORT Convention.   Live at the L. A. Troubadour.   Is-
       land HELP 28 (E)
          RS   May 19   150w.   3½

2585   FARMSTEAD.   The Sheep and the Hay.   Fellside FE 005
          FR   Oct.   p25.   250w.   2

2586   FARRIERS.   Brummagem Ballads.   Broadside Records BRO
       119 (E)
          EDS   Winter   p113.   350w.   3
          FR   Aug.   p24.   200w.   2

2587   FELDMAN, Peter.   How to Play Carter-Style Guitar.   Sonya-
       tone STI 105
          PIC   July   p64.   225w.   4½

2588   FENWICK, Nick.   Looks a Lot Like Me.   Ran-Tans Records
       Rant 001
          FR   Aug.   p24.   100w.   3

2589   FISHER, Archie.   The Man with a Rhyme.   Folk Legacy
       FSS 61
          RSP   March-April   p14.   400w.   5

2590   FISHER, Betty.   I Got a Song to Sing.   Atteiram API-L-
       1534
          BGU   Feb.   p24.   75w.   5

2591   FISHER, Cillia and Artie Trezise.   Balcanquhal.   Trailer
       LER 2100

EDS Summer p74. 225w. 4
FR June p29. 150w. 4

2592 FIVE Hand Reel. Rubber RUB 019
FOL March p23. 600w. 4

2593 FIVE Hand Reel. For a' That. RCA PL 25066 (E)
FR Aug. p24. 300w. 4
GR Aug. p354. 50w. 2
MM June 25 p24. 400w. 4

2594 FIVEPENNY Piece. Telling Tales. EMI EMC 3183 (E)
CAC Aug. p166. 100w. $3\frac{1}{2}$
GR Nov. p920. 25w. 4

2595 FOSTER, Chris. Layers. Topic 12 TS 329 (E)
FR Aug. p25. 300w. 4

2596 FRANKE, Bob. Love Can't Be Bitter All the Time. Fretless 116
FOL Feb. p25. 450w. 5

2597 GABERLUNZIE. Wind and Water, Time and Tide. MWSLS
507 (E)
FR April p27. 200w. 3

2598 Le GALANT Noye. Ballades et Chansons. Le Chant du
Monde 74576 (France)
RSP 1:3 p13. 225w. $3\frac{1}{2}$

2599 GARBUTT, Vin. King Gooden. Trailer LER 2102 (E)
EDS Summer p73. 300w. 0
RSP 1:3 p12. 150w. 2

2600 GAUGHAN, Dick. Coppers and Brass. Topic 12TS 5315 (E)
MM May 14 p14. 125w. $3\frac{1}{2}$
RSP 1:3 p15. 250w. 4

2601 GAUGHAN, Dick. Kist o' Gold. Trailer LER 2103 (E)
FR May p21. 250w. $4\frac{1}{2}$
MM April 2 p26. 300w. $3\frac{1}{2}$
RSP 1:3 p10-11. 300w. 5
SO Sept./Oct. p50. 150w. 4

2602 GAVIN, Frankie and Alec Finn. Shanadie 29008 (E)
FR Nov. p31. 400w. 3

2603 GEAR, Robert. Steel Guitar and Dobro. Physical Records
PR32-007
GP Feb. p113. 125w. 4
PIC May p69. 150w. $2\frac{1}{2}$

2604 GILFELLON, Tommy. In the Middle of the Tune. Topic

12TS283 (E)
>   EDS   Spring   p32.   150w.   2½

2605   GILMOUR Brothers. A Good Time Is a Good Time. Michigan Archives NA 103
>   CFS   Autumn   p25.   75w.   4

2606   GILTRAP, Gordon. Perilous Journey. Electric (E)
>   MM   Dec. 3   p23.   200w.   5

2607   GLACKIN, Paddy. Gael Linn CEF 060 (E)
>   MM   Oct. 15   p30.   125w.   5

2608   GLAZER, Tom with Pat Moffitt. The Musical Heritage of
America, Vol. 1.   CMS 650 (4 discs)
>   RC   July   p16.   300w.   3

2609   GLICK, Michael. City Dreams. New Morning
>   SO   March/April   p50.   250w.   2½

2610   GOLDING, John. Another. Cottage COT 401 (E)
>   FR   Jan.   p29.   100w.   2

2611   GOODLUCK, John. Monday's Childe. Tradition TSR 028 (E)
>   FR   Dec.   p33.   200w.   3

2612   GRAHAM, Davey. All That Moody. Eron Records 007 (E)
>   FR   Feb.   p25.   100w.   2

2613   GRAHAM, Len. Wind and Water. Topic 12TS534 (E)
>   FR   Oct.   p27.   250w.   4

2614   GREEN, Gary. These Six Strings Neutralize the Tools of
Oppression. Folkways FH 5351
>   FR   June   p35.   500w.   1
>   PIC   Aug.   p71.   200w.   2
>   RSP   1:3   p21-2.   50w.   0

2615   GROSSMAN, Stefan. Country Blues Guitar. Kicking Mule
SNKF 129
>   FR   Aug.   p25.   350w.   2
>   MM   June 25   p24.   250w.   3½

2616   GROSSMAN, Stefan. Finger Picking Guitar Techniques.
Kicking Mule 112
>   PIC   Oct.   p59.   200w.   3½

2617   GROSSMAN, Stefan. Hot Dogs. Kicking Mule KM 131
>   CFS   Summer   p22.   150w.   4

2618   GROSSMAN, Stefan. Memphis Jellyroll. Kicking Mule 118
>   PIC   May   p63.   625w.   4

2619   GROSSMAN, Stefan.   My Creole Belle.   Transatlantic TRA
        326 (E)
            FR   Feb.   p25.   300w.   4

2620   GRUBSTAKE.   Biscuit City BC 1310
            CFS   Summer p21.   125w.   5

2621   GRUPO Folk Lorico y Experimental Neuvayorquino.   Lo Dice
        Todo.   Salsoul SAL-4110
            DB   March 24 p49.   375w.   5
            HF   March p139.   250w.   4
            SR   Feb.   p111.   200w.   5

2622   GUTHRIE, Woody.   Original Recordings, 1940-46.   Warner
        BS 2999 (Reissue)
            AU   Aug.   p81.   100w.   3
            CRA   April p102.   200w.   3
            FR   Aug.   p26.   400w.   2
            MM   July 16 p21.   600w. $4\frac{1}{2}$

2623   HADLEY, Bob.   Tunes from the Well.   Kicking Mule Records
        KM 103
            FR   July p23.   200w.   3
            GP   Jan.   p97.   125w. $4\frac{1}{2}$
            VV   Aug.   1 p51.   50w.   3

2624   HALEY, Ed.   Parkersburg Landing.   Rounder 1010
            FOL   May p4.   225w.   5

2625   HALL, Tony.   Fieldvole Music.   Free Reed FRR 012 (E)
            FR   July p23.   400w.   4

2626   HAMMOND, John.   Solo.   Vanguard VSD 79380
            GP   March p112.   275w. $3\frac{1}{2}$
            SR   April p90.   132w.   5

2627   HAMMOND, Lawrence.   Coyote's Dream.   Takoma C 1047.
        Cart. 10478TRK
            CM   May p61.   150w.   3

2628   HARDING, Michael.   Old Four Eyes Is Back.   Phonogram
        6308 290 (E)
            FR   Aug.   p27.   300w.   4

2629   HARDY, Dave.   Leaving the Dales.   Red Dog RRR 008
            FR   March p21.   250w.   2

2630   HARRIS, Roy.   By Sandback Fields.   Topic 12TS 327 (E)
            FR   Oct.   p27.   100w.   4

2631   HARRIS, Woody.   After Dinner Mints.   Kicking Mule KM
        133
            GP   Nov.   p137.   150w.   4

2632   HENDERSON, Hamish.   Freedom Come All Ye.   Claddagh
        CCA 7 (E)
            MM Dec. 3 p31.   250w.   4½

2633   HERON.   Diamond of Dreams.   Bronze 460 (E)
            FOL May p3.   75w.   2½
            MM March 26 p19.   350w.   3
            RS Aug. 11 p55.   50w.   2

2634   HICKERSON, Joe.   Drive Dull Care Away.   Folk-Legacy FSI-
        58/59 (2 discs)
            FOL June p24.   550w.   4
            RSP Jan. -Feb. p28-9.   200w.   3½
            SO Sept. /Oct. p49-50.   175w.   4

2635   HIGGINS, Lizzie.   Up and Awa' wi' the Love Rock.   Topic
        12TS260 (E)
            TM No. 6 p22-3.   625w.   5

2636   HINCHCLIFFE, Frank.   In Sheffield Park.   Topic 12TS308
        (E)
            FR May p22.   350w.   4
            RSP V1/#3 p11.   200w.   2½
            TM No. 6 p20-2.   1200w.   4

2637   HOLMES, Joe and Len Graham.   Chaste Muses, Bards and
        Sages; Traditional Songs, Ballads Lilts and Fiddletunes from
        Northern Ireland.   Free Reed FRR 007 (Ireland)
            FR March p21.   350w.   4
            TM No. 6 p10.   525w.   3½

2638   HORSLIPS.   Book of Invasions.   DJM DJM 10
            FOL May p3.   25w.   2½
            RSP May-June p60.   250w.   4½
            MM April 30 p30.   275w.   3½
            RC Dec. p8.   250w.   4
            TP June/July p37.   350w.   2½

2639   HORSLIPS.   Live.   Horslips MOO 10 (E) (2 discs) (Reissue)
            TP June/July p37.   350w.   3

2640   HOW to Change a Flat Tire.   A Point of Departure.   Front
        Hall FHR 09
            FR July p25.   200w.   2
            FS Nov. p22-3.   350w.   1½

2641   HUGHES, Carolyne.   Black Dog and Sheep Crook.   Folk-
        tracks FSA 043 (E) (Cassette Only)
            TM No. 6 p13-4.   225w.   3

2642   HURLEY, Michael.   Have Moicy!   Rounder 3010
            FR July p25.   250w.   5

2643   HURLEY, Michael. Long Journey. Rounder 3011
       FOL   May p2.   100w.   4½
       RS   Aug. 25 p57.   325w.   3

2644   HUTCHINGS, Ashley. Rattlebone and Ploughjack. Island
       HELP 24 (E)
       RS   Jan. 27 p68.   75w.   3

2645   HUTCHINGS, Ashley. Son of Morris on. Harvest Heritage
       SHSM 2012 (E)
       RS   May 19 125w.   3

2646   IMLACH, Hamish. Transatlantic TRA SAM 43 (E) (Reissue)
       FR   July p27.   50w.   2½

2647   IMLACH, Hamish. Hamish Imlach-All Round Entertainer
       (Vol. 2). TRASAM 31 (Reissue)
       EDS   Spring p33.   150w.   0

2648   INCREDIBLE String Band. Seasons They Change. Island
       ISLD 9 (E) (2 discs)
       FOL   May p3.   75w.   0
       FR   July p27.   300w.   3

2649   INTI-ILLIMANI. Viva Chile. Monitor
       VV   Nov. 28 p66.   50w.   3½

2650   IRVINE, Andy & Paul Brady. Mulligan LUN 008 (Ireland)
       FR   May p23.   450w.   5
       RS   Aug. 25 p55.   75w.   3
       RSP   1:3 p12.   200w.   3½
       SO   Jan. -Feb. p48.   300w.   4

2651   JACOB'S Reunion. Towne Crier Reel. Chelsea Records CHR
       2001
       FOL   June p5.   200w.   5
       RSP   1:3 p23.   125w.   3½

2652   JADE and Sarsaparilla. Submaureen
       SO   Jan. /Feb. p49.   75w.   4½

2653   JAMES, John. Guitar Jump. Kicking Mule SNKF 128
       FR   June p33.   350w.   4
       MM   May 28 p27.   200w.   3

2654   JANSCH, Bert. Early Bert. Xtra 1170 (Reissue)
       RR   June p94.   50w.   3

2655   JANSCH, Bert. A Rare Conundrum. Charisma
       MM   July 9 p23.   250w.   3½

2656   JAY and Lyn. Songs, Ballads, and Fiddle Tunes. Philo 1023
       PIC   April p70.   150w.   5

2657   JIMINEZ, Flaco.   Teardrop 2051
        RSP   1:3   p40-1.   200w.   2½

2658   JIMINEZ, Flaco.   A Mis Amigos.   DLP LP 1034
        RSP   1:3   p40.   200w.   4

2659   JIMINEZ, Flaco.   Polkas, Vals, Redovas, Shotis.   Disco
        Grande 4031
        RSP   1:3   p41.   100w.   0

2660   JOHNSON, Bob and Peter Knight.   The King of England's
        Daughter.   Chrysalis CHR 1137 (E)
        FR   Sept.   p27.   600w.   4

2661   JONES, Davis.   Easy and Slow.   Minstrel JD 201
        RC   Aug.   p6.   350w.   2½

2662   JONES, Nic.   The Noah's Ark Trip.   Trailer LER 2091 (E)
        EDS   Winter   p114.   50w.   3
        FR   March   p23.   250w.   4
        MM   April 2   p26.   250w.   3½
        RSP   1:3   p15-6.   250w.   4
        SO   Sept/Oct.   p50.   150w.   4

2663   KAIRO, Peter.   Playing It Safe.   Physical PR 32-006
        FOL   June   p7.   450w.   4½
        GP   Aug.   p120.   150w.   4
        SO   Jan./Feb.   p49.   75w.   4

2664   KATZMAN, Nick and Ruby Green.   Mississippi River Blues.
        Kicking Mule 111
        BSR   No. 7   unpaged   300w.   3

2665   KATZMAN, Nick and Ruby Green.   Panic When the Sun Goes
        Down.   Kicking Mule
        MM   Nov. 19   p23.   250w.   3½

2666   KEANE, Sean.   Gusty's Frolicks.   Claddagh CC 17 (E)
        RSP   Jan.-Feb.   p14.   200w.   3

2667   KELLY, Jo-Ann and Peter Emery.   Do It.   Red Rag RRR
        006
        FR   Jan.   p29.   450w.   4

2668   KEMPION.   Broadside Records BRO 123
        EDS   Winter   p113.   150w.   3
        FR   Aug.   p27.   100w.   3½

2669   KEMPION.   Come Ye O'er Froe France.   Sweet Folk and
        Country SFA 044 (E)
        RSP   March-April   p15.   100w.   2

2670   KIRKPATRICK, John.   Plain Capers.   Free Reed FRR 010

(E)
  FR   Feb.   p28.   350w. $4\frac{1}{2}$
  RS   May 19   125w.   3

2671   KIRKPATRICK, John and Sue.   Among the Many Attractions
       at the Show Will Be a Really High Class Band.   Topic
       12TS295 (E) (Reissue)
         EDS   Spring   p33.   200w.   2

2672   KIRWAN, Danny.   DJM DJL PA 9
         SR   Dec.   200w.   4

2673   KLEZMORIM.   East Side Wedding.   Arhoolie 3006
         SO   Sept./Oct.   p49.   350w.   4

2674   KOLOC, Bonnie.   Close-Up.   Epic 34184
         FOL   Feb.   p15, 23-25.   700w.   4

2675-6 KOTTKE, Leo.   Did You Hear Me?, 1971-76.   Capitol ST
       11576 (Reissue)
         AU   Feb.   p86.   100w.   5
         CAC Aug.   p163.   300w.   3
         CMR June   p15.   200w.   3
         RSP May-June   p59.   200w.   3

2677   KOTTKE, Leo.   Leo Kottke.   Chrysalis CHR 1106
         AU   April   p87.   150w.   4
         CRA May   p77-8.   300w.   3
         FOL Aug.   p26.   200w. $3\frac{1}{2}$
         GP   May   p128.   100w.   4
         GR   April   p1617.   75w. $3\frac{1}{2}$
         RR   May   p86-7.   50w. $2\frac{1}{2}$
         SR   April   p90, 94.   125w.   4

2678   KREW Brothers.   Yes, We Are All Brothers.   WAM W4037
         RC   Dec.   p12.   100w.   2

2679   The LAGGAN.   Scottish Folk Songs.   Arfolk SB 346
         FR   March   p23.   200w.   4

2680   LARIE, Mick.   La Mandoline Americaine.   Le Chant Du
       Monde LDX 74618 (France)
         BGU Sept.   p16.   125w.   4
         PIC Dec.   p59.   125w. $3\frac{1}{2}$

2681   LAT and Trall.   YTF EFG 501 6082 (Sweden)
         EDS Spring   p33.   200w.   0

2682   LEONARD, John and John Squire.   Broken Down Gentlemen.
       Rugger 018
         RSP Jan.-Feb.   p20.   350w. $3\frac{1}{2}$

2683   LESLIE, John and Chris Leslie.   The Ship of Time.   Cot-

tage COT 901 (E)
      FR   March   p25.   200w.   3

2684   LIMELIGHTERS.   Reunion, Vols. 1, 2.   Brass Dolphin (2
       discs)
      FR   July   p27.   250w.   5

2685   LING Family.   Singing Traditions of a Suffolk Family.   Topic
       12TS 292 (E)
      FR   Oct.   p27.   150w.   3
      MM   June 25 p24.   200w. $3\frac{1}{2}$

2686   LOCKHEART, Paula.   Flying Fish 045
      RC   Dec.   p16.   100w. $2\frac{1}{2}$

2687   LONDON, Lew.   Swingtime in Springtime.   Philo 1032
      CAD   May   p13.   50w.   3
      FOL   June p21.   575w.   3
      GP   Aug.   p119.   100w.   3
      PIC   Dec.   p58.   200w.   5
      RSP   1:3   p25.   250w. $2\frac{1}{2}$
      SO   May/June p47-9.   225w.   4

2688   LOUDERMILK, John.   The Early Styles of.   Country Classics
       Library CCL 1111 (Reissue)
      RSP   Jan. -Feb. p34.   250w.   2

2689   LOUDERMILK, John.   The Rocking Style of.   Country Clas-
       sics Library CCL 1112 (Reissue)
      RSP   Jan. -Feb. p34-5.   250w. $2\frac{1}{2}$

2690   McCALMANS.   McCalman's Folk.   One-Up (E)
      FR   March   p25.   250w.   3

2691   McCALMANS.   Side by Side by Side.   Transatlantic TRA
       346 (E)
      MM   Oct. 15 p30.   125w. $2\frac{1}{2}$

2692   McCASLIN, Mary.   Old Friends.   Philo 1046
      MG   Nov.   p51.   25w. $3\frac{1}{2}$
      RC   Oct.   p9.   150w. $3\frac{1}{2}$

2693   McCASLIN, Mary.   Prairie in the Sky.   Philo 1024
      CS   April 7 p19.   200w. $4\frac{1}{2}$

2694   McCASLIN, Mary.   Way Out West.   Philo 1011
      CS   April 7 p19.   200w.   4

2695   McCLATCHY, Debby.   Green Linnet 1003
      FOL   Dec.   p26.   450w.   5
      RSP   Jan. -Feb. p32.   200w. $1\frac{1}{2}$

2696   McCONNELL, Cathal and Robin Morton.   An Irish Jubilee.

Topic 12TS290 (E)
FR Feb. p28. 200w. 2

2697 MacDERMOTT, Josie. Darby's Farewell. Topic 12TS325 (E)
FR Oct. p29. 300w. 2

2698 McDONALD, Alastair. Polydor 2383 404 (E)
FR March p25. 150w. 2

2699 McGANN, Andy & Paddy Reynolds. Shanachie 29004
RSP March-April p12-3. 175w. 4
SO Jan./Feb. p48. 275w. 5

2700 McGINN, Matt. Transatlantic TRA SAM 41 (Reissue)
FR July p29. 100w. 4

2701 McGLINCHEY, Brendan. Music of a Champion. Silver Hill
PSH 100 (E)
RSP 1:3 p13. 225w. 3

2702 McGREVY and Cooley. Philo 2005
BGU Feb. p25. 150w. 4

2703 McKENNA, Mae. Everything That Touches Me. Transatlantic (E)
CAC Feb. p437. 75w. 2

2704 McKENNA, Mae. Walk on Water. Transatlantic TRA 345
(E)
MM Nov. 12 p29. 50w. 2

2705 McMORLAND, Alison. Belt wi' Colours Three. Tangent
TGS 125 (E)
FR Oct. p29. 400w. $4\frac{1}{2}$
MM Jan. 18 p42. 225w. 5

2706 MacNEIL, Flora. Craobh nan Ubhal. Tangent TGS 124 (E)
FR Oct. p31. 450w. 4

2707 MacPHERSON, Donald. Pibroch Masterpieces. Polydor
2384 087 (E)
FR May p23. 200w. $2\frac{1}{2}$

2708 McTELL, Ralph. Collection, Vol. 2. Transatlantic (E)
(Reissue)
CAC Jan. p392. 250w. 3

2709 McTELL, Ralph. Ralph, Albert and Sydney. Warner
K56399 (E)
FR Nov. p33. 150w. 3
MM Sept. 10 p26. 275w. $4\frac{1}{2}$

2710 McTELL, Ralph. Right Side Up. Warner K56296 (E)

FR   Jan.   p30.   100w.   2

2711   MAIRS, Julie and Chris Stowell.   Soft Sea Blue.   Cottage
       COT 211 (E)
       FR   Aug.   p27.   50w.   4

2712   MAKEM, Tommy and Liam Clancy.   Blackbird.   Columbia
       ELS 384 (Canada)
       OLR   Dec.   p293.   50w.   4

2713   MANN, Steve.   'Live' at the Ash Grove.   Pacific Perceptions
       HBC-001
       GP   March   p113.   150w.   4

2714   MANUEL, Ian.   The Dales of Caledonia.   Topic 12TS301 (E)
       FR   May   p25.   250w.   4

2715   MARTIN, Juan.   Flamenco Soul.   Decca SKL 5256 (E)
       GP   June   p137.   100w.   4

2716   MAZLYN-JONES, Nigel.   Ship to Shore.   Isle of Light [no
       no.] (E)
       FR   March   p27.   350w.   3

2717   MENSAH, Joe.   The Afrikan Hustle.   Mezumbah ME-D1000
       BM   March   p24.   100w.   4

2718   MIKRON Theater Company.   Last Run.   PBR International
       PBR 5001
       FR   Sept.   p29.   300w. $3\frac{1}{2}$

2719   MILLER, Dale.   Finger Picking Rags and Other Delights.
       Sonet SNKF 110
       CMR   June   p9.   100w.   2

2720   MILLER, Dale.   Guitarist's Choice.   Kicking Mule KM 137
       CFS   Autumn   p25.   100w.   4
       GP   Dec.   p152.   50w.   3

2721   MILLER, John.   How About Me.   Blue Goose 2012
       FOL   April   p22.   425w.   3

2722   MITCHELL, Kevin.   Free and Easy.   Topic 12TS314 (E)
       FR   July   p29.   250w.   4
       MM   April 2   p26.   100w.   4

2723   MITCHELL, Sam.   Bottleneck and Slide Guitar.   Kicking Mule
       SNKF 121
       FR   July   p29.   350w. $4\frac{1}{2}$

2724   MITHRAS.   For We Trade in Fun.   Cottage COT 801 (E)
       FR   March   p27.   500w.   1

2725   MOLLOY, Matt. Mulligan Records LUN 004 (Ireland)
          FOL   May p3, 9. 50w. 5
          FR   May p25. 300w. 4
          RSP   March-April p12-3. 175w. $3\frac{1}{2}$
          SO   Jan./Feb. p48. 125w. 5

2726   MOORE, Christy. Polydor 2383 426 (E)
          FR   Oct. p33. 150w. 1
          MM   May 14. p34. 300w. $3\frac{1}{2}$
          RSP   1:3 p10. 150w. $2\frac{1}{2}$

2727   MOORE, Michael. The Tallest Man in the World. Plant
        Life PLR 007
          MM   Oct. 15 p30. 200w. $3\frac{1}{2}$

2728   MORSE, Kendall. Lights along the Shore. Folk Legacy
        FS1 57
          CFS   Autumn p26. 125w. 4
          FS   Nov. p26-7. 400w. $3\frac{1}{2}$

2729   MUCKRAM Wakes. Trailer LER 2043 (E)
          FR   Jan. p30. 150w. 2

2730   MULCAHY, Mick. Gael-Linn KEF 050 (E)
          FR   July p31. 400w. 3

2731   MURPHY, Noel. Plant Life PLR 002 (E)
          FR   July p33. 100w. 3
          MM   Jan. 29 p27. 150w. 4

2732   MURPHY, Rose. Milltown Lass. Topic 12TS 1316 (E)
          FR   Nov. p33. 200w. 3
          TM   No. 6 p8. 500w. 4

2733   NiDHOMNAIL, Triona. Gael Linn 043 (E)
          RSP   Jan.-Feb. p15. 350w. 5

2734   NULL, Lisa and Bill Shute. The Feathered Maiden and Oth-
        er Ballads. Green Linnet 1006
          FOL   Dec. p27. 375w. 4
          FR   Sept. p31. 200w. 4

2735   OCHS, Phil. Chords of Fame. A&M SP 4599. Cart. 8T-
        4599. Cass. CS-4599. (2 discs) (Reissue)
          AU   Oct. p174. 150w. 5
          CIR   March 17 p16-7. 575w. $3\frac{1}{2}$
          HF   March p140. 300w. 3
          RC   May p4. 250w. $4\frac{1}{2}$
          RSP   Jan.-Feb. p29. 150w. $3\frac{1}{2}$
          SR   April p104. 750w. 4
          VV   April 11 p53. 400w. $4\frac{1}{2}$

2736   OCHS, Phil. Sings for Broadside. Folkways FD 5320

FOL   Feb.   p10.   325w.   4

2737   ODETTE, Paul.   Parklane PR 002
       CC   Nov.   p36.   100w.   3

2738   O'HALLORAN Brothers.   The Men of the Island.   Topic
       12TS305 (E)
       FR   March   p29.   200w.   1
       RSP   Jan. -Feb.   p14.   250w. $3\frac{1}{2}$

2739   OLD Swan Band.   No Reels.   Free Reed FRR 011 (E)
       FR   July   p33.   250w. $4\frac{1}{2}$
       FS   Nov.   p23-4.   550w.   4
       MM   May 14   p34.   150w.   3

2740   OLDHAM Tinkers.   Sit Thee Down.   Topic 12TS323 (E)
       FR   Aug.   p29.   300w.   2

2741   OSBORNE, Brian.   Ae Fond Kiss.   Tradition 024
       RSP   March-April   p15.   175w.   3

2742   OSSIAN.   Springthyme SPR 1004
       FR   Oct.   p33.   200w.   4
       MM   Sept. 24   p31.   200w.   4

2743   O'SULLIVAN, Bernard and Tommy McMahon.   Clare Con-
       certinas.   Topic 12TFRS502 (E)
       TM   No. 6   p28-9.   575w.   4

2744   O'SULLIVAN, Bernard and Tommy McMahon.   Play Irish
       Traditional Music of County Clare.   Topic 12TFRS 505 (E)
       TM   No. 6   p27-9.   575w.   3

2745   PACO Pena.   Fabulous Flamenco.   London SPC 22135
       SR   Feb.   p111.   200w.   5

2746   PAGE, Jim.   Shot of the Usual.   Whid-Isle Records
       FOL   Sept.   p23.   350w. $3\frac{1}{2}$

2747   PALEY, Tom.   Hard Luck Papa.   Kicking Mule KM-201
       BGU   Aug.   p32.   200w.   4
       CAD   May   p13.   25w. $2\frac{1}{2}$
       CFS   Summer   p20.   150w.   4
       FOL   Aug.   p4.   125w.   4
       FR   Feb.   p29.   300w.   4
       MM   Feb. 19   p28.   100w.   4
       RSP   March-April   p22-3.   125w.   3

2748   PARDON, Walter.   Our Side of the Baulk.   Leader LED
       2111 (E)
       MM   Aug. 13   p42.   200w.   4

2749   PAXTON, Tom.   New Songs from the Briarpatch.   Vanguard

VSD-79395
    CFS Autumn p24-5. 125w.   4
    MG Oct. p60. 50w. 1
    RC Dec. p12. 100w. 3
    SR Nov. p83. 300w. 5

2750   PAXTON, Tom. Saturday Night. MAM MAMS 1003
        CMR April p35. 75w. 0
        MM Jan. 8 p18. 250w. $1\frac{1}{2}$

2751   PAZ, Suni. Canciones Para El Recreo. Folkways FC 7850
        SO Sept./Oct. p49. 175w. 4

2752   PAZ, Suni. Entre Hermanas. Folkways FW8768
        SO Sept./Oct. p49. 175w. 4

2753   PENFOLD, Rebecca. Sweet Primroses. Folk Tracks FSA
    30-042 (E) (Cassette Only)
        TM No. 6 p13-4. 225w. 3

2754   PENTANGLE. Cruel Sister. XTRA 1172 (E) (Reissue)
        FR July p33. 50w. 1

2755   PEOPLES, Tommy. Comhaltas Ceoltoiri Eirann CL 13
        FR March p31. 250w. 2

2756   PEOPLES, Tommy and Paul Brady. The High Part of the
    Road. Shanachie 29003
        AU Nov. p134. 500w. 5
        FR Sept. p31. 700w. 3
        RSP March-April p12-3. 175w. 3

2757   PETTYJOHN, Bunk and Becky. Arizona Friends of Folklore
    AFF 33-4
        AU June p124. 600w. $3\frac{1}{2}$
        RC Aug. p7. 300w. 4

2758   PHILLIPS, Utah. El Capitan. Philo PH 1016
        CM June p48. 300w. 3

2759   PINNEY, Dick. Devil Takes My Shiny Coins. Mountain
    Railroad MR 52777
        CFS Summer p19. 125w. 4

2760   PLANT, Richard. Better Be Sane. Tradition TSR 022
        EDS Spring p32. 100w. 0

2761   PLANXTY. Collection. Polydor (Reissue) (E)
        CAC Jan. p392. 200w. 3

2762   PLANXTY. The Well Below the Hill. Antilles AN 7042
        AU Oct. p187. 100w. 5

2763   POST, Jim. Back on the Street Again--Live.   Mountain
        Railroad MR 52778
                CFS   Summer   p19.   100w. $4\frac{1}{2}$

2764   POWER, Jimmy. Irish Fiddle Player.   Topic 12T306
                EDS   Summer   p73.   200w. $2\frac{1}{2}$
                FR   April   p30.   350w.   4
                MM   Feb. 19   p28.   125w.   4
                RSP   March-April   p16.   150w. $1\frac{1}{2}$
                TM   No. 6   p24-5.   700w. $2\frac{1}{2}$

2765   PRIOR, Maddy & June Tabor.   Silly Sisters.   Chrysalis CHR
        1101
                AU   Sept.   p99.   200w.   5
                CRA   Aug.   p68.   150w. $2\frac{1}{2}$
                FOL   March   p22-3.   500w.   5
                RC   July   p9-10.   200w.   4
                SR   Nov.   p124.   250w.   5

2766   PURVIS, Geoff.   The Border Fiddler.   Fellside FE 003 (E)
                FR   Aug.   p29.   200w. $4\frac{1}{2}$

2767   RAVEN, John, John Kirkpatrick and Sue Harris.   The Eng-
        lish Canals.   Broadside BRO 118 (E)
                FR   May   p27.   100w.   4

2768   RAVEN, Mike. A Miscellany of Guitar Music.   Broadside
        BRO 124 (E)
                FR   Aug.   p29.   100w.   4

2769   REDHEAD.   Legend Records (no serial number)
                CFS   Summer   p19.   100w.   4

2770   REDPATH, Jean.   Jean Redpath.   Philo 2015
                FOL   March   p13, 22.   450w.   5

2771   REDPATH, Jean.   The Songs of Robert Burns.   Philo PH
        1037
                CFS   Summer   p23.   200w.   5
                FR   July   p33.   350w.   4
                PIC   Oct.   p57.   100w.   3
                RSP   March-April   p12.   275w.   2
                SR   June   p116, 120.   125w.   4

2772   REDPATH, Jean.   There Were Minstrels.   Trailer LER 2106
        (E)
                FR   March   p32.   200w.   5

2773   REED, Ray.   Sings Traditional Frontier and Cowboy Songs.
        Folkways FD 5329
                PIC   Oct.   p60.   300w.   3

2774   RENBOURN, John.   The Hermit.   Transatlantic TRA 336

CAC March p475.   300w.   3
EDS Summer p72.   150w. $2\frac{1}{2}$
FOL May p3.   25w.   4
FR Feb. p29.   250w.   4

2775 RIDDLE, Almeda. Ballads and Hymns from the Ozarks.
Rounder 0017
CMR Feb. p33.   200w.   4

2776 RINGER, Jim. Any Old Wind that Blows.   Philo 1021
CS April 21 p18.   200w. $3\frac{1}{2}$

2777 RINGER, Jim. Tramps and Hawkers.   Philo 1047
RC Nov. p16.   200w.   3

2778 RITCHIE, Jean. None but One.   Sire SA 7530.   Cart.
8147 7530H.   Cass. S147 7530H
HF Sept. p145.   75w.   3
PIC Nov. p56.   150w.   2
RS Sept. 8 p116-7.   450w. $4\frac{1}{2}$
SR Dec.   250w. $3\frac{1}{2}$

2779 RIZETTA, Sam. Trapezoid.   Skyline DD 107
SO March/April p51.   300w. $4\frac{1}{2}$

2780 ROARING Jelly. Golden Grates.   Free Reed FRR 13 (E)
FR July p35.   150w.   4
FS Nov. p24.   300w.   4
MM April 23 p50.   200w.   3

2781 ROBERTS, John and Tony Barrard.   Nowell Sing We Clear.
Front Hall FHR 013
CFS Autumn p25.   150w.   4

2782 ROGERS, Gamble. Mountain Railroad Records MR 52779
CFS Autumn p25.   125w.   5
GP Nov. p137.   225w. $4\frac{1}{2}$
MM Oct. 22 p22.   200w.   4
RC Dec. p5.   150w. $4\frac{1}{2}$

2783 ROGERS, Stan. Fogarty's Cove.   Barn Swallow BS 1001
(Canada)
CFS Summer p20.   200w.   4

2784 RONK, Dave Van. Sunday Street.   Philo 1036
SR May p79.   525w.   5

2785 ROONEY, Jim. Rounder 3008
FOL Sept. p13.   75w.   1

2786 ROSE, Tony. On Banks of Green Willow.   Trailer LER
2101 (E)
EDS Summer p73.   200w.   4

        FR   Feb.   p31.   100w. $4\frac{1}{2}$
        RSP   1:3   p13.   100w. $3\frac{1}{2}$

2787   ROSENBAUM, Art.   The Art of the Mountain Banjo.   Kicking
      Mule 203
        PIC   May   p69.   175w.   4

2788   ROTH, Kevin.   The Mountain Dulcimer Instrumental Album.
      Folkways FS 3570
        FR   Aug.   p31.   100w.   2

2789   ROTH, Kevin.   The Other Side of the Mountain.   Folkways
      31045
        CFS   Summer   p23.   100w. $3\frac{1}{2}$
        PIC   May   p62-3.   75w.   4

2790   ROTH, Kevin.   Somebody Give Me Direction.   Folkways FTS-
      31050
        BGU   July   p36.   50w.   2
        FR   Aug.   p31.   100w.   2
        PIC   Aug.   p72-3.   275w.   4
        RSP   March-April   p25.   50w. $1\frac{1}{2}$

2791   ROUND, Jay.   One-Time Friend.   Turnaround TR 5003
        CFS   Autumn   p25.   125w.   4
        PIC   Nov.   p54.   150w.   2

2792   ROWSOME, Leo.   Volume 2.   Topic (E)
        MM   June 25   p24.   150w.   4

2793   RUSKIN, Richard.   The Six String Conspiracy.   Takoma
      C-1057
        CAD   July   p22.   50w.   3
        FOL   Aug.   p25-6.   350w. $4\frac{1}{2}$
        GP   July   p129.   125w.   4

2794   RUSSELL, Micho.   Traditional Country Music of County
      Clare.   Free Reed FFR 004 (E)
        FR   May   p27.   350w. $4\frac{1}{2}$
        SO   July/Aug.   p50.   200w.   4

2795   RUSTIC Parts.   Don't You Wish You Were Here.   Sweet
      Folk and Country SFA 075 (E)
        FR   Nov.   p33.   100w.   3

2796   SAHLSTROM, Eric and Gosta Sandstrom.   Fiddle Music from
      Uppland.   Philo 2017
        BGU   Feb.   p25.   150w.   5
        SO   July/Aug.   p50.   100w. $4\frac{1}{2}$

2797   SANDBURG, Carl.   Sings His "American Songbag."   Caed-
      mon TC 2025 (2 discs)
        FR   April   p31.   200w.   5

2798   SEEGER, Nick. Sail on Flying Dutchman. Biograph RC-
       6010
           FOL   Sept. p22-3.   550w.   5
           RSP   1:3   p26.   175w.   4

2799   SEEGER, Pete. Fifty Sail on Newburgh Bay. Folkways
       FH 5237
           FOL   May p11, 13.   800w.   5
           PIC   Aug. p66, 68.   175w.   4

2800   SHANAHAN, John and Steve Gordon. Dance of Flies. Sweet
       Folk and Country SFA 077 (E)
           FR   Nov. p35.   50w.   1

2801   SHORTWAVE Band. Greatest Hats. Crescent ARS 111
           FR   May p29.   150w.   4

2802   SILLY Wizard. Xtra 1158 (E)
           RSP   March-April p13.   175w.   3

2803   SIMPSON, Martin. Golden Vanity. Trailer LER 2099 (E)
           FR   Jan. p31.   300w.   4
           RSP   March-April p13.   125w.   2

2804   SKINNER, James. The Music of James Scott Skinner. Topic
       12TS268 (E) (Reissue)
           EDS   Spring p32.   125w.   4

2805   SKINNER, Scott. Strathspeg King. Topic 12T280 (E) (Re-
       issue)
           TM   No. 6 p10-3.   500w.   4

2806   SKINNER, Scott/Bill Hardie. Music of. Topic 12TS268 (E)
       (partial reissue)
           TM   No. 6 p11-7.   500w. $3\frac{1}{2}$

2807-8 SMITH, Bob. Better Than an Orchestra. Topic 12T320 (E)
       (Reissue)
           FR   Aug. p31.   150w.   3

2809   SMITH, Bob. Ideal Music for All the Year Round. Topic
       12T319 (Reissue)
           FR   Aug. p31.   150w.   3

2810   SMITH, Jasper. The Travelling Songster. Topic 12TS304
       (E)
           FR   April p31.   350w.   3

2811   SMITH, Phoebe and Joe Smith. I Am a Romany. Folktracks
       FSA 60-100 (E) (Cassette Only)
           TM   No. 6 p13-4.   225w.   4

2812   SORRELS, Rosalie. Always a Lady. Philo 1029

PIC   May   p64.   150w.   4

2813   SPENCE, Bill.   The Hammered Dulcimer.   Front Hall FHR
       010
           CFS   Autumn   p26.   150w.   5
           RC   Dec.   p6-7.   100w. $4\frac{1}{2}$

2814   SPINNERS.   All-Day Singing.   EMI EMC 3167 (E)
           CAC   May   p51.   25w. $2\frac{1}{2}$
           FR   May   p29.   100w.   4
           GR   April   p1617.   25w. $2\frac{1}{2}$

2815   SPRAGUE, Carl T.   The First Popular Singing Cowboy.   Folk
       Variety FV 12001
           CMR   April   p36.   175w.   4

2816   SPRIGUNS.   Revel Weird and Wild.   Decca SKL 5262 (E)
           CAC   Feb.   p437.   100w.   3
           FR   May   p29.   100w.   3
           MM   Feb. 19   p28.   200w.   3

2817   SPRUNG, Joan.   Sixty Ballads and Butterflies.   Folk Legacy
       FSI60
           RSP   Jan. -Feb.   p32.   125w. $1\frac{1}{2}$

2818   STARBOARD List.   Songs of the Tall Ships.   Adelphi AD
       1025
           FOL   March   p24-6.   650w.   0
           SR   March   p116.   150w.   3

2819   STEELEYE Span.   Commoner's Crown.   Chrysalis CHR 1071
           AU   Jan.   p78.   200w. $4\frac{1}{2}$

2820   STEELEYE Span.   Original Masters.   Chrysalis CH2 1136
       (2 discs) (Reissue)
           AU   Nov.   p116.   250w.   4
           FR   July   p36.   150w.   3
           MM   June 18   p21.   150w.   3
           RR   Aug.   p83.   75w. $2\frac{1}{2}$

2821   STEELEYE Span.   Rocket Cottage.   Chrysalis CHR 1123
           AU   Jan.   p78.   200w.   4
           CRA   Jan.   p78-9.   175w. $3\frac{1}{2}$
           FR   Jan.   p31.   200w.   1
           RC   May   p9.   150w. $3\frac{1}{2}$
           RS   Feb. 24   p65.   200w. $1\frac{1}{2}$

2822   STEELEYE Span.   Story.   Chrysalis CHR CH2-1136 (2 discs)
           RC   Aug.   p11.   150w.   4

2823   STEELEYE Span.   Time Span.   Mooncrest CRDI (2 discs)
       (Reissue)
           MM   Jan. 18   p21.   150w. $3\frac{1}{2}$

2824   STEWART, Belle.   Queen among the Heather.   Topic 12TS307
       (E)
           FR   June p37.   500w.   3
           TM   No. 6 p22-3.   625w.   5

2825   STIVELL, Alan.   Before Landing.   Fontana 9286 999 (E)
           FR   Oct.   p33.   250w.   3

2826   STRAWHEAD.   Farewell Musket, Pike and Drum.   Tradition
       TSR 026 (E)
           FR   June p39.   100w.   3

2827   SWARBRICK, Dave.   Swarbrick.   Transatlantic TRA 337
           CAC   March p475.   100w. $3\frac{1}{2}$
           EDS   Summer p72.   150w.   2
           FR   April p33.   200w.   4
           RS   May 19 125w. $3\frac{1}{2}$

2828   SWARBRICK, Dave.   2.   Transatlantic TRA 341 (E)
           FR   Sept.   p33.   300w.   3
           MM   June 4 p58.   250w. $3\frac{1}{2}$

2829   SWARBRICK, Dave and Martin Carthy.   Selections.   Antilles
       AN 7041
           AU   Oct.   p181.   100w. $4\frac{1}{2}$

2830   SWEENEY'S Men.   Tracks of the Sweeney.   Transatlantic
       TRA SAM 40 (Reissue)
           MM   April 2 p26.   100w. $1\frac{1}{2}$

2831   TABOR, James.   Airs and Graces.   Topic 12TS298 (Reissue)
           AU   Oct.   p181.   100w. $4\frac{1}{2}$
           EDS   Spring p33.   150w.   4
           FR   Dec.   p34.   300w.   2
           MM   Oct. 15 p30.   300w. $3\frac{1}{2}$
           RSP   Jan. -Feb.   p18.   350w. $4\frac{1}{2}$

2832   TAIL Toddle.   Tot Leeringhe Ende Vermaeck.   Stoof MU
       7424 (Netherlands)
           FR   Jan.   p33.   100w.   3

2833   TANNAHILL Weavers.   Are Ye Sleeping, Maggie.   Plant
       Life PLR 001 (E)
           FR   May p29.   150w.   4

2834   THACKRAY, Jake.   Live Performance.   Note NTS 105
           FR   May p31.   50w.   3

2835   THACKRAY, Jake.   On Again, On Again.   EMI EMC 3166
       (E)
           FR   May p31.   50w.   3

2836   THERAPY.   Almanac.   DJM DJF 20492

FR   June   p33.   200w.   2

2837   THOMASSON, Benny.   Omac 1
       CFS   Autumn   p27.   100w. $3\frac{1}{2}$

2838   TILSTON, Steve.   Songs from the Dress Rehearsal.   Cornu-
       copia Records [no. number]
       FR   May   p31.   200w. $4\frac{1}{2}$

2839   TRAUM, Artie.   Life on Earth.   Rounder 3014
       RS   Aug.   25   p58.   225w. $2\frac{1}{2}$

2840   TRAUM, Happy.   Relax Your Mind.   Kicking Mule KM-110
       BGU   Aug.   p35.   100w.   4
       FOL   May   p14, 27.   300w.   2
       RSP   Jan. -Feb.   p30.   150w.   3

2841   TRAUM, Happy and Artie Traum.   Hard Times in the Country.
       Rounder 3007
       MN   V7/#7   p16.   150w. $3\frac{1}{2}$

2842   TRIONA.   Gael-Linn CEF 043 (Ireland)
       FR   March   p32.   200w.   2

2843   TROTTO.   Free Reed FRR 005 (E)
       EDS   Summer   p74.   175w.   0
       FR   Feb.   p31.   300w.   2

2844   TRULL, Teresa.   The Ways Woman Can Be.   Olivia LF910
       SO   July/Aug.   p49.   100w. $3\frac{1}{2}$

2845   TUFT, Harry.   Across the Blue Mountain.   Folk Legacy
       FSI-63
       CFS   Summer   p22.   150w.   4
       FOL   Sept.   p21-2.   550w. $4\frac{1}{2}$
       RSP   1:3   p19.   225w.   2

2846   TYSON, Willie.   Debutante.   Urana.
       SO   Sept. /Oct.   p50.   150w.   4

2847   VAN Ronk, Dave.   Sunday Street.   Philo 1036
       AU   Sept.   p90.   100w. $4\frac{1}{2}$
       CAD   April   p27. $4\frac{1}{2}$
       FOL   June   p25.   450w.   5
       FR   April   p33.   250w.   1
       GP   June   p137.   50w.   4
       RS   March   10   p68.   300w. $3\frac{1}{2}$
       RSP   March-April   p19.   100w.   3
       SO   May/June   p47.   100w. $4\frac{1}{2}$

2848   VOSS, Jane.   An Album of Songs.   Bay Records Bay 207
       BGU   June   p40.   50w.   2
       OTM   Winter   p30.   200w.   3

PIC   Aug.   p70.   75w.   2
RSP   Jan. -Feb.   p23.   150w.   4
SR   June   p120.   150w.   4

2849   WALKER, Sammy.   Song for Patty.   Folkways BR 5310
FOL   Aug.   p24-5.   500w.   4½

2850   WALTERS, Dave.   Comes Sailing In.   Fellside FE004
FR   Oct.   p35.   100w.   2

2851   WARD, Jean.   Stay Not Late.   Folksound FS104
FR   Feb.   p35.   100w.   3

2852   WARM Gold.   A Taste of Cornwall.   Hurler Records HURLS
009
FR   Jan.   p37.   100w.   2

2853   WARNER, Frank.   Come All You Good People.   Minstrel
JD 204
CFS   Summer   p20.   250w.   5
FOL   Sept.   p20-1.   550w.   4
FR   June   p39.   200w.   3
RC   July   p11-2.   200w.   4

2854   WARNER, Frank.   Listen to America Sing.   Folktracks
FSV90 901
FR   Apr.   p35.   200w.   4

2855   WARNES, Jennifer.   Arista 4062
CIR   May 17   p18.   175w.   3
CRA   May   p78.   175w.   3
FOL   June   p22-3.   650w.   4½
HF   May   p128.   600w.   3
MG   May   p51.   100w.   1
MM   June 25   p21.   250w.   3

2856   WATERSON, Mike.   Topic 12TS332 (E)
FR   Nov.   p37.   150w.   4

2857-8   WATERSON, Norma and Lal Waterson.   A True-Hearted
Girl.   Topic 12TS 331 (E)
FR   Nov.   p37.   150w.   3
MM   Sept.   10   p28.   175w.   3

2859   WATT, John and Davey Steward.   Shores of the Forth.
Springthyme SPR 1002 (E)
FR   June   p40.   500w.   4

2860   WEISSMAN, Dick.   Five String Banjo, Vol. 2.   Music Minus
One 187
PIC   May   p60.   175w.   2

2861   WEISSMAN, Dick and Dan Fox.   How to Play the Five String

Banjo. Music Minus One 186
PIC May p60. 175w. 2

2862 WEST, Hedy. Love, Hell and Biscuits. Bear Family 15003
(West Germany)
SO March/April p50. 200w. 5
FR Dec. p35. 250w. 3

2863 WEST, Hedy and Bill Clifton. Getting Folk Out of Country.
Bear Family 15008
CMP Sept. p35-6. 225w. 4

2864 WHELLANS, Mike. Dirtwater Fox. Dara MPA 016
FR May p33. 400w. 5

2865 WHITE, Jeff. Grey Lord. Stovepipe ST0001
CC Sept. p34. 50w. 3

2866 WIJNKAMP, Leo, Jr. Rags to Riches. Kicking Mule 117
RSP Jan. -Feb. p27. 200w. 4

2867 WILLIAMS, Tommy. Springtime in Battersea. Free Reed
FRR 008 (E)
FR Jan. p27. 300w. 4

2868 WILLIAMSON, Robin and His Merry Men. Journey's Edge.
Flying Fish 033
AU Sept. p98. 200w. 4
GP Dec. p153. 25w. 3

2869 WOOD, Hywel and Manfri Wood. Harps and Hornpipes.
Folktracks FSA 053 (E) (Cassette Only)
TM No. 6 p14. 450w. 5

2870 WOOD, Royston and Heather Wood. No Relation. Transat-
lantic TRA 342 (E)
FR Aug. p32. 400w. 2
MM April 23 p24. 250w. 2½

2871 WOOTTON, Brenda. Children Singing. Sentinel SENS 1036
FR March p33. 400w. 4

2872 WOOTTON, Brenda and Robert Bartlett. Tin in the Stream.
Stockfish SF 7001
FR Jan. p37. 100w. 2

2873 WRIGLEY, Bernard. Songs, Stories and Elephants. Trans-
atlantic TRA 327 (E)
FR Jan. p37. 50w. 1
RSP March-April p15. 175w. 3

2874 YETTIES. Up Market. Decca SKL 5282 (E)
FR Oct. p37. 150w. 2

2875   YETTIES.   Village Band.   Decca SKL 5253 (E)
          FR   Feb.   p35.   100w.   2

JAZZ

This section contains material from diverse origins: Dixieland, ragtime, instrumental blues, swing, avant-garde, and so forth. Music of a light "cocktail jazz" texture usually performed by non-jazz musicians will be found in MOOD--POP. Similarly, the employment of jazz in ROCK will be found in the ROCK category. BLUES has its own section, although the 12-bar construction and the "blue" notes are employed extensively in jazz.

Of all the popular music fields, jazz is the best documented. There are sufficient discographies, journals, exchange markets, record stores and mail-order outlets to meet the demand, but work continues into the esoteric reaches of descriptive writings and performances. Unfortunately, measured against "classical music" standards, jazz is far behind in critical and scholarly writing ventures. Articles and books thus far have been of the survey type, employing biographies and personal experiences, histories of ventures, discographic information, and photography, but while there have been lots of words about the subject of jazz, there has been little written about the actual jazz music. Many writers and critics do not play any instrument, and some cannot even read or write music. This is completely opposite from the situation with writers in folk and blues music.

Jazz is an aural music; its written score represents a skeleton of what actually takes place during a performance. Thus, there appears to be no need for the "classical music" approach. Yet it cannot be denied that written transcriptions are valuable for instrumental purposes and for structural analysis. Such data are usually not available in published form, and the demand for it at the present time is slight. Educational use is limited to original transcriptions, often not yet published. Often, too, critics and reviewers will argue against systematic analysis of jazz, for then the music will not be enjoyable anymore. This visceral reaction, also common to rock music writers, is negated by the continual enjoyment people derive from classical music. What is really meant is that the writers would not be able to understand the musicological terms for they cannot play jazz. Reaction of this kind is missing in folk and blues, for the use of the solo instrument enables detailed study by the listener in order to emulate his favorite performers. One reason advanced for musicological discussions within jazz is that such writings will enhance the level of jazz criticism and make it more acceptable for classical music writers. Yet the other side of

the coin is that the performers themselves cannot usually read or
write music, playing only by ear and by a feel for it.   Both argu-
ments are specious.

        For the moment, then, jazz critics and reviewers are in-
tensely interested in discovering and disseminating all facts they can
locate about the performers and the performances of the music per
se.   The British publication Jazz Journal often contains discographical information consuming more lineage than the review itself, and
even within the review there are plenty of informative bits of data
that appear to have no relevance to the music at hand.   Virtually
every jazz record released gets reviewed somewhere and there is
also a proliferation of reissues, and new releases of recently discovered unreleased material never before commercially available.
"Bootleggers" have emerged to sell the previously unreleased material, most of it very old and rare.   It is not our intention to probe
this matter of ethical issues, for that battle is being waged in the
media.   But "unauthorized" versions--usually selling 500 or fewer
copies--serve the purpose of meeting the demand for keeping in
print virtually every worthwhile (and some not-so-worthwhile) jazz
recording, and this matter of availability is constantly being referred
to in the media.   1977 has also seen a proliferation of original issues based on taped transcriptions from the 1940's, 1950's and
1960's.

        America is thought of as the home of jazz, yet the leading
magazines and scholars are European.   Europe is now the scene of
exciting new jazz and many reissues of earlier material.   England
and France have the key reissues, all nicely packaged and often re-
taining the original monophonic sound.   Sweden is close behind, and
so is Japan.   The International Jazz Federation is well organized
and is certain to expand.   In the lists of "best" records below the
reader should note that the bulk of the reissues come from England
and France and that much post-Parker material comes initially from
Europe.   That jazz is neglected at home is evidenced by both the
lack of issued product and by the lack of review media devoted to
jazz.   Cadence and Down Beat concentrate on American modern jazz
labels, while Jazz Report, a mimeographed alternative, concentrates
on traditional material.   General review publications, such as Stereo
Review or Audio have jazz sections, while Rolling Stone will review
the occasional jazz record.   Canada, on the other hand, has probably
the best jazz magazine in the world in Coda, put out by two immi-
grants from Britain.   And Britain itself has the prestigious Jazz
Journal International plus excellent sections in Gramophone, Records
and Recording, and Storyville.

        We have noted a tendency for non-jazz magazine reviews to
go overboard on "black jazz" (e.g., Rolling Stone) with the resulting
swings of 0 to 5 on the rating scales when compared with the jazz
magazines.   This is easily proved with regularity as the jazz review magazines give a wide range of rankings to individual records
(from low to high), while the non-jazz publications give a consistently high rating that smacks of appeasement.

The greatest single influence on jazz has been Charlie Parker and his early followers. By changing chord progressions, Parker's innovative style had set jazz free from the printed score and the ar- ranged notes. Some may argue that other musicians were influential at other times, but such influences only took the shape of imitation plus modest refinement. Parker influenced whole schools of jazz, and brought on bop, cool, time changes, and free jazz. To many fans, there was no jazz before Parker. Thus, we have divided the "best" items in the jazz category (based on the reviews themselves) into "Pre-Parker" and "Post-Parker" (including Parker himself). According to the 1977 reviews, the following appear to be the best discs:

PRE-PARKER STYLE:

> BASIE, Count. Basie Jam No. 2. Pablo 2310-786
> BELLSON, Louis. Louis Bellson Seven. Concord CJ25
> GUARNIERI, Johnny. Superstride. Taz-Jaz Records TJZ 1001
> HERMAN, Woody. The 40th Anniversary Carnegie Hall Con-
>   cert. RCA BGL2-2203 (2 discs)
> JOHNSON, Plas. Positively. Concord Jazz CJ 24
> KESSEL, Barney. Soaring. Concord Jazz CJ 33
> PASS, Joe. Virtuoso, No. 2. Pablo 2310.788
> PIZZARELLI, Bucky, and Bud Freeman. Buck and Bud. Fly-
>   ing Dutchman BDL1-1378
> WELLSTOOD, Dick. Live at the Cookery. Chiaroscuro CR
>   139

POST-PARKER STYLE:

> AKIYOSHI-Tabackin Big Band. Road Time. RCA CPL2-2242
>   (2 discs)
> BLEY, Paul, Gary Peacock, and Barry Altschul. Japan Suite.
>   Improvising Artists IAI 373849
> BRAXTON, Anthony. The Montreux/Berlin Concerts. Arista
>   AL 5002 (2 discs)
> CARTER, Benny and Dizzy Gillespie. Carter, Gillespie, Inc.
>   Pablo 2310.781
> CHERRY, Don. A & M Horizon SP 717
> COLEMAN, Ornette. Dancing in Your Head. A & M Horizon
>   SP 722
> COREA, Chick. My Spanish Heart. Polydor PD2-9003 (2
>   discs)
> EVANS, Bill. Quintessence. Fantasy F 9529
> GORDON, Dexter. Homecoming: Live at the Village Vanguard.
>   Columbia PG 34650 (2 discs)
> HANCOCK, Herbie. V.S.O.P. Columbia PG 34688 (2 discs)
> JARRETT, Keith. Staircase. ECM 2-1090 (2 discs)
> LEWIS, Mel. And Friends. A & M Horizon SP 716
> McLAUGHLIN, John. A Handful of Beauty. Columbia PC
>   34372

TAYLOR, Cecil. Dark to Themselves. Inner City 3001
WOODS, Phil. "Live" from The Showboat. RCA BGL2-2202
(2 discs)

2876   ABADI, Marden. Classic Joplin. Orion ORS 76217
       RA July-Aug. p8. 125w. 0

2877   ABERCROMBIE, John and Ralph Towner. Sargasso Sea.
       ECM-1-1080. Cart. 8T-1-1080
       AU Jan. p88. 350w. 5
       CAD Jan. p25, 26. 200w. $4\frac{1}{2}$
       JF No. 48 p51. 250w. 3
       MG Jan. 100w. $4\frac{1}{2}$
       SR Feb. p107. 100w. 0

2878   ADAMS, Arthur. Midnight Serenade. Fantasy F-9523
       CAD June p22. 100w. 2

2879   ADAMS, George. Jazz A Confronto: Vol. 22. Horo H11
       101-22 (Italy)
       CAD Sept. p17. 150w. 5

2880   ADAMS, George. Suite for Swingers. Horo HZ-03 (Italy)
       CAD Sept. p17-8. 100w. 2
       CO April p20. 250w. 3

2881   ADAMS, Pepper and Donald Byrd. Stardust. Bethlehem
       BCP 6029 (Reissue)
       CAD Dec. p54. 100w. $1\frac{1}{2}$

2882   ADDERLEY, Cannonball. Beginnings. Mercury Emarcy
       EMS 2-404 (2 discs) (Reissue)
       DB April 21 p38. 150w. 4

2883   ADDERLEY, Cannonball. Cannonball, Vol. 1. Dobre 1008
       (Reissue)
       CAD Nov. p50. 100w. 3

2884   ADDERLEY, Cannonball. Coast to Coast. Milestone M-47039
       (2 discs)
       CAD Sept. p45. 175w. 5
       MM May 21 p28. 300w. 4

2885   ADDERLEY, Nat. Hummin'. Little David 1012
       CAD April p16. 125w. 5
       DB April 21 p32. 250w. $1\frac{1}{2}$
       MG Feb. p57. 125w. 3
       MM Feb. 19 p29. 300w. $3\frac{1}{2}$

2886   AGUDO, Luis and Afonso Viera. Jazz A Confronto: Vol. 33.

Horo HLL 101-33 (Italy)
CAD Sept. p19. 100w. $3\frac{1}{2}$

2887 AKENDENGUE, Pierre. Nandipo. Saravan SH 10045 (France)
JF No. 46 p67, 69. 75w. $4\frac{1}{2}$

2888 AKETAGAWA, Shoji. This Here Is Aketa, Vol. 2. Offbeat
ORLP-1004 (Japan)
CO Aug. p20-1. 275w. 3

2889 AKIYOSHI, Toshiko. Tales of a Courtesan. RCA JPL 10723
(Japan)
SOU March p42. 50w. 4

2890 AKIYOSHI-TABACKIN Big Band. Road Time. RCA CPL2-
2242 (2 discs) Cart. CPS2-2242
CAD July p37. 300w. $4\frac{1}{2}$
DB Oct. 6 p25. 500w. 4
RFJ Nov. p17-8. 450w. 4
SR July p71. 625w. 5

2891 ALBANY, Joe. Birdtown Birds. Inner City IC 2003 (Reis-
sue)
CAD May p15, 18. 150w. 3
CK Dec. p73. 25w. 2

2892 ALBANY, Joe. Two's Company. Steeplechase SCS1019
(Denmark)
JJ May p41. 200w. 5

2893 ALCORN, Alvin. An Original New Orleans Jazz Brunch.
Sandcastle SCR 1030
CAD Oct. p47-8. 100w. 4
MJ Dec. p25. 75w. $3\frac{1}{2}$

2894 ALEXANDER, Monty. Love and Sunshine. MPS BASF G
22620
AU May p95. 300w. 5

2895 ALEXANDER, Monty. Montreux Alexander. MPS 68-170
(E)
MM Oct. 22 p28. 250w. $3\frac{1}{2}$

2896 ALI, Rashied and Leroy Jenkins. Swift Are the Winds of
Life. Survival SR 112
CAD April p37. 250w. 4

2897 ALKE, Bjorn. Fine & Mellow. EMI 062-35291 (E)
CAD Oct. p51. 225w. $2\frac{1}{2}$

2898 ALLEN, Henry. 1936, V. 3/4. Collector's Classics CC 51
(Sweden) (2 discs) (Reissue)
RR Dec. p88. 50w. 3

2899   ALLEN, Red. 1956, V. 5.   RCA FXM1-7326 (Reissue)
       JJ   April   p29.   200w.   2½

2900   ALLISON, Mose. Your Mind Is on Vacation.   Atlantic SD
       1691
       CAD   Feb.   p38.   150w.   3
       CK   Jan.   p51.   100w.   4½
       MG   Jan.   100w.   3

2901   ALLRED, Bill. Rosie O'Grady's Good Time Jazz Band.   TC
       1149
       CAD   Sept.   p21-2.   225w.   3½

2902   ALLRED, Bill and Al Winters.   Jazz Trombones.   Jim Tay-
       lor Presents JTP-101
       CAD   Oct.   p57-8.   225w.   3

2903   ALTSCHUL, Barry. Virtuosi.   Improvising Artists 383844
       MM   Feb. 26 p33.   400w.   4
       SR   Sept.   p120.   125w.   5

2904   ALTSCHUL, Barry. You Can't Name Your Own Tune.
       Muse 5124
       CAD   Sept.   p30-1.   300w.   4
       MM   Sept. 17 p28.   400w.   4½

2905   AMALGAM. Another Time.   Vinyl VS 100 (E)
       JJ   Feb.   p28.   200w.   2
       MM   April 23 p26.   450w.   3

2906   AMBROSETTI, Franco. Jazz A Confronto: Vol. 11.   Horo
       HLL 101-11 (Italy)
       CAD   Sept.   p15-6.   150w.   0

2907   AMMONS, Gene. The Gene Ammons Story: Organ Combos.
       Prestige P-24071 (2 discs) (Reissue)
       CAD   Aug.   p45.   200w.   4
       GR   Dec.   p1162.   25w.   3
       RFJ   Nov.   p15.   450w.   3½

2908   AMMONS, Gene. Jug Sessions.   Mercury Emarcy MMS 2
       400 (Reissue)
       DB   April 21 p38.   150w.   4

2909   AMMONS, Gene. Red Top.   Savoy SJL 1103 (Reissue)
       CAD   Feb.   p36.   50w.   2
       CO   Feb.   p22.   125w.   2½
       SOU   Jan.   p48.   100w.   4

2910   AMMONS, Gene and Sonny Stitt.   Together Again for the Last
       Time.   Prestige P10100
       BM   March p52.   200w.   4

2911   ANDERSON, Arild. Shimri. ECM 1-1082
        CAD Sept. p32.   300w.   0
        DB   Nov. 3 p22.   300w.   4
        JF   No. 48 p23.   50w. $3\frac{1}{2}$
        MG   Sept. p53.   75w.   3

2912   ANDERSON, Ernestine. Hello Like Before. Concord Jazz
        CJ-31
        SR   June p120.   150w.   5
        VV   May 16 p55, 59.   300w. $2\frac{1}{2}$

2913   ANDERSON, T. J. Classic Rags and Ragtime Songs. Smith-
        sonian Collection N001 (Reissue)
        RA   March-April p5-6.   125w. $2\frac{1}{2}$

2914   ARMSTRONG, Louis. GNP Crescendo 11001 (2 discs) (Re-
        issue)
        CAC Feb. p432.   150w. $4\frac{1}{2}$
        MJ   Nov. p24.   100w.   3
        MJ   Dec. p25.   125w.   4

2915   ARMSTRONG, Louis. Storyville SLP 236 (Reissue)
        RR   Aug. p84.   50w.   4

2916   ARMSTRONG, Louis. And His Friends. Phonogram (E) (Re-
        issue)
        CAC Feb. p418.   50w. $1\frac{1}{2}$

2917   ARMSTRONG, Louis. In Concert, Vols. 1, 2. Rarities 18/
        19 (2 discs) (Reissue)
        JM   Summer p63.   100w. $2\frac{1}{2}$

2918   ARMSTRONG, Louis. Live Recording. Muxa SXL 1158
        (Poland)
        CAD March p40-1.   125w. $2\frac{1}{2}$

2919-20 ARMSTRONG, Louis. Rarest Performances, V. 2. Kings
        of Jazz KLJ 20026 (Reissue)
        JM   1:2 p65.   100w. $3\frac{1}{2}$

2921   ARMSTRONG, Louis. Satchmo. Varese International VS
        81006
        CAD June p39.   250w. $4\frac{1}{2}$

2922   ARMSTRONG, Louis. Snake Rag. Chiaroscuro CR 2002
        CAD April p35-6.   222w. $2\frac{1}{2}$

2923   ARMSTRONG, Louis. Young Louis Armstrong, 1932-1933.
        RCA Bluebird AXM2-5519 (2 discs) Cart. AXS2-5519 (Reissue)
        CAD May p28.   50w.   2
        DB   Oct. 6 p35-7.   100w.   4
        MJ   Dec. p25.   150w. $3\frac{1}{2}$
        MR   May p6.   400w.   4

SR   July p108.   200w.   5

2924   ARMSTRONG, Louis and Bunny Berigan.   Bunny/Louie (sic).
       Shoestring 103
            CAD   Feb.   p32.   250w.   3

2925   ARMSTRONG, Louis and the Dukes of Dixieland.   Great Al-
       ternatives.   Chiaroscuro CR 2003
            AU   Oct.   p186.   400w.   5
            CAD   April p35-6.   225w.   3
            SOU   June p46.   200w.   4

2926   ARMSTRONG, Louis and the Dukes of Dixieland.   Sweetheart/
       Definitive Alternatives.   Chiaroscuro CR 2006
            CAD   Dec.   p44.   125w.   3

2927   ARMSTRONG, Louis and Earl Hines.   Armstrong and Hines,
       1928.   Smithsonian Collection R002 (Reissue)
            AU   Oct.   p186.   400w.   4

2928   ARMSTRONG, Walter Zuber.   Alpha and Omega.   World
       Artists WA 1001
            JF   No. 48 p52-3.   200w.   4

2929   ARMSTRONG, Walter Zuber.   High Places.   World Artists
       WA 1003
            CAD   July p18.   200w.   4
            CAD   July p45.   350w. $4\frac{1}{2}$
            MM   Nov. 5 p31.   200w.   3

2930   ARMSTRONG, Walter Zuber.   Hitana.   World Artists WA
       1002
            JF   No. 48 p52-3.   200w. $3\frac{1}{2}$

2931   ARPIN, John.   Solo Piano.   Eubie Blake Music EBM 10
            MJ   Jan.   p28.   50w. $3\frac{1}{2}$
            RA   Jan.-Feb.   p5, 7.   100w.   5

2932   ART Ensemble of Chicago.   Fanfare for the Warriors.   At-
       lantic ATL 50 304 (West Germany) (Reissue)
            JJ   May p41-2.   250w.   5

2933   ARTISTS' Jazz Band.   AJB ST57427-57430 (Canada)
            CO   Feb.   p16-7.   500w.   2

2934   ASHBY, Irving.   Memoirs.   Accent Records ACS-5091
            CAD   Nov.   p28.   50w.   4
            GP   Oct.   p129.   150w. $3\frac{1}{2}$

2935   AUSTRALIAN Jazz Quartet.   Bethlehem BLP 6002 (Reissue)
            JR   V9/#3 unpaged 75w.   4

2936   AYERS, Roy, Ubiquity.   Everybody Loves the Sunshine.

Polydor PD1 6070
DB   March 10 p23.   350w. $1\frac{1}{2}$
MM   April 2 p19.   100w.   3
RS   Feb. 24 p71.   225w. $1\frac{1}{2}$
SOU Feb. p44. 50w. 1

2937   AYERS, Roy, Ubiquity. Lifeline.   Polydor PD1 6108
BS   Oct. p27. 150w. 3
CRA Sept. p69. 250w. 1

2938   AYERS, Roy, Ubiquity. Vibrations.   Polydor PD1 2391 256
BM   May p51-2. 200w. 2
CAC June p91-2. 200w. $2\frac{1}{2}$
PRM Feb. p41. 350w. $1\frac{1}{2}$

2939   AYLER, Albert. Nuits de la Fondation Maeght.   Shandar
83503/04 (France) (2 discs)
CAD June p44. 350w. 5

2940   BAILEY, Benny. How Deep Is the Ocean.   EMI Harvest
7C-362-35278 (E)
CAD Oct. p40. 250w. 5

2941   BAILEY, Derek and Andres Centazzo. Drops. Incus 003
(E)
MM   Nov. 12 p34. 150w. $3\frac{1}{2}$

2942   BAILEY, Derek and Evan Parker. London Concert. Incus
16 (E)
MM   Jan. 1 p17. 350w. 3

2943   BAILEY, Derek and Tristan Honsinger. Duo. Incus 20 (E)
JJ   April p28. 200w. 3
MM   Jan. 29 p28. 550w. $4\frac{1}{2}$

2944   BAKER'S, Tom, San Francisco Jazz Band. Volume I.   Jazz
& Jazz J&J001
ST   Oct.-Nov. p38-9. 150w. 3

2945   BALABAN, Red. A Night at the New Eddie Condon's.
Classic Jazz 17
CAD Feb. p28. 200w. 4

2946   BALES, Burt. New Orleans Ragtime.   Euphonic ESR 1210
RA   Sept./Oct. p6. 100w. 1

2947   BARBER, Chris. The Great Reunion Concert.   Black Lion
BLP 12140/1 (2 discs) (E)
JJ   May p42. 100w. $4\frac{1}{2}$
MM   Oct. 1 p26. 550w. $3\frac{1}{2}$
RR   June p95. 75w. $3\frac{1}{2}$

2948   BARBER, Chris. In Concert.   Golden Hour GH 633 (E)

(Reissue)
    RR   April p88.   25w.   3
    RR   June   p95.   25w.   3

2949   BARBER, Chris. Petite Fleur. Hallmark HMA 213 (E)
    (Reissue)
    RR   April p88.   50w.   3

2950   La BARBERA, Pat. Pass It On. PM PMR 009
    JF   No. 50 p20.   75w. $3\frac{1}{2}$

2951   BARBIERI, Gato. Caliente. A&M SP 4597
    CRA April p98.   375w.   2

2952   BARBIERI, Gato. Ruby, Ruby. A&M 4655
    CAD Nov.   p31.   50w. $4\frac{1}{2}$
    VV   Dec. 5 p61.   200w.   4

2953   BARBIERI, Gato and Dollar Brand. Confluence. Freedom
    FLP 41003
    MM   Oct. 1 p28.   200w.   4

2954   BARDUHN, Dave. Barduhn RL5135
    CAD Aug.   p22.   350w. $4\frac{1}{2}$
    CAD Aug.   p41.   150w.   3

2955   BAREFIELD, Eddie. The Indestructible. Famous Door HC
    113
    MJ   Dec.   p24.   125w. $3\frac{1}{2}$

2956   BARNES, George. And His Octet, 1946. Hindsight HSR 106
    (Reissue)
    GP   Dec.   p152.   50w.   3

2957   BARRON, Kenny. Lucifer. Muse MS 5070
    RFJ Jan.   p15-6.   550w. $3\frac{1}{2}$

2958   BARTZ, Gary. Ju Ju Man. Catalyst 7610
    CAD Jan.   p41-2.   275w. $3\frac{1}{2}$
    DB   June 16 p36, 38.   300w.   4
    RRE May-June p40.   400w.   4
    SR   May p97.   150w.   5

2959   BARTZ, Gary. Music Is My Sanctuary. Capitol ST-11647
    CAD July p24.   150w. $4\frac{1}{2}$
    DB   Dec. 15 p28.   250w.   3

2960   BASCOMB, Paul. Bad Bascomb. Denmark DL-431 (Reissue)
    CAD April p29.   120w.   3
    CO   Sept./Oct. p24.   50w.   3
    DB   Nov. 17 p26.   325w.   3
    JR   V9/#4 unpaged 50w.   3
    MJ   May p31.   200w. $3\frac{1}{2}$

RSP   March-April   p35.   250w.   4

2961   BASIE, Count.   Basie Jam #2.   Pablo 2310-786
       CAD   April   p24.   96w.   5
       DB   April 7   p26, 28.   200w.   4
       GR   Sept.   p525.   150w. $3\frac{1}{2}$
       JJ   May   p42.   150w.   5
       MM   Aug. 27   p24.   225w. $3\frac{1}{2}$
       MR   Feb.   p13.   250w.   3
       RFJ   June   p20.   650w. $2\frac{1}{2}$
       RR   April   p88.   50w. $3\frac{1}{2}$
       SR   May   p97, 99.   50w.   5

2962   BASIE, Count.   Best of.   MCA 2-4050 (2 discs) (Reissue)
       JM   1:2   p56.   350w. $3\frac{1}{2}$

2963   BASIE, Count.   Blues by Basie, 1942.   Tax M 8025
       AU   Dec.   p126.   150w.   4

2964   BASIE, Count.   Good Morning Blues.   MCA 2 4108 (2 discs)
       (Reissue)
       AU   Dec.   p126.   150w.   4
       DB   Oct. 6   p35-7.   75w.   5
       MJ   Nov.   p22, 24.   100w. $2\frac{1}{2}$
       MR   April   p12.   200w. $3\frac{1}{2}$

2965   BASIE, Count.   Great Concert of.   Festival 231 (France)
       (Reissue)
       AU   Dec.   p126.   150w.   4

2966   BASIE, Count.   I Told You So.   Pablo 2310-767
       AU   Dec.   p126.   150w.   4
       CAC   Feb.   p432.   250w.   3
       CAD   Jan.   p26.   200w.   4
       JJ   Feb.   p28.   500w.   5
       MM   Feb. 19   p29.   250w. $3\frac{1}{2}$
       MR   Feb.   p13.   250w.   3
       SOU   March   p42.   50w. $4\frac{1}{2}$

2967   BASIE, Count.   Live.   DJM DJML 068 (E)
       GR   Sept.   p525.   75w. $4\frac{1}{2}$

2968   BASIE, Count.   Montreux '77.   Pablo 2308 207
       MM   Dec. 21   p16.   250w. $4\frac{1}{2}$

2969   BASIE, Count.   Prime Time.   Pablo 2310 797
       CAD   Oct.   p49-50.   200w.   4
       DB   Nov. 17   p23-4.   225w. $3\frac{1}{2}$
       HF   Oct.   p144.   200w. $2\frac{1}{2}$
       MM   Oct. 8   p38.   250w.   4
       RFJ   Oct.   p17-8.   900w. $3\frac{1}{2}$
       RR   Oct.   p90.   25w.   3

2970   BASIE, Count.   Sixteen Swinging Men.   Verve VE2-2517 (Re-
       issue)
           AU   Dec.   p126.   150w.   4
           CAD   Aug.   p57.   225w.   4
           DB   July 14   p45-7.   50w.   4

2971   BASIE, Count.   The V-Discs Volume 2.   Jazz Society 506
       (Reissue)
           AU   Dec.   p126.   350w.   4
           CO   Sept./Oct.   p23.   250w.   5

2972   BASIE, Count and Zoot Sims.   Basie and Zoot.   Pablo 3210
       745
           GR   March   p1471.   100w. $4\frac{1}{2}$

2973   BASSINI, Piero.   "Tonalita."   Red Records VPA 109 (Italy)
           CO   Sept./Oct.   p18-20.   225w.   4

2974   BASSO, Gianni.   Jazz A Confronto: Vol. 3.   Horo HLL
       101-3 (Italy)
           CAD   Sept.   p14.   200w.   4

2975   BASSO, Gianni.   Jazz A Confronto: Vol. 4.   Horo HLL 101-
       4 (Italy)
           CAD   Sept.   p14.   200w.   5

2976   BECHET, Sidney.   Blackstick.   MCA 510.100 (French Issue)
           ST   Aug.-Sept.   p233-4.   300w.   2

2977   BECHET, Sidney.   His Way.   Pumpkin 102
           CAD   Aug.   p43.   150w.   4

2978   BECHET, Sidney.   Sidney Bechet Album.   Sagapan 6900 (E)
       (Reissue)
           SR   Jan.   p104.   225w.   2

2979   BECHET, Sidney and Mezz Mezzrow.   Classic Jazz 28 (Re-
       issue)
           CO   Feb.   p23.   125w.   3

2980   BECK, Joe.   Watch the Time.   Polydor PD-1-6092
           DB   Oct. 6   p33.   250w.   2
           GP   Oct.   p129.   150w.   4
           MM   July 16   p22.   250w. $2\frac{1}{2}$

2981   BEIDERBECKE, Bix.   The Golden Days of Jazz.   CBS
       88030 (E) (2 discs) (Reissue)
           RR   June   p95.   50w.   4

2982   BELLSON, Louis.   Louis Bellson's Seven.   Concord CJ-25
           CAD   Jan.   p35.6.   225w.   4
           DB   June 16   p34.   225w. $3\frac{1}{2}$
           JF   No. 47   p69.   50w.   3

JJ   May   p42, 44. 200w.   5
SR   May   p99.   100w.   5

2983   BENSON, George.   Benson Burner.   Columbia 33569
       DB   March 24 p31.   600w. $2\frac{1}{2}$
       GP   March p113.   25w. $2\frac{1}{2}$
       MJ   March p44.   100w. $2\frac{1}{2}$
       SR   April p110.   150w.   5

2984   BENSON, George.   Blue Benson.   Polydor PD-1-6084 (Reissue)
       CAD   Jan.   p27-9.   225w.   3

2985   BENSON, George.   In Concert--Carnegie Hall.   CTI CTI-6072
       BM   July   p50.   175w.   4
       CAD   March p44.   75w. $2\frac{1}{2}$
       RS   May 19   450w. $3\frac{1}{2}$
       SR   June   p120, 122.   400w.   5

2986   BENSON, George.   In Flight.   Warner Bros. BSK 2983
       CAD   March p45-6.   75w. $2\frac{1}{2}$
       DB   April 7 p21.   200w.   3
       GR   April p1617.   50w.   2
       HF   April p138.   250w.   3
       MM   Feb. 26 p29.   600w. $1\frac{1}{2}$
       PRM   April p44-5.   250w.   3
       RS   May 19   450w. $3\frac{1}{2}$
       SR   June   p120, 122.   400w.   5

2987   BENSON, George.   New Bass Guitar.   Prestige, P-24072
       (2 discs) (Reissue)
       CK   Aug.   p49.   25w. $2\frac{1}{2}$

2988   BENSON, George and Jack McDuff.   Prestige P-24073 (Reissue)
       CAD   Aug.   p45.   125w.   4
       GR   Dec.   p1162.   50w.   3
       MM   Sept. 3 p25.   200w.   3

2989   BENSON, George and Joe Farrell.   Benson and Farrell.
       CTI CTI 6069   CT8-6069
       BM   April p51.   150w.   4
       SMG   May   p27.   100w.   4
       SR   March p177.   150w.   3

2990   BENTLEY, John and His Buddies.   Euphonic 1211
       CAD   Jan.   p41.   125w.   2
       TR   V9/#3   unpaged 275w.   5

2991   BENTLEY, John and Guy Richards.   Mostly Blues.   Euphonic
       1214
       CAD   Dec.   p51.   100w.   3

2992   BERGER, Karl and David Holland.   All Kinds of Time.
        Sackville 3010 (Canada)
            CAD   April   p34.   192w.   3
            OLR   Sept.   p225.   50w.   4
            SOU   Feb.   p46.   100w.   4

2993   BERIGAN, Bunny.   1938-39, Vol. 1/2.   Shoestring SS 100/1
        (2 discs) (Reissue)
            MR   July   p10.   250w. $3\frac{1}{2}$
            DB   April 7   p31-33.   100w. $2\frac{1}{2}$
            ST   Oct. -Nov.   p39.   25w. $1\frac{1}{2}$

2994   BERIGAN, Bunny.   Take It, Bunny!   Epic JLN 3109 (Re-
        issue)
            CAD   May   p26-7.   175w.   4
            MR   May   p6.   450w. $3\frac{1}{2}$

2995   BERIGAN, Bunny and Louis Armstrong.   Bunny and Louis.
        Shoestring SS 103 (Reissue)
            JM   Summer   p63.   100w. $2\frac{1}{2}$

2996   BERIGAN, Bunny and the ODJB.   Fanfare #3   (Reissue)
            CAD   Jan.   p21, 22.   200w. $3\frac{1}{2}$

2997   BERKOW, Peter.   Faculty Recital.   Second Pressing
            GP   May   p129.   75w.   3

2998   BERRY, Bill.   Hello Rev.   Concord CJ-27
            CAD   Jan.   p35-6.   225w.   4
            DB   Nov. 3   p26-7.   225w.   3
            SOU   March   p42.   100w.   4

2999   BERRY, Bill.   L. A. Big Band.   Concord CJ-27
            JJ   May   p44.   250w. $4\frac{1}{2}$

3000   BICKERT, Ed.   Ed Bickert.   PM-010 (Canada)
            CAD   Aug.   p41.   150w.   4
            SOU   Nov.   p63.   300w.   4

3001   BIGARD, Barney.   Barney Goin' Easy.   Tax 8023 (Reissue)
            CO   Aug.   p23.   150w.   3

3002   BIGARD, Barney.   Black and White.   Storyville SLP 807
        (Denmark)
            RR   Aug.   p84.   50w.   3

3003   BIGARD, Barney.   Clarinet Gumbo.   RCA APL1-1744
            AU   Nov.   p122.   250w.   4

3004   BILK, Aker.   Best of.   Golden Hour (E) (Reissue)
            CAC   Feb.   p415.   100w.   3

3005   BILK, Aker.   Invitation.   Pye NSIPX41054 (E)

GR   April   p1688.   25w. $2\frac{1}{2}$

3006   BISHOP, Walter, Jr.   Bish Bash.   Xanadu 114
       CAD   Sept.   p30.   150w.   3

3007   BLAKE, Ran.   Breakthru.   Improvising Artists 373842
       CAD   Jan.   p37.   500w. $3\frac{1}{2}$
       CK   April   p49.   100w.   4
       DB   June 16   p31, 34.   600w.   5
       MG   June   p53.   150w.   3
       MM   Feb.   19   p29.   425w.   4
       SR   Feb.   p108.   150w.   4
       VV   Aug.   22   p58.   250w.   3

3008   BLAKE, Ran.   Wende.   Owl 05 (France)
       CAD   Nov.   p42.   350w. $4\frac{1}{2}$
       JF   No. 49   p21.   50w.   3
       VV   Aug.   22   p58.   100w.   3

3009   BLAKEY, Art.   Catalyst CAT-7-902
       JF   No. 47   p69.   100w.   3
       JJ   Feb.   p28.   250w.   5
       SR   Jan.   p104.   300w.   3

3010   BLAKEY, Art.   The Finest of.   Bethlehem BCP 6015 (Re-
       issue)
       CAD   Dec.   p48.   300w. $3\frac{1}{2}$

3011   BLAKEY, Art.   Gypsy Folk Tales.   Roulette SR5008
       CAD   Sept.   p43-4.   275w.   5

3012   BLAKEY, Art.   A Night in Tunisia.   RCA Masters FXL1-
       7318 (France) (Reissue)
       JJ   March   p30.   425w.   4

3013   BLAKEY, Art and John Coltrane.   CBS 82109 (E) (Reissue)
       MM   Aug.   13   p22.   200w.   3
       RR   Oct.   p90.   50w. $3\frac{1}{2}$

3014   BLAKEY, Art and Max Roach.   Chess ACACJ 406 (2 discs)
       (Reissue)
       JF   No. 47   p69.   100w.   3

3015   BLAKEY, Art and Max Roach.   Drum Suite.   DBS 88042
       (France)
       JJ   Feb.   p28.   250w.   5

3016   BLANKE, Toto.   Electric Circus.   Bellaphon BAC 2048
       (W. Germany)
       JF   No. 49   p50-1.   700w. $3\frac{1}{2}$

3017   BLEY, Carla.   Dinner Music.   Watt #6
       CAD   July   p19.   500w. $4\frac{1}{2}$

MG   Dec.   p59.   175w.   3
SR   Nov.   p126, 128.   325w.   5

3018   BLEY, Paul.   Inner City 2005
       CK   Nov.   p64.   75w.   4½

3019   BLEY, Paul.   Alone Again.   Improvising Artists 373840
       JF   No. 46   p59-60.   175w.   2

3020   BLEY, Paul.   Pastorius/Metheny/Ditmas/Bley.   Improvising
       Artists 373846
       DR   March 24   p17.   325w.   4

3021   BLEY, Paul.   Virtuosi.   Improvising Artists IAI 373844
       CK   Aug.   p48.   85w.   4

3022   BLEY, Paul and Ornette Coleman.   Live at the Hillcrest
       Club, 1958.   Inner City IC 1007 (Reissue)
       JM   V1/#3   p51.   700w.   3½

3023   BLEY, Paul; Bill Connors; Jimmy Giuffre.   Quiet Song.   Im-
       provising Artists 373839
       JF   No. 46   p59-60.   175w.   2

3024   BLEY, Paul, Gary Peacock and Barry Altschul.   Japan Suite.
       Improvising Artists IAI 373849
       CAD   July   p36.   150w.   3½
       CK   Aug.   p48.   85w.   4
       HF   Sept.   p142.   100w.   4
       JM   Summer   p49.   400w.   5
       SR   Sept.   p120.   125w.   5

3025   BLEY, Paul; Paul Motian; Gary Peacock.   Turning Point.
       Improvising Artists 373841
       JF   No. 46   p59-60.   175w.   3

3026   BLUE Notes.   Blue Notes for Mongezi.   Ogun OGD 001/2
       (E) (2 discs)
       MM   Jan. 22   p25.   800w.   3

3027   BLUIETT, Hamiet.   Endangered Species.   India Navigation
       IN 1025
       CAD   June   p37.   100w.   2
       DB   Sept. 8   p34-5.   250w.   3½
       JJ   Feb.   p28.   325w.   4
       MM   June 25   p25.   225w.   2½
       VV   March 14   p81.   50w.   2

3028   BOBO, Willie.   Tomorrow Is Here.   Blue Note LA 711-G
       CAD   April   p10.   40w.   2½
       SR   July   p108.   50w.   5

3029   BOLAND, Francy, Orchestra.   Blue Flame.   MPS DC 229106

MM   Jan. 1   p17.   250w.   4

3030   BOLCOM, William/William Albright.   Ragtime: Back to
Back.   University of Michigan School of Music SM0004
ARG   Aug.   p41.   300w.   4

3031   BOLLING, Claude.   Original Ragtime.   Columbia PC 33277
JR   V9/#3   unpaged   125w.   3

3032   BOLLING, Claude.   Suite for Flute and Jazz Piano.   Columbia M33233
JR   V9/#3   unpaged   200w.   4

3033   BONNER, Joe.   Angel Eyes.   Muse MR 5114
DB   Feb. 24   p31.   275w.   4

3034   BORRARO, Chivo.   Buenos Aires Blues.   Catalyst CAT 7917
MG   Nov.   p53.   25w. $1\frac{1}{2}$

3035   BORTHEN, Per and Laila Dalseth.   Swinging Departure.
Talent TLS 3020 (Norway)
JF   No. 48   p23.   50w. $3\frac{1}{2}$
ST   April/May   p154.   100w.   2

3036   BOSS Brass.   Big Band Jazz.   Umbrella UMB DD4
SOU   Sept.   p64.   150w.   5
SOU   Dec.   p58.   350w.   5

3037   BOWIE, Joseph and Oliver Lake.   Sackville 2010 (Canada)
CAD   March   p38.   100w.   4
MM   June 11   p20.   300w. $3\frac{1}{2}$
OLR   Sept.   p225.   50w.   5
SOU   Feb.   p46.   100w.   4

3038   BOWIE, Lester.   Rope-a-Dope.   Muse MR 5081
CO   Feb.   p12.   525w.   4

3039   BRACKEEN, JoAnne.   Snooze.   Choice CRS 1009
JM   V1/#2   p51-2.   650w. $3\frac{1}{2}$

3040   BRADFORD, Bobby.   Love's Dream.   Emanem 3302
CAD   March   p32.   150w.   3
CAD   April   p14.   325w.   4

3041   BRADY, Victor.   Classical Soul.   Inner City IC 1006
CAD   April   p8.   75w. $2\frac{1}{2}$

3042   BRAFF, Ruby.   Bugle Call Rag.   Vogue Double VJD 524
(France) (2 discs)
JJ   Feb.   p29.   500w. $3\frac{1}{2}$
MM   Feb. 12   p28.   425w.   5
RR   April   p88.   75w. $4\frac{1}{2}$

3043   BRAFF, Ruby.   Them Three Eyes.   Sonet SNTF 713 (E)
          RR April p88.   25w.   3

3044   BRAND, Dollar.   African Portraits.   Sackville 3009 (Canada)
          OLR Sept. p225.   25w. $4\frac{1}{2}$

3045   BRAND, Dollar.   Capetown Fringe.   Chiaroscuro CR 2004
          CAD Sept. p38.   200w.   4
          MG Sept. p53.   75w.   3
          RS Oct. 20 p96.   200w.   2
          VV Oct. 3 p65.   50w.   4

3046   BRAND, Dollar.   The Children of Africa.   Inner City 3003
       (Reissue)
          CAD Oct. p55.   300w.   5
          CO Feb. p12.   425w.   4
          RS Oct. 20 p96.   200w.   3

3047   BRAND, Dollar.   Peace.   Soultown KRS 110 (South Africa)
          OLR Dec. p292.   50w.   5

3048   BRAND, Dollar.   With Kippie Moketsi.   Soultown KRS 113
       (South Africa)
          OLR Dec. p292.   50w.   5

3049   BRAXTON, Anthony.   Ring Records 01010-11 (West Germany)
          CAD Nov. p18.   175w. $3\frac{1}{2}$

3050   BRAXTON, Anthony.   Creative Orchestra Music 1976.   Aris-
       ta AL 4080
          CO Feb. p13-4.   1225w.   4
          RR July p97.   100w. $3\frac{1}{2}$

3051   BRAXTON, Anthony.   Five Pieces 1975.   Arista 4064
          CO Feb. p12-3.   925w. $2\frac{1}{2}$

3052   BRAXTON, Anthony.   In the Tradition.   Inner City IC 2015
          CAD June p34.   150w.   4

3053   BRAXTON, Anthony.   The Montreux/Berlin Concerts.   Aris-
       ta AL 5002 (2 discs)
          CAD July p35.   350w.   4
          CRA Aug. p70, 72.   475w. $3\frac{1}{2}$
          DB Oct. 20 p22-4.   500w.   5
          MG July p53.   125w.   3
          MM Aug. 6 p19.   400w.   4
          RRE May-June p45.   300w. $4\frac{1}{2}$
          SR Aug. p103.   125w. $4\frac{1}{2}$

3054   BRAXTON, Anthony.   Recital Paris '71.   Musica B2004 (E)
       (Reissue)
          MM Jan. 8 p20.   100w. $3\frac{1}{2}$

3055   BRAXTON, Anthony.   Saxophone Improvisations.   Inner City
        IC 1008
            JF No. 45 p64.   600w.   2½

3056   BRAXTON, Anthony.   Solo.   Ring Records 01002 (West Ger-
        many)
            CAD Nov. p18.   175w.   3½

3057   BRAXTON, Anthony.   Three Compositions of New Jazz.
        Delmark DS 415
            CAD Dec. p38.   200w.   3

3058   BRAXTON, Anthony/Joseph Jarman.   Together Alone.   Del-
        mark DS 428
            MM Nov. 19 p33.   250w.   3½

3059   BRAXTON, Anthony and Muhal Richard Abrams.   Duets
        1976.   Arits Arista AL 4101
            BM March p52.   350w.   4
            CK May p48.   100w.   2½
            DB Feb. 10 p20.   250w.   4
            HF April p128.   250w.   3
            RS March 24 p72.   500w.   2½
            SOU Jan. p47.   200w.   4½
            SR April p110.   100w.   4

3060   BREUKER, Willem.   Kollektief Live in Berlin.   Bvhaast 008
        (Netherlands)
            CAD March p35.   75w.   3

3061   BREUKER, Willem.   Kollektief, the European Scene.   MPS
        68-168
            JF No. 50 p51-2.   325w.   4
            MM Jan. 7 p18.   200w.   4½

3062   BREUKER, Willem.   20 Minutes in the Life of Bill Moons.
        Bvhaast 006 (Netherlands)
            CAD May p24.   150w.   3

3063   BREUKER, Willem and Leo Cuypers.   Live in Shaffy.
        Bvhaast 005 (Netherlands)
            CAD March p34-5.   375w.   4

3064   BRIDGEWATER, Dee Dee.   Atlantic SD 18188.   Cart. TP
        18188.   Cass. CS18188
            DB April 21 p22-3.   200w.   1½
            JM V1/#1 p52.   475w.   1½
            SR July p93.   150w.   3½

3065   BRITT, Pat.   Starrsong.   Catalyst 7612
            CAD Jan. p44-5.   150w.   3
            DB Nov. 17 p28.   75w.   3
            SR May p99.   50w.   4

3066   BRONSTEIN, Stan.   Living on the Avenue.   Muse MR 5113
        CAD   June   p37.   200w.   3½

3067   BROOMER, Stuart.   Conversation Pieces.   Onari Records
        002 (Canada)
              CC   June   p28.   50w.   3
              CK   Nov.   p65.   25w.   1

3068   BROTHER Aah (Robert Northern).   Move Ever Onward.
        Divine Records 52134 A
              CAD   Nov.   p25.   100w.   0

3069   BROTZMANN, Peter.   Solo.   FMP 0360 (West Germany)
              CAD   July   p14.   200w.   4

3069a   BROTZMANN, Peter.   Wolke in Hosen.   Free Music Pro-
        ductions FMP 0360 (West Germany)
              JF   No. 49   p53.   400w.   4

3070   BROTZMANN, Peter; Van Hove; Bennick.   Outspann #2.
        FMP 0200 (West Germany)
              CAD   Feb.   p35-6.   200w.   4½

3071   BROWN, Clifford.   The Complete Paris Collection.   Pye
        Vogue VJ 3001 (3 discs) (E) (Reissue)
              GR   Sept.   p525.   200w.   4

3072   BROWN, Clifford.   The Quinete Vol. 1.   Emory EMT-8-2-
        403 (Reissue)
              DB   April 21   p36.   150w.   5
              SR   April   p110.   350w.   4

3073   BROWN, Reuben and Richie Cole.   Starburst.   Adelphi 5001
              CAD   Feb.   p30.   200w.   3½
              CK   Sept.   p58.   75w.   3

3074   BRUBECK, Dave.   25th Anniversary Reunion.   A&M SP-714
              AU   Nov.   p124.   350w.   4
              CAD   April   p44.   168w.   3
              CK   May   p49.   100w.   5
              DB   May 19   425w.   4
              MM   April 16   p23.   450w.   4
              SOU   April   p62.   100w.   2
              SR   July   p108.   225w.   5

3075   BRUNINGHAUS, Rainer.   The Following Morning.   ECM
        1-1084
              CK   May   p49.   25w.   4

3076   BRUNO, Levita.   Work of Love.   Nucleus 121
              DB   April 21   p30.   200w.   2

3077   BRUNO, Tom and Ellen Christi.   The Sounds of Life.   New

York City Artists Co-op 501
  CAD May p11. 225w. 4

3078 BRYANT, Ray. Solo Flight. Pablo 2310-798
  CAD Oct. p43. 100w. 4
  MM Aug. 27 p24. 175w. 4
  RR Oct. p90. 25w. 3½

3079 BUCKNER, Milt and Jo Jones. Buck and Jo. Jazz Odyssey
  007 (2 discs) (E)
  RR Feb. p68. 75w. 2½

3080 BUCKNER, Teddy. On the Air, Volume 1. Aircheck 10
  ST Aug. -Sept. p237-8. 225w. 4

3081 BUNCH, John. Chiaroscuro 144
  MJ Jan. p29. 50w. 2½

3082 BUNCH, John. John's Other Bunch. Famous Door HL 114
  MJ Dec. p24. 125w. 3½

3083 BURKE, Raymond. A Self Portrait. Land O' Jazz LOJ
  4115
  ST June-July p195-6. 250w. 4

3084 BURRELL, Dave. Dreams. Trio. PAP-9010 (Japan)
  CO Feb. p14-5. 575w. 4

3085 BURRELL, Dave. High Won - High Two. Arista Freedom
  AL 1906 (2 discs) (Reissue)
  CO Feb. p15-6. 575w. 4
  DB Feb. 24 p30. 500w. 3

3086 BURRELL, Duke. Louisiana Shakers Band. Cresent Jazz
  Productions CJP-3
  CAD July p35. 150w. 4

3087 BURRELL, Kenny. Ellington Is Forever, V 2. Fantasy F
  79008 (2 discs)
  CAD Dec. p49-50. 150w. 3½

3088 BURRELL, Kenny. Recapitulation. Chess 2ACMJ-408
  CAD April p29. 275w. 4½

3089 BURTON, Gary. Turn of the Century. Atlantic SD 2-321
  (2 discs) (Reissue)
  CAD Feb. p30, 32. 100w. 4½
  DB June 16 p38-9. 425w. 4
  GP Jan. p97. 25w. 2½
  MG Jan. 150w. 3½
  RSP March-April p39-40. 100w. 4½

3090 BURTON, Gary and Eberhard Weber. Passengers. ECM

1092.   Cart. 8T-1-1092
    CAD   July   p34.   100w.   4
    CRA   Sept.   p72.   200w. $2\frac{1}{2}$
    JF   No. 49   p20.   50w.   4
    MG   July   p53.   100w.   3
    MM   May 21   p28.   600w. $4\frac{1}{2}$
    SR   Oct.   p126.   150w.   5

3091   BYAS, Don.   Savoy Jam Party.   Savoy SJL 2213 (Reissue)
    CAD   Feb.   p40.   175w.   4
    CO   Feb.   p22-3.   125w.   4
    MJ   Nov.   p22.   100w.   3
    MR   Feb.   p12.   400w.   3

3092   BYRD, Charlie.   Charlie Byrd Swings Downtown.   Improv
7116
    CAD   June   p36.   75w.   2
    RFJ   April   p14.   350w.   3
    SR   June   p122.   150w.   4

3093   BYRD, Charlie, Barney Kessel and Herb Ellis.   Great Guitars.   Concord JAZZ CJ-23
    CAD   Jan.   p27-9.   225w.   3
    RFJ   July   p15.   300w. $3\frac{1}{2}$

3094   BYRD, Donald.   Caricatures.   Blue Note LA633-G
    BS   June   p17.   125w.   3
    CAD   March   p78.   50w.   1
    DB   Aug. 11   275w. $2\frac{1}{2}$
    SR   June   p122.   100w.   0

3095   BYRD, Donald.   House of Byrd.   Prestige PR 24066 (2
discs) (Reissue)
    AU   April   p89.   250w.   4
    JJ   Jan.   p26.   300w.   4
    MM   Jan. 8   p20.   100w.   4
    RR   Feb.   p94.   25w. $2\frac{1}{2}$

3096   BYRD, Donald.   Long Green.   Savoy SJL 1101 (Reissue)
    GR   May   p1758.   100w.   4
    JJ   Feb.   p29.   200w.   4
    MM   March 26   p22.   300w. $4\frac{1}{2}$
    RR   April   p88.   50w. $2\frac{1}{2}$

3097   CALLOWAY, Cab.   'Mr. Hi-De-Ho' 1930-1931.   MCA 510.
174 (France) (Reissue)
    ST   June-July   p199.   300w. $3\frac{1}{2}$

3098   CANADIAN Creative Music Collective.   CCMC: Vol. 1/2.
Music Gallery Editions Records CCMC 1002 (Canada)
    CAD   Jan.   p15.   350w.   5

3099   CAPP, Frankie and Nat Pierce.   Juggernaut.   Concord CJ-40

CAD Oct. p34. 175w. 5
MM Nov. 19 p33. 350w. 4

3100 CARTER, Benny. The King. Pablo 2310 768
GR Jan. p1198. 75w. $3\frac{1}{2}$
RR Jan. p85. 58w. $3\frac{1}{2}$

3101 CARTER, Benny and Dizzy Gillespie. Carter, Gillespie, Inc.
Pablo 2310-781
CAD March p32-3. 75w. 4
DB April 7 p30. 200w. 5
JJ May p44. 250w. $4\frac{1}{2}$
RFJ May p15. 500w. 5
SR May p99. 50w. 5

3102 CARTER, Kent. Beauvais Cathedral. Emanem 3306
CAD Jan. p20, 21. 200w. 5
CAD Jan. p21. 200w. 5
CAD Feb. p21. 175w. $4\frac{1}{2}$

3103 CARTER, Ron. Pastels. Milestone M-9073
BM April p50. 150w. 4
CAD April p20, 22. 144w. 3
DB May 19 300w. $3\frac{1}{2}$
JJ April p28. 150w. 2
RR Sept. p96. 50w. 3
RS April 7 p83. 250w. $3\frac{1}{2}$

3104 CARTER, Ron. Piccolo. Milestone M-55004
CAD Nov. p39. 400w. 5
MG Dec. p57. 100w. 3
RS Dec. 29 p77. 425w. 3
VV Sept. 19 p66. 400w. $3\frac{1}{2}$

3105 CARTER, Ron. Yellow and Green. CTI 6064
DB Feb. 10 p19. 200w. 2
SMG May p27. 100w. 4

3106 CATALYST. A Tear and a Smile. Muse MR 5069
CAD March p41. 50w. $2\frac{1}{2}$
DB April 21 p25-6. 150w. $1\frac{1}{2}$

3107 CELESTIN, Oscar "Papa" and Sharkey Bonano. Battle of
the Bands. Fairmont 103
CAD July p38. 175w. 3

3108 CENTAZZO, Andrea. Duetti. OLP 10009 (Italy)
JF No. 47 p67-8. 150w. $3\frac{1}{2}$

3109 CENTAZZO, Andrea. Fragments. PDW 6020 (Italy)
JF No. 47 p67-8. 150w. $3\frac{1}{2}$

3110 CENTAZZO, Andrea. Solos. OLP 10008 (Italy)

JF No. 47 p67-8. 175w. $3\frac{1}{2}$

3111 CHADBOURNE, Eugene. Volume One: Solo Acoustic Guitar.
Parachute Records P. 001 (Canada)
CO Feb. p17. 500w. 4

3112 CHADBOURNE, Eugene. Volume 2. Parachute P002 (Canada)
CAD March p26. 75w. 2

3113 CHADBOURNE, Eugene. Volume 3, Guitar Trios. Parachute P-003
GP Nov. p137. 175w. 4

3114 CHAMBERLAND, Linc. A Place Within. Muse MR 5064
CAD June p41. 150w. 3

3115 CHAMBERS, Joe. New World. Finite 1976-2
CAD April p30. 120w. $2\frac{1}{2}$

3116 CHARIG, Marc. Pipedream. Ogun OG 710
MM Aug. 20 p24. 275w. 4

3117 CHARLESTON Chasers. 1929-1931. VJM VLP 44 (Reissue)
RR June p95. 50w. $3\frac{1}{2}$

3118 CHARTERS, Ann. Ragtime Compositions. Sierra Wave SW
101
CAD May p13. 50w. 4

3119 CHERRY, Don. A & M Horizon SP-717
CAD April p23-4. 275w. 4
DB May 19 400w. $4\frac{1}{2}$
GR Sept. p525. 125w. $3\frac{1}{2}$
JJ May p45. 200w. 4
MM March 12 p25. 550w. 5
RR May p88. 225w. 4
RSP May-June p45. 200w. 5
SOU April p62. 100w. 2
VV Oct. 3 p65. 125w. 4

3120 CHERRY, Don. Eternal Now. Sonet SNTF 653 (E)
JF No. 48 p22. 50w. 4

3121 CHERRY, Don. Hear and Now. Atlantic SD 18217
CAD Aug. p47. 150w. 2
MG Nov. p53. 25w. $3\frac{1}{2}$
MM Oct. 22 p26. 125w. 1

3122 CHERRY, Don. Old and New Dreams. Black Saint BSR
0013
CAD Aug. p55. 200w. 4
CAD Sept. p44. 175w. 4

MG Sept. p53. 125w. $3\frac{1}{2}$
MM June 4 p32. 300w. 4

3123 CHERRY, Don and Gato Barbieri. Inner City 1009
CAD Aug. p48. 125w. 4

3124 CHILDREN at Play. JAPO 60009 ST
JF No. 48 p51. 600w. 3

3125 CHRISTLIEB, Pete. Jazz City. Rahmp #2
CAD June p22. 200w. 5

3126 CHRISTMANN, Gunter and Detlef Schonenberg. Live at
Moers Festival '76. Ring Records 01012 (West Germany)
CAD Nov. p20. 50w. 3

3127 CLARKE, Stanley. School Days. Nemperor NE 900
CIR June 17 p17. 200w. 2

3128 CLAYTON, Buck. The Essential. Vanguard VSD 103/104
(2 discs) (Reissue)
CO Dec. p22. 150w. $1\frac{1}{2}$

3129 CLAYTON, Buck. Golden Days of Jazz--Jams with Basie
and Goodman. CBS 88031 (2 discs) (Reissue)
MM Jan. p16. 375w. 4

3130 CLAYTON, Buck. Jam Sessions, Vols. 1/2. Chiaroscuro
132/143 (2 discs)
JM V1/#3 p52-3. 700w. 3

3131 CLAYTON, Buck and Frankie Laine. Jazz Spectacular.
Columbia JC2 808 (Reissue)
DB April 7 p31-3. 100w. 4

3132 CLAYTON, Buck, and Jimmy Witherspoon. Live in Paris.
Vogue VJD 527 (2 discs) (E)
JJ Feb. p29. 700w. 5
MM April 23 p26. 400w. $3\frac{1}{2}$
RR April p88. 50w. $3\frac{1}{2}$

3133 CLAYTON, Buck and Roy Eldridge. Trumpet Summit.
Pumpkin 101
CAD Aug. p52. 300w. 5

3134 CLEWS, Dud. Who's Blue. Neovox Jazzman 513 (Cassette
Only) (E)
RR Dec. p87. 100w. $3\frac{1}{2}$

3135 CLIMAX Jazz Band. Live at Harbourfront. Climax J 18606
SOU Sept. p64. 200w. $3\frac{1}{2}$

3136   COBB, Arnett.   The Fabulous Apollo Sessions.   Vogue
        CLKAP 768 (Reissue) (France)
             RSP 1:3 p34. 175w. 3

3137   COBB, Arnett.   Jumpin' the Blues.   Jazz Circle 01 (Reissue)
             CO Aug. p24. 75w. 4

3138   COBHAM, Billy.   Magic.   Columbia JC 34939
             DB Dec. 1 p22. 425w. 3

3139   COBHAM, Billy and George Duke.   Live on Tour in Europe.
        Atlantic SO 18194
             BM March p22. 150w. 3
             CAD Jan. p42. 100w. $2\frac{1}{2}$
             MM Jan. 22 p23. 250w. 3

3140   COHEN, Alan.   Black, Brown and Beige.   Monmouth Ever-
        green MES 7077 (Reissue)
             MJ Jan. p28. 50w. 3

3141   COHEN, Mark.   Open Four Doors.   All Season Records 001
             CAD Aug. p21. 100w. 4

3142   COHN, Al.   Al Cohn's America.   Xanadu 138
             CAD Oct. p30. 125w. 4
             RFJ Nov. p16-7. 300w. 3

3143   COHN, Al.   Play It Now.   Xanadu 110 (Reissue)
             MJ March p77. 25w. 3

3144   COHN, Al.   True Blue.   Xanadu 136
             CAD Oct. p30. 125w. 3

3145   COKER, Dolo.   Dolo!   Xanadu 139
             CAD Sept. p30. 150w. 4
             MM Oct. 15 p27. 300w. $3\frac{1}{2}$

3146   COLE, Richie.   Starburst.   Adelphi 5001
             RFJ May p18-9. 350w. $3\frac{1}{2}$

3147   COLE, Richie.   Trenton Makes - The World Takes.   Pro-
        gressive Records 1001
             CAD Jan. p14. 275w. $3\frac{1}{2}$

3148   COLEMAN, Hadley.   Projecting.   Catalyst CAT 7604
             RSP March-April p60-1. 300w. $3\frac{1}{2}$

3149   COLEMAN, Ornette.   Dancing in Your Head.   A & M Hori-
        zon SP-722
             CAD Oct. p34. 300w. 4
             CRA Sept. p81. 125w. 4
             DB Oct. 6 p24. 400w. 5
             JF No. 50 p18-9. 50w. 4

MJ   Sept. p28. 50w. 2
MM   Aug. 13 p22. 500w. 4
RR   Nov. p116. 175w. 3½
RS   Sept. 22 p72, 77. 250w. 3
SR   Oct. p128. 300w. 2
VV   July 4 p45. 400w. 5

3150   COLEMAN, Ornette.   Free Jazz.   Atlantic KSD 1364
       SOU Sept. p66. 50w. 4

3151   COLLETTE, Buddy.   Block Buster.   R. G. B. Records RGB
       2001
       CAD Aug. p50. 275w. 4

3152   COLLIE, Max.   At the Beiderbecke Fest.   Bix Lives, Vol. 6
       MR   Jan. p13. 200w. 3

3153   COLLIER, Graham.   New Conditions.   Mosaic GMC 761 (E)
       MM   Jan. 7 p18. 425w. 1½
       RR   July p97. 100w. 3

3154   COLLIER, Graham.   Symphony of Scorpions.   Mosaic GCM
       773 (E)
       RR   Nov. p116. 50w. 3½

3155   COLLINS, Lee and Ralph Sutton.   Jazzola Six, Volume 1 &
       2.   Rarities 31/32 (2 discs) (Reissue)
       CO   Sept. /Oct. p23. 75w. 3
       JJ   Jan. p26. 250w. 4

3156   COLTRANE, Alice.   Radha-Krsna Nama Sankirtana.   Warner
       Bros. , BS 2968
       CAD March p45-6. 75w.   2½
       CK   May p49. 25w.   2½
       DB   July 14 p42-3. 300w.   0
       MG   May p53. 125w. 3

3157   COLTRANE, John.   Impulse AS 21 (Reissue)
       BM   Jan. p53. 150w. 5

3158   COLTRANE, John.   Afro Blue Impressions.   Pablo 2620 101
       (Reissue)
       DB   Dec. 15 p28, 30. 400w. 5
       MM   Oct. 22 p28. 175w.   4½
       RR   Sept. p96. 100w.   2½
       RSP May-June p44. 200w.   3½
       SOU Sept. p66. 100w. 4

3159   COLTRANE, John.   Black Pearl.   Prestige P 24037 (2
       discs) (Reissue)
       RRE March-April p35-6. 100w. 3

3160   COLTRANE, John.   Creation.   Blue Parrot AR 700 (E)

JJ   May   p46.   150w.   5
MM   May 21   p28.   200w.   4

3161   COLTRANE, John.   Giant Steps.   Atlantic SD 1311 (Reissue)
       RSP   March-April   p36.   100w.   4
       SOU   Sept.   p66.   50w.   4

3162   COLTRANE, John.   Interstellar Space.   Impulse ASD-9277
       CO   Feb.   p17-8.   725w.   3

3163   COLTRANE, John.   Live at Birdland.   Impulse A 50 (Reissue)
       RSP   March-April   p37.   300w.   5

3164   COLTRANE, John.   Live at Village Vanguard.   Impulse A
       10 (Reissue)
       RSP   March-April   p36-7.   75w.   4

3165   COLTRANE, John.   A Love Supreme.   Impulse A 77 (Reis-
       sue)
       RSP   March-April   p37.   75w. $3\frac{1}{2}$

3166   COLTRANE, John.   My Fantastic Things.   Atlantic SD 1361
       (Reissue)
       RSP   March-April   p36.   100w.   4

3167   COLTRANE, John.   The Other Village Vanguard Tapes.   Im-
       pulse AS 9325 (Reissue)
       CAD   May   p21-2.   225w.   4
       DB   Sept. 8   p30, 32.   400w.   5
       RFJ   July   p15.   500w.   5
       RS   May 19   500w. $2\frac{1}{2}$
       RSP   May-June   p40.   300w.   4

3168   COLTRANE, John.   The Turning Point.   Bethlehem 6024
       (Reissue)
       CO   Dec.   p22.   150w.   2

3169   COLTRANE, John.   Wheelin'.   Prestige PR-24069 (2 discs)
       (Reissue)
       CAD   Sept.   p45.   150w.   4
       CO   Dec.   p22.   75w. $1\frac{1}{2}$
       GR   Dec.   p1162.   50w.   3
       MM   Oct. 22   p28.   175w.   4
       RR   Oct.   p90.   75w. $3\frac{1}{2}$
       RR   Nov.   p116.   50w. $2\frac{1}{2}$

3170   COLTRANE, John and Wilbur Harden.   Dial Africa.   Savoy
       SJL 1110 (Reissue)
       CAD   Oct.   p42.   200w. $2\frac{1}{2}$
       CO   Dec.   p22.   150w.   2
       MM   Oct. 22   p28.   175w.   4
       RR   Oct.   p90.   25w.   4

3171   COMPANY. One. Incus 21
        MM April 30 p32. 325w. $3\frac{1}{2}$

3172   COMPANY. Two. Incus 23
        MM July 16 p30. 300w. $3\frac{1}{2}$

3173   COMPOSERS' Workshop Ensemble. We've Been Around.
        Strata-East SES 7422
        JM V1/#3 p53-4. 650w. 3

3174   CONDON, Eddie. Eddie Condon Concerts, Town Hall, 1944-.
        Storyville SLP 509 (Reissue)
        RR April p88. 50w. $3\frac{1}{2}$

3175   CONDON, Eddie. Golden Days of Jazz. CBS 88032 (France)
        (2 discs) (Reissue)
        MM Jan. 1 p17. 375w. 4

3176   CONDON, Eddie. One Night Stand. Joyce 1035
        CAD March p35. 75w. 3

3177   CONFREY, Zez. Folkways RF 28 (Reissue)
        RA July-Aug. p5-6. 100w. 4
        RT May p24. 250w. 5

3178   COREA, Chick. Polydor, PD-2-9003
        CK March p56. 300w. 4

3179   COREA, Chick. Musicmagic. Columbia PC 34682
        CAD June p43. 300w. 4
        RFJ May p18. 100w. $\frac{1}{2}$

3180   COREA, Chick. My Spanish Heart. Polydor PD-2-9003.
        Cart. POL-8T2-9003. Cass. POL-CT2-9003 (2 discs)
        AU June p132. 250w. 5
        CAC July p142. 500w. $4\frac{1}{2}$
        CAD March p31. 150w. 4
        DB March 24 400w. $3\frac{1}{2}$
        RS April 7 p78, 80. 450w. 3
        SOU May p62. 100w. 2
        SR May p99. 75w. 4

3181   COREA, Chick, David Holland and Barry Altschul. A. R. C.
        ECM-1-1009
        CAD Oct. p53. 175w. 4
        CK Nov. p65. 25w. $4\frac{1}{2}$
        SR Dec. 150w. $3\frac{1}{2}$

3182   COREA, Chick, Herbie Hancock, Keith Jarrett, McCoy Tyner.
        Atlantic SD 1696
        CRA Aug. p65. 500w. 3
        DB May 5 p22. 400w. $4\frac{1}{2}$
        MG April p53. 125w. 3

3183   CORYELL, Larry. Basics. Vanguard VSD 79375
        CAD March p33. 75w. $2\frac{1}{2}$
        JM Summer p55-6. 150w. 0

3184   CORYELL, Larry. The Lion and the Ram. Arista AL 4108
        CRA May p77-8. 300w. $2\frac{1}{2}$
        DB April 21 p26, 27. 350w. 3
        JM Summer p55-6. 150w. $2\frac{1}{2}$
        MG May p53. 125w. 3
        SR May p99-100. 75w. 3

3185   CORYELL, Larry and Alphonse Mouzon. Back Together
        Again. Atlantic SP 18220
        CAD Aug. p24. 100w. $3\frac{1}{2}$
        GP Sept. p118-9. 200w. 4
        MG Sept. p53. 75w. 3
        SR Dec. 75w. $1\frac{1}{2}$

3186   The COTTON PICKERS. Grannyphone 03304/5 (2 discs) (Re-
        issue)
        ST Dec.-Jan. p74-5. 175w. 4

3187   COUNCE, Curtis. Exploring the Future. Dooto DTL 247
        (Reissue)
        MM June 4 p32. 125w. 5

3188   COWELL, Stanley. Ancestral Streams. Strata-East SES
        19743
        JJ April p28. 200w. $3\frac{1}{2}$

3189   COWELL, Stanley. Blues for the Viet Cong. Arista Free-
        dom 1032
        DB Dec. 15 p27-8. 250w. 4
        MG Aug. p63. 100w. $2\frac{1}{2}$
        RFJ Nov. p15. 400w. $3\frac{1}{2}$

3190   COWELL, Stanley. Regeneration. Strata-East SES 1976/5
        JJ April p28-9. 225w. $3\frac{1}{2}$

3191   COXHILL, Lol. Diverse. Ogun OG 510 (E)
        MM April 23 p26. 275w. $3\frac{1}{2}$

3192   CRAWFORD, H. Ray. It's About Time. Dobre 1010
        CAD Nov. p38, 39. 200w. $4\frac{1}{2}$

3193   CRAWFORD, Hank. Hank Crawford's Back. Kudu 333
        CAD April p8. 180w. 2
        DB April 7 p21-2. 200w. 1
        MM June 25 p25. 200w. 3

3194   CREATIVE Construction Company. CCC. Muse MR 5071
        CO Feb. p19. 675w. $2\frac{1}{2}$

3195   CREATIVE Construction Company.   Vol. 2.   Muse 5097
       CAD   Feb.   p22.   300w.   3
       MG   April   p53.   125w.   3

3196   CRISS, Sonny.   The Joy of Sax.   Impulse AS 9326
       CAD   July   p23.   100w.   3
       CRA   Sept.   p69.   250w. $2\frac{1}{2}$
       DB   Nov. 17   p22-3.   275w.   2

3197   CRISS, Sonny.   Out of Nowhere.   Muse MR 5089
       RFJ   April   p16.   400w.   5

3198   CROTHERS, Connie.   Perception.   Inner City 2022
       CAD   May   p26.   100w.   1
       CK   Oct.   p65.   100w. $2\frac{1}{2}$

3199   CRUMB, D. George.   Makrokosmos, Vol. II.   Columbia Zo-
       diac Y34135
       DB   April 21   p22.   200w.   4

3200   CUBER, Ronnie.   Cuber Libre.   Xanadu 135
       ARG   Aug.   p41-2.   175w.   4
       CAD   March   p46-7.   150w.   1
       DB   June 16.   p40-3.   225w. $4\frac{1}{2}$
       JM   Summer   p49-50.   400w. $3\frac{1}{2}$
       RFJ   June   p15.   300w.   3
       SOU   April   p58.   100w.   4
       VV   March 14   p81.   50w.   3

3201   CULLUM, Jim, Jr.   Look Over There...Happy Jazz.   Amer-
       ican Jazz 125
       CAD   April   p33.   108w.   3

3202   CULLUM, Jim, Sr.   Jazz: The Muse of....   Audiophile
       AP117
       CAD   April   p33.   108w. $3\frac{1}{2}$

3203   CUNIMONDO, Frank.   Sagittarius.   Mondo Records (M-105)
       CAD   Nov.   p29.   50w.   3

3204   CUNIMONDO, Frank.   The Top Shelf Collection.   Sound Idea
       90175
       CAD   Nov.   p30.   50w.   3

3205   CUNNINGHAM, David.   Grey Scale.   Piano 001 (E)
       MM   Nov. 5   p31.   150w.   3

3206   CURSON, Ted.   Flip Top.   Arista-Freedom AL1030
       CAD   July   p41.   200w. $3\frac{1}{2}$

3207   CURSON, Ted.   Jazz Meeting 1.   Four Leaf Records FLC
       5019 (Sweden)
       CAD   Oct.   p26.   125w.   4

3208   CURSON, Ted.   Jubilant Power.   Inner City 1017
       CAD   March   p33.   200w.   4
       DB   May 5   p20.   325w.   4½
       RFJ   May   p18.   300w.   3

3209   CURSON, Ted.   Typical Ted.   Trident 503
       CAD   July   p31.   250w.   4

3210   CUYPERS, Leo.   Live in Shafty.   Bvhasst 001 (Netherlands)
       CAD   May   p24.   150w.   4

3211   CYRILLE, Andrew.   Junction.   IPS 003
       CAD   Feb.   p14-5.   325w.   4
       JF   No. 48   p21.   75w.   3½

3212   CYRILLE, Andrew and Milford Graves.   Dialogue of Drums.
       IPS 001 (Reissue)
       JF   No. 47   p69.   50w.   3½

3213   DACOSTA, Paulinho.   Agora.   Pablo 2310-785
       CAD   April   p36-7.   86w.   2½
       GR   Aug.   p354.   100w.   3
       JJ   March   p30.   400w.   4
       MM   Feb. 26   p33.   75w.   1½
       SR   June   p96.   150w.   5

3214   DAHLANDER, Bert.   A Swedish Accent.   Everyday 31309
       CAD   Nov.   p28.   75w.   3½

3215   DALLWITZ, Dave.   Midnight Crawl.   Swaggie S-1343 (Aus-
       tralia) (Reissue)
       ST   Dec. -Jan.   p75.   250w.   4

3216   DANDRIDGE, Putney.   Putney Dandridge, Volume 3.   Rari-
       ties 34
       JJ   Jan.   p27.   400w.   4

3217   DAPOGNY, James.   Piano Music of Ferdinand "Jelly Roll"
       Morton.   Smithsonian Collection N003
       RA   March-April   p5.   100w.   3

3218   DAUGHERTY, Jack.   Carmel by the Sea.   Monterey MS-100
       CAD   Feb.   p36-7.   300w.   3

3219   DAUGHERTY, Keith.   Let My Heart Be My Home.   Fantasy
       F 9515
       SR   March   p95.   100w.   3

3220   DAVIS, Charles.   Ingia.   Strata East SES 7425
       JJ   March   p30.   225w.   4

3221   DAVIS, Eddie "Lockjaw."   Straight Ahead.   Pablo 2310-778
       CAD   Feb.   p44-5.   225w.   4

DB Feb. 24 p25. 150w. 3
GR Sept. p525. 75w. 3
JJ May p46. 50w. 3
MM April 16 p25. 250w. 4

3222 DAVIS, Eddie "Lockjaw." Swingin' Till the Girls Come
      Home. Inner City 2058
      CAD Nov. p39, 40. 125w. 5

3223 DAVIS, Miles. Facets. CBS Special Prod. JP 13811
      CAD Oct. p36, 38. 275w. 4

3224 DAVIS, Miles. Green Haze. Prestige PR 24064 (2 discs)
      (Reissue)
      JJ Jan. p27. 450w. 4
      RSP Jan. -Feb. p35-6. 550w. 3

3225 DAVIS, Miles. Water Babies. Columbia PC-34396. Cart.
      PCA-34396. Cass. PCT-34396
      CAD May p18. 150w. 4
      CRA April p96-7. 800w. 4
      DB May 5 p20. 400w. 4
      GR Sept. p525. 125w. 3
      HF June p119. 400w. 4
      JM Summer p50. 400w. $2\frac{1}{2}$
      MG June p53. 100w. $4\frac{1}{2}$
      MM June 4 p32. 200w. $3\frac{1}{2}$
      RS April 7 p83. 50w. $3\frac{1}{2}$
      RS April 21 650w. 4
      RSP May-June p36-8. 1100w. $3\frac{1}{2}$
      SR July p87-8. 550w. 5

3226 DAVIS, Rev. Gary. Ragtime Guitar. Kicking Mule 106
      CAD Nov. p17. 50w. $4\frac{1}{2}$

3227 DAVIS, Richard. As One. Muse 5093
      CAD April p24-5. 192w. $2\frac{1}{2}$
      MJ Sept. p30. 50w. $3\frac{1}{2}$

3228 DAVIS, Wayne. Black Fire 19752
      JF No. 50 p20. 50w. 3

3229 DAVISON, Wild Bill. Storyville SLP 248
      JJ Jan. p27. 325w. 5

3230 DAVISON, Wild Bill. But Beautiful. Storyville SLP 248
      (Denmark)
      GR March p1471. 150w. 4
      MM March 19 p32. 250w. $3\frac{1}{2}$

3231 DAVISON, Wild Bill. Drifting Down the River with. Story-
      ville SLP 264
      RR Dec. p88. 25w. $1\frac{1}{2}$

3232   DAVISON, Wild Bill.   Up Top.   RCA Masters FXL 1-7317
       (France) (Reissue)
           JJ   April   p29.   150w.   1½

3233   DAVISON, Wild Bill and Fessor's Big City Band.   Birthday.
       Horekiks HKLP5
           MR   June   p8-9.   100w.   3

3234   DAVISON, Wild Bill and Freddy Randall.   Black Lion BLP
       30187 (E)
           RR   Oct.   p89.   50w.   2½

3235   DEAN, Elton.   Happy Daze.   Ogun OG 910 (E)
           MM   Nov. 12   p34.   175w.   4

3236   DEAN, Elton.   Oh! For the Edge.   Ogun OG 900 (E)
           CO   Feb.   p19-20.   400w.   4

3237   DEAN, Elton.   They All Be on This Old Cool.   Ogun OG
       410 (E)
           MM   July 9   p24.   250w.   3

3238   DEAN, Elton and Alan Skidmore.   El Skid.   Vinyl VS 103
       (E)
           MM   Nov. 12   p34.   175w.   4½

3239   DEAN, Elton, Joe Gallivan, and Kenny Wheeler.   The Cheque
       Is in the Mail.   Ogun OG 610
           MM   July 23   p22.   125w.   3½

3240   DEGEN, Bob.   Sequoia Song.   Enja 2072 (West Germany)
           MM   Jan. 1   p16.   50w.   3

3241   DE JOHNETTE, Jack.   ECM ECM-1074.   Cart. 1-1074
           JF   No. 47   p65.   225w.   2½
           JM   V1/#2.   p54.   350w.   3½
           SR   Feb.   p108.   150w.   2

3242   DE JOHNETTE, Jack.   New Rags ECM-1-1103
           CAD   Nov.   p34.   300w.   2
           DB   Dec. 1   p22.   350w.   4
           MM   Oct. 1   p28.   300w.   3

3243   DE JOHNETTE, Jack.   Pictures.   ECM 1079
           CAD   May   p23.   75w.   3
           DB   July 14   p36.   300w.   3
           JF   No. 47   p65.   225w.   3
           MG   June   p53.   150w.   3
           MM   Jan. 18.   p24.   150w.   2
           RFJ   May   p18.   250w.   4

3244   DELLA GROTTA, Roberto.   Jazz A Confronto: Vol. 31.
       Horo HLL 101-31 (Italy)

CAD Sept. p19. 150w. 3

3245 DE PAULA, Irio. Jazz A Confronto: Vol. 1. Horo HLL
101-1 (Italy)
CAD Sept. p14. 125w. 5

3246 DESEO, Csabu. Ultraviola. Pepita SLPX 17504 (Hungary)
JF No. 49 p23. 75w. 3

3247 DESMOND, Paul, and Gerry Mulligan. Two of a Mind. RCA
Masters FXL 1-7311 (France) (Reissue)
JJ March p31. 225w. 3

3248 DE SOUZA, Paul. Sweet Lucy. Capitol ST-11648
CAD July p24. 150w. 3
DB Oct. 20 p26. 250w. 2

3249 DICKENSON, Vic. Essential. Vanguard VSD 99/100 (2
discs)
CAD March p44-5. 125w. 5
CO Dec. p23-4. 125w. $3\frac{1}{2}$
MJ Sept. p32. 50w. $3\frac{1}{2}$
MJ Nov. p24. 50w. 3
MR May p6-7. 250w. 3
RSP May-June p40. 200w. 2

3250 DICKENSON, Vic. In Session. Jazzways 106/3
CO Feb. p20. 750w. 3

3251 DICKENSON, Vic. Plays Bessie Smith. Sonet 720 (E)
CAD Aug. p51. 200w. $3\frac{1}{2}$

3252 DICKENSON, Vic. Trombone Charly. Sonet SNTF 720 (E)
MM March 19 p32. 400w. 4

3253 DICKERSON, Walt. Peace. Steeplechase 1042
CAD Sept. p42. 150w. $4\frac{1}{2}$

3254 DICKIE, Neville. Back to Boogie. Music for Pleasure MFP
50194 (E)
RA March-April p7. 125w. 3
RT Jan. p4. 200w. $3\frac{1}{2}$

3255 DIKKER-Waterland Ensemble. Tan Tango. Waterland Records WM 001 (Netherlands)
CAD March p26. 150w. $3\frac{1}{2}$

3256 DI MEOLA, Al. Elegant Gypsy. Columbia PC34461
CAD June p20. 100w. $3\frac{1}{2}$
DB Aug. 11 275w. 3
GP July p129. 150w. 5

3257 DI MEOLA, Al. Land of the Midnight Sun. Columbia PC

34074
GP   Jan.   p97.   150w.   4

3258   DIXON, Bill.   Intents and Purposes.   RCA FXLI-7331
(France) (Reissue)
CO   Aug.   p24.   100w.   3

3259   DODGE, Bill.   Swinging '34, vol. 1.   Melodeon 7328 (Reissue)
CAD   Dec.   p58.   425w.   3

3260   DODGE, Charles.   Synthesized Speech Music.   CRI SD 348
DB   May 19   325w.   5

3261   DOLPHY, Eric.   Memorial.   DJM 22041 (E)
BM   Jan.   p53.   150w.   4

3262   DOLPHY, Eric.   Status.   Prestige P-24070 (2 discs) (Reissue)
CAD   Sept.   p36-7.   300w.   4
CO   Dec.   p22.   75w.   2
GR   Dec.   p1162.   150w.   3
MM   Sept. 10.   p29.   225w.   4
RR   Oct.   p90.   75w. $3\frac{1}{2}$
RR   Nov.   p116.   50w.   3
VV   May 30   p63.   250w. $3\frac{1}{2}$

3263   DOLPHY, Eric and Misja Mendelberg.   Epistrophy/Eeko.
ICP 015
CO   Feb.   p20-1.   525w. $2\frac{1}{2}$

3264   DONEGAN, Dorothy.   Four Leaf Clover FLC 5006
CAD   Oct.   p26.   175w.   5

3265   DORHAM, Kenny.   But Beautiful.   Milestone M 47036 (2
discs) (Reissue)
DB   April 21   p26-30.   250w.   4
JF   No. 46   p60-1.   575w. $3\frac{1}{2}$
JM   1:2   p62-3.   325w.   3

3266   DOROUGH, Bob.   Beginning to See the Light.   Laissez-faire
SD-02
CAD   April   p6.   300w.   4

3267   DOROUGH, Bob.   Just About Everything.   Inner City 1023
CAD   Oct.   p59.   150w.   4

3268   DREW, Kenny.   Duo with Neils Henning Orsted-Pedersen.
SteepleChase 1002
CAD   March   p34.   50w. $1\frac{1}{2}$
CK   Sept.   p59.   150w.   3
CO   Feb.   p21.   150w. $2\frac{1}{2}$
CO   Feb.   p21.   150w.   3

3269   DREW, Kenny. Everything I Love. Inner City 2007
       CAD April p30.   50w.   3
       CK   Sept. p59.   150w. 3
       CO   Feb.   p21.   300w. 4

3270   DREW, Kenny. If You Could See Me Now. Inner City Rec-
       ords 2002
       CK   Sept. p59.   150w. 3

3271   DREW, Kenny. Morning. Inner City 2048
       CAD Nov.   p37, 38.   175w.   3

3272   DUDEK, Les. Say No More. Columbia PC34397
       GP   July   p129.   50w. $2\frac{1}{2}$
       MM   July 16 p22.   250w.   3
       RC   July   p10.   250w. $3\frac{1}{2}$

3273   DUDZIAK, Urszula. Midnight Rain.   Artista 4132
       CAD Nov.   p34.   125w.   1
       HF   Dec.   p142.   300w.   3
       MG   Dec.   p57.   50w.   3
       RSP Nov. -Dec.   p37.   450w. $3\frac{1}{2}$
       SOU Dec.   p56.   300w.   3

3274   DUKE, George. From Me to You. Epic PE-34469. Cart.
       PEA-34469. Cass. PET-34469
       DB   July 14 p39-40.   200w.   4
       SR   Sept. p120.   100w.   1
       VV   May 2 p61.   200w.   2

3275   DUKE, George. Liberated Fantasies.   MPS G-22835
       CAD Jan.   p18-9.   75w. $2\frac{1}{2}$
       MG   Feb.   p57.   100w. $2\frac{1}{2}$
       RS   Feb. 24 p69, 71.   250w.   3

3276   DUKE, George. Reach for It.   Epic J4 34883
       CK   Dec.   p73.   100w. $3\frac{1}{2}$

3277   DUKES of Dixieland. Creole Gumbo.   Sandcastle 1035
       MJ   Dec.   p24-5.   75w. $3\frac{1}{2}$

3278   DYANI, Johnny. Music for Xaba.   Antilles AN 7035
       AU   Dec.   p129.   350w.   3
       JF   No. 48 p22.   75w. $3\frac{1}{2}$

3279   DYKSTRA, Brian. Something Like a Rag.   Advent 5021
       RA   March-April p6.   100w. $2\frac{1}{2}$

3280   E. M. T. Canadian Cup of Coffee.   SAJ 02
       CAD March p37.   225w.   3

3281   EASTMAN Jazz Ensemble. Eastman Jazz Ensemble: Live.
       Mark Records MES 54600

CAD April p10. 100w. 3

3282 EASTON, Ted. Hefty Jazz. Riff 659. 025 (Holland)
      JJ Jan. p30. 800w. 5
      MM Jan. 22 p25. 425w. 3
      ST April-May p158. 325w. 4

3283 EDELHAGEN, Kurt. Big Band Jazz. Big Band International
      2701
      CAD Feb. p33. 100w. 0

3284 EDELHAGEN, Kurt. Concert Jazz. Golden Era 15017
      CAD Feb. p33. 100w. 0

3285 EDISON, Harry. After You've Gone. Concord Jazz CJ6
      CO April p13-4. 175w. 4

3286 EDISON, Harry. Blues for Basie. Verve 2332082 (E)
      RR Oct. p90. 25w. 3

3287 EDISON, Harry. Edison's Lights. Pablo 2310-780.
      CAD Feb. p44-5. 225w. 4
      DB March 10 p24. 275w. 4
      GR Sept. p525. 50w. $3\frac{1}{2}$
      JJ May p46. 200w. $4\frac{1}{2}$
      MM June 25 p25. 250w. $3\frac{1}{2}$
      RR April p88. 25w. 3

3288 EDISON, Harry. Sweets, Lips and Lots of Jazz. Xanadu
      123
      CO April p13. 300w. 4
      HF Jan. p146. 200w. 4
      SOU Jan. p48. 300w. $4\frac{1}{2}$

3289 EDWARDS, Teddy. Feelin's. Muse 5045
      CO April p14. 250w. 5

3290 EDWARDS, Teddy. The Inimitable Teddy Edwards. Xanadu
      134
      CAD April p14. 375w. 5
      DB June 16 p40-3. 225w. 5
      RFJ May p16-7. 600w. $3\frac{1}{2}$
      SOU April p56. 100w. 3

3291 ELDRIDGE, Roy. Hecklers Hop. Tax 8020 (Reissue)
      CO Aug. p23. 225w. 4

3292 ELDRIDGE, Roy. Little Jazz, Record 1. Vogue VJD 533-2
      (2 discs) (France) (Reissue)
      MM May 14 p36. 450w. $3\frac{1}{2}$

3293 ELDRIDGE, Roy. What's It All About. Pablo 2310 766
      BM Jan. p53. 100w. 3

         JM May p54-5.   650w. $3\frac{1}{2}$
         RR Jan. p85.   58w.   3

3294   ELLINGTON, Duke.   The Afro-Eurasian Eclipse.   Fantasy
       F-9498
         CO April p14.   700w. $2\frac{1}{2}$

3295   ELLINGTON, Duke.   The Age of.   RCA PC 42086 (3 discs)
       (Reissue)
         RR June p94.   100w.   3

3296   ELLINGTON, Duke.   All-Time Great Orchestra of 1943, Vols.
       1, 2, 3.   Hall of Fame JG 625/7 (3 discs)
         JM Summer p63.   100w. $3\frac{1}{2}$

3297   ELLINGTON, Duke.   The Bethlehem Years, Vol. 1.   Bethle-
       hem BCP 6013 (Reissue)
         JR V9/#3 unpaged 150w. $3\frac{1}{2}$
         RR Oct. p90.   25w.   3

3298   ELLINGTON, Duke.   Carnegie Hall Concerts, 1943.   Prestige
       P 34004 (3 discs)
         RS Feb. 9. p91, 93.   250w. $3\frac{1}{2}$

3299   ELLINGTON, Duke.   Carnegie Hall Concerts, 1944.   Pres-
       tige P-24073 (2 discs) (Reissue)
         RS Feb. 9 p91, 93.   250w. $3\frac{1}{2}$

3300   ELLINGTON, Duke.   Carnegie Hall Concerts, 1946.   Pres-
       tige P-24074 (2 discs) (Reissue)
         RS Feb. 9 p91, 93.   250w. $3\frac{1}{2}$

3301   ELLINGTON, Duke.   Carnegie Hall Concerts, 1947.   Pres-
       tige P-24075 (2 discs)
         RS Feb. 9 p91, 93.   250w. $3\frac{1}{2}$

3302-3 ELLINGTON, Duke.   The Complete, Vol. 1, 1925-28.   CBS
       67264 (2 discs) (France) (Reissue)
         MM June 4 p30.   350w.   4

3304   ELLINGTON, Duke.   The Complete, Vol. 2, 1928-30.   CBS
       68275 (2 discs) (France) (Reissue)
         MM June 4 p30.   350w.   4

3305   ELLINGTON, Duke.   The Complete, Vol. 3, 1930-32.   CBS
       88000 (2 discs) (France) (Reissue)
         MM June 4 p30.   350w.   4

3306   ELLINGTON, Duke.   The Complete, Vol. 4, 1932.   CBS
       88035 (2 discs) (Reissue)
         MM Jan. 18 p24.   550w.   4

3307   ELLINGTON, Duke.   A Date with the Duke Volumes 1-8.

Fairmont FA-1001/4, 1007/10
    CAD June p28. 175w. 4
    SR Oct. p132. 1350w. 5

3308 ELLINGTON, Duke. The Duke 1940. Jazz Society 520/521
    (2 discs) (Reissue)
    CO Sept./Oct. p23-4. 125w. 4

3309 ELLINGTON, Duke. Ellington Is Forever. Fantasy F-79008
    RSP Nov.-Dec. p41. 150w. $3\frac{1}{2}$

3310 ELLINGTON, Duke. Ellington, 1938. Smithsonian R003 (2
    discs) (Reissue)
        CO Feb. p23-4. 300w. 3
        DB April 7 p31-3. 100w. $4\frac{1}{2}$
        HF Feb. p142. 300w. 4
        MJ March p44. 150w. $2\frac{1}{2}$
        MR Feb. p12. 450w. $2\frac{1}{2}$
        RFJ May p11. 700w. $4\frac{1}{2}$

3311 ELLINGTON, Duke. Fargo Encores, 1940. Jazz Guild 1006
    (Reissue)
        CAD March p39-40. 125w. $2\frac{1}{2}$
        JM Summer p63. 100w. 3

3312 ELLINGTON, Duke. Film Sound Track, Vol. 1. Storyville
    702 (Reissue)
        RR Dec. p87. 50w. $2\frac{1}{2}$

3313 ELLINGTON, Duke. Here Is. Kings of Jazz KLJ 20003
    (Italy) (Reissue)
        JM 1:2 p65. 100w. $2\frac{1}{2}$

3314 ELLINGTON, Duke. His Most Important Second War Con-
    cert. Saga 6902 (E) (Reissue)
        SR Jan. p106. 230w. 4

3315 ELLINGTON, Duke. The Hollywood Bowl Concert. Unique
    Jazz UJ 001 (Reissue)
        MM Nov. 5 p32. 375w. 4

3316 ELLINGTON, Duke. The Intimate Ellington. Pablo 2310-
    787
        CAD April p31-2. 456w. $2\frac{1}{2}$
        JJ March p31. 400w. 4
        RR April p88. 50w. $2\frac{1}{2}$

3317 ELLINGTON, Duke. On the Air. Aircheck #4 (3 discs)
    (Reissue)
        CAD Jan. p34, 35. 125w. $3\frac{1}{2}$
        CO Feb. p23. 175w. 3

3318 ELLINGTON, Duke. One Night Stand with. Joyce 1023

AU Jan. p88. 200w. $4\frac{1}{2}$

3319 ELLINGTON, Duke. The Works of, Vol. 18. RCA FXM1-
      7301 (Reissue)
      RR Aug. p84. 50w. $2\frac{1}{2}$

3320 ELLINGTON, Duke. World of, Vol. 2. Columbia KG
      33341 (Reissue) (2 discs)
      JR V9/#3 unpaged 75w. 4
      RR Feb. p94. 200w. 4

3321 ELLINGTON, Duke. The World of, Vol. 3. Columbia CG
      33961 (Reissue)
      CAD Feb. p27. 200w. $3\frac{1}{2}$
      CO Aug. p22. 175w. 2
      DB April 7 p31-3. 100w. $2\frac{1}{2}$
      JR V9/#3 unpaged 75w. 4
      MJ March p44. 50w. $2\frac{1}{2}$

3322 ELLINGTON, Duke and Horace Henderson. Ridin' in Rhythm.
      World Records SHB 42 (E) (2 discs)
      ST Oct. -Nov. p34-5. 200w. $3\frac{1}{2}$

3323 ELLIS, Herb and Barney Kessel. Poor Butterfly. Concord
      CJ-34
      CAD Sept. p37. 175w. 4

3324 ELLIS, Herb and Ray Brown. Hot Tracks. Concord Jazz
      CJ-12
      GP Feb. p113. 50w. 4

3325 ELLIS, Lloyd. Las Vegas 3 a.m. Famous Door HL 110
      CAD March p31. 125w. 4

3326 ELLIS, Pee Wee. Home in the Country. Savoy SJL 3301
      DB Dec. 1 p31. 325w. 3

3327 ELLISON, Mel. Friends. New Jazz Records MRC-1001-B
      CAD July p18. 300w. $3\frac{1}{2}$
      CAD Nov. p28. 50w. 3

3328 ELSDON, Alan. Jazz Journeyman. Black Lion BLP 12163
      (E)
      MM Dec. 3 p32. 250w. 3

3329 EMERALD City Jazz Band. Maiden Flight. Tri-AD 901
      CAD June p12. 200w. 2

3330 ERICSON, Rolf. Oh Pretty Little Neida. Four Leaf Clover
      FLC 5003 (Sweden)
      CAD Oct. p27. 150w. 4

3331 ERVIN, Booker. Back from the Gig. Blue Note LA 488-H2

          CAD   April   p17.   300w.   4
          DB   Aug. 11   200w.   5

3332   ERVIN, Booker.   Lament for B. E.   Inner City 3006
          CAD   Oct.   p50.   200w.   4
          JJ   Jan.   p28.   350w.   4
          MM   Jan. 1   p16.   50w.   3

3333   ESCOVEDO, Sheila and Pete Escovedo.   Solo Two.   Fantasy
          F-9524
          CAD   June   p22.   75w.   4

3334   EVANS, Bill.   Empathy.   Verve 2332 087 (Reissue)
          MM   Oct. 8   p38.   225w.   3

3335   EVANS, Bill.   Quintessence.   Fantasy F-9529
          CAD   Sept.   p44.   150w.   4
          CK   Oct.   p64.   100w. $3\frac{1}{2}$
          DB   Dec. 1   p26-7.   275w. $4\frac{1}{2}$
          MJ   Sept.   p32.   25w. $2\frac{1}{2}$
          RFJ   Oct.   p19.   650w.   3
          SR   Nov.   p128.   100w.   5

3336   EVANS, Bill.   Spring Leaves.   Milestone M 47034 (2 discs)
          (Reissue)
          DB   April 21   p26-30.   250w.   5
          MM   Jan. 8   p20.   100w.   4
          RSP   Jan.-Feb.   p36.   450w.   4

3337   EVANS, Bill.   Trio and Duo.   Verve VE 2-2509 (2 discs)
          (Reissue)
          SR   May   p98-9.   150w. $2\frac{1}{2}$
          FOL   June   p23.   325w.   5

3338   EVANS, Bill and Eddie Gomez.   Montreux III.   Fantasy F-
          9510
          CAD   Feb.   p39-40.   175w. $3\frac{1}{2}$
          DB   Feb. 24   p27.   300w.   4
          MG   Feb.   p57.   100w. $2\frac{1}{2}$

3339   EVANS, Frank.   Noctuary.   Blue Bag BB 101 (E)
          GP   Feb.   p113.   175w.   4
          GR   July   p237.   50w.   4
          ST   Feb.-March   p112-3.   375w.   5

3340   EVANS, Frank.   Soiree.   Blue Bag BB102 (E)
          MM   Sept. 17   p18.   175w.   1

3341   EVANS, Gil and Miles Davis.   The Arrangers Touch.   Pres-
          tige PR 24049 (2 discs) (Reissue)
          RR   Jan.   p63.   150w.   3

3342   EXTRA Ball.   Musa SX 1414

JF No. 46 p64-5.   750w.   3

3343 EYERMANN, Tim. Unity.   Juldane DB SLP 20039
      CAD Oct.   p24.   100w. $3\frac{1}{2}$

3344 FADDIS, Jon. Youngblood.   Pablo 2310 765
      GR March p1471.   100w. $3\frac{1}{2}$

3345 FAHEY, John. The Best of John Fahey.   Takoma C-1058
      CAD July p22.   100w.   4
      MM Dec. 21 p15.   250w.   3
      PIC Dec.   p60.   125w. $3\frac{1}{2}$

3346 FARLOW, Tal. Second Set.   Xanadu 119
      CAD July p39.   125w. $4\frac{1}{2}$
      DB Oct. 20 p24.   400w.   5
      HF Sept. p142.   100w. $3\frac{1}{2}$

3347 FARLOW, Tal. A Sign of the Times.   Concord JAZZ CJ-26
      CAD June p36.   150w.   4
      DB July 14 p36.   200w. $4\frac{1}{2}$
      GP May p129.   50w.   3
      JJ May p46, 48.   150w. $4\frac{1}{2}$
      MM July 2 p24.   175w. $3\frac{1}{2}$

3348 FARMER, Art. Crawl Space.   CTI 7073
      CAD June p38.   150w. $4\frac{1}{2}$
      JM Summer p51-2.   175w.   2
      RFJ May p18.   100w.   3
      SR Nov. p128, 129.   225w.   2

3349 FARMER, Art. A Sleeping Bee.   Sonet SNTF 715 (E)
      CAD Aug. p46.   100w. $4\frac{1}{2}$

3350 FARMER, Art. Something You Got.   CTI 7080
      CAD Dec. p61.   100w.   2
      RSP Nov.-Dec. p41.   100w. $2\frac{1}{2}$

3351 FARMER, Art. To Duke with Love.   East Wind EW-7012
      (Japan)
      CO April p12.   225w.   5

3352 FARMER, Art. Yesterday's Thoughts.   East Wind EQ-8025
      (Japan)
      CO April p12.   225w.   5

3353 FARRELL, Joe. Song of the World.   CTI 6067
      DB June 16 p34, 36.   350w.   5
      RT Sept. p4.   150w.   4
      ST Aug.-Sept. p239.   400w.   1

3354 FAVERO, Alberto. Suite Trane (In Memoriam John Coltrane).
      Catalyst CAT-7914

CAD   July p44.   275w.   4

3355   FAYS, Raphael.   Gerard Tournier GT 36 516 (France)
       GP Nov. p137.   100w.   3

3356   FELDMAN, Victor.   The Artful Dodger.   Concord Jazz CJ-
       38
       CAD Oct. p41-2.   200w.   3

3357   FELDMAN, Victor.   Rockabibabe.   DJM 22058 (E)
       MM Feb. 28. p34.   350w. $3\frac{1}{2}$

3358   FERGUSON, Maynard.   Conquistador.   Columbia 34457
       CAD April p11.   195w. $2\frac{1}{2}$
       DB July 14 p40, 42.   225w. $2\frac{1}{2}$

3359   FEW, Bobby, Alan Silva and Frank Wright.   Solo et Duets.
       Sun 102
       CAD Feb. p35-6.   200w.   3

3360   FINE, Milo.   Hah! Hat Hut E
       CAD Oct. p52.   275w.   4

3361   FIRST Cosins Jazz Ensemble.   For the Cos of Jazz.   Capi-
       tol ST-11589.   Cart. 8XT-11589
       CAD March p28.   50w.   0
       SR Aug. p103.   125w.   2

3362   FISHER, Elliott.   In the Land of Make Believe.   Dobre 1003
       CAD Feb. p20.   100w.   0

3363   FISHER, John.   Interface.   Composer Collective CC 722
       CAD Feb. p14.   150w. $3\frac{1}{2}$

3364   FISHER, John.   Poum.   Composer Collective CC 721
       CAD Feb. p14.   175w.   3

3365   FOL, Raymond.   Duke's Moods.   Blue Star XBLY-80710
       (France)
       ST June-July p195.   175w.   3

3366   FOL, Raymond.   Piano Solos.   Blue Star XBLY-80702
       (France) (Reissue)
       ST April-May p157-8.   350w.   4

3367   FOREFRONT.   In.   AFI U-64389
       CAD June p38.   150w.   4

3368   FOREFRONT.   Incantation.   AFI U-57415
       CAD June p38.   150w.   4

3369   FORRESTER, Bobby.   Organist.   Dobre 1012
       CAD Nov. p31.   25w.   2

3370   FORTUNE, Sonny.   Serengeti Minstrel.   Atlantic SD 18225
       CAD Oct. p60. 225w. 4

3371   FORTUNE, Sonny.   Waves of Dreams.   Horizon SP 711
       CRE March p63. 50w. 4
       DB March 10 p22. 300w. 4
       JJ Jan. p28. 400w. 4
       RR March p97. 150w. 3

3372   FOSTER, Frank.   Here and Now.   Catalyst CAT 7613
       DB Oct. 6 p26-7. 225w. 2

3373   FRANKLIN, Henry.   Blue Lights.   Ovation OV-1801 (Re-
       issue)
       CAD July p36. 100w. 2

3374   FRANKLIN, Henry.   Tribal Dance.   Catalyst 7618
       CAD Sept. p29. 550w. 4
       DB Nov. 17 p29. 75w. $3\frac{1}{2}$

3375   FREEMAN, Bud.   Chicagoans in New York.   Dawn Club DC
       12009
       CO April p14-5. 350w. 4

3376   FREEMAN, Bud and Jess Stacy.   The Joy of Sax.   Chiaro-
       scuro CR 135
       CO April p15. 300w. $2\frac{1}{2}$

3377   FREEMAN, Van.   Have No Fear.   Nessa N-6
       CO April p15-6. 500w. $2\frac{1}{2}$

3378   FRENCH Market Jazz Band.   Flying Dutchman BDL 1-1239
       AU March. p97. 250w. 1

3379   FRIEDMAN, David.   Future's Passed.   Enja 2068 (West
       Germany)
       MM Jan. 1 p16. 50w. 1

3380   FRIESEN, Dave.   Star Dance.   Inner City 1019
       CAD April p43. 180w. 5
       DB May 19 375w. 5

3381   FRISBERG, Dave.   Getting Some Fun Out of Life.   Concord
       Jazz CJ 37
       CAD Oct. p42-3. 350w. 3
       CK Oct. p65. 100w. $3\frac{1}{2}$
       HF Oct. p144, 146. 400w. $3\frac{1}{2}$
       MJ Sept. p31. 100w. 3

3382   FROG Island Jazz Band.   Oliver Frogge HMVR 001/77 (E)
       RR Dec. p87. 50w. $2\frac{1}{2}$

3383   The FUNKY New Orleans Jazz Band.   Make Me a Pallet on

the Floor. Herwin 301
CAD Aug. p38. 100w. 3½

3384   GAFA, Al. Leblon Beach.   Pablo 2310-782
CAD March p42, 44. 75w. 3
GP June p136. 75w. 3½
GR Aug. p354. 50w. 3½
JJ April p29. 200w. 3
MM July 9 p24. 225w. 4
SMG May p27. 100w. 4
SR April p110, 112. 50w. 0

3385   GAILLARD, Slim. Son of McVouty.   HEP 11
ST June-July p199. 125w. 4

3386   GAILLARD, Slim and Slam Stewart.   Slim and Slam.   Tax
M-8028 (Sweden) (Reissue)
MM Dec. 21 p16. 300w. 3½

3387   GALE, Eric. Ginseng Woman.   Columbia PC 34421
DB July 14 p42, 44. 250w. 3
GP Oct. p129. 75w. 3
MM Sept. 10 p20. 250w. 1½

3388   GALLIVAN, Joe and Charles Austin.   Expression to the Winds.
Spitball SB6
CAD June p26. 275w. 4½

3389   GALLIVAN, Joe and Charles Austin.   Intercontinental Express. Compendium Fidardo 8
CAD Aug. p42. 250w. 3

3390   GALLOWAY, Jim, Dick Wellstood and Pete Magadini.   Three
Is Company. Sackville 2007 (Canada)
ST June-July p198-9. 275w. 4

3391   GANELIN, Vyacheslav. Con Anima.   Melodia C60-07361-2
(Lithuania)
JF No. 49 p22-3. 50w. 3

3392   GANNON, Jim. Gannon's Back in Town.   Catalyst 7605
CAD Jan. p42. 75w. 2
DB Nov. 17 p29. 75w. 2½

3393   GARBAREK, Jan. Dis.   ECM 1093
CAD Aug. p34. 300w. 3½
DB Nov. 3 p21. 250w. 4
JF No. 50 p19. 75w. 2½
MG Aug. p63. 100w. 3
SR Nov. p129. 250w. 5

3394   GARBER, Lloyd. Energy Patterns.   Onari Series 001
CAD Sept. p42-3. 225w. 2½

          GP   Sept.   p119.   150w.   5
          OLR Dec.   p292.   25w.   5

3395   GARNER, Erroll. Early Erroll, Vol. 1, 1945 Stride. Jazz
       Connoisseur JC 001 (Italy) (Reissue)
          MM   Oct. 8 p36.   225w.   4

3396   GARNER, Erroll. The Elf. Savoy SJL 2207 (2 discs) (Re-
       issue)
          JJ   Jan.   p28.   300w.   4

3397   GARNET, Carlos. Cosmos Nucleus. Muse MR 5104
          CAD Feb.   p46.   125w.   2
          DB   April 7.   p22, 26.   300w.   3
          MG   April p53.   125w.   3

3398   GARTHWAITE, Terry. San Francisco Ltd. Crystal Clear
       CCS 5004
          CAD May   p12.   75w.   3

3399   GAULT, Billy. When Destiny Calls. Inner City 2027
          CAD Oct.   p55-6.   100w.   0

3400   GEOBBELS, Heiner and Alfred Harth. Hommageivier Fauste
       Fue Hanns Eisler. SAJ-08
          CAD July   p12.   125w. $3\frac{1}{2}$

3401   GETZ, Stan. Best of Both Worlds. CBS 81207 (E)
          RR   Jan.   p85.   50w. $1\frac{1}{2}$

3402   GETZ, Stan. Captain Marvel. Columbia KC 32706
          AU   Sept.   p92.   400w.   5

3403   GETZ, Stan. The Chick Corea/Bill Evans Sessions. Verve
       VE2-2510 (2 discs) (Reissue)
          SR   May   p98-9.   150w.   3

3404   GETZ, Stan. Opus de Bop. Savoy 1105 (Reissue)
          CAD June   p14.   100w.   4
          DB   Sept. 8.   p38-41.   50w.   4
          GR   July   p237.   75w. $3\frac{1}{2}$
          SOU May   p62.   100w.   3

3405   GETZ, Stan. Special Magic of..., Vol. 2. Verve 2317 135
       (E) (Reissue)
          CAC July   p142.   175w. $4\frac{1}{2}$

3406   GETZ, Stan. Sweet Rain. Verve Select 2317 115 (E) (Reis-
       sue)
          CAC Jan.   p390.   300w. $3\frac{1}{2}$
          GR   Jan.   p1198.   75w. $4\frac{1}{2}$
          JJ   Jan.   p28.   425w.   5

3407   GIGER, Peter.   Family of Percussion.   Nagara MX 1010-N
        (West Germany)
        JF No. 47.   p67.   450w.   3½

3408   GILBERTO, Joao.   Amorso.   Warner Bros. 3053
        CAD July p22.   50w.   3
        DB Aug. 11 425w.   4
        GP Sept. p119.   50w.   2½

3409   GILLESPIE, Dizzy.   Bahiana.   Pablo 2625 708 (2 discs)
        GR March p1471.   200w.   4

3410   GILLESPIE, Dizzy.   Dee Gee Days - The Savoy Sessions.
        Savoy SJL 2209 (2 discs) (Reissue)
        GR April p1618.   100w.   3
        JJ Feb. p31.   700w.   5
        MM Jan. 1 p17.   300w.   4

3411   GILLESPIE, Dizzy.   The Development of an American Artist.
        Smithsonian Collection R004 (Reissue)
        CAD April p22-3.   480w.   5
        DB July 14 p40.   400w.   5
        JM Summer p52-3.   100w.   4½
        MJ July p72.   200w.   3
        RFJ June p14-5.   600w.   3
        SR Aug. p103, 104.   375w.   5

3412   GILLESPIE, Dizzy.   Dizzy's Party.   Pablo 2310-784
        CAD April p23.   180w.   2
        GR Aug. p354.   100w.   3
        MM Feb. 26 p33.   75w.   2

3413-4 GILLESPIE, Dizzy.   Good Bait.   Spotlite SPJ 122 (Reissue)
        CO Dec. p24.   100w.   3½

3415   GILLESPIE, Dizzy.   Live at the Spotlite.   Hi Fly H01
        JF No. 49 p46.   550w.   3

3416   GILLESPIE, Dizzy and Machita.   Afro-Cuban Jazz Moods.
        Pablo 2310-771
        BM March p52.   150w.   3
        CAD Jan. p29, 30.   225w.   4
        CO April p16.   500w.   4
        DB Feb. 24 p22.   300w.   5
        JJ Feb. p32.   300w.   4
        SR Jan. p110.   700w.   4

3417   GILLESPIE, Dizzy and Stan Getz.   Diz and Getz.   Verve
        VE2-2521 (E) (Reissue)
        CAD Oct. p53.   325w.   3
        GR Dec. p1162.   50w.   3
        RR Oct. p90.   25w.   3

3418 GISMONTI, Egberto. Danca das Cabecas. ECM 1089
       CAD July p40. 175w. 3½
       DB Dec. 1 p24. 250w. 5
       JF No. 49 p20. 50w. 4
       MM May 14 p27. 350w. 5

3419 GLENN, Roger. Reachin'. Fantasy 9516
       CAD Jan. p18. 75w. 3
       DB March 24 150w. 3½
       MG Feb. p57. 100w. 3

3420 GOGGERTY, Patrick. Classical Rags of Joseph F. Lamb.
       Sound Current (no no.)
       RA July-Aug. p7-8. 100w. 4

3420a GOLDEN Age Jazz Band. Arhoolie 4007
       AU Feb. p86. 250w. 3

3421 GOLSON, Benny. Killer Joe. Columbia PC-34678. Cart.
       PCA-34678. Cass. PCT-34678
       SR Sept. p98. 250w. 4

3422 GONSALVES, Paul. The Buenos Aires Session. Catalyst
       7913
       CAD Oct. p28. 275w. 3
       HF Sept. p142. 75w. 3½
       MJ July p73. 150w. 2½

3423 GONSALVES, Paul. In Paris. Blue Star XBLY-80 703
       (France) (Reissue)
       ST Dec. -Jan. p76-7. 225w. 5

3424 GONZALEZ. Our Only Weapon Is Our Music. EMI EMC
       3100 (E)
       RR Jan. p63. 50w. 2

3425 GORDON, Dexter. Spotlite 10
       CAD Nov. p48. 100w. 4

3426 GORDON, Dexter. The Apartment. Inner City IC 2025
       CAD June p33. 100w. 4

3427 GORDON, Dexter. Blues Walk. Black Lion 309
       MJ Jan. p29. 50w. 3

3428 GORDON, Dexter. The Chase. Spotlite SPJ 130 (Reissue)
       MM Jan. 29 p28. 200w. 3½

3429 GORDON, Dexter. Homecoming-Live at the Village Vanguard.
       Columbia PG 34650 (2 discs)
       CAD June p27. 300w. 5
       DB April 21 p23. 550w. 5
       JM Summer p50. 300w. 5

MJ   July   p72.   100w.   2½
MM   Aug.   20   p23.   325w.   5
RS   June 2   p78, 80.   350w.   2
RSP   May-June   p39.   700w.   5
SR   July   p110.   550w.   5

3430   GORDON, Dexter.   Long Tall Dexter.   Savoy SJL 2211 (2 discs) (Reissue)
       GR   April   p1618.   75w.   3½
       JJ   March   p32.   750w.   4
       MM   April 2   p28.   400w.   3½
       RR   March   p97.   50w.   3

3431   GORDON, Dexter.   More Than You Know.   Inner City 2030
       CAD   June   p29.   175w.   3½
       SR   Sept.   p121.   100w.   4

3432   GORDON, Dexter.   Stable Mable.   SteepleChase SCS-1040
       CO   April   p16.   175w.   2

3433   GORDON, Dexter.   Swiss Nights.   Inner City 2050
       CAD   June   p34.   200w.   4½
       DB   Nov. 3   p23, 26.   400w.   5
       MM   Jan. 29   p28.   200w.   4

3434   GORDON, Dexter and Blue Mitchell.   True Blue.   Xanadu 136
       JM   Summer   p50-1.   300w.   4

3435   GORDON, John.   Step by Step.   Strata East SES 19760
       CAD   Jan.   p39.   125w.   4
       RFJ   May   p17.   450w.   3½

3436   GRAPPELLI, Stephane.   Homage to Django.   Classic Jazz 23 (Reissue)
       CAD   Feb.   p40.   75w.   3½
       CO   Aug.   p24.   75w.   3
       DB   June 2   p22.   125w.   4

3437   GRAPPELLI, Stephane and Bill Coleman.   Classic Jazz 24 (Reissue)
       CAD   Aug.   p48.   175w.   4½
       DB   June 2   p22.   125w.   3½
       RSP   March-April   p33-4.   275w.   4½

3438   GRAPPELLI, Stephane and Earl Hines.   The Giants.   Black Lion BLP 30193
       RR   Oct.   p89.   25w.   3

3439   GRAVES, Milford.   Babi.   IPS ST 004 (E)
       MM   Dec. 21   p16.   350w.   4

3440   GRAVES, Milford.   Nommo.   SRP LP 299

CAD   June   p36.   150w.   4

3441   GRAWE, Georg.   New Movements.   FMP 0320
CAD   July   p14.   150w.   3

3442   GRAY, Wardell.   And Friends.   Spotlite 134 (Reissue)
CAD   Dec.   p36.   300w. $4\frac{1}{2}$
MM   April 2   p28.   225w.   3

3443   GRAY, Wardell.   Central Avenue.   Prestige PR 24062 (Re-
issue)
CO   April   p16-8.   1375w. $2\frac{1}{2}$
JJ   Jan.   p28.   700w.   5
RR   Feb.   p94.   50w. $2\frac{1}{2}$

3444   GREAT Excelsior Jazz Band.   Hot Jazz from the Territory.
Voyager VRLP 202
CAD   Dec.   p60.   300w. $2\frac{1}{2}$

3445   GREEN, Bunky.   Transformations.   Vanguard VSD 79389
CAD   Aug.   p57.   150w.   2
DB   Nov. 3   p26.   300w.   4

3446   GREEN, Grant.   Iron City.   Muse MR 5120
CAD   June   p41.   75w.   2

3447   GREEN, Grant.   The Main Attraction.   Kudu KU29
SMG   May   p27.   75w. $3\frac{1}{2}$

3448   GREEN, Urbie.   The Fox.   CTI CTI-7070.   Cart. CT8-7070.
Cass. CTC-7070
CAD   June   p20.   75w.   3
DB   Sept. 8   p34.   200w.   2
JM   Summer   p51-2.   175w.   3
MM   Oct. 1   p28.   50w.   1
RR   Sept.   p96.   75w. $2\frac{1}{2}$
SR   Sept.   p121.   175w. $3\frac{1}{2}$

3449   GREEN, Urbie.   Senor Blues.   CTI 7079
CAD   Dec.   p61.   100w.   2

3450   GREY, Al.   Basic Grey.   Chess Jazz Masters 2ACMJ-409
(2 discs) (Reissue)
CAD   June   p34.   100w. $3\frac{1}{2}$

3451   GRIFFEN, Johnny.   Big Soul.   Milestone 47014 (2 discs)
(Reissue)
CO   Feb.   p23.   100w.   3

3452   GRIFFEN, Johnny.   Blues for Harvey.   Inner City 2004
CAD   Feb.   p44.   200w.   3
DB   Dec. 1   p22.   325w.   5

3453   GRIFFIN, Johnny.   Jazz A Confronto: Vol. 10.   Horo HLL
       101-10 (Italy)
           CAD Sept. p15.   175w.   5

3454   GRIFFIN, Johnny.   You Leave Me Breathless.   Black Lion
       304
           MJ Jan.   p29.   25w.   3

3455   GRIFFIN, Johnny and Eddie Lockjaw Davis.   The Toughest
       Tenors.   Milestone M 47035 (2 discs) (Reissue)
           AU July p100.   200w.   5
           BM Jan.   p53.   125w.   3

3456   GROSSMAN, Steve.   Stone Alliance.   PM PMR 013
           RFJ May p18.   100w.   3

3457   GRUSIN, Dave.   Discovered Again.   Sheffield LAB-5
           CAD Aug.   p48.   200w.   4

3458   GRUSIN, Dave.   Phantasia.   Blue Note BN-LA 736-14
           CK Sept. p58.   75w.   2

3459   GUARNIERI, Johnny.   Superstride.   Taz-Jaz Records TJZ-
       1001
           CAD May p20.   125w.   5
           CK   April p48.   100w. $4\frac{1}{2}$
           JJ   Feb. p32.   400w.   5
           JR   V9/#3 unpaged 175w.   5
           MR   Feb. p12-3.   300w. $3\frac{1}{2}$
           RT   March p4.   1950w.   5
           SR   June p122, 124.   150w.   0

3460   GUIFFRE, Jimmy.   Music for People, Butterflies and Mos-
       quitoes.   Choice 1001
           AU July p101.   200w.   5

3461   GUIFFRE, Jimmy with Marty Paich.   Tenors West.   Crescendo
       Gps 9040
           CAD July p31.   150w. $3\frac{1}{2}$

3462   GULLIN, Lars.   Aeros Aromatic Atomica Suite.   EMI CO62-
       35282 (Denmark)
           CAD Oct. p58-9.   200w.   3

3463   GULLIN, Lars.   Like Glass.   Odeon E 062-34874 (Denmark)
           CAD Oct. p58-9.   200w.   3

3464   GUY, Garry.   Statements V-XI for Double Bass and Violence.
       Incus 22
           MM Sept. 17 p28.   350w. $3\frac{1}{2}$

3465   GYLLANDER, Dick.   Nobody Knows.   Dragon 8 (Sweden)
           CAD Nov. p47, 48.   215w. $3\frac{1}{2}$

3466   HACKETT, Bobby. Live at the Roosevelt Grill, Vol. 2.
        Chiaroscuro CR 138
            AU   March p97.   200w. 2
            CAD Dec.   p44.   125w. 3

3467   HACKETT, Bobby. String of Pearls. Vogue VJD 531 (2
        discs) (France)
            MM   Aug. 6 p19.   350w. $3\frac{1}{2}$
            RR   Aug.   p84.   50w. $3\frac{1}{2}$

3468   HACKETT, Bobby. Thanks Bobby. Dobre 1004
            CAD June p39.   100w. 4

3469   HADEN, Charlie. Closeness. Horizon SP 710
            AU   Jan.   p88.   350w. $4\frac{1}{2}$
            CRA March p81.   100w. $2\frac{1}{2}$
            DB   Feb. 24 p22, 24.   300w.   5
            JJ   Jan.   p29.   425w.   5
            RR   May   p88.   150w.   4
            SOU Jan.   p49.   50w.   4
            SR   March p117.   300w.   4

3470   HAIG, Al. Chelsea Bridge. East Wind EW-8023 (Japan)
            CO   April p12.   225w. 4

3471   HAIG, Al. Four! GI Records GSS 1 (E)
            JJ   March p32.   225w. 4

3472   HALE, Corky. Plays Gershwin and Vernon Duke. GNP
        9035
            CAD Oct.   p23.   75w. $2\frac{1}{2}$

3473   HALES, Bobby. One of My Bags. Centre Line 0975
            CAD July p20.   400w. $3\frac{1}{2}$

3474   HALL, Herb. Old Tyme Modern. Sackville 3003 (Canada)
            ST   June-July p193-4.   150w.   2

3475   HALL, Jim. Committment. Horizon SP-715
            CAD Jan.   p27-29.   225w.   3
            DB   Feb. 10 p19.   200w.   4
            GP   March p113.   200w.   4
            JJ   Jan.   p30.   350w.   5
            JM   1:2 p55.   500w.   4
            MM   Jan. 29 p28.   200w.   3
            RFJ April p17.   300w. $3\frac{1}{2}$
            SOU Jan.   p48.   100w.   4

3476   HALL, Jim. Live! Horizon SP-705
            CO   April p18.   475w. 4
            OLR Sept. p225.   50w. 4

3477   HALL, Kenny and the Sweets Mill String Band. Vol. 2.

Bay 103
    CAD   Sept.   p43.   225w.   2
    FOL   Aug.   p5.   125w. $4\frac{1}{2}$
    RSP   1:3   p22-3.   400w. $3\frac{1}{2}$

3478   HAMILTON, Chico.   Blue Note LA 622G
    CR   Feb.   p115.   125w.   4

3479   HAMILTON, Chico.   Catwalk.   Mercury SRM 1-1163
    CAD   Aug.   p24.   150w.   3
    MG   Aug.   p63.   125w.   3
    SR   Dec.   100w.   3

3480   HAMPTON, Lionel.   The Complete, 1937-41.   RCA Bluebird AXM6-5536 (6 discs) (Reissue)
    AU   Sept.   p93.   700w.   5
    BSR   No. 7   unpaged   400w.   5
    DB   June 16   p36.   550w.   5
    HF   April   p136.   350w.   3
    RSP   March/April   p38.   1200w. $4\frac{1}{2}$

3481   HAMPTON, Lionel.   Ring Dem Vibes.   Blue Star XBLY-
80706 (France) (Reissue)
    ST   Feb.-March   p117-8.   250w.   4

3482   HAMPTON, Slide.   Jazz A Confronto: Vol. 18.   Horo HLL
101-18 (Italy)
    CAD   Sept.   p17.   125w. $3\frac{1}{2}$

3483   HANCOCK, Herbie.   Secrets.   Columbia PC 34180
    AU   April   p88.   200w.   1
    RR   Jan.   p85.   50w.   3
    RSP   Jan.-Feb.   p38-40.   2000w.   3

3484   HANCOCK, Herbie.   V.S.O.P.   Columbia PG 34688 (2 discs)
    AU   Sept.   p93.   250w.   5
    BM   July   p50.   400w.   5
    CAD   June   p30.   525w. $4\frac{1}{2}$
    CAD   Dec.   p46-7.   300w.   3
    CK   Aug.   p48.   300w. $4\frac{1}{2}$
    CRA   Aug.   p70, 72.   475w. $3\frac{1}{2}$
    DB   Aug. 11   450w.   3
    MG   July   p53.   150w. $3\frac{1}{2}$
    MM   July 9   p24.   300w. $1\frac{1}{2}$
    RSP   May-June   p37.   650w. $4\frac{1}{2}$
    VV   June 13   p49.   300w.   3

3485   HANDY, John.   Ali Akbar Khan.   Karun Supreme.   MPS/
BASF G 22791
    SR   March   p121.   350w.   4

3486   HANDY, John.   Carnival.   Impulse AS 9324
    AU   June   p132.   150w.   2

CAD   April   p10.   120w.   2
DB   July 14   p38-9.   200w.   3
RSP   May-June   p30-2.   1650w. $3\frac{1}{2}$

3487   HANDY, John.   In the Vernacular.   Vogue VJD 530 (2 discs)
(France) (Reissue)
JJ   April   p29.   250w. $3\frac{1}{2}$
RFJ   April   p16.   600w. $2\frac{1}{2}$
RR   April   p88.   25w. $2\frac{1}{2}$
RSP   March-April   p60.   400w.   4

3488   HANNA, Jake.   Jake Takes Manhattan.   Concord CJ-35
CAD   Sept.   p41.   200w.   4
MJ   Sept.   p31.   50w.   3

3489   HANNA, Jake.   Kansas City Express.   Concord Jazz CJ-
22
HF   Jan.   p146.   200w. $2\frac{1}{2}$
JF   No. 47   p69.   50w.   3
SR   March   p121.   150w.   3

3490   HANNA, Jake.   Live at the Concord.   Concord CJ 11
JF   No. 47   p69.   50w.   3

3491   HANNA, Roland.   Perugia.   Arista Freedom 1010
AU   Feb.   p84.   200w.   5

3492   HARPER, Billy.   Black Saint.   Black Saint BSR 0001 (Italy)
JF   No. 45   p64-5.   500w.   3

3493   HARRIOTT, Joe/Joe Mayer.   Indo-Jazz Fusions: Duo 123.
EMI (E) (Reissue)
RR   July   p97.   100w.   2

3494   HARRIS, Barry.   Live in Tokyo.   Xanadu 130
DB   June 16   p40-3.   225w.   5
JM   1:2   p56-7.   500w.   5

3495   HARRIS, Eddie.   How Can You Live Like That?   Atlantic
SD 1698
CAD   May   p12.   150w. $2\frac{1}{2}$

3496   HARRIS, Gene.   Tone Tantrum.   Blue Note BNLA 760 H
CAD   Oct.   p23.   50w.   1

3497   HARTMAN, Johnny.   Johnny Hartman, Johnny Hartman.
Musicor MUS-2502
CAD   April   p10.   180w.   2
VV   May 16   p55.   100w.   2

3498   HAWES, Hampton.   The Challenge.   RCA JPL 1-1508
SR   Feb.   p108.   50w.   2

3499   HAWKINS, Coleman. Blowin' Up a Breeze.   Spotlite SPJ
       137
              MM   June 18   p24.   250w.   3½

3500   HAWKINS, Coleman. Centerpiece.   Phoenix LP 13 (Reissue)
              DB   Oct. 6   p35-7.   100w.   5

3500a HAWKINS, Coleman. The Complete... Body and Soul, Vol. 1,
       1924-40.   RCA B&W FXM 17325 (Reissue)
              JJ   April   p30.   250w.   3½
              RR   June   p95.   50w.   3½

3501   HAWKINS, Coleman. The Tenor Sax Album.   Savoy SJL
       2220 (2 discs) (Reissue)
              HF   Nov.   350w.   3½

3502   HAYNES, Roy. Jazz A Confronto: Vol. 29.   Horo HLL 101-
       29 (Italy)
              CAD   Sept.   p18-9.   150w.   4½

3503   HEATH Brothers. Marchin' On.   Strata East SES19766
              JJ   May   p48.   150w.   4½

3504   HEMPHILL, Julius. Blue Boyé.   Mbari Records 1000X (2
       discs)
              CAD   Oct.   p20.   500w.   4½
              VV   Nov. 18   p61.   300w.   4½

3505   HEMPHILL, Julius. Coon 'Bidness.   Arista-Freedom 1012
              MM   May 28   p32.   300w.   4½

3506   HEMPHILL, Julius. Dogon A.D.   Arista-Freedom 1028
              CAD   July   p32.   225w.   4½
              MM   Oct.   p28.   400w.   4
              SOU   Sept.   p66.   100w.   4
              VV   June 13   p49.   125w.   3½

3507   HENDERSON, Fletcher. Volumes 1-3.   RCA 730-584, 741-
       071, FPM1-7011 (3 discs) (France) (Reissue)
              CO   April   p18-9.   225w.   3

3508   HENDERSON, Fletcher. Complete, 1927-1936.   RCA Blue-
       bird AXM2-5507 (2 discs) (Reissue)
              CO   April   p18-9.   225w.   3

3509   HENDERSON, Fletcher. Developing an American Orchestra,
       1923-37. The Smithsonian Collection, R006 (Reissue)
              CAD   Aug.   p52.   25w.   4½
              CK   Aug.   p48.   75w.   3½
              CO   Dec.   p23.   250w.   3
              JF   No. 50   p18.   50w.   4
              JM   Summer   p52-3.   100w.   3½
              MJ   Sept.   p28.   100w.   3

3510   HENDERSON, Joe.   Black Narcissus.   Milestone M-9071
       BM   March   p52.   225w.   2
       CAD   Feb.   p34.   150w.   4
       CK   March   p57.   25w.   3
       DB   Feb.   24   p30-1.   275w.   2
       JJ   March   p32-3.   400w.   3
       MG   April   p53.   100w.   1½
       MM   Jan.   1   p16.   425w.   4

3511   HENDERSON, Wayne.   Big Daddy's Place.   ABC AB 1020
       CAD   June   p20.   75w.   2

3512   HERBOLZHEIMER, Peter.   Jazz Gala Concert.   Atlantic K
       50277 (West Germany)
       JJ   Feb.   p32.   350w.   4

3513   HERMAN, Woody.   The 40th Anniversary Carnegie Hall Con-
       cert.   RCA BGL2-2203 two discs.   Cass. BGS2-2203.   Cart.
       BGK2-2203
       AU   Aug.   p89.   500w.   4
       CAD   July   p38.   350w.   5
       DB   Aug.   11   525w.   4
       MJ   Sept.   p28.   100w.   4
       MM   Oct.   22   p26.   550w.   4½
       RFJ   Oct.   p16.   750w.   3½
       RR   Aug.   p84.   100w.   3½
       SR   Sept.   p87-88.   550w.   5
       VV   March   28   p81.   350w.   3½

3514   HILL, Andrew.   Invitation.   Inner City 2026
       CAD   Oct.   p31.   300w.   3

3515   HINES, Earl.   At Saralee's.   Fairmont Fa-1101
       CAD   May   p14, 75.   125w.   4
       JJ   April   p30.   250w.   3
       JR   V9/#3 unpaged 100w.   4
       MJ   July   p73.   125w.   3½
       SR   May   p100.   75w.   5

3516   HINES, Earl.   Dinah.   RCA FXL1-7290
       JJ   March   p33.   525w.   3

3517   HINES, Earl.   An Evening with...   Vogue Jazz VDJ 534 (2
       discs) (France) (Reissue)
       RR   Aug.   p84.   50w.   3½

3518   HINES, Earl.   In New Orleans.   Biograph BLP 12056
       CAD   Dec.   p59.   150w.   2½

3519   HINES, Earl.   Live at the Downtown Club.   Improv IMP 7114 .
       JJ   Feb.   p32.   275w.   4
       MJ   Jan.   p28.   50w.   3½
       RFJ   Jan.   p15.   400w.   3

3520   HINES, Earl. Live at the New School. Chiaroscuro CR 157
          CAD   Dec.   p53-4.   100w. $3\frac{1}{2}$
          RSP   Nov.-Dec.   p41.   200w.   4

3521   HINES, Earl. The New Earl Hines Trio. Columbia JCS
       9120
          CAD   June   p43.   300w.   3

3522   HINES, Earl. Plays Duke Ellington (Piano Solos Volume 4).
       Master Jazz Recordings MJR 8132
          CAD   Jan.   p25.   200w. $4\frac{1}{2}$
          MJ   Jan.   p28.   50w. $3\frac{1}{2}$

3523   HINES, Earl. Plays George Gershwin. Classic Jazz CJ 31
       (2 discs)
          CAD   June   p43.   300w.   2
          DB   Dec. 1   p28-9.   250w.   3
          MJ   July   p73.   125w. $3\frac{1}{2}$

3524   HINES, Earl. The Quintessential. Chiaroscuro CR 131
          AU   Feb.   p84.   200w.   5

3525   HINES, Earl. Solo Walk in Tokyo. Biograph BLP-12055
          CAD   June   p45.   300w. $4\frac{1}{2}$
          MJ   July   p73.   125w. $3\frac{1}{2}$

3526   HINES, Earl. Swingin' Away. Black Lion BLP 30190
          RR   Oct.   p89.   25w. $3\frac{1}{2}$

3527   HINES, Earl and Roy Eldridge. At the Village Vanguard.
       Xanadu 106
          CO   April   p18.   250w.   3

3528   HINES, Earl and Marva Josie. Jazz Is His Old Lady. Cata-
       lyst CAT 7622
          MM   Nov. 12   p34.   300w.   3

3529   HINO, Terumasa. Hino at Berlin Jazz. Festival '71. Cata-
       lyst CAT-7910
          CAD   July   p32.   175w. $3\frac{1}{2}$

3530   HODES, Art. Plays Bessie Smith and Ma Rainey. Euphonic
       1213
          CAD   Dec.   p51.   100w.   3
          RSP   1:3   p36-7.   350w.   3

3531   HODGES, Johnny. Rarities 38
          JJ   April   p30.   125w. $1\frac{1}{2}$

3532   HODGES, Johnny. Love in Swingtime. Tax 8022 (Reissue)
          CO   Aug.   p23.   150w.   3

3533   HODGES, Johnny. Mellow Tone. Vogue VJD 528 (2 discs)

(France) (Reissue)
>> JJ   April   p30, 32.   400w.   2
>> RR   April   p88.   25w.   3

3534   HOLDSWORTH, Allan.   Velvet Darkness.   CTI 6068
>> GP   Sept.   p118.   150w.   4

3535   HOLIDAY, Billie.   A Day in the Life of....   Different Drummer DD 1003
>> JR   V9/#4   unpaged   100w.   1

3536   HOLIDAY, Billie.   I Wonder Where Our Love Has Gone.
Giants of Jazz 1001
>> CAD   June   p32.   300w.   4
>> JR   V9/#4   unpaged   75w.   3

3537   HOLIDAY, Billie.   The Lady Day Story.   DJM 22047 (E)
(Reissue)
>> BM   Jan.   p53.   75w.   3
>> CAC   Jan.   p390.   150w. $1\frac{1}{2}$

3538   HOLIDAY, Billie.   Stormy Blues.   Verve VE 2-2515 (2 discs)
(Reissue)
>> DB   July 14   p45-7.   50w.   2
>> MG   June   p53.   100w. $3\frac{1}{2}$
>> RFJ   Sept.   p12-3.   450w.   4

3539   HONSINGER, Tristan and Maarten Van Rigteren.   Live Performance.   SAJ 10
>> CAD   July   p12.   150w.   3
>> MM   April 30   p30.   325w. $3\frac{1}{2}$

3540   HOOD, Ernest.   Neighbourhoods.   Thistlefield Records RR
5120
>> CAD   April   p7-8.   300w.   5

3541   HOOPER, Les.   Dorian Blue.   Churchill 67234
>> CAD   Dec.   p51-2.   100w. $2\frac{1}{2}$

3542   HOOPER, Les.   Hoopla.   Churchill 67235
>> CAD   Dec.   p51-2.   100w. $2\frac{1}{2}$

3543   HOPE, Elmo.   The All-Star Sessions.   Milestone M-47037
(2 discs) (Reissue)
>> DB   April 21   p26-30.   250w. $3\frac{1}{2}$

3544   HOPE, Elmo.   Last Sessions.   Inner City 1018
>> CAD   April   p31.   204w. $2\frac{1}{2}$
>> CK   May   p49.   25w. $2\frac{1}{2}$
>> HF   Aug.   p114, 118.   350w.   3
>> MM   June 4   p32.   125w. $3\frac{1}{2}$

3545   HOPKINS, Claude.   Singin' in the Rain.   Jazz Archives JA-27

CO April p19. 350w. $2\frac{1}{2}$

3546 HORN, Paul. Inside the Great Pyramid. Mushroom MRS-5507
CAD Sept. p33-4. 175w. 0
HF Oct. p146, 148. 450w. $4\frac{1}{2}$
SOU Nov. p56. 200w. 3
SR Dec. 250w. $2\frac{1}{2}$

3547 HORN, Paul and Egberto Gismonti. Altura Do Sol. Epic PE 34231. Cass. PEA 34231
SR Feb. p108. 150w. 4

3548-9 HOT Peppers of Jazz. A Bicentennial Jubilation. Black Boy Records
MR April p13. 400w. $3\frac{1}{2}$

3550 HOWARD, Bob. A Chronological Study, Vol. 1. Rarities 48 (Reissue)
MM Dec. 21 p16. 300w. 3

3551 HOWARD, Noah. Berlin Concert. SAJ-07
CAD July p13. 200w. 4

3552 HOWARD, Noah. Patterns. Altsax AMC 100
CAD July p18. 200w. 3

3553 HOWELL, Michael. Alone. Catalyst CAT-7615
CAD June p23. 550w. 3
DB Nov. 17 p29. 75w. 4
GP Dec. p152-3. 125w. $3\frac{1}{2}$

3554 HUBBARD, Freddie. Bundle of Joy. Columbia JC 3 4 902. Cart. JCT 34902. Cass. JACA 34902
HF Dec. p143-4. 325w. $2\frac{1}{2}$
RSP Nov.-Dec. p41. 150w. 1

3555 HUBBARD, Freddie. Here to Stay. Blue Note LA 496-H2
CAD April p17. 240w. 3
DB Aug. 11 200w. 5

3556 HUMPHREY, Percy. Climax Rag. Pearl PS-3
JR V9/#4 unpaged 50w. 3
SR Sept. p121. 125w. $2\frac{1}{2}$

3557 HUTCHERSON, Bobby. Knucklebean. Blue Note LA 789
CAD Dec. p40-1. 150w. 4

3558 HUTCHERSON, Bobby. The View from Inside. Blue Note 7106
CAD July p34. 200w. 4
OB Nov. 3 p28-9. 350w. 4
SR May p100. 100w. 4

3559   IACOUCCI, Gerardo.   Jazz A Confronto: Vol. 30.   Hol HLL
       101-30 (Italy)
           CAD Sept. p19. 100w. 3
           CO Sept./Oct. p18-20. 225w. 4

3560   IBRAHIM, Abdul Rahim.   Al Rahman! Cry of the Floridian
       Tropic Son.   Tablight TBL 100
           CAD Aug. p57. 275w. 4

3561   IMADA, Masaru.   Piano.   Three Blind Mice TBM 60 (Japan)
           CO Dec. p20-1. 100w. $3\frac{1}{2}$

3562   The IMPERIAL Brass Funeral Jazz Band.   A New Orleans
       Street Parade Live in Paris.   Sandcastle SCR 1034
           CAD Oct. p48. 100w. 4

3563   INTERFACE.   NY Composers Collection CC722
           JF No. 48 p22. 50w. 3

3564   IOWA Ear Music Ensemble.   Corn Pride 1
           DB April 21 p30, 32. 300w. 5

3565   ISAACS, Ike.   Ike Isaacs at Pied Piper.   RBG 2000
           CAD Aug. p56. 150w. $2\frac{1}{2}$

3566   ISKRA.   Caprice CAP 2006 (2 discs) (Sweden)
           JF No. 46 p65-6. 550w. $3\frac{1}{2}$

3567   J. A. T. P.   The Historic Recordings.   Verve 22504
           MR Aug. p13-3. 375w. 3

3568   J. A. T. P.   In Tokyo, 1953.   Pablo 2620 104 (Reissue)
           DB Oct. 6 p24-5. 325w. $3\frac{1}{2}$
           MJ Sept. p32. 100w. 3
           RR Aug. p84. 50w. 3

3569   JACKSON, Milt.   All-Star Bags.   Blue Note LA 590-H2
           CAD April p17. 264w. $2\frac{1}{2}$
           CO Aug. p23. 175w. 3
           DB Aug. 11 200w. 5

3570   JACKSON, Milt.   At the Kosei Nenkin.   Pablo Live 2620-
       103
           CAD Aug. p39. 375w. 4
           RFJ Nov. p14. 600w. $4\frac{1}{2}$
           SOU Sept. p66. 100w. 4

3571   JACKSON, Milt.   The Atlantic Years.   Atlantic SD 2319 (E)
       (Reissue)
           RR Jan. p63. 25w. $2\frac{1}{2}$

3572   JACKSON, Milt.   The Big Three.   Pablo 2310 757
           GR March p1471. 100w. $4\frac{1}{2}$

3573   JACKSON, Milt. The First Q. Savoy 1106 (Reissue)
        CAD June p15. 100w. 3
        DB Sept. 8 p38-44. 50w. 4
        SOU May p62. 100w. 3

3574   JACKSON, Milt. Second Nature. Savoy SJL2204 (2 discs)
        (Reissue)
        GR May p1758. 100w. 3½

3575   JACKSON, Willis. In the Alley. Muse MR 5100
        CAD Oct. p56. 100w. 4

3576   JACQUET, Illinois. Fabulous Apollo Sessions. Vogue
        CLDAP 858 (France) (Reissue)
        RSP 1:3 p34. 175w. 3

3577   JACQUET, Illinois. Illinois Jacquet's Birthday Party. JRC
        Records (114-34)
        CAD Nov. p30. 100w. 3

3578   JAMAL, Ahmad. Sun Set. Chess Jazz Masters 2ACMT-407
        (2 discs) (Reissue)
        CAD June p34. 150w. 4
        RSP 1:3 p36. 200w. 3½

3579   JAMES, Harry. Comin' from a Good Place. Sheffield Lab
        6
        CAD Dec. p59. 200w. 3½

3579a   JAMES, Harry. Harry James and His Music Makers, 1945-
        49. First Heard 9
        AU June p130. 200w. 5

3580   JAMES, Harry. Harry James and His Orchestra, 1954.
        Sunbeam SB 217
        AU June p130. 200w. 3½

3581   JAMES, Harry. The King James Version. Sheffield Lab 3
        AU May p92. 600w. 3
        HF July p123. 100w. 4
        SR March p121. 200w. 4

3582   JAMES, Harry. One Night Stand with Harry James, 1954.
        Joyce 1034 (Reissue)
        AU June p130. 200w. 4

3583   JAMES, Harry. Radio Discs of Harry James. Joyce 2002
        (Reissue)
        AU June p130. 200w. 4

3584   JAMES, Harry. Texas Chatter: Harry James, 1937-38.
        Tax m8015 (Reissue)
        AU June p130. 200w. 4½

3585   JAMES, Harry.   The Young Harry James, 1939-41.   Jazz
       Archives JA 31
           AU   June p130.   200w.   4

3586   JAMES, Stafford.   Jazz A Confronto: Vol. 26.   Horo HLL
       101-26 (Italy)
           CAD   Sept.   p18.   125w.   0

3587   JANSA, Tone.   RTB LP4202 (Yugoslavia)
           JF   No. 50   p21.   50w.   3

3588   JARMAN, Joseph.   Song for.   Delmark DS 408
           CAD   Dec.   p38.   200w.   3

3589   JARREAU, Al.   Look to the Rainbow.   Warner Bros. 2BZ
       3052
           CAD   Aug.   p46.   300w.   4
           DB   Oct. 6   p24.   400w. $3\frac{1}{2}$
           HF   Sept.   p138-9.   400w. $2\frac{1}{2}$
           MM   June 4   p24.   300w. $4\frac{1}{2}$
           SR   Oct.   p86.   300w. $4\frac{1}{2}$

3590   JARRETT, Keith.   Byablue.   Impulse AS 9331
           CAD   Dec.   p59-60.   150w. $2\frac{1}{2}$
           CK   Dec.   p73.   50w. $3\frac{1}{2}$
           MG   Nov.   p52-3.   50w. $3\frac{1}{2}$
           SOU   Nov.   p64.   350w.   3

3591   JARRETT, Keith.   Hymns/Spheres.   ECM-2 1086
           CAD   June   p42.   100w.   3
           CK   May   p48.   100w. $3\frac{1}{2}$
           DB   June 2   p20, 22.   200w. $2\frac{1}{2}$
           MG   May   p53.   125w. $3\frac{1}{2}$
           MM   Jan. 15   p20.   300w.   2
           SR   July   p109.   125w.   3

3592   JARRETT, Keith.   Shades.   ABC Impulse, ASD-9322
           CAD   May   p20.   100w.   1
           CK   May   p48.   100w.   4
           DB   May 19   275w.   5
           HF   Feb.   p143.   400w.   4
           RFJ   June   p17.   400w. $4\frac{1}{2}$
           RSP   May-June   p39.   400w.   5

3593   JARRETT, Keith.   Staircase.   ECM-2-1090 (2 discs)
           CAD   Aug.   p42.   175w.   4
           CK   Sept.   p58.   150w.   5
           DB   Oct. 6   p27.   225w.   4
           HF   Sept.   p139, 141.   400w.   3
           JF   No. 50   75w.   4
           MG   Aug.   p63.   150w.   4
           MM   May 14   p36.   400w. $4\frac{1}{2}$
           RS   Nov. 3   p110, 115.   400w.   4

SR Nov. p129, 130. 275w. 3

3594   JARRETT, Keith. The Survivors Suite. ECM 1-1085
       CAD Dec. p59-60. 150w. $4\frac{1}{2}$
       MG Dec. p57. 200w. $2\frac{1}{2}$
       MM Nov. 5 p32. 250w. $4\frac{1}{2}$

3595   JARRETT, Keith. Tales of Another. ECM1-1101
       CK Dec. p73. 50w. $3\frac{1}{2}$

3596   JASEN, Dave. Rip-Roaring Ragtime. Folkways FG 3561
       RT Sept. p4. 175w. 4

3597   JAZZ Co-Op. Live at the Basement. 44 Records 6357-706
       CAD Jan. p14-5. 250w. 5

3598   JAZZ Lips. Metronome MLP 15.563
       ST April-May p152-3. 275w. 4

3599   JEANNEAU, Francois. Such a Weird Planet. Palm 22
       JJ Feb. p33. 300w. 5

3600   JEANNEAU, Francois. Techniques Douces. Owl 04 (France)
       CAD Feb. p35-6. 200w. 5
       CO April p21. 300w. 3

3601   JEFFERSON, Billy. Still on the Planet. Muse MR 5063
       DB Feb. 24 p24-5. 300w. 4

3602   JEFFERSON, Eddie. The Jazz Singer. Inner City 1016
       CAD April p28. 120w. 3
       CO Sept./Oct. p24. 125w. 4
       SR Aug. p104-5. 325w. 5

3603   JENKINS, Leroy. Solo Concert. India Navigation 1n1028
       CAD Nov. p35. 225w. $3\frac{1}{2}$
       MM Nov. 19 p34. 200w. 4

3604   JOHNSON, Bunk. NoLa LP3 (Reissue)
       RR Oct. p89. 25w. $2\frac{1}{2}$

3605   JOHNSON, Bunk. The Last Testament of a Great Jazzman.
       Columbia JCL829 (Reissue)
       CO April p20-1. 350w. 4

3606   JOHNSON, Dink. Din's Good Time Music. NoLa LP 12
       JR V9,/#4 unpaged 225w. 4
       MR Aug. p12. 275w. $3\frac{1}{2}$
       RR Dec. p87-8. 100w. $2\frac{1}{2}$
       ST June-July p192-3. 400w. $2\frac{1}{2}$

3607   JOHNSON, J. J., Kai Winding and Bennie Green. Early
       Blues. Prestige P-24067 (2 discs) (Reissue)

RSP   Jan. -Feb.   p36-7.   900w. $3\frac{1}{2}$

3608   JOHNSON, James P.   Father of Stride Piano.   Columbia CC 1780 (Reissue)
       MR   Aug.   p8.   50w.   4

3609   JOHNSON, James P.   New York Jazz.   Stinson SLP 21
       MR   Aug.   p8.   50w.   3

3610   JOHNSON, James P.   The Original.   Folkways FJ 2850 (Reissue)
       MR   Aug.   p8.   100w. $2\frac{1}{2}$
       RSP   Jan. -Feb.   p46.   200w. $3\frac{1}{2}$

3611   JOHNSON, James P.   Piano Rolls.   Biograph BLP 1003Q/ 1009Q (2 discs)
       MR   Aug.   p8-9.   200w. $3\frac{1}{2}$

3612   JOHNSON, James P.   W. C. Handy Blues.   Folkways FG 3540
       MR   Aug.   p9.   50w. $3\frac{1}{2}$

3613   JOHNSON, James P.   Yamekraw.   Folkways FJ 2842
       MR   Aug.   p9.   50w.   3

3614   JOHNSON, James P. and Perry Bradford.   1921-1929.   Arcadia 2009 (Reissue)
       RA   May-June   p4-5.   125w.   4
       RT   March   p6.   250w.   4
       ST   Feb. -March   p116.   425w.   3

3615   JOHNSON, Pete/Cozy Cole.   All Star Swing Groups.   Savoy 2218
       CAD   June   p15.   150w. $3\frac{1}{2}$
       DB   Sept. 8   p38-41.   50w.   2
       MM   July 2   p24.   400w. $3\frac{1}{2}$

3616   JOHNSON, Plas.   The Blues.   Concord CJ 15
       SOU   March   p42.   50w.   5

3617   JOHNSON, Plas.   Positively.   Concord Jazz CJ-24
       CAD   Jan.   p30.   275w. $4\frac{1}{2}$
       SOU   March   p44.   100w.   5
       SR   March   p11.   150w.   4

3618   JONES, Elvin.   Vanguard VSD 79389
       MG   Sept.   p53.   100w.   3

3819   JONES, Elvin.   Live at the Town Hall.   PM PMR 004
       JF   No. 47   p64.   800w.   3

3620   JONES, Elvin.   Oregon.   Vanguard VSD 79377
       SR   Feb.   p108.   100w.   4

3621   JONES, Elvin.   The Prime Element.   Blue Note BN LA 506
       (Reissue)
            DB   Aug. 11   200w.   5
            JF   No. 47   p69.   100w.   3

3622   JONES, Elvin.   Time Capsule.   Vanguard VSD 79390
            CAD   Oct.   p35-6.   275w.   4

3623   JONES, Hank.   'Bop Redux.   Muse MR 5123
            CAD   Nov.   p36.   125w.   3½

3624   JONES, Hank.   Hanky Panky.   East Wind EW-8021 (Japan)
            CO   April   p12.   225w.   4

3625   JONES, Hank.   Jones-Brown-Smith.   Concord CJ 32
            CAD   May   p15, 18.   150w.   3
            JJ   May   p48.   200w.   5
            JM   Summer   p52.   300w.   4
            SR   Aug.   p105.   75w.   5

3626   JONES, Jo.   The Essential.   Vanguard VSD 101/2 (2 discs)
       (Reissue)
            CAD   Dec.   p49.   250w.   3
            MJ   Nov.   p24.   100w.   3

3627   JONES, Jo.   The Main Man.   Pablo 2310-799
            CAD   Oct.   p49-50.   200w.   4
            DB   Nov. 17   p26, 28.   300w.   4

3628   JONES, Quincy.   I Heard That.   A&M 3705 (2 discs)
            CAC   May   p49-50.   500w.   3½

3629   JONES, Quincy.   We Had a Ball.   Philips SON 033 BS (E)
            BM   March   p52.   150w.   3

3630   JONES, Sam.   Cello Again.   Xanadu 129
            DB   June 16   p40-3.   225w.   4

3631   JONES, Sam.   Seven Minds.   East Wind ED-7012 (Japan)
            CO   April   p12.   225w.   4

3632   JONES, Thad.   Greetings and Salutations.   Four Leaf Clover
       5001 (Sweden)
            CAD   Oct.   p27.   150w.   3

3633   JONES, Thad and Aura.   Four Leaf Clover 5020 (Sweden)
            CAD   Oct.   p27.   150w.   3

3634   JONES, Thad and Mel Lewis.   New Life.   Horizon A&M
       SP707
            CO   April   p21.   175w.   4

3635   JONES, Thad and Mel Lewis.   Suite for Pops.   A&M SP-701

CO   April   p21.   350w.   3

3636   JORDAN, Clifford.   The Highest Mountain.   Inner City 2047
       CAD   Nov.   p44.   200w.   3

3637   JORDON, Clifford.   Night of the Mark 7.   Muse MR 5076
       CO   April   p22.   275w. $2\frac{1}{2}$

3638   JORDAN, Clifford.   Remembering Me-Me.   Muse MR 5105
       CAD   June   p45.   450w. $4\frac{1}{2}$

3639   JORDAN, Duke.   Flight to Denmark.   Inner City 2011
       CAD   Dec.   p56.   200w.   3

3640   JORDON, Duke.   Two Loves.   Inner City 2024
       CAD   Aug.   p40.   150w.   4

3641   JOYCE, Johnny.   Joyce's Choice Mixture.   Freedom FLP
       99003
       MM   May 14   p34.   125w.   4

3642   KAMUCA, Richie.   Drop Me Off in Harlem.   Concord Jazz
       CJ-39
       CAD   Sept.   p31.   250w.   4
       MJ   Sept.   p30-1.   50w.   3

3643   KAMUCA, Richie.   Richard Kamuca: 1976.   Jazzz 104
       CO   April   p21-2.   375w.   5
       RFJ   Jan.   p14-5.   350w. $3\frac{1}{2}$

3644   KARMA.   Celebration.   Horizon SP 713
       CAD   Jan.   p18.   75w. $3\frac{1}{2}$
       RR   March   p97.   50w.   3
       RSP   March-April   p28.   100w.   3

3645   KARUSH, Larry and Glen Moore.   May 24, 1976.   Japo
       60014
       CAD   Feb.   p26-7.   175w. $2\frac{1}{2}$
       MG   Oct.   p60.   75w.   3

3646   KASAI, Kimiko and Mal Waldron.   One for Lady.   Catalyst
       CAT 7900
       DB   May 19   250w.   5

3647   KELLIN, Orange.   In New Orleans.   Biograph-Center CEN
       7
       RR   June   p95.   75w. $3\frac{1}{2}$

3648   KENO, Duke.   Crest of the Wave.   Trident TRS-501
       CAD   June   p12.   200w. $4\frac{1}{2}$

3649   KENTON, Stan.   Greatest Hits.   Capitol CAPS 1002 (E) (Re-
       issue)

GR   April   p1608.   75w. $3\frac{1}{2}$
MM   June 4   p32.   200w. $3\frac{1}{2}$

3650   KENTON, Stan. The Jazz Compositions Stan Kenton. Cre-
ative World ST 1078 (Reissue)
CAD   June   p13.   200w.   4
RFJ   Sept.   p14.   400w.   4

3651   KENTON, Stan. Journey to Capricorn. Creative World ST
1077
CAD   Feb.   p32.   100w.   4
DB   May 5   p24.   250w.   4
HF   April   p145.   100w.   4
MJ   Sept.   p28.   50w.   3
SOU   March   p42.   50w.   2

3652   KENTON, Stan. Kenton '76. Creative World ST 1076
HF   April   p145.   100w.   4

3653   KENTON, Stan. Live in Europe. Decca PFS 43993
GR   July   p234.   100w. $3\frac{1}{2}$
HF   April   p145.   100w. $4\frac{1}{2}$

3654   KENTON, Stan. One Night Stand at the Click. Joyce 1040
CAD   Aug.   p49.   125w. $3\frac{1}{2}$

3655   KENTON, Stan. One Night Stand at the Commodore. Joyce
1030
CAD   March   p36-7.   50w. $3\frac{1}{2}$

3656   KERR, Bob, Hugh Crozier, Phil Franklin. Blues, Jazz,
Boogie Rags. Whoopee 11
MM   March 12   p24.   300w.   4

3657   KERR, Brooks. Soda Fountain Rag. Chiaroscuro CR 2001
JM   1:2   p66.   150w. $3\frac{1}{2}$

3658   KESSEL, Barney. Slow Burn. Phil Spector International
2307 011 (E) (Reissue)
SMG   May   p27.   150w.   4

3659   KESSEL, Barney. Soaring. Concord Jazz CJ-33
CAD   June   p36.   100w.   4
DB   July 14   p36.   200w.   4
GP   May   p129.   25w. $2\frac{1}{2}$
JJ   May   p48.   150w. $4\frac{1}{2}$
MM   May 21   p28.   250w.   4
SR   Sept.   p121.   125w.   5

3660   KESSEL, Barney. Straight Ahead. Contemporary S75635
GP   May   p129.   25w.   3

3661   KESSEL, Barney and Herb Ellis. Poor Butterfly. Concord

CJ 34
　SR Dec. 75w. 3

3662 KESSEL, Barney, Herb Ellis and Charlie Byrd. Great Guitars. Concord JAZZ CJ 23
　　GP May p129. 25w. $2\frac{1}{2}$

3663 KIKUCHI, Masabumi. Matrix. Catalyst 7916
　　CAD Nov. p32. 200w. 0

3664 KINCH, Don. Conductors Ragtime Band. Rexius RL 5123
　　JR V9/#3 unpaged 175w. $3\frac{1}{2}$

3665 KIRBY, John. Boss of the Bass. Columbia CG 33557 (2 discs) (Reissue)
　　AU Dec. p125. 450w. 4
　　CAD March p36. 100w. 4
　　CO Aug. p22. 375w. 5
　　DB April 7 p31-3. 100w. 4
　　JR V9/#4 unpaged 100w. 4
　　MJ March p44. 100w. $3\frac{1}{2}$
　　MR Feb. p12-3. 375w. 3

3666 KIRBY, Roy, Paragon Jazz Band. (no serial number)
　　ST April-May p155. 150w. 4

3667 KIRK, Andy. Best of. MCA 2-4105 (2 discs) (Reissue)
　　JM 1:2 p56. 100w. 3

3668 KIRK, Andy and His Clouds of Joy 1936-1942. MCA (French) 510033, 510121, 510133 (3 discs)
　　ST Aug.-Sept. p232-3. 325w. 1

3669 KIRK, Rahsaan Roland. Early Roots. Bethlehem BCP 6016 (Reissue)
　　CAD Dec. p52. 200w. 4
　　RSP Nov.-Dec. p41. 200w. $3\frac{1}{2}$

3670 KIRK, Rahsaan Roland. Kirkatron. Warner BS 2982
　　CAD March p45-6. 75w. $2\frac{1}{2}$
　　DB June 2 p20. 200w. 4

3671 KIRK, Rahsaan Roland. Other Folks Music. Atlantic SD 1686
　　RFJ Jan. p15. 750w. 3

3672 KLEMMER, John. Barefoot Ballet. ABC ABCL 5198
　　MM Jan. 1 p16. 50w. $1\frac{1}{2}$

3673 KLEMMER, John. Lifestyle (Living & Loving). ABC Records AB-1007
　　CAD Oct. p40-1. 150w. 2
　　DB Nov. 3 p21. 250w. $2\frac{1}{2}$

RSP   Nov. -Dec. p36.   350w. $2\frac{1}{2}$

3674   KLOSS, Eric. Essence. Muse 5038
       CO   April p22.   275w. $3\frac{1}{2}$

3675   KLOSS, Eric & Barry Miles. Together. Muse MR 5112
       CAD   Feb. p29.   150w.   4
       MG   April p53.   75w.   4

3676   KLOSS, Eric and Richie Cole. Battle of the Saxes, Vol. 1.
       Muse MR5082
       CAD   Sept. p38.   200w.   4

3677   KLOTCHKOFF, Michel and Chris Woods. Full Space. Pro-
       mophone Records 13
       CAD   Aug. p55.   250w. $3\frac{1}{2}$

3678   KLUGH, Earl. Finger Painting. Blue Note BNLA 737H
       BM   Oct. p44.   250w.   4
       DB   Dec. 1 p28.   350w.   3
       MM   Oct. 1 p26.   225w. $4\frac{1}{2}$

3679   KLUGH, Earl. Living Inside Your Love. Bluenote BNLA
       667-G
       BM   April p50.   200w.   3
       GP   May p128.   50w.   3
       SR   March p122.   100w.   2

3680   KNAACK, Donald. Duchamp: The Bride Stripped Bare by
       Her Bacheloy, Even. Erratum Musical
       DB   Dec. 15 p28.   100w.   3

3681   KONITZ, Lee. Jazz A Confronto: Vol. 32. Horo HLL
       101-32 (Italy)
       CAD   Sept. p19.   150w.   5
       CO   April p22-3.   200w.   4

3682   KONITZ, Lee. The Lee Konitz Nonet. Roulette SR 5006
       AU   Nov. p121.   350w.   4
       DB   Dec. 1 p27-8.   400w.   5

3683   KONITZ, Lee and Warne Marsh. Atlantic 50298 (West Ger-
       many) (Reissue)
       RR   May p87-8.   300w. $3\frac{1}{2}$

3684   KONITZ, Lee and Warne Marsh. London Concert. Wave LP
       16 (E)
       JF   No. 49 p46-7.   550w.   4

3685   KONITZ, Lee and Warne Marsh. Meet Again. Produttori
       Associati LP 72 (Italy)
       CO   April p22-3.   200w.   4

3686   KRIEGEL, Volker.   Tropical Harvest.   MPS 20228274 (West Germany)
         JF No. 46 p64.   400w. $3\frac{1}{2}$

3687   KROECKEL, Dick.   Echoes from Lulu White's Mahogany Hall.
Ragtime CA 94101
         CK Dec. p73.   25w.   2

3688   KRUPA, Gene.   Monmouth Evergreen MES 7072 (Reissue)
         JF No. 47 p69.   50w.   3
         MJ Jan. p29.   50w.   3

3689   KRUPA, Gene.   1945-1949.   First Heard Records FHR 1947-7 (E) (Reissue)
         SMG May p27.   200w.   3

3690   KRUPA, Gene.   One Night Stand.   Joyce 1029
         SMG Sept. p27.   25w.   3

3691   KRUPA, Gene.   The Radio Discs of.   Joyce LP 2008 (Reissue)
         MM June 11 p20.   450w.   4
         SMG Sept. p27.   25w.   3

3692   KRUPA, Gene.   The Second Big Band Sound.   Verve (E)
         CAD Jan. p390.   300w.   3

3693   KRUPA, Gene and Buddy Rich.   Film Tracks.   Joyce 3002
         SMG Sept. p27.   25w.   3

3694   KUHN, Joachim.   Hip Elegy.   MPS/BASF G22794
         SR March p122.   50w.   0

3695   KUHN, Joachim.   Springfever.   Atlantic SD 1695
         CAD Jan. p42.   150w.   3
         CK Jan. p51.   75w.   4
         DB March 24 200w.   3
         MG Jan. 75w.   3
         MM April 9 p23.   150w. $3\frac{1}{2}$

3696   KUHN, Rolf.   The Day After.   MPS-BASF G21604
         CAD April p45.   336w.   4
         SOU June p46.   100w.   4

3697   KUHN, Steve.   Ecstacy.   ECM ECM-L-1058.   CT-L-1058
         CRA March p80-1.   250w.   2
         DB Dec. 15 p30, 32.   200w.   4
         SR Feb. p108.   100w.   4

3698   KUHN, Steve and Ecstasy.   Motility.   Polydor ECM 1-1094
         CAD July p40.   250w.   4
         CK Sept. p58.   125w. $4\frac{1}{2}$
         JF No. 49 p20.   50w.   4

SR Oct. p128. 150w. 4½

3699 KURITA, Hachiro. Sky to Sing to Me. Offbeat ORLP-1006
(Japan)
CO Aug. p20-1. 275w. 2½

3700 KURUSH, Larry. May 24, 1097. ECM 1-1901
CK Nov. p65. 74w. 4½

3701 KUSTBANDET. Star Dust. Kenneth KS 2039 (Reissue)
JJ April p32-3. 200w. 3
ST Dec.-Jan. p78-9. 650w. 5

3702 LA BARBARA, Joan. Voice Is the Original Instrument.
Wizard Records RVW 2266
CAD Jan. p15. 225w. 3

3703 LA BARBERA, Pat. Pass It On. PM 009 (Canada)
CAD Aug. p34. 200w. 3½
RFJ May p18. 100w. 3

3704 LACY, Steve. Raps. Adelphi 5004
CAD Nov. p37. 250w. 4

3705 LACY, Steve. Saxaphone Special. Emanem 3310
CO April p23. 375w. 2½

3706 LACY, Steve. School Days. Emanem 3316
CO April p23. 750w. 4

3707 LACY, Steve. Scraps. Saravah SH 10049 (France)
JF No. 46 p67, 69. 75w. 4½

3708 LACY, Steve. Stabs - Solo in Berlin. Free Music Production SAJ-05 (E)
CO April p23-4. 275w. 4

3709 LACY, Steve and Andrea Centazzo. Clangs. Ictus Records
0001
CO April p23-4. 275w. 3

3710 LACY, Steve and Michael Smith. Sidelines. Improvising
Artists Inc. IAI 37347
Cad Oct. p38. 125w. 2
MG Sept. p53. 75w. 3½

3711 LACY, Steve and Roswell Rudd. Trickles. Black Saint
0008 (Italy)
CAD Feb. p43. 150w. 4
SR Dec. 150w. 4

3712 LAKE, Oliver. Holding Together. Black Saint BSR 0009
(Italy)

CAD   May p19-20.   150w.   5
MM   Jan. 22 p25.   425w.   4
SR   Aug. p105-6.   200w.   5

3713   LAKE, Oliver and Joseph Bowie.   Sackville 2010 (Canada)
       CO   June p14.   325w.   5

3714   LAMBERT, Donald.   Harlem Stride Classics.   Pumpkin 104
       CAD   Dec. p53-4.   100w. $3\frac{1}{2}$

3715   LAMBERT, Donald.   Meet the Lamb.   IAJRC 23 (Reissue)
       RA   May-June p5.   125w. $3\frac{1}{2}$
       RT   March p6.   250w. $3\frac{1}{2}$
       ST   Feb.-March p119.   400w.   2

3716   LANDE, Art.   Rubisa Patrol.   ECM 1081
       CAD   Jan. p30, 31.   75w. $2\frac{1}{2}$
       DB   March 10 p22-3.   250w.   4
       MG   Jan.   100w.   3
       PRM   Feb. p41.   300w.   4
       SR   March p122.   150w.   4

3717   LANDRY, Richard.   4 Cuts.   Chatham Square LP 10
       CAD   Aug. p21.   200w.   4

3718   LANDRY, Richard.   Solos.   Chatham Square STLP 17
       CAD   Aug. p21.   400w.   4

3719   LANE, Steve and His Southern Stompers.   My Blue Heaven.
       Halcyon SHAL 10
       RR   June p94.   50w.   1

3720   LANG, Eddie.   Jazz Guitar Virtuoso.   Yazoo L-1059 (Reis-
       sue)
       GP   Sept. p118.   175w.   3

3721   LARKIN, Milt.   Down Home Saturday Night.   Copasetic Rec-
       ords 933
       CAD   Jan. p14.   200w.   4
       JM   1:2 p57.   200w.   3

3722   LATEEF, Yusef.   Morning.   Savoy SJL 2208 (2 discs) (Re-
       issue)
       GR   May p1758.   200w.   5

3723   LAURENCE, Baby.   Dancemaster.   Classic Jazz CJ30
       AU   Oct. p194.   350w.   5
       CAD   April p8.   180w.   2
       RFJ   Sept. p11.   600w. $3\frac{1}{2}$
       SR   July p109-10.   175w.   3

3724   LAVIN, Bud.   Moods in Jazz.   Vantage 501
       CAD   Jan. p24, 25.   100w.   2

3725   LAWRENCE, Azar. People Moving. Prestige P-10099
        DB   April 21 p26. 300w. 1

3726   LAWS, Hubert. Romeo and Juliet. Columbia PC 34330.
        Cart. PCA34330
        SR   March p123. 150w. 3

3727   LAWS, Hubert. The San Francisco Concert. CTI 7071
        CAD   May p12. 75w. $2\frac{1}{2}$
        MM   Oct. 1 p28. 50w. 1

3728   LAWS, Ronnie. Friends and Strangers. Blue Note LA 730-H
        CAD   July p23. 100w. 2
        DB   Nov. 17 p20. 300w. 3
        HF   Sept. p142. 75w. 2

3729   LEE, David R. Original Rags. Jazz Studies JS-4 (Canadian
        issue)
        CC   May p34. 75w. 3
        MR   June p9. 300w. 4
        RA   May-June p5-6. 125w. 3
        RT   March p6. 250w. 3
        ST   Aug.-Sept. p234, 236. 400w. 4

3730   LEE, Jeanne. Conspiracy. Earthforms 1
        CAD   Sept. p34-5. 350w. 4
        CO   June p14. 625w. 4

3731   LEE, Tom. Lee Lambert Records 3416
        CAD   Nov. p47. 125w. $4\frac{1}{2}$

3732   LEGENDS of Jazz. Starring Barney Bigard. Crescent Jazz
        Productions CJP 2
        JR   V9/#3 unpaged 200w. 5

3733   LEIGH, Carol and Original Salty Dogs Jazz Band. Wild
        Women Don't Have the Blues. Jazzology GHB-88
        SR   Sept. p121-2. 325w. 5

3734   LENZ, Klaus. Aufbruch. Amiga 855 509 (West Germany)
        JF   No. 48 p54. 600w. 3

3734a   LEVIN, March. Sound Sketches. Enja 2058
        JF   No. 48 p52. 300w. $3\frac{1}{2}$

3735   LEVINE, James. Plays Scott Joplin. RCA ARL1-2243
        CK   Oct. p65. 50w. $2\frac{1}{2}$

3736   LEVINE, Mark. Up 'Til Now. Catalyst CAT 7614
        CAD   June p31. 250w. $3\frac{1}{2}$
        CK   Nov. p65. 33w. 3
        DB   Nov. 17 p29. 75w. 4
        RSP   May-June p45. 225w. 2

3737   LEWIS, George. In Japan. Storyville SLP (E)
        RR Dec. p88. 50w. $2\frac{1}{2}$

3738   LEWIS, George. New Orleans All-Stars. Catalyst 7905
        (Reissue)
        CO Dec. p23. 50w. $3\frac{1}{2}$

3739   LEWIS, George. Solo Trombone. Sackville 3012
        CAD Sept. p44-5. 325w. $4\frac{1}{2}$
        OLR Dec. p292. 50w. $4\frac{1}{2}$
        VV Nov. 28 p61. 200w. $3\frac{1}{2}$

3740   LEWIS, John. Traveling. Finite 1976-1
        CAD April p30. 120w. $3\frac{1}{2}$

3741   LEWIS, John and Helen Merrill. Mercury SRMI-1150
        CAD June p31. 125w. $4\frac{1}{2}$

3742   LEWIS, Mel. And Friends. Horizon SP716
        CAD April p27. 325w. 4
        CO June p14. 300w. $2\frac{1}{2}$
        DB July 14 p36, 38. 300w. 4
        JJ May p49. 150w. 5
        JM Summer p54-5. 350w. $4\frac{1}{2}$
        MJ Sept. p28. 50w. 3
        RFJ May p14-5. 550w. $3\frac{1}{2}$
        RSP May-June p44. 225w. 3
        SOU April p62. 150w. 4
        SR June p124, 125. 175w. 5

3743   LIEBMAN, Dave. Father Time. Enja 2056
        CO June p15-6. 525w. 4

3744   LIEBMAN, Dave. Lighten Up, Please! A&M Horizon SP-
        721
        CAD July p22. 100w. 2
        DB Nov. 3 p21-2. 325w. $2\frac{1}{2}$

3745   LIEBMAN, Dave. Sweet Hands. Horizon SP-702
        CO June p14-5. 525w. 4

3746   LISTEN. Inner City 1025
        CAD Sept. p36. 225w. 4
        DB Nov. 17 p20. 200w. 3

3747   LITTLE, Booker. Legendary Quartet Album. Island ILPS
        9454 (E) (Reissue)
        RR May p88. 150w. 4

3748   LOEVENDIE, Theo. Quartet. Universe Productions UP1-27
        (Netherlands)
        JF No. 46 p66. 325w. $4\frac{1}{2}$

3749   LOLAX, Paul.   Ragtime Guitar.   Titanic TI-13
       SO Jan./Feb.   p50.   50w.   4

3750   LONGO, Mike.   Talk with the Spirits.   Pablo 2310-769
       CAD Jan.   p18.   75w.   0
       CK   Jan.   p51.   25w.   4
       GR   Aug.   p354.   75w.   3
       JJ   Feb.   p33.   400w.   4
       RR   Jan.   p85.   25w. $1\frac{1}{2}$

3751   The LOUISIANA Dandies Orchestra.   Feeling the Spirit.   CBS
       81753 (Swiss)
       ST Aug. -Sept.   p239.   150w. $4\frac{1}{2}$

3752   LOUISIANA Shakers Band.   Crescent Jazz Productions CJP 3
       JR V9/#3 unpaged 200w.   4

3753   LOWE, Frank.   The Flam.   Black Saint BSR 0005 (Italy)
       CO June p16.   400w. $3\frac{1}{2}$

3754   LOWE, Mundell.   Guitar Player.   Dobre 1007
       CAD Nov.   p45.   150w. $3\frac{1}{2}$

3755   LUCIEN, Jon.   Premonition.   Columbia PC 34255
       DB April 21 p24-5.   300w. $3\frac{1}{2}$

3756   McBEE, Cecil.   Strata East "Mutima" SES 7417
       CAD Feb.   p16.   175w.   4
       JJ April p33.   250w.   4

3757   McCANN, Les.   River High, River Low.   Atlantic SD 1690
       CK   Jan.   p50.   100w. $4\frac{1}{2}$
       DB April 21 p22.   300w. $1\frac{1}{2}$

3758   McCANN, Les and Wayne Henderson.   Music Lets Me Be.
       Impulse AS9329
       BS Aug.   p27.   150w.   3
       CAD June p20.   75w.   2
       CK Aug.   p48.   100w.   5

3759   McCONNELL, Rob & the Boss Brass.   The Jazz Album.
       Attic LA 1015 (Canada)
       CAD Jan.   p34.   175w. $3\frac{1}{2}$

3760   McCRAE, Gwen.   Something So Right.   Catalyst CAT 2608
       RS Feb. 10 p100, 103.   400w.   2

3761   McDOUGAL, E. Parker.   Initial Visit.   Grits Records 2001
       CAD Oct.   p20-1.   200w.   4

3762   McGHEE, Howard.   Cookin' Time.   ZIM 2004
       CAD Nov.   p46, 47.   250w.   5

3763   McGHEE, Howard. Maggie, the Savoy Sessions. Savoy Rec-
        ords SJL 2219
            CAD Oct. p38-40. 475w. 2½
            CO Dec. p22. 125w. 3
            MJ Nov. p22. 50w. 3
            MM Dec. 3 p32. 250w. 3
            RR Oct. p90. 25w. 2½

3764   McGHEE, Howard. Trumpet at Tempo. Spotlite 131
            CAD Nov. p48, 49. 200w. 2½
            CO Aug. p24. 125w. 3
            MM April 2 p28. 200w. 3½

3765   McGHEE, Howard and Illinois Jacquet. Here Comes Freddy.
        Sonet SNTF 714 (E)
            CAD Aug. p47. 250w. 3½
            MM March 26 p22. 275w. 3
            RR April p88. 25w. 3

3766   McGREGOR, Chris. Blue Notes for Mongezi. Ogun 001/002
        (2 discs)
            CAD Feb. p37-8. 225w. 2½
            CO Aug. p16. 500w. 4
            JF No. 49 p50. 525w. 4
            JJ Jan. p32. 550w. 4

3767   McGREGOR, Chris. Live at Willisau. Ogun OG 100 (E)
            CO Feb. p14. 225w. 5

3768   McGRIFF, Jimmy. Red Beans. Groove Merchant GM 3314
            CAD Jan. p18. 25w. 2

3769   McINTYRE, Ken. Hindsight. Inner City 2014
            CAD Nov. p37, 38. 275w. 3

3770   McINTYRE, Ken. Home. Inner City IC 2039
            SR Nov. p130. 175w. 5

3771   McKENNA, Dave. By Myself. Shiah MK-1
            CO June p18. 250w. 4

3772   McLAUGHLIN, John. A Handful of Beauty. Columbia PC
        34372
            CAD April p11. 75w. 4
            DB June 16 p30. 300w. 5
            GP Aug. p119. 125w. 4
            RSP May-June p33-6. 2550w. 4½
            SR Sept. p122. 125w. 5

3773   McLAUGHLIN, John. Natural Elements. Column JC 34980
            MM Dec. 21 p15. 350w. 5

3774   McLEAN, Jackie. A Ghetto Lullaby. Inner City 2013

(Reissue)
    CAD Feb. p34-5. 100w. 3
    DB   Dec. 1 p31. 300w. 3
    VV   Nov. 28 p66. 50w. 4

3775   McLEAN, Jackie. Live at Montmartre. Inner City OC 2001
    CAD May p30. 50w. 2

3776   McLEAN, Jackie and Dexter Gordon. The Meeting. Vol. 1
    Inner City 2006
    CAD June p29. 225w. 3

3777   McLEAN, Jackie and Dexter Gordon. The Source. Inner
    City IC 2020
    CAD April p32. 122w. 4

3778   McLEAN, Jackie and Gary Bartz. Ode to Super. Inner City
    IC 2009
    CAD May p30. 50w. 2

3779   McLEAN, Rene. Watch Out. Inner City 2037
    CAD Oct. p51-2. 150w. 5

3780   McNEILL, Lloyd. Treasures. Baobab No. 1
    CAD April p26. 264w. 4

3781   McPARTLAND, Marion. A Fine Romance. Improv 7115
    CAD May p15, 18. 150w. 3
    DB   Aug. 11 200w. $3\frac{1}{2}$
    RFJ April p17. 300w. 4
    SR   May p100. 125w. 4

3782   McPARTLAND, Marion. Solo Concert at Haverford. Halcyon
    LP111
    CO   June p17-8. 300w. 4

3783   MacPARTLAND, Jimmy/Bobby Hackett. Shades of Bix. MCA
    2-4110. Tape. MCAT 2-4110. Cass. MCAC 2-4110
    CO   June p17. 375w. 3
    DB   Oct. 6 p35-7. 100w. 3
    HF   Oct. p152, 156. 350w. 4
    MJ   Nov. p24. 100w. 3
    MR   April p12. 200w. 3

3784   McPHEE, Joe. Black Magic Man. Hat Hut HAT-A
    CO   June p18. 250w. 3
    SN   April p11. 275w. $3\frac{1}{2}$

3785   McPHEE, Joe. Nation Time. CJR 2
    CAD Jan. p29. 250w. 3

3786   McPHEE, Joe. On Tour II. World Jazz Records WJLP-
    S-10

CAD   Sept.   p21.   350w.   5

3787   McPHEE, Joe.   Rotation.   Hat Hut D
CAD   Sept.   p22.   350w.   5
CAD   Oct.   p48-9.   425w.   4

3788   McPHEE, Joe.   Tenor.   Hat Hut C. (Switzerland)
CAD   March   p23.   150w.   4
CAD   June   p43.   150w. $3\frac{1}{2}$
CAD   March   p23.   150w.   4
JF   No. 50   p52.   200w.   4

3789   McPHEE, Joe.   The Willisau Concert.   Hat Hut B.
CAD   Jan.   p23, 24.   200w.   5
CO   June   p18.   250w.   3
SN   April   p11.   275w.   4

3790   McPHEE, Joe and John Snyder.   Pieces of Light.   CJR 4
CAD   Jan.   p23, 24.   200w. $3\frac{1}{2}$

3791   McPHERSON, Charles.   Beautiful.   Xanadu 15 (Reissue)
MJ   March   p77.   50w.   3

3792   McPHERSON, Charles.   Live in Tokyo.   Xanadu 131
CAD   April   p30-1.   108w. $4\frac{1}{2}$
DB   June 16   p40-43.   225w. $4\frac{1}{2}$
SOU   April   p56.   100w.   4

3793   MacPHERSON, Fraser.   Live at the Planetarium.   West End
101 (Canada)
CAD   May   p14.   225w.   5
CO   June   p16.   350w. $3\frac{1}{2}$
HF   Jan.   p147.   200w.   3
OLR   Dec.   p292.   25w.   5
SR   Jan.   p85.   200w.   4

3794   McSHANN, Jay and Charlie Parker.   Early Bird, 1940-43.
RCA B&W FXM1-7334 (France) (Reissue)
JJ   April   p33.   450w.   3
RR   June   p95.   50w.   3

3795   McSHANN, Jay and Buddy Tate.   Crazy Legs and Friday
Steve.   Sackville 3011 (Canada)
CAD   July   p45.   300w.   4
HF   Oct.   p156.   300w.   2
OLR   Dec.   p292.   50w. $4\frac{1}{2}$
SOU   Sept.   p64.   200w.   4

3796   MAGADINI, Peter.   Polyrhythms.   Briko 1000
CAD   April   p6.   300w.   4
CO   June   p18.   175w.   3

3797   MAKOWICZ, Adam.   Piano Vistas Unlimited.   Helicon HT

001 (Poland)
    JF No. 49 p45-6.   550w.   5

3798 MALFATTI, Radu and Stephen Wittwer.   Thrumblin.   FMP
      0350
          CAD July p14.   200w.   4
          MM March 5 p32.   450w.   4

3799 MANGELSDORFF, Albert.   Tromboneliness.   MPS 68-129
      (West Germany)
          JF No. 50 p19.   75w.   4

3800 MANGELSDORFF, Albert.   The Wide Point.   MPS/BASF G
      22561
          SOU Feb. p44.   150w.   5

3801 MANGELSDORFF, Albert, Gunter Hampel, Joachim Kuhn,
      Pierre Favre.   Solo Now.   MPS BASF DC 226298
          MM Feb. 12 p27.   400w. $3\frac{1}{2}$

3802 MANGUAL, José.   Buyu.   Turnstyle T 433
          CAD Oct. p23.   100w.   4
          DB Dec. 1 p30.   400w. $3\frac{1}{2}$

3803 MANN, Herbie.   Bird in a Silver Cage.   Atlantic SD 18209.
      Cart. TP-18209
          BM June p47.   150w.   2
          DB March 10 p24, 26.   250w. $1\frac{1}{2}$
          MM Oct. 1 p48.   50w.   2
          SR June p125.   75w.   4

3804 MANN, Herbie.   Fire Island.   Atlantic 19112
          CAD Nov. p30.   75w.   4

3805 MANN, Herbie.   Gagaku and Beyond.   Finnadar SR 9014
          CAD Jan. p43-4.   100w. $3\frac{1}{2}$
          HF Jan. p146.   150w.   4
          SOU Feb. p44.   50w.   1
          SR March p123.   150w.   3

3806 MANN, Herbie and Buddy Collette.   Just for Kicks - 1957.
      Vintage Jazz 101657
          CAD June p26.   100w. $3\frac{1}{2}$

3807 MANNE, Shelly.   ABC Impulse IMP 8044 (E)
          RR Aug. p84.   50w.   4

3808 MANNE, Shelly.   Perk Up.   Concord Jazz CT-21
          CAD Jan. p19.   400w.   3
          DB April 7 p29.   200w.   3
          SR April p112.   150w.   4

3809 MANTLER, Mike.   Silence.   Watt Records #5

       CAD April p10. 84w. 2
       DB Nov. 17 p23. 400w. 3
       MG May p53. 125w. 3
       MM March 12 p23. 450w. 0
       RR July p96. 200w. 2

3810   MANTRA, Michael. First Time In. PM PMR 7601
       RFJ April p16. 400w. 3

3811   MANUSARDI, Guido. "Blue & New Things." Carosello CLE
      21018 (Italy)
       CO Sept./Oct. p18-20. 225w. 4

3812   MARIANO, Charlie. Helen Twelve Trees. MPS G22941
       CAD April p20. 180w. 2
       HF June p122. 350w. 4
       MG May p53. 125w. $3\frac{1}{2}$
       SR July p110. 150w. 3

3813   MARIANO, Charlie. Jazz A Confronto: Vol. 15. Horo HLL
      101-15 (Italy)
       CAD Sept. p16. 150w. 3
       JF No. 50 p49. 250w. $3\frac{1}{2}$

3814   MARIANO, Charlie. Reflections. Catalyst CAT - 7915
       CAD Nov. p36. 225w. $2\frac{1}{2}$
       MG Dec. p57. 150w. $2\frac{1}{2}$
       RS Nov. 3 p110. 250w. $3\frac{1}{2}$

3815   MARKOWITZ, Mark. Marky's Vibes. Famous Door HL-111
       CAD June p28. 100w. $3\frac{1}{2}$
       SR Aug. p106. 150w. $4\frac{1}{2}$

3816   MARSH, Warne. All Music. Nessa N7
       CAD May p20-1. 150w. 4
       DB June 16 p30. 375w. 5
       MM June 25 p25. 300w. $3\frac{1}{2}$
       RSP March-April p36. 250w. 4

3817   MARTINO, Pat. Exit. Muse MR 5075
       CAD Dec. p36-7. 225w. 3

3818   MARTINO, Pat. Joyous Lake. Warner Bros. BS-2977
       CAD March p45-6. 75w. $2\frac{1}{2}$
       DB June 2 p22, 26. 300w. 4
       GP Aug. p119. 200w. 5
       JM Summer p55-6. 150w. 3
       MG May p53. 125w. 3

3819   MARTINO, Pat. We'll Be Together Again. Muse MR 5090
       AU Jan. p88. 350w. 3
       CO June p16-7. 150w. 4
       DB March 10 p24. 250w. $4\frac{1}{2}$

3820   MAS, Jean Pierre. Rue de Lourmie. Inner City IC 1014
        CAD   March   p34. 50w. 1

3821   MATTHEWS, Dave. Night Flight. Muse MR 5098
        CAD   Sept.   p41. 125w. 4
        MG   Sept.   p53. 75w. 2

3822   MAUPIN, Bennie. Slow Traffic to the Right. Mercury SRM-
        1-1148
        CAD   June   p21. 125w. 2
        DB   Oct. 20 p28. 250w. $3\frac{1}{2}$
        MG   July   p53. 100w. $3\frac{1}{2}$

3823   MAYERL, Billy. Syncopated Impressions. Folkways RF 30
        (Reissue)
        JJ   March   p33-4. 300w. 4
        RA   July-Aug. p6. 125w. $2\frac{1}{2}$
        RT   May   p24. 350w. $4\frac{1}{2}$

3824   MAYL, Gene. Down South. Red Onion 3
        MJ   Dec.   p24. 125w. $3\frac{1}{2}$

3825   MELIS, Marcello. The New Village on the Left. Black Saint
        0012
        CAD   Aug.   p48. 150w. 4
        MM   July 23 p22. 250w. 4

3826   MEMPHIS Nighthawks. Jazz Lips. Delmark DS-216
        CAD   Nov.   p45. 225w. 4
        MJ   Dec.   p25. 50w. $3\frac{1}{2}$

3827   MENZA, Don. First Flight. Catalyst CAT 7617
        CAD   June   p28. 300w. 4
        DB   Nov. 17 p28. 75w. 3
        SR   Nov.   p130, 132. 200w. 5

3828   METHENY, Pat. Bright Size Life. ECM 1-1073. Cart.
        1-1073
        SR   Jan.   p106. 50w. 4

3829   METHENY, Pat. Watercolors. ECM 1097
        CAD   Aug.   p34. 20w. 3
        CRA   Sept.   p72. 200w. $2\frac{1}{2}$
        GP   Aug.   p120. 150w. 4
        JF   No. 50 p19. 50w. 4
        MG   Aug.   p63. 100w. 2
        VV   Sept. 12 p53. 500w. $4\frac{1}{2}$

3830   MIDORIKAWA, Keiki. Five Pieces of Cake. Offbeat ORLP-
        1002 (Japan)
        CO   Aug.   p20-1. 275w. 3

3831   MIKI, Bingo. Scandinavian Suite. Three Blind Mice TBM

1005 (Sweden)
    AU Dec. p139. 350w. 3½

3832 MILES, Barry. Sky Train. RCA BGL1-2200
      RFJ May p200. 150w. 3

3833 MILLER, Artie with No-Gap Generation Jazz Band. No-Gap
      7444-002
      CAD Dec. p44. 200w. 3

3834 MILLER, Eddie. Soft Jive. Golden Era 15023
      CAD Feb. p28-9. 100w. 0

3835 MILLER, Harry. Family Affair. Ogun OG 310
      MM Nov. 5 p32. 325w. 4½

3836 MILLER, Kid Punch. Jazz Rareties 1929-1930. Herwin 108
      (Reissue)
          CO June p19. 350w. 2½
          JR V9/#4 unpaged 100w. 4
          MR Jan. p13. 325w. 3½
          ST Feb.-March p116-7. 100w. 5

3837 MILO Fine Free Jazz Ensemble. Improvisations (Being
      Free). Shih Shih Wu Ai SSWA 2
          AU Jan. p87. 800w. 3½

3838 MINGUS, Charlie. Blues and Roots. Atlantic KSD 1305
          SOU Sept. p66. 50w. 4

3839 MINGUS, Charlie. East Coasting. CBS 82110 (E) (Reissue)
          RR Oct. p90. 50w. 4

3840 MINGUS, Charlie. Live with Eric Dolphy. Byg YX 7099
      (Japan) (Reissue)
          MM Nov. 5 p31. 150w. 4½

3841 MINGUS, Charlie. 3 or 4 Shades of Blues. Atlantic 1700.
      Cart. SDT 1700. Cass. SDC 1700
          CAD Sept. p33. 175w. 5
          DB Oct. 20 p22. 300w. 5
          MG Oct. p60. 75w. 3½
          MM Nov. 5 p31. 150w. 3
          RS Oct. 6 p96, 102. 400w. 2

3842 MINGUS, Charlie. Tijuana Moods. RCA FXL1-7295 (France)
      (Reissue)
          JJ March p34. 375w. 4

3843 MITCHELL, Billy. Now's the Time. Catalyst CAT 7611
          CAD April p19. 444w. 3
          DB Nov. 17 p28-9. 75w. 2

3844   MITCHELL, Red.   Red Mitchell Meets Guido Manusardi.
       Produttori Associati PA/LP73 (Italy) (Reissue)
          CO   June   p19-20.   250w.   4

3845   MITCHELL, Roscoe.   Quartet.   Sackville 2009 (Canada)
          CO   June   p20.   325w.   3½
          OLR   Sept.   p225.   25w.   4

3846   MITCHELL, Roscoe.   Sound.   Delmark DS 408
          CAD   Dec.   p38.   200w.   2½
          RS   Nov. 17   p96.   600w.   3½

3847   MODERN Jazz Quartet.   The Last Concert.   Atlantic 2SD-
       909 (2 discs)
          CO   June   p20.   225w.   5
          RR   Jan.   p63.   125w.   2

3848   MOLE, Miff.   The Early Years.   Jazz Studies JS-2
          CO   Aug.   p16.   475w.   5
          OLR   Dec.   p292-3.   50w.   3½

3849   MONK, Thelonious.   The Complete Genius.   Blue Note BN
       LA 579 (Reissue)
          DB   Aug. 11   200w.   5

3850   MONK, Thelonious.   In Person.   Milestone PR 47033 (2
       discs) (Reissue)
          AU   July   p102.   250w.   3½
          BM   Jan.   p53.   150w.   4
          DB   April 21   p26-30.   250w.   3½
          MM   Jan. 8   p20.   100w.   4
          RSP   Jan.-Feb.   p34-5.   800w.   4

3851   MONTEROSE, J. R.   Straight Ahead.   Xanadu 126
          CO   Aug.   p16-7.   350w.   5
          DB   June 16   p40-3.   225w.   5

3852   MONTGOMERY, Buddy.   Ties.   Bean BW-102
          CAD   July   p23.   225w.   3½
          CK   Nov.   p64.   75w.   4

3853   MONTGOMERY, Wes.   Movin'.   Milestone M-47040 (2 discs)
       (Reissue)
          CAD   Aug.   p45.   175w.   4
          CO   Dec.   p22.   50w.   3
          GP   July   p129.   50w.   3

3854   MONTGOMERY, Wes.   The Small Group Recordings.   Verve
       VE-2-2513 (2 discs) (Reissue)
          CAD   Feb.   p26.   175w.   5
          DB   July 14   p45-7.   50w.   5
          GR   Dec.   p1162.   125w.   4
          JR   May   p98-9.   150w.   3½

SOU Nov. p62.   350w.   5

3855 MONTOLIU, Tete. Inner City 2029
      CAD Aug. p40.   150w.   4

3856 MONTOLIU, Tete. Catalonian Fire.   Inner City 2017
      CK Nov. p64.   75w. $4\frac{1}{2}$

3857 MONTOLIU, Tete. Music for Perla.   Inner City IC 2021
      CAD Sept. p41.   150w.   4

3858 MONTOLIU, Tete. "Songs for Love." Enja 2040
      CO Sept./Oct. p18-20.   225w.   4
      JJ Jan. p34.   300w.   3
      MM Jan. 1 p16.   50w.   3

3859 MONTOLIU, Tete. Yellow Dolphin Street.   Temeliss SJP
      107 (E)
      MM Nov. 19 p33.   150w. $2\frac{1}{2}$

3860 MOODY, James. Moody's Mood.   Chess Jazz Masters
      2ACMJ-403 (Reissue)
      RSP 1:3 p36.   200w.   2

3861 MOODY, James. Sun Journey.   Vanguard VSD 79381
      RFJ July p15-6.   500w.   4

3862 MOONSTRUCK. Lunatunes Records.   Sar 2003
      CAD Nov. p33.   200w. $2\frac{1}{2}$
      CC April p36.   50w.   3

3863 MOORE, Glen and David Frieson. In Concert.   Vanguard
      BSD 79383
      CAD July p44.   100w.   4

3864 MORATH, Max. Plays Ragtime.   Vanguard VSD 83/84 (2
      discs)
      AU March p97.   200w.   2

3865 MORATH, Max. The Ragtime Women.   Vanguard VSD 79402
      RT Nov. p4.   350w.   5

3866 MOREIRA, Airto. "I'm Fine, How Are You?" Warner Bros.
      B.S. 3084
      CAD Nov. p32.   75w. $2\frac{1}{2}$
      MG Nov. p53.   25w.   3

3867 MOREIRA, Airto. Promises of the Sun.   Arista AL 4116
      CAD June p22.   25w.   2
      DB April 21 p23.   400w.   3

3868 MORGAN, Frank. Frank Morgan.   GNP Crescendo 9041
      CAD July p43.   200w. $3\frac{1}{2}$

3869   MORGAN, Lee and Hank Mobley.   A-1.   SJI 1104 (Reissue)
       CAD   Feb.   p34.   75w. $3\frac{1}{2}$
       CO   Feb.   p22.   75w. $2\frac{1}{2}$

3870   MORITZ, Lori.   Lorelie on the Rocks.   Tri-ad 907
       CAD   Aug.   p23.   150w. $3\frac{1}{2}$

3871   MORRIS, Byron.   Byron and Gerald.   EPI-01
       CAD   Nov.   p29.   125w.   4

3872   MORRIS, Thomas.   Complete Set of 1923 Recordings.   Foun-
       tain FJ-113 (Reissue)
       JJ   March p34.   700w.   4
       MM   April 30 p32.   300w. $3\frac{1}{2}$
       ST   April-May p158-9.   350w.   3

3873   MOSES, Bob/Stanley Free.   Bittersuite in the Ozone.   Mo-
       town MZ001
       CAD   May   p10.   300w.   4

3874   MOSES, Kathryn.   CBC (Canada)
       SOU   May   p62.   150w.   4

3875   MOSS, Mike.   Upstream.   Fourth Stream ERG 013
       CAD   May   p10-1.   225w. $2\frac{1}{2}$
       JF   No. 48   p21.   75w.   4

3876   MOST, Sam.   But Beautiful.   Catalyst CAT 7609
       CAD   April   p40.   504w.   4
       DB   Nov. 17   p28.   75w.   3

3877   MOST, Sam.   Mostly Flute.   Xanadu 133
       CO   Aug.   p17.   275w.   5
       DB   June 16   p40-3.   225w. $4\frac{1}{2}$
       JM   1:2   p57-8.   400w. $3\frac{1}{2}$

3878   MOTHER Mallard's Portable Masterpiece Co.   Like a Duck
       to Water.   Earthquack EQ0002
       CAD   June   p12.   200w. $4\frac{1}{2}$
       CK   Oct.   p64-5.   100w.   3

3879   MOTIAN, Paul.   Conception Vessel.   ECM-1-1028
       CAD   Oct.   p54-5.   175w.   4
       MG   Oct.   p60-1.   50w. $3\frac{1}{2}$

3880   MOUZON, Alphonse.   Virtue.   MPS 68-130
       JF   No. 50   p19.   100w.   3
       MM   Sept. 10   p23.   250w.   4

3881   MTUME.   Alkebu-Lan.   Strata East SES 19724
       CAD   Feb.   p16-7.   200w.   4

3882   MULLIGAN, Gerry.   Idol Gossip.   Chiaroscuro CR-155

       CAD April p36. 240w. $4\frac{1}{2}$
       HF May p118. 250w. 4
       SR July p110-1. 250w. 5
       VV March 14 p81. 50w. $1\frac{1}{2}$

3883 MURIBUS, George. Brazilian Tapestry. Catalyst CAT 7602
       CK Oct. p65. 50w. 3

3884 MURIBUS, George. Trio '77. Catalyst CAT-7619
       CAD Aug. p45. 150w. 3
       CK Oct. p65. 50w. 3
       DB Nov. 17 p29. 75w. 3

3885 MURO, Don. It's Time. Sine Wave 0077
       CK Dec. p72. 200w. $3\frac{1}{2}$

3886 MURPHY, Turk. Live at Easy Street, Volume 2/3. Dawn
     Club 12018/9 (2 discs) (Reissue)
       ST April-May p156. 375w. 1

3887 MURPHY, Turk. Live from the Cinegrill, Vol. 1/2. Fair-
     mont F 111/2
       CAD Oct. p61-2. 200w. 4
       JR V9/#4 unpaged 150w. $3\frac{1}{2}$

3888 MURRAY, David. Flowers for Albert. India Navigation
     1026
       CAD April p42. 240w. $4\frac{1}{2}$
       JJ Feb. p34. 275w. 4
       MM March 26 p22. 600w. 4
       VV Feb. 28 p47. 200w. $1\frac{1}{2}$

3889 MURRAY, David. Low Class Conspiracy. Adelphi AD 5002
       CAD May p28, 30. 100w. 4
       CO Aug. p17-8. 650w. 4
       HF Sept. p142. 75w. 3
       JM Summer p56. 600w. 2
       MM Sept. 10 p29. 350w. $3\frac{1}{2}$
       MM Dec. 21 p16. 250w. $3\frac{1}{2}$
       RFJ July p17-8. 500w. $3\frac{1}{2}$
       VV Feb. 28 p47. 200w. $4\frac{1}{2}$

3890 MUSIC Improvisation Co. 1969-1971. Incus 17 (E)
       MM Jan. 1 p17. 350w. 3

3891 NAKAMURA, Terou. Rising Sun. Polydor PD-1-6097
       CAD April p44. 72w. 3
       DB Sept. 8 p38. 200w. $2\frac{1}{2}$
       GP June p137. 25w. 3

3892 NAMYSLOWSKI, Zbigniew. Kuyaniak Goes Funky. Muza
     SX 1230
       JF No. 45 p65-6. 600w. $4\frac{1}{2}$

3893   NANA.   Saravah SH 10044 (France)
       JF No. 46 p67, 69.   75w.   4

3894   NANA.   Africadeus.   Saravah SH 10039 (France)
       JF No. 46 p67, 69.   75w.   4

3895   NAPOLEON, Phil.   Featuring the Original Memphis Five.
       IAJRC 26
       CAD Nov. p41, 42.   275w. $3\frac{1}{2}$

3896   NATIONAL Jazz Ensemble.   Volume 2.   Chiaroscuro CRD
       151
       CAD Dec. p61-2.   300w.   3

3897   NATURAL Life.   All Music AS1-5006.   AS1 5006
       GP Dec. p153.   25w.   3

3898   NAUGHTON, Bobby.   The Haunt.   OTIC 1005
       CAD Feb. p14.   150w. $4\frac{1}{2}$
       CO Aug. p18.   950w.   5
       RFJ April p14.   600w.   3

3899   NAVARRO, Fats.   Milestone M-47041 (2 discs) (Reissue)
       CAD Aug. p38.   250w. $3\frac{1}{2}$
       RS Aug. 11 p66.   225w.   3

3900   NAVARRO, Fats.   Fat Girl.   Savoy 2216 (2 discs) (Reissue)
       CAD June p14.   125w.   5
       DB Sept. 8 p38-41.   50w.   5
       RS Aug. 11 p66.   225w.   3
       SOU May p62.   50w. $3\frac{1}{2}$

3901   NAVARRO, Fats.   Prime Source.   Blue Note BN LA 507 H2
       (2 discs) (Reissue)
       RS Aug. 11 p66.   225w.   3

3902   NAVARRO, Fats and Allen Eager.   Saturday Night Swing
       Session.   GI Records GSS 2
       JJ March p35.   250w.   4

3903   NEIL, Al.   The Al Neil Trio Retrospective: 1965-1968.
       Lodestone Records LR 7001 (Canada)
       CO Feb. p16.   500w. $2\frac{1}{2}$

3904   NELSON, Louis.   In Denmark, Vol. 1.   Storyville SLP 241
       RR Dec. p88.   50w.   3

3905   The NEW Black Eagle Jazz Band.   GHB 59
       CAD Jan. p38.   100w. $3\frac{1}{2}$

3906   NEW Black Eagle Jazz Band.   The N. B. E. J. B. in Manassas.
       Fat Cat 166
       CAD Jan. p38.   100w. $2\frac{1}{2}$

3907   NEW Black Eagle Jazz Band.   The N. B. E. J. B. on the River.
Dirty Shame 2002
CAD   Jan.   p38.   100w.   4

3908   NEW Dalta Ahkri.   Song of Humanity.   Kabell Records (K-3)
CAD   Nov.   p29.   150w.   4

3909   NEW Leviathan Oriental Foxtrot Orchestra.   Old King Tut.
Camel Race CR 19327
MR   July   p10.   350w. $3\frac{1}{2}$
RT   July   p9.   200w.   4

3910   NEW Orleans Rascals.   World Is Waiting for the Sunrise.
RCA JRS 7265 (Japan)
JR   V9/#3   unpaged   200w.   4

3911   NEW York Mary.   A Piece of the Apple.   Arista AL 1035
DB   Feb. 24   p22.   300w.   3

3912   NEWBORN, Phineas Jr.   Solo Piano.   Atlantic SD 1672
AU   Feb.   p84.   200w.   5

3913   NEWMAN, David.   Front Money.   Warner BS 2984
CAD   June   p20.   100w.   3
CRA   Sept.   p69.   250w.   2

3914   NEWTON, James.   Flute Music.   Flute Music Productions
FMP 001
CAD   Nov.   p28.   150w. $3\frac{1}{2}$
CO   Sept./Oct.   p16.   350w.   5
VV   June 13   p49.   100w. $4\frac{1}{2}$

3915   NEWTON All Stars.   Black Lion 303 (E)
MJ   Jan.   p29.   50w.   3

3916   NICHOLS, Herbie.   Bethlehem BCP 6028 (Reissue)
CAD   Dec.   p52.   200w.   4

3917   NICHOLS, Herbie.   The Third World.   Blue Note LA-485-H2
(2 discs) (Reissue)
CO   Aug.   p19-20.   1150w.   5

3918   NICHOLS, Red.   Class of '39.   Blue Lantern 1000
CAD   Sept.   p32-3.   200w.   4

3919   NICHOLS, Red.   Early Red Nichols.   Jazz Studies JS-3
(Reissue)
CO   Aug.   p20.   600w.   5

3920   NICRA.   Listen/Hear.   Ogun OG 010 (E)
MM   Aug. 20   p24.   275w.   4

3921   NIEMEN.   Katharsis.   Muza SX 1202

JF No. 48 p53-4.   650w.   4

3922 NIEWOOD, Gerry. Timepiece.   A & M Horizon SP-719
        CAD April p23.   108w.   2
        DB Oct. 6 p28.   200w.   3
        SOU April p62.   150w. $3\frac{1}{2}$

3923 NIGHTHAWKS. Live.   Adelphi AD 4110
        FOL Aug. p23-4.   350w. $3\frac{1}{2}$
        SR Jan.   p82.   200w.   4

3924 NIGHTHAWKS. Side Pocket Shot.   Adelphi AD 4115
        AU Dec.   p113.   400w.   4
        CAD Dec.   p39-40.   150w. $2\frac{1}{2}$
        RC Nov.   p8.   100w.   3

3925 NISTICO, Sal. Jazz A Confronto: Vol. 16.   Horo HLL 101-
        16 (Italy)
        CAD Sept.   p16-7.   150w. $4\frac{1}{2}$
        JF No. 50 p20-1.   50w.   4

3926 NISTICO, Sal. Just for Fun.   Ego 4002
        JF No. 46.   p60.   300w.   3

3927 NOONE, Jimmie. V. 4.   'Another Date with Jimmie. '   MCA
        510-138 (French Issue)
        ST June-July p194-5.   300w. $3\frac{1}{2}$

3928 NOONE, Jimmie. Chicago Rhythm, 1928-1930.   MCA510. 110
        (France) (Reissue)
        ST April-May p151.   450w.   4

3929 NOONE, Jimmie. 'Softly with Feeling. '   MCA 510120
        (France) (Reissue)
        ST June-July p194-5.   300w. $3\frac{1}{2}$

3930 NOONE, Jimmie and Earl Hines.   At the Apex Club, 1928.
        MCA510. 039 (France) (Reissue)
        ST April-May p151.   450w.   4

3931 NORMAN, Neil. Not of This Earth.   GNP GNPS 2111 (E)
        GP Dec.   p153.   50w.   3

3932 NORVO, Red. Savoy 2212 (2 discs) (Reissue)
        CAD Feb.   p42.   150w.   4
        CO Feb.   p22.   150w.   3
        DB March 10 p26-7.   100w. $3\frac{1}{2}$
        MJ Nov.   p22.   125w.   3
        RSP March-April p33.   350w. $4\frac{1}{2}$
        SOU Jan.   p48.   50w. $3\frac{1}{2}$

3933 NORVO, Red. Wartime Vibe-rations.   IAJRC 24
        CAD March p41.   50w. $3\frac{1}{2}$

3934   NOTO, Sam.   Act One.   Xanadu 127
       CAD   Feb.   p30.   200w. $3\frac{1}{2}$
       CO   Sept./Oct.   p16.   300w. $4\frac{1}{2}$
       DB   June 16   p40-3.   225w. $4\frac{1}{2}$

3935   NOVI.   Five, Four, Three....   Muza SX 1120 (Poland)
       JF   No. 50   p49, 51.   225w.   3

3936   NUNEZ, Flip.   My Own Time and Space.   Catalyst Cat-7603
       CK   Nov.   p65.   33w. $3\frac{1}{2}$

3937   O. D. J. B.   O. D. J. B. Revisited.   Rarities 36 (Reissue)
       CO   Sept./Oct.   p23.   150w.   5

3938   O. M. C. I.   Contro.   L'Orchestra OLP 10-004 (Italy)
       JF   No. 49   p22.   50w.   3

3939   OGERMAN, Claus.   Gate of Dreams.   Warner BS 3006
       CAD   March   p45-6.   75w. $2\frac{1}{2}$
       DB   Sept. 8   p35.   250w.   3
       MG   June   p53.   125w. $4\frac{1}{2}$

3940   OLD Time Jungle Cats.   In Jubilee.   Swiss Jazz ATLP 6320
       (Switzerland)
       JF   No. 50   p21.   50w. $2\frac{1}{2}$

3941   OLIVER, King.   Smithsonian Collection 001 (Reissue)
       CO   Aug.   p21-2.   350w.   4

3942   OLIVER, King.   Volume One.   Classic Jazz Masters CJM
       19 (Reissue)
       CO   Sept./Oct.   p23.   200w.   4
       RSP   March-April   p34-5.   425w. $4\frac{1}{2}$

3943   OLIVER, Sy.   Above All.   Above All Records 10001
       CAD   Oct.   p43-4.   125w.   2
       MJ   July   p73.   200w.   3

3944   OLIVER, Sy.   Easy Walker.   Jazz Club JC 3802 (Reissue)
       JF   No. 46   p61-2.   650w. $3\frac{1}{2}$

3945   OM.   Rautionaha.   Japo 60016 (West Germany)
       JF   No. 49   p22.   50w.   4

3946   ONENESS of Ju Ju.   African Rhythms.   Blackfire BF 19751
       CAD   May   p22.   50w. $2\frac{1}{2}$

3947   ONENESS of Ju Ju.   Space Jungle Luv.   Blackfire 19754
       CAD   May   p22.   50w. $2\frac{1}{2}$

3948   OPA.   Goldenwings.   Milestone 9069
       CAD   Jan.   p18.   100w. $3\frac{1}{2}$
       CK   Jan.   p50.   100w.   4

DB   Feb. 10 p21.   200w.   3
RR   March   p97.   200w.   4

3949   OPA.   Magic Time.   Milestone M9078
       CAD   Aug.   p28.   125w.   3½
       MG   Sept.   p53.   75w.   3

3950   OREGON.   Friends.   Vanguard VSD 79370
       CAD   July   p44.   100w.   3
       DB   Nov. 3 p21.   325w.   5
       MG   July   p53.   125w.   3½

3951   ORIGINAL Memphis Five.   Folkways RBF 26 (Reissue)
       CO   Sept. /Oct.   p16-7.   450w.   3
       RA   Nov. /Dec.   p6.   25w.   3

3952   ORTEGA, Anthony.   A Delanto.   Jazz Records 108
       CAD   Feb.   p37.   175w.   3

3953   OSBORNE, Mike.   Marcel's Muse.   Ogun OG 810 (E)
       MM   Oct. 15 p27.   250w.   4

3954   OSBORNE, Mike and Stan Tracey.   Tandem.   Ogun OB 210
       (E)
       JJ   May   p50.   200w.   4½

3955   OSCARSSON, Ivan.   Ivan the Terrible.   Dragon 7 (Sweden)
       CAD   Nov.   p47, 48.   215w.   3

3956   Les OUBLIES de Jazz Ensemble.   That Nigger Music.   Touche
       TRLPS 101
       SN   April   p11.   600w.   3

3957   OUSLEY, Harold.   The People's Groove.   Muse MR 5107
       CAD   Dec.   p37.   100w.   1½

3958   OWENS, Jimmy.   Young Man on the Move.   Horizon SP 712
       JJ   Jan.   p34.   200w.   0
       RR   March   p97.   100w.   3½

3959   OXLEY, Tony.   February Papers.   Incus 18 (E)
       MM   Oct. 29 p28.   200w.   3

3960   PACIFIC Salt.   Live.   Little Mountain LMP 105
       CAD   Nov.   p36, 37.   275w.   4

3961   PALAME, Emil.   Make Room.   Mark Records MES 51213
       CAD   April   p8.   180w.   5

3962   PAPAI, Roy.   Seeds.   Ultra-Nova UN 1002/7
       CAD   March   p26.   175w.   3

3963   PARIS Quartet.   Jazz A Confronto: Vol. 28.   Horo HLL

101-28 (Italy)
CAD Sept. p18. 150w. $3\frac{1}{2}$

3964   PARKER, Charlie. Apartment Jam Sessions. Zim 1006
CAD Nov. p48. 125w. $3\frac{1}{2}$
DB Oct. 6 p35-7. 100w. $4\frac{1}{2}$

3965   PARKER, Charlie. At the Pershing Ballroom. ZIM 1003
DB Oct. 6 p35-7. 100w. 3
MM July 16 p28. 150w. 3
RSP March-April p35-6. 300w. $3\frac{1}{2}$
VV March 21 p55. 100w. $4\frac{1}{2}$

3966   PARKER, Charlie. Bird at the Roost. Savoy SJL-1108
(Reissue)
CAD Oct. p41. 200w. $2\frac{1}{2}$
CO Dec. p24. 75w. 3
RR Oct. p90. 75w. 3

3967   PARKER, Charlie. Bird with Strings. CBS HG 34832 (Reissue)
VV Dec. 19 p80-1. 250w. 2

3968   PARKER, Charlie. Bird's Next. Vogue (France)
BM Jan. p53. 125w. 5

3969   PARKER, Charlie. Encores Savoy 1107 (Reissue)
CAD June p14. 125w. 5
DB Sept. 8 p38-41. 50w. 3
MM Oct. 8 p36. 100w. 3
SOU May p62. 100w. $4\frac{1}{2}$
VV March 21 p55. 100w. $2\frac{1}{2}$

3970   PARKER, Charlie. One Night in Birdland. CBS JG 34808
(2 discs) (Reissue)
VV Dec. 19 p80-1. 250w. 4

3971   PARKER, Charlie. The Verve Years, 1950-1. Verve VE-
2-2512 (2 discs) (Reissue)
CAD Feb. p40-1. 225w. $3\frac{1}{2}$
DB July 14 p45-7. 75w. 4
SR May p98-9. 150w. 3
VV March 21 p55. 100w. 3

3972   PARKER, Charlie. Yardbird in Lotus Hand. Spotlite SPJ
123
MM March 5 p32. 350w. 3

3973   PARKER, Errol and the Contemporary Jazz Ensemble. African Samba. Sahara 1006
CAD Feb. p32-3. 200w. 2

3974   PARKER, Evan. Saxophone Solos. Incus 19 (E)

JJ Jan.   p34.   400w.   4

3975 PARKER, Evan and Paul Lytton.   Ra 1+2.   Ring Records
      016016 (West Germany)
          CAD Nov.   p20.   150w.   4

3976 PARLAN, Horace.   Arrival.   Inner City Records IC 2012
          CAD   March p30.   150w.   3
          CK   March 11 p56.   100w. $4\frac{1}{2}$

3977 PARLAN, Horace.   No Blues.   Inner City 2056
          CAD   Dec.   p37-8.   100w.   3

3978-9 PARSONS, Will.   Iowa Ear Music.   Cornpride 28155
          CAD   May p11.   175w.   3

3980 PASCOAL, Hermeta.   Slaves Mass.   Warner Bros., BS
      2980
          CAD   March p45-6.   75w. $2\frac{1}{2}$
          CK   May p49.   150w. $4\frac{1}{2}$
          HF   March p146.   250w.   4
          MG   May p53.   125w. $3\frac{1}{2}$
          RS   June 2 p83.   100w.   2

3981 PASS, Joe.   Virtuoso.   Pablo 2310 708
          CO   Sept. /Oct.   p17.   300w.   3

3982 PASS, Joe.   Virtuoso #2.   Pablo 2310 788
          CAD   June p42.   125w.   4
          DB   May 5 p22, 24.   475w.   5
          GP   Sept.   p119.   125w. $2\frac{1}{2}$
          GR   July p237.   50w.   4

3983 PASTORIUS, Jaco.   Epic PE 33949
          JM   1:2 p58.   200w. $4\frac{1}{2}$

3984 PASTORIUS, Jaco, Pat Metheny, Bruce Ditmas, Paul Bley.
      Improvising Artists 373846
          GP   March p112.   175w.   4
          MM   Feb. 26 p33.   400w. $3\frac{1}{2}$
          SR   March p123.   150w.   2

3985 PATTERSON, Don.   Movin' Up.   Muse 5121
          CAD   Nov.   p33.   125w.   3

3986 PAUNETTO, Bobby.   Commit to Memory.   Pathfinder 1776
          HF   Oct.   p158.   450w. $3\frac{1}{2}$

3987 PAUVROS, Jean-Francois, Gabby Bizien.   No Man's Land.
      Un-Deux-Trois Records 6 (France)
          MM   Jan. 1 p16.   75w. $3\frac{1}{2}$

3988 PAYNE, John.   The John Payne-Louis Levin Band.   Mercury

SRM 1-1166
  CAD   Aug.   p24.   100w.   2
  MG   Aug.   p63.   100w. $2\frac{1}{2}$

3989   PAYNE, John.   The Razor's Edge.   Arista-Freedom 1036
  CK   Aug.   p49.   100w.   4
  DB   April 21   p24.   350w. $3\frac{1}{2}$
  MG   Jan.   75w. $2\frac{1}{2}$
  RS   Feb. 24   p69.   200w.   3

3990   PEACOCK, Gary.   Tales of Another.   ECM-1-1101
  CAD   Nov.   p44, 45.   400w. $4\frac{1}{2}$
  MG   Nov.   p53.   25w. $3\frac{1}{2}$
  MM   Sept. 3   p25.   350w. $3\frac{1}{2}$

3991   PEPPER, Art.   Discoveries.   Savoy 2217 (2 discs) (Reissue)
  CAD   June   p14.   125w.   4
  DB   Sept. 8   p38-41.   50w. $3\frac{1}{2}$
  SOU   May   p62.   50w.   4

3992   PEPPER, Art.   Early Art.   Blue Note BN-LA591-H2 (2
  discs) (Reissue)
  CO   Sept./Oct.   p17.   425w.   4
  DB   Aug. 11   200w.   5

3993   PEPPER, Art.   The Early Show.   Xanadu 108
  CAD   March   p42.   150w.   3
  CO   Sept./Oct.   p17.   225w. $3\frac{1}{2}$
  RFJ   Oct.   p17.   600w. $3\frac{1}{2}$
  SOU   April   p58.   200w.   4

3994   PEPPER, Art.   Living Legend.   Contemporary S7633
  CAD   Jan.   p40.   300w. $3\frac{1}{2}$

3995   PEPPER, Art.   The Trip.   Contemporary S 7638
  CAD   Sept.   p46.   250w.   3
  MM   Aug. 27   p24.   300w. $3\frac{1}{2}$

3996   PEPPER, Art.   The Way It Was - 1950's.   Vintage Jazz
  VJR 111453
  CAD   June   p26.   175w.   4

3997   PERKINS, Bill.   On Stage.   Pacific Jazz 1221
  CAD   Feb.   p17.   325w.   5

3998   PERSON, Houston.   Harmony.   Mercury SRM 1-1151
  CAD   Aug.   p24.   100w.   3

3999   PERSON, Houston.   Stolen Sweets.   Muse MR 5110
  CAD   June   p32.   100w. $3\frac{1}{2}$

4000   PETERSON, Hannibal Morium.   Hannibal in Berlin.   MPS
  68152

MM   July 23 p22.   378w.   4

4001   PETERSON, Oscar.   Verve 2332088 (E) (Reissue)
       RR Oct.   p89-90.   25w.   3

4002   PETERSON, Oscar.   In Russia.   Pablo 2625 711 (2 discs)
       AU April p88.   250w.   5
       SMG Jan.   p27.   100w.   4

4003   PETERSON, Oscar.   Rockin' in Rhythm.   RCA FXMI-7327
       (Reissue)
       CO Aug.   p23-4.   100w.   4

4004   PETERSON, Oscar.   Special Magic of.   Verve 2317 136 (E)
       (Reissue)
       MM Aug. 20 p23.   150w.   4

4005   PETERSON, Oscar.   Travelin' On.   MPS 20693 (Reissue)
       CO Feb.   p23.   100w.   4

4006   PETERSON, Oscar.   Trio in Transition.   Mercury EMS
       2-405 (2 discs) (Reissue)
       DB April 21 p38.   150w. $3\frac{1}{2}$

4007   PETERSON, Oscar and Joe Pass.   Porgy & Bess.   Pablo
       2310-779
       CAD Jan.   p27-9.   225w.   4
       CK Jan.   p50.   100w.   5
       DB Feb. 10 p19-20.   250w. $2\frac{1}{2}$
       GP Jan.   p97.   50w.   4
       JJ Feb.   p34.   500w.   5
       JM 1:2 p55.   275w.   5
       SR Feb.   p109.   200w.   0

4008   PETERSON, Oscar, Joe Pass and Ray Brown.   The Giants.
       Pablo 2310-796.   Cart. K10-796.   Cass. S10-796
       CAD Oct.   p35.   175w.   3
       DB Oct. 20 p24-5.   300w.   3
       MM Sept. 24 p32.   250w. $3\frac{1}{2}$
       RR Oct.   p89.   25w.   3
       SR Dec.   150w.   3

4009   PETTIFORD, Oscar.   Finest of.   Bethlehem BCP 6007 (Re-
       issue)
       CAD Dec.   p54-5.   100w.   2

4010   PHILLIPS, Barre.   Mountainscapes.   ECM 1076
       CAD March p42.   100w. $2\frac{1}{2}$
       JF No. 45 p66.   450w. $3\frac{1}{2}$
       PRM April p45.   275w. $3\frac{1}{2}$
       SOU March p44.   50w.   3

4011   PHILLIPS, Flip.   Phillips' Head.   Choice 1013

CAD Jan. p36-7. 175w. 2
SR May p101. 175w. 4

4012 PHILLIPS, Sonny. My Black Blower. Muse 5118
      CAD Oct. p56. 100w. 4

4013 PHOENIX Symphony Ragtime Ensemble. World Jazz Records
      S-12
      MJ Dec. p25-6. 75w. $3\frac{1}{2}$

4014 PIANO Choir. Handscapes. Strata-East SES 10750
      JJ April p34. 200w. $3\frac{1}{2}$

4015 PIERANUNZI, Enrico. "The Day After the Silence. " EDI-
      PAN SML 103 (Italy)
      CO Sept./Oct. p18-20. 225w. 4

4016 PIERCE, DeDe and His New Orleans Stompers. Biograph
      Center CEN 5 (Reissue)
      RR June p95. 50w. $3\frac{1}{2}$

4017 PIERCE, Nat; Freddie Cap. Juggernaut. Concord CJ 40
      DB Nov. 3 p26-7. 225w. 4
      MJ Sept. p30. 200w. $3\frac{1}{2}$

4018 PIG'S Eye Jass. Fidelity First Vol. 2
      AU Jan. p93. 350w. $4\frac{1}{2}$

4019 PIZZARELLI, Bucky and Bud Freeman. Buck & Bud. Fly-
      ing Dutchman BDL 1-1378
      CAD Jan. p27-8. 225w. $3\frac{1}{2}$
      DB April 21 p22. 300w. 5
      GP Jan. p97. 225w. 4
      HF Jan. p145. 150w. 4
      JM 1:2 p58, 60, 62. 400w. $4\frac{1}{2}$
      SR Feb. p84. 400w. 4

4020 PIZZI, Ray. Conception. Pablo 2310-795
      CAD Aug. p43. 350w. 4
      MM Sept. 17 p28. 200w. $4\frac{1}{2}$

4021 The PLAYERS Association. Vanguard VSD 79384
      CAD April p43. 75w. 2
      MG May p53. 125w. $3\frac{1}{2}$

4022 PLETCHER, Tom. Sons of Bix. Fairmont F110
      CAD May p22-3. 50w. $2\frac{1}{2}$

4023 POINTER, Noel. Phantazia. Blue Note BN LA 736
      DB Sept. 8 p33-4. 250w. 3
      MJ Sept. p32. 50w. $1\frac{1}{2}$
      SOU Oct. p59. 100w. 5

4024   The POLLWINNERS.   Straight Ahead.   Contemporary S7635
        SOU   May   p60.   200w. $4\frac{1}{2}$

4025   PONDER, Jimmy.   White Room.   Impulse 9327
        CAD   May   p12.   50w.   3

4026   PONTY, Jean-Luc.   Canteloupe Island.   Blue Note BN LA
        632 (Reissue)
        DB   Aug.   11   200w.   5

4027   PONTY, Jean-Luc.   Enigmatic Ocean.   Atlantic 19110
        CAD   Nov.   p30.   25w.   4
        GP   Dec.   p153.   75w.   4
        MG   Dec.   p57.   150w.   3
        RSP   Nov.-Dec.   p35.   600w. $2\frac{1}{2}$

4028   PONTY, Jean-Luc.   Imaginary Voyage.   Atlantic SD 18195
        DB   Feb.   24   p28.   275w.   3
        GP   June   p137.   50w. $3\frac{1}{2}$
        MG   Feb.   p57.   125w.   3
        RS   March   24   p74.   200w. $3\frac{1}{2}$

4029   PONTY, Jean-Luc.   Sonata Erotica.   Inner City IC 1003
        DB   June   2   p22.   125w.   3

4030   PONTY, Jean-Luc and Stephane Grappelli.   Ponty/Grappelli.
        Inner City IC 1005
        DB   June   2   p22.   125w. $4\frac{1}{2}$
        SR   Jan.   p106.   50w.   2

4031   PORT of Dixie Ragtime Band.   Showcase.   P. O. D. Records
        P. O. D.   101
        CAD   Sept.   p42.   175w. $4\frac{1}{2}$
        CAD   Sept.   p22.   125w.   5

4032   PORTER, Roy.   Inner Feeling.   Bel-ad 1006
        CAD   July   p23.   200w. $3\frac{1}{2}$

4033   POWELL, Baden.   Brazilian Rhythms.   Philips SON032
        GR   April   p1608.   50w. $2\frac{1}{2}$
        MM   Jan.   1   p16.   50w. $1\frac{1}{2}$

4034   POWELL, Bud.   Bud in Paris.   Xanadu 102
        CO   Feb.   p20-1.   525w.   3

4035   POWELL, Bud.   Swingin' with Bud.   RCA VXM1-7312
        (France) (Reissue)
        JJ   May   p50, 52.   250w.   4

4036   PRIESTER, Julian and Marine Intrusian.   Polarization.   ECM-
        1-1098
        CAD   Aug.   p41.   150w. $3\frac{1}{2}$
        MM   July   2   p22.   400w.   5

4037   PULLEN, Don.   Five to Go.   Horo H202 (Italy)
       CAD Sept.   p17.   150w.   4½
       CO   April p19-20.   250w.   5

4038   PULLEN, Don.   Healing Force.   Black Saint 0010
       CAD Feb.   p38-9.   150w.   2½
       CO   Sept./Oct.   p18-20.   225w.   4
       MM   May 14 p36.   300w.   4½

4039   PULLEN, Don.   Jazz A Confronto: Vol. 21.   Horo HLL
       101-21 (Italy)
       CAD Sept.   p17.   125w.   4

4040   PULLEN, Don.   Solo Piano Album.   Sackville 3008
       CO   Sept./Oct.   p18.   450w.   4½

4041   PULLEN, Don.   Tomorrow's Promises.   Atlantic SP 1699
       CAD July p22.   200w.   3
       CK   Aug.   p49.   25w.   2½
       MM   Sept. 3 p24.   300w.   3

4042   PURIM, Flora.   Encounter.   Milestone M-9077
       CAD Aug.   p26.   125w.   3½
       MG   Aug.   p63.   125w.   3

4043   PURIM, Flora.   500 Miles High at Montreux.   Milestone
       M-9070
       CAD Jan.   p32.   100w.   2½
       CRA Jan.   p69.   600w.   2
       MM   March 19 p31.   375w.   2½
       RR   March p97.   150w.   4

4044   PURIM, Flora.   Nothing Will Be as It Was ... Tomorrow.
       Warner Bros. BS 2985
       CAD May p13.   50w.   1
       DB   May 19 250w.   3
       HF   June p127.   300w.   3
       MM   June 18 p21.   150w.   3
       RR   Sept.   p96.   50w.   3

4045   QUEEN City Ragtime Ensemble.   Zeno HZ99
       RA   Sept./Oct.   p5-6.   100w.   2½

4046   RADUCANU, Johnny.   Jazz in My Country.   Electrecord STM
       EDE 01186 (Rumania)
       JF   No. 50 p21.   50w.   3

4047   RAI, Vasant.   Spring Flowers.   Vanguard VSD 79379
       DB   April 21 p26.   250w.   5
       MG   April p53.   75w.   3

4048   RANEY, Charles.   Live in Tokyo.   Xanadu 132
       CAD April p30-1.   168w.   4½

4049   RANEY, Jimmy. Live in Tokyo.   Xanadu 132
       DB June 16 p40-3. 225w. 5
       GP May p129. 25w. 3
       SOU April p56. 100w. 4

4050   RAVA, Enrico. Il Giro del Giorno in 80 Mondi.   Black Saint
       0011 (Italy)
       CAD May p18-9. 150w. 3

4051   RAVA, Enrico. Jazz A Confronto: Vol. 14.   Horo HLL 101-
       14 (Italy)
       CAD Sept. p16. 150w. $3\frac{1}{2}$

4052   RAVA, Enrico. The Plot. ECM-1-1078
       CAD Oct. p42. 125w. $2\frac{1}{2}$
       DB Nov. 17 p20. 300w. 4
       JF No. 48 p23. 75w. 4

4053   REFORM Art Unit. R. A. U. 1005
       CAD April p38. 144w. 3
       JF No. 46 p66. 450w. 4

4054   REICHEL, Hans. Bonobo. FMP 0280
       CO Sept. /Oct. p20. 450w. 3

4055   REID, Steve. Nova. Mustevic Sound MLS 2001
       JF No. 47 p69. 25w. 2
       JF No. 48 p49. 250w. 3
       SR Jan. p106. 250w. 4

4056   REID, Steve. Rhythmatism. Mustevic 1001
       DB June 2 p29. 225w. $2\frac{1}{2}$
       JF No. 47 p69. 50w. 2
       JF No. 48 p49-50. 250w. 3

4057   REILLY, Jack. Carousel ATM 1001
       JR V9/#3 unpaged 25w. 2

4058   REILLY, Jack. Blue-Sean-Green. Carousel 1001
       JF No. 49 p48. 400w. $2\frac{1}{2}$

4059   REILLY, Jack. Tributes. Carousel CLP 1002
       DB March 24 p51. 250w. 3
       SR Jan. p108. 150w. 3

4060   REINHARDT, Django. GNP 9039 (Reissue)
       CAD Oct. p23-4. 75w. 4

4061   REINHARDT, Django. Django -- The Later Years. La
       Roulotte MA3
       GP Jan. p97. 50w. 3
       RSP March-April p33-4. 300w. 4

4062   REINHARDT, Django. Swing It Lightly. Columbia KC 31479
       JR V9/#4 unpaged 75w. 4

4063   RENDELL, Don. Just Music. Spotlite 502
       CAD Nov. p45, 46. 150w. 4½

4064   RETURN to Forever. Musicmagic. Columbia PC 34682
       BM Oct. p50. 175w. 2
       CK June p49. 125w. 4
       DB June 2 p20. 300w. 3½
       HF July p154. 500w. 2
       MM July 16 p26. 250w. 1
       RS May 19 325w. 2

4065   RICH, Buddy. Both Sides. Mercury EMS 2-402 (2 discs)
       (Reissue)
       DB April 21 p40. 150w. 3

4066   RICH, Buddy. One Night Stand, Vol. 2. Joyce 1025 (Re-
       issue)
       JM 1:2 p66. 50w. 3

4067   RICH, Buddy. Plays and Plays and Plays. RCA CPL 1-
       2273
       CAD Oct. p49. 175w. 4
       DB Nov. 17 p23-4. 225w. 3½
       MM Oct. 8 p36. 450w. 2½

4068   RICH, Buddy. Speak No Evil. RCA 1503
       JF No. 47 p69. 25w. 2

4069   RICH, Buddy and Gene Krupa. Drum Battle. Verve 2317.116
       (E) (Reissue)
       CAD Feb. p432-3. 200w. 4

4070   RICHARDS, Trevor. On Tour USA. Crescent Jazz Produc-
       tions CJP-4
       CAD July p41. 225w. 4
       JR V9/#3 unpaged 150w. 3½

4071   RICHMOND, Donnie. Jazz A Confronto, Vol. 25. Horo HLL
       101-25 (Italy)
       CO April p20. 250w. 4

4072   RIDGLEY, Tommy. Through the Years. SONO 1007
       CAD Dec. p41-2. 100w. 2½

4073   RILEY, Doug. Dreams. PM PMR 007 (Canada)
       SOU Jan. p49. 100w. 3

4074   RIMMINGTON, Sammy. Storyville SLP 255
       GR March p1471. 100w. 1½
       JJ Jan. p34. 625w. 3

4075   RIVERS, Sam. The Quest. Red Record VPA 106
            CO Sept./Oct. p20-1. 700w. 5
            JF No. 49 p48. 275w. 4

4076   RIVERS, Sam and Dave Holland. Vol. 2. IAI 373848
            CAD May p24, 26. 100w. 5
            CK Aug. p49. 25w. $2\frac{1}{2}$
            RFJ May p18-9. 275w. 5

4077   RIZZI, Tony. Disco Pacific. Morrhythm 006
            CAD April p11. 120w. $2\frac{1}{2}$

4078   RIZZI, Tony. Surfin' Pacific. MorRhythm 010
            CAD Oct. p23. 50w. 1

4079   ROACH, Max. The Many Sides of. Trip TLP 5599 (Reissue)
            RFJ July p16. 450w. 4

4080   ROBINSON, Jim. Biograph-Center CEN 8 (Reissue)
            RR June p95. 50w. $3\frac{1}{2}$

4081   ROBINSON, Jim. Economy Hall Breakdown. Pearl PS-5
            CAD May p27. 50w. $2\frac{1}{2}$
            HF June p132. 350w. 3
            MJ May p31. 50w. 3
            JR V9/#4 unpaged 50w. 3
            SR June p125 . 100w. 0

4082   ROBINSON, Joyce. The Amazing Mrs. Robinson. Big Ben
        BB 0008 (E)
            RR Feb. p67. 75w. 2

4083   RODNEY, Red. The Red Tornado. Muse MR 5088
            CO Sept./Oct. p21-2. 500w. 4

4084   ROGERS, Shorty. Blues Express. RCA FXL 17234 (France)
        (Reissue)
            JJ April p34. 250w. $3\frac{1}{2}$

4085   ROLLINS, Sonny. The Way I Feel. Milestone M-9074
            BM June p48. 175w. 2
            CAD April p43-4. 128w. $2\frac{1}{2}$
            DB June 16 p30-1. 400w. $3\frac{1}{2}$
            MM Aug. 13 p22. 175w. 3
            RFJ July p18. 300w. 3

4086   ROMAO, Dom Um. Hotmosphere. Pablo 2310-777
            CAD Jan. p32. 100w. 3
            DB June 2 p26-7. 200w. $3\frac{1}{2}$
            JJ Feb. p34-6. 300w. 4

4087   ROSE, Wally. Whippin' the Keys. Blackbird C 12010
            JR V9/#4 unpaged 100w. $3\frac{1}{2}$

MR   Feb.   p12.   400w.   2

4088   ROSOLINI, Frank and Conte Candoli.   Conversation.   MPS
        20 227 146
              MM   March 5   p32.   225w.   3½

4089   ROSS, Arnold.   Barbed Wire, Bums and Beans.   Jazz Chron-
        icle JLS 76 3/4 (2 discs) (Reissue)
              CAD   March   p28-9.   100w.   3
              MM   Aug.   27   p24.   175w.   3

4090   ROUSE, Charlie.   Cinnamon Flower.   Douglas Recordings
        NBLP 7044
              CAD   April   p10.   100w.   2½
              MG   June   p53.   100w.   3
              RFJ   Sept.   p12.   300w.   4
              SR   Aug.   p106.   125w.   5

4091   ROUSE, Charlie.   Two Is One.   Strata East SES 19746
              CAD   Feb.   p16.   75w.   2

4092   ROWLES, Jimmy.   Grandpaws.   Choice 1014
              CAD   Jan.   p45.   200w.   3½
              RFJ   July   p16-7.   450w.   3½
              SR   April   p112, 113.   260w.   4

4093   ROYAL Blue.   N.Y. Aint So Bad.   Survival 111
              CAD   April   p40-1.   168w.   2

4094   RUDD, Roswell.   Inside Job.   Arista AL 1029
              CO   Dec.   p14.   200w.   3½
              DB   Feb.   10   p19.   200w.   4

4095   RUIZ, Hilton.   Piano Man.   Inner City 2036
              CAD   Aug.   p40.   150w.   3½

4096   RUIZ, Jorge Lopez.   Amor Buenos Aires.   Catalyst CAT-
        7908
              MJ   July   p73.   200w.   3
              SR   Oct.   p130.   225w.   3½

4097   RUSSELL, George.   Electronic Sonata for Souls Loved by
        Nature.   Strata East SES 19761
              JJ   March   p35.   225w.   3

4098   RUSSELL, George.   Guitar.   Dobre 1002
              CAD   June   p22.   100w.   2

4099   RUTHERFORD, Paul.   The Gentle Harm of the Bourgeosie.
        Emanem 3305
              CO   Dec.   p14.   200w.   3½
              VV   July   25   p49, 51.   500w.   5

4100   RUTHERFORD, Paul. Old Moers Almanac. Ring Records
       01014 (West Germany)
              CAD Nov. p18. 100w. $3\frac{1}{2}$

4101   RYPDAL, Terje. After the Rain. ECM ECM-1-1083. Cart.
       8T1-1083. Cass. CT1-1083
              CAD March p39. 100w. 3
              DB March 24 300w. 3
              GP June p137. 100w. 4
              JF No. 48 p50-1. 325w. 3
              MM Jan. 8 p20. 425w. $4\frac{1}{2}$
              SOU March p44. 100w. $2\frac{1}{2}$
              SR July p111. 150w. 3

4102   RZEWSKI, Frederic. No Place to Go but Around. Finnador
       SR 9011
              DB May 5 p24. 250w. 4

4103   SALVADOR, Don. My Family. Muse MR 5085
              CAD Feb. p39. 75w. $4\frac{1}{2}$
              MG April p53. 100w. $3\frac{1}{2}$

4104   SANBORN, David. Warner BS 2957
              DB April 21 p23-4. 300w. 3
              MM Jan. 1 p15. 250w. $2\frac{1}{2}$

4105   SANBORN, David. Promise Me the Moon. Warner Bros.
       BS 3051
              CAD Aug. p26. 100w. $2\frac{1}{2}$
              CRA Sept. p69. 250w. $2\frac{1}{2}$
              DB Dec. 1 p30-1. 300w. 3
              MG Aug. p63. 125w. 3
              RS Sept. 8 p118. 450w. 2

4106   SANTAMARIA, Mongo. Skins. Milestone M 47038 (Reissue)
              DB April 21 p26-30. 250w. $2\frac{1}{2}$

4107   SANTAMARIA, Mongo Safrito. Voya JMVS-53
              CRA March p70-2. 450w. 5

4108   SAVOY Orpheans and Havana Band. Volume 1, 1923-24.
       Neovox (Reissue)
              CAC March p475-76. 100w. 3

4109   SAYLES, Charlie. The Raw Harmonica Blues of. Dusty
       Road 701
              CAD April p32-3. 216w. 3
              LB Nov./Dec. p31. 175w. 3
              RSP V1/#3 p4. 300w. 4

4110   SCHARF, Stuart. The Disguises Album. Laissez-Faire
       SD-01
              CAD April p6. 275w. $2\frac{1}{2}$

Jazz   389

4111   SCHIAFFINA, Giancarlo. Jazz A Confronto: Vol. 5. Horo
       HLL 101-5 (Italy)
           CAD Sept. p14-5. 200w. 4

4112   SCHIANO, Mano. Jazz A Confronto: Vol. 8. Horo HLL
       101-8 (Italy)
           CAD Sept. p15. 250w. 4

4113   SCHIFRIN, Lalo. Black Widow. CTI 5000
           SMG May p27. 100w. 3

4114   SCHIFRIN, Lalo. Towering Toccata. CTI 7-5003
           CAD Aug. p164. 250w. 3
           CAD June p20. 75w. $3\frac{1}{2}$
           CK Aug. p49. 25w. 3

4115   SCHLIPPENBACK, Alex and Svenake Johansson. Live at the
       Latin Quarter. FMP 0310
           CAD July p13. 200w. $3\frac{1}{2}$
           CO Dec. p16. 300w. 3

4116   SCHNITTER, Dave. Invitation. Muse 5108
           CAD April p18. 216w. 5

4117   SCHOENBERG, Eric. Acoustic Guitar. Rounder Records
       3017
           GP Nov. p137. 175w. 4

4118   SCHOOF, Manfred. Scales. Japo 60013 (West Germany)
           CAD Feb. p26-7. 175w. 3
           JF No. 46 p63-4. 550w. $4\frac{1}{2}$
           MM Feb. 12 p28. 350w. $3\frac{1}{2}$

4119   SCHWEIZER, Irene. Wilde Senoritas. FMP 0330
           CAD July p13. 200w. $4\frac{1}{2}$

4120   SCHWEIZER, Irene and Rudiger Carl. Messer. FMP 0290
           JF No. 50 p53, 55. 375w. 4

4121   SCOTT, Shirley. One for Me. Strata East SES 7430
           CAD Feb. p16. 125w. 5
           CO Dec. p16-7. 300w. $3\frac{1}{2}$

4122   SCOTT-HERON, Gil and Brian Jackson. Winter in America.
       Strata East SES 19742
           CAD Feb. p17. 50w. 2

4123   SEALY, Joe. Sailin' Home. Solar SAR 2004
           CAD Oct. p56. 75w. 4

4124   SEAWIND. CTI 5002
           CAD April p43. 84w. 2
           DB April 1 p28-9. 225w. 3

HF April p148. 50w. 3
MM May 14 p33. 50w. 1
SR May p101. 150w. 3

4125 SEIFERT, Zbigniew. Capitol ST-11618
      CAD June p21. 100w. 3
      CK Aug. p49. 25w. $2\frac{1}{2}$
      DB Oct. 6 p34. 200w. $2\frac{1}{2}$
      JF No. 50 p20. 75w. $2\frac{1}{2}$

4126 SENENSKY, Bernie. New Life. PM Records PMR006
      (Canada)
      CO Dec. p16. 500w. 3

4127 SHANK, Bud. Sunshine Express. Concord Jazz CJ-20
      SR Jan. p108. 150w. 4

4128 SHANKAR, Ravi. Grazing Dreams. ECM 1096
      RR Nov. p116. 25w. 4

4129 SHARP, Randy and Orchestra. First in Line. Nautilus NR1
      AU May p92. 600w. $2\frac{1}{2}$
      HF July p123. 200w. $2\frac{1}{2}$
      SOU Oct. p63. 250w. 5

4130 SHAVERS, Charlie and Budd Johnson. The Last Session.
      Black and Blue 33032 (France)
      CO Dec. p14-5. 325w. 3

4131 SHAVERS, Charlie and Budd Johnson. Ya! Ya! Black and
      Blue (France)
      CO Dec. p14-5. 325w. 3

4132 SHAW, Charles Bobo. Concere Ntasia. Justice JU 101
      CAD March p31-2. 100w. $3\frac{1}{2}$

4133 SHAW, Woody. Concert Ensemble at the Berliner Jazzstage.
      Muse MR 5139
      CAD June p41. 150w. $4\frac{1}{2}$
      CO Dec. p17-8. 300w. 3
      DB Nov. 17 p22. 400w. $4\frac{1}{2}$
      MG July p53. 100w. 4

4134 SHAW, Woody. Love Dance. Muse MR 5074
      CO Dec. p17. 300w. $3\frac{1}{2}$

4135 SHELDON, Jack. GNPS 9036 (Reissue)
      CAD Oct. p23. 100w. 4

4136 SHEPP, Archie. Bijou. Musica Records 3001
      CAD Feb. p35-6. 200w. 4

4137 SHEPP, Archie. Jazz A Confronto: Vol. 27. Horo HLL

101-27 (Italy)
>CAD Sept. p18. 125w. 5
>CO Sept./Oct. p22. 175w. 4

4138 SHEPP, Archie. Mariamar. Horo HZ 01 (Italy)
>CAD Sept. p18. 125w. 5
>CO Sept./Oct. p22. 175w. 4

4139 SHEPP, Archie. Montreux One. Freedom FLP 41027
>MM Aug. 20 p23. 450w. 4

4140 SHEPP, Archie. Steam. Inner City 3002
>CAD Oct. p57. 250w. 4
>CO Sept./Oct. p22. 175w. 4
>JJ Jan. p36. 525w. 5

4141 SHEPP, Archie and Karin Krog. Hi-Fly. Compendium
Fidardo 2 (Norway)
>CAD April p39. 216w. 5
>JF No. 48 p22-3. 50w. 4
>JF No. 49 p47-8. 600w. 4

4142 SHULMAN, Joel. Nowhere but Here. Attic 1014 (Canada)
>CAD Jan. p34. 175w. 4
>SR June p93. 200w. 5

4143 SIDRAN, Ben. The Doctor Is In. Arista 4131
>DB Oct. 20 p25. 200w. 2

4144 SILVER, Horace. Silver 'n Voices. Blue Note BN-LA708G
>CAD April p34. 144w. 2
>CK May p49. 75w. 3
>DB June 2 p28. 200w. 4
>SOU May p60. 150w. 3
>SR June p125. 75w. 0

4145 SILVER, Horace. The Trio Sides. Blue Note BA 474-H2
(2 discs) (Reissue)
>CAD April p16-7. 120w. 4
>CK May p49. 75w. 4
>CO Aug. p23. 125w. 5
>DB Aug. 11 200w. 5

4146 SILVERTONES. One Chance with You. Blind Pig 002
>CAD Dec. p39-40. 150w. $2\frac{1}{2}$

4147 SIMMONS, Norman. Ramira the Dancer. Spotlite Records
LP13 (E)
>CK Nov. p65. 25w. 3
>MM May 28 p32. 250w. 4

4148 SIMS, Zoot. And Friend. Classic Jazz 21 (Reissue)
>CO Dec. p14. 250w. 3

4149   SIMS, Zoot.   Dream Dancing.   DJM DJM 22059 (E)
       GR   July   p237.   75w.   3½
       MM   Feb.   26   p33.   250w.   3½

4150   SIMS, Zoot.   Hawthorne Nights.   Pablo 2310-783
       CAD   April   p39-40.   192w.   3
       DB   Aug.   11   450w.   3½
       GR   July   p237.   125w.   3½
       RFJ   June   p15, 17.   550w.   5
       RR   April   p88.   25w.   1½
       SMG   May   p27.   75w.   3
       SR   June   p125.   125w.   3

4151   SIMS, Zoot.   Soprano Sax.   Pablo 2310-770
       AU   Feb.   p82.   500w.   4
       GR   Jan.   p1198.   100w.   4
       MM   Jan.   22   p25.   200w.   4
       SMG   Jan.   p27.   100w.   5

4152   SIMS, Zoot.   Zootcase.   Prestige PR 24061 (2 discs) (Re-
       issue)
       JJ   Feb.   p36.   400w.   5
       RR   Feb.   p94.   75w.   3
       RR   March   p97.   50w.   3

4153   SIX and Seven-Eights String Band of New Orleans.   Folkways
       FLW-2671 (Reissue)
       CM   March   p56.   50w.   2½

4154   SMALLS, Cliff.   Swing and Things.   Master Jazz MJR 8131
       CAD   Jan.   p30.   100w.   3½
       CO   Dec.   p15-6.   325w.   3
       HF   March   p147.   300w.   4
       MJ   Jan.   p28.   50w.   3

4155   SMITH'S, Art, K. C. Jazz Band.   K. C. Jazz on 12th Street.
       Cavern 42523
       JJ   March   p35.   300w.   4
       ST   Feb.-March   p113-4.   575w.   4

4156   SMITH, Bill and Stuart Broomer.   Conservation Please.   On-
       ari 002 (Canada)
       CAD   June   p12.   250w.   3
       CO   Dec.   p18.   650w.   2
       OLR   Dec.   p293.   50w.   5
       SOU   June   p46.   150w.   4

4157   SMITH, Jabbo.   Volumes 1 and 2.   Melodeon MLP 7326/7
       (2 discs) (Reissue)
       RRE   May-June   p40.   300w.   2½

4158   SMITH, Lonnie Liston.   Renaissance RCA APL1-1822
       AU   May   p90.   350w.   3½

      CK   March p57.   25w.   3
      DB   April 7 p21.   300w.   3
      JJ   April p34, 36.   200w. $2\frac{1}{2}$
      RS   June 16 p58-60.   400w. $2\frac{1}{2}$

4159   SMITH, Lonnie Liston. Live. RCA APL 1-2433
      CAD Oct. p35-6.   275w.   3
      CK Nov. p65.   25w.   3

4160   SMITH, Michael. Austin Stream. SAJ 09
      CAD July p12.   200w.   3

4161   SMITH, Michael. Sidelines. Improvising Artists 37-38-47
      CK Oct. p65.   100w. $1\frac{1}{2}$

4162   SMITH, Paul. The Art Tatum Touch. Outstanding 004
      CAD April p25-6.   120w.   3
      CK April p48, 49.   125w.   4

4163   SMITH, Paul. The Art Tatum Touch, Vol. 2. Outstanding
    007
      CAD Oct. p41.   150w. $2\frac{1}{2}$
      CK Aug. p49.   50w. $4\frac{1}{2}$

4164   SMITH, Paul. The Ballad Touch. Outstanding Records 003
      CK Aug. p49.   50w. $4\frac{1}{2}$

4165   SMITH, Paul. Heavy Jazz. Outstanding Records 009
      CK Nov. p65.   50w. $3\frac{1}{2}$

4166   SMITH, Paul. The Master's Touch. Outstanding 002
      CAD April p25-6.   120w.   3

4167   SMITH, Tab. Because of You. Denmark DL-429
      CAD April p28.   96w. $2\frac{1}{2}$
      CO Sept./Oct. p24.   50w.   3
      DB Nov. 17 p24, 26.   325w.   3
      HF Aug. p122.   250w. $3\frac{1}{2}$
      JR V9/#4 unpaged 50w.   3
      MJ May p31.   200w. $3\frac{1}{2}$
      SR July p111.   175w.   4

4168   SMITH, Terry. British Jazz Artists, Vol. 2. Lee Lambert
    LAM002 (E)
      MM Sept. 3 p24.   300w. $3\frac{1}{2}$

4169   SNOW, Michael. Music for Piano, Whistling Microphone and
    Tape Recorder. Chatham Square LP 1009/10 (2 discs) (Can-
    ada)
      CAD Aug. p22.   300w.   4
      CO Feb. p17.   475w.   4

4170   SOLAL, Martial. Nothing but Piano. MPS 20-226808

SN May p11. 500w. 5

4171   The SONS of Bix's. A Legend Revisited. Fairmont F-110
        JR V9/#3 unpaged 150w. $4\frac{1}{2}$
        MR Feb. p11. 400w. 3
        SR April p113. 350w. 5

4172   SPANIER, Mugsy. Jazum 34 (Reissue)
        JM 1:2 p66. 75w. $2\frac{1}{2}$

4173   SPANIER, Mugsy. Little David Play Your Harp. Jazz
        Archives JA 30 (Reissue)
        JM 1:2 p66. 75w. 3
        MR June p9-10. 400w. 4

4174   SPONTANEOUS Music Ensemble. Face to Face. Emanem
        303
        CO Feb. p17-8. 725w. 3

4175   STEIG, Jeremy. Firefly. CTI 7075
        CAD Aug. p24. 125w. 3

4176   STEIN, Lou. Tribute to Tatum. Chiaroscuro 149
        MJ Jan. p29. 58w. 2

4177   STERN, Bobby. Libra - Bobby Stern & Head, Heart and
        Hands. Phonogramvertigo 6360-632
        CAD Jan. p17. 100w. $2\frac{1}{2}$
        JF No. 50 p52. 200w. 4

4178   STEWART, Jimmy. Fireflower. Catalyst 7621
        CAD Aug. p40. 125w. 4
        DB Nov. 17 p29. 75w. $3\frac{1}{2}$
        GP Oct. p129. 150w. 4
        RC Nov. p14. 200w. 3

4179   STILES, Danny. In Tandem. Famous Door HL 103
        DB Sept. 8 p36. 450w. 4

4180   STILES, Danny and Bill Watrous. One More Time. Famous
        Door HL 112
        CAD July p42. 175w. 4

4181   STITT, Sonny. I Remember Bird. Catalyst 7616
        CAD April p35. 75w. 3
        DB Nov. 17 p28. 100w. $3\frac{1}{2}$
        SR May p101. 262w. 5

4182   STITT, Sonny. Interaction. Chess Jazz Masters 2ACMJ405
        (2 discs) (Reissue)
        RSP 1:3 p36. 200w. 3

4183   STITT, Sonny. Plays for Gene Ammons, My Buddy. Muse

MR 5091
    CAD April p33. 262w. 2½
    MJ Sept. p30. 50w. 3

4184 STITT, Sonny. A Tribute to Duke Ellington. Catalyst CAT-7620
    CAD Aug. p33. 150w. 2
    MJ Sept. p30. 50w. 3

4185 STITT, Sonny. With Strings. Catalyst CAT 7620
    DB Nov. 17 p26. 75w. 3½

4186 STITT, Sonny and Red Holloway. Forecast: Sonny & Red. Catalyst 7608
    CAD Feb. p34. 100w. 4½
    SR Jan. p108. 100w. 4

4187 STIVIN, Jiri and Rudolph Dasek. System Tandem. Japo 60008 (West Germany)
    CO Dec. p19-20. 200w. 2

4188 STOBART, Kathy and Joe Temperley. Saxploitation. Spotlite SPJ 503 (E)
    JJ April p36. 250w. 3

4189 STONE Alliance. PM PMR 013 (Canada)
    JF No. 49 p21. 100w. 4
    MG June p53. 225w. 3
    SOU Nov. p64. 450w. 1

4190 STORMY Six. L'Apprendista. L'Orchestra OLP 10012 (Italy)
    MM Jan. 7 p16. 200w. 2

4191 STRAZZERI, Frank. After the Rain. Catalyst CAT 7607
    CK Nov. p65. 33w. 3

4192 STRAZZERI, Frank. Frames. Glendale Records 6002
    CAD Aug. p37. 100w. 4

4193 STROZIER, Frank. Dance, Dance. Trident TRS-502
    CAD June p21. 100w. 3½

4194 STROZIER, Frank. Remember Me. Steeplechase SCS 1066
    MM June 18 p24. 250w. 4

4195 SUDLER, Monette. Time for a Change. Inner City IC 2062
    CAD Dec. p57-8. 250w. 3

4196 SULLIVAN, Charles. Genesis. Inner City 1012 (Reissue)
    CAD Jan. p35. 300w. 4
    JJ Feb. p36. 225w. 5

4197   SUMMER, Bill. Feel the Heat.   Prestige P10102
        CAD   May   p13.   75w.   1

4198   SUN Ra.   Cosmos.   Inner City 1020
        CAD   Aug.   p42.   200w.   3
        CK   Dec.   p73.   50w. $2\frac{1}{2}$

4199   SUN Ra.   Solo Piano.   Improvising Artists IAI 37. 3. 8. 50
        HF   Nov.   550w.   4
        MG   Oct.   p61.   100w.   5

4200   SUTTON, Ralph.   Changes.   77 Records 77S57 (E) (Reissue)
        GR   Jan.   p1198.   200w. $3\frac{1}{2}$
        ST   Dec. -Jan.   p75-6.   550w.   4

4201   SUTTON, Ralph.   Six.   Rarities 32 (Reissue)
        CO   Sept. /Oct.   p23.   75w.   3

4202   SUZUKI, Isao.   Blue City.   Three Blind Mice TBM 2524
        (Japan)
        CO   Dec.   p20-1.   100w.   4

4203   SUZUKI, Isao.   Black Orpheus.   Three Blind Mice TBM63
        (Japan)
        CO   Dec.   p20-1.   100w. $3\frac{1}{2}$

4204   SWIFT, Duncan.   Piano Ragtime.   Black Lion BL 301
        RA   March-April   p7.   125w.   0

4205   The SWING Machine.   Blue Star XBLY-80701 (France) (Re-
        issue)
        ST   Feb. -March   p114-5.   275w.   3

4206   The SWING Machine.   Vol. 2.   Blue Star 80 709 (France)
        ST   Aug. -Sept.   p236.   200w. $1\frac{1}{2}$

4207   SWOPE, Earl.   The Lost Session.   Jazz Guild JG 108 (E)
        MM   Dec. 3   p32.   425w. $4\frac{1}{2}$

4208   SZABO, Gabor.   Faces.   Mercury SRM 1-1141
        CAD   Aug.   p24.   50w.   2

4209   SZABO, Gabor.   Small World.   Four Leaf Clover EFG-7230
        (Sweden)
        CAD   Oct.   p26.   125w.   4

4210   TAKAYANAGI, Masayuki.   Axis/Another Revolvableething.
        Offbeat ORLP-1005 (Japan)
        CO   Aug.   p20-1.   275w.   3

4211   TATE, Buddy and Joy McShann.   Crazy Legs and Friday
        Street.   Sackville 3011 (Canada)
        CO   Dec.   p20.   400w.   4

4212   TATE, Buddy and Jay McShann.   Kansas City Joys.   Sonet
        716 (E)
            CAD   Aug.   p51.   175w. $4\frac{1}{2}$
            DB   Oct. 20   p27-8.   250w.   4

4213   TATUM, Art.   DJM (E) (Reissue)
            CAC   Feb.   p432.   100w.   4

4214   TATUM, Art.   Get Happy.   Black Lion BLP 30194 (E)
            RR   Oct.   p90.   25w.   4

4215   TATUM, Art.   The Keystone Sessions.   Varese International
        VS 81021
            CAD   June   p39.   200w.   4
            DB   Oct. 6   p35-7.   100w. $4\frac{1}{2}$

4216   TATUM, Art.   Tatum Group Masterpieces.   Pablo 2625 706
        (8 discs) (Reissue)
            BM   March   p52.   350w.   5
            MM   Sept. 10   p29.   400w.   5
            MM   Oct. 15   p28.   150w.   5
            MM   Oct. 8   p36.   225w.   4
            MM   Oct. 1   p26.   100w.   4

4217   TATUM, Art and James P. Johnson.   Tatum Group Master-
        pieces, Vol. 2: Plays Fats Waller.   MCA MCA2-4113 (2
        discs)
            DB   Oct. 6   p35-7.   100w. $3\frac{1}{2}$
            MJ   Nov.   p24.   100w. $3\frac{1}{2}$
            MR   April   p13.   200w.   3

4218   TAYLOR, Cecil.   Dark to Themselves.   Inner City 3001
            CAD   Feb.   p23.   200w.   5
            CK   Oct.   p64.   100w.   3
            DB   Oct. 20   p22.   200w.   4
            CO   Dec.   p20.   400w.   3
            MM   July 16   p28.   200w.   4
            RS   Oct. 6   p89-90.   300w. $2\frac{1}{2}$
            VV   Aug. 15   p51-2.   400w. $3\frac{1}{2}$

4219   TAYLOR, Cecil.   The Great Concert of.   Prestige P-34003
        (3 discs) (Reissue)
            DB   Dec. 15   p27.   300w.   5
            MG   Dec.   p57, 59.   100w.   2

4220   TAYLOR, Cecil.   Indent.   Arista/Freedom AL 1038 (Reissue)
            DB   Oct. 20   p22.   200w.   5
            MM   Nov. 19   p34.   250w. $3\frac{1}{2}$
            RS   Oct. 6   p89-90.   300w.   3
            SR   Nov.   p132.   250w.   5

4221   TAYLOR, Cecil.   Nuits de la Fondation Maeght.   Shandar
        88507-9 (France)

CAD   June p40.   350w.   5

4222   TAYLOR, Cecil.   Solo.   Trio PA-7067 (Japan)
       MM July 16 p28.   200w. $4\frac{1}{2}$

4223   TAYLOR, Keith.   Ragtime Piano.   Sami 1001
       RT Nov. p4.   150w.   3

4224   TEAGARDEN, Jack.   The Great Soloists 1929-36.   Biograph
       BLP-C2
       CAD Nov. p37.   250w.   4

4225   TEAGARDEN, Jack.   King of the Blues Trombone.   Epic
       JSN 6044 (3 discs) (Reissue)
       CAD May p26-7.   175w.   5

4226   TEAGARDEN, Jack.   Let's Start with Jack Teagarden.   Har-
       rison C (E)
       ST June-July p191-2.   250w.   4

4227   TEAGARDEN, Jack.   Spotlight On.   Joyce 4003
       CAD Aug. p49.   175w. $3\frac{1}{2}$

4228   TEAGARDEN, Jack.   A Standard Library of Jazz, Vol. 1.
       Storyville SLP 700 (Reissue)
       RR April p88.   50w. $1\frac{1}{2}$

4229   TEAGARDEN, Jack and Bobby Hackett.   Hollywood Bowl Con-
       cert.   Shoestring 102
       CAD Feb. p42.   200w.   4
       JM Summer p63.   100w. $2\frac{1}{2}$
       ST Oct.-Nov. p33.   200w.   3

4230   TEAGARDEN, Jack/Teddy Buckner.   Sessions, Live.   Calli-
       ope CAL 3004
       SR Dec. 150w.   1

4231   TEITELBAUM, Richard.   Time Tones.   Arista-Freedom AL
       1037
       AU Dec. p130.   300w.   4
       CAD July p44.   175w.   3
       DB Oct. 20 p29.   250w.   5

4232   TEMIZ, Okay.   Turkis Folk Jazz.   Sonet SNTF 668
       JF No. 50 p21.   50w.   3

4233   TERRY, Clark.   Big B-a-d Band Live! at Buddy's Place.
       Vanguard VSD 79373
       CAD Feb. p33-4.   150w. $2\frac{1}{2}$
       RFJ May p15-6.   550w. $4\frac{1}{2}$

4234   TERRY, Clark.   The Globetrotter.   Vanguard VSD 79303
       CAD Oct. p55.   200w.   4

4235   TERRY, Clark. Live on 57th Street.
        SMG Jan. p27. 175w. 4

4236   TERRY, Clark. Professor Jive.   Inner City 1015
        CAD June p42. 250w. $3\frac{1}{2}$
        MJ Sept. p32. 50w. $3\frac{1}{2}$

4237   TERRY, Clark. Wham. MPS G22676
        CAD April p20. 180w. 2
        SOU June p46. 150w. 3

4238   THIGPEN, Ed. Action-ne-Action. GNP Crescendo 2195
        DB Sept. 8 p35-6. 200w. $2\frac{1}{2}$

4239   THOMAS, Kid, Dixieland Band.   Nola 14
        MR Aug. p12. 275w. $3\frac{1}{2}$
        RR Oct. p89. 75w. 3

4240   THOMPSON, Butch. Biograph Center CEN4 (Reissue)
        RR June p95. 25w. 2

4241   THOMPSON, Don. Country Place. PM PMR 008 (Canada)
        SOU Jan. p49. 150w. 3

4242   THORTON, Clifford. The Gardens of Harlem.   JCOA 1008
        DB May 19 425w. $2\frac{1}{2}$
        SN May p11. 300w. 3

4243   360° Music Experience. In: Sanity.   Black Saint BSR 0006/7
        (2 discs)
        DB Sept. 8 p30. 450w. 5
        MM Feb. 12 p28. 300w. $3\frac{1}{2}$
        RFJ Sept. p13-4. 500w. $3\frac{1}{2}$
        VV March 7 p45. 325w. $4\frac{1}{2}$

4244   TIRABASSO, John. Plays Pearls. Fairmont 106
        CAD June p29. 75w. 3

4244a   TOMPKINS, Fred. Somesville.   Festival 9002
        RFJ May p16. 600w. $3\frac{1}{2}$

4245   TOMPKINS, Ross. Scrimshaw.   Concord Jazz CJ 28
        CAD Jan. p31. 225w. $2\frac{1}{2}$
        DB May 19 225w. 2
        RFJ June p17. 400w. 5
        SOU March p44. 100w. $4\frac{1}{2}$

4246   TONEFF, Radka. Winter Poem.   Zavepta 1439 (Norway)
        JF No. 49 p22. 50w. 3

4247   TOWNER, Ralph. Diary. ECM ECM-1032 ST.   Cart. 8T-
        1-1032. Cass. CT-1-1032
        CAD May p23. 75w. 3

MG   June   p53.   100w. $3\frac{1}{2}$
SR   Aug.   p106.   125w. $4\frac{1}{2}$

4248   TOWNER, Ralph.   Solstice/Sound and Shadows.   ECM-1-1095
       CAD   Dec.   p60-1.   150w. $2\frac{1}{2}$
       MG   Dec.   p59.   100w.   3
       MM   Nov.   12   p34.   200w. $4\frac{1}{2}$

4249   TOWNER, Ralph and John Abercrombie.   Sargasso Sea.   ECM
       1-1095
       CRE   March   p63.   25w.   3

4250   TRACEY, Stan.   The Bracknell Connection.   Steam SJ 103
       JJ   March   p36.   350w.   4
       MM   April 9   p29.   550w.   5

4251   TRACEY, Stan.   Captain Adventure.   Steam Records SJ 102
       CK   April   p49.   25w.   4

4252   TRACEY, Stan and Keith Tippett.   TNT.   Emanem 3307
       CAD   Feb.   p21.   250w. $4\frac{1}{2}$
       CAD   Feb.   p21.   125w. $3\frac{1}{2}$
       CK   March   p56.   100w.   5
       MM   March 19   p32.   650w. $4\frac{1}{2}$

4253   The TRADITIONAL Jazz Union.   Christmas New Orleans
       Style.   Dawn Club DC 12020 (E) (Reissue)
       ST   Dec.-Jan.   p76.   100w.   3

4254   TRANSCENDPROVISATION.   Trans.   Trans Museq 1
       CAD   Oct.   p21.   250w.   5

4255   TREMBLE Kids.   Hats Off to Eddie Condon.   MPS 2122367-1
       JF   No. 50   p55.   500w.   4

4256   TROPEA, John.   Short Trip to Space.   Marlin 2204
       CAD   June   p20.   50w.   2
       DB   Dec. 1   p29-30.   400w.   3
       GP   Nov.   p137.   125w.   5
       MM   Sept. 3   p22.   25w. $2\frac{1}{2}$

4257   TROUP, Bobby.   Makin' Whoopee.   Vintage Jazz VJR 9313
       CAD   June   p26.   125w.   3

4258   TUCKER, Mickey.   Triplicity.   Xanadu 128
       DB   June 16   p40-3.   225w.   5

4259   TURETZKY, Bertram.   New Music for Contrabass.   Finna-
       dar SR 9015
       CAD   April   p44-5.   324w. $4\frac{1}{2}$

4260   TURNER, Bruce and Johnny Barnes.   Jazz Masters.   Cadil-
       lac SGC 10056

MM   March 12 p25.   250w. $3\frac{1}{2}$

4261   TURNER, Joe.   Another Epic Stride Piano.   Pablo 2310-763
       AU Nov. p121. 350w. 4
       GR March p1471. 150w. 4

4262   TURNER, Joe.   King of Stride.   Chiaroscuro CR 147
       AU Feb. p89. 250w. $3\frac{1}{2}$
       MJ Jan. p29. 50w. 3

4263   TURRENTINE, Stanley.   The Man with the Sad Face.   Fan-
       tasy F9519
       DB March 10 p22. 250w. $1\frac{1}{2}$

4264   TURRENTINE, Stanley.   Night Wings.   Fantasy 9534
       CAD Oct. p23. 100w. 3
       RSP Nov. -Dec. p33. 400w. 2

4265   TYLER, Charles.   Live in Europe.   AK-BA 1010
       CAD April p7. 300w. 3
       CO Dec. p21-2. 225w. $3\frac{1}{2}$
       VV March 14 p81. 50w. $3\frac{1}{2}$

4266   TYLER, Charles.   Voyage from Jericho.   Ak-Ba AK100
       CO Dec. p21-2. 225w. $3\frac{1}{2}$

4267   TYNER, McCoy.   Cosmos.   Blue Note BN-LA 460 (Reissue)
       DB Aug. 11 200w. 5

4268   TYNER, McCoy.   Echoes of a Friend.   Milestone M-9055
       AU Feb. p84. 200w. 5

4269   TYNER, McCoy.   Focal Point.   Milestone M-9072
       BM March p52. 150w. 4
       CAD Feb. p23, 26. 175w. 3
       CK April p48. 180w. 4
       JJ Feb. p36. 400w. 4
       MG April p53. 125w. $3\frac{1}{2}$
       MM Jan. 15 p20. 350w. 5
       RFJ Sept. p14. 300w. $2\frac{1}{2}$
       RS March 24 p58. 500w. 2
       RSP March-April p30-33. 2000w. 3

4270   TYNER, McCoy.   Supertrios.   Milestone M-5503
       AU Dec. p124. 600w. $4\frac{1}{2}$
       CAD Aug. p44. 275w. $4\frac{1}{2}$
       CK Oct. p64. 100w. $2\frac{1}{2}$
       DB Nov. 3 p22-3. 450w. 4
       MM Aug. 6 p19. 450w. $3\frac{1}{2}$

4271   UM ROMAO, Dom.   Hotmosphere.   Pablo 2310 777
       RR Jan. p85. 75w. $1\frac{1}{2}$

4272   UNITY.   Blow Through Your Mind.   EPI-02
       CAD   Nov.   p25, 28.   50w. $3\frac{1}{2}$

4273   UNIVERSITY of Illinois Jazz Band.   World of Jazz.   Golden
       Crest CRS 4161
       HF   Dec.   p144.   300w.   4

4274   URBANI, Massimo.   Jazz A Confronto: Vol. 13.   Horo HLL
       101-13 (Italy)
       CAD   Sept.   p16.   250w.   4

4275   URBANIAK, Michal.   The Beginning.   Catalyst CAX7909 (2
       discs) Cart. CLT 8XT-7909
       CAD   April   p20-7.   375w. $3\frac{1}{2}$
       SR   July   p111.   75w.   1

4276   VACHE, Warren, Jr.   First Time Out.   Monmouth Ever-
       green 7087
       CAD   July   p36.   175w.   4
       HF   Sept.   p142.   100w.   3
       MJ   Sept.   p28.   75w.   3

4277   VALDAMBRINI, Oscar.   Jazz A Confronto: Vol. 34.   Horo
       HLL 101-34 (Italy)
       CAD   Sept.   p19.   150w. $2\frac{1}{2}$

4278   VALENTINE, Thomas.   At Kohlman's Tavern.   New Orleans
       NOR 7201 (E)
       RR   Feb.   p67.   125w.   3

4279   VANESSA.   Black and White.   Compendium Fidardo 3 (Nor-
       way)
       CAD   April   p39.   216w. $2\frac{1}{2}$
       JF   No. 49   p22.   50w.   3

4280   VENUTI, Joe.   Boot Records BOS-7149 (Canada)
       CAD   Sept.   p31-2.   100w.   3

4281   VENUTI, Joe.   In Milan.   Vanguard VSD 79396
       CAD   Sept.   p31-2.   100w.   3

4282   VENUTI, Joe.   S'Wonderful.   Flying Fish FF035
       CAD   Sept.   p31-2.   100w.   4
       CM   Nov.   p40.   300w.   4
       DB   Oct. 6   p34.   150w. $2\frac{1}{2}$

4283   VENUTI, Joe and Earl Hines.   Hot Sonatas.   Chiaroscuro
       CR 145
       AU   Feb.   p83.   350w.   5

4284   VENUTI, Joe and Eddie Lang.   Stringing the Blues.   CBS

JCL-24 (2 discs) (Reissue)
    CAD Oct. p58. 175w. 5
    MJ Nov. p24. 25w. 3
    MM Feb. 26 p34. 700w. 3

4285   VENUTI, Joe and Dave McKenna.   Alone at the Palace.
      Chiaroscuro CR 160
      CAD Dec. p62. 100w. 3

4286   VENUTI, Joe and George Barnes.   Live at the Concord Sum-
      mer Festival.   Concord CJ30
      CAD May p26. 75w. $3\frac{1}{2}$
      GP May p129. 25w. 3
      HF July p148. 300w. 4
      MM July 9 p24. 300w. $3\frac{1}{2}$
      RR Oct. p89. 50w. 4
      RR Dec. p88. 75w. 5

4287   VENUTI, Joe and Mariam McPhartland.   The Maestro and
      Friend.   Holycon 112
      MJ Jan. p28. 50w. 3

4288   VESALA, Edward.   I'm Here.   Blue Master Special SPEL
      311 (Finland)
      JF No. 47. p65, 67. 325w. $2\frac{1}{2}$

4289   VESALA, Edward.   Satu.   ECM 1-1088
      CAD Oct. p56. 150w. 4
      JF No. 47 p65, 67. 325w. $3\frac{1}{2}$
      JF No. 49 p51, 53. 600w. 4
      MM Feb. 26 p34. 525w. $3\frac{1}{2}$

4290   VICK, Harold.   Don't Look Back.   Strata East SES
      7431
      CAD Feb. p16. 125w. 5

4291   VITOUS, Miroslav.   Majesty Music.   Arista AL 4099
      CAD Jan. p41. 100w. $2\frac{1}{2}$
      DB Feb. 10 p20-7. 225w. 3
      SOU Feb. p44. 50w. 1

4292   VOERKEL, Urs.   S'Grschank.   FMP0300
      CAD July p13. 125w. 4
      MM Feb. 5 p22. 250w. 3

4293   VOERKEL, Urs.   Voerkel-Frey-Lovens.   FMP 0340
      CAD July p13. 200w. 3
      MM Feb. p22. 250w. 4

4294   VOICE.   Ogun OG 110 (E)

JF No. 50 p49, 51. 225w. 3
MM April 16 p23. 350w. 2

4295 VON SCHLIPPENBACH, Alexander. The Living Music.
      FMP 0100
          CAD April p38. 300w. 5

4296 WALCOTT, Colin. Grazing Dreams. ECM 1-1096
          CAD Nov. p38. 100w. 4
          DB Dec. 15 p27. 275w. 5
          MG Nov. p53. 50w. 3

4297 WALDEN, Narada Michael. Garden of Love Light. Atlantic
      SD 18199
          BM April p50. 150w. 4
          DB May 5 p20, 22. 250w. 2
          GP Aug. p120. 50w. $2\frac{1}{2}$
          GR April p1617. 50w. 2
          MG Feb. p57. 125w. $3\frac{1}{2}$
          RS March 24 p69. 300w. $3\frac{1}{2}$

4298 WALDO, Terry. Blackbird C 6002
          JR V9/#4 unpaged 125w. 4

4299 WALDRON, Mal. One and Two. Prestige P-24068 (2 discs)
      (Reissue)
          AU April p90. 300w. 5
          JM 1:2 p62-3. 325w. 3

4300 WALDRON, Mal. Jazz A Confronto: Vol. 19. Horo HLL
      101-19 (Italy)
          CAD Sept. p17. 150w. $3\frac{1}{2}$
          CO Sept./Oct. p18-20. 225w. 4

4301 WALDRON, Mal and Gary Peacock. First Encounter. Cata-
      lyst CAT-7906
          CAD June p45. 300w. $4\frac{1}{2}$
          DB Oct. 20 p25-6. 350w. 5
          HF Sept. p142. 50w. $2\frac{1}{2}$
          JM Summer p58-9. 400w. 3
          MG July p53. 125w. 3

4302 WALLER, Fats. DJM (E) (Reissue)
          CAD Feb. p432. 100w. $3\frac{1}{2}$

4303 WALLER, Fats. Complete Recordings (1939) Vol. 18. RCA
      FXM1-7316 (France) (Reissue)
          RR June p95. 25w. $3\frac{1}{2}$

4304 WALLER, Fats. Fractious Fingering. RCA Starcall NL
      42011 (Reissue)
          CAD July p142. 225w. 4
          JJ April p37-8. 200w. $3\frac{1}{2}$

RR June p95. 50w. 4

4305 WALLER, Fats. Piano Solos 1929-1941. Bluebird AXM2-
5518 (2 discs) (Reissue)
CO Sept./Oct. p23. 150w. 4
MR July p10-11. 300w. $3\frac{1}{2}$
RSP May-June p44. 200w. $3\frac{1}{2}$
VV Aug. 1 p47. 300w. 4

4306 WALTON, Ceder. From Roots. Muse Records 5059
CK April p49. 25w. 3

4307 WALTON, Cedar. Pit Inn. East Wind EW-7009 (Japan)
CO April p12. 225w. 4

4308 WALTON, Cedar and Hank Mobley. Breakthrough. Muse
MR-5132
CAD Nov. p46. 400w. 4

4309 WATANABE, Sadas and Charlie Mariano. Nebesada and
Charlie. Catalyst CAT-7911
CAD July p40. 150w. $3\frac{1}{2}$

4310 WEATHER Report. Heavy Weather. Columbia PC-34418.
Cass. CT-34418. Cart. CA-34418
AU July p99. 500w. 4
CAD May p13-4. 50w. $1\frac{1}{2}$
CK May p48. 400w. $4\frac{1}{2}$
CRA July p70. 500w. $3\frac{1}{2}$
DB May 19 625w. 5
GR May p1758. 50w. 3
HF July p156. 450w. 4
JM Summer p59-60. 400w. 5
MG June p53. 200w. 3
MM April 9 p27. 850w. 2
RR July p97. 150w. $3\frac{1}{2}$
RSP May-June p38. 1000w. 4
SR Oct. p130. 225w. $3\frac{1}{2}$

4311 WEBB, Art. Love Eyes. Atlantic SD 18226
CAD Nov. p30. 25w. $2\frac{1}{2}$

4312 WEBB, Art. Mr. Flute. Atlantic SD 18202
CAD April p10. 80w. 4

4313 WEBB, Chick. Best. MCA2-4107 (2 discs) (Reissue)
CAD Oct. p25. 125w. $2\frac{1}{2}$

4314 WEBB, Chick. Bronzeville Stomp. Jazz Archives JA-33
CAD April p41-2. 222w. 2
JM Summer p61. 175w. 3

4315 WEBER, Eberhard. The Following Morning. ECM-1-1084

       CAD   April   p16.   450w.   3
       JM   Summer p60.   400w. $3\frac{1}{2}$
       RSP   May-June p45.   225w. $4\frac{1}{2}$

4316   WEBSTER, Ben.   ... and Friends.   Verve 2332-086 (E)
       (Reissue)
       GR   Dec.   p1162.   50w. $3\frac{1}{2}$
       RR   Oct.   p90.   50w. $3\frac{1}{2}$

4317   WEBSTER, Ben.   Ben and the Boys.   Jazz Archives JA35
       CAD   May   p27-8.   125w.   4
       DB   April 7   p31-3.   100w.   5
       JM   Summer p61.   200w.   3
       RSP   1:3   p37.   450w. $3\frac{1}{2}$

4318   WEBSTER, Ben.   Makin' Whoopee.   Spotlite 9
       CAD   Nov.   p50.   65w.   5
       MM   April 23   p26.   125w. $3\frac{1}{2}$

4319   WEBSTER, Ben.   My Man.   Inner City 2028
       CAD   Aug.   p47.   125w.   4

4320   WEBSTER, Ben.   See You at the Fair.   Impulse IMPL 8034
       BM   Jan.   p53.   75w.   3

4321   WEBSTER, Ben and Coleman Hawkins.   Tenor Giants.
       Verve 2-2520 (Reissue)
       CAD   Oct.   p45.   175w.   5
       HF   Nov.   375w.   3

4322   WEBSTER, Ben and Harry "Sweets" Edison.   Walkin' with
       Sweets.   Verve (E) (Reissue)
       BM   Jan.   p53.   125w.   4

4323   WEIN, George and the Newport All-Stars.   ABC/Impulse
       IMPL 8046 (E) (Reissue)
       RR   Aug.   p84.   50w.   3

4324   WELLSTOOD, Dick.   From Dixie to Swing.   Music Minus
       One CJ 10
       CAD   Aug.   p50.   150w. $3\frac{1}{2}$
       JJ   Jan.   p37.   300w.   4

4325   WELLSTOOD, Dick.   Live at the Cookery.   Chiaroscuro CR
       139
       AU   May   p94.   200w.   5
       MM   Feb. 5   p22.   225w.   4
       RA   Nov./Dec.   p6.   25w.   4

4326   WELLSTOOD, Dick.   This Is the One.   Audiophile AP120
       HF   Nov.   300w.   3

4327   WELLSTOOD, Dick and Peter Ind.   Some Hefty Cats!

Hefty Jazz HJ 100
    ST June-July p198-9. 275w. 4½

4328 WELSH, Alex. In Concert. Black Lion BLPX 12115/6 (2 discs)
    MM Oct. 1 p27. 375w. 3½
    RR Oct. p89. 25w. 2½

4329 WERNER, Lasse. Saxafonsymfonin. Dragon 6 (Sweden)
    CAD Nov. p47, 48. 215w. 3

4330 WERTMAN, David. Kara Suite. Mustevic Sound Records MS 3001
    CAD Jan. p40-1. 150w. 3½
    JF No. 47 p69. 50w. 3
    MG Feb. p57. 100w. 3½

4331 WESTBROOK, Mike. Love/Dream and Variations. Transatlantic TRA 323 (E)
    JF No. 45 p66-7. 500w. 3½

4332 WESTON, Randy. African Nite. Inner City IC 1031
    CK April p49. 100w. 3
    CO Feb. p23. 75w. 4
    JM 1:2 p63. 450w. 3

4333 WESTON, Randy. Berkshire Blues. Arista/Freedom AL 1026
    DB Nov. 17 p20. 400w. 4
    RFJ Oct. p18-9. 450w. 4
    SOU Sept. p66. 200w. 4
    SR Nov. p132. 225w. 4
    VV Nov. 7 p53, 59. 100w. 3

4334 WESTON, Randy. Little Niles. Blue Note LA 598-H2
    CAD April p17-8. 450w. 2½
    CK May p49. 25w. 4
    DB Aug. 11 200w. 5

4335 WESTON, Randy. "Meets Himself." Produttori Associati PA/LP 70 (Italy)
    CO Sept./Oct. p18-20. 225w. 4

4336 WHITE, Andrew. Red Top, Vol. 3. Andrew's Music AM 26
    CAD Nov. p25. 150w. 2½

4337 WHITE, Andrew. Seven Giant Steps for Coltrane, Vol. 7. Andrew's Music AM 30
    CAD Nov. p25. 50w. 2½

4338 WHITE, Andrew. Spotts, Maxine and Brown. Andrew's Music No. 24
    CAD July p19. 225w. 2

CAD   July   p43.   300w.   5

4339   WHITNEY, Dave.   When Somebody Thinks You're Wonderful.
       Dave's Jazz Records 6024N7
       CAD   March   p27.   125w.   3½

4340   WILBER, Bob and Kenny Davern.   Chalumeau Blue.   Chiaro-
       scuro CR 148
           CO   Dec.   p18-9.   750w.   3½
           DB   April 7   p21.   250w.   3
           HF   Jan.   p146.   200w.   4
           JJ   Jan.   p36.   900w.   5
           MJ   Jan.   p29.   50w.   3½
           SR   March   p93.   600w.   4

4341   WILBER, Bob and Kenny Davern.   Soprano Summit in Con-
       cert.   Concord Jazz CJ29
           AU   Nov.   p122.   350w.   4
           CAD   Jan.   p35-6.   225w.   4
           JJ   April   p36.   225w.   3
           MM   May 28   p32.   450w.   3½
           SOU   May   p60.   250w.   4½

4342   WILKINS, Jack.   Chiaroscuro CR156
           CAD   Dec.   p41.   200w.   5

4343   WILLEN, Barney.   Moshi.   Saravah SH 10028/29 (2 discs)
       (France)
           JF   No. 46   p67, 69.   75w.   4½

4344   WILLIAMS, Buster.   Crystal Reflections.   Muse MR 5101
           CAD   April   p42.   168w.   4

4345   WILLIAMS, Clarence.   1933/35 Volume 3.   Classic Jazz
       Masters CJM 16 (Reissue)
           CO   Dec.   p23.   50w.   1½
           ST   Dec. -Jan.   p72.   150w.   4

4346   WILLIAMS, Clarence.   Music Man, 1927-1934.   MCA 510
       144 (France) (Reissue)
           ST   Oct. -Nov.   p33-4.   325w.   1

4347   WILLIAMS, Jessica.   The Portal of Antrem.   Adelphi AD
       5003
           CAD   May   p22.   500w.   0
           CK   Sept.   p58.   125w.   4
           MG   Aug.   p63.   125w.   3

4348   WILLIAMS, Mary Lou.   The Ash Recordings 1944-47.   Folk-
       ways 2966 (Reissue)
           CAD   Nov.   p42, 43.   550w.   5

4349   WILLIAMS, Mary Lou.   Live at the Cookery.   Chiaroscuro

146
    MJ Jan. p29. 50w. 3

4350 WILLIAMS, Tony. Million Dollar Legs. Columbia PC
34263
    BM March p23. 200w. 3
    GP Jan. p97. 50w. 5
    JF No. 47 p69. 25w. 0

4351 WILSON, Gary. You Think You Really Know Me. 7042N11
    CAD Aug. p23. 75w. 2

4352 WILSON, Phil. That's All. Famous Door HL-109
    CAD Jan. p31. 275w. $3\frac{1}{2}$
    DB Oct. 6 p27-8. 225w. $2\frac{1}{2}$
    MJ Dec. p24. 75w. $3\frac{1}{2}$
    SR March p123. 150w. 5

4353 WILSON, Teddy. DJM DJB 26076 (E) (Reissue)
    JF No. 50 p48-9. 375w. 4
    SMG May p27. 125w. 4

4354 WILSON, Teddy. Chiaroscuro CR150
    CR Aug. p490. 125w. 4
    SOU Feb. p44. 100w. 4

4355 WILSON, Teddy. 1944, Vol. II. Jazz Archives JA 36
    CAD April p44-5. 276w. $4\frac{1}{2}$
    JM Summer p61. 200w. $3\frac{1}{2}$

4356 WILSON, Teddy. Jazz A Confronto, Vol. 12. Horo HLL
101-12 (Italy)
    CO Sept./Oct. p18-20. 225w. 4

4357 WILSON, Teddy. Moonglow. Black Lion BLP 30133 (Reissue)
    JJ April p38. 250w. 2

4358 WILSON, Teddy. Revamps Rodgers and Hart. Chiaroscuro
CR168
    CAD Dec. p53-4. 100w. 2

4359 WILSON, Teddy. Statements & Improvisations, 1934-1942.
Smithsonian Collection R 005
    CAD June p41. 200w. $4\frac{1}{2}$
    CK Aug. p48. 75w. $4\frac{1}{2}$
    CO Sept./Oct. p23. 250w. 4
    JF No. 50 p18. 50w. 4
    JM Summer p52-3. 100w. 4
    MJ Sept. p28, 30. 100w. 3

4360 WILSON, Teddy. Striding After Fats. Black Lion BL 308
    AU Feb. p84. 200w. 5

MJ   Jan.   p38.   50w. $2\frac{1}{2}$

4361   WINDING, Kai.   Caravan.   Glendale 6004
       CAD   Aug.   p33.   325w.   4

4362-3 WOFFORD, Mike.   Scott Joplin: Interpretations.   Flying
       Dutchman BDL1-1372
       AU   Oct.   p195.   200w.   4

4364   WOLVERINES.   The Complete.   Fountain FJ 114
       ST   Oct. -Nov.   p34.   200w.   3

4365   WOOD, George Scott.   World Record Club SH249 (Reissue)
       RR   Dec.   p87.   50w. $1\frac{1}{2}$

4366   WOOD, John.   Until Goodbye.   Los Angeles Records LAPR
       1002
       CAD   May   p19.   75w. $2\frac{1}{2}$
       CR   Dec.   p73.   75w.   3
       DB   Nov. 3   p30.   150w.   2
       MG   June   p53.   100w.   3

4367   WOODING, Sam.   Bicentennial Jazz Vistas.   Twin Signs TS-
       1001
       JJ   Feb.   p36-8.   300w.   5

4368   WOODS, Chris.   Somebody Done Stole My Blues.   Delmark
       DL-434
       CAD   April   p29.   216w.   3
       CO   Sept./Oct.   p24.   50w.   3
       DB   Nov. 17   p26.   325w.   3
       JR   V9/#4   unpaged   50w.   4
       MJ   May   p31.   100w. $3\frac{1}{2}$
       RFJ   May   p18.   150w. $2\frac{1}{2}$
       RSP   1:3   p37.   300w.   2

4369   WOODS, Chris and Marcodi Marco.   Together in Paris.
       Disques Esperance ESP155518 (France)
       RFJ   May   p18.   50w.   3

4370   WOODS, Chris and Michel Klotchkoff.   Free Space.   Promo-
       phone PROM 13 (France)
       RFJ   May   p18.   100w. $3\frac{1}{2}$

4371   WOODS, Phil.   Floresta Canto.   RCA BGL1-1800
       DB   March 10   p22.   300w. $2\frac{1}{2}$
       CRE   March   p63.   50w.   2
       RR   June   p94.   50w.   3

4372   WOODS, Phil.   The Phil Woods Six 'Live' from the Showboat.
       RCA BGL2-2202 (2 discs)   Cart. BGS2-2202.   Cass. BGK2-
       2202
       CAD   July   p42.   225w.   4

          CK   Aug. p48.   100w.   5
          DB   Oct. 20 p28.   350w.   5
          RS   Sept. 8 p119.   325w.   3
          SR   Sept. p122.   100w.   5

4373   WOODS, Phil and Michel Legrand.   Images.   RCA BGL1-
       1027
          AU   Nov. p122.   500w. $4\frac{1}{2}$

4374   WORLD'S Greatest Jazz Band.   In Concert at Lawrenceville
       School.   Flying Dutchman BDL1-1371
          DB   April 21 p26.   150w. $2\frac{1}{2}$

4375   WORLD'S Greatest Jazz Band.   Music by Rodgers and Hart.
       World Jazz WJLPS 7
          CR   Feb. p115.   250w.   4
          DB   April 21 p26.   150w.   3
          MM   April 2 p28.   200w. $2\frac{1}{2}$

4376   WORLD'S Greatest Jazz Band.   On Tour.   World Jazz S-8
          HF   Sept. p142.   75w. $2\frac{1}{2}$
          MR   June p8-9.   50w.   3

4377   WORLD'S Greatest Jazz Band.   Plays Duke Ellington.   World
       Jazz WJLP-S-9
          CAD   Feb. p41.   100w.   4
          JF   No. 50 p47-8.   400w. $3\frac{1}{2}$
          MM   Sept. 3 p25.   350w.   3
          MR   June p8.   50w.   3
          SOU   Feb. p44.   150w.   4

4378   WRIGHT, Denny and Danny Moss.   Jazz at the New Theatre.
       Joyce JC003
          MM   July 2 p24.   300w.   4

4379   WYBLE, Jimmy.   Classical/Jazz.   Jazz Chronicles JCS 77-
       1&2
          CAD   July p41.   175w.   3
          GP   Aug. p120.   125w.   4

4380   WYBLE, Jimmy.   Diane.   Vantage 502
          CAD   Jan. p25.   100w.   0

4381   YAMASHITA, Yosuki.   Chiasma.   MPS20 22678-6 (West
       Germany)
          JF   No. 46 p62-3.   500w.   2

4382   YOUNG, Lester.   Jammin' with Lester, Vol. 2.   Jazz
       Archives JA-34
          CAD   June p35.   100w. $3\frac{1}{2}$
          DB   April 7 p31-3.   100w.   3
          JM   Summer p61.   200w.   4

4383   YOUNG, Lester.   Lester Swings.   Verve VE-2-2516 (2 discs)
        (Reissue)
            CAD   June p35.   100w. $3\frac{1}{2}$
            DB   July 14 p45-7.   50w. $3\frac{1}{2}$
            GR   Jan. p1198.   200w. $2\frac{1}{2}$

4384   YOUNG, Lester.   Pres: The Complete Savoy Recording.
        Savoy SJL2202 (E) (2 discs) (Reissue)
            GR   April p1618.   200w. $3\frac{1}{2}$
            RR   Feb. p94.   50w.   4
            RR   March p97.   50w.   3

4385   YOUNG, Lester.   Pres Lives.   Savoy SJL 1109 (Reissue)
            CAD   Oct. p43.   175w.   3
            CO   Dec. p24.   75w. $2\frac{1}{2}$
            RR   Oct. p90.   25w.   3

4386   YOUNG, Lester.   Story, Vol. 1.   Columbia CG 33502 (Re-
        issue)
            CAD   Feb. p45-6.   200w. $4\frac{1}{2}$
            CO   Aug. p22.   200w.   3
            DB   April 7 p31-3.   100w.   5
            GR   Sept. p525.   150w. $4\frac{1}{2}$
            JJ   April p39.   200w.   4
            JR   V9/#4 unpaged 125w.   4
            MJ   March p44.   100w. $3\frac{1}{2}$
            MM   May 28 p32.   275w. $4\frac{1}{2}$
            MR   Feb. p12-3.   375w.   3
            RFJ   May p13-4.   550w. $4\frac{1}{2}$
            RR   June p95.   50w. $3\frac{1}{2}$

4387   ZADLO, Leszek.   Thoughts.   Ego 4003
            JF   No. 45 p67.   350w.   3

4388   ZAWINUL, Joe.   Concerto Retitled.   Atlantic SD 1694
            CAD   Feb. p30.   100w. $3\frac{1}{2}$
            CK   Jan. p50.   125w.   4
            MG   Jan. p61.   100w. $2\frac{1}{2}$
            SOU   Jan. p48.   50w. $3\frac{1}{2}$

4389   ZEITLIN, Denny.   Syzygy.   1750 Arch Records 1759
            CAD   Sept. p45-6.   200w. $2\frac{1}{2}$
            CK   Sept. p58.   350w. $4\frac{1}{2}$

4390   ZOLLER, Attila.   Dream Bells.   Inner City IC 3008
            CAD   Dec. p52.   150w.   1
            JJ   Jan. p38.   225w.   5
            MM   Jan. p16.   50w.   3

BLUES

This section comprises material generally classifed by collectors as pre-World War II or post-World War II vocal blues, and based on the two major discographies of Godrich and Dixon, and Leadbitter and Slavens. Blues music is often of two types--country, rural, solo, and acoustic; or electric, amplified, and urban with ensemble playing. The former has been around since before the turn of the century; however, the latter is a more recent development, often called "Chicago blues" and generally attributed to Muddy Waters but also having roots in the string bands and the Mississippi Delta. Heavy white blues bands are in the ROCK category, for they have used the technical aspects of blues as a format, not as a life style. Instrumental blues is more properly JAZZ, although the odd instrumental turns up on an album of vocals.

Scholars and collectors have tried to break blues into manageable forms with partial success. Regional styles, time periods, format of presentation, type of instrumentation, individuals--the blues get worked over as much as the grieving performer. This accounts for the vast number of anthologized offerings and the responses of the so-called "bootleggers."

Anyone can play the blues, for it is a simple technical form of music. Thus, all interest in the blues is dependent on the performer. But not everyone can feel the blues, with the message to be conveyed being essentially one of emotion. Real blues singers used the blues therapeutically to escape from their situation. They stood outside, looking in while singing about their problems. It always felt so good to a blues singer when he finished his song, for he "talked it out" as many people in therapy do. Most typical white blues singers cannot feel the blues because they have not experienced it. They see injustices and become disturbed; the typical black blues singer is the actual recipient of those injustices. He not only sees it, but also he lives it. Thus, for all purposes, the typical white singer cannot get into the blues.

Many blues records are reviewed only once or twice in a well-covered field. Besides the British publication Blues Unlimited and the American Living Blues, blues music is proportionately well off in all jazz magazines, some folk, some rock, and some general publications. Foreign language magazines exist in Japan, France, Germany, Sweden and other countries. "The blues is everywhere" is a true statement indeed. While Blues Unlimited stands out for its

convincing rave reviews, ephemeral publications present their fair
share of glossies that only serve notice to collectors that records
exist and are now on the market.   Many such publications exist for
a short period of time, ceasing to exist for a multitude of reasons.

For reissued material, the reviews themselves often tend
only to be notices explaining that certain records are now available
for purchase; hence, on our rating scale, there is a heavy prepond-
erance of $2\frac{1}{2}$ to $3\frac{1}{2}$ ratings.   The collector knows what he wants,
and the reviews only interest him for consideration of sound quality,
duplicated tracks on existing albums, and additional biographical information not easily obtained elsewhere.

New material seems to be exceedingly difficult to evaluate.
Reviewers appear to be on safe ground with reissues, but uncertain
with new post-war material.   The case has been made, quite suc-
cessfully, that electric blues has not matured beyond its mid-50's
development.   Nothing new is being played and the hordes of white
imitators are prolonging the status quo.   The jazz magazines tend
to be more realistic about the music; if it is good, then it is ranked
as such; if it is bad, then it is shot down.   Tainted by white com-
mercialism, certain "Chicago bluesmen" are virtually ignored or
condemned by the blues press while given rave send-ups by the rock
media.   Thus, these groups are regarded by both types of media as
having sold out from one side to another.   All the media seems to
have agreed that original electric blues have oversaturated the market.   Artists such as B. B. King, James Cotton, Buddy Guy and
Junior Wells, and even Muddy Waters himself have been battered
around by the critics who are still waiting for that "definitive, next
album. "   Yet the records sell well and this is yet another example
of there being no correlation between critical acclaim and sales.
And in recent years the number of new titles has declined as older
bluesmen die.

According to the 1977 reviews, the following are the best
discs:

CHENIER, Clifton.   Cajun Swamp Music Live.   Tomato 2-7002
    (2 discs)
DAWKINS, Jimmy.   Blisterstring.   Delmark DS 641
ELLIS, Big Chief.   Trix 3316
MUDDY Waters.   Hard Again.   Blue Sky PZ 34449
RUSH, Otis.   Right Place, Wrong Time.   Bullfrog 301
SEALS, Son.   Midnight Son.   Alligator AL 4708
TARHEEL, Slim.   No Time at All.   Trix 3310
WILSON, Edith.   He May Be Your Man But He Comes to See
    Me Sometimes.   Delmark DS 637

4391   ACES.   With Their Guests.   MCM 900. 293 (France)

CZM   June p61.   25w. $2\frac{1}{2}$
LB   March-April   p37-8.   200w.   1

4392   ARNOLD, Billy Boy.   Sinners Prayer.   Red Lightnin' RL0014
(E) (Reissue)
BM   March p53.   150w.   4

4393   ARNOLD, Kokomo.   Bad Luck Blues, 1934-38.   MCA 510-
116 (France) (Reissue)
ST   Oct. -Nov.   p39.   300w. $3\frac{1}{2}$

4394   ARNOLD, Kokomo.   Set Down Gal.   Magpie PY 1802 (Reissue)
RSP   Jan. -Feb.   p3.   200w. $3\frac{1}{2}$

4395   BAKER, Mickey.   Kicking Mule SNKF 127
FR   Sept.   p23.   200w.   3
MM   Aug. 27 p22.   250w.   4

4396   BARBECUE Bob.   Chocolate to the Bone.   Mamlish S-3808
(Reissue)
JJ   March p30.   400w.   5
MM   April 2 p26.   450w. $3\frac{1}{2}$
RSP   Jan. -Feb.   p9.   300w. $3\frac{1}{2}$

4397   BENTLEY, Gladys/Mary Dixon.   Collector's Classics CC52
(Sweden) (Reissue)
ST   Aug. -Sept.   p233.   275w. $4\frac{1}{2}$

4398   BERNARD, Rod and Clifton Chenier.   Boogie in Black &
White.   JIN 9014
CAD   Aug.   p56.   125w.   4
RSP   1:3   p6.   100w. $1\frac{1}{2}$

4399   BIG Maceo.   Chicago Breakdown.   RCA AXM2-5506 (2 discs)
(Reissue)
LB   May-June   p35, 36.   325w. $4\frac{1}{2}$

4400   BLIND Blake.   1926-1930.   Biograph BLP 12050 (Reissue)
JR   V9/#4   unpaged 100w.   4

4401   BOOGIE Woogie Red.   Live at the Blind Pig.   Blind Pig 001
CAD   Dec.   p42-3.   125w. $2\frac{1}{2}$

4402   BOOGIE Woogie Red.   Red Hot.   Blind Pig 003
CAD   Dec.   p42-3.   125w.   3

4403   BOOKER, James.   The Piano Prince from New Orleans.
Aves 69. 031 (West Germany)
CZM   June p30.   50w.   5

4404   BOYD, Eddie.   Brotherhood.   Finnish Blues Society FBS 101
(Finland)

LB   Sept./Oct.   p38.   150w.   3

4405   BOYD, Eddie.   For Sincere Listening.   Bluebeat S 77331 (E)
        MM   Dec. 31   p31.   275w. $2\frac{1}{2}$

4406   BOYD, Eddie.   The Legacy of the Blues.   Sonet SNTF 670
        (E)
        LB   Sept./Oct.   p38.   150w.   3

4407   BOYD, Eddie.   Live.   Storyville SLP 268
        RR   Dec.   p87.   50w. $3\frac{1}{2}$

4408   BOYD, Eddie.   Praise to Helsinki.   Love LRLP-25 (Finland)
        LB   Sept./Oct.   150w.   p38.   3

4409   BOYD, Eddie.   Vacation from the Blues.   Jefferson 601
        (Sweden) (Reissue)
        CZM   June   p69-71.   250w. $4\frac{1}{2}$

4410   BROONZY, Big Bill.   RCA FXM1-7275 (France) (Reissue)
        LB   May-June   p35, 36.   325w.   5

4411   BROWN, Arlean.   The Blues in the Loop.   Simmons 1317
        LB   Nov./Dec.   p31-2.   225w.   4

4412   BROWN, Gabriel.   Gabriel Brown and His Guitar.   Policy
        Wheel PW 4592
        CZM   June   p67.   75w. $2\frac{1}{2}$
        RSP   March-April   p9.   200w.   4

4413   BROWN, Olive.   Olive Brown Sings!   GHB GHBS-86
        SR   Nov.   p128.   200w.   5

4414   BROWN, Roy.   Laughin' But Crying.   Route 66 KIX2 (Sweden)
        (Reissue)
        CAD   July   p32.   150w. $3\frac{1}{2}$
        CZM   June   p74.   100w.   5
        HBS   June/Sept.   p22.   100w.   4
        LB   Sept./Oct.   p34.   275w.   4
        NK   Summer   p37.   225w.   4
        SMG   Sept.   p28.   50w.   4

4415   BUMBLE Bee Slim, 1931-1937.   Vintage Country Blues.
        Magpie PY 1801 (E)
        BM   Jan.   p49.   200w.   4
        JJ   Jan.   p26.   300w.   5
        MM   Jan. 29   p27.   450w.   3
        RSP   Jan.-Feb.   p10-11.   300w. $3\frac{1}{2}$

4416   BUTLER, George "Wild Child."   Funky Butt Lover.   Roots
        1003
        CAD   Feb.   p39.   150w. $3\frac{1}{2}$
        LB   July-Aug.   p33, 34.   375w.   4

RSP March-April p5-6. 200w. $1\frac{1}{2}$

4417 BUTTERBEANS and Suzie. Classic Jazz 29 (Reissue)
CAD June p22. 125w. 5
CO Sept./Oct. p24. 50w. 3
SR Oct. p126, 128. 350w. 4

4418 CARTER, Joe. Mean and Evil Blues. Barrelhouse BH-07
CZM June p69. 250w. 0
JJ May p44-5. 150w. 4
LB July-Aug. p34, 35. 425w. $4\frac{1}{2}$
RSP March-April p7. 125w. $1\frac{1}{2}$

4419 CHARITY, Pernell. The Virginian. Trix 3309
LB March-April p36-7. 225w. 4

4420 CHENIER, Clifton. Bayou Blues. Specially SNTF 5012 (E)
CMR June p16. 150w. 3

4421 CHENIER, Clifton. Bogalusa Boogie. Arhoolie 1076
LB July-Aug. p35, 36. 325w. 5

4422 CHENIER, Clifton. Boogie 'n Zydeco. Maisonde Soul LP
1003
CAD Oct. p40. 150w. 3

4423 CHENIER, Clifton. Cajun Swamp Music Live. Tomato 2-
7002 (2 discs)
CAD Dec. p55. 125w. 4
CZM Dec. p51. 125w. 4

4424 COX, Ida. Volume 2. Fountain FB-304 (Reissue)
ST Dec.-Jan. p74. 275w. 5

4425 CRUDUP, Arthur. That's Alright Mama. DJM DJSLM 2025
(E)
SMG May p24. 75w. 3

4426 DAVIS, Blind John. Stomping on a Saturday Night. Alligator
AL 4709 (Reissue)
CAD Oct. p50-1. 225w. 4
CFS Autumn p24. 250w. 4
CZM Dec. p52-4. 250w. $4\frac{1}{2}$
LB Nov./Dec. p33-4. 200w. 4
RC Oct. p12-3. 125w. 4
VV Nov. 28 p66. 50w. $3\frac{1}{2}$

4427 DAVIS, Walter. Bluebird No. 9. RCA FXM1-7330 (France)
(Reissue)
RR June p94. 50w. 3
RSP V1/#3 p3. 300w. 4

4428 DAWKINS, Jimmy. Blisterstring. Delmark DS 641

AU   Aug.   p91.   500w. $3\frac{1}{2}$
CZM   June   p68.   200w. $2\frac{1}{2}$
DB   June 2   p29-31.   200w.   5
SO   March/April   p52.   75w.   4

4429   DAWKINS, Jimmy.   I Want to Know.   MCM 900. 290 (France)
CZM   June   p61.   25w. $2\frac{1}{2}$
LB   March-April   p36-7.   200w.   4

4430   DELSANTO, Don.   White Feathers in the Coop.   Trix 3314
CAD   July   p33.   200w.   4

4431   DIXON, Floyd.   Opportunity Blues.   Route 66 KIX-1 (Sweden)
(Reissue)
LB   Sept./Oct.   p34.   275w.   4
NK   Winter   p33.   250w.   4

4432   DUNN, Roy.   Know'd Them All.   Trix 3312
CAD   July   p33.   175w.   4
GP   Dec.   p153.   25w. $3\frac{1}{2}$
LB   March-April   p36-7.   225w.   4

4433   DUPREE, Champion Jack.   Happy to Be Free.   GNP Crescendo 10005
LB   March-April   p36.   225w.   4

4434   DUPREE, Champion Jack.   Legacy of the Blues, Vol. 3.
GNP Crescendo 10013
LB   March-April   p36.   225w.   3

4435   DUPREE, Champion Jack.   Tricks.   GNP Crescendo 10001
LB   March-April   p36.   225w.   5

4436   EAGLIN, Snooks.   Blues from New Orleans.   Storyville SLP
140
RR   Aug.   p84.   100w. $3\frac{1}{2}$

4437   EALEY, Robert.   Live at the New Blue Bird Nite Club.   Blue
Royal 300
CZM   June   p72-3.   250w.   2
LB   Nov./Dec.   p33.   200w.   3

4438   ELLIS, Big Chief.   Big Chief Ellis.   Trix 3316
CAD   July   p33.   150w.   4
CK   Nov.   p65.   25w.   4
DB   June 2   p29-31.   200w.   4
RSP   Jan.-Feb.   p10.   300w.   5

4439   FULSON, Lowell.   Hung Down Head.   Chess 408
CZM   June   p66.   125w.   5

4440   FULSON, Lowell.   Lowell Fulson.   Chess 2ACMB-205 (2
discs) (Reissue)

BM Nov. p51. 75w. 4
CZM June p66. 125w. 5
GP March p113. 75w. $4\frac{1}{2}$

4441 FULSON, Lowell. The Ol' Blues Singer. Granite 1006
RC June p5. 100w. $3\frac{1}{2}$

4442 GAINES, Roy. Superman. Black & Blue 33-088 (France)
RSP March-April p6. 325w. $3\frac{1}{2}$

4443 GAITHER, Bill. Leroy's Buddy 1935-1941. Magpie PY-
1804 (E)
ST Aug.-Sept. p232. 250w. 4

4444 GILLUM, Jazz. Vol. 1. RCA FXM1-7231 (France) (Reissue)
LB May-June p35, 36. 325w. $4\frac{1}{2}$

4445 GLENN, Lloyd. Old Time Shuffle. Black and Blue 33-077
(France)
RSP March-April p8. 275w. $3\frac{1}{2}$

4446 GOOD Rockin' Charles. Mr. Blues MB 7601 (E)
BSR No. 7 unpaged 450w. $3\frac{1}{2}$

4447 GUITAR Shorty. Alone. Trix 3306
JR V9/#3 unpaged 75w. $2\frac{1}{2}$

4448 HARPO, Slim. Blues Hangover. Flyright LP520 (E) (Reis-
sue)
CZM June p57. 100w. 4
JJ Jan. p30. 300w. 5
MM Oct. 15 p30. 300w. 3
NK Autumn p49. 150w. 4
RSP March-April p5. 200w. 4

4449 HARRIS, Wynonie. Good Rockin' Blues. King KS 1086 (Reissue)
NK Winter p33. 50w. 5

4450 HARRIS, Wynonie. Mr. Blues Is Coming to Town. Route
66 KIX 3 (Sweden) (Reissue)
CAD Dec. p56-7. 2
CZM Dec. p56. 100w. 4
NK Autumn p42. 200w. 5

4451 HAYES, Clifford and the Dixieland Jug Blowers. Yazoo 1054
(Reissue)
CO Feb. p22. 175w. 3
RR June p94. 100w. 3

4452 HILL, Blind Joe. Boogie in the Dark. Barrelhouse BH-08
CZM June p73. 100w. 5
LB Sept./Oct. p39. 225w. 4

4453   HILL, Joe. Boogie in the Dark.   Barrelhouse BH 08
        RSP March-April p7.   125w. $2\frac{1}{2}$

4454   HOLMES, Groove and Jimmy Witherspoon.   Cry the Blues.
        Bulldog BDL 0112
        BM Jan. p49.   75w.   1

4455   HOMESICK James.   Goin' Back Home.   Trix 3315
        CAD July p33.   100w.   3
        CFS Autumn p24.   250w. $3\frac{1}{2}$
        DB June 2 p29-31.   200w.   4

4456   HOOKER, Earl Jody Williams.   The Leading Band.   Red
        Lightnin' RL 0018 (E) (Reissue)
        CZM Dec. p59.   25w.   4

4457   HOOKER, John Lee.   Black Snake.   Fantasy F24722 (2 discs)
        (Reissue)
        AU Dec. p128.   500w.   4
        CAD Nov. p40.   225w.   5

4458   HOOKER, John Lee.   Dimples.   DJM DJD 28026 (E) (2 discs)
        (Reissue)
        BM May p53.   300w.   5
        MM Jan. 8 p28.   350w.   4
        NK Spring p40.   125w.   4

4459   HOOKER, John Lee.   Moanin' & Stompin' the Blues.   King
        KS 1085 (Reissue)
        JJ March p33.   325w.   4

4460   HOPKINS, Lightnin'.   Lightnin'.   Tomato 2-7004 (2 discs)
        (Reissue)
        CAD Dec. p55.   125w. $4\frac{1}{2}$

4461   HORTON, Walter and Floyd Jones.   Do Nothing Till You Hear
        from Us.   Magnolia MLP 301
        CZM June p63.   125w.   2
        RSP Jan.-Feb. p6.   250w. $1\frac{1}{2}$

4462   HOVINGTON, Frank.   Lonesome Road Blues.   Rounder 2017
        CAD Nov. p33.   350w.   4
        JJ Jan. p31.   300w.   3
        RSP Jan.-Feb. p8.   300w.   4

4463   HOWLIN' Wolf.   Chess Blues Masters Series 2ACMB-201 (2
        discs) (Reissue)
        BM Aug. p49.   150w.   5
        DB May 5 p28-32.   225w.   5
        GP March p113.   75w. $4\frac{1}{2}$

4464   HOWLIN' Wolf.   Legendary Sun Performer.   Charly CR
        30134 (E) (Reissue)

        CZM Dec. p59.   25w.   4
        NK   Autumn p43. 100w.   4

4465   HUTTO, J. B. Blues for Fonessa. Amigo AMLP 823
      (Sweden) (Reissue)
        RSP Jan. -Feb. p13.   250w. $2\frac{1}{2}$

4466   JACKSON Blue Boys. Policy Wheel PW 4593 (E) (Reissue)
        BM May p53.   300w.   2
        JJ April p32.   300w.   2
        RSP 1:3 p7-8.   250w. $3\frac{1}{2}$

4467   JAMES, Elmore. Shake Your Money Maker. DJM (E)
        CAD Feb. p434.   200w. $1\frac{1}{2}$

4468   JOHNSON, Jimmy and Luther Johnson Jr. Ma Bea's Rock.
      MCM 900. 294 (France)
        CZM June p61-2.   75w.   3
        LB March-April p38.   200w.   4

4469   JOHNSON, Luther Jr. Luther's Blues. Black and Blue 33-
      579 (France)
        CZM Dec. p55.   150w. $4\frac{1}{2}$

4470   JOHNSON, Pete and Joe Turner. 1944-1949. Jackson 1207
      (Reissue)
        BM May p53.   300w.   3
        CO Dec. p23.   100w.   2
        JJ April p32.   250w.   4

4471   KENT, Willie and Willie James Lyon. Ghetto. MGM 900291
      (France)
        LB March-April p37-8.   200w.   4

4472   KING, Albert. Albert Live. Utopia BUL 1-1731
        AU May p96.   400w. $3\frac{1}{2}$
        CAD May p23-4.   175w.   3
        DB June 2 p29-31.   200w.   5
        GP Aug. p119.   150w.   5
        LB March-April p32.   425w. $2\frac{1}{2}$
        LB Nov. /Dec. p34.   450w. $3\frac{1}{2}$
        RSP 1:3 p7.   225w.   3
        SR June p104.   200w.   3

4473   KING, Albert. King Albert. Tomato 6002
        CAD Dec. p55.   125w. $1\frac{1}{2}$

4474   KING, Albert. The Pinch. Stax STX 4104 (Reissue)
        RS Feb. 9 p95-6.   325w. $1\frac{1}{2}$

4475   KING, B. B. King Size. ABC AB-977
        AU May p94.   250w.   2
        CAD April p8.   168w.   4

DB   June 2 p29-31.   200w.   1
GP   June p137.   50w. $2\frac{1}{2}$
LB   Nov./Dec. p28.   150w.   2
RSP   March-April p6.   125w. $1\frac{1}{2}$

4476   KING, Bobby.   Chaser.   MCM 900. 292 (France)
CZM   June p61.   25w. $2\frac{1}{2}$
LB   March-April p37-8.   200w. $2\frac{1}{2}$

4477   KING, Freddie.   Freddie King (1934-1976).   RSO RS-1-3025
(Reissue)
GP   Nov.   p127.   225w. $4\frac{1}{2}$
HF   Nov.   p101.   375w.   3
NK   Autumn p49.   50w.   3

4478   LAZY Lester.   They Call Me Lazy.   Flyright 526 (E) (Re-
issue)
NK   Autumn p49.   150w.   4
RSP   1:3 p8-9.   300w. $3\frac{1}{2}$

4479   LEADBELLY.   Midnight Special.   Folkways FTS 31046
ARG   May p51-2.   150w.   3

4480   LEAVY, Calvin.   Cummins Prison Farm.   P-Vine Special
PLP 701 (Japan)
LB   Nov./Dec. p29, 31.   250w.   3

4481   LENOIR, J. B.   Chess Blues Masters 2ACMB 208 (2 discs)
(Reissue)
BM   Nov.   p50.   400w.   5
CZM   Dec.   p51-2.   225w.   4

4482   LEWIS, Furry.   The Fabulous.   Southland SLP-3
CAD   Oct.   p60-1.   125w.   4

4483   LEWIS, Furry.   In His Prime, 1927-1928.   Yazoo 1050
(Reissue)
ST   Dec.-Jan. p77-8.   275w.   5

4484   LEWIS, Smiley.   I Hear You Knocking.   Liberty 70075
(Reissue)
LB   March-April p32.   425w.   4

4485   LEWIS, Smiley.   Lonesome Road Blues.   G. P. 5000
CZM   June p37, 40.   100w.   5

4486   LIGGINS, Joe/Jimmy Liggins.   Saturday Night Boogie Woogie
Man.   Specialty SNTF5020
BM   Aug. p49.   125w.   3
CZM   June p30.   25w. $2\frac{1}{2}$
MM   March 5 p24.   75w.   3
NK   Winter p38.   75w.   4
SMG   May p25.   125w.   4

4487   LIGHTNIN' Slim.   The Early Years.   Flyright LP524 (E)
        (Reissue)
            BM   March   p53.   150w.   4
            CZM   June   p57-8.   200w.   4
            JJ   Jan.   p36.   200w.   2
            NK   Autumn   p49.   150w.   4
            RSP   March-April   p5.   200w.   4

4488   LITTLE Milton.   Chess Blues Masters Series 2ACMB-204
        (2 discs) (Reissue)
            BM   Nov.   p51.   50w.   4
            GP   March   p113.   75w. $4\frac{1}{2}$

4489   LITTLE Milton.   Friend of Mine.   Glades 7506
            LB   Nov./Dec.   p28-9.   225w.   4

4490   LITTLE Milton.   Me for You, You for Me.   Glades 7511
            LB   Nov./Dec.   p28-9.   225w.   4

4491   LITTLE Walter.   Chess Blues Masters Series 2ACMB-202
        (2 discs) (Reissue)
            BM   Nov.   p51.   75w.   5
            DB   May 5   p28-32.   225w.   5
            GP   March   p133.   75w. $4\frac{1}{2}$

4492   LITTLEFIELD, Little Willie.   K. C. Loving.   K. C. 101 (Re-
        issue)
            CZM   Dec.   p59.   50w. $3\frac{1}{2}$

4493   LOCKWOOD, Robert Jr.   Blues Live in Japan.   Advent
        2807
            GP   May   p128.   100w.   4

4494   LOCKWOOD, Robert Jr.   Contrasts.   Trix 3307
            JR   V9/#3   unpaged   75w. $3\frac{1}{2}$

4495   LOCKWOOD, Robert Jr.   Does 12.   Trix 3317
            CAD   Dec.   p54.   150w. $3\frac{1}{2}$

4496   LONESOME Sundown.   Been Gone Too Long.   Joliet 6002
            CZM   Dec.   p60.   25w.   4

4497   LONESOME Sundown.   Legendary Jay D. Miller Sessions.
        Flyright LP 529 (E) (Reissue)
            NK   Autumn   p49.   150w.   5

4498   LOUISIANA Red.   Dead Stray Dog.   Blue Labor BL 107
            CAD   Dec.   p42.   150w.   3
            LB   Sept./Oct.   p34, 37.   475w.   4
            RSP   1:3   p5-6.   100w.   1

4499   LYONS, Willie James and Kent Willie.   Ghetto.   MCM 900.
        291

CZM   June p61.   25w. $2\frac{1}{2}$

4500   MABON, Willie.   Willie Mabon Sings "I Don't Know" and
Other Chicago Blues Hits.   Antilles AN-7013
CAD   Oct.   p48.   200w.   2

4501   McDOWELL, Fred and Johnny Woods.   Rounder 2007
RR   Oct.   p89.   25w.   3
RSP   1:3   p9.   200w.   3

4502   McGHEE, Brownie.   Blues Is Truth.   Blue Labor BL 117
CAD   Dec.   p42.   150w.   3
RSP   V1/#3   p3   200w. $1\frac{1}{2}$
SR   Aug.   p98.   150w.   4

4503   MARS, Johnny.   Oakland Boogie.   Big Bear BEAR 12
SMG   Jan.   p27.   200w.   3

4504-5 MARTIN, Bogan and Armstrong.   Sonet SNTF 711
CMR   April   p33.   100w.   3

4506   MARTIN, Bogan and Armstrong.   The Barnyard Dance.
Rounder 2003
CAD   Nov.   p16.   50w.   4

4507   MEMPHIS Minnie and the McCoy Brothers.   MCA 3529 (Reissue)
RSP   March-April   p4-5.   325w.   5

4508   MEMPHIS Slim.   Inner City 1011
CAD   April   p34.   108w.   4

4509   MEMPHIS Slim.   Everyday I Have the Blues.   DJM (E) (Reissue)
CAC   Feb.   p434.   250w.   2

4510   MEMPHIS Slim.   Messin' Around with the Blues.   King KS
1082 (Reissue)
SMG   Sept.   p27.   50w. $2\frac{1}{2}$

4511   MILTON, Roy.   Roy Milton and His Solid Senders.   Specialty
SNTF5019 (E) (Reissue)
BM   Aug.   p49.   125w.   3
CZM   June   p30.   25w. $2\frac{1}{2}$
MM   March 5   p24.   75w. $3\frac{1}{2}$
SMG   May   p25.   125w.   4

4512   MONTGOMERY, Little Brother.   Crescent City Blues.   RCA
AXM2-5522 (2 discs) (Reissue)
CAD   Nov.   p40, 41.   125w.   5
CODA   Sept./Oct.   p23.   150w.   5

4513   MUDDY Waters.   Chess Blues Masters 2ACMB-203 (2 discs)

(Reissue)
    BM   Nov. p51. 75w. 5
    DB   May 5 p28-32. 225w. 5

4514   MUDDY Waters. Hard Again.   Blue Sky PX 34449
    AU   May p94. 250w. 4
    BM   July p48. 50w. 4
    CAD April p24. 216w. 4
    CIR April 28 p16. 300w. $4\frac{1}{2}$
    DB   May 19 225w. 4
    GP   March p113. 75w. $4\frac{1}{2}$
    GP   June p136-7. 150w. $4\frac{1}{2}$
    HBS April/May p21. 125w. 4
    LB   March-April p32, 34. 450w. $2\frac{1}{2}$
    MM   April 2 p26. 350w. $3\frac{1}{2}$
    RR   June p95. 25w. $3\frac{1}{2}$
    RS   March 24 p65. 450w. 3
    RS   April 7 p83. 50w. $3\frac{1}{2}$
    RSP March-April p6. 125w. 1
    RSP May-June p24, 62. 750w. 4
    SR   May p94. 150w. 4

4515   MUSCLES. Big Bear BBR 1001
    BM   April p52-3. 150w. 3

4516   MUSE, Lewis "Rabbit" Anderson. Muse Blues. Outlet STLP
1005
    RSP March-April p4. 125w. 4

4517   The NEW Mississippi Sheiks. Rounder 2004
    CAD Nov. p16. 25w. $3\frac{1}{2}$

4518   ODOM, Andrew "B. B." Sings and Sings and Sings. WASP
Music 26761
    LB   May-June p39, 40. 225w. $4\frac{1}{2}$
    RSP Jan.-Feb. p11. 125w. 2

4519   PARKER, Junior. The ABC Collection. ABC AC-30010
(Reissue)
    CZM June p64. 175w. 4
    RSP Jan.-Feb. p10. 300w. 3

4520   PARKER, Junior. The Best of Junior Parker. Dule DLP
83 (Reissue)
    CZM June p64. 25w. 5

4521   PARKER, Junior/Billy Love. Legendary Sun Performers.
Charly CR 30135 (Reissue)
    CZM Dec. p59. 25w. 4
    NK   Autumn p45. 100w. 4

4522   PIANO Red. Ain't Goin' to Be Your Lowdown Dog No More.
Black Lion BLP 311

426 Record Reviews, 1977

AU   Jan.   p89.   600w.   2½
MJ   Jan.   p38.   50w.   1½
```

4523   PIANO Red.   Percussive Piano.   Euphonic 1212
```
CAD   Jan.   p43.   100w.   4½
JR   V9/#3   unpaged   250w.   3
RSP   Jan. -Feb.   p8.   150w.   2½
```

4524   PLEASANT, Cousin Joe.   From New Orleans.   Riverboat 900-265 (Reissue)
```
RSP   March-April   p9.   300w.   3½
```

4525   PRICE, Sammy with Fessor's Big City Band.   Copenhagen Boogie.   Storyville SLP 266
```
GR   March   p1471.   125w.   4
JJ   Jan.   p34.   250w.   4
MR   June   p8-9.   100w.   2½
```

4526   REED, Jimmy.   Big Boss Man, Memorial Album, Vol. 1. DJM DJD 28033 (2 discs) (Reissue)
```
BM   March   p53.   325w.   5
MM   Jan. 29   p27.   400w.   3½
NK   Winter   p34.   150w.   4
RSP   1:3   p5.   325w.   3
```

4527   ROBERTSON, William.   South Georgia Blues.   Southland SLP-5
```
CAD   Oct.   p46-7.   275w.   5
```

4528   ROCKIN' Sidney.   They Call Me Rockin'.   Flyright LP 515 (E) (Reissue)
```
LB   Nov. /Dec.   p36.   150w.   3
```

4529   ROGERS, Buddy.   Buddy Rogers Sings the Greatest Songs of Jimmy Reed.   Teem LP 5006
```
LB   July-Aug.   p36.   325w.   ½
```

4530   RUSH, Otis.   Cold Day in Hell.   Delmark DS 638
```
BM   Jan.   p49.   125w.   2
```

4531   RUSH, Otis.   Right Place, Wrong Time.   Bullfrog 301
```
AU   Jan.   p118.   100w.   4
CAD   March   p39.   150w.   4
CZM   June   p56.   250w.   5
DB   April 7   p22.   300w.   4½
GP   May   p128.   125w.   4
LB   May-June   p35.   750w.   4½
MM   Sept. 10   p28.   250w.   3½
RSP   Jan. -Feb.   p8-9.   450w.   4½
SO   March/April   p51, 52.   175w.   5
```

4532   SEALS, Son.   Midnight Son.   Alligator AL 4708
```
AU   Dec.   p135.   450w.   4
```
```

BM   Aug. p49. 250w. 5
CAD   March p29-30. 150w. 4
CRA   April p112. 300w. $3\frac{1}{2}$
CZM   June p61. 175w. 5
DB   June 2 p29-31. 200w. $4\frac{1}{2}$
GP   July p129. 125w. 5
JJ   April p34. 200w. $1\frac{1}{2}$
LB   March-April p34. 375w. 2
MM   June 25 p24. 300w. 3
RS   June 16 p64. 850w. $4\frac{1}{2}$
RSP   Jan. -Feb. p5. 300w. $3\frac{1}{2}$
SO   March/April p52. 100w. 4
SR   July p100-1. 225w. $4\frac{1}{2}$
VV   March 7 p45, 47. 350w. $3\frac{1}{2}$

4533 SHINES, Johnny. And Company. Biograph BLP 12048
ARG   March p48. 100w. 5

4534 SIMMONS, Little Mac. Blue Lights. Black & Blue 33.514
(France)
CZM   June p58. 125w. 4

4535 SMALL, Drink. I Know My Blues Are Different ... Cause
I'm the One Who Has Them. Southland SLP-1
CAD   Oct. p60-1. 125w. 3

4536 SMITH, Dan. Now Is the Time. Biograph BLP 12053
AU   Jan. p90. 500w. 3

4537 SPIVEY, Victoria. The Blues Is Life. Folkways FS 3541
(Reissue)
CAD   Jan. p22, 23. 200w. 4
JJ   March p36. 400w. 3
LB   Sept. /Oct. p34. 400w. 4
RSP   Jan. -Feb. p5. 175w. 2

4538 STIDHAM, Arbee. There's Always Tomorrow. Folkways
ST531033
CAD   Aug. p36. 100w. $3\frac{1}{2}$
LB   May-June p39. 225w. $1\frac{1}{2}$

4539 STOKES, Frank. Creator of the Memphis Blues. Yazoo
1056 (Reissue)
FR   Nov. p35. 350w. 4
RSP   Jan. -Feb. p12. 300w. 4

4540 SUNNYLAND Slim. Blues Jam. Storyville SLP 245
RR   Aug. p84. 50w. 2

4541 SUNNYLAND Slim. She's Got That Jive. Slim's Airway Records 3220
CAD   April 275w. 3

4542   SYKES, Roosevelt.   Bluebird No. 10.   RCA PM 42048
        (France) (Reissue)
            RSP   V1/#3   p4-5.   250w.   3½

4543   SYKES, Roosevelt.   Boogie Honky Tonk.   Oldie Blues 2818
        (Netherlands) (Reissue)
            RSP   March-April   p3.   300w.   4

4544-5 SYKES, Roosevelt.   Is Blue and Ribald.   Southland SLP-2
            CAD   Oct.   p60-1.   125w.   4

4546   SYKES, Roosevelt.   The Meek Roosevelt Sykes.   Inner City
        IC 1010 (Reissue)
            CAD   April   p34.   156w.   3½
            CK   April   p49.   100w.   4

4547   TAJ Mahal.   Anthology, Vol. 1.   Columbia 34466 (Reissue)
            MG   July   p55.   150w.   3
            VV   April 25   p55.   200w.   4½

4548   TAJ Mahal.   Music fuh Ya.   Warner BS 2994
            AU   April   p85.   150w.   4
            BM   May   p51.   300w.   5
            CAD   Feb.   p20.   75w.   2
            CIR   March 17   p17.   250w.   4
            RS   March 24   p62, 65.   400w.   3
            SR   May   p86.   150w.   2½
            VV   April 25   p55.   75w.   2

4549   TAMPA Red.   You Can't Get That Stuff No More.   Oldie
        Blues 2816 (Reissue)
            CZM   June   p68.   200w.   4
            RSP   March-April   p7-8.   200w.   3

4550   TARHEEL Slim.   No Time at All.   Trix 3310
            CAD   July   p33.   100w.   4
            DB   June 2   p29-31.   200w.   4
            GP   Dec.   p153.   25w.   3½
            LB   July-Aug.   p33.   475w.   5

4551   TAYLOR, Eddie.   I Feel So Bad.   DJM DJM2265 (E)
            BM   Aug.   p49.   150w.   4

4552   TAYLOR, Eva.   Maggie's Blue Five.   Kenneth KS 2042
            MR   Aug.   p16.   100w.   4
            ST   June-July   p196.   300w.   5

4553   TAYLOR, Hound Dog.   Beware of the Dog.   Sonet SNTF 701
            BM   Jan.   p49.   200w.   4

4554   TAYLOR, Koko.   I Got What It Takes.   Alligator 4706
            SO   March/April   p52.   150w.   5

4555   TERRY, Sonny & Brownie McGee.   Midnight Special.   Fantasy F24721 (2 discs) (Reissue)
        CAD   Nov.   p40.   225w.   5

4556   THOMAS, Henry.   Ragtime Texas.   Herwin 209 (Reissue)
        CAD   Aug.   p37.   200w.   4
        JR   V9/#4   unpaged   200w.   4

4557   TRICE, Willie.   Blue and Ragged.   Trix 3305
        JR   V9/#3   unpaged   100w.   4

4558   TURNER, Ike.   I'm Tore Up.   Red Lightnin' 0016 (E) (Reissue)
        CAD   Oct.   p62.   250w.   4
        HBS   April/May   p17.   125w.   4
        LB   May-June   p36.   575w.   5
        NK   Spring   p37.   200w.   4
        SMG   May   p24.   150w.   5

4559   TURNER, Joe.   The Boss of the Blues.   Atlantic ATC 50 244 (E) (Reissue)
        BM   Aug.   p49.   200w.   4
        SOU   Sept.   p66.   50w.   4

4560   TURNER, Joe.   In the Evening.   Pablo 2310-776
        AU   Nov.   p120.   250w.   3
        DB   Oct. 20   p28.   200w.   4
        CAD   March   p36.   100w.   3
        JJ   April   p36.   250w.   3
        LB   May-June   p37.   350w.   3
        MM   March 5   p32.   350w. $2\frac{1}{2}$
        NK   Spring   p40.   50w. $3\frac{1}{2}$
        SR   April   p113.   75w.   2

4561   TURNER, Joe.   Nobody in Mind.   Pablo 2310-760
        LB   May-June   p36, 37.   175w.   0

4562   TURNER, Joe.   Things That I Used to Do.   Pablo 2310-800
        CAD   Oct.   p46.   175w.   4
        NK   Autumn   p49.   50w.   4
        RR   Oct.   p89.   25w.   3

4563   TURNER, Joe.   The Trumpet King Meets.   Pablo 2310-717
        AU   Nov.   p120.   250w.   4

4564   TURNER, Johnny and Zaven Jambazian.   Blues with a Feeling.   Testament 2227
        CAD   Nov.   p49.   175w.   4
        RSP   1:3   p9.   350w. $3\frac{1}{2}$

4565   WALKER, Philip.   Someday You'll Have These Blues.   Joliet 6001
        CAD   July   p36.   150w.   2

CZM June p71-2. 300w. 5
GP Nov. p137. 125w. 3
LB Sept./Oct. p38-9. 375w. 4
RSP 1:3 p6-7. 600w. $3\frac{1}{2}$

4566   WASHBOARD Sam. Bluebird No. 7. RCA FXM1-7297
(France) (Reissue)
RSP V1/#3 p4-5. 250w. $3\frac{1}{2}$

4567   WEBSTER, Katie. Whoee Sweet Daddy. Flyright LP530 (E)
(Reissue)
CZM Dec. p55-6. 150w. 4

4568   WELLS, Junior. Blues Hit Big Town. Delmark DC 640 (Re-
issue)
CAD Dec. p50. 350w. 3
CZM Dec. p54-5. 425w. 5
JR V9/#4 unpaged 50w. 4

4569   WHITE, Bukka. Big Daddy. Biograph BLP 12049
JR V9/#4 unpaged 75w. 4

4570   WILLIAMS, Big Joe. Bluebird Vol. 8. RCA FXM1-7323
(France) (Reissue)
CZM June p58. 150w. 5
JJ May p52. 300w. 5
RR June p94. 25w. 3

4571   WILLIAMS, Blind Connie. Philadelphia Street Singer. Testament 2225
CAD Nov. p49. 225w. 5

4572   WILLIAMSON, Sonny Boy No. 1. RCA FXM1-7203 (France)
(Reissue)
LB Nov./Dec. p28. 300w. 4

4573   WILLIAMSON, Sonny Boy No. 2. Sonny Boy Williamson.
Chess 2ACMB-206 (2 discs) (Reissue)
CZM June p37. 75w. 2
GP March p113. 75w. $4\frac{1}{2}$

4574   WILSON, Edith. He May Be Your Man. Delmark DS-637
CAD April p18-9. 180w. 5
CFS Autumn p24. 250w. 4
DB June 2 p29-31. 200w. 5
JR V9/#4 unpaged 125w. 5
LB Sept./Oct. p34. 400w. 4
MJ May p31. 100w. $2\frac{1}{2}$
MR Feb. p13. 300w. 4

4575   WILSON, Joe Lee. What Would I Be without You. Survival
SR 110
CAD April p40-1. 264w. 3

4576   WILSON, Smokey. Blowin' Smoke.   Big Town BT1001
           CZM   Dec. p60.   25w.   3

4577   WISMER, Steve. Bring Me Another Half a Pint.   Barrel-
           house BH-09
           CZM   June p73.   175w.   4

4578   WITHERSPOON, Jimmy and Ben Webster.   Warner WB56295
           (E) (Reissue)
           JJ   April p38-9.   250w. $3\frac{1}{2}$
           MM   May 14 p34.   250w.   4

4579   YANCEY, Jimmy. The Immortal Jimmy Yancey, Vol. 2.
           Oldie Blues 2813 (Netherlands) (Reissue)
           CZM   June p68.   150w.   5
           MM   Feb. 19 p28.   500w. $3\frac{1}{2}$

SOUL, REGGAE, and SALSA

This section covers the basic soul market--the black and ethnic alternative to rock music. Included here are rhythm 'n' blues music, reggae, salsa and other gospel-inspired and inflected artists or records. Most of this music is vocal. Attempts have been made to pass rock and jazz records off as soul (to sell the record); those sections should be consulted for those records which usually include in their titles the words: "funky," "right on," "dues," "soul," "dig it," and other forms of jive talk. This is not to say that this music is not soul--but certainly it is not pure soul and as a hybrid it is best placed where it originated, as is much of disco music.

There are few American review media for soul. Ebony has a few watered-down reviews (mostly of the New Jazz). SMG and Black Music, two British magazines, are not very critical; indeed, they present reviews that include blues material more adequately handled elsewhere. No rhythm and blues fanzines contain record reviews. Mention is often made of albums, but no serial number of title is given. What are often reviewed (as in Soul Cargo, Blues Unlimited, and Living Blues) are the 45-rpm singles, and this is where the soul market lies, in the three-minute miniature. Singles are important because they all sound the same, with no extended lengths for improvisation, and the guaranteed formula seems to strike pay dirt each time. Artists rarely play around with success. Many performers go into the studio to cut singles, with few ideas or plans for albums; consequently, the music is mainly a variation on a few hit themes at the same tempo. Such speeds and other technical devices (riffing horns, for example) render a whole album monotonous if one number follows another in the same manner and mode. The best purchases in this category are the anthologies, for a selection of different stylings. All male vocalists may sound like James Brown, but they don't sound like the Temptations, Diana Ross or Aretha Franklin, or vice versa.

A blues magazine and a good rock magazine will always review a good soul disc, but the reviewer may come from a white background. Such periodicals as the British Blues Unlimited, and the American Rolling Stone, Living Blues, and Creem appear to be fair, although the records never seem to come in as raves. This is still an independent label's field, but the best of the smaller majors come from the Mowest complex, Atlantic (and Atco), Philadelphia International, and Epic.

According to the reviews, the best records for 1977 appear
to be:

SOUL

ARMATRADING, Joan. Show Some Emotion. A & M SP 4663
EMOTIONS. Rejoice. Columbia PC 34762
FACTS of Life. Sometimes. Kayvette 802
HOLLOWAY, Loleatta. Gold Mind GZS 7500
ISLEY Brothers. Go for Your Guns. T-Neck PZ 34432
JACKSON, Millie. Feelin' Bitchy. Spring SP1-6715
METERS. New Directions. Warner Brothers BS 3042
PERSUASIONS. Chirpin'. Elektra 7E-1099
PHILLIPS, Esther. Capricorn Princess. Kudu KU 31
RUFUS. Ask Rufus. ABC 975

REGGAE

BURNING Spear. Dry and Heavy. Mango MLPS 9431
HEPTONES. Party Time. Island ILPS 9456
MARLEY, Bob, and the Wailers. Exodus. Island ILPS 9498
TOSH, Peter. Equal Rights. Columbia PC 34670

4580   ABIODUN, Admiral Dele. Adawa Super 5. Olumo ORPS 56
            BM April p20. 50w. 3

4581   ADE, Sunny and His African Beats. Festac '77. Alade
        SALPS 14 (E)
            BM June p19. 25w. 4

4582   AFRICAN Brothers Band. Afrahili to USA. Afribros AB001
        (E)
            BM April p20. 50w. 4

4583   AGROVATORS and Revolutionaires. At Channel One. Third
        World TWS 900 (E)
            BM Aug. p51. 75w. 4

4584   ALCAPONE, Dennis. Investigator Rock. Third World TWS
        911 (E)
            BM Oct. p51. 75w. 2

4585   ALLSPICE. AT-HOME Ah-401
            BS Nov. p64. 250w. $3\frac{1}{2}$
            SR Dec. 150w. 3

4586   ALTON, Roy. Don't Stop the Carnival. Tackle TAK 004 (E)
            BM Dec. p51. 100w. 3

4587   ANDY, Bob.   The Music Inside Me.   Tropical Sound Tracs
        1003 (E)
            BM   Feb.   p51.   150w.   4

4588   AREMU, Durojaiye.   Sunny Ade.   Yinka Esho Records ESLP
        70 (E)
            BM   Nov.   p24.   200w.   5

4589   ARMATRADING, Joan.   A&M SP 4588
            RM   Jan.   p14-5.   200w.   5

4590   ARMATRADING, Joan.   Shoe Some Emotion.   A&M 4663
            BM   Nov.   p46.   300w.   5
            GR   Nov.   p920.   75w.   3½
            MG   Dec.   p61.   100w.   3
            MM   Sept. 10 p20.   450w.   5
            RR   Nov.   p115.   75w.   4½
            RS   Dec. 29 p65.   500w.   2½

4591   ARMATRADING, Joan.   Whatever's for Us.   CUBE HIFLY
        12 (E) (Reissue)
            BM   March p22.   150w.   3
            CAC Feb.   p415.   300w.   4

4592   ASHFORD and Simpson.   Send It.   Warner Bros. BS 3088
            BS   Dec.   p48.   225w.   2½
            RS   Dec. 29 p74, 77.   400w.   2½

4593   ASHFORD and Simpson.   So So Satisfied.   Warner Bros. BS
        2992.   Cart. M82992.   Cass. M52992
            HF   April p136.   250w.   4
            MG   May p55.   125w.   2
            RS   March 24 p69.   400w.   2
            SR   July p92.   100w.   2

4594   ASSALAM Aleikoum Africa.   Progressive and Popular Music
        of West Africa.   Antilles 7032
            MG   Sept.   p55.   100w.   3
            RS   Sept. 22 p72, 77.   250w.   3

4595   AUSTIN, Patti.   End of the Rainbow.   CT1 5001
            BM   April p50-1.   150w.   3
            DB   Feb. 24 p25.   300w.   3

4596   AUTOMATIC Man.   Visitors.   Island ILPS 9429
            MG   Dec.   p55.   50w.   2
            MG   Dec.   p61.   100w.   3
            MM   Jan. 7 p16.   50w.   0

4597   BAR Kays.   Too Hot to Stop.   Mercury SRM 1-1099
            MG   April p54.   125w.   2½

4598   BEE, Celi and the Buzzy Bunch TK XL 14060

    BM   Oct.   p47.   75w.   2
    MG   July   p55.   75w.   1
    MM   Sept. 3 p46.   50w. $2\frac{1}{2}$

4599   BELL, Archie and the Drells.   Hard Not to Like It.   Phila-
       delphia International PZ 34855
       BM   Dec.   p48.   300w.   3
       MM   Nov. 19 p24.   200w. $3\frac{1}{2}$

4600   BELL, Archie and the Drells.   Where Will You Go When the
       Party's Over.   Philadelphia International PZ 34323
       BM   Feb.   p49.   200w.   4
       MG   April   p54.   100w. $2\frac{1}{2}$
       MM   Jan. 22 p24.   350w. $2\frac{1}{2}$

4601   BELL, William.   Coming Back for More.   Mercury 1-1146
       BM   Oct.   p44.   325w.   5

4602   BELL, William.   Relating.   Stax (E)
       CAC   Jan.   p477-8.   150w.   2

4603   BENTON, Brook.   Mister Bartender.   Phonogram (E)
       CAC   Feb.   p417.   50w.   3

4604   BERRY, Chuck.   Greatest Hits.   Archive of Folk and Jazz
       Music FS 321
       SR   March   p94.   150w.   0

4605   BERRY, Chuck.   Motorvatin'.   Chess 9286 (E) (Reissue)
       MM   May 14 p33.   50w.   3
       NK   Winter   p37.   50w.   4
       SMG   May   p22.   50w.   5

4606   BERRY, Chuck.   Six Two Five.   Maybelline MBL 676 (Re-
       issue)
       RSP   1:3   p30.   100w. $3\frac{1}{2}$

4607   BIDDU.   Eastern Man.   Epic PE 34723
       BM   June   p49.   125w.   2
       HBS   April/May   p21.   100w.   2

4608   BIG Youth.   Hit the Road, Jack.   Trojan 137 (E)
       BM   Feb.   p51.   200w.   3

4609   BIG Youth.   Reggae Phenomenon.   Trojan BYD 1 (E)
       BM   Aug.   p50.   100w.   3

4610   BILLION Dollar Band.   TK XL14051 (E)
       MM   Oct. 1 p48.   50w.   2

4611   BLACK Blood.   Blood Brothers, Blood Sister.   Chrysalis
       CHR 1144
       MM   Oct. 1 p23.   50w.   3

RC   Nov.   p2-3.   200w.   4

4612   BLACKBYRDS.   Unfinished Business.   Fantasy F9518
       BM   March   p23.   150w.   4
       DB   May 5   p28.   250w.   2
       HBS   April/May   p20.   100w. $2\frac{1}{2}$
       MG   April   p54.   75w. $2\frac{1}{2}$

4613   BLAND, Bobby.   Reflections in Blue.   ABC 1018
       CAD   June   p20.   50w.   2
       SOU   July   p39.   400w.   2
       SR   Sept.   p94.   100w.   4

4614   BOND, Angelo.   Bondage.   ABC D-889
       SR   Aug.   p73.   225w.   5

4615   BONEY, M.   Love for Sale.   Atlantic SD 19145
       BM   Oct.   p47.   75w.   1
       MM   Aug. 6   p16.   200w.   2

4616   BONEY, M.   Take the Heat Off Me.   Atlantic SD36-143
       BM   Feb.   p50.   150w.   2
       MG   June   p55.   125w. $3\frac{1}{2}$
       MM   Jan. 22   p24.   150w.   2
       RC   April   p10.   200w.   4

4617   BOOKER T and the MGs.   Melting Pot.   Stax (E) (Reissue)
       CAC   June   p92.   100w.   3

4618   BOOKER T and the MGs.   Universal Language.   Asylum 7E
       1093.   Cart. ET8 1093.   Cass. TC5 1093
       MM   April 2   p24.   250w. $3\frac{1}{2}$
       SMG   Sept.   p27.   125w.   3
       SR   May   p83.   300w.   5

4619   BOOTSY'S Rubber Band.   Ahh ... the Name Is Bootsy, Baby.
       Warner Bros. BS 2972
       BM   April   p53.   450w.   5
       MG   May   p55.   125w. $3\frac{1}{2}$
       MM   April 23   p21.   200w. $3\frac{1}{2}$
       RS   April 7   p72, 75.   500w. $3\frac{1}{2}$
       VV   Aug. 1   p51.   50w. $3\frac{1}{2}$

4620   BOOTSY'S Rubber Band.   Stretchin' Out in Bootsy's Rubber
       Band.   Warner Bros. BS 2920
       RS   April 7   p72-5.   500w. $3\frac{1}{2}$

4621   BOYLE, Gary.   The Dancer.   Gull GULP 1020 (E)
       BM   Nov.   p47.   75w.   2
       RR   Sept.   p93.   100w.   4

4622   BRAINSTORM.   Stormin'.   Tabu BQL 1-2048
       BM   Sept.   p49.   100w.   3

4623   BRASS Construction. II.   United Artists LA677G
        BM   Jan. p42. 475w. 4
        CAC April p11. 25w. $2\frac{1}{2}$
        HBS June/Sept. p21. 150w. $3\frac{1}{2}$
        MM   Jan. 29 p23. 200w. 3

4624   BRICK.   Bang Records BLP 409
        BS   Nov. p65. 225w. 3
        RC   Dec. p5. 50w. 5

4625-6 BRICK.   Good High.   Bang Records 408
        RC   April p5. 150w. $4\frac{1}{2}$

4627   BRISTOL, Johnny.   Bristol's Creme.   Atlantic SD 18197
        BM   Feb. p50. 200w. 4
        CAC Feb. p416. 300w. $3\frac{1}{2}$
        MG   Jan. 100w. $2\frac{1}{2}$
        MM   Jan. 22 p24. 225w. 2

4628   BROWN, James.   Bodyheat.   Polydor 3177 258 (E)
        CAC April p10. 150w. 3
        HBS April/May p19, 20. 125w. 4

4629   BROWN, James.   Get Up Offa That Thing.   Polydor 2391
        228 (E)
        HBS Feb./March p20. 100w. 4

4630   BROWN, James.   Mutha's Nature.   Polydor PD1-6111
        BM   Nov. p49. 200w. 3
        HF   Nov. 50w. $2\frac{1}{2}$
        MM   Nov. 5 p25. 200w. 3
        RS   Oct. 20 p88. 550w. 3

4631   BROWN, James.   Solid Gold.   Polydor 2679 044 (2 discs)
        (E) (Reissue)
        BM   July p48. 100w. 5
        MM   June 4 p29. 250w. $3\frac{1}{2}$

4632   BROWN, James.   30 Golden Hits.   Polydor 2679 044 (E)
        (Reissue)
        SMG Sept. p28. 25w. 5

4633   BROWN, Shirley.   Arista AL 4129
        BM   Nov. p46. 250w. 4
        MG   July p55. 125w. $3\frac{1}{2}$
        MM   Oct. 8 p32. 275w. $3\frac{1}{2}$
        RS   Aug. 25 p57. 350w. 2
        SC   No. 2 p15. 75w. 4

4634   BULLOCKS, Lester "Dillinger" and Wade "Trinity" Brommer.
        Dillinger vs Trinity: Clash.   Burning Sounds BS 1003
        BM   Nov. p50. 200w. 4

4635   BURCH, Vernon. I'll Be Your Sunshine. UA-LA 342-G
        SR   Aug.   p73.   200w.   4

4636   BURKE, Kevin.   Dark Horse DH 3022.   Cass. M5 3022.
        Cart. M8 3022
        BS   Nov.   p64.   225w.   3
        HF   Nov.   50w.   1½

4637   BURNING Spear.   Dry and Heavy.   Mango MLPS 9431.   Cart.
        Y8M-9431
        BM   Oct.   p50.   175w.   4
        MG   Oct.   p63.   100w.   4
        MM   Sept. 3 p17.   350w.   2½
        RR   Nov.   p116.   125w.   2
        SR   Nov.   p87.   300w.   5
        VV   Aug. 15 p51.   25w.   1½
        ZZ   Sept.   p31.   400w.   4

4638   BUTLER, Jerry.   It All Comes Out in My Song.   Motown
        6-892-51
        RS   Feb. 9 p99.   400w.   0

4639   BUTLER, Jerry.   Make It Easy on Yourself.   DJM DJD
        28027 (2 discs) (E) (Reissue)
        BM   Jan.   p43.   225w.   4
        HBS Feb./March p19.   50w.   5
        NK   Winter p37.   100w.   4

4640   BUTLER, Jerry.   Suite for the Single Girl.   Motown 6-87851
        BM   May   p51.   300w.   4
        CAC June p92.   200w.   2½
        GR   May   p1757.   50w.   2½
        MM   April 2 p20.   250w.   4½

4641   BYLES, Junior.   Micron
        VV   Aug. 15 p51.   25w.   3

4642   C. J. & Co.   Devil's Gun.   Atlantic/Westbound 6100
        MM   Sept. 10 p20.   50w.   4½

4643   CACHAO.   Volume 1.   Salsoul SAL 4111
        SR   Aug.   p86.   200w.   4

4644   CAMERON, G. C.   You're What's Missing in My Life.   Mo-
        town 6-88051
        BM   July p49.   250w.   3
        MM   June 4 p29.   125w.   3

4645   CAMPBELL, Cornell.   Stalowatt.   Third World 301 (E)
        BM   Feb.   p51.   200w.   3

4646   CAMPBELL, Cornell.   Turn Back the Hands of Time.   Third
        World TWS 913 (E)

BM Dec. p51. 150w. 4

4647 CARLETON, Carl. I Wanna Be with You. ABC D-910.
Cart. 8022-910H. Cass. 5022-910H
SR Aug. p73. 200w. 4½

4648 CARN, Jean. Philadelphia International PZ-34394
CAD Jan. p17. 50w. 3
JR V9/#4 unpaged 50w. 2½
MG April p54. 125w. 1
RSP March-April p28. 100w. 3½
SR April p89. 70w. 2

4649 CARTER, Betty. Now Its My Turn. Roulette SR 5005
CRA Jan. p72. 350w. 4½

4650 CARTER, Betty. What a Little Moonlight Can Do. ABC
Impulse ASD 9321/2 (2 discs) (Reissue)
CRA Jan. p72. 350w. 4½
DB Feb. 24 p24. 300w. 4½
MG Jan. 275w. 3½

4651 CHAIN Reaction. Indebted to You. Gull GULP 1021 (E)
BM Oct. p49. 225w. 3

4652 CHANDELL, Tim. Loving Moods. Orbitone OLP 011 (E)
BM Aug. p51. 75w. 3
MM Sept. 10 p20. 50w. 2½

4653 CHANDLER, Gene. Duke of Earl. DJM DJB 26077 (E) (Re-
issue)
BM Jan. p45. 175w. 3
HBS Feb./March p19. 50w. 3

4654 CHARLENE. Prodigal P6-10015
MM July 16 p27. 50w. 1

4655 CHARLES, Ray. True to Life. Atlantic SD 19142
CAD Nov. p31. 50w. 4½
RS Feb. 9 p96. 500w. 3

4656 CHARLES, Tina. Heart 'n' Soul. CBS 82180 (E)
BM Oct. p47. 75w. ½
MM Sept. 10 p20. 50w. 2

4657 CHARLES, Tina. I Love to Love. Columbia PC 34424
SR May p88. 375w. 4

4658 CHARLES, Tina. Rendezvous. Columbia PC-34807. Cart.
PCA-34807. Cass. PCT-34807
SR Sept. p119. 175w. 5

4659 CHI-LITES. Chi-lite Time. Brunswick BBLS B023 (E)

(Reissue)
   BM   Feb.   p43.   300w.   4
   HBS Jan.   p17.   50w.   4
   MM   Jan. 8 p18.   75w.   3

4660   CHI-LITES.   The Fantastic.   Mercury SRM 1-1147
   BM   Oct.   p48.   350w.   3
   GR   Dec.   p1162.   25w. $2\frac{1}{2}$

4661   CHI-LITES.   Happy Being Lonely.   Mercury SRM1-1118
   BM   Jan.   p47, 50.   175w.   3
   MM   Jan. 8 p18.   75w.   2
   VV   March 14 p83.   300w.   5

4662   CHOCOLATE Milk.   Comin'.   RCA APL 1-1830
   BM   April   p51.   200w.   4
   MM   Feb. 12 p25.   50w.   2

4663   CLARKE, Johnny.   Authorized Version.   Virgin V2076
   BM   June   p50.   100w.   4

4664   CLARKE, Johnny.   Don't Stay Out Too Late.   Paradise
   PDLP 001 (E)
   BM   Dec.   p51.   150w.   4

4665   CLARKE, Johnny.   Girl, I Love You.   Justice JUSLP 06 (E)
   BM   Oct.   p50.   125w.   4

4666   CLIFF, Jimmy.   Island ILPS 9414
   BM   June   p50.   100w.   2

4667   CLIFF, Jimmy.   In Concert: The Best of Jimmy Cliff.
   Reprise MS 2256.   Cart. M82256
   AU   March   p78.   400w. $4\frac{1}{2}$
   BM   March   p51.   200w.   4
   CIR May 12 p19.   200w.   2
   SR   March   p95.   400w.   0

4668   COASTERS.   The World Famous.   DJM 22053 (E) (Reissue)
   BM   Jan.   p45.   75w.   2
   NK   Winter   p38.   75w. $2\frac{1}{2}$

4669   COBBETT, Rupert.   Sensitive Cat.   Soul Deep 764
   CAD   June   p36.   200w.   2

4670   COLE, Natalie.   Unpredictable.   Capitol SO-11600
   BM   June   p49.   150w.   4
   CAC July   p130.   125w. $2\frac{1}{2}$
   CRA July   p71.   300w. $3\frac{1}{2}$
   GR   June   p110.   75w.   3
   HF   May   p114.   250w.   3
   MG   May   p55.   125w. $2\frac{1}{2}$
   PRM April   p45.   250w. $2\frac{1}{2}$

RS May 19 325w. 2
SR June p91, 92. 300w. 5

4671 COMMODORES. Motown M7-884RI
      MG June p55. 100w. 3
      RSP May-June p22. 450w. 2
      VV May 30 p63, 65. 250w. 1½

4672 COMMODORES. Live. Motown M984A2 (2 discs)
      RC Dec. p2. 50w. 5

4673 COMMODORES. Zoom. Motown STML 12057
      BM June p49. 125w. 3
      SMG Sept. p27. 75w. 3

4674 CONNORS, Norman. Romantic Journey. Buddah BDLP
      4045
      BM July p50. 75w. 3

4675 CONNORS, Norman. You Are My Starship. Buddah 4043
      HBS April/May p20. 100w. 4

4676 COOKE, Sam. The Golden Age of. RCA RS 1054 (E) (Re-
      issue)
      BM Feb. p50. 300w. 5

4677 COOKIE and the Cupcakes. Goldband GRLP 7757
      CAD Aug. p25. 50w. 3
      LB Nov. /Dec. p31. 225w. 3½

4678 COUNT Bishops. Chiswick WIK 1 (E)
      MM Sept. 3 p22. 200w. 2½
      TP Oct. p44. 300w. 3
      ZZ Sept. p31-2. 225w. 2

4679 CROWN Heights Affair. Do It Your Way. Dep 2002
      MG July p55. 125w. 2½

4680 The CRUSADERS. The Best of the Crusaders. Blue Thumb
      BTSY 6027/2 (2 discs) (Reissue)
      BM March p22-3. 250w. 3
      CAD Jan. p17-8. 175w. 4½
      MM Jan. 8 p18. 50w. 3

4681 CRUSADERS. Free as the Wind. ABC BT 6029
      CAD July p24. 75w. 2
      BM Aug. p49. 375w. 4
      DB Nov. 17 p20, 22. 300w. 5
      GR Oct. p715. 50w. 3½
      MM July 9 p22. 250w. 3½

4682 CRYSTALS. Sing Their Greatest Hits. Phil Spector Interna-
      tional 2307 006 (E) (Reissue)

        SR   June   p118-9.   125w.   3

4683   DAVIS, John.   Up Jumped the Devil.   Polydor 2353 455
        SC   No. 2   p16.   50w.   4

4684   DAVIS, Tyrone.   Let's Be Closer Together.   CBS 82178 (E)
        BM   Oct.   p44.   325w.   5
        VV   July 4   p69.   100w.   3

4685   DEADLY Nightshade.   F and W the Deadly Nightshade.   Phan-
        tom BPL 1-1370.   Cart.   BPS 1-1379
        RC   May   p2.   200w.   3
        SR   Jan.   p86.   30w.   4

4686   DEBANGO, Manu.   Manu '76.   Fiesta 326 001
        BM   March   p24.   50w.   4

4687   DEES, Rick.   The Original Disco Duck.   RSO 3017
        MM   May 14   p33.   50w.   0

4688   DELLS.   Cornered.   DJM 23032 (E) (2 discs) (Reissue)
        BM   April   p53.   200w.   4
        HBS April/May   p17.   125w.   5
        NK   Spring   p39.   50w.   4

4689   DELLS.   They Say It Can't Be Done.   Mercury 1145
        VV   May 9   p59.   350w.   3½

4690   DETROIT Emeralds.   Feel the Need.   Westbound
        BM   Sept.   p49.   200w.   2
        GR   Oct.   p715.   50w.   2½
        MG   July   p55.   200w.   3
        MM   Aug. 20   p18.   200w.   3
        VV   Aug. 1   p51.   50w.   3

4691   DILLINGER.   Bionic Dread.   Black Swan 9455
        BM   March   p51.   150w.   3

4692   DILLINGER.   Talking Blues.   Magnum DEAD 1001
        BM   Oct.   p50.   125w.   5
        MM   Oct. 22   p21.   125w.   3

4693   DILLINGER and Trinity.   Clash.   Burning Sounds Records
        [no serial number] (E)
        MM   Oct. 22   p21.   125w.   3½

4694   DISCO Tex and His Sexolettes.   Manhattan Millionaire.   Chel-
        sea 2306 (E)
        BM   Jan.   p47.   125w.   3

4695   DOMINO, Fats.   Fantastic Fats.   Music for Pleasure MFP
        50294 (E) (Reissue)
        NK   Winter   p37.   50w.   3

4695a DOMINO, Fats. Fats Domino Story, Vols. 1-6. United
       Artists UAS 30067/9, 30099, 30117/8 (6 discs) (E) (Reissue)
       MM   May 28 p26. 600w. 4
       MM   Aug. 20 p17. 300w. 4
       NK   Spring p40. 75w. 5
       NK   Autumn p43. 100w. 5
       SMG Sept. p28. 100w. 5

4696   DOMINO, Fats. 20 Greatest Hits. United Artists UAS
       29967 (E) (Reissue)
       MM   May 14 p33. 50w. $3\frac{1}{2}$
       NK   Spring p37. 125w. 5

4697   DOUBLE Exposure. 10%. Salsoul SZS 5503 (E)
       BM   May p51. 200w. 3

4698   DOUGLAS, Carol. Full Bloom. Midsong BKL1-222
       SR   Nov. p120. 50w. $1\frac{1}{2}$

4699   DOUGLAS, Carol. Midnight Love Affair. RCA BKL1-1798
       BM   Jan. p42. 200w. 2
       RC   April p11. 150w. 3

4700   DOZIER, Lamont. Peddlin' Music on the Side. Warner
       Bros. BS 3039. Cart. M83039. Cass. M53039
       MM   Oct. 1 p26. 125w. 3
       SR   Sept. p96. 125w. 3

4701   DRIFTERS. Every Nite's a Saturday Night. Arista ARTY
       140
       BM   Jan. p43. 175w. 2

4702   DYNAMIC Superiors. Give and Take. Motown MG 8791
       MG   Aug. p61. 50w. 2
       RS   Oct. 6 p90, 93. 300w. $2\frac{1}{2}$

4703   DYNAMIC Superiors. Nowhere to Run. Motown STML 12065
       BM   Nov. p46-7. 325w. 3
       SC   No. 1 p16. 100w. $2\frac{1}{2}$

4704   DYNAMIC Superiors. You Name It. Motown M6-875
       BM   April p50. 200w. 2
       MG   Jan. 150w. 2
       SMG May p24. 75w. 3

4705   DYSON, Ronnie. Love in All Flavours. Columbia COL PC-
       34866
       BS   Dec. p49. 200w. $3\frac{1}{2}$

4706   EARLAND, Charles and Odyssey. Revelation. Mercury
       BS   Aug. p27. 150w. 3

4707   EARTH Wind and Fire. Spirit. Columbia PC 34241. Cart.

PCA 34241
BM   Feb.   p48.   400w.   4
CAC Feb.   p417. 100w.   2
CIR Jan.   17 p14.   150w.   3
MM   Jan.   22 p74.   150w.   2
SMG May   p24.   100w.   0
SR   Feb.   p92.   100w.   2

4708   EL Coco. Let's Get It Together.   Pye (E) NSPL 28229
MM   June 4 p20.   25w.   0

4709   ELLIS, Kwamena Roy. Keyboard Africa.   Agora AGL 005
BM   Aug.   p17.   150w.   3½

4710   EMOTIONS. Flowers. CBS 81639 (E)
BM   Oct.   p48.   200w.   4

4711   EMOTIONS. Rejoice. Columbia PC 34762.   Cart. PCT
34762.   Cass. PCA 34762
BS   Aug.   p26.   150w.   3
MG   Sept. p55.   100w.   2
MM   Nov.   12 p20.   200w.   4
RC   Aug.   p8.   200w.   4½
SC   No. 2 p16.   100w.   4
SR   Dec.   150w.   3½

4712   EMOTIONS. Sunshine. Stax STX 4100
RS   Feb. 9 p95-6.   325w.   1½

4713   ENCHANTMENT. United Artists UAS 30089 (E)
BM   July   p49.   150w.   3
BS   June   p17.   175w.   3
MM   Aug. 6 p16.   125w.   3½

4714   ETHIOPIANS. Slave Call.   Third World TWS 15 (E)
BM   Nov.   p50.   450w.   5
MM   Nov. 5 p22.   200w.   3½

4715   EVERETT, Betty. It's in His Kiss.   DJM 22042 (E) (Reis-
sue)
HBS Feb./March p19.   50w.   4
NK   Winter p38.   75w.   4

4716   EXCITERS. Heaven Is Where You Are.   Twentieth Century
BT-472
BM   Jan.   p50.   225w.   3
HBS Jan.   p18.   50w.   1

4717   FACTS of Life. Sometimes.   Kayvette 802
BM   Oct.   p49.   300w.   4
MM   Oct. 8 p35.   200w.   3
SC   No. 1 p15.   100w.   5
SR   Aug.   p72.   200w.   4

4718   FAITH, George.   To Be a Lover.   Island ILPS 9504
          BM   Nov.   p50.   200w.   3
          MM   Sept. 10   p26.   375w.   5

4719   FANIA All Stars.   Delicate and Jumpy.   Columbia PC 34283
          CRA   March   p70-2.   450w.   0

4720   FANIA All Stars.   Rhythm Machine.   Columbia PC 34711.
       Cart. PCT 34711.   Cass. PCA 34711
          HF   Sept.   p145.   50w.   2
          VV   June 27   p71.   300w.   3

4721   FANTASTIC Four.   Got to Have Your Love.   Westbound 306
          SC   No. 2   p17.   75w.   4

4722   FARAGHER Brothers.   Family Ties.   ABC 941
          MM   May 14   p33.   50w.   4

4723   FARRA, Maryann and Satin Soul.   Never Gonna Leave You.
       Brunswick BRLS 3022
          BM   Jan.   p50.   50w.   2
          CAC   Jan.   p378.   100w. $2\frac{1}{2}$
          GR   Jan.   p1194.   25w.   3
          HBS   Jan.   p17.   50w.   4

4724   FAT Larry's Band.   Feel It.   WMOT K50330 (E)
          BM   April   p51-2.   100w.   3

4725   FATBACK Band.   Best of.   Polydor 2391 246 (E) (Reissue)
          BM   Feb.   p48-9.   75w.   4

4726   FATBACK Band.   NYCNYUSA.   Spring SP 1-6714
          CAC   Aug.   p166.   150w.   3
          BM   July   p49.   300w.   3
          MG   June   p55.   100w. $2\frac{1}{2}$

4727   FELA and the Afrika 70s.   Before I Jump Like Monkey, Give
       Me Banana.   Coconut PMLP 1001
          BM   Aug.   p17.   50w.   3

4728   FIRST Choice.   Delusions.   Gold Mind GZS 7501
          MG   Nov.   p54.   125w.   3

4729   FISHER, Bruce.   Red Hot.   Mercury 1168
          BS   Nov.   p65.   250w. $3\frac{1}{2}$

4730   FLAMINGOES.   Chess ACRR 702 (2 discs) (Reissue)
          NK   Spring   p39.   50w.   3
          RSP   March-April   p30.   325w. $3\frac{1}{2}$
          SMG   Sept.   p25.   100w.   5

4731   FLAVOR.   In Good Taste.   Motown 6-1002
          MM   Sept. 3   p46.   150w.   3

4732   FLOATERS. ABC 5229
       BM Oct. p44. 250w. 3
       MM Sept. 24 p28. 150w. 2
       SC No. 2 p15. 100w. 1

4733   FLOATERS. Float on. ABC 1030
       RC Dec. p6. 100w. 3

4734   FOUNDERS 15. EMI NEMI 0175 (E)
       BM June p19. 25w. 1

4735   FOUR Tops. Motown Special STMX 6004 (E) (Reissue)
       HBS April/May p21. 25w. $2\frac{1}{2}$

4736   FOXY. Dash 3001
       MG July p55. 75w. 1

4737   FRANKLIN, Aretha. Sweet Passion.   Atlantic SD 19102
       BM Aug. p49. 300w. 2
       BS Aug. p26. 150w. 3
       CAD July p24. 150w. 5
       HF Sept. p138. 400w. $2\frac{1}{2}$
       MG Aug. p57. 500w. 2
       MG Aug. p61. 100w. $2\frac{1}{2}$
       MM July 2 p21. 300w. $3\frac{1}{2}$
       RR Sept. p92-3. 50w. 3
       SR Nov. p100. 300w. 3
       VV July 11 p47-8. 500w. 3

4738   FRANKLIN, Aretha. Ten Years of Gold.   Atlantic SD 18204
       (Reissue)
       CAC April p12. 125w. 4
       RC April p3. 100w. $4\frac{1}{2}$

4739   FUNKADELIC. The Best of the Early Years, Vol. 1. West-
       bound WB 303
       RS Aug. 25 p56-7. 200w. 3

4740   FUNKADELIC. Hardcore Jollies. Warner 2973
       VV Aug. 1 p51. 75w. 4

4741   FUNKERS. Now I'm a Man. EMI NEM 10204 (E)
       BM June p19. 50w. 3

4742   FUNKY Kings. Arista (E)
       ZZ June p40-1. 175w. 3

4743   GAP Band. Tattoo FL 12168
       BM Sept. p46. 250w. 4

4744   GAYE, Marvin. Best of.... Tamla 6-348 (Reissue)
       BM Jan. p45. 50w. 5
       HRS Feb./March p19. 50w. $2\frac{1}{2}$

      SMG Jan. p28. 100w. 4

4745 GAYE, Marvin. Live at the London Palladium. Tamla
     T7-352R (2 discs). Cart. 9-352NT. Cass. 9-352NC
       BM June p46. 350w. 3
       MG June p55. 100w. $3\frac{1}{2}$
       MM May 28 p29. 400w. 1
       RS June 2 350w. 3
       RSP May-June p28. 400w. $3\frac{1}{2}$
       SMG Sept. p27. 25w. 4
       SR Aug. p93. 125w. 2

4746 GAYNOR, Gloria. Glorious. Polydor PD-1-6095. Cart.
     8T-1-6095. Cass. CT-1-6095
       MG June p55. 200w. $3\frac{1}{2}$
       MM June 4 p20. 50w. 3
       SR July p105. 125w. 4

4747 GIBSON Brothers. Non-Stop Dance/Come to America. Poly-
     dor 2383 468 (E)
       BM Dec. p47. 150w. 2

4748 GIORGIO. From Here to Eternity. Casablanca NBLP 7065.
     Cart. NBLP8 7065. Cass. NBLP5 7065
       BM Dec. p49. 125w. 2
       HF Nov. 50w. 3
       MG Dec. p62. 100w. 3
       RS Oct. 6 p96. 250w. $2\frac{1}{2}$

4749 GOLDEN Eagles. Awa ti Danfi. EMI NEM1 0190 (E)
       BM June p19. 25w. 2

4750 GRAHAM, Ralph. Wisdom. RCA APL1-1918-A
       MG Jan. 100w. 3

4751 GRAHAM Central Station. Now Do You Wanna Dance. Warn-
     er BS 3041
       BM June p46. 250w. 5
       MM May 28 p30. 350w. $3\frac{1}{2}$
       RR Sept. p92. 50w. 3

4752 GRANT, Eddy. Message Man. Ice (E)
       MM Jan. 7 p17. 300w. 2

4753 GRAY, Owen. Fire and Bullets. Trojan TRLS 139 (E)
       BM Aug. p50. 125w. 3

4754 GREEN, Al. The Belle Album. Hi(Cream) 6004
       VV Dec. 26 p55, 57. 450w. $3\frac{1}{2}$

4755 GREEN, Al. Greatest Hits. Hi London SHL 32105 (Reissue)
       MG Sept. p55. 50w. 3

4756   GREEN, Al. Have a Good Time. Hi SHL 32103
        BM   Feb.   p49.   300w.   4
        CAC May   p51.   200w. $2\frac{1}{2}$
        CAD March p28.   100w.   3
        CIR Jan. 17 p14.   400w. $3\frac{1}{2}$
        MG   Feb.   p55.   125w.   3
        MM   Jan. 22 p24.   250w. $2\frac{1}{2}$
        RS   Jan. 27 p70.   275w. $2\frac{1}{2}$
        SR   April p90.   75w.   2

4757   GREEN, Johnny and the Greenmen. Seven Over from Mars.
        Barak BARL 100 (E)
        MM   Sept. 17 p22.   250w.   2

4758-9 GRIFFITHS, Marcia. Naturally. High Note DB 1003
        BM   Oct.   p50-1.   175w.   3

4760   HAMMOND, Johnny. Forever Taurus. Milestone 9068
        CAD Jan. p18.   50w.   2
        CK   Jan. 11 p51.   100w.   6
        JJ   March p32.   100w.   2

4761   HAMMOND, Johnny. Storm Warning. Millstone M-9076
        CAD Aug. p28.   125w.   3
        CK   Nov. p65.   25w. $2\frac{1}{2}$

4762   HASKINS, Fuzzy. A Whole Nother Thing. Westbound W 229
        MG   Nov. p54.   25w.   3
        MG   Jan. p47.   75w. $2\frac{1}{2}$

4763   HAYES, Isaac and Dionne Warwick. A Man and a Woman.
        ABC 996 (2 discs)
        BS   May   p25.   150w. $3\frac{1}{2}$

4764   HEAT Wave. Too Hot to Handle. Epic PE 34761
        MG   Oct. p61.   50w. $1\frac{1}{2}$

4765   HEINZ. Remembering. Decca REM 7 (E) (Reissue)
        SMG Sept. p25.   75w.   1

4766   HENDERSON, Eddie. Comin' Through. Capitol ST 11671
        BS   Oct. p26.   200w.   3

4767   HENDRYX, Nona. Epic PE 34863
        BM   Nov. p47-8.   25w.   1
        MM   Oct. 15 p23.   200w. $1\frac{1}{2}$

4768   HEPTONES. Cool Rasta. Trojan TRLS 128 (E)
        CRA April p101.   50w. $4\frac{1}{2}$

4769   HEPTONES. Party Time. Island ILPS 9456
        BM   June p50.   150w.   4
        RS   Aug. 11 p65-6.   550w.   4

VV   Aug. 15 p51.   100w. $3\frac{1}{2}$

4770   HI Rhythm.   On the Loose.   London SHU 8506
       BM   April p52.   150w.   2
       HBS April/May p21.   100w.   3
       MM   April 2 p26.   250w. $1\frac{1}{2}$

4771   HINES, Justin and the Dominoes.   Jezebel.   Island ILPS
       9416
       CRA April p100-1.   400w. $4\frac{1}{2}$

4772   HITCHHIKERS.   ABC ABC 973
       BM   April p52.   150w.   4

4773   HODGES, James and Smith.   What's on Your Mind.   London
       SHU 8507 (E)
       BM   Dec. p49.   125w.   2
       MM   Nov. 12 p26.   50w. $3\frac{1}{2}$
       SC   No. 1 p15.   75w.   4

4774   HOLLOWAY, Loleatta.   Loleatta.   Gold Mind GZS 7500
       BM   July p4, 6.   300w.   4
       SR   Aug. p73.   225w.   5

4775   HOLMAN, Eddie.   A Night to Remember.   Salsoul SZS 5511.
       Cart. S8Z 5511
       MM   Nov. 5 p26.   225w.   3
       SR   Nov. p102, 105.   175w.   4

4776   HOLMES, Rupert.   Singles.   Epic PE 34288
       HF   Feb. p144.   50w.   2
       RS   Jan. 27 p68.   200w.   2

4777   HOLT, John.   2000 Volts of Holt.   Trojan 134 (E)
       BM   March p51.   175w.   3

4778   HOLT, John.   Up Park.   Channel One
       BM   Oct. p51.   100w.   2

4779   HONEYBOY.   Strange Thoughts.   Trojan TRLS 125 (E)
       BM   Oct. p51.   125w.   3

4780   HOPKINS, Linda.   Me and Bessie.   Columbia PC 34032
       JR   V9/#4 unpaged 150w.   4

4781   HOT Chocolate.   XIV Greatest Hits.   Rak 524 (E) (Reissue)
       HBS Jan. p17.   50w.   4

4782   HOT Chocolate.   Ten Greatest Hits.   Big Tree TT 76002
       (Reissue)
       MG   Dec. p61.   100w. $3\frac{1}{2}$

4783   HOUSTON, Thelma.   Anyway You Like It.   Tamla T-34551

CAC   May   p51-2.   100w.   4
GR   July   p237.   50w. $3\frac{1}{2}$
HBS   April/May   p19.   100w. $3\frac{1}{2}$
MG   April   p54.   150w.   3
RC   Aug.   p6.   150w.   3
SMG   May   p24.   100w.   3

4784   HOUSTON, Thelma and Jerry Butler.   Thelma and Jerry.
Motown M6-887-S1.   Cass. M5-887-H.   Cart. M8-887-H
BM   Sept.   p48.   225w.   3
SMG   Sept.   p27.   75w.   4
SR   Oct.   p98, 100.   250w.   3

4785   HUES Corporation.   Best of.   RCA APL12408 (Reissue)
RC   Aug.   p14.   100w. $2\frac{1}{2}$

4786   HUES Corporation.   I Caught Your Act.   Warner BS 3034
MG   Nov.   p54.   25w.   3

4787   HUMPHREY, Bobbi.   Tailor Made.   Epic PE 34704
BS   Aug.   p27.   200w.   3

4788   HUNT, Tommy.   A Sign of the Times.   Spark SRLP 120
BM   Jan.   p45.   50w.   2

4789   HUNTER, Ivory Joe.   7th Street Boogie.   Route 66 KIX 4
(Sweden) (Reissue)
CAD   Dec.   p56-7.   150w.   3
CZM   Dec.   p56.   100w.   3
NK   Autumn   p45.   100w.   4

4790   HUTCH, Willie.   Havin' a House Party.   Motown M6-874
BM   Nov.   p49.   300w.   2

4791   HYMAN, Phyllis.   Phyllis Hyman.   Buddah BDS 5681
BS   June   p17.   200w.   3
SR   Nov.   p105.   250w.   4

4792   IMPRESSIONS.   For Your Precious Love.   DJM DJB 26086
(E) (Reissue)
BM   Jan.   p44-5.   275w.   3
HBS   Feb./March   p19.   50w.   3

4793   IMPRESSIONS.   28 Original Hits.   ABCD 303 (2 discs) (Re-
issue)
BM   Jan.   p42-3.   200w.   5
HBS   Feb./March   p19.   50w.   3

4794   INNER Circle.   Reggae Thing.   Capitol ST 11574
BM   Feb.   p51.   225w.   4
RS   Jan. 27   p70.   150w. $1\frac{1}{2}$

4795   ISLEY Brothers.   Forever Gold.   T-Neck PZ 34452

          BM   Dec. p48.   150w.   5
          RC   Oct. p7.   50w.   3½

4796   ISLEY Brothers.   Go for Your Guns.   T-Neck PZ34432.
       Cart. PZA-34432.   Cass. PZT-34432
          BM   June p46.   350w.   4
          BS   June p17.   225w.   3
          CRA July p68, 70.   325w.   3
          MG   June p55.   150w.   3
          SR   Sept. p102, 104.   200w.   5

4797   J. A. L. N. Band.   Just Another Lonely Night.   Magnet MAG
       5014 (E)
          MM   Dec. 3 p20.   200w.   1½

4798   J. A. L. N. Band.   Life Is a Fight.   Magnet MAG 5017 (E)
          BM   Jan. p43.   200w.   3
          MM   Jan. 22 p24.   150w.   3½

4799   JACKSON, Chuck.   Any Day Now.   DJM 22074 (E) (Reissue)
          MM   Sept. 10 p20.   50w.   3½
          NK   Autumn p42.   25w.   2½
          SC   No. 2 p15.   50w.   4

4800   JACKSON, Jermaine.   Feel the Fire.   Motown M888P1
          BM   Nov. p47.   250w.   3
          MM   Aug. 20 p17.   225w.   3½
          SC   No. 1 p16.   50w.   2½
          SOU Sept. p62.   300w.   4

4801   JACKSON, Jermaine.   My Name Is.   Motown M6-842S1
          MM   Jan. 8 p18.   150w.   2
          RS   Jan. 27 p70.   100w.   2

4802   JACKSON, Millie.   Best of.   Polydor 2391 247 (E) (Reissue)
          BM   Feb. p48.   125w.   5
          CAC March p454.   100w.   2½

4803   JACKSON, Millie.   Feelin' Bitchy.   Spring SP1-6715.   Cart.
       8T1-6715.   Cass. CT1-6715
          BM   Dec. p47.   400w.   5
          HF   Nov. 75w.   3½
          MG   Oct. p61.   50w.   3

4804   JACKSON, Millie.   Lovingly Yours.   Spring 6712
          BM   June p48.   200w.   4
          RR   July p95.   100w.   3

4805   JACKSON, Vivian.   Chant Down Babylon Kingdom.   Nation-
       wide PRO 001
          BM   Sept. p50.   100w.   5

4806   JACKSON, Vivian.   Deliver Me from My Enemies.   Grove

GMLP 0010
   BM   Sept.   p50.   100w.   5
   MM   Dec. 3   p24.   400w. $3\frac{1}{2}$

4807   JACKSON, Walter.   Feeling Good.   Chi-Sound LA 656-G
   BM   April   p52.   225w.   4
   MG   Jan.   175w. $3\frac{1}{2}$

4807a   JACKSON, Walter.   Greatest Hits.   Epic E 34657
   HBS   Jan.   p18.   125w.   4

4807b   JACKSON, Walter.   I Want to Come Back as a Song.   United
   Artists CH LA 733G
   MG   June   p55.   50w. $2\frac{1}{2}$

4808   JACKSON 5.   Anthology.   Motown TMSP 6004 (E) (2 discs)
   (Reissue)
   CAC   May   p52.   250w. $2\frac{1}{2}$
   MM   April 2   p24.   50w.   3
   SMG   May   p24.   100w. $3\frac{1}{2}$

4809   JACKSON 5.   Joyful Jukebox Music.   Motown M6-865
   BM   Feb.   p49.   125w.   3
   HBS   Feb./March   p21.   100w. $2\frac{1}{2}$
   MM   Jan. 8   p18.   150w.   3

4810   JACKSONS.   Epic PE 34229
   BM   March   p22.   150w.   3
   CAC   April   p12, 14.   200w.   3
   HF   Feb.   p144.   50w.   2
   MM   Jan. 8   p18.   150w.   3
   RS   Jan. 27   p70.   100w.   2

4811   JACKSONS.   Going Places.   Epic JE 34835
   MM   Dec. 3   p23.   200w.   4
   RS   Dec. 29   p77.   300w. $3\frac{1}{2}$
   SC   No. 2   p17.   100w.   4

4812   JAH Stitch.   No Dread Can't Dead.   Third World 401
   BM   Feb.   p51.   225w.   3

4813   JAH Woosh.   The World Marijuana Tour.   Carib Gem
   ZZ   Oct.   p31, 34.   100w.   3

4814   JAZZBO, Prince.   Natty Passing Through.   Black Wax 1
   BM   Jan.   p51.   200w.   3

4815   JOHNSON, Alphonso.   Yesterday's Dreams.   Epic PE-34364
   CAD   Jan.   p18.   100w.   2
   DB   April 7   p29-30.   125w.   2
   GP   Aug.   p120.   50w.   3
   MG   Feb.   p57.   100w. $2\frac{1}{2}$

4816-18 JOHNSON Brothers.   Right on Time.   A&M SP 64644
        BM   July p46.   300w.   4
        BS   Aug. p26.   150w.   3
        CAC Feb. p417. 125w.   3
        DB   Nov. 3 p23. 300w.   3
        MM   July 16 p22. 300w.   4
        VV   June 27 p73. 175w.   3

4819   JONES, Barbara.   Best of.   Trojan 136 (E) (Reissue)
        BM   Jan. p51.   200w.   3

4820   JONES, Etta.   Ms. Jones to You.   Muse MR 5099
        CAD Feb. p38.   150w.   5
        SOU Feb. p44.   100w.   4

4821   JONES, Grace.   Portfolio.   Island ILPS 9470
        MG   Dec. p62.   100w.   3
        SOU Dec. p54.   150w.   4
        VV   Nov. 28 p66.   50w.   2

4822   JONES, Tamiko.   Cloudy.   Contempo 602
        SC   No. 2 p15.   75w.   4

4823   JORDAN, Louis.   Big Band Sessions.   MCA Coral 6-22418
        (Reissue)
        RSP March-April p36.   125w.   4

4824   JORDAN, Louis.   And His Tympani, Vol. 1.   Jazz Club 123
        (Reissue)
        RSP March-April p36.   125w.   4

4825   JORDAN, Louis.   Swings.   Black Lion BLP 30175
        BM   Jan. p49.   75w.   3

4826   JOY.   Cadillac SGC 10006
        MM   June 4 p32.   200w. $3\frac{1}{2}$

4827   K. C. and the Sunshine Band.   Part Three.   TK 4021
        HBS June/Sept. p21.   100w. $3\frac{1}{2}$
        MG   Feb. p55.   125w.   3
        RS   Feb. 10 p100, 103.   400w.   2

4828   KALYAN.   MCA 2245
        BM   June p50.   125w.   3
        CAC Aug. p167.   100w.   2
        HF   April p148.   50w.   2
        SOU April p56.   400w.   5

4829   KELLY, Paul.   Stand on the Positive Side.   Warner BS 3026
        RS   Aug. 11 p69.   325w.   3

4830   KENDRICKS, Eddie.   Goin' Up in Smoke.   Tamla T6-346
        BM   Jan. p43-4.   300w.   1

4831   KENDRICKS, Eddie. Slic. Tamla T6-356
       MM Dec. 3 p20. 300w. 4
       RS Nov. 17 p96. 250w. 3

4832   KING, Ben E. and the Average White Band. Benny and Us.
       Atlantic 19105
       GR Oct. p715. 25w. 3½

4833   KING, Earl. New Orleans Rock 'n' Roll. Sonet SNTF 719
       (E)
       NK Summer p38. 25w. 3

4834   KIRKLAND, Bo and Ruth Davis. Bo & Ruth. EMI Interna-
       tional INS 3007 (E)
       BM Aug. p48. 200w. 2
       MM Aug. 20 p15. 175w. 3

4835   KITAJIMA, Osama. Island ILPS 9426
       AU Oct. p172. 250w. 5
       MG Oct. p61. 100w. 3

4836   KNIGHT, Gladys. Pipe Dreams. Buddah BDS5676 ST
       MG   Feb. p55. 125w. 1
       RS Feb. 24 p66. 250w. 1½

4837   KNIGHT, Gladys and the Pips. Still Together. Buddah BDS
       5689
       BM June p47-8. 325w. 3
       CAC June p95. 275w. 5
       GR Aug. p353. 50w. 3
       HF July p149. 300w. 4
       RS June 2 p78. 200w. 3
       SR Oct. p100. 250w. 3

4838   KOOL and the Gang. Live at the Sex Machine. Polydor (E)
       CAC Feb. p416. 50w. 2

4839   KUTI, Fela Anikulapo. Up Side Down. Decca PFS 4411 (E)
       MM Jan. 7 p16. 50w. 2

4840   LABELLE, Patti. Epic PEC 8226. Cart. PET 34847. Cass.
       PEA 34847
       BM Dec. p48. 350w. 4
       CRA Oct. p72. 400w. 1½
       HF Nov. 425w. 2½
       MG Nov. p54. 25w. 4½
       MM Oct. 15 p23. 200w. 3½
       RS Oct. 6 p86. 375w. 4
       SR Dec. 175w. 2

4841   LABELLE, Patti. Chameleon. EPIC PE 34189 PEa 34189
       BM Jan. p42. 325w. 4
       SR Jan. p88, 92. 100w. 4

4842 LADY Flash. Beauties in the Night.   RSO 3002
      BM April p52. 150w. 3
      CAC April p14. 150w. $2\frac{1}{2}$

4843 LAMONT, Dozier. Peddlin' Music on the Side.   Warner SB
      3039
      MG Aug. p61. 100w. $2\frac{1}{2}$

4844 LARUE, D. C. Ca-the-drals.   Pye NSPL 28225 (E)
      BM Feb. p50. 300w. 3
      HBS Feb./March p20. 50w. 3
      MM Jan. 22 p24. 250w. $\frac{1}{2}$
      RC April p6. 250w. $4\frac{1}{2}$

4845 LARUE, D. C. Tea Dance.   Pye International 28228 (E)
      HBS June/Sept. p22. 100w. 3
      RC June p3-4. 300w. $4\frac{1}{2}$

4846 LA SALLE, Denise. Second Breath.   ABC ABCD 966
      RS Feb. 24 p68. 200w. $1\frac{1}{2}$

4847 LATIMORE, Benny. It Ain't Where You Been.   TK 14034
      BM May p53. 150w. 5
      HBS June/Sept. p22. 100w. 4
      MG Jan. 100w. 3
      MM July 9 p22. 300w. 4
      RS Feb. 10 p100, 103. 400w. 2

4848 LEWIS, Linda. Woman Overboard.   Arista 1003
      HBS June/Sept. p21. 125w. 4

4849 LEWIS, Ramsay. Love Notes.   Columbia PC 34696
      CAD June p21. 100w. $3\frac{1}{2}$
      CK Aug. p49. 100w. 4
      GR Sept. p522. 75w. 3

4850 LEWIS, Ramsay. Tequila Mockingbird.   Columbia JC 35018
      MM Dec. 21 p14. 50w. $2\frac{1}{2}$

4851 LEWIS, Webster. On the Town.   Epic PE 34186
      RS March 24 p71. 200w. 3

4852 LINDO, Willie. Far and Distant.   Klik 9019
      BM March p51. 150w. 3

4853 LITTLE Sonny. New Orleans Rhythm and Blues.   CSA
      CLPS 1017
      BM May p53. 175w. 3

4854 LITTLE Richard. Get Down with.   Redita 114
      RSP March-April p28-9. 200w. 3

4855 LITTLE Richard. Now.   Creole CRLP 570

NK Autumn p4-6. 150w. 4

4856 LITTLE Richard. Whole Lotta Shakin' Goin' On. DJM
      28036 (E) (Reissue)
          HBS June/Sept. p22. 125w. 4
          NK Summer p37. 100w. 4

4857 LITTLE Richard and Jimi Hendrix. Friends from the Be-
      ginning. Ember 3434 (E) (Reissue)
          HBS April/May p19. 125w. 5

4858 LITTLE Tina. This Little Bird. Rockhouse 7704
          NK Spring p39. 50w. $3\frac{1}{2}$

4859 LIZZARD. Satta I. Trojan 138 (E)
          BM Aug. p50. 125w. 3

4860 LOVE and Kisses. Casablanca NBLP 7063
          MG Dec. p62. 150w. $2\frac{1}{2}$
          MM Jan. 7 p16. 50w. 0
          RC Dec. p11. 50w. $3\frac{1}{2}$

4861 LOVE Childs Afro-Cuban Blues Band. Span Disco. RCA
      Midsong BKL1 2292
          MG Sept. p53. 125w. 3

4862 LOVE Unlimited. He's All I've Got. Twentieth Century BT
      101
          BM July p47. 300w. 2
          HBS June/Sept. p22. 75w. 3
          MG Dec. p61. 100w. 2
          MM April 9 p24. 75w. $2\frac{1}{2}$

4863 LOVE Unlimited. My Summer Suite. Twentieth Century BT
      517
          BM Jan. p47. 125w. 2

4864 LYNN, Barbara. Here Is. Oval OVLM 5002
          BM Jan. p45. 150w. 3
          HBS Jan. p17. 50w. 5

4865 MX-80 Sound. Hard Attack. Island ILPS 9520
          ZZ Nov. p33. 400w. $3\frac{1}{2}$

4866 McCOO, Marilyn & Billy Davis Jr. I Hope We Get to Love
      in Time. ABC ABCD-952
          BM April p52. 125w. 2
          SR April p94. 100w. 4

4867 McCOO, Marilyn and Billy Davis. The Two of Us. ABC
      1026
          BS Oct. p26. 150w. 3
          MM Oct. 15 p24. 150w. 2

4868 McCOOK, Tommy. Instrumental. Justice JUSLP 07
       BM Oct. p51. 25w. 2

4869 McCRAE, George. Diamond Touch. TK XL 14042
       BM Oct. p48. 175w. 1
       MM Aug. 6 p16. 200w. $1\frac{1}{2}$

4870 McDONALD, Ralph. Sound of a Drum. TK XL 14030
       BM July p50. 75w. 4
       DB March 10 p24. 250w. 4
       HBS June/Sept. p20. 150w. 4

4871 McDUFF, Jack. Hot Barbeque. Prestige P-24072 (Reissue)
       CK Aug. p49. 25w. $2\frac{1}{2}$

4872 McDUFF, Jack. Sophisticated Funk. Chess 19004
       CAD Feb. p20. 50w. 2

4873 McNEIR, Ronnie. Love's Comin' On. Motown M6-870
       BM Jan. p42. 300w. 4

4874 MANDRE. Motown M7-900
       BM Oct. p48. 150w. 2
       RSP May-June p61. 250w. 3

4875 MANHATTANS. I Wanna Be Your Everything. DJB 26084
       (E) (Reissue)
       BM Jan. p50. 75w. 2
       HBS Feb./March p19. 50w. 4

4876 MANHATTANS. It Feels So Good. Columbia PC34450
       BM May p52. 150w. 4
       GR April p1617. 25w. 2
       HBS April/May p20. 200w. 5

4877 MARCUS. United Artists 30000 (E)
       BM Jan. p44. 125w. 1

4878 MARLEY, Bob and the Wailers. The Birth of a Legend.
       Calla ZX 34759
       BM Sept. p50. 200w. 3
       CIR Sept. 15 p66. 100w. 3

4879 MARLEY, Bob and the Wailers. Exodus. Island ILPS 9498.
       Cart. Y8I-9498. Cass. ZCI-9498
           AU Aug. p82. 200w. $4\frac{1}{2}$
           BM Aug. p50. 150w. 5
           CIR Sept. 15 p65-6. 4
           CRA Aug. p64. 375w. $3\frac{1}{2}$
           DB Sept. 8 p30. 500w. 3
           GR Aug. p354. 50w. $4\frac{1}{2}$
           HF Aug. p119. 100w. 3
           MG Sept. p51. 250w. 3

         MM   May 14 p27.   325w.   4
         RC   Aug.   p9.   250w.   3
         RR   July   p97.   200w.   4
         RS   July 14 p63.   1050w. $2\frac{1}{2}$
         SR   Sept.   p96.   275w.   2
         VV   June 27 p71.   300w.   2
         VV   Aug. 1 p51.   50w. $3\frac{1}{2}$

4880   MARLEY, Bob and the Wailers.   Live.   Island ILPS 9376
         SR   Feb.   p97.   200w.   4

4881   MASON, Barbara and Bunny Sigler.   Locked in This Position.
       Curtom 5014
         RC   Aug.   p14.   50w.   2

4882   MASS Production.   Believe.   Cotillon 9918
         MM   Oct. 15 p24.   150w.   3

4883   MASS Production.   Welcome to Our World.   Cotillon 9910
         BM   April   p51.   200w.   1
         MG   Jan.   p55.   50w. $3\frac{1}{2}$
         MM   Feb. 12 p25.   50w. $1\frac{1}{2}$

4884   MATTHEWS, David.   Dune.   CTI 75005
         CAD Oct.   p23.   50w.   0
         MG   Oct.   p61.   100w. $1\frac{1}{2}$

4885   MATTHEWS, David.   Shoogie Wanna Boogie.   Kudu 30
         MM   Feb. 12 p25.   50w.   2

4886   MATUMBI.   Best of.   Trojan (E) (Reissue)
         MM   Dec. 21 p14.   200w. $2\frac{1}{2}$

4887   MAXI.   Blue Note LA 738-H
         BS   Oct.   p27.   150w.   3

4888   MAYFIELD, Curtis.   Never Say You Can't Survive.   Curtom
       CU 5013
         BS   May   p24.   150w.   3
         RS   June 2 600w.   2

4889   MAZE Featuring Frankie Beverly.   Capitol ST 11607
         BM   July   p48-9. 300w.   5
         BS   Sept. p16.   200w.   3   .
         RC   Dec.   p5.   50w.   4

4890   MBULU, Letta.   There's Music in the Air.   A & M SP 4609
         BM   April p20.   150w.   5
         BS   May   p24.   150w.   3
         SR   June   p104, 109.   125w.   3
         VV   April 18 p70.   100w. $2\frac{1}{2}$

4891   MELVIN, Harold and the Blue Notes.   Reaching for the World.

ABC 969
    BM April p52. 200w. 2
    RS May 5 275w. 2

4892   The METERS. New Directions. Warner Bros. BS 3042
    BM Sept. p46. 350w. 4
    CAD Aug. p28. 125w. $3\frac{1}{2}$
    CRA Sept. p81. 250w. 2
    MG Sept. p55. 75w. $2\frac{1}{2}$
    RS Sept. 8 p114, 116. 175w. $2\frac{1}{2}$
    SR Nov. p108, 110. 200w. 5

4893   MIGHTY Diamonds. Ice on Fire. Virgin PZ-34454. Cart.
PZT-34454. Cass. PZA-34454
    AU Aug. p82. 200w. 2
    BM June p50. 100w. 4
    HF Aug. p119. 100w. $2\frac{1}{2}$
    MG Sept. p55. 100w. 3
    MM March 26 p20. 550w. $3\frac{1}{2}$
    RS June 16 p69. 575w. 2
    VV Aug. 1 p51. 50w. 3

4894   MIGHTY Sparrow. King of the Caribbean. DJM 26087 (E)
    MM Jan. 22 p46. 50w. $2\frac{1}{2}$

4895   MIRACLES. Love Crazy. Columbia PC 34460
    BM May p51. 200w. 3
    GR April p1617. 25w. 2

4896   MIRACLES. The Power of Music. Tamla T6-344
    SMG May p24. 150w. 4

4897   MITTOO, Jackie. Hot Blood. Third World TWS 912 (E)
    BM Oct. p51. 25w. 2

4898   MITTOO, Jackie. The Keyboard King. Third World 501 (E)
    BM Aug. p50. 200w. 3

4899   MOHAWK, Essra. Private Stock PS 2024
    MM May 14 p28. 300w. 3
    RS March 24 p74. 450w. 2

4900   MOMENTS. Best of. All Platinum 9109 305 (E) (Reissue)
    BM Nov. p48. 50w. 4
    MM Oct. 29 p27. 150w. 4

4901   MOMENTS. Greatest Hits. Stang 1033 (E) (Reissue)
    VV Sept. 5 p59-60. 350w. $3\frac{1}{2}$

4902   MONTGOMERY, James. Island ILPS 5419
    RS Feb. 24 p65. 175w. $1\frac{1}{2}$

4903   MOONGLOWS. Chess ACRR 701 (Reissue)

                NK   Spring p39.   50w.   3
                RSP   March-April p30.   325w. $3\frac{1}{2}$
                SMG   Sept.   p25.   100w.   5
                VV   July 11 p48.   400w.   4

4904   MOORE, Dorothy.   TK Malaco Records 6353
                BS   Nov.   p65.   200w. $3\frac{1}{2}$
                MG   Dec.   p62.   100w. $3\frac{1}{2}$

4905   MOORE, Melba.   Melba.   Buddah BDS 5677 8320-5677
                BM   June   p48.   225w.   3
                SR   March p112. 200w.   3

4906   MORNING, Noon and Night.   United Artists UAS 30114 (E)
                BM   Oct.   p46.   200w.   4

4907   MOTHER'S Finest.   Epic PE 34179
                BM   Jan.   p44.   125w.   3

4908-9 MOTHER'S Finest.   Another Mother Further.   Epic PE34699
                MG   Dec.   p61.   100w. $3\frac{1}{2}$

4910   MUHAMMAD, Idris.   Turn this Mutha Out.   Kudu 34
                CAD   July   p23.   75w.   3
                MG   Oct.   p61.   75w.   3
                SC   No. 2 p16.   50w.   4

4911   MURPHY, Walter.   A Fifth of Beethoven.   Private Stock PS
        2015.   Cart. PVS 830-2015H
                BM   Jan.   p42.   150w.   3
                CAC   Feb.   p419. 125w.   2
                SR   Jan.   p91, 96. 50w.   0

4912   MURVIN, Junior.   Police and Thieves.   Island ILPS 9499
                BM   June   p50.   200w.   3
                CIR   Sept. 15 p66. 75w. $3\frac{1}{2}$
                RR   July   p95.   50w. $3\frac{1}{2}$

4913   NASCIMENTO, Milton.   Milton.   A&M SP 4611.   Cart. 8T-
        4611
                BM   June   p48-9. 225w.   4
                CRA   April p98.   375w.   3
                DB   May 5 p20.   250w.   4
                JM   Summer p56, 58. 350w.   4
                RRE   March-April p28.   150w.   4
                RS   June 2 p83.   100w.   3
                RS   May   p90-1. 100w.   4

4914   NASH, Johnny.   What a Wonderful World.   Epic EPC 81783
        (E)
                BM   July   p49.   75w.   3
                HBS   April/May p19.   100w.   4

4915   NEWBEATS. Bread and Butter. Hickory (E)
       HBS   Jan.   p17.   50w.   4

4916   NIGHTINGALE, Maxine.   Nightlife.   United Artists UA LA
       731-G
       BM   Dec.   p49.   50w.   1
       MG   Oct.   p63.   75w.   3½
       MM   Oct. 8 p35.   225w.   2

4917   90 Degrees Inclusive.   Vertigo 6360 139 (E)
       BM   Jan.   p51.   150w.   2

4918-19 NORTH, Freddie. 'Cuss the Wind.   Contempo CLP 544 (E)
       BM   March   p23.   150w.   4

4920   OBEY, Ebenezer.   Eda to Mose Okunkun.   Decca WAPS 358
       (E)
       BM   April   p20.   50w.   4

4921   OBEY, Ebenezer. Immortal Songs for the Traveller.   Decca
       WAPS 378 (E)
       BM   Aug.   p17.   150w.   4

4922   OCEAN, Billy.   GTO GTLP 015 (E)
       BM   Jan.   p45, 47.   75w.   2

4923   OGUN, Lammy and the Rock Mountain Band.   Volume 1.
       Panorama PRLPS 2 (E)
       BM   June   p19.   25w.   2

4924   OHIO Players.   Angel.   Mercury SRM-1-3701
       BM   Oct.   p46.   250w.   3
       CRA   July   p68, 70.   325w.   3
       MG   June   p55.   100w.   3
       VV   June 29   p71, 73.   175w.   1½

4925   OHIO Players.   The Best of the Early Years, Vol. 1.   West-
       bound 304 (Reissue)
       MG   Aug.   p61.   125w.   3
       RS   Aug. 25   p56-7.   200w.   2½

4926   OHIO Players.   Gold.   Mercury SRM1-1122 (Reissue)
       CIR   March 31   p19-20.   225w.   3
       RR   May   p87.   25w.   3½
       SMG   May   p25.   100w.   4

4927   O'JAYS.   Message in the Music.   Philadelphia International
       PZ 34245
       CIR   Feb. 28   p11.   375w.   4
       SR   March   p112.   50w.   0

4928   O'JAYS.   Travellin' at the Speed of Thought.   Philadelphia In-
       ternational PZ-34684.   Cart. PZA-34684.   Cass. PZT-35684

        BM   Aug.   p48.   400w.   4
        HF   Aug.   p119, 121.   350w. $2\frac{1}{2}$
        MG   July   p55.   150w.   2
        RS   July 14   p70.   400w.   3
        SR   Sept.   p110.   125w.   3

4929   OLYMPIC Runners.   Hot to Trot.   Chipping Norton NOR 1
       (E)
        BM   March   p23.   250w.   3

4930   OMOVURA, Alhaji Ayinla.   Abode Mecca.   EMI NEMI 0218
       (E)
        BM   June   p19.   25w.   3

4931   ONE World.   Peace.   EMI NEMI 0180 (E)
        BM   June   p19.   25w.   2

4932   ONYIA, Zeal.   Returns.   Tabansi TRL110 (E)
        BM   Aug.   p16.   150w.   5

4933   ORIGINALS.   Down to Love Town.   Motown Soul S6-749
        BM   July   p49.   150w.   3
        HBS   June/Sept.   p23.   125w.   3
        MM   June 4   p29.   125w.   3

4934   ORLONS.   Best.   London 8504 (E) (Reissue)
        HBS   June/Sept.   p20.   75w.   4
        NK   Spring   p42.   50w. $3\frac{1}{2}$

4935   OSIBISA.   Black Magic Night: Live at the Royal Festival
       Hall.   Bronze (2 discs) (E)
        MM   Dec. 21   p15.   200w.   4

4936   OSIBISA.   Ojah Awake.   Antilles 7058
        BM   Jan.   p43.   250w.   2
        SOU   April   p52.   300w.   4

4937   OZO.   Listen to the Buddah.   DJM 4
        BM   Jan.   p52.   75w.   3

4938   PABLO, Augustus.   King Tubby Meets Rockers Uptown.
       Clock Tower LPCT 0085
        BM   Sept.   p50.   50w.   5

4939   PARLIAMENT.   Chocolate City.   Casablanca 7014
        MM   Aug. 20   p18.   175w.   3

4940   PARLIAMENT.   The Clones of Dr Frankenstein.   Casablanca
       CAC 2003
        BM   Aug.   p47.   225w.   4
        CAC   July   p134.   100w. $1\frac{1}{2}$
        CRA   Jan.   p78.   300w. $2\frac{1}{2}$
        MM   May 28   p30.   200w. $2\frac{1}{2}$

RC June p2. 150w. 4

4941 PARLIAMENT. Live--P. Funk Earth Tour. Casablanca
CALD 5002 (2 discs)
    BM Aug. p47. 225w. 5
    MG Nov. p54. 25w. 3
    MM July 9 p23. 175w. 2
    RSP May-June p25. 400w. 2
    VV Aug. 1 p51. 50w. $3\frac{1}{2}$

4942 PARLIAMENT. Mothership Connection. Casablanca 7022
    MM June 4 p29. 50w. $3\frac{1}{2}$

4943 PARLIAMENT. Up for the Down Stroke. Casablanca 7002
(Reissue)
    MM June 4 p29. 50w. 3

4944 PATTERSON, Kellee. Turn on the Lights--Be Happy. Shady-
brook Records 33007
    BS Sept. p16. 200w. 3

4945 PAUL, Billy. Let 'Em In. Philadelphia International PZ
34389
    BM April p52. 100w. 3

4946 PEACHES and Herb. MCA MCF2802 (E)
    GR Nov. p920. 50w. 3
    MM Sept. 3 p22. 200w. 2

4947 PENDERGRASS, Teddy. Philadelphia International PZ 34390
    BS May p24. 150w. 3
    MM April 2 p20. 250w. $4\frac{1}{2}$
    RS May 5 350w. 3

4948 PEOPLE Star. Festac Explosion. Emperor EMLP 001 (E)
    BM March p24. 100w. $4\frac{1}{2}$

4949 PERSUASIONS. Chirpin'. Elektra 7E-1099
    AU July p90. 150w. $4\frac{1}{2}$
    SR Oct. p118. 225w. 5
    VV May 30 p63. 650w. 4

4950 PHILLIPS, Esther. Capricorn Princess. KUDU KU-31
    BM July p47. 300w. 4
    CAC April p15. 125w. 4
    CAD March p44. 75w. $3\frac{1}{2}$
    MG April p54. 150w. 3
    RC April p7. 200w. $4\frac{1}{2}$
    SR April p96. 125w. 4

4951 POCKETS. Come Go with Us. Columbia PC 34879
    BS Dec. p49. 250w. $2\frac{1}{2}$

4952   POINTER Sisters.   Best of.   ABC ABCD 611 (Reissue)
       BM   March   p23.   100w.   3

4953   POOLE, Brian.   Remembering.   Decca REM 5 (E) (Reissue)
       SMG   Sept.   p28.   25w. $2\frac{1}{2}$

4954   PRESTON, Billy.   A&M SP 4587
       BM   Jan.   p52.   125w.   3
       CAC   March   p455.   250w.   2
       RS   Jan. 13   p55.   325w.   2

4955   PRESTON, Billy.   Billy's Boy.   DJM 26082 (E) (Reissue)
       HBS   Feb./March   p19.   50w.   4

4956   PURIFY, James & Bobby.   Purify Bros.   Mercury 9100028
       (E)
       BM   July   p47.   150w.   3
       HBS   June/Sept.   p21.   125w. $4\frac{1}{2}$
       MM   May 28   p30.   125w.   3

4957   QUANSAH, Edi.   Che Che Kule.   Island ILPS 9446
       BM   June   p19.   150w.   4

4958   RAMBLERS.   Doin' Our Own Thing.   Decca WAPS 35 (E)
       (Reissue)
       BM   April   p20.   50w. $3\frac{1}{2}$

4959   RAWLS, Lou.   The Best of Lou Rawls.   Capitol SKBB-11585
       (Reissue)
       CAD   Jan.   p17.   125w. $4\frac{1}{2}$

4960   RAWLS, Lou.   Unmistakably Lou.   Philadelphia International
       PZ 34488
       BM   June   p49.   100w.   2
       BS   June   p16.   150w.   3
       HF   July   p153.   200w.   3
       MM   June 4   p29.   200w.   3
       SR   Aug.   p100.   175w. $3\frac{1}{2}$

4961   RECORD, Eugene.   Warner Brothers BS 3018
       BS   May   p25.   125w.   3

4962   REED, Herb.   Sweet River.   PVK 002 (E)
       BM   Nov.   p49.   150w.   2

4963   REEVES, Martha.   The Rest of My Life.   Arista AL 4105
       RS   Feb. 10   p103, 105.   325w. $1\frac{1}{2}$
       SR   April   p99.   300w.   4

4964   REEVES, Martha and the Vandellas.   Anthology.   Motown
       12060 (E) (Reissue)
       BM   Nov.   p48.   50w.   4
       NK   Summer   p40.   25w.   4

SMG Sept. p27. 125w. $3\frac{1}{2}$

4965 RHYTHM Makers. Soul on Your Side. Vigor V17002
    MG Jan. 50w. 4

4966 RIPERTON, Minnie. Stay in Love. Epic PE-34191. Cart.
    PEA-34191. Cass. PET-34191
    BM May p52. 250w. 4
    BS May p25. 150w. 3
    PRM April p43. 250w. $3\frac{1}{2}$
    RSP May-June p59-60. 275w. 3
    SR Aug. p100. 75w. 2

4967 RITCHIE Family. African Queens. Marlin 2206
    BM Oct. p47. 125w. 0
    MG Oct. p61. 50w. 1
    MM Oct. 15 p23. 50w. 1
    RC Dec. p15-6. 100w. 3

4968 RITCHIE Family. Arabian Nights. Polydor 2383 416 (E)
    BM Jan. p44. 200w. 2
    CAC Jan. p381. 100w. 2
    HBS Feb./March p18. 50w. 2
    MM Jan. 29 p24. 300w. 1

4969 RITCHIE Family. Life Is Music. Marlin 2203
    BM June p48. 25w. 1
    MG May p55. 125w. $2\frac{1}{2}$
    MM April 9 p24. 75w. 2

4970 ROBINSON, Smokey. Deep in My Soul. Tamla T6-350S1.
    Cart. T8-350-H. Cass. T75-350-H
    BM July p46. 150w. 3
    CAC Aug. p168. 225w. $2\frac{1}{2}$
    MG May p55. 125w. $3\frac{1}{2}$
    MM May 28 p24. 425w. $3\frac{1}{2}$
    RS April 21 p98. 375w. 3
    SR June p112-3. 175w. 4

4971 ROBINSON, Vicky Sue. RCA RS 1095
    BM March p22. 250w. 3
    MM Jan. 1 p15. 50w. 0

4972 RODRIGUES, Rico. Man from Wareika. Island ILPS 9485
    BM June p50. 100w. 5

4973 ROGERS, D. J. Love, Music and Life. RCA APL1-2218
    BM Nov. p46. 250w. 5
    CK Sept. p58. 75w. 3
    MM Nov. 19 p27. 200w. 4

4974 ROGERS, D. J. On the Road Again. RCA APL 42021 (E)
    MM Feb. 12 p26. 50w. 3

4975 ROMEO, Max. Reconstruction. Mango MLPS 9503
      BM Oct. p51. 125w. 2
      MG Oct. p63. 75w. $3\frac{1}{2}$
      MM Oct. 22 p21. 150w. $1\frac{1}{2}$
      RR Nov. p116. 50w. $2\frac{1}{2}$
      VV Sept. 5 p59. 450w. 3

4976 ROMEO, Max. War Ina Babylon. Island ILPS 9392. Cart.
      Y8L 9392
      CAR April p100-1. 400w. 4
      RS March 24 p69, 71. 300w. 2
      SR March p93. 500w. 3

4977 RONDO, Gene. Memories. Venture VNLP 8862 (E)
      BM Aug. p51. 150w. 3

4978 RONETTES. Sing Their Greatest Hits. Phil Spector Inter-
      national 2307 003 (E) (Reissue)
      SR June p118. 125w. 3

4979 ROSE Royce. Car Wash. MCA MCSP 278 (E) (2 discs)
      BM Feb. p48. 400w. 4

4980 ROSE Royce. In Full Bloom. Whitfield WH 3074. Cart.
      M8 3074. Cass. M5 3074
      BM Oct. p49. 250w. 3
      HF Nov. 75w. $2\frac{1}{2}$
      MM Oct. 8 p26. 275w. 3
      RS Oct. 6 p93. 325w. 2

4981 ROSS, Diana. Motown Special STMX 6001 (E) (Reissue)
      HBS April/May p21. 25w. $2\frac{1}{2}$
      HBS April/May p21. 25w. $2\frac{1}{2}$

4982 ROSS, Diana. Baby, It's Me. Motown M7-890
      BM Dec. p48-9. 250w. 2
      BS Dec. p48. 225w. 3
      HF Dec. p140. 300w. 3
      MG Dec. p59. 75w. 2
      MM Nov. 5 p22. 450w. $3\frac{1}{2}$
      RS Dec. 1 p78. 600w. $3\frac{1}{2}$
      RSP Nov.-Dec. p24. 300w. $2\frac{1}{2}$

4983 ROSS, Diana. An Evening with Diana Ross. Motown M7-
      877R2 (2 discs). Cart. 9-840NT. Cass. 9-840NC
      BM April p53. 125w. 2
      CAC June p96. 200w. 3
      MG May p55. 200w. 2
      MM April 2 p22. 100w. $1\frac{1}{2}$
      SMG May p25. 250w. 1
      SR July p88-9. 450w. 5

4984 ROSS, Diana and the Supremes. 20 Golden Greats. Motown

EMTV5 (E) (Reissue)
BM Nov. p48. 50w. 5
MM Oct. 8 p30. 100w. $3\frac{1}{2}$

4985 ROUTERS. The Chuck Berry Songbook. Reprise 26047 (E)
NK Autumn p48. 25w. $2\frac{1}{2}$

4986 RUFFIN, David. In My Stride. Motown M6-885
BM Sept. p47. 250w. 2
SMG Sept. p27. 50w. 3

4987 RUFUS. Ask Rufus. ABC AB-975
BM April p51. 150w. 4
RS May 19 p99. 325w. $4\frac{1}{2}$
RSP May-June p60. 300w. $3\frac{1}{2}$
SR June p113. 62w. 4

4988 RUSHEN, Patrice. Shout It Out. Prestige P10101
CAD May p13. 75w. 1
DB Dec. 15 p27. 150w. 2
MM Oct. 15 p25. 200w. $3\frac{1}{2}$

4989 SALSOUL Orchestral. Magic Journey. Salsoul SZS 5515
BM Sept. p48-9. 100w. 3
MG Nov. p54. 25w. $3\frac{1}{2}$
SR Aug. p87. 225w. $4\frac{1}{2}$

4990 SALSOUL Orchestra. Nice 'n' Nasty. Salsoul 5502
HBS Jan. p17. 50w. 3

4991 SCOTT-HERON, Gil. It's Your World. Arista AL 5001
MG Jan. 125w. 3

4992 SCOTT-HERON, Gil/Brian Jackson. Bridges. Arista 4147
MM Jan. 7 p17. 550w. $4\frac{1}{2}$

4993 SECRET Place. Kudu KU 32
DB March 24 250w. 2

4994 SHALAMAR. Uptown Festival. Soul Train BVLI1-2289
BM Sept. p49. 200w. 3
MG Aug. p61. 75w. $2\frac{1}{2}$
MM Aug. 6 p16. 200w. $2\frac{1}{2}$

4995 SHARP, Dee Dee. Happy 'bout the Whole Thing. Philadelphia
International PZ-33839. Cart. PZA-33839
SR Aug. p72-3. 225w. 5

4996 SHAW, Marlena. Sweet Beginnings. Columbia PC 34458
BM Sept. p47. 150w. 4
DB Sept. 8 p33. 250w. 3
MM Aug. 20 p17. 200w. 3
SR Aug. p100. 100w. $2\frac{1}{2}$

4997   SIGLER, Bunny. My Music. Philadelphia International PIR
        81765 (E)
            BM   April p50.   250w.   4
            HBS   April/May p19.   100w. $3\frac{1}{2}$

4998   SILVER. Arista (E)
            MM   Feb. 12 p25.   50w.   0

4999   SIMON, Joe. Easy to Love. Spring 6713
            BM   July p48.   200w.   3
            CAC   Aug. p168.   150w. $4\frac{1}{2}$
            MM   June 4 p29.   150w. $3\frac{1}{2}$

5000   SISTER Sledge. Together. Cotillon SD 9199.   Cart. SDC
        9199. Cass. SDT 9199
            HF   Nov.   50w. $3\frac{1}{2}$
            MG   Nov. p54.   25w. $2\frac{1}{2}$

5001   SLY & the Family Stone. Heard Ya Missed Me, Well I'm
        Back. EPIC PE 34348
            BM   March p22.   150w.   3
            CIR   Feb. 14 p13.   225w. $2\frac{1}{2}$
            CRE   March p59.   375w.   1
            HBS   Feb./March p20.   100w.   3
            SR   April p100.   175w.   4

5002   SMART, Leroy. Superstar. Third World TWLP 601 (E)
            BM   Aug. p51.   100w.   5

5003   SMITH, Jimmy. Sit on It. Mercury SRM-1-1127
            CAD   Oct. p36.   100w.   2
            DB   July 14 p38.   150w. $1\frac{1}{2}$

5004   SMITH, Lonnie. Keep on Lovin'. Groove Merchant GM 3312
            CAD   Jan. p18.   25w.   2

5005   SMITH, O. C. Together. Caribou PZ-34471.   Cart. PZA-
        34471. Cass. PZT-34471
            BM   Sept. p47.   100w.   2
            SR   Sept. p112, 115. $5\frac{1}{2}$

5006   SOUL Syndicate. Harvest Uptown/Famine Downtown. Epiphany
        EPLP 101
            RC   Oct. p12.   150w. $3\frac{1}{2}$
            VV   Aug. 15 p51.   25w.   3

5007   SOUL Train Gang. RCA APL1-1844
            MM   July 16 p23.   100w. $2\frac{1}{2}$

5008   SPARTACUS. Watching You Grow. Zara AMRL 101 (E)
            BM   Jan. p52.   150w.   3
            MM   June 25 p21.   250w. $3\frac{1}{2}$

5009   SPIDERS Webb. I Don't Know What's on Your Mind. Fantasy Records 9517
        BM   March   p23, 50.   200w.   4
        CAD Jan.   p18.   50w.   2
        GP   Feb.   p113.   100w. $4\frac{1}{2}$
        MG   April   p54.   125w. $2\frac{1}{2}$

5010   SPINNERS. Smash Hits. Atlantic SD 19179 (Reissue)
        BM   July   p48.   100w.   5
        MM   May 28   p30.   300w. $3\frac{1}{2}$

5011   SPINNERS. Yesterday, Today and Tomorrow. Atlantic SD 19100
        MG   July   p55.   150w.   3
        RS   June 2   500w.   3

5012   STATON, Candi. Music Speaks Louder than Words. Warner Brothers BS 3040
        BM   Sept.   p47.   225w.   4
        CRA Sept.   p78.   200w. $3\frac{1}{2}$
        HF   Oct.   p162-3.   300w.   5
        MG   Sept.   p55.   125w. $3\frac{1}{2}$
        MM   Aug. 13   p20.   200w. $3\frac{1}{2}$
        RR   Sept.   p93.   25w.   3
        RS   Aug. 25   p56.   300w. $3\frac{1}{2}$

5013   STONE, R & J. RCA PL 25069 (E)
        CAC Aug.   p170.   50w. $2\frac{1}{2}$
        MM   Sept. 24   p27.   50w. $2\frac{1}{2}$

5014   STREET Corner Symphony. Bang 406
        RC   Nov.   p15.   50w. $3\frac{1}{2}$

5015   STYLISTICS. Once Upon a Jukebox. H&L 69015
        RC   May   p10.   150w.   3

5016   STYLISTICS. Spotlite on. H&L 6641-622 (E) (2 discs) (Reissue)
        SMG Sept.   p27.   50w.   3

5017   STYLISTICS. Sun and Soul. Phonogram 9109 014 (E) (Reissue)
        CAC June   p98.   100w. $1\frac{1}{2}$

5018   SUMMER, Donna. Four Seasons of Love. Casablanca NBLP 7038
        BM   Feb.   p48.   200w.   4
        RS   Jan. 27   p68, 70.   300w. $3\frac{1}{2}$

5019   SUMMER, Donna. I Remember Yesterday. Casablanca NBLP 7056. Cass. NBL5-7056. Cart. NBL8-7056
        BM   Sept.   p46-7.   300w.   3
        MG   Aug.   p61.   125w.   3

      RS   Aug. 11 p63. 275w. 4
      SOU Oct. p60. 400w. 4
      SR   Oct. p122, 124. 225w. 3

5020 SUPREMES. Mary, Scherrie and Susaye. Motown M6-873
      BM   Feb. p48. 250w. 4
      CAC June p98. 200w. $1\frac{1}{2}$
      HBS Feb./March p21. 100w. $4\frac{1}{2}$

5021 SWANN, Bettye. Make Me Yours. Contempo CLP 541
      BM   April p51. 150w. 3

5022 SWEET Talks. Adam and Even. Philips MEZ100 (E)
      BM   March p24. 50w. $3\frac{1}{2}$

5023 SWEET Talks. Kusum Beat. Philips MEZ101 (E)
      BM   March p24. 50w. $3\frac{1}{2}$

5024 SYLVERS. Something Special. Capitol ST 11580
      CIR Jan. 31 p14. 300w. 3
      HBS Feb./March p18. 125w. 4
      MG   Feb. p55. 75w. 2
      RS   July 14 p69. 400w. 3

5025 SYLVESTER. Fantasy F 9531
      RS   Oct. 6 p90, 93. 300w. 2

5026 SYREETA. One to One. Tamla T6-349
      BM   June p46. 125w. 3
      GR   July p237. 50w. $2\frac{1}{2}$
      PRM April p43. 300w. $2\frac{1}{2}$
      RSP March-April p28. 150w. $2\frac{1}{2}$

5027 SYREETA and G. C. Cameron. Rich Love, Poor Love. Mo-
    town M6-891
      RS   Nov. 3 p110. 375w. 3

5028 T-CONNECTION. Magic. Dash TK14054 (E)
      MM   Sept. 3 p46. 250w. 3
      SC   No. 1 p15. 75w. 4

5029 TATA Vega. Full Speed Ahead. Tamla Motown STML 12039
    (E)
      BM   Jan. p43. 250w. 3

5030 TATE, Grady. Master Grady Tate. ABC
      BS   Dec. p49. 200w. 3

5031 TATTOO. Prodigal POL 2003 (E)
      SMG May p22. 100w. 1

5032 TAVARES. Best of. Capitol ST 11701 (Reissue)
      MM   Dec. 3 p24. 200w. 4

5033 TAVARES. Check It Out. Capitol (E)
        CAC May p54. 125w. 2½
        MM April 2 p24. 50w. 3

5034 TAVARES. Love Storm. Capitol STAO-11628
        BM July p49. 250w. 3
        BS June p16. 150w. 3
        MG July p55. 150w. 3½
        MM May 28 p29. 300w. 3
        RS July 14 p69. 400w. 3

5035 TAYLOR, Johnnie. Chronicle--The Twenty Greatest Hits.
      Stax STX 88001 (2 discs) (Reissue)
        RS Feb. 9 p95-6. 325w. 3½
        SC No. 2 p15. 100w. 5

5036 TAYLOR, Johnnie. Rated Extraordinaire. Columbia PC
      33401
        MM April 2 p20. 250w. 3½

5037 TAYLOR, Ted. 1976. Contempo 538 (E)
        HBS Feb./March p18. 125w. 5

5038 TEE, Willie. Anticipation. United Artists 655
        RS Feb. 10 p105. 225w. 3

5039 TEMPTATIONS. Motown Special STMX 6002 (E) (Reissue)
        HBS April/May p21. 25w. 2½

5040 TEMPTATIONS. Greatest Hits, Vol. 3. Motown STML
      12061 (Reissue)
        BM Oct. p46. 650w. 4
        MM Oct. 8 p30. 100w. 4

5041 TEX, Joe. Bumps and Grinds. Epic PE-34666. Cart. PEA-
      34666. Cass. PET-34666
        BM July p46. 300w. 5
        GR Aug. p353. 125w. 2
        HF July p156. 250w. 3
        MG Sept. p55. 75w. 2½
        MM June 4 p29. 200w. 3½
        SR Sept. p120. 200w. 5

5042 THIRD World. 96° in the Shade. Island ILPS 9443
        BM Nov. p50. 50w. 4
        MM Nov. 5 p26. 250w. 2½

5043 THOMAS, Irma. Live. Island HELP 29
        BM July p46-7. 100w. 3

5044 THOMAS, Joe. Feelin's from Within. Groove Merchant
      3315
        CAD Feb. p20. 75w. 0

5045   THOMAS, Rufus. If There Were No Music. AVI AVL 6015
       RC   Oct.   p6.   50w.   3

5046   THREE Degrees. Standing Up for Love. Epic PE 34385
       BM   June   p47.   125w.   3
       GR   April   p1617.   25w.   2
       MG   July   p55.   150w.   3
       MM   April 9 p24.   75w.   3

5047   TOSH, Peter. Equal Rights. Columbia PC-34670. Cart.
       PCA-34670. Cass. PCT-34670
       AU   Aug.   p84.   100w.   4
       BM   Aug.   p50.   200w.   5
       CIR   Sept. 15 p66.   100w. $3\frac{1}{2}$
       CRA   Aug.   p64.   350w.   3
       HF   Aug.   p119.   100w.   3
       MG   Aug.   p61.   75w. $3\frac{1}{2}$
       MG   Sept.   p51.   250w.   3
       MM   May 14 p30.   350w. $3\frac{1}{2}$
       RR   July   p95.   100w.   4
       RS   July 14 p63.   450w.   4
       SR   Sept.   p96.   275w.   5
       VV   June 6 p49.   450w. $3\frac{1}{2}$
       VV   Aug. 1 p51.   50w. $3\frac{1}{2}$

5048   TOWER of Power. Ain't Nothin' Stoppin' Us Now. Columbia
       PC 34302
       BM   Jan.   p47.   125w.   3

5049   TRADITION. In Duo. BP1 BLP 808IA (E)
       BM   Aug.   p51.   150w.   3

5050   TRAMMPS. Disco Inferno. Atlantic SD 18211
       MG   April   p54.   100w. $2\frac{1}{2}$
       RC   Oct.   p2.   250w.   3
       RS   April 7 p80.   300w.   4

5051   TRINITY. Up Town Girl. Magnum DEAD 1003 (E)
       BM   Dec.   p51.   250w.   5

5052   TWINKLE Brothers. Do Your Own Thing. Carib Gems
       CGLP 1001 (E)
       BM   Nov.   p50.   100w.   4
       ZZ   Oct.   p34.   50w.   3

5053   The TYMES. Diggin' Their Roots. RCA APL1-2406
       MM   Dec. 3 p27.   250w.   2

5054   The TYMES. Turning Point. RCA RS 1091 (E)
       BM   Feb.   p50.   100w.   2
       CAC   Jan.   p381.   100w.   3
       MM   Jan. 22 p24.   175w. $2\frac{1}{2}$

5055   UNDISPUTED Truth.   Best of.   Motown STMC 8029 (Reissue)
       BM Nov. p49. 50w. 4
       MM Oct. 1 p23. 250w. 4
       SC No. 1 p15. 75w. 4

5056   UNDISPUTED Truth.   Method to Madness.   Whitfield 2967
       BM May p51. 300w. 3
       HBS Feb./March p20. 125w. 4

5057   VALOR, Tony, Sounds Orchestra.   Gotta Get It.   Brunswick
       (E)
       MM Sept. 3 p22. 25w. 0

5058   VANDERBILT, Lee.   Get into What You're in.   Twentieth
       Cent. T-529
       BM Nov. p48. 150w. 3
       MM Oct. 15 p23. 50w. 1½

5059   VIS-A-VIS.   Best of ... in Congo Style.   Ride Away RAL
       015 (E)
       BM March p24. 50w. 3

5060   WAILER, Bunny.   Blackheart Man.   Island ILPS-9415
       AU Jan. p77. 200w. 4½

5061   WAILER, Bunny.   Protest.   Island ILPS 9512
       BM Dec. p51. 200w. 5
       MM Nov. 12 p29. 300w. 2

5062   WALKER, Junior.   Motown Special STMX 6005 (E) (Reissue)
       HBS April/May p21. 25w. 2½

5063   WALKER, Junior.   Whopper Bopper Show Stopper.   Motown
       STML 12048 (E)
       BM April p50. 100w. 3
       MM Feb. 26 p25. 200w. 3
       SMG May p24. 100w. 3

5064   WAR.   Platinum Funk.   Island ILPS 9507
       BM Dec. p49. 200w. 4
       MM Nov. 5 p22. 250w. 3

5065   WAR.   Platinum Jazz.   Blue Note BNLA-690J2
       MG Sept. p55. 75w. 3
       SR Nov. p85. 250w. 5

5066   WAR, Featuring Eric Burdon.   Live Is All Around.   ABC 988
       MM Feb. 12 p25. 100w. 3

5067   WARWICK, Dionne.   Love at First Sight.   Warner Brothers
       3119
       MM Nov. 12 p23. 200w. 3½

5068   WASHINGTON, Delroy. Rasta.   Virgin V2088
       BM   Nov. p50. 50w. 4
       MM   Nov. 5 p22. 250w. 3
       RR   Nov. p116. 50w. $2\frac{1}{2}$

5069   WASHINGTON, Grover, Jr.   A Secret Place.   Kudu KU32
       BM   May p52. 150w. 4
       MG   April p53. 75w. $3\frac{1}{2}$
       RSP March-April p61. 150w. 2

5070   WASHINGTON, Grover. Soul Box.   Kudu Soul 001
       SC   No. 1 p16. 75w. 4

5071   WATSON, Johnny Guitar. Ain't That a Bitch. DJM DJLPA-3
       LB   May-June p38, 39. 275w. 4

5072   WATSON, Johnny Guitar.   A Real Mother for Ya.   DJM
       DJLPA-7
       BM   Sept. p48. 300w. 3
       BS   Sept. p16. 150w. $3\frac{1}{2}$
       HBS June/Sept. p20. 150w. 4
       LB   July-Aug. p35. 475w. 4

5073   WATSON, Wah Wah. Elementary. Columbia PC 34328
       BM   Jan. p50, 52. 350w. 4
       DB   Feb. 24 p27-8. 300w. 2
       GP   Jan. p97. 50w. 3

5074   WELL Charged. Vital Dub. Virgin V2055 (E)
       BM   Aug. p51. 50w. 4

5075   WENA, Lulu. Rhapsody in Black. CBS 81806 (E)
       BM   July p47. 100w. 3

5076   WHISPERS. One for the Money. Soul Train 1-1450
       BM   Feb. p49. 150w. 3

5077   WHISPERS. Open Up Your Love. Soultrain BVL1-2270.
       Cart. BVS1-2270
       BS   Oct. p26. 150w. $3\frac{1}{2}$
       SR   Nov. p116. 300w. 5

5078   WHITE, Barry. Is this Watcha Won't? Twentieth Century
       T516
       CAC May p54. 150w. 2
       HBS Jan. p18. 75w. $2\frac{1}{2}$
       MM   Jan. 1 p15. 400w. $3\frac{1}{2}$

5079   WHITE, Barry. Sings for Someone You Love.   Twentieth
       Century T-543
       BM   Dec. p49. 300w. 3
       BS   Nov. p64. 225w. $3\frac{1}{2}$
       MG   Nov. p54. 25w. $4\frac{1}{2}$

      MM Oct. 22 p22. 150w. $\frac{1}{2}$

5080 WHITE, Lenny. Big City. Nemperor NE 441
      BM July p50. 75w. 3
      CK June p49. 150w. $4\frac{1}{2}$
      DB May 19 350w. 3
      GP Aug. p120. 50w. 3
      RS June 16 p50, 60. 400w. $1\frac{1}{2}$

5081 WHITE, Tony Joe. Eyes. Twentieth Century T-523
      MM May 14 p33. 50w. $3\frac{1}{2}$
      ZZ May p38. 250w. $2\frac{1}{2}$

5082 WILLIAMS, Carol. 'Lectric Lady. Salsoul SZS 5506
      BM Sept. p48-9. 100w. 2
      MM May 14 p33. 50w. $1\frac{1}{2}$

5083 WILLIAMS, Deniece. Songbird. Columbia JC 34911
      MM Dec. 21 p14. 200w. $3\frac{1}{2}$

5084 WILLIAMS, Deniece. This Is Niecy. Columbia PC 34242
      BM July p47. 300w. 4

5085 WILLIAMS, Lenny. Choosing You. ABC ABC 1023
      BM Dec. p49. 175w. 4
      SC No. 2 p16. 100w. 4

5086 WILSON, Delroy. 20 Golden Hits. Third World TWD001
(E) (Reissue)
      BM Aug. p51. 50w. 5

5087 WILSON, Jackie. Nobody But You. Brunswick (E) (Reissue)
      MM Sept. 10 p20. 50w. 2

5088 WING Prayer Fife and Drum Corps. Baby Face Strikes
Again. Wing and a Prayer HS3026
      BM Oct. p47. 125w. 0

5089 WITHERS, Bill. Menagerie. Columbia JC 34903. Cart.
JCT 34903. Cass. JAC 34903
      BS Dec. p48. 200w. $3\frac{1}{2}$
      HF Dec. p139. 75w. 1

5090 WITHERS, Bill. Naked and Warm. Columbia 34327. Cart.
PCA 34327
      BM March p23. 250w. 4
      MG Jan. 125w. $2\frac{1}{2}$
      MM Jan. 22 p24. 250w. $2\frac{1}{2}$
      RSP Jan.-Feb. p30-2. 1750w. $2\frac{1}{2}$
      SR Feb. p106. 150w. 4

5091 WOMACK, Bobby. Home Is Where the Heart Is. Columbia
PC34384

MG   April   p54.   125w.   2

5092   WONDER, Stevie.   Songs in the Key of Life.   Tamla T13-
       340C2 (2 discs).   Cart. T15-340ET
          AU   March p87.   200w.   4
          HF   Feb. 1 p141.   120w.   4
          RSP Jan. -Feb.   p26-9.   2400w. $4\frac{1}{2}$
          SR   Jan.   p94.   500w.   4

5093   WRIGHT, Betty.   This Time for Real.   Alston 4406
          BM   Oct.   p47.   200w.   3
          MM   Sept. 3   p46.   150w.   3
          RS   Nov. 3   p115.   450w. $3\frac{1}{2}$

5094   WYNSOR, Lance.   I'll Be Around.   Decca SKL 5244
          BM   Jan.   p43.   50w.   2

POPULAR RELIGIOUS MUSIC

Without regard to genre, this section comprises all religious items except for classically based church music such as cantatas, masses, "authorized" hymns, and soundtracks. Here will be found those items expressed in another genre: the country and western hymn, the old timey call, the spiritual and gospel elements, the jazz masses, the "Jesus Rock," and so forth. In other words, "secular" or "vulgar" religious music.

There is no one review medium for this music as there is for classical church music reviewed under "Classical" sections in magazines. Secular items are reviewed when they appear in a genre format. Jazz Journal International seems to be the best for jazz, and both Blues Unlimited and Jazz Journal International are the best for gospel. The latter, plus country and western hymns, are still underdeveloped areas in the recording field. Most blues and country albums have a smattering of religious music, but seldom are the tracks ever compiled into one specific disc. This is still a big singles market. There are, though, two distinct markets of appeal, based on the dichotomy between the styles of the happy black gospel and the solemn white country hymn. Bluegrass magazines usually give much information on sacred music, as well as the British Country Music People.

5095   ALAMO, Tony and J. D. Summer. Susan, I Love You So Much, It Hurts Me ... Love Tony. Alamo TSA 777
      CMR June p11. 155w. 3

5096   ALL-Star Brass. Carols at Christmas. EMI One-Up OU2154
      GR Dec. p1161. 50w. $4\frac{1}{2}$

5097   BAILEY, Charlie and the Happy Valley Boys. Everlasting Joy-Early Bluegrass Gospel. Old Homestead OHCS 102
      PIC July p64-5. 225w. $3\frac{1}{2}$

5098   BARRETT, T. L. Do Not Pass Me By. Gospel Roots GR 5002
      CAD Feb. p20. 75w. $3\frac{1}{2}$

5099   BARTON Brothers. Gospel. Galleon G-1408

BGU Jan. p25. 100w. 3

5100 BLACK Dyke Mills Band. Christmas Festival. Pye TB 3013
       (Reissue)
       GR Dec. p1161. 125w. 4½

5101 BLUEGRASS Gospel Four. Come Over & Join Me. River-
       side Records RSR 429
       BGU June p40. 50w. 2

5102 BOONE, Pat. Country Lace. DJM (E)
       MM Jan. 4 p20. 50w. 3

5103 BOWLING, Vernon and Joe Isaacs. Enter into the Joy of the
       Lord. Gospel Shore 770442
       BGU Sept. p18. 200w. 4

5104 BROWN, Rev. Pearly. It's a Mean Old World to Try and
       Live In. Rounder 2011
       CAD Nov. p16. 25w. 4½

5105 BURKE, John. Ain't That What It's All About. Layman
       Records
       BGU June p41. 50w. 2½
       PIC Aug. p74-5. 250w. 3½

5106 BURKE, John. Bluegrass Gospel Songs. Jalyn 137
       PIC Feb. p53-4. 75w. 3

5107 BURKE, John. It's a Beautiful Life. Jalyn 141
       PIC Feb. p53-4. 75w. 3

5108 BURKE, John. Over the Clouds of Glory. Jalyn 133
       PIC Feb. p52-4. 75w. 2

5109 CAESAR, Shirley. First Lady. United Artists RS-LA 744-R.
       Cart. RS-EA 744-H
       CRA Sept. p78. 200w. 2½
       RC Oct. p4-5. 125w. 3½
       SR Oct. p100. 300w. 4

5110 CHESTNUT Grove Quartet. Another Friend's Gone. LSRL
       73405
       BGU May p38. 125w. 4

5111 CHESTNUT Grove Quartet. We've Travelled a Long Way for
       the Lord. LSS 76250 T
       BGU May p38. 125w. 4

5112 CLINE, Charlie & the Lonesome Pine Fiddlers. Bluegrass
       Gospel. Shiloh Records 6054N18B
       BGU Sept. p23. 75w. 0

5113   COLCLASURE, George.   The World Is Not My Home.   Lem-
        co 760645
        BGU   Jan.   p30.   50w.   3

5114   CRANK, Tommy.   Tommy Crank Sings Revival Songs.   Pine
        Tree 525
        PIC   May   p61.   150w. $2\frac{1}{2}$

5115   CROUCH, Andrea and the Disciples.   Take Me Back.   Light
        LS 5637
        RC   July   p8.   300w. $3\frac{1}{2}$

5116   CROUCH, Andrea and the Disciples.   This Is Another Day.
        DJM DJF 20496 (E)
        BM   March   p51.   150w.   4

5117   DALE, Archie.   Testify for Jesus.   Jewel LPS 0133
        RC   Dec.   p3.   50w.   2

5118   DARVIN and Randy, The Byrd Family.   America! Where
        Do You Stand with God?   Grand DB 3006
        PIC   Feb.   p56-7.   75w.   3

5119   DAVIS, Rev. Gary.   Children of Zion.   Kicking Mule 101
        CAD   Nov.   p17.   50w.   5

5120   DAVIS, Rev. Gary.   O Glory.   Adelphi AD 1008
        AU   Dec.   p131.   100w. $4\frac{1}{2}$

5121   DAVIS, Rev. Gary.   Sun Is Going Down.   Folkways 3542
        (Reissue)
        CAD   Jan.   p22, 23.   200w.   3
        JJ   March   p30.   300w.   3
        LB   Nov./Dec.   p33.   300w.   3
        RSP   Jan.-Feb.   p9.   300w.   3

5122   DIXIE Hummingbird.   Live.   ABC/Peacock PL 59231
        HF   June   p119.   300w.   4

5123   DRANES, Arizona.   Barrel House Piano with Sanctified Sing-
        ing 1926-1928.   Herwin 210
        CAD   Aug.   p35.   275w. $4\frac{1}{2}$

5124   DUCK Creek Quartet.   Just Got to Heaven (Golden Shoes).
        TSRC-681227
        BGU   May   100w.   p38, 39.   4

5125   DUCK Creek Quartet.   That's the Reason.   TSRC 701289
        BGU   May   100w.   p38, 39.   4

5126   EANES, Jim.   (Original) Shenandoah Valley Quartet.   Outlet
        Recordings Collectors Series 400
        BGU   Sept.   p16.   100w.   4

RSP 1:3 p25. 125w. 3

5127 EASTER Brothers & the Green Valley Quartet. Hold on.
      Old Homestead OHS 70008
          BGU April p23. 150w. 2½
          OTM Winter p26. 100w. 2½
          PIC June p71. 175w. 4
          RSP Jan.-Feb. p25. 100w. 1½

5128 The EVANGEL Temple Choir. Trinity TR 101
          CMP March p41. 100w. 3
          CMR March p28. 50w. 4

5129 FANTASTIC Family Aires. I'm So Glad. Gospel Roots GR
      5004
          CAD Feb. p20. 50w. 3

5130 FRANKLIN, C. L. What Is Your Life? Gospel Roots GR
      5003
          CAD Feb. p20. 50w. 3½

5131 GIRL Guides. 20 Traditional Christmas Carols. BBC REC
      288 (E)
          GR Dec. p1161. 75w. 3

5132 GOINS Brothers. On the Way Home. Rebel SLP 1557
          BGU April p18. 100w. 3

5133 The GOLDEN Echoes. Heaven on My Mind. Rounder 2002
          CAD Nov. p16. 50w. 5

5134 GOSPEL Ramblers. Most of All. King Bluegrass Records
      KB-546
          BGU April p24. 75w. 2½

5135 GRANT, Bill and Delia Bell. The Last Christmas Tree.
      Kiamichi KMB 105
          BGU Aug. p30. 200w. 5
          CMR Sept. p7. 300w. 4
          PIC Aug. p64. 200w. 3

5136 GRANT, Bill and Delia Bell. There Is a Fountain. Kiamichi
      KMB 103
          CMR March p30. 350w. 4

5137 HALL, Jennie. He Walks Beside Me. Jessup MB-110
          BGU May p42. 100w. 2½

5138 HARRIS, Pete/Smith Casey. Library of Congress Field Re-
      cordings from Texas. Hermin 211
          JR V9/#4 unpaged 75w. 3½

5139 JACKSON, Mahalia. Gospel. Vogue VJD 537 (France)

(Reissue)
RR Dec. p87. 75w. 4

5140   JIM & Jesse. A Handful of Good Seeds. Canaan CGS 8512
       CMP May p38. 125w. 5

5141   KALLMAN, Gunter, Choir. Christmas Sing-In with. Poly-
       dor 2418 203 (E)
       GR Dec. p1161. 50w. 3

5142   The KELLEY Family. While Eternal Ages Roll. Sun Ray
       SR 1009
       BGU March p23. 175w. 4

5143   KENNEDY, Hal. Best of. Canaan CGS 511
       CMP May p39. 125w. 5

5144   KENNEDY, Hal. Welcome Home. Sacred SAC 5090 (E)
       CMP March p41. 100w. 4

5145   KING'S College Choir. Christmas Music for Kings. HMV
       Greensleeves ESD 7050
       GR Dec. p1156. 200w. $4\frac{1}{2}$

5146   LEWIS, Little Roy. Entertainer. Canaan 9811
       PIC Nov. p52. 225w. $1\frac{1}{2}$

5147   The LEWIS Family. We'll Keep Praising His Name. Canaan
       CAS 9795
       BGU Jan. p23. 95w. 4

5148   McDOWELL, Fred. Somebody Keeps Callin' Me. Antilles
       AN7022
       CAD Aug. p55. 100w. $3\frac{1}{2}$

5149   MAINER, Wade. From the Maple to the Hill. Old Home-
       stead OHTRS 4000
       BGU Sept. p19. 150w. 5

5150   MARSHALL, David. King Bluegrass 555 5151
       PIC April p64. 200w. 3

5151   MARSHALL, David. Song of Poverty. King Bluegrass 562
       BGU Dec. p19. 125w. $2\frac{1}{2}$

5152   MARSHALL Family. The Lifeguard. Rebel SLP-1567
       BGU Sept. p20. 175w. 4

5153   MARSHALL Family. Requests. Rebel Recording Co., SLP
       1553
       BGU Feb. p27. 200w. 5

5154   MIGHTY Clouds of Joy. Truth Is the Power. ABC AB 986

HF April p145. 250w. 4

5155 MILLS, Walt. Peace. Word WST 9566
      CMP March p44. 100w. 4

5156 MITCHELL, Geoffrey, Choir. The Joy of Christmas. HMV
      CDS 3784
      GR Dec. p1156. 275w. $3\frac{1}{2}$

5157 MONTGOMERY, Little Brother. Church Songs. Folkways
      FTS 31042
      ST Oct. -Nov. p37-8. 300w. $3\frac{1}{2}$

5158 MORMON Tabernacle Choir. White Christmas. CBS 73630
      (E)
      GR Dec. p1161. 125w. 3

5159 OMARTIAN, Michael. Adam Again. Myrrh Records MSA-
      6576
      CK Sept. p58. 75w. $3\frac{1}{2}$

5160 OZARK Bible Bluegrass Revival. Lemco 761218
      PIC Aug. p73. 150w. 2

5161 PRICE, Ray. Precious Memories. Word WST 9565
      CMP Feb. p39. 125w. 5

5162 ST. George's Canzona. A Tapestry of Music for King
      Wenceslas and His Page. Enigma VAR 1046
      GR Dec. p1156, 1161. 200w. 3

5163 SALSOUL Orchestra. Christmas Jollies. Salsoul SZS 5507
      BM Feb. p49-50. 225w. 4
      HBS Jan. p17. 50w. 3

5164 SHIVELEY, Carl, Faithful Travelers. Two Groups in One.
      [no label given]
      PIC Aug. p76. 125w. $3\frac{1}{2}$

5165 The SHUFFLER Family. Gospel. Rebel 1556
      BGU March p26. 125w. 4
      RSP March-April p23. 100w. 2

5166 SNOW, Hank and Jimmy. Live from Evangel Tabernacle.
      RCA APL1-1361
      CMR Aug. p23. 50w. 3

5167 The SONS of the Gospel. Hold On. Pine Tree 531
      PIC June p74. 100w. 3

5168 SOUL Stirrers. Heritage, Vol. II. Jewel LPS 0113
      AU June p127. 500w. 4

5169   SPARKS, Larry and the Lonesome Ramblers.   Christmas in
        the Hills.   King Bluegrass 559
           BGU   March p24.   225w.   5
           RSP   Jan.-Feb.   p23.   300w. $3\frac{1}{2}$

5170   SPARKS, Larry and the Lonesome Ramblers.   Thank You
        Lord.   Old Homestead 90060
           BGU   Jan.   p28-9.   350w.   4
           MN   V8/#1   p16.   300w. $3\frac{1}{2}$
           OTM   Winter   p26.   50w.   3
           PIC   April   p70.   150w.   5
           RSP   Jan.-Feb.   p22.   150w.   3

5171   STANLEY Brothers, Vol. 4.   County 754 (Reissue)
           BGU   Feb.   p26.   150w.   5
           JEMF   No. 45   p47.   100w.   5
           PIC   April   p65-6.   175w.   4

5172   STAPLE Singers.   Stand by Me.   DJM 28028 (E) (2 discs)
           MM   April 2   p24.   25w. $3\frac{1}{2}$

5173   The STAPLES.   Family Tree.   Warner Brothers BS 3064.
        Cart. M5 3064.   Cass. M8-3064
           BS   Oct.   p27.   150w. $2\frac{1}{2}$
           HF   Nov.   75w.   2
           MG   Oct.   p63.   50w. $2\frac{1}{2}$

5174   The STAPLES.   Pass It On.   Warner Bros. BS 2945 M8
        2945
           SR   March   p114.   100w.   4

5175   STORY, Carl and His Rambling Mountaineers.   The Blue-
        grass Gospel Collection.   CMH Bluegrass Classics CMH 9005
           BGU   Jan.   p30.   50w. $3\frac{1}{2}$

5176   STORY, Carl and His Rambling Mountaineers.   Just a Rose
        Will Do.   Old Homestead HCS 105 (Reissue)
           PIC   Dec.   p61.   200w.   3

5177   STORY, Carl and His Rambling Mountaineers.   Mountain Mu-
        sic.   CMH 6204
           BGU   Jan.   p25.   125w.   4
           OTM   Spring   p26-7.   200w.   3
           PIC   Aug.   p66.   100w.   2

5178   STUBB Family Singers.   Since You Gave Me a Song.   Old
        Homestead OHG 70005
           PIC   May   p62.   150w. $2\frac{1}{2}$

5178a   THOMAS, B. J.   Home Where I Belong.   Myrrh MYR 1060
           CMP   Aug.   p36.   150w.   4

5179   WALDRON, Cliff.   Gospel.   Rebel SLP-1558

AU Dec. p138. 200w. 4
BGU Aug. p34. 275w. 5
RSP 1:3 p21. 175w. 3

5180 WESTMINSTER Cathedral Choir. Christmas Carols. Enigma
Classics VAR 1016 (E)
GR Dec. p1156. 200w. 3

5181 WHITEWATER Gospel Singers. Harvest Time for Mama.
Pine Tree 537
PIC Feb. p51. 175w. $2\frac{1}{2}$

5182 WILKIN, Marijohn. Reach Up and Touch God's Hand. Word
WST 9572
CMP May p38. 150w. 4

5183 WILLIAMS, Jimmy & the Gospel Grass. Oh Yes, Lord.
Gospel Grass 1003
BGU May p35. 100w. 2

5184 WISEMAN, Mac. Shenadoah Valley Memories. Canaan CGS
8510
CMP May p38. 125w. 5

SHOW and HUMOR

Included here are soundtracks from films, radio and television; original cast stage productions; studio recordings of the original item; and reissues of original soundtracks. The chief criterion is music, but those soundtracks which have little or no music will be found here. Additional albums are conveniently located here when the performers have associations with the media.

There is no proper review medium for soundtracks. Reviews are scattered, often depending on content for inclusion among regular records. Consistently good, well-thought-out reviews appear in the Gramophone, with Stereo Review and High Fidelity not far behind. Stage shows are reviewed most often, followed by film soundtracks. Television and radio music is virtually non-existent. Reviews of any kind are usually harsh and the lack of an audience usually precludes tape release. At best, most soundtracks serve as mementoes, except for the outstanding stage musicals and classically-derived film soundtracks.

5185   ALL This and World War Two. Twentieth Century 2T-522
        (2 discs) (Original film soundtrack)
            RS   Jan. 27   p68.   400w. $2\frac{1}{2}$
            SR   March   p124.   200w. $2\frac{1}{2}$

5186   ALLARD, Louis-Paul.   200 Histoires de Newfie.   RCA KXL1-
        0156 (Canada)
            OLR   Sept.   p224.   25w.   2

5187   ANNIE.   (Charles Strouse - Martin Charnin)   Columbia PS
        34712 (Original Broadway cast)
            ARG   Oct.   p51.   200w.   2
            RC   Nov.   p2.   100w.   2
            SR   Aug.   p102.   975w.   5

5188   L'APOCALYPSE des Animaux (Papathanassiou).   Tele-Hachette
        RAI (France) (Original film soundtrack recording)
            RR   Feb.   p92.   125w. $2\frac{1}{2}$

5189   BAGLEY, Ben.   Vincent Youmans Revisited.   Painted Smiles
        PS 1352

485

SR Sept. p100. 350w. 5

5190   The BAKER'S Wife (Swartz). Take Home Tunes THT 772
       (Original cast)
            SR Nov. p121. 325w. 4

5191   BARKER, Les. Mrs. Acroyd, Superstar. Free Reed Frr
       015 (E)
            FR Dec. p26. 150w. 3

5192   BARKER, Ronnie and Ronnie Corbett. The Two Ronnies.
       BBC (E)
            MM Feb. 12 p26. 50w. 3

5193   BEN Hur (Rozsa). Decca PFS 4394 (E) (Original film sound-
       track recording)
            GR Aug. p350. 350w. 4
            RR Aug. p82. 1100w. 3

5194   BIG Time. Motown Tamla T6-355 (Original film soundtrack
       recording with Smokey Robinson)
            BM Nov. p46. 325w. 4

5195   BOUND for Glory (Woody Guthrie and Leonard Rosenman).
       United Artists UALA 695H. Cart. EA 695. Cass. CA 695
       (Original film soundtrack recording)
            RR Dec. p84. 100w. $2\frac{1}{2}$
            RRE March-April p58. 200w. $3\frac{1}{2}$
            SR May p96. 375w. 4

5196   A BRIDGE Too Far (Addison). United Artists 30097 (Orig-
       inal film soundtrack)
            RR Dec. p85. 225w. 4

5197   BROADWAY Brass. Takes "Guys and Dolls" Disco. Twen-
       tieth Century T-514
            CAC Feb. p420. 100w. 3

5198   BUBBLING Brown Sugar. H & L 69011 (Original London
       cast)
            MM Dec. 3 p20. 200w. 3

5199   CALL Me Madam (Berlin). RCA CBM 1-2206 (Reissue)
       (Original Broadway cast)
            VV Aug. 22 p55. 50w. $2\frac{1}{2}$

5200   CALL Me Madam (Irving Berlin). RCA CBM1-2032 (Studio
       recording with Dinah Shore)
            SR May p95, 96. 175w. 2

5201   CARROTT, Jasper. Carrott in Notts. DJM (E)
            CAC Feb. p436. 100w. 3

5202   CHEECH and Chong.   Sleeping Beauty.   Ode SP 77040.   Cart.
        8T 4591.   Cass. CS 4591
            SR Feb. p109. 150w. 4

5203   A CHORUS Line (Marvin Hamlish and Edward Klehan).   (NY
        Shakespearian cast) Columbia PS 33581
            CAC March p477. 200w. 5

5204   CHULAS Fronteras (Blank).   Arhoolie 3005 (Original sound-
        track recording)
            AU June p122. 500w. 4
            RSP March-April p37. 400w. 5
            SO Jan./Feb. p48. 225w. 5

5205   CONNOLLY, Bill.   Atlantic Bridge.   Polydor 2383-419 (E)
            MM Jan. 15 p34. 300w. $3\frac{1}{2}$

5206   CONNOLLY, Bill.   Raw Meat for the Balcony.   Polydor (E)
            MM Jan. 7 p16. 350w. 3

5207   CROSS of Iron (Gold).   EMI EMA 782 (E) (Original film
        soundtrack recording)
            RR June p92. 200w. 2

5208   The DEEP (Barry).   Casablanca NBLP 7060
            BM Nov. p47. 100w. 1
            CRA Oct. p73. 125w. $2\frac{1}{2}$

5209   DESERT Song/New Moon (Romberg).   World Records SH 254
        (E) (Reissue) (Original 1927 and 1929 London casts)
            GR Dec. p1155. 150w. 4

5209a   DONAGGIO, Pino.   United Artists UAS 30033 (E)
            RR June p92. 200w. 3

5209b   EMANUELLE II (Lai).   Warner K 56231 (E) (Original film
        soundtrack recording)
            RR Feb. p92. 175w. $2\frac{1}{2}$

5209c   ESCAPE from the Dark.   EMI EMC 3148 (E) (Original film
        soundtrack recording)
            GR Jan. p1188. 100w. $3\frac{1}{2}$

5209d   EVITA (Webber and Rice).   MCA 2-11003 (2 discs).   Cart.
        MCATZ-11003.   Cass. MCACZ-11003
            CIR March 31 p20-1. 550w. 2
            CRA March p81. 250w. 3
            RS April 7 p76. 350w. $2\frac{1}{2}$
            SOU April p53. 500w. 4
            SR April p108. 700w. 2

5209e   EXORCIST II: The Heretic (Morricone).   Warner Brothers
        BSK 3068

MM   Oct. 8 p29.   50w.   1
RR   Dec.   p84.   125w.   2

5209f   FARQUHARSON, Charlie.   Doesn't Anyone Here Know It's
        Christmas?   Harrae HR 5050 (Canada)
              CC   Dec.   p34.   50w.   3
              OLR Dec.   p290. 25w.   3

5209g   FIRESIGN Theater.   The Best of.   Columbia PG 34391 (2
        discs) (Reissue)
              AU   March p88.   50w.   4

5210   FIRESIGN Theater.   Forward into the Past.   Sire SASH (Re-
        issue) (2 discs)
              RS   Jan. 13 p51.   50w. $2\frac{1}{2}$

5211   FIRESIGN Theater.   Just Folks ... a Firesign Chat.   Butter-
        fly FLY 001
              RS   Aug. 25 p58.   300w. $3\frac{1}{2}$
              VV   Oct. 3 p65.   50w.   2

5212   FITZGERALD, Ella.   The Cole Porter Songbook.   Verve VE-
        22511 (2 discs) (Reissue)
              CAD Feb.   p27.   225w.   2
              DB   July 14 p45-7.   75w.   5
              SR   May   p98-9.   150w.   5

5213   FITZGERALD, Ella.   Jerome Kern and Johnny Mercer Song-
        book.   Verve VE 2610 025 (2 discs) (E) (Reissue)
              GR   Feb.   p1336.   50w. $3\frac{1}{2}$

5214   FITZGERALD, Ella.   Rodgers and Hart Songbook.   Verve VE
        2-2519 (2 discs) (Reissue)
              CAD Oct.   p25.   100w.   4

5215   FLANDERS, Michael and Donald Swann.   Tried by the Center
        Court.   EMI Note NTS 116 (E)
              GR   May   p1750.   225w.   4

5216   FLO and Eddie.   Moving Targets.   Columbia PC 34262
              ZZ   Feb.   675w.   4

5217   FOR Colored Girls Who Have Considered Suicide When the
        Rainbow Is Enuf (Ntozake Shange--Bill Eaton).   Buddah BDS
        95007-OC (Original Broadway cast recording)
              SR   July   p105, 107.   325w.   5

5218   FUN in Acapulco.   RCA AFL1-2756 (Reissue) (Original Elvis
        Presley film soundtrack)
              MM   Nov. 19 p28.   50w. $2\frac{1}{2}$
              NK   Autumn p40.   25w. $2\frac{1}{2}$

5219   GERHARDT, Charles and National Philharmonic Orchestra.

Citizen Kane and Others by Herrmann.   RCA ARD 1-0707
    AU March p94. 400w. 4

5220   GERHARDT, Charles and National Philharmonic Orchestra.
Lost Horizon/Guns of Navarone--classic film scores of
Dimitri Tiomkin.   RCA ARL 1-1669
    GR Sept. p521. 175w. 2
    HF Feb. p116. 300w. 3
    RR Oct. p87. 300w. 3

5221   GERHARDT, Charles and National Philharmonic Orchestra.
The Private Lives of Elizabeth and Essex; the classic film
score of Erich Wolfgang Komgold.   RCA ARL 1-2792
    AU Feb. p92. 300w. $2\frac{1}{2}$

5222   GERSHWIN, George. Plays.   Columbia Masterworks 76509
    JJ April p29. 250w. $3\frac{1}{2}$

5223   GIRLS, Girls, Girls.   RCA PL 42354 (E) (Reissue) (Original
Elvis Presley film soundtrack)
    MM Nov. 19 p28. 50w. $2\frac{1}{2}$
    NK Autumn p40. 25w. $2\frac{1}{2}$

5224   GOON Show Classics, Vol. 3.   BBC (E)
    CAC Feb. p434. 100w. $3\frac{1}{2}$

5225   The GREATEST (Benson, Masser).   Arista AL 7000 (Original film soundtrack)
    BM Oct. p49. 225w. 3
    CRA Oct. p73. 125w. 3
    MM Sept. 3 p22. 50w. 1

5226   GRENFELL, Joyce. Collection.   EMI One-Up OU 2149 (E)
    GR Jan. p1194. 50w. $3\frac{1}{2}$

5227   HAZEL Flagg. RCA CBM1-2207 (Reissue) (Original cast)
    VV Aug. 22 p55. 50w. 3

5228   HEARTS and Flowers (Richmond).   DJM 22073 (E) (Original
film soundtrack recording)
    MM Dec. 21 p14. 200w. $2\frac{1}{2}$

5229   HERMANN, Bernard. The Mysterious Film World of....
Decca PFS 4337 (E)
    RR June p92. 225w. $3\frac{1}{2}$

5230   HISTOIRE d'O (Bachelet).   Decca SKLR 5235 (E) (Original
film soundtrack recording)
    RR Feb. p92. 75w. $2\frac{1}{2}$

5231   I Love My Wife (Coleman and Stewart).   Atlantic SD 19107
(Original Broadway cast)
    SR Nov. p118. 550w. 4

5232   IDLE, Eric and Neil Innes.   The Rutland Weekend Television
        Songbook.   Passport PPSD 98018
            SR   Feb.   p109, 111.   175w.   4½

5233   INNES, Neil.   Taking Off.   Arista SPARTY 1004 (E)
            MM   April 23   p22.   250w.   3½
            TP   Sept.   p37-8.   200w.   4

5234   IPI-Tombi (Bertha Egnos--Gail Lakier).   Ashtree 26000 (2
        discs) (Original cast)
            SR   May   p95.   250w.   3

5235   JESUS of Nazareth (Jarré).   Pye NSPH 28504 (E)
            RR   Oct.   p87.   150w.   3½

5236   KENTON, Stan.   Film Tracks.   Joyce 3003
            CAD   Aug.   p49.   175w.   4

5237   KING Kong (Steiner).   Entre' acte ERS 6504 (E) (Original
        film score, National Philharmonic Orchestra cond. by Fred
        Steiner)
            HF   July   p124.   250w.   3
            RR   Oct.   p87.   150w.   2½

5238   KING Kong (Barry).   Reprise MS 2260.   Cart. M8 2260.
        Cass. M5 2260 (Original 1977 film soundtrack)
            HF   July   p124.   250w.   2½

5239   KING'S Singers.   Sing Flanders and Swann and Noel Coward.
        EMI EMC 31960 (E)
            GR   Dec.   p1162.   50w.   3

5240   KISSIN' Cousins.   RCA AFL 1-2894 (Reissue) (Original Elvis
        Presley film soundtrack)
            MM   Nov. 19   p28.   50w.   2½
            NK   Autumn   p40.   25w.   2½

5241   KOSTELANETZ, Andre.   Plays Gershwin's Greatest Hits.
        Harmony H30090 (Reissue)
            GR   March   p1468.   50w.   2½

5242   KOSTELANETZ, Andre.   Plays "A Chorus Line," "Tree-
        monisha" and "Chicago."   Columbia KC 33954
            AU   Feb.   p92.   100w.   1

5243   KOVACS, Ernie.   Columbia PC 34250
            CIR   Jan. 31   p16.   200w.   1½
            CRA   Jan.   p78.   175w.   3
            SR   March   p116-7.   200w.   3½

5244   LONDON Philharmonic Orchestra.   Great Movie Thrillers.
        London SPS 44126
            AU   Jan.   p92.   500w.   4½

5245   LUCKY Lady.   Arista AL 4069 (Original soundtrack)
        AU Feb. p93. 250w. 3

5246   McCORKLE, Susannah. The Music of Harry Warren. World
        Records WRS 1001 (E)
        JJ Feb. p33-4. 500w. 5
        MM Feb. 5 p22. 325w. $3\frac{1}{2}$
        ST April-May p151-2. 200w. 4

5247   MAKE a Wish (Hugh Martin).   RCA CBM1-2033 (Original
        cast)
        SR May p95, 96. 200w. 3

5248   A MAN and a Woman (Lai).   United Artists UAS 5147 (Orig-
        inal French soundtrack recording)
        RR Dec. p85. 100w. $2\frac{1}{2}$

5249   MARTIN, Steve. Let's Get Small.   Warner BSK 3090
        CAD Oct. p24. 50w. $2\frac{1}{2}$
        RS Nov. 17 p94, 96. 375w. $1\frac{1}{2}$
        VV Oct. 3 p65. 75w. $2\frac{1}{2}$

5250   MOYES, Fred. Sings Satire.   FM Records FM 1000 (Canada)
        CC Nov. p36. 75w. 3

5251   MULL, Martin. I'm Everyone I've Ever Loved.   ABC AB-
        997
        AU July p95. 250w. 4
        CRA May p74, 76. 600w. 1
        SR May p90. 75w. 0

5252   NEW Faces of 1952.   RCA CBM1-2206 (Reissue) (Original
        Broadway cast)
        SR Dec. p116. 350w. $3\frac{1}{2}$
        VV Aug. 22 p55. 50w. $3\frac{1}{2}$

5253   NEW York, New York (Kanden--Ebb).   United Artists UA-LA
        750-L2 (2 discs). Cart. UA-EA 750-L. Cass. UA-CA 750-L
        (Original motion-picture score)
        CAD Aug. p24. 200w. $4\frac{1}{2}$
        RR Dec. p84-5. 175w. 3
        SR Sept. p110. 600w. 5

5254   NOT Ready for Prime Time Players. Saturday Night Live.
        Arista
        CIR Feb. 28 p15-6. 650w. 1
        CRE March p61-2. 450w. 3

5255   NOVE Cento. RCA TBL 1-1221 (Italy) (Original film sound-
        track)
        HF July p126. 250w. 4

5256   OBSESSION (Herrmann).   London SPCS 21160

        AU Jan. p92. 500w. $4\frac{1}{2}$
        GR Feb. p92. 300w. $3\frac{1}{2}$

5257 O'CONNOR, Tom. Ace of Clubs. DJM 22055 (E)
        CAC Feb. p436. 125w. $2\frac{1}{2}$

5258 OF Thee I Sing (Gershwin). Capitol T 11651 (Original cast
      recording)
        RC Nov. p9. 100w. $3\frac{1}{2}$

5259 PELE (Mendes). Atlantic 18231 (Original film soundtrack
      recording)
        CAD Nov. p30. 50w. 4

5260 PINK Panther Strikes Again (Mancini). United Artists LA
      694G (Original film soundtrack)
        GR March p1468. 100w. 4
        HF April p119. 200w. 3
        RR April p86. 50w. $2\frac{1}{2}$

5261 PORGY and Bess (Gershwin). London OSA 13116 (3 discs)
      (Studio recording)
        ARG Sept. p10. 700w. $4\frac{1}{2}$

5262 PORGY and Bess (Gershwin). RCA ARL 3-2109 (3 discs)
      (Studio recording)
        ARG Sept. p10. 700w. 4

5263 PORGY and Bess (Gershwin). RCA CPL2-1831 (2 discs)
      (Studio version with Ray Charles and Cleo Laine)
        CAC Feb. p433. 100w. 2
        CK Jan. p50. 150w. 5
        DB March 24 475w. 5
        GR Feb. p1332. 300w. 4
        JJ Feb. p29. 400w. 4
        JM 1:2 p55. 275w. $2\frac{1}{2}$

5264 PORGY and Bess (Gershwin). Verve VE 2-2507 (2 discs)
      (Reissue) (Studio version with Ella Fitzgerald and Louis Arm-
      strong)
        SR May p98-9. 150w. 4

5265 PORTER, Cole. Classic Cole. Columbia M34533
        SR Dec. 300w. 2

5266 PRYOR, Richard. Bicentennial Nigger. Warner Brothers
      BS 2690
        MG Feb. p55. 125w. 3

5267 PRYOR, Richard. Greatest Hits. Warner Brothers BSK
      3057
        MG Sept. p53. 100w. $2\frac{1}{2}$

5268   RAGGEDY Ann and Andy (Raposo).   Columbia 534686 (Orig-
       inal film soundtrack recording)
          SR   Oct.   p124, 126.   250w.   4

5269   RETURN of a Man Called Horse (Rosenthal).   United Artists
       LA 692G (Original film soundtrack)
          HF   April   p120.   250w.   3
          RR   Feb.   p92.   125w.   3

5270   ROCKY.   United Artists LA 693G.   Cart.   EA693H (Original
       soundtrack)
          HF   July   p126.   250w.   3

5271   ROLLERCOASTER (Schifrin).   MCA 2284 (Original film sound-
       track)
          CRA   Oct.   p73.   125w. $1\frac{1}{2}$
          RC   Aug.   p5.   25w. $2\frac{1}{2}$

5272   ROOTS (Jones).   A&M 4626 (Original TV soundtrack record-
       ing)
          BM   June   p46-7.   200w.   2

5273   ROUSTABOUT.   RCA AFL1-2999 (Reissue) (Original Elvis
       Presley film soundtrack)
          MM   Nov. 19   p28.   50w. $2\frac{1}{2}$
          NK   Autumn   p40.   25w. $2\frac{1}{2}$

5274   ROZSA, Miklos.   Conducts Rozsa.   Polydor 2383 440 (E)
          GR   June   p109.   200w.   4
          MM   May 14   p33.   50w.   2
          RR   June   p92.   300w.   4

5275   SCOTT Joplin (Joplin; arr. Hyman).   MCA 2098 (Original
       film soundtrack)
          CAD   April   p22.   198w.   4
          RT   March   p7.   375w. $3\frac{1}{2}$

5276   SEVENTEEN (Kim Gannon--Walter Kent).   RCA CBM1-203
       (Original cast)
          SR   May   p95, 96.   75w.   4
          VV   Aug. 22   p55.   50w. $2\frac{1}{2}$

5277   SHOWBOAT/Sunny (Kern).   World Records SH 240 (E) (Orig-
       inal London casts)
          GR   Aug.   p350.   250w. $3\frac{1}{2}$

5278   SIDE by Side by Sondheim.   RCA Red Seal CBL 2-1851 (2
       discs).   Cart. CBS2-1851 (Original London cast)
          CAC   Feb.   p437.   300w. $1\frac{1}{2}$
          HF   Feb.   p116.   300w.   3
          RC   Oct.   p14.   125w.   5
          SR   Jan.   p102.   700w.   4

5279   SILENT Movie (Morris).   United Artists UALA 672-G (Orig-
        inal film soundtrack recording)
            RR   April   p86.   200w.   3½

5280   SILK Stockings.   RCA CBM1-2208 (Reissue) (Original Broad-
        way cast)
            VV   Aug. 22   p55.   50w.   3½

5281   SMOKEY and the Bandit (Reed).   MCA 2099 (Original film
        soundtrack)
            CRA   Oct.   p73.   125w.   2½
            CMP   Oct.   p41.   150w.   3
            MM   Sept. 3   p22.   25w.   3½
            RSP   Nov.-Dec.   p30.   275w.   3

5282   The SPIRIT of St. Louis (Waxman).   Entr'acte ERS0507-ST
        (E) (Reissue) (Original film soundtrack recording)
            RR   Dec.   p84.   375w.   3½

5283   The SPY Who Loved Me (Hamlisch).   United Artists UALA
        774-H (Original film soundtrack)
            MM   Sept. 3   p46.   50w.   3½
            RR   Dec.   p85.   100w.   1½

5284   A STAR Is Born (Arlen--Gershwin).   Columbia SPACS 8740
        (Original soundtrack recording with Judy Garland)
            SR   March   p110.   50w.   4

5285   A STAR Is Born (Kristofferson, Streisand).   Columbia JS-
        34403.   Cart. JSA-34403 (Original 1977 film soundtrack with
        Barbra Streisand and Kris Kristofferson)
            CAC   April   p16.   125w.   2½
            CIR   March 31   p18.   200w.   0
            CM   April   p54.   350w.   1
            MG   April   p55.   50w.   0
            MM   Feb. 19   p224.   200w.   0
            RS   Feb. 24   p66.   175w.   0
            SOU   Feb.   p42.   600w.   1
            SR   March   p110.   800w.   3

5286   STAR Wars (John Williams).   20th Century Records 2T-541
        (2 discs).   Cart. 8-2T-541.   Cass. C-2T-541 (Original sound-
        track recording)
            CIR   Sept. 8   p60.   250w.   3
            CK   Dec.   p72.   125w.   2½
            CRA   Oct.   p73.   125w.   3
            RC   Oct.   p3-4.   100w.   4
            SR   Sept.   p95.   550w.   5

5287   STARTING Here, Starting How (Shire--Maltby).   RCA ABL1-
        2360 (Original cast recording)
            SR   Oct.   p124.   800w.   4½

5288   SWASHBUCKLER (Addison).   MCA MCF 2779 (E) (Original
        film soundtrack)
            RR   April p86.   300w. $3\frac{1}{2}$

5289   THIEF of Baghdad (Rozsa).   Film Music Collection FMC 8
            HF   Sept.   p116.   400w.   3
            RR   Oct.   p87.   325w.   4

5290   TO Kill a Mockingbird (Bernstein).   Film Music Collection 7
        (Original film score)
            HF   April p119.   350w.   4
            RR   Feb.   p92.   300w.   3

5291   TOMLIN, Lily.   On Stage.   Arista AB-4142
            RS   Nov. 17 p93-4.   750w. $3\frac{1}{2}$

5292   VIVA Zapata/Death of a Salesman (North).   Film Music Col-
        lection Series FMC-9
            RR   Dec.   p85.   250w. $3\frac{1}{2}$

5293   VOYAGE of the Damned (Schifrin).   Entr'acte ERS6508-ST
        (E) (Original film soundtrack)
            RR   Dec.   p84.   125w.   2

5294   WHITE Rock (Wakeman).   A & M SP 4614 (Original film
        soundtrack)
            CAC   April p9.   150w.   3
            CIR   May 26 p56.   600w. $4\frac{1}{2}$
            CK   May   p49.   150w.   4
            GR   May   p1757.   50w. $2\frac{1}{2}$
            MM   Feb. 19 p22.   350w. $4\frac{1}{2}$
            RR   April p86.   50w. $3\frac{1}{2}$

5295   YOUR Arms Too Short to Box with God (Alex Bradford,
        Micki Grant, Vinnette Carrol).   ABC AB-1004.   Cart. 8020-
        1004N.   Cass. 5020-1004N (Original cast)
            SR   Aug.   p101, 103.   200w.   5

ANTHOLOGIES and CONCERTS

"Anthology" is derived from Greek words meaning "flower gathering." Presumably, this means either the best that is available or a mixed bag, with some parts showing off the rest by means of contrast. Certainly the display should be stunning, for why else anthologize?

In the music world, anthologies serve as samplers or introductions to a company's products. These collections of popular performers sell to a captured audience that is used to having preselected and convenience items before their eyes. At the same time they are invaluable for rapidly building up a music record library, or for fleshing out an area of popular music not already covered in the library. There will be little duplication among the collections if the library does not already have the originals.

Within the past three years, aided by the soaring costs of studio time and performers' fees plus the recognized fad for nostalgia of the past, more anthologies and collections than ever before have been released. From a manufacturer's point of view, they are cheap to produce: the material has virtually paid for itself already; the liner notes are few, if any, or standardized; there is uniform packaging and design; there is a ready market which the rackers and jobbers love, and hence little advertising is necessary; and anthologies act as a sampler of the performer or to the catalogue, hence promoting future sales. Selection of the program depends on the cooperation of music publishers in granting reduced rates.

Personally, we are quite partial to anthologized performances. For a pure musical experience there has been nothing quite like, say, on a hot and humid night, throwing on a pile of 45 RPM singles and sitting back guzzling beer while tapping to the rhythms. At this point, our attention span is about three minutes; thus a new record with a new voice comes on just as our minds start to wander. With older records the effect is familiarity and fond, past memories. For the sake of convenience and better musical reproduction, it is easier to do all this with a stack of anthologized long play records. Most new records today can be quite boring between the highlights, and it is not uncommon for a group to have an album with a hit single, fleshed out with 9 duds. You really wouldn't want to hear it all again. While most people might all like or remember one or two particular numbers, they also like other tracks individually. An anthology or "best" album attempts to take those most popular selec-

496

tions which we all enjoy and market them so that most people might like the whole reissue album. One man's meat is not another man's poison in the case of the anthology.

There are many reservations about compilations. In many instances, there are only 10 tracks to a disc. These may have fewer tracks than the original albums, and certainly it makes each number more expensive at a per selection cost. Yet there are distinct advantages for a certain market that has low-fidelity equipment; the wider grooves give a full range of sound and increase the bass proportionately, thus making this particular disc virtually ideal for home stereo consoles and for older "heavier" cartridges. As the wider grooves don't wear out as quickly as compressed ones, the records may be played over and over again with less wear than an "original" disc. In other instances, some "best" collections (especially multi-volume sets) almost equal the catalogue material from which they are drawn, and hence cost more in the long run.

A number of gimmicks such as "electronic enhancement" for stereo has a vast echoing sound being reminiscent of a train station lobby. These types are dying out as it costs money to re-channel, some of the public are demanding original monophonic sound, and-- the biggest marketing blow of all--these discs have been relegated to the semi-annual Schwann-2 Catalog with the mono discs. Sometimes the informative print was very small, or it was printed as, say, yellow on orange, and the consumer virtually couldn't read the notice "enhanced for stereo. "

Another problem with the vinyl product is that anthologies are mostly regional pressings. Duplicate masters are used in factories not as careful as the home plant. Then they are shipped directly to the regional distributor. Of course, a careless pressing sounds worse than a skillfully crafted product, and the polyvinyl chloride content can drop to below 85%. This is important, for the extender in a disc can be exposed to the stylus riding on the otherwise soft plastic, and great harm can occur. Classical records are generally 95-99% vinyl, with pop recordings being around 90%. Anything lower than 90% can be detrimental to sound reproduction.

The material is usually selected by the producer or company, so that it may have no relation to what the performers themselves think is their best material. Many such groups are anthologized after they leave the company for greener pastures, and the manufacturer can keep churning out the reissues year after year, relying on the groups' future success to advertise the old reissued product. Some anthologies are passed off as shoddy memorials after death. This keeps the name in front of the record buying public, but too often the album is at full list price and the cover only mentions that it is a reissue in passing.

With the new packaging gatefold, it is likely that all notes will be inside the shrink-wrapped cellophane parcel, and the consumer will not know what he is supposed to buy until he reads a review, ad, or opens the package (thus forfeiting a "return" if he already has the item). As these records rarely get reviewed or advertised, there is no certain way of knowing what is on them. Schwann does not often give track listings for them. England is the best place to go for inexpensive reissues in all fields, and more so if the reissue is not available on the North American market.

Mail order houses are a direct development from the recording companies, and some of the latter have gone into the business themselves. By leasing the material for a one-shot appearance, the selected items are pure gravy for the companies. Thus, with groove compression of $2\frac{1}{2}$ minute songs, 18-24 titles can appear on some of these albums. Usually these discs are only promoted by television commercials or direct mail. Other reissue companies (mostly prevalent in England) lease material from the original companies and repackage it as they see fit. Pickwick International is most successful at this, drawing on the large Capitol and Mercury catalogues (which is one reason why these two companies do not do much disc reissuing).

The records listed below consist of reissued material, either in the form of anthologies, or "live" versions of studio tracks which enjoy reasonably good sound. Concerts in this same context refers to issued (or reissued) recordings of several artists or groups that performed as part of a show or benefit. They are anthologies in the sense that no one artist predominates; most of these recordings come from music festivals. All are listed by title entry, and exhaustive artist indexing is beyond the time available to the compilers. Recent examples have included CTI Summer Jazz at the Hollywood Bowl (5348), Fifth Annual Pee Wee Russell Memorial Stomp (5401), and San Diego Jazz Club (5610).

5296   A-1: The Savoy Sessions. Savoy SLP 1104 (Reissue)
        SOU Jan. p48. 50w. 3

5297   AC/DC: Gay Jazz Reissues. Stash ST 106 (Reissue)
        CAD June p33. 300w. 4
        RSP V1/#3 p34-5. 350w. $1\frac{1}{2}$

5298   AFRICAN Dances. Authentic 601
        MG May p55. 100w. $2\frac{1}{2}$

5299   AFRO-Cuban Jazz. Verve VE-2-2522 (2 discs) (Reissue)
        CAD Oct. p54. 400w. 3
        MG Oct. p60. 75w. $3\frac{1}{2}$

5300   ALL Star Swing Groups. Savoy 2218 (2 discs) (Reissue)
        MJ Nov. p22. 100w. 3
        MM May 14 p34. 450w. $3\frac{1}{2}$
        SOU May p62. 100w. 4

5301   ALL This and WWII. Twentieth Century 2-T522 (2 discs)
        RC May p4-5.   225w. $3\frac{1}{2}$
        RRE Jan. -Feb. p23-4. 150w.   3

5302   ALL Time Bloopers: Radio and Television's Most Hilarious
        Boners, Six Vol. MCA2-4116-8 (2 discs)
        RC Nov. p7-8.   100w. $3\frac{1}{2}$

5303   ALLA Blues: Country Blues in California, 1947-1954. Muska-
        dire 104 (Reissue)
        DB May 5 p28-32.   225w.   4

5304   AMERICAN Teenage Classics.   Roulette (E) (Reissue)
        HBS June p17. 50w.   4

5305   ANTHOLOGY of American Folk Music.   Folkways FA-2951-
        1253 (9 discs)
        CM March p56.   75w. $2\frac{1}{2}$

5306   ASSALAM Aleikoum Africa, Volume 1.   Antilles
        VV Aug. 1 p51.   50w. $3\frac{1}{2}$

5307   BBC TV Nationwide Carols: Winners 1976.   Decca MOR506
        (E)
        GR Dec. p1161.   125w. $3\frac{1}{2}$

5308   BACK in the Country-40 Country Greats.   DJM DJD 28025
        (E) (2 discs) (Reissue)
        CMR Jan. p28.   400w.   5
        NK Winter p33.   100w.   4

5309   BACK in the Streets Again.   DJM 22051 (E) (Reissue)
        BM Jan. p52.   200w.   4
        CAC Feb. p420.   350w.   2
        HBS Jan. p17.   50w.   4
        NK Winter p38.   50w.   4

5310   The BANDS Played On.   Decca DDV5001/2 (E) (2 discs) (Re-
        issue)
        GR Sept. p522.   225w. $3\frac{1}{2}$

5311   BAYOU Rock.   Goldband FR 7764
        CAD Aug. p26.   125w. $3\frac{1}{2}$

5312   BEALE Street Mess Around.   Rounder 2006
        CAD Nov. p16.   75w.   5

5313   BEAT Merchants.   United Artists 101/2 (E) (2 discs) (Reis-
        sue)
        MM April 16 p21.   200w. $2\frac{1}{2}$
        RS July 14 p65.   300w.   3

5314   BEBOP.   New World Records 271

MJ Dec. p23. 50w. 3

5315   BEER Parlour Jive. String STR 801 (E) (Reissue)
       CMP May p34. 125w. 5
       JEMF No. 46 p102-3. 100w. 5
       MM Feb. 26 p30. 50w. 4

5316   BEGGARS Hill. Moonshine MS60 (E)
       FR Jan. p33. 100w. 1

5317   BELGIAN Ragtime. EMI 4CO54-96707 (Belgium)
       CAD Oct. p53-4. 150w. 4
       JR V9/#3 unpaged 225w. 3½
       MR Feb. p12. 300w. 2

5318   BEN Bagley's Oscar Hammerstein Revisited. Painted Smiles
       PS 1365
       SR Feb. p98. 700w. 4

5319   BEST of "Car Wash." MCA (E) (2 discs)
       MM July 16 p22. 200w. 3

5320   BEST Disco in Town. Tee Vee TA-1059 (2 discs)
       RC June p3. 300w. 3½

5321   The BEST of Irish Folk. EMI One-Up OU 2180 (E) (Reissue)
       FR Oct. p35. 200w. 3

5322   BEST of Sun Rockabilly, V. 1/2. Charly CR 30-123/4 (E)
       (2 discs) (Reissue)
       NK Autumn p50. 150w. 5

5323   BIG Bands and Territory Bands of the Twenties. New World
       Records 256 (Reissue)
       MJ Dec. p23. 100w. 4

5324   BIG Bands and Territory Bands of the Thirties. New World
       Records 217 (Reissue)
       MJ Dec. p23. 100w. 4

5325   BIONIC Gold. Big Sound BLSP-001
       RS Nov. 3 p115. 250w. ½
       TP Oct. p41. 300w. 3½

5326   BLACK and White Connection. Valer (E)
       MM Aug. 13 p20. 50w. 3

5327   BLACK and White Masters. Storyville SLP 806 (Denmark)
       (Reissue)
       CO Aug. p24. 125w. 3

5328   BLACK California. Savoy SJL 2215 (2 discs) (Reissue)
       CAD Feb. p41. 325w. 3

CO   Feb.   p23.   325w.   2½
DB   March 10 p26.   350w.   3
MG   Feb.   p57.   100w.   3½
MJ   Nov.   p22.   100w.   3
SOU Jan.   p49.   100w.   4

5329   BLUE Note Live at the Roxy.   Blue Note BN-LA663-J2 (2
       discs)
       CAD   Jan.   p43.   325w.   3
       DB   Feb. 10 p20.   250w.   2½
       MJ   Sept.   p32.   25w.   1

5330   BLUEGRASS on Campus.   Vol. 1/2.   Outlet 0-1000/01 (2
       discs)
       CAD   Aug.   p25.   100w.   3½
       RSP   1:3   p18.   250w.   3

5331   BLUES and More Blues.   Spivey LP 1015
       CAD   Aug.   p37.   100w.   4

5332   BLUES Box, 2.   MCA PCOX 7758/1-4 (4 discs) (West Ger-
       many) (Reissue)
       RSP   Jan. -Feb.   p6-7.   600w.   3

5333   The BLUES Came Down from Memphis.   Charly CR 30-125
       (E) (Reissue)
       NK   Autumn   p45.   75w.   4
       SMG   Sept.   p28.   25w.   4

5334   BLUES Come to Chapel Hill.   Flyright 504 (E)
       LB   Sept./Oct.   p37.   250w.   2½

5335   BLUES from the Windy City.   Chicago in Transition, 1946-
       1952.   Flyright FLYLP 4713 (E) (Reissue)
       BM   Jan.   p49.   325w.   4
       JJ   Jan.   p26.   400w.   5
       RSP   Jan. -Feb.   p3.   400w.   4

5336   BLUES Is Killing Me.   Juke Joint Records 1501 (Reissue)
       CZM   Dec.   p60.   50w.   4½

5337   BLUES-Southside Chicago.   Flyright LP 521 (E) (Reissue)
       JJ   Jan.   p26.   200w.   2
       RSP   Jan. -Feb.   p5.   300w.   3

5338   BLUESVILLE.   Goldband 7774
       CAD   Aug.   p25.   125w.   3½

5339   BOBBY Sox to Blue Jeans.   WEA K56315 (E) (Reissue)
       NK   Winter   p37.   100w.   4

5340   BOOGIE Woogie Session '76 Live in Vienna.   EMI 12 CO58-
       33190 (E)

MR   Aug.   p16.   125w. $3\frac{1}{2}$

5341   BOOT That Thing.   Flyright-Matchbox SDM 258 (E)
LB   Sept./Oct.   p37-8.   225w.   3

5342   BREAKFAST Special.   Rounder 3012
CS   Nov.   p19.   200w. $1\frac{1}{2}$

5343   BRING Me Another Half-a-Pint.   Barrelhouse BH-09 (Reissue)
RSP   March-April   p7.   125w.   0

5344   BRITISH Beat Groups, 1963-64.   United Artists UDM101/2
(E) (2 discs) (Reissue)
TP   June-July   p36, 38.   300w.   5

5345   BRITISH Music for Brass Bands.   RCA (E)
CAC   Sept.   p217.   100w. $3\frac{1}{2}$

5346   BROTHERS and Other Mothers.   Savoy SJL 2210 (2 discs)
(Reissue)
JJ   Feb.   p30.   600w.   5
RR   March   p97.   50w. $2\frac{1}{2}$

5347   A BUNCH of Stiff Records.   Stiff SEEZ-22 (E)
AU   Aug.   p85.   500w.   4
CRA   July   p78.   350w. $3\frac{1}{2}$
GR   July   p234, 237.   50w. $2\frac{1}{2}$
MM   May 14   p31.   200w.   4
RC   Oct.   p9.   150w. $4\frac{1}{2}$
RS   July 14   p65.   350w.   3
TP   June/July   p39.   150w. $2\frac{1}{2}$

5348   CTI Summer Jazz at the Hollywood Bowl, Vol. 1/3.   CTI
7076/8 (3 discs)
CAD   Oct.   p59-60.   375w.   4
MG   Oct.   p61.   100w.   2
RSP   Nov.-Dec.   p34.   300w. $3\frac{1}{2}$

5349   CAJUN Home Music.   Folkways FA 2620
CFS   Summer   p22.   150w.   4
PIC   Oct.   p59.   250w.   4

5350   CAJUN Music of the Early 1950s.   Arhoolie 5008 (Reissue)
CM   March   p56.   25w. $2\frac{1}{2}$

5351   CALIFORNIA Rockabilly.   Rollin' Rock LP012
RC   Oct.   p8.   200w.   2

5352   CAPITOL Country Kicks.   Capitol CAPS 1005 (E) (Reissue)
CMP   May   p39.   125w.   5
CMR   July   p22.   300w.   3
MM   May 14   p31.   50w.   4

5353   CAPITOL Rockabilly Originals.   Capitol CAPS 1009 (E) (Reissue)
          CMP   Dec.   p36.   200w.   3

5354   CAROLINA Country Blues.   Flyright 505 (E)
          LB   Sept./Oct.   p37.   250w. $2\frac{1}{2}$

5355   CELEBRATION!   Old Time Music at Berea.   Appalachian Centre AC-DO1
          OTM   Spring   p24.   400w. $2\frac{1}{2}$

5356   CHARTBUSTERS Salute the Shadows.   Precision (E)
          CAC   June   p98.   50w.   3

5357   CHICAGO Blues at Home.   Advent 2806
          CAD   Sept.   p37-8.   175w.   5
          GP   Sept.   p119.   200w.   3

5358   CHICAGO Boogie.   Barrelhouse 04 (Reissue)
          DB   May 5   p28-32.   225w.   3

5359   CHICAGO Slickers, 1948-53.   Nighthawk 102 (Reissue)
          CAD   April   p37-8.   150w.   4
          DB   May 5   p28-32.   225w.   4
          LB   March-April   p34-5.   400w.   4

5360   CHILE Vencera!:   An Anthology of Chilean New Song 1962-1973.   Rounder 4009/4010 (2 discs)
          FOL   Aug.   p27-8.   800w. $3\frac{1}{2}$
          RSP   1:3   p38-9.   850w.   4
          VV   May 2   p59.   350w. $4\frac{1}{2}$

5361   CLASSICS for Brass Band.   Decca (E)
          CAC   Sept.   p217.   100w. $3\frac{1}{2}$

5362   CLWT y ddawns 1 (Selection of Welsh Dances 1).   Sain 1035 D
          EDS   Summer   p74.   200w.   4

5363   COME All You Coal Miners.   Rounder 4005
          CMR   July   p23.   300w.   3

5364   COOK Book.   Warner PRO 660 (2 discs)
          RC   Aug.   p14.   50w.   2

5365   COOLEY High.   Motown (E) (Reissue)
          MM   Jan. 29   p25.   25w. $2\frac{1}{2}$

5366   COPULATIN' Blues.   Stash ST-101 (Reissue)
          JF   No. 46   p62.   450w. $3\frac{1}{2}$
          JM   1:2   p66.   125w. $2\frac{1}{2}$
          LB   July-Aug.   p34.   150w. $3\frac{1}{2}$
          ST   Feb.-March   p117-8.   425w.   4

5367   COTTON City County.   Charly CR 30104 (E) (Reissue)
       CM   Feb.   p57.   300w.   4

5368   COUNTRY Artists.   Peerless DT013 (2 discs) (Reissue)
       CMR   Sept.   p16-7.   225w.   0

5369   COUNTRY Classics - Volume 8.   Capitol 5COf2-81441X
       (Dutch Issue)
       CMR   July   p24.   500w.   4

5370   COUNTRY Comes to Carnegie Hall.   ABC ABCD 614 (2
       discs)
       CMP   Nov.   p38.   350w.   5
       MM   Dec. 3   p28.   100w. $3\frac{1}{2}$
       NK   Autumn   p43.   100w.   4

5371   COUNTRY Comfort.   K-Tel NE 924 (Reissue)
       CMR   Feb.   p33.   75w.   4

5372   COUNTRY Comment.   Charly CR 30118 (E) (Reissue)
       CMP   March   p41.   150w.   5
       MM   March 19   p31.   50w.   3
       NK   Spring   p39.   50w. $2\frac{1}{2}$
       SMG   May   p26.   150w. $3\frac{1}{2}$

5373   COUNTRY Meets Rock 'n' Roll.   ABC 28082 ET (West Ger-
       many) (Reissue)
       CMR   June   p13.   350w.   4
       NK   Spring   p37.   125w.   5
       SMG   May   p26.   200w.   4

5374   COUNTRY Music's Golden Hit Parade.   Reader's Digest GMUS
       6AR
       CMP   April   p55.   150w.   5

5375   COUNTRY Round-Up.   Polydor (E)
       CAC   Feb.   p433.   125w. $2\frac{1}{2}$

5376   COWBOY Image.   MCA VIM 4010 (Japan) (Reissue)
       JEMF   Autumn   p157-60.   200w.   5
       OTM   Summer   p30-4.   500w.   4

5377   CUT! Out Take from Hollywood Musicals.   Out Take OTF-1/
       OTF-2
       SR   April   p106.   325w.   4

5378   DANCE Bands on the Air, Vol. 1 & 2.   BBC TV (E) (2
       discs) (Reissue)
       CAC   Feb.   p434.   250w. $3\frac{1}{2}$

5379   The DANCING Twenties.   Folkways RBF 27 (Reissue)
       RA   Nov./Dec.   p6.   50w.   4
       RT   Jan.   p4.   200w.   3

5380   DEALING with the Devil, Vol. 1.   EMI One-Up OU2164 (E)
            MM   June 25 p24.   250w. $3\frac{1}{2}$
            RR   June p94-5.   75w.   3

5381   DEALING with the Devil, Vol. 2.   EMI One-Up 2192 (E)
            MM   Nov. 19 p31.   350w. $3\frac{1}{2}$

5382   DETROIT After Hours, Vol. 1.   Trix 3311
            JR   V9/#3 unpaged 300w.   4

5383   DETROIT Ghetto Blues, 1948-1954.   Nighthawk 104 (Reissue)
            CAD   April p37-8.   150w.   4
            DB   May 5 p28-32.   225w.   4
            LB   March-April p34-6.   400w. $3\frac{1}{2}$

5384   DINGLE'S Regatta.   Dingle's DIN 301 (E)
            FR   Jan. p35.   150w.   3

5385   DIRECT from New Orleans ... All the Classic Rhythm in
        Blues Songs of Mardis Gras.   Mardis Gras 1-1001
            MG   Dec. p61.   125w. $2\frac{1}{2}$

5386   DISCO Dancers, Vol. 2.   CBS 81816 (E)
            BM   April p52.   100w.   3
            MM   Feb. 26 p30.   50w. $1\frac{1}{2}$

5387   DISCO Party.   Contempo CLP 540 (E)
            BM   Sept. p48.   150w.   4

5388   DO the Hula.   Waikiki ST 325
            RC   May p10.   100w.   3

5389   DON'T Step on My Blue Suede Shoes.   Charly CR 30-119 (E)
        (Reissue)
            NK   Autumn p40.   50w.   4
            SMG   Sept.   p26.   75w.   5
            ZZ   Oct.   p32-3.   200w.   4

5390   DOWN Home Blues.   Specialty SNTF 5024
            CZM   June p30, 37.   75w.   5

5391   The EARLY Days of Bluegrass, Vol. 1.   Rounder 1013 (Re-
        issue)
            CMR   Jan.   p29-30.   250w.   5

5392   EARLY Days of Bluegrass, Vol. 2.   Rounder 1014 (Reissue)
            OTM   Winter p25.   200w. $3\frac{1}{2}$

5393   The EARLY String Bands: Nashville, Volume 1 & Volume 2.
        Country 541, 542 (Reissue)
            BGU   April p18.   300w.   4

5394   EARLY Viper Jazz (Rare Scat Vocals 1927-33).   Stash ST-

105 (Reissue)
ST April-May p154-5. 450w. 4

5395 ECHOES of the Sixties. Polydor PSI 2307-013 (E) (Reissue)
      NK Autumn p48. 25w. $2\frac{1}{2}$

5396 The ELECTRIC Muse; The Story of Folk into Rock. Island
      Folk 1001 (E) (4 discs) (Reissue)
      SR Feb. p110. 450w. 4

5397 The ENTERTAINER. Kicking Mule KM 122
      RA July-Aug. p7. 100w. $3\frac{1}{2}$

5398 EUBIE Blake's Song Hits. EBM-9
      MJ Jan. p28. 50w. 3

5399 FESTIVAL Jazz, Volume 1/2. Jim Taylor Presents JTF
      106/7 (2 discs)
      JJ March p31. 300w. 3

5400 FIDDLE Music from Uppland. Philo 2017
      FOL June p6. 200w. 3

5401 FIFTH Annual Pee Wee Russell Memorial Stomp. Jersey
      Jazz 1001
      JF No. 48 p21. 50w. $3\frac{1}{2}$

5402 FIFTIES Rarest Jazz Performances, Vol. 1/2. Kings of
      Jazz, KLJ 20030/1 (2 discs) (Reissue)
      JM V1/#2 p65. 200w. $2\frac{1}{2}$

5403 FIFTY All Time Country Hits. Pickwick SODA 300
      CMP July p37. 100w. 3

5404 50 Years of Jazz Guitar. Columbia CG33566 (2 discs) (Re-
      issue)
      CAD March p37-8. 225w. 4
      CO Sept./Oct. p24. 450w. 4
      CRA May p77-8. 300w. 3
      DB April 7 p31-3. 100w. $3\frac{1}{2}$
      GP May p129. 150w. $3\frac{1}{2}$
      GR July p237. 250w. $4\frac{1}{2}$
      HF March p139. 300w. 4
      JR V9/#4 unpaged 100w. 4
      MJ March p44. 50w. $2\frac{1}{2}$
      MM April 9 p29. 500w. 3
      RR June p95. 100w. $2\frac{1}{2}$
      RSP 1:3 p35. 350w. $3\frac{1}{2}$

5405 The FILE Series. Pye File FILD 006 (E) (Reissue)
      NK Autumn p46. 25w. $3\frac{1}{2}$

5406 The FINEST of Folk Bluesmen. Bethlehem BCP 6017 (Reissue)

JR   V9/#7   unpaged   200w.   4
LB   May-June p38.   925w. $3\frac{1}{2}$
RSP   March-April p3.   150w. $1\frac{1}{2}$

5407   FIRST Annual Brandywine Mountain Music Convention.   Heritage VI
AU   Dec.   p136.   450w. $3\frac{1}{2}$

5408   FLAT Pickin' Guitar Festival.   Kicking Mule SNKF 1
FR   April   p35.   200w.   3
MM   March 5   p31.   250w. $2\frac{1}{2}$

5409   FOLK Festival.   Transatlantic TRA 324 (2 discs) (Reissue)
RSP   Jan. -Feb.   p16.   300w. $3\frac{1}{2}$

5410   FOLK Music in America, Vol. 1/5.   Archives of Folk Song,
Library of Congress, LBC 1/5 (5 discs) (Reissue)
CFS   Summer p16.   800w.   5
JEMF   No. 45 p45-6.   500w.   4
OTM   Spring p21-2.   1700w. $3\frac{1}{2}$

5411   FOR Canadian Fields.   Leader LEE 4057 (E)
OTM   Spring   p23.   200w. $2\frac{1}{2}$

5412   FOUR World Champion Fiddlers.   Benny Thomasson; Texas
Shorty; Terry Morris; Mark O'Connor.   OMAC-1
PIC   Aug.   p61.   300w.   4

5413   FRANKLIN County's Second Annual Fiddlers.   Convention:
Vol. 2.   Outlet 1-1001
CAD   Aug.   p25.   100w. $3\frac{1}{2}$

5414   FROM Ragtime to No Time.   3600 Records (Reissue)
JF   No. 47 p69.   50w. $3\frac{1}{2}$

5415   FULLstrengthsockittomeknockmeoutmakemeboogiejustlovethat-
disco.   Decca Soul-RZ (E)
BM   Jan.   p42.   100w.   3
HBS   Jan.   p17.   50w.   4

5416   GENNETT-Champion Collection.   Harrison B (Reissue)
ST   April-May p152.   275w. $4\frac{1}{2}$

5417   GEORGE Davis Is Innocent-ok.   Sweet Folk and Country SFA
054 (E)
FR   Jan.   p35.   350w.   2

5418   GEORGIA Blues.   Rounder 2008
CAD   Nov.   p16.   25w. $4\frac{1}{2}$

5419   GET Down and Boogie.   Casablanca NB7402
MG   May   p55.   125w. $2\frac{1}{2}$

5420   GET Your Ass in the Water and Swim Like Me.   Rounder
       2014
          CAD   Nov.   p16.   25w.   4

5421   GOIN' Back to Memphis.   Bopcat 400 (Netherlands)
          RSP   Jan.-Feb.   p38.   350w.   2½

5422   GOLDEN Age of British Dance Bands.   World Records
       SH361/6 (E) (6 discs) (Reissue)
          GR   Feb.   p1335.   400w.   5

5423   GOLDEN Favourites Country and Western.   MCA 6. 22551 AF
       (West German Issue) (Reissue)
          CMR   July   p24.   25w.   3

5424   GOLDEN Hour of Disco Soul.   Golden Hour GH 648 (E) (Re-
       issue)
          BM   Nov.   p48-9.   25w.   0

5425   GOLDEN Hour of Simon Says.   Pye Golden Hour (E) (Reissue)
          MM   May 14   p33.   50w.   0

5426   GOLDEN Hour of Stax Soul.   Pye Golden Hour GH 851 (E)
       (Reissue)
          BM   Jan.   p43.   125w.   4

5427   GOLDEN Hour of Trad Jazz, Vol. 3.   Pye Golden Hour
       GH644 (E) (Reissue)
          RR   Dec.   p87.   50w.   2½

5428-9 GOLDEN Soul.   Atlantic K50332 (E) (Reissue)
          BM   Sept.   p50.   50w.   5

5430   GOLDEN Sounds of the Big Bands, Vol. 1.   Contour CN 2010
       (E) (Reissue)
          RR   April   p88.   25w.   2

5431   GOLDEN Summer.   United Artists LA 627-H2 (2 discs) (Re-
       issue)
          RC   July   p13.   200w.   3

5432   GONNA Head for Home.   Flyright LP517 (E) (Reissue)
          NK   Autumn   p49.   150w.   5

5433   GOOD 'n Country.   London HSU 5031 (E)
          CMP   Sept.   p35.   200w.   3

5434   GOSPEL Music, Vol. 1: 1926-40.   MCA 3530 (Japan) (Reis-
       sue)
          RSP   V1/#8   350w.   3½

5435   The GREAT American Singing Cowboys.   Republic IRDA
       LPNR 6016

CMP   Jan.   p35.   225w.   5
CMR   Jan.   p28.   125w.   2
CM   Jan.   p54-5.   425w.   3
OTM   Winter p25.   150w.   1
RC   Aug.   p16.   150w. $2\frac{1}{2}$

5436   GREAT Bluesmen: Golden Hour.   Golden Hour GH864 (E)
(Reissue)
CAC   June p108.   200w.   3
MM   April 23 p24.   450w.   4
RR   June p95.   25w. $3\frac{1}{2}$

5437   GREAT Bluesmen.   Vanguard VSD 77/78 (2 discs) (Reissue)
RSP   Jan. -Feb.   p12-3.   400w.   4

5438   The GREAT British All-Star Country Music Sampler.   Sweet
Folk and Country SFA050 (E) (Reissue)
CMP   April p58.   150w.   4

5439   The GREAT Canadian Fiddle.   Springwater 56
CC   Feb.   p32.   50w.   3
RSP   March-April p20.   250w. $4\frac{1}{2}$

5440   GREAT Continental Marches.   Decca SB713 (E)
GR   Feb.   p1329.   325w. $4\frac{1}{2}$

5441   GREAT Film Composers.   Polydor (E)
MM   Feb. 19 p22.   50w.   4

5442   GREAT Moments at the Grand Ole Opry.   RCA CPL 2-1904
(2 discs)
CMR   June p15.   200w.   3
CS   April 21   p19.   325w. $2\frac{1}{2}$

5443   The GREATER Antilles Sampler.   Antilles SX7000 (Reissue)
SOU   May p58.   400w.   4

5444   GREATEST of the Greats.   Goldband LP7766 (Reissue)
RC   Nov.   p12.   150w. $4\frac{1}{2}$

5445   GREEN Grow the Laurels.   Topic 12TS285 (E) (Reissue)
EDS   Spring p33.   200w.   4

5446   The GUITAR Album.   Polydor (E) (2 discs)
MM   June 4 p20.   400w.   3

5447   GUITAR Player.   MCA2-6002 (2 discs)
CAD   June p40.   300w.   4

5448   GUITAR Star.   Red Lightnin' RL0017 (E) (Reissue)
BM   Nov.   p51.   200w.   4
CAD   Oct.   p62.   250w.   3
CZM   Dec.   p50.   400w.   3

5449   GUITAR Tapestry.   Project 3 PR2-6019/20 (2 discs) (Reissue)
        CAD   July   p22.   100w. $3\frac{1}{2}$
        GP   May   p129.   75w.   3

5450   GUITAR Workshop, Vol. 2.   Transatlantic TRA 315 (E) (Re-
        issue)
        CMP   May   p52.   200w.   3

5451   HARD Times in the Country.   Rounder 3007
        FOL   May   p14.   350w. $4\frac{1}{2}$

5452   HARMONICA Blues.   Yazoo L1053 (Reissue)
        LB   Nov./Dec.   p34.   200w.   4
        RR   June   p94.   50w.   3
        ST   Dec.-Jan.   p79-80.   375w.   4

5453   HARVEST Heritage of 20 Greats.   Harvest (E) (Reissue)
        MM   Dec. 21   p14.   50w.   4

5454   HEATH, Kenton and Goodman.   Sounds Brassy.   Decca (E)
        (Reissue)
        MM   Dec. 21   p14.   50w.   3

5455   HEATH, Kenton and Goodman.   Sounds of.   Decca (E) (Re-
        issue)
        MM   Dec. 21   p14.   50w.   3

5456   HEAVY Timbre; Chicago Boogie Piano.   Sirens Records 102
        AU   Dec.   p130.   600w.   4
        CAD   Jan.   p26.   175w.   4
        LB   Nov./Dec.   p34, 6.   200w.   3
        RSP   Jan.-Feb.   p11.   250w. $3\frac{1}{2}$

5457   HERE and Now.   Catalyst CAT 7613
        CAD   April   p35.   120w.   2

5458   HERE'S a Health to the Man and the Maid.   Living Folk LFR
        103
        FOL   March   p25.   400w.   5

5459   HERMAN Smith's Annual Tall Trees Bluegrass Festival.
        King Bluegrass KB 558
        BGU   Jan.   p29.   125w.   3

5460   HEY la Bas pas Partout.   Goldband GRLP 7771
        AU   June   p125.   500w.   2
        RC   Oct.   p16.   150w. $3\frac{1}{2}$
        RSP   1:3   p41.   400w. $2\frac{1}{2}$

5461   HIGH Water Blues.   Flyright 512 (E) (Reissue)
        LB   July-Aug.   p33.   200w.   4

5462   HILLBILLY Jazz, Volume 1/2.   Sonet SNTF 721

    CMP April p52. 100w. 5
    CMR June p16. 25w. 3

5463 HILLBILLY Rock. DJM DJM22069 (Reissue)
    CMP Aug. p40. 300w. 4
    MM July 16 p27. 50w. $3\frac{1}{2}$
    NK Summer p37. 150w. 4

5464 HILLS and Home: Thirty Years of Bluegrass. New World
   Records NW 225
    BGU March p22. 450w. 5

5465 HISTORY of Bell, U. K. (1970-1975). Arista 4112 (E) (Reissue)
    RC Aug. p12. 150w. 3
    TP Feb./March p30-1. 425w. 4

5466 HITS from the Golden West. Capitol 148-50211 (2 discs)
   (West Germany) (Reissue)
    CMR Aug. p23. 50w. 3

5467 HITS of the Mersey Era, Vol. 1. EMI NUT 1 (E) (Reissue)
    MM Jan. 8 p18. 75w. $2\frac{1}{2}$
    RR Feb. p93. 200w. 3
    TP Feb./March p33. 350w. 4

5468 HITSVILLE: The New Direction in Country Music. Hitsville
   HVS 3001 (Reissue)
    CMR June p8. 100w. 3
    NK Spring p39. 50w. $2\frac{1}{2}$
    SMG May p26. 425w. $2\frac{1}{2}$

5469 HOLLYWOOD Rock 'n' Roll. Chiswick CHI (E) (Reissue)
    MM May 14 p33. 50w. $3\frac{1}{2}$
    NK Spring p40. 100w. 3
    RC Nov. p10. 150w. 3

5470 HOMAGE to Hugues Panassie. Flame 1003/4 (2 discs)
    CAD Dec. p47. 425w. 2

5471 HOMESPUN America. Vox SVBX 5309 (3 discs)
    SR April p103. 400w. 5

5472 I Got Rhythm. Kicking Mule KM 132
    CFS Autumn p26-7. 150w. 4

5473 IF Beale Street Could Talk: A Selection of Pre-War Memphis
   Blues Favorites, 1928-1939. Magnolia 501 (Sweden) (Reissue)
    LB Nov./Dec. p31. 475w. $3\frac{1}{2}$

5474 I'M Coming from Seclusion. Collectors Items 005 (E) (Reissue)
    BM May p53. 300w. 3

          JJ April p37.   250w. $3\frac{1}{2}$
          ST April-May p159.   375w.   4

5475   I'M Moving On. Bopcat 300 (Netherlands) (Reissue)
          NK Summer p40.   50w.   3

5476   IMPERIAL Rockabillies.   United Artists UAS 30101 (E) (Re-
       issue)
          MM Sept. 10 p24.   475w. $3\frac{1}{2}$
          NK Summer p40.   100w.   5

5477   IN an Arizona Town.   Arizona Friends of Folklore 33-3 (Re-
       issue)
          RC Aug. p13.   150w.   4

5478   INTERNATIONAL Jam Sessions.   Xanadu 102 (Reissue)
          CO Feb. p23.   175w. $2\frac{1}{2}$
          RSP Jan.-Feb.   p46.   300w.   3

5479   IRISH Traditional Concertina Styles.   Topic 12 TFRS 506 (E)
          TM No. 6 p27-9.   575w.   5

5480   IT'S Rock and Roll.   Beeb BEMP 001 (E) (Reissue)
          CAD June p99.   250w. $2\frac{1}{2}$
          NK Spring p39.   50w. $2\frac{1}{2}$

5481   JACK O' Diamonds.   Herwin 211 (Reissue)
          CAD Sept. p35.   325w.   4

5482   JACKSON Blue Boys (and Two Frown New Orlean).   Policy
       Wheel PW 4593
          CZM June p67.   75w. $2\frac{1}{2}$

5483   JAZZ Ambassadors, Vol. 2.   Verve 2610 022 (E) (2 discs)
       (Reissue)
          GR Jan. p1198.   200w.   4

5484   JAZZ at the New School.   Storyville SLP 515
          RR Dec. p88.   50w.   3

5485   JAZZ at the Philharmonic.   Bird and Pres, The '46 Concerts.
       Verve VE-2-2518 (2 discs) (Reissue)
          CAD June p34.   100w. $3\frac{1}{2}$
          GR Jan. p1198.   225w. $3\frac{1}{2}$
          DB July 14 p45-7.   50w.   5
          RR Jan. p85.   125w.   3

5486   JAZZ at the Philharmonic in Tokyo.   Live at the Nickegeki
       Theatre.   Pablo 2620 104 (3 discs) (Reissue)
          CAD Aug. p36.   350w.   4

5487   JAZZ Gala Concert.   Atlantic SD 1693
          RSP Jan.-Feb.   p46.   200w.   4

5488   JAZZ Giants. Vol. 1. Giants of Jazz 1002
       CAD   June p29.   300w.   4
       JM   Summer p63.   100w. $2\frac{1}{2}$

5489   JAZZ in Harlem, 1926-1931. Arcadia 2008 (Reissue)
       JJ   Jan. p31.   550w.   4

5490   JAZZ in Revolution: The Big Band in the 1940's. New
       World NW284 (Reissues)
       CAD   July p39.   250w.   4

5491   JAZZ in the Thirties. World Records SHB 39 (E) (2 discs)
       (Reissue)
       ST   June-July p191.   275w. $4\frac{1}{2}$

5492   Le JAZZ Parisien, 1945-1947. Barclay 81004/81005 (France)
       (2 discs) (Reissue)
       ST   Aug. -Sept. p238.   450w. $3\frac{1}{2}$

5493   JAZZ Piano Masters. Chiaroscuro CR 170
       CAD   Dec. p53-4.   100w. $3\frac{1}{2}$

5494   JAZZTIME USA. MCA MCA2-4113 (2 discs) (Reissue)
       MJ   Nov. p24.   75w.   2
       MR   April p13.   200w.   3

5495   The JOE Meek Story. Decca DPA 3053/6 (E) (2 discs)
       (Reissue)
       MM   April 16 p21.   200w. $1\frac{1}{2}$
       NK   Spring p39.   75w.   3

5496   JUKE Joint Blues Piano. MCA 3529 (Japan) (Reissue)
       RSP   Jan. -Feb. p11.   250w. $3\frac{1}{2}$
       RSP   March-April p8.   200w.   4

5497   JUMPING on the Hill: Memphis Blues & Hokum 1928-1941.
       Policy Wheel PW 459-1
       CZM   June p67.   50w.   3

5498   KICKING Mule's Flat Picking Festival. Kicking Mule KM 206
       FOL   Sept. p12.   50w.   0

5499   KINGS of the Twelve String. Flyright 101
       LB   July-Aug. p33.   200w. $4\frac{1}{2}$

5500   LAS Vegas-3 a. m. Famous Door HL-110
       MJ   Dec. p24.   150w. $3\frac{1}{2}$

5501   LET'S All Go Wild. Dial LP 003 (Netherlands) (Reissue)
       NK   Spring p37.   100w. $3\frac{1}{2}$

5501a LET'S Clean Up the Ghetto. Philadelphia International 34659
       BM   Oct. p44.   450w.   4

BS   Sept.   p16.   400w. $3\frac{1}{2}$
MG   Oct.   p61.   75w. $2\frac{1}{2}$
MM   Oct. 8 p32.   200w.   2
RC   Oct.   p14.   75w. $2\frac{1}{2}$
RS   Oct. 6 p94, 96.   400w. $2\frac{1}{2}$
VV   Aug. 15 p51.   400w.   3

5502   LIVE at CBGB's, Vol. 1.   Atlantic 2SA-508 (2 discs)
       SOU   July   p39.   250w.   3
       RR   Feb.   p93.   150w.   3

5503   LIVE at McClure, Virginia.   Rebel SLP 1554/55 (2 discs)
       CMR   June   p14.   450w.   4

5504   LIVE at the Rat.   Rat Records 528
       MM   Aug. 6 p17.   300w. $1\frac{1}{2}$
       RC   Oct.   p13.   250w.   4

5505   LIVE at the Vortex.   Vortex/NEMS (E)
       MM   Dec. 21 p15.   300w.   0

5506   The LONGHORN Jamboree Presents Willie Nelson and His
       Friends.   Plantation PLP 24 (Reissue)
       CMP   March   p40.   150w.   5
       CMR   June   p12.   200w.   4

5507   LOUISIANA Cajun French Music; Vol. 1, 1964-1967.   Rounder
       6001 (Reissue)
       OTM   Spring   p30.   300w. $2\frac{1}{2}$

5508   LOWDOWN Memphis Harmonica Jam 1950-1955.   Nighthawk
       103 (Reissue)
       DB   May 5 p28-32.   225w.   4
       LB   March-April p34-5.   400w. $3\frac{1}{2}$

5509   The MGM Rockabilly Collection.   Polydor 2315-394 (E) (Re-
       issue)
       MM   Nov. 5 p26.   300w. $3\frac{1}{2}$
       NK   Summer   p40.   125w.   5

5510   MASSED Bands of the Guards.   EMI EMSP 321 (E) (2 discs)
       GR   Dec.   p1155.   225w.   4

5511   MASTERS of the Modern Piano.   Verve VE-2-2514 (2 discs)
       (Reissue)
       CAD   Feb.   p22-3.   350w. $3\frac{1}{2}$
       CRA   Aug.   p65.   500w.   3
       DB   July 14 p45-7.   50w. $3\frac{1}{2}$
       SR   May   p98-9.   150w. $3\frac{1}{2}$

5512   MAX'S Kansas City, 1976.   Ram Records 1213
       CIR   March 31 p15-6.   575w.   3
       CRA   Jan.   p71.   125w.   1

5513   MEDIUM Rare. Polydor 2482 381 (E) (Reissue)
        MM May 14 p33. 50w. 4
        TP Nov. p42. 75w. 2

5514   MEMPHIS Blues Sounds. Charly CR30-126 (E) (Reissue)
        SMG Sept. p28. 25w. 4

5515   MEMPHIS Harmonica, 1950-1953. Nighthawk 103 (Reissue)
        CAD April p37-8. 150w. 4

5516   MEXICO. Tiestas of Chiapas and Oaxaca. Nonesuch H-
        72070
        SR Jan. p100. 200w. 4

5517   MIRAGE: Avant-Garde & Third Stream Jazz. New World
        NW216 (Reissue)
        CAD July p39. 200w. $3\frac{1}{2}$

5518   MR. Charlie's Blues, 1926-1938. Yazoo L-1024 (Reissue)
        CM March p56. 25w. $2\frac{1}{2}$

5519   The MODERN Country Sound. RCA (E) (Reissue)
        CAC Jan. p393. 250w. 2

5520   MONSTER Soul. DJM 28031 (E) (2 discs) (Reissue)
        BM Jan. p44. 150w. 3
        HBS Jan. p17. 50w. 4
        NK Winter p38. 50w. 3

5521   MORE Latin Delights. Verve (E)
        MM April 16 p23. 50w. 2

5522   MORE Path Rent. Eckerworks EW 001
        RSP V1/#3 p26. 225w. 1

5523   MOTOWN Disco-Tech, Vol. 3. Motown STML 12044 (E)
        (Reissue)
        BM Feb. p50. 75w. 3
        MM Jan. 29 p25. 25w. $2\frac{1}{2}$

5524   MOTOWN Extra Special. Motown Special STMX 6007 (E)
        (Reissue)
        HBS April/May p21. 25w. $2\frac{1}{2}$
        CAC July p134. 125w. 5

5525   MOTOWN Gold, Vol. 2. Motown STMC 12070 (E) (Reissue)
        BM Dec. p48. 150w. 4

5526   MOVIN' to Music. Philips (E) (Reissue)
        CAC Feb. p418. 50w. 3

5527   MUD Acres. Music among Friends. Rounder 3001
        CMR June p17. 250w. 3

5528   MUSIC from Round Peak.   Heritage X
       OTM Spring p24.   400w. $2\frac{1}{2}$
       RSP V1/#3 p25.   300w. $2\frac{1}{2}$

5529   MUSIC from Royal Occasions.   Decca (E)
       CAC Sept.   p217.   100w. $3\frac{1}{2}$

5530   MUSIC from Sliabh Luachra.   Vol. 1 Kery Fiddles.   Topic
       12T 309 (E)
       EDS Winter p114.   100w.   4

5531   MUSIC from Sliabh Luachra.   Vol. 2 The Star of Munster
       Trio.   Topic 12TS 310 (E)
       EDS Winter p114.   100w.   4

5532   MUSIC from Sliabh Luachra.   Vol. 3 The Humours of Lisheen.
       Topic 12TS 311 (E)
       EDS Winter p114.   100w.   3

5533   A MUSICAL Tour of New Orleans.   Storyville SLP 103 (Den-
       mark)
       RR Aug. p84.   50w.   3

5534   MY Generation.   EMI Nut 4 (E) (Reissue)
       MM Jan. 8 p18.   50w. $3\frac{1}{2}$
       RS July 14 p65.   300w. $2\frac{1}{2}$
       TP Feb./March p33.   400w.   4

5535   NASHVILLE: The Early String Bands, Vol. 1/2.   Country
       541/2 (2 discs) (Reissue)
       OTM Summer p29.   1000w.   5
       PIC Aug. p60.   300w. $4\frac{1}{2}$
       RSP Jan.-Feb. p29.   350w.   3

5536   NEGRO Songs of Protest.   Rounder 4004
       CAD Nov. p16.   50w.   5

5537   NEW American Music.   Folkways FTS 33901
       JJ April p34.   300w. $2\frac{1}{2}$

5538   A NEW Approach to Jazz Improvisation, Vol. 8/10.   Jazz
       Archives 1216/9 (3 discs)
       DB Dec. 1 p24-6.   1000w.   4

5539   The NEW Beehive Songster, Vol. 2: New Recordings of Utah
       Folk Music.   Okehdokee 76004
       RSP March-April p25.   225w.   3

5540   NEW Orleans Bounce, Vol. 1-2: New Orleans R & B Gui-
       tarists.   Liberty LLS70076/77 (2 discs) (Japan) (Reissue)
       RSP Jan.-Feb. p4.   700w.   4

5541   NEW Orleans Jazz & Heritage Festival, 1976.   Island 9424

(2 discs)
    CAD   July   p22.   150w. $4\frac{1}{2}$
    DB   Nov. 3   p29-30.   425w.   3
    SOU   June   p42.   700w.   5
    SR   Nov.   p132.   425w.   4

5542 NEW Wave.   Vertigo 6300902 (E)
    GR   Oct.   p715.   50w. $2\frac{1}{2}$
    MM   Aug. 6   p17.   300w.   3
    RC   Nov.   p6.   200w.   4
    TP   Oct.   p43-4.   400w.   3
    RSP   Nov.-Dec.   p26.   300w. $2\frac{1}{2}$

5543 NEW York Jazz, 1925.   Neovox (E) (Reissue)
    CAC   March   p475-76.   100w.   2

5544 NEW York Jazz, 1927-30.   VJM VLP 41 (E) (Reissue)
    ST   Aug.-Sept.   p236.   300w.   4

5545 NEW York Really Has the Blues, Vol. 1.   Spivey LP 1018
    CAD   Aug.   p37.   150w.   4
    RSP   March-April   p4.   350w.   1

5546 NICA'S Dream: Small Jazz Groups of 50s and Early 60s.
    New World Records NW 242
    CAD   Dec.   p46.   125w.   3

5547 1930s Decca Hillbilly Records.   MCA MCX 16 (Japan) Re-
    issue)
    JEMF   Autumn   p157-60.   200w.   5
    OTM   Summer   p30-4.   500w.   4

5548 NON-STOP Rock 'n' Roll.   MCA COLM 8049 (E) (Reissue)
    NK   Winter   p38.   100w.   4

5549 NORMAN Granz Jam Sessions: The Charlie Parker Sides.
    Verve VE2-2508 (2 discs) (Reissue)
    SR   May   p98-9.   150w.   5

5550 NOTHING but a Worried Mind; the Piano Blues, Vol. 2.
    Magpie PY 4402
    MM   Oct. 15   p30.   400w. $3\frac{1}{2}$

5551 NOVELTY Guitar Instrumentals.   Kicking Mule Records KM
    127
    CAD   April   p11.   90w.   3
    CMR   June   p9.   25w.   2

5552 NUGGETS: Original Artifacts from the First Psychedelic
    Era, 1965-68.   Sire SASH 3716-2 (Reissue) (2 discs)
    AU   Aug.   p88.   50w. $3\frac{1}{2}$
    CIR   Aug. 4   p59-60.   350w.   3
    CRE   March   p62.   550w.   4

GP   June   p137.   25w. $2\frac{1}{2}$
RS   Jan. 13 p51.   100w. $3\frac{1}{2}$
TP   Feb./March p31.   350w.   4

5553   OLD Grey Whistle Test, Take 2.   BBC (E) (2 discs)
       CAC   March p476.   200w.   4

5554   OLD Time Southern Dance Music.   Old Timey 100-102 (3
       discs) (Reissue)
       CM   March p56.   25w. $2\frac{1}{2}$

5555   OLD Time Tunes from Coal Creek.   Heritage V
       BGU   Feb.   p28.   125w.   4

5556   OLD Timey Music.   MCA VIM 4013 (Japan) (Reissue)
       JEMF   Autumn p157-60.   200w.   5
       OTM   Summer p30-4.   500w.   4

5557   ON the Halls.   World Records SHB43 (E) (2 discs)
       GR   Sept.   p522, 525.   300w.   4

5558   ONENESS of Juju.   African Rhythms.   Blackfire 19751
       JF   No. 49 p21.   50w.   4
       JF   No. 50 p47.   450w.   3

5559   ORKNEY Fiddle Music.   One-Up OU 2157 (E)
       FR   March p31.   300w.   3

5560   OUT in the Cold Again.   Library of Congress Series Vol. 3/
       Flyright-Matchbox SDM 257
       LB   March-April p37.   350w.   3

5561   OUT on the Streets Again.   ABC ABCL 5192 (E)
       BM   Jan. p52.   200w.   3

5562   PACIFIC Rim Dulcimer Project.   Biscuit City 1314
       PIC   Dec.   p56-7.   225w.   3

5563   PARAMOUNT Cornet Blues Rarities, 1924-1927.   Herwin 111
       (Reissue)
       JR   V9/#4 unpaged 100w.   4

5564   PARAMOUNT Hot Jazz Rarities 1926-1928.   Herwin 110 (Re-
       issue)
       ST   Aug.-Sept. p231.   575w. $4\frac{1}{2}$
       JM   Summer p63.   125w.   3
       JR   V9/#4 unpaged 100w.   4

5565   PERCUSSIVE Jazz.   Ovation 1714
       CAD   July p42.   100w.   2

5566   PERSONAL Choice.   Trojan TRLS 140 (E) (Reissue)
       BM   Aug. p50.   50w.   2

5567   PHIL Spector's 20 Greatest Hits.   Warner Brothers/Phil
       Spector 2SP9104
           CAC   Feb.   p420.   250w.   4
           CIR   May 26 p55-6.   300w. $4\frac{1}{2}$
           GP   May   p129.   75w. $3\frac{1}{2}$
           HF   June   p132.   500w.   4
           NK   Winter   p37.   75w.   4
           RS   April 21   2000w. $3\frac{1}{2}$
           SMG   Jan.   p26.   100w.   5
           SOU   April   p52.   400w.   5
           SR   June   p118-9.   125w.   4
           VV   April 11   p55.   400w. $4\frac{1}{2}$

5568   PHILADELPHIA Freedom.   London HAU8501 (2 discs) (E)
       (Reissue)
           BM   March   p51.   250w.   3
           HBS   Feb./March   p20.   50w.   3

5569   PHILLYBUSTERS, Vol. IV.   Philadelphia International PIR
       81658 (E) (Reissue)
           BM   Feb.   p49.   50w.   3

5570   PHILLYBUSTERS, Vol. X.   Philadelphia International (E)
       (Reissue)
           MM   Feb. 5   p23.   50w.   3

5571   PIANO Blues, Vol. 1: Paramount 1929-30.   Magpie PY 4401
       (E) (Reissue)
           MM   Sept. 10   p28.   450w.   4
           ST   Oct.-Nov.   p38.   300w.   3

5572   PIANO Ragtime of the 40's.   Herwin 403 (Reissue)
           CAD   Aug.   p25.   125w. $3\frac{1}{2}$

5573   PIANO Ragtime of the 50's.   Herwin 404 (Reissue)
           CAD   Aug.   p25.   75w.   3
           CO   Sept./Oct.   p18.   300w.   1
           JR   V9/#4   unpaged   100w.   5
           RA   Nov./Dec.   p5.   100w.   3

5574   PIANO Summit.   77 Records 77S58 (E) (Reissue)
           GR   Jan.   p1198.   200w.   4
           ST   Dec.-Jan.   p75-6.   550w.   4

5575   PIONEERS of the Jazz Guitar.   Yazoo L-1057
           GP   Sept.   p118.   175w.   3
           RSP   1:3   p35.   350w.   3

5576   PIPE, Spoon, Pot and Jug.   Stash ST 102 (Reissue)
           JF   No. 48   p54-5.   600w.   4

5577   PLAINCAPERS.   Free Reed 10
           FS   Nov.   p24.   300w.   3

5578   POLISH Jazz, 1946-1950, Vol. 1.   Muza SX 1322 (Poland)
       (Reissue)
           JF No. 50 p21.   50w. $2\frac{1}{2}$

5579   PREMIER Festival Pop Celtique.   Le Chant du Monde 74513
       (France)
           RSP Jan. -Feb. p19.   325w. $2\frac{1}{2}$

5580   PRIDE of the Rhondda.   EMI One-Up OU2165 (E)
           GR April p1607.   150w. $4\frac{1}{2}$

5581   RAGS to Jazz, 1913-27.   New World Records 269 (Reissue)
           MJ Dec. p23.   75w. $3\frac{1}{2}$

5582   RAGTIME and Cakewalks Played by Antique Musical Boxes.
       Musical Wonder Hour Album 1103
           RA March-April p4-5.   100w.   4

5583   RAGTIME and Novelty Music, Vol. 1, 1906-34.   RCA FXMI-
       7185 (France) (Reissue)
           GR Feb. p1336.   550w. $2\frac{1}{2}$

5584   RAGTIME in Rural America.   New World Records 235 (Re-
       issue)
           MJ Dec. p23.   75w.   3

5585   RARE Big Band Gems, 1932-1947.   Nostalgia Book Club 1004
       (3 discs) (Reissue)
           CAD July p30.   475w.   4
           JR V9/#4 unpaged 100w.   4

5586   RARE Hot Chicago Jazz 1925-1929.   Herwin 109 (Reissue)
           JR V9/#4 unpaged 100w.   5
           MR Jan. p13.   325w.   3
           ST Feb. -March p111-2.   1100w.   5

5587   RARE Masters, Vol. 1-2.   Phil Spector International 2307
       00819 (E) (2 discs) (Reissue)
           CAC June p378.   100w. $4\frac{1}{2}$
           SR June p18.   125w.   4

5588   RARE Rockabilly, Vol. 2.   MCA MCFM 2789 (E) (Reissue)
           CAC Aug. p170-1.   200w. $3\frac{1}{2}$
           CMP Aug. p40.   200w.   5
           MM May 14 p28.   300w. $3\frac{1}{2}$
           NK Spring p40.   125w.   5
           RSP 1:3 p32.   300w. $2\frac{1}{2}$

5589   REDNECK Mothers.   RCA APL1-2438 (Reissue)
           RS Dec. 29 p73.   475w.   3
           RSP Nov. -Dec. p31.   250w.   3

5590   REEFER Songs.   Stash ST-100 (Reissue)

LB   July-Aug.   p34.   150w.   4

5591   REGGAE: Sweet and Smooth.   Tackle TAK LP003 (E)
       BM   Dec.   p51.   100w.   3

5592   REPUBLIC Records: Good 'n' Country.   London HSU 5031
       (E) (Reissue)
       NK   Autumn   p43.   50w. $2\frac{1}{2}$

5593   RESIDENTS' Night Out.   Fo'c'sle Records FOR1001 (E)
       FR   Dec.   p35.   150w.   3

5594   RHYTHM and Blues.   New World Records 261 (Reissue)
       MJ   Dec.   p23.   100w. $3\frac{1}{2}$

5595   ROCK Follies of '77.   Polydor 2302 072 (E)
       GR   Sept.   p522.   125w. $1\frac{1}{2}$
       TP   Oct.   p44.   350w. $3\frac{1}{2}$

5596   ROCK 'n' Roll at the Capitol Towers, Vol. 2.   Capitol 2C150-
       85029/30 (France) (2 discs) (Reissue)
       CM   March   p59.   250w.   4
       NK   Spring   p40.   100w. $3\frac{1}{2}$

5597   ROCK 'n Roll Dance Party of the 50's.   Specialty SNTF
       5022 (E) (Reissue)
       CZM   June   p30.   25w. $2\frac{1}{2}$
       MM   March 5   p24.   75w.   3
       NK   Spring   p39.   50w. $3\frac{1}{2}$
       SMG   May   p25.   125w.   4

5598   ROCK On.   Arcade ADEP 27 (E) (Reissue)
       NK   Summer   p37.   50w. $2\frac{1}{2}$

5599   ROCKABILLY Originals.   Capitol CAPS1009 (E) (Reissue)
       NK   Summer   p40.   125w.   4

5600   ROCKING from Hollywood to Gronnigen.   Dial LP002 (Nether-
       lands)
       NK   Autumn   p45.   100w. $3\frac{1}{2}$

5601   ROOSTER Crowed for Day.   Flyright LP518 (E) (Reissue)
       BM   March   p53.   200w.   4
       CZM   June   p56-7.   25w. $2\frac{1}{2}$
       NK   Autumn   p49.   150w.   4

5602   ROOTS: Soul Sounds of a Proud People.   Kent KTS-700 (Re-
       issue)
       CAD   Sept.   p41-2.   250w.   4

5603   ROOTS of British Rock.   Sire SASH 3711-2 (2 discs) (Reis-
       sue)
       SMG   Jan.   p25.   200w.   4

5604   ROOTS of the Blues. New World Records NW-252
        CAD Dec. p44-5. 200w. 3

5605   The ROOTS of Rock 'n Roll. Savoy SJL 2221 (2 discs) (Re-
        issue)
                CAD Sept. p35-6. 325w. 4
                CRA Oct. p65-6. 800w. 3
                MJ Nov. p22. 125w. $2\frac{1}{2}$
                MM Aug. 13 p21. 650w. 4
                RS Oct. 6 p93-4. 450w. 3
                RSP 1:3 p33. 650w. $4\frac{1}{2}$
                SR Nov. p112. 275w. 4

5606   ROSKO--So Ya Wanna Hear Another? Atlantic K50305 (E)
        (Reissue)
                BM March p22. 100w. 3

5607   The ROXY London, W.C. 2. Harvest SHSP 4069 (E)
                MM June 25 p20. 675w. $2\frac{1}{2}$
                TP Sept. p39. 300w. 0

5608   SKAP Golden Anniversary Album. Phono Swecia (Sweden)
                MM March 12 p23. 350w. $3\frac{1}{2}$

5609   SALUTE to Satchmo. Black Lion BLPX 12161/2 (E) (2 discs)
                CAC Sept. p221. 300w. $3\frac{1}{2}$
                RR Oct. p89. 25w. 3

5610   SAN Diego Jazz Club. Sound of Jazz. SDJC 22477
                CAD Oct. p45-6. 125w. 5

5611   SAN Francisco Blues Festival. Jefferson BL 602 (Sweden)
                GP Dec. p153. 50w. 3
                MM Sept. 17 p21. 300w. $3\frac{1}{2}$

5612   SAVOY Jam Party. Savoy SJL 2213 (2 discs) (Reissue)
                SOU Jan. p49. 50w. 4

5613   SIMPLE Gifts. Pine Breeze Records 2
                PIC Dec. p61. 125w. $2\frac{1}{2}$

5614   SIX Five Special. BBC REB 252 (E) (Reissue)
                NK Winter p37. 25w. $2\frac{1}{2}$
                SMG May p21. 75w. 3

5615   16 Country Greats, Vol. 2. MCA Coral CDL 8048 (E) (Re-
        issue)
                CMP Jan. p36. 125w. 4

5616   16 Number 1 Country Hits. CBS EMB 31456 (E) (Reissue)
                CMP July p40. 100w. 3

5617   SMALL Groups of the 30s. New World Records 250 (Reissue)

MJ   Dec.   p23.   125w. $2\frac{1}{2}$

5618   SMALL Jazz Groups of the 50s & Early 60s.   New World
       Records 242 (Reissue)
       MJ   Dec.   p23.   50w. $2\frac{1}{2}$

5619   SMOKEY Mountain Ballads.   RCA LPV-507 (Reissue)
       CM   March   p56.   25w.   3

5620   SODA Pop, Vol. 2.   DJM 22070 (E) (Reissue)
       MM   Aug. 13   p20.   50w.   3
       NK   Summer   p38.   75w.   4

5621   SOME Hefty Cats.   Hefty Jazz HJ100
       MM   June 11   p20.   300w.   3

5622   SON of Morris On.   Harvest SHSM 2012 (E)
       FR   Feb.   p33.   100w.   4

5623   SONGS about Elvis.   Songs About Elvis 8135 (E)
       NK   Autumn   p48.   50w.   3
       RSP   March-April   300w.   3

5624   SONGS about Thanksgiving and Harvest Time.   Classroom Ma-
       terials CM1023
       RC   Oct.   p11.   150w. $1\frac{1}{2}$

5625   SONGS and Southern Breezes; Country Singers from Hamp-
       shire and Sussex.   Topic 12T 317 (E)
       EDS   Winter   p113.   100w.   3
       FR   May   p31.   300w. $4\frac{1}{2}$
       MM   April 23   p24.   100w.   3
       TM   No. 6   p24.   900w.   3

5626   SORROW Come Pass Me Around: A Survey of Rural Black
       Religious Music.   Advent 2805
       MG   Dec.   p62.   50w. $2\frac{1}{2}$

5627   SOUL Food.   ABC 5179 (E)
       HBS   Jan.   p17.   50w.   4

5628   SOUL on Fire.   DJM 28038 (E) (Reissue)
       SC   No. 2   p16.   100w. $4\frac{1}{2}$

5629   SOUNDS of Indian America: Plains & Southwest.   Indian
       House IH 9501
       RC   Oct.   p7-8.   400w.   5

5630   SOUTHERN Feelings.   DJM DJD 28837 (E)
       CMP   Dec.   p37.   150w.   3
       MM   Oct. 15   p23.   50w.   4

5631   The SOUTH'S Greatest Hits.   Capricorn CP 0187 (Reissue)

MG   Sept.   p51.   125w.   1
RC   Aug.   p11-2.   150w.   3

5632   SPECIAL Motown Disco Album.   Motown 12059 (E) (Reissue)
       BM   Sept.   p47.   200w.   5
       HBS   June/Sept.   p23.   25w.   4

5633   SPIVEY'S Blues Showcase.   Spivey LP 1017A
       CAD   Aug.   p37.   100w.   4

5634   STARS of Modern Jazz Concert.   IAJRC 20 (Reissue)
       CAD   Jan.   p39-40.   275w.   4

5635   STEAMBOAT'S A-Comin'.   National Geographical Society
       07787
       SR   May   p94, 95.   262w.   3

5636   STRINGBEAN Memorial Bluegrass Festival.   Old Homestead
       80005
       BGU   Jan.   p29.   100w.   3
       PIC   March   p54-5.   75w.   0

5637   STYLE-Makers of Jazz, 1920s & 1940s.   New World Records
       274 (Reissue)
       MJ   Dec.   p23.   100w.   3

5638   SUBMARINE Tracks and Fool's Gold.   Chiswick Ch 2 (E)
       MM   Aug.   6 p17.   300w. $3\frac{1}{2}$
       TP   Nov.   p41.   250w. $2\frac{1}{2}$

5639   SUN--The Roots of Rock.   Charly (13 discs) (E) (Reissue)
       BM   March   p53.   450w.   4
       CM   March   p62-3.   75w.   3
       MM   Sept.   24 p27.   250w. $3\frac{1}{2}$
       RSP   Jan.-Feb.   p37.   775w. $2\frac{1}{2}$

5640   SUPER Country and Western Festival.   MCA Coral 628347
       (2 discs) (Holland) (Reissue)
       CMR   May   p37.   200w.   5

5641   SWAMPLAND Soul.   Goldband LP 7754
       CAD   Aug.   p25.   50w.   3

5642   SWEETS, Lips and Lots of Jazz.   Xanadu 123
       DB   April 7   p31-3.   100w. $3\frac{1}{2}$
       MJ   March   p77.   50w. $2\frac{1}{2}$

5643   SWING Street: Volume 1.   Tax 8026 (Reissue)
       CO   Aug.   p23.   150w.   3

5644   SWINGTIME Jive.   Stash 108 (Reissue)
       CAD   Dec.   p48.   300w.   3

5645   T. T. Ross and Friends.   Third World 201 (E)
       BM   Jan.   p51.   200w.   3

5646   TAHREEL Stomp.   Flyright 511 (E) (Reissue)
       LB   Sept./Oct.   p37.   250w. $2\frac{1}{2}$

5647   TENNESSEE Guitar.   Starday SLP 176
       CMR   June   p9.   300w.   4

5648   The TENOR Sax Album.   Savoy SJL2220 (2 discs) (Reissue)
       CAD   Oct.   p35.   300w.   3
       CO   Dec.   p24.   100w. $3\frac{1}{2}$
       MJ   Nov.   p22.   125w. $3\frac{1}{2}$
       MM   Aug. 20   p24.   550w. $3\frac{1}{2}$
       RR   Oct.   p90.   25w.   3

5649   The TERRITORIES, Vol. 2.   Arcadia 2007 (Reissue)
       ST   Oct.-Nov.   p35, 37.   500w.   4

5650   The TERRITORY Bands.   Classic Jazz Masters CJM 10 (Den-
       mark) (Reissue)
       ST   April-May   p153-4.   250w. $4\frac{1}{2}$

5651   TEXAS Country.   United Artists UALA574-H2 (2 discs) (Re-
       issue)
       NK   Winter   p37.   75w. $3\frac{1}{2}$

5652   TEXAS Jam Session Featuring Four World Champion Fiddlers.
       OMAC-1
       BGU   Aug.   p30.   200w.   4

5653   TEXAS-Mexico Border Music.   Folklyric 9007
       SR   Jan.   p100.   200w.   3

5654   THEY All Played Bango.   Retrieval FG 403 (E) (Reissue)
       RSP   V1/#3   p20.   200w.   3

5655   THIRD World Disco, Vol. 1-2.   Third World (E) (2 discs)
       MM   Sept. 10   p24.   200w.   3

5656   THIS Is Jazz Vol. 2.   Rarities 35 (E) (Reissue)
       CO   Sept./Oct.   p22-3.   200w.   3

5657   THIS Is Loma, Vol. 1-7.   Warner Brothers K 56265/71 (E)
       (7 discs) (Reissue)
       BM   March   p50.   350w.   2
       HBS   Feb./March   p2-13.   2500w.   4
       MM   Jan. 22   p22.   1200w.   2
       NK   Winter   p33.   125w.   3

5658   THOSE Classic Years, 1948-1956.   Capitol E-ST 23368 (E)
       (Reissue)
       CMR   July   p22.   150w.   3

5659   THOSE Dance Band Years.   World SH 361/66 (E) (6 discs)
        (Reissue)
            RR   Feb.   p94.   125w. $3\frac{1}{2}$

5660   THOSE Ragtime Years, 1899-1916.   World Records SHB 41
        (2 discs) (E) (Reissue)
            GR   Sept.   p522.   300w. $3\frac{1}{2}$
            RT   Sept.   p4.   300w.   5

5661   'TILL the End of Time.   Realm 8030/31 (2 discs)
            RC   April   p7.   300w. $3\frac{1}{2}$

5662   TIMES and Traditions for Dulcimer.   Trailer LER 2094 (E)
            EDS   Spring   p32.   200w. $4\frac{1}{2}$

5663   TOP of the Pops, Vol. 4.   BBC Records (E)
            CAC   March   p476-7.   200w.   3

5664   TOWN Hall Party.   Columbia 1072 (Reissue)
            CMR   Aug.   p24.   350w.   3

5665   TRADITIONAL Instrumental Music from Flanders.   Omega
        International LP2 538 (E)
            FR   Nov.   p35.   200w.   4

5666   TRAVELLING Folk.   Erin 006 (Ireland)
            FR   Jan.   p33.   100w.   3

5667   The TRAVELLING Songster.   Topic 12TS304 (E)
            EDS   Summer   p73.   300w.   4
            RSP   V1/#3   p12-3.   250w.   3

5668   TRIBUTE to Woody Guthrie.   Warner Brothers 2W-3007 (2
        discs) (Reissue)
            CRA   April   p102.   200w.   3
            RRE   March-April   p58-9.   500w.   4

5669   TRIP to Harrogate.   Tradition TSR 027 (E)
            FR   Sept.   p34.   300w.   4

5670   TROJAN Story.   Trojan 402 (E) (Reissue)
            BM   Feb.   p51.   100w.   2

5671   20 Country and Western Greats.   BBC Records and Tapes
        REC 276 (E) (Reissue)
            CMR   July   p19.   50w.   3

5672   20 Golden Hits Country and Western.   MCA MOPS 8465 (West
        Germany) (Reissue)
            CMR   May   p33, 34.   50w.   4

5673   20 Great Truck Drivin' Songs.   K-Tel NE990 (Reissue)
            CMP   Nov.   p36.   225w.   3

5674   200 Years of American Heritage in Song.   CMH Records
       CMH-1776 (5 discs)
              BGU   March   p25.   625w.   5
              OTM   Spring   p29.   300w.   1

5675   UKRAINIAN Folk Songs.   APA 2347
              RC   April   p6-7.   250w. $2\frac{1}{2}$

5676   UNFINISHED Boogie: Western Blues Piano, 1946-52.   Muska-
       dine 104 (Reissue)
              CAD   Sept.   p37-8.   175w.   3
              CK   Nov.   p65.   25w. $4\frac{1}{2}$
              LB   Nov./Dec.   p32-3.   600w.   5

5677   UNION Avenue Breakdown.   Charly CR 30-127 (E) (Reissue)
              NK   Autumn   p50.   75w.   4
              SMG   Sept.   p28.   25w.   4

5678   UNION Grove Convention 1976.   Union Grove SS-11
              PIC   Nov.   p55.   150w. $2\frac{1}{2}$

5679   URBAN Blues.   Specialty SNTF 5023 (E) (Reissue)
              BM   Aug.   p49.   125w.   4
              CZM   June   p30.   50w. $2\frac{1}{2}$
              NK   Winter   p38.   75w.   4

5680   VARRY Canny--Canny Fettle.   Tradition TSR 023 (E)
              EDS   Spring   p32.   200w.   4

5681   VICTORIA Spivy Presents the All Star Blues World of Maestro
       Willie Dixon & His Chicago Blues Band.   Spivey LP 1016
              CAD   Aug.   p37.   150w.   4

5682   The VOICE of the Blues; Bottleneck Guitar.   Yazoo L-1046
       (Reissue)
              ST   Dec.-Jan.   p72, 74.   450w.   2

5683   VOICES of Bluegrass, V. 2.   Revonah 5918
              MN   V8/#1   p17.   200w. $2\frac{1}{2}$

5684   VOLUNTEER Jam.   Capricorn CPO172
              CM   March   p63.   50w.   3

5685   The WALNUT Valley Spring Thing.   Takoma D-1054
              BGU   May   p34.   200w.   3
              GP   Feb.   p113.   25w. $2\frac{1}{2}$
              PIC   May   p61-2.   200w.   5
              RSP   March-April   p24.   125w. $2\frac{1}{2}$
              SR   April   p102.   150w.   4

5686   The WAY They Were Back When.   Shasta LP 517 (Reissue)
              CMR   June   p8.   250w.   4

5687   WEED: A Rare Batch.   Stash ST-107 (Reissue)
       CAD   Aug.   p26.   150w. $3\frac{1}{2}$

5688   WESTERN Swing, Vol. 2/3.   Old Timey LP 116/7 (2 discs)
       (Reissue)
       JEMF   No. 46   p102-3.   200w.   5
       OTM   Winter   p24.   600w.   3

5689   WESTERN Swing and Country Jazz.   MCA VIM 4015 (Japan)
       (Reissue)
       JEMF   Autumn   p157-60.   200w.   5
       OTM   Summer   p30.   50w.   4

5690   WHEN Lights Are Low.   Philips 6612 103 (E)
       GR   March   p1468.   50w. $3\frac{1}{2}$

5691   WHEN Women Sand the Blues.   Arhoolie Blues Classics 26
       (Reissue)
       SR   Feb.   p107.   200w.   2

5692   WILDFLOWERS--The New York Loft Jazz Sessions, V. 1-5.
       Douglas Records NBLP 7045-7049 (5 discs)
       CAD   June   p10, 11.   1400w.   4
       DB   Aug. 11   p19-20.   1000w.   4
       MM   May 28   p33.   900w. $3\frac{1}{2}$
       RFJ   June   p12-3.   2500w.   2

5693   WINDY City Blues: 1935-1953.   Nighthawk 101 (Reissue)
       CAD   April   p37-8.   150w.   4
       DB   May 5   p28-32.   225w. $4\frac{1}{2}$
       LB   March-April   p34-5.   400w.   4

5694   WOODSTOCK Mountains; More Music from Mud Acres.
       Rounder 3018
       BGU   Sept.   p21.   200w.   4
       CS   Nov.   p19.   300w. $4\frac{1}{2}$

5695   The WORLD of Swing.   Columbia KG 32945 (2 discs) (Reissue)
       CO   Aug.   p22-3.   650w.   5

5696   WORRIED All the Time, Country Blues, 1929-40.   Whoopee
       104 (Reissue)
       RSP   V1/#3   p6.   600w.   5

5697   YESTERDAY'S Hits--Today.   Phil Spector International 2307
       007 (E) (Reissue)
       SR   June   p118-9.   125w.   3

DIRECTORY OF RECORD LABELS

This address directory is divided by three countries--the United States, England, and Canada. "See" references will direct the searcher to the appropriate distributor for a manufacturer that does not distribute for itself. Each distributor listing also contains the names of the labels that it distributes. Certain names which are not labels but series lines (such as "Explorer") were added to these lists for purposes of clarification; the "See" references will direct the searcher to the manufacturer (in this case, for example, "Elektra," which distributes "Nonesuch," the producer of the "Explorer" series). Ownership of the labels has not been determined. The name of the manufacturer has not been repeated in the listing address.

These lists are given in terms of the following restrictions: (a) only record labels which were indexed for 1976 are included; (b) only English and Canadian labels and records which were not also released in the United States are listed; and (c) no addresses are provided for labels manufactured outside the three countries. It is suggested that a record store or record importer could deal with the foreign pressings, perhaps better than a library or an individual could. There were many addresses that proved virtually impossible to find; try the specialty stores for these two. Most of these latter records are bootleg issues and they would rather not be found.

United States

A & M   1416 North LaBrea Ave., Hollywood, Cal. 90028

ABC   see   MCA

ABKCO   1700 Broadway, New York, N.Y. 10019

ACCENT   6533 Hollywood Blvd., Hollywood, Cal. 90028

ADELPHI   P. O. Box 288, Silver Spring, Md. 20907   Distributes: Hope, Piedmond, Skyline

ADITI   2266 Cambridge St., Los Angeles, Cal. 90006

ADVENT PRODUCTIONS   P. O. Box 635, La Habra, Cal. 90631 Distributes: Muskadine

ADVENT RECORDS (RAGTIME) 4150 Mayfield Rd., Cleveland, Ohio
  44121

ALADDIN 101 North Columbus St., Alexandria, Va. 22314

ALL PLATINUM 96 West St., Englewood, N.J. 07631 Distributes:
  Cadet, Checker, Chess, Custom, Janus, Kent

ALLEN-MARTIN 9701 Taylorsville Rd., Louisville, Ky. 40299
  Distributes: Bridges

ALLIGATOR P.O. Box 11741, Fort Dearborn Sta., Chicago, Ill.
  60611

ALSHIRE INTERNATIONAL P.O. Box 7107, Burbank, Cal. 91505

AMERICAN HERITAGE 1208 Everett St., Caldwell, Idaho 83605

AMERICAN MUSE 130 W. 57th St., New York, N.Y. 10019

AMPEX 555 Madison Ave., New York, N.Y. 10022

AMSTERDAM see RCA

ANGEL see CAPITOL

ANITA O'DAY Box 442, Hesperia, Cal. 92345

ANVIL Rt. 1, Olin, N.C. 28660

APPLE see CAPITOL

ARBOR P.O. Box 946, Evanston, Ill. 60204

ARCADIA 7200 Cresheim Rd. B-6, Philadelphia, Pa. 19119

ARCANE Maple Leaf Club, 6388 Ivarene, Hollywood, Cal. 90068

ARCHIVE OF FOLK AND JAZZ MUSIC see EVEREST

ARHOOLIE 10341 San Pablo Ave., El Cerrito, Cal. 94530 Distributes: Blues Classics, Folylyric, Old Timey

ARISTA 6 W. 57th St., New York, N.Y. 10019 Distributes: Haven, Savoy

ASCH see FOLKWAYS

ASYLUM see ELEKTRA/ASYLUM/NONESUCH

ATCO see ATLANTIC

ATLANTIC 75 Rockefeller Plaza, New York, N.Y. 10019 Dis-

tributes: Atco, Big Tree, Cotillion, Embryo, Little David, Nemperor, Rolling Stone

ATTEIRAM P.O. Box 606, Marietta, Ga. 30061

AUDIOFIDELITY 221 W. 57th St., New York, N.Y. 10019 Distributes: BASF, Black Lion, Chiaroscuro, World Jazz

AUDIOPHILE see HAPPY JAZZ

AVCO EMBASSY 1301 Ave. of the Americas, New York, N.Y.
10019

BASF see AUDIOFIDELITY

BANANA see STACY-LEE

BANG/BULLET 2107 Fawkner Rd. N.E., Atlanta, Ga. 30324
Distributes: Bang

BANON 11 Dogwood Lane, Larchmount, N.Y. 10538

BARNABY 816 N. La Cienga Blvd., Los Angeles, Cal. 90064

BATTERY 116 Nassau St., New York, N.Y. 10038 Distributes:
Painted Smiles

BAY 1516 Oak St., Alamenda, Cal. 94501

BEARS 3459 Nakoma Lane, Las Vegas, Nev. 89109

BEARSVILLE see WARNER BROTHERS

BENSON 365 Great Circle Rd., Nashville, Tenn. 37228

BERKELEY RHYTHM 3040 Benevenue, Berkeley, Cal. 94705

BESERKLEY RECORDS see PLAYBOY

BEVERLY HILLS P.O. Box 4009, Hollywood, Cal. 90028

BIG STAR 4228 Joy Rd., Detroit, Mich. 48204

BIG TREE see ATLANTIC

BIOGRAPH 16 River St., Chatham, N.Y. 12037 Distributes: Center, Melodeon

BIRCH Box 92, Wilmette, Ill. 60091

BISCUIT CITY 1106 E. 17th Ave., Denver, Col. 80218

BIZARRE see WARNER BROTHERS

BLACK EAGLE   128 Front St., Marblehead, Mass. 01945

BLACK FIRE   4409 Douglas St. N.E., Washington, D.C. 20019
Distributes: IPS, Tribe

BLACK JAZZ see OVATION

BLACK LION see AUDIOFIDELITY

BLACKBIRD   Lakco Record Co., 3902 N. Ashland Ave., Chicago,
Ill. 60613

BLINET RECORDS   Box 11366, Denver, Col. 80211

BLUE CANYON   1037 7th St., Las Vegas, Nev. 87701

BLUE GOOSE   245 Waverly Place, New York, N.Y. 10014

BLUE GRASS REVUE   3608 Ann Arbor Place, Oklahoma City, Okla.
73122

BLUE HORIZON see ABC

BLUE NOTE see UNITED ARTISTS

BLUE RIDGE   Box 19820, Milwaukee, Wis. 53219

BLUE SKY see COLUMBIA

BLUEGRASS EXPRESS   6808 Robin Dr., Chattanooga, Tenn. 37421

BLUEGRASS SEED   1443 S. Main St., Wichita, Kan. 67213

BLUEGRASS SOUTHLAND   2704 Haley Ave., Fort Worth, Tex.
76117

BLUES CLASSICS see ARHOOLIE

BLUETICK   Box 793, Parkesbury, W.Va. 26101

BLUGRAS   Rt. 2, Box 397, Princeton, W.Va. 24740

BOB THIELE MUSIC see RCA

BOUNTIFUL   12311 Gratiot Ave., Detroit, Mich. 48205

BRASS DOLPHIN   2835 Woodstock Rd., Los Angeles, Cal. 90046

BRIAR see TAKOMA

BRIDGES see ALLEN-MARTIN

BRIKO   P.O. Box 15075, Phoenix, Ariz. 85060

BRUNSWICK   888 Seventh Ave., New York, N.Y. 10019

BRUT   1345 Avenue of the Americas, New York, N.Y. 10019

BUCKSHOT RECORDS   see   JEREE

BUDDAH/KAMA SUTRA   810 Seventh Ave., New York, N.Y. 10019
Distributes: Celebration, Kama Sutra

BURCHETTE BROTHERS   P.O. Box 1363, Spring Valley, Cal.
92077

CBGB/OMFUG   315 Bowery, New York, N.Y. 10003

CK RECORDS   1000 S. 7th St., Ann Arbor, Mich. 48203

CMH RECORDS   P.O. Box 39439, Los Angeles, Cal. 90039

CMS   14 Warren St., New York, N.Y. 10007

CTI   see   MOTOWN

CADENCE   119 W. 57th St., New York, N.Y. 10019

CADET   see   ALL PLATINUM

CAMBRIDGE   125 Irving St., Framingham, Mass. 01701

CAMDEN   see   RCA

CAMEL RACE   5153 Mt. Revarb Ct., Marrew, La. 70072

CANAAN   see   WORD

CANEYCREEK   1418 E. Portland, Springfield, Mo. 65804

CAPITOL   1750 N. Vine St., Hollywood, Cal. 90028   Distributes:
Angel, Apple, Harvest, Melodiya/Angel

CAPRICE   907 Main St., Nashville, Tenn. 37206

CAPRICORN   see   WARNER BROTHERS

CAROUSEL   1273$\frac{1}{2}$ N. Crescent Heights Blvd., Los Angeles, Cal.
90046

CASABLANCA   8255 Sunset Blvd., Los Angeles, Cal. 90046   Distributes: Douglas

CASCADE   Box 512, Chester, Va. 23831

CASSANDRA   2027 Parker St., Berkeley, Cal. 94704

CATALYST   see   SPRINGBOARD

CELEBRATION   see   BUDDAH/KAMA SUTRA

CELESTE   45 Cherry St. , Cambridge, Mass. 01139

CENTER   see   BIOGRAPH

CENTURY PRODUCTIONS   171 Washington Rd. , Sayreville, N. J.
     08872

CHAIRMAN   Box 4413   Sunnyside Station, New York, N. Y. 11104

CHECKER   see   ALL PLATINUM

CHELSEA HOUSE   Box 1057, Brattleboro, Vt. 05301

CHESS/JANUS   see   ALL PLATINUM

CHIAROSCURO   see   AUDIOFIDELITY

CHOICE   245 Tilley Place, Sea Cliff, N. Y. 11579

CHRYSALIS   9255 Sunset Blvd. , Suite 212, Los Angeles, Cal. 90069

CHYTOWNS   1410 E. 72nd St. , Chicago, Ill. 60619

CINNAMON   1805 Hayes St. , Nashville, Tenn. 37203

CLASSIC JAZZ   see   MUSIC MINUS ONE

CLUB OF SPADE   Box 1771, Studio City, Cal. 91604

COLLEGIUM   35-41 72nd St. , Jackson Heights, N. Y. 11372 Dis-
     tributes: Minstrel

COLUMBIA   51 W. 52nd St. , New York, N. Y. 10019 Distributes:
     Blue Sky, Daffodil, Epic, Harmony, Kirshner, Philadelphia In-
     ternational, Portrait, Spindizzy, T-Neck, Virgin

COMBINED MKTG.   10 Boston Sq. , Fort Smith, Ark. 72901 Dis-
     tributes: Testament

CONCERT   3318 Platt Ave. , Lynwood, Cal. 90262

CONCORD JAZZ   P. O. Box 845, Concord, Cal. 94522

CONNOISSEUR   390 B West End Ave. , New York, N. Y. 10024

CONTEMPORARY   8481 Melrose Place, Los Angeles, Cal. 90069
     Distributes: Good Time Jazz

COPLIX   152 W. 42nd St. , Suite 536, New York, N. Y. 10036

CORAL   see   MCA

COTILLION   see   ATLANTIC

COUNTRY LIFE   C. P. O. 1322, Berea, Ky. 40403

COUNTRY MUSIC HISTORY   Box 39439, Los Angeles, Cal. 90039

COUNTRY   Box 191, Floyd, Va. 24091

COUNTRYSIDE   Box 7155, Tampa, Fla. 38673

CREAM   8025   8025 Melrose Ave., Los Angeles, Cal. 90046   Dis-
    tributes: HI

CREATIVE WORLD   1012 S. Robertson Blvd., Los Angeles, Cal.
    90035

CREED   see   NASHBORO

CREED TAYLOR INC.   see   MOTOWN

CRESCENDO   3725 Crescent St., Long Island City, N. Y. 11101

CRESCENT JAZZ   P. O. Box 60244, Los Angeles, Cal. 90054

CURTOM   5915 N. Lincoln Ave., Chicago, Ill. 60645

CUSTOM   see   ALL PLATINUM

D RECORDS   c/o H. W. Daily Inc., 314 11th Ave. E., Houston,
    Tex. 77088

DGJ   P. O. Box 010772, Miami Fla. 33101   Distributes: Sami

DAFFODIL   see   COLUMBIA

DAKAR   see   BRUNSWICK

DAVIS UNLIMITED   Route 11, 16 Bond St., Clarkesville, Tenn.
    37040

DAWN   P. O. Box 535, Main St., Belair, Md. 21014

DAYBREAK   6725 Sunset Blvd., Suite 504, Hollywood, Cal. 90028

DECCA   see   MCA

DELITE   200 W. 57th St., New York, N. Y. 10019

DELMARK   4243 N. Lincoln, Chicago, Ill. 60618

DELUXE   see   GUSTO

DEMO RECORDS Trails End, 1893 San Luis, Mountain View, Cal.
94040

DERAM see LONDON

DEUTSCHE GRAMMOPHON see POLYDOR

DEVI see TAKOMA

DIAL P. O. Box 1273, Nashville, Tenn. 37202

DIRTY SHAME 4552 Shenandoah, St. Louis, Mo. 63110

DISCREET see WARNER BROTHERS

DOBRE see RAY LAWRENCE

DOMINION P. O. Box 993, Salem, Va. 24153

DOT see MCA

DOUGLAS see CASABLANCA

DOWN HOME J. D. Jarvis, Box 3113, Hamilton, Ohio 45013

DRIFTWOOD P. O. Box 579, Mineral Wells, Tex.

DUKE see MCA

DUNHILL see MCA

DUTCHLAND 1860 W. Main St., Ephrata, Pa. 17522

EBM see EUBIE BLAKE MUSIC

EGM Lothlovien Co., 2111 Vanderbilt Lane, Austin, Tex. 78723

EPI RECORDS G. P. O. Box 2301, New York, N. Y. 10001

ESP 5 Riverside Drive, Krumville, N. Y. 12447

ELEKTRA/ASYLUM/NONESUCH 962 N. LaCienega, Los Angeles,
Cal. 90069 Distributes: Asylum, Nonesuch

EMANEN P. O. Box 362, Highland, N. Y. 12528 Distributes:
Steam

EMBASSY see AVCO EMBASSY

EMBRYO see ATLANTIC

ENVY c/o Norm Vincent Sound Recording Studios, 4541 Brown Ave.,
Jacksonville, Fla. 32207

EPIC   see   COLUMBIA

ETHELYN   13240 Fidler Ave., Downey, Cal. 90242

EUBIE BLAKE MUSIC   284A Stuyvesant Ave., Brooklyn, N.Y. 11221

EUPHONIC   P. O. Box 476, Ventura, Cal. 93001

EVEREST   10920 Wilshire Blvd. W., Los Angeles, Cal. 90024
   Distributes: Archive of Folk and Jazz Music, Olympic

EVERYMAN   see   VANGUARD

EXCELLO   see   NASHBORO

EXPLORER (NONESUCH)   see   ELEKTRA/ASYLUM/NONESUCH

EXTREME RARITIES   Ken Crawford, 215 Steuben Ave., Pittsburgh,
   Pa. 15205

F & W   see   ROUNDER

FAMILY   see   REQUEST

FAMOUS DOOR   40-08 155th St., Flushing, N.Y. 11354

FANIA   888 Seventh Ave., New York, N.Y. 10019 Distributes: International, Vaya

FANTASY   10th and Parker Sts., Berkeley, Cal. 94710 Distributes:
   Milestone, Prestige

FARGO   1419 Fargo Ave., Chicago, Ill. 60626

FAT CAT'S JAZZ   Box 458, Manassas, Va. 22110

FIDDLER'S GROVE   P. O. Box 38, Union Grove, N.C. 28689 Distributes: Union Grove

FIRST TIME   P. O. Box 03202-R, Portland, Ore. 97203

FLAT TOWN   P. O. Drawer 10, Ville Platte, La. 70586 Distributes:
   Swallow

FLYING DUTCHMAN   see   RCA

FLYING FISH   3320 N. Halstead, Chicago, Ill. 60657 Distributes:
   Kaleidoscope, Mountain Railroad

FOLK HERITAGE   University of West Virginia, Morgantown, W. Va.
   26505

FOLK LEGACY   Sharon Mt. Rd., Sharon, Conn. 06069

FOLKLYRIC see ARHOOLIE

FOLKWAYS 43 W. 61st St. , New York, N. Y. 10023 Distributes:
Asch, Mankind (Asch), RBF

FOREFRONT 1945 Wilmette Ave. , Wilmette, Ill. 60091

400 11 Dogwood Lane, Larchmount, N. Y. 10588

FOX HOLLOW RD 1, Petersburg, N. Y. 12138

FOX-ON-THE-RUN P. O. Box 40553, Washington, D. C. 20016

FREEDOM P. O. Box 888, Easley, S. C. 29640

FRETLESS see PHILO

FRONT HALL see SWALLOW TAIL

FRONT PORCH 1934 E. Treetop Lane, Birmingham, Ala. 35216

GHB see JAZZOLOGY

GNP CRESCENDO 8560 Sunset Blvd. , Hollywood, Cal. 90069

GRC Greater Recording Co. , 164 Manhattan Ave. , Brooklyn, N. Y.
11206

GRC GENERAL 174 Mills St. , Atlanta, Ga. 30313

GALAX MOOSE LODGE Box 665, Galax, Va. 24333

GITFIDDLE 114 W. Montclair Ave. , Greenville, S. C. 29609

GLORYLAND 1414 E. Broad St. , Columbus, Ohio

GOINS W. Prestonburg, Ky. 41668

GOLDBAND P. O. Box 1485, Lake Charles, La. 70601

GOLDEN CIRCLE Sharpsbury, Md. 21782

GOLDEN CREST 220 Broadway, Huntington Station, N. Y. 11746

GOOD TIME JAZZ see CONTEMPORARY

GORDY see MOTOWN

GOSPEL GRASS Box 534, Elba, Ala. 36323

GOSPEL SHORE 2397 N. Snyder Rd. , Dayton, Ohio 45426

GRANITE 6255 Sunset Blvd. , Los Angeles, Cal. 90028

GRASSROOTS 2737 N. E. 25th St. , Portland, Ore. 97212

GRATEFUL DEAD see UNITED ARTISTS

GREEN LINNET see INNISFREE

GRITZ 4012 Tuxedo Rd. N. W. , Atlanta, Ga. 30342

GROOVE MERCHANT Suite 3701, 515 Madison Ave. , New York, N. Y. 10022

GRUNT see RCA

GUITAR WORLD see MUSIC MINUS ONE

GUSTO 220 Boscobel St. , Nashville, Tenn. 37213 Distributes: Deluxe, King, Starday

HALCYON 302 Clinton St. , Bellmore, N. Y. 11710

HALO Township Group, Box 7084, 10 Michael Dr. , Greenville, S. C. 29610

HAM AND EGGS RFT 1, Box 220, Mountain Green, Utah 84050

HAPPY JAZZ P. O. Box 66, San Antonio, Tex. 78291 Distributes: Audiofidelity, Paseo Stereo

HARMONY see COLUMBIA

HARRISON 229 Oak St. , Wakefield, Mass. 01880

HARVEST see CAPITOL

HAVEN see ARISTA

HERITAGE Rt. 3, Box 278, Galax, Va. 74333

HERITAGE PRODUCTIONS P. O. Box 2284, West Lafayette, Ind. 47906

HERWIN 45 First St. , Glen Cove, N. Y. 11542

HI see CREAM

HICKORY 2510 Franklin Rd. , Nashville, Tenn. 37204

HILLTOP see PICKWICK INTERNATIONAL

HISTORICAL P. O. Box 4204, Jersey City, N. J. 07304

HOME COMFORT Box 33, Marion, Ore. 97359

HOPE   see   ADELPHI

HYANNISPORT   Box 337, Hyannisport, Mass. 02647

I. A. J. R. C.   1284 Old Johnson Ferry Road N. E. , Atlanta, Ga.
   30319

I. P. S.   RECORDS   see   BLACK FIRE

IMPROVISING ARTISTS   26 Jane St. , New York, N. Y. 10014

IMPULSE   see   MCA

INDIA NAVIGATION   P. O. Box 559, Nyack, N. Y. 10960

INNER CITY   see   MUSIC MINUS ONE

INNISFREE   70 Turner Hill Rd. , New Canaan, Conn. 06840   Distributes: Green Linnet

INTERNATIONAL   see   FANIA

INTERNATIONAL ASSOCIATION OF JAZZ RECORD COLLECTORS
   see   I. A. J. R. C.

IRMA   see   MELODY

ISLAND   7720 Sunset Blvd. , Los Angeles, Cal. 90046

JACK RABBIT   4323 Woodglen Dr. , Moorpark, Cal. 93021

JALYN   1806 Brown St. , Dayton, Ohio 45409

JANUS   see   ALL PLATINUM

JAZUM   5808 Northcumberland St. , Pittsburgh, Pa. 15217

JAZZ ARCHIVES   P. O. Box 194, Plainview, N. Y. 11805

JAZZ CHRONICLE   6226 Santa Monica Blvd. , Hollywood, Cal.
   90038

JAZZ COMPOSERS' ORCHESTRA ASSOCIATION   6 W. 95th St. ,
   New York, N. Y. 10025

JAZZOLOGY   3008 Wadsworth Mill Pl. , Decatur, Ga. 30032   Distributes: GHB, Paramount, Southland

JEREE   1469 Third St. , New Brighton, Pa. 15066   Distributes:
   Buckshot

JESSUP   3150 Francis St. , Jackson, Mich. 49203   Distributes:
   Michigan Bluegrass

JEWEL 728 Texas St., Shreveport, La. 71163 Distributes: Paula, Ronn

JEWEL 1594 Kinney Ave., Cincinnati, Ohio 45231

JEZEBEL 1233 Greenleaf St., Allentown, Pa. 18102

JIM TAYLOR PRESENTS 12311 Gratiot Ave., Detroit, Mich. 48205

JOHN EDWARDS MEMORIAL FOUNDATION c/o Center for Study of Folklore & Mythology, U.C.L.A., Los Angeles, Cal. 90024

JOHN T. BENSON see BENSON

JOLIET Box 67201, Los Angeles, Cal. 90067

JUNE APPAL RECORDS Box 743, Whitesburg, Ky. 41858

KPL c/o Lin Michael, Rt. 2, Killen, Ala. 35645

KALEIDOSCOPE see FLYING FISH

KAMA SUTRA see BUDDAH/KAMA SUTRA

KANAWHA P.O. Box 267, Dayton, Ohio 45420

KENT see ALL PLATINUM

KIAMICHI Rt. 2, Box 114, Hugo, Okl. 74743

KICKING MULE P.O. Box 3233, Berkeley, Cal. 94703

KILMARNOCK 300 W. 57th St., New York, N.Y. 10019

KIM-PAT P.O. Box 654, Fayetteville, Tenn. 37344

KING see GUSTO

KING BLUEGRASS 6609 Main St., Cincinnati, Ohio 45244 Distributes: Lemco

KINGFISH P.O. Box 427, Oak Lawn, Ill. 60454

KIRSHNER see COLUMBIA

KLAVIER 10515 Burbank Blvd., N. Hollywood, Cal. 91601

KO-KO 888 Seventh Ave., New York, N.Y. 10019

KUDU see MOTOWN

LAB Box 5038, North Texas Sta., Denton, Tex. 76203

LAND O' JAZZ P. O. Box 26393, New Orleans, La. 70126

LANDERS ROBERTS 9255 Sunset Blvd., Los Angeles, Cal. 90048
Distributes: Mums

LAVAL 266 N. Burdick St., Kalamazoo, Mich. 49006

LAWRENCE, RAY see RAY LAWRENCE

LEGACY see OWL

LEGEND see MCA

LEMCO see KING BLUEGRASS

LIBRARY OF CONGRESS Washington, D. C.

LIFESTORY 488 Madison Ave., New York, N. Y. 10022

LIGHT see WORD

LITTLE DAVID see ATLANTIC

LIVE OAK P. O. Box 1094, Charleston, S. C. 29402

LIVING FOLK RECORDS 65 Mt. Auburn St., Cambridge, Mass.
02128

LONDON 539 W. 25th St., New York, N. Y. 10001 Distributes:
Deram, Hi, Parrot, Threshold

LONG NECK 6004 Bull Creek Rd., Austin, Tex. 78757

LOTUS Box 5606, Las Vegas, Nev. 89102

LYRICHORD 141 Perry St., New York, N. Y. 10014

MBA 8914 Georgian Dr., Austin, Tex. 78753

MCA 100 Universal City Plaza, Universal City, Cal. 91608 Distributes: Decca, Legend, Rocket, Uni, ABC, Dot, Duke, Dunhill,
Impulse, Peacock, Shelter, Sire

MGM see POLYDOR

MAINSTREAM 1700 Broadway, New York, N. Y. 10019

MAJOR 151 W. 46th St., New York, N. Y. 10036

MAMLISH Cathedral Sta., Box 417, New York, N. Y. 10025

MANKIND (ASCH) see FOLKWAYS

MANMADE 812 N. W. 57th St., Miami, Fla.

MASTER JAZZ RECORDINGS   955 Lexington Ave., New York, N.Y.
  10024

MEADOWLANDS   3135 Sedgwick Ave., Bronx, N.Y. 10463

MEGA   1605 Hawkins St., Nashville, Tenn. 37203 Distributes:
  Caprice

MELODEON   see   BIOGRAPH

MELODIYA/ANGEL   see   CAPITOL

MELODY   1912 St. Clair St., Hamilton, Ohio 45011 Distributes:
  Irma, Pine Tree

MERCURY   see   PHONOGRAM

MESSAROUND   Box 1392, Burlingame, Cal. 94010

METROMEDIA   1700 Broadway, New York, N.Y. 10019

MICHIGAN ARCHIVES   6116 Dixie Highway, Bridgeport, Mich. 48722

MICHIGAN BLUEGRASS   see   JESSUP

MILESTONE   see   FANTASY

MINSTREL   see   COLLEGIUM

MIR-A-DON   5333 Astor Pl. S.E., Washington, D.C. 20019 Distributes: Solid Soul

MISSION RECORDS   General Delivery, Floyd, Va. 24091

MISTLETOE   see   SPRINGBOARD

MONMOUTH/EVERGREEN   1697 Broadway, Suite 1201, New York,
  N.Y. 10019

MONUMENT   21 Music Sq. E., Nashville, Tenn. 37203

MOON   P.O. Box 4001, Kansas City, Kan. 66104

MORNINGSTAR   see   SPRINGBOARD

MOTOWN   6255 Sunset Blvd., Hollywood, Cal. 90028 Distributes:
  CTI, Gordy, Kudu, Mowest, Rare Earth, Soul, Tamla

MOUNTAIN   Box 231A, Rt. 3, Galax, W.Va. 24333

MOUNTAIN RAILROAD   see   FLYING FISH

MOWEST   see   MOTOWN

MUMS   see   LANDERS ROBERTS

MUSE   Blanchris Inc., 160 W. 71st St., New York, N.Y. 10023

MUSIC CITY WORKSHOP   38 Music Sq. E., Suite 115, Nashville,
   Tenn. 37203

MUSIC MINUS ONE   43 W. 61st St., New York, N.Y. 10023   Distributes: Classic Jazz, Guitar World, Inner City

MUSICAL WONDER HOUSE   18 High St., Wiscasset, Me. 04578

MUSICORE   see   SPRINGBOARD

MUSKADINE   see   ADVENT

MYRRH   see   WORD

NASHBORO   1011 Woodland St., Nashville, Tenn. 37206 Distributes:
   Creed, Excello

NASHVILLE INTERNATIONAL   20 Music Sq. W., Nashville, Tenn.
   37203

NATIONAL GEOGRAPHIC SOCIETY   Dept. 100, Wash., D.C. 20036

NEMPEROR   see   ATLANTIC

NEW MORNING   641 W. 169th St., New York, N.Y. 10032

NEW ORLEANS   1918 Burgundy, New Orleans, La. 70116

NEW WORLD   3 East 54th St., New York, N.Y. 10022

NONESUCH   see   ELEKTRA/ASYLUM/NONESUCH

NORTH TEXAS LAB BAND   see   LAB

ODE   1416 N. LaBrea, Hollywood, Cal. 90028

OKEHDOKEE   370 West 1st St. South, Salt Lake City, Utah 84101

OLD DOMINION   P.O. Box 27, Gallatin, Tenn. 37066

OLD HOMESTEAD   P.O. Box 100, Brighton, Mich. 48116   Distributes: Pretzel Bell

OLD TIMEY   see   ARHOOLIE

OLIVIA   Box 70237, Los Angeles, Cal. 90070

OLYMPIC   200 W. 57th St., New York, N.Y. 10019

OMNISOUND Delaware Water Gap, Pa. 18327

ORIGIN JAZZ LIBRARY Box 863, Berkeley, Cal. 94701

ORIGINAL SOUND 7120 Sunset Blvd. , Los Angeles, Cal. 90046

ORION 5840 Busch Dr. , Malibu, Cal. 90265

ORK P. O. Box 159, Cooper Stn. , New York, N. Y. 10003

OUTLET Box 594, Rocky Mountain, Va. 24151

OUTSTANDING Box 2111, Huntington Beach, Cal. 92647

OVATION 1249 Waukegan, Glenview, Ill. 60025 Distributes:
Black Jazz

OWL P. O. Box 557, Lithia Springs, Ga. 30057 Distributes:
Legacy

OWL P. O. Box 711 Sebastopol, Cal. 95472

OYSTER see POLYDOR

P. M. RECORDS 20 Martha St. , Woodcliff Lake, N. J. 07675

PA DA 27 Washington Sq. N. , Suite 4D, New York, N. Y. 10011

PABLO see RCA

PACIFIC PERCEPTIONS 1906 Parkwell Ave. , Los Angeles, Cal.
90025

PACIFICIA 1628 E. 24th St. , Eugene, Ore. 97403

PAINTED SMILES see BATTERY

PALOMINO Box 6, Fairlawn, N. J. 07410

PANINI Box 15808, Honolulu, Hawaii 96813

PARAGON 1265 Broadway, New York, New York. 10001

PARAMOUNT see JAZZOLOGY

PAREDON P. O. Box 889, Brooklyn, N. Y. 11202

PARROT see LONDON

PAULA see JEWEL

PEACABLE Box 77038, Los Angeles, Cal. 90007

PEACOCK   see   MCA

PEERLESS   Record Distributors of America, 780 W. 27th St. , Hialeah, Fla. 33010

PELICAN   P. O. Box 34732, Los Angeles, Cal. 90034

PEOPLE   see   POLYDOR

PERCEPTION   165 W. 46th St. , New York, N. Y. 10036

PETER PAN   145 Kormon St. , Newark, N. J. 07105 Distributes:
Power

PHILADELPHIA INTERNATIONAL   see   COLUMBIA

PHILIPS   see   PHONOGRAM

PHILO   c/o The Barn, North Ferrisburg, Vt. 05473 Distributes:
Fretless

PHOENIX JAZZ   P. O. Box 3, Kingston, N. J. 08528

PHONOGRAM   1 IBM Plaza, Chicago, Ill. 60611 Distributes:
Mercury, Philips, Smash, UK, Vertigo

PHYSICAL   see   ROUNDER

PICKWICK INTERNATIONAL   135 Crossways Park Dr. , Woodbury,
Long Island, N. Y. 11797 Distributes: Hilltop

PIEDMONT   see   ADELPHI

PINE MOUNTAIN   Box 584, Barbourville, Ky.

PINE TREE   see   MELODY

PLAYBOY   Playboy Music Inc. , 8560 Sunset Blvd. , Los Angeles,
Cal. 90169 Distributes: Beserkley

PLAYHOUSE   Box 61, Monroe, N. C. 28110

POLYDOR   810 Seventh Ave. , New York, N. Y. 10019 Distributes:
Deutsche Grammophon, MGM, Oyster, People, RSO, Spring,
Verve

POPPY   see   UNITED ARTISTS

PORTRAIT   see   COLUMBIA

POWER   see   PETER PAN

PRESTIGE   see   FANTASY

PRETZEL BELL see OLD HOMESTEAD

PRINCESS 8127 Elrita Dr., Los Angeles, Cal. 90046

PRIORITY 2300 Lincoln Ave., Fort Worth, Tex. 76106

PRIZE JEM Entertainment, 707 18th Ave. S., Nashville, Tenn.
  37203

PROJECT THREE Total Sound Inc., 1133 Ave. of the Americas,
  New York, N.Y. 10036

PURITAN P.O. Box 946, Evanston, Ill. 60204

PYRAMID 5930 Genoa, Oakland, Cal. 94608

RBF see FOLKWAYS

RCA 1133 Ave. of the Americas, New York, N.Y. 10036 Distributes: Amsterdam, Bob Thiele Music, Camden, Chelsea, Daybreak, Flying Dutchman, Grunt, Pablo, Signature

RCS P.O. Box 362, Tacoma, Washington 98409

RSO see POLYDOR

RACCOON see WARNER BROTHERS

RAM 397 Saundersville Rd., Old Hickory, Tenn. 37138

RANWOOD 9034 Sunset Blvd., Los Angeles, Cal. 90069

RARE EARTH see MOTOWN

RAY LAWRENCE P.O. Box 1987, Studio City, Cal. 91604 Distributes: Dobre, Sheba

REAL EARTH 6207 Brooke Jane Dr., Clinton, Md. 20735

REBEL Rt. 12, Asbury, W. Va. 24916 Distributes: Zap

REFLECTION SOUND 1018 Central Ave., Charlotte, N.C. 28204
  Distributes: Revelation

REM 3805 White Creek Pike, Nashville, Tenn. 37207

REPRISE see WARNER BROTHERS

REQUEST 3800 S. Ocean Dr., 2nd Floor, Hollywood, Fla. 33019
  Distributes: Family

REVELATION see REFLECTION SOUND

REVONAH   Box 217, Ferndale, N. Y. 12734

RICH-R-TONE   3713 Benham Ave., Nashville, Tenn. 37215

RICO   748 10th Ave., New York, N. Y. 10019   Distributes: Solo

RIDGE RUNNER   3035 Townsend Dr., Fort Worth, Tex. 76110

RIM ROCK   Concord, Ark. 72523

RISING STAR   see   TREEHOUSE

ROB LEE MUSIC   P. O. Box 1385, Merchantville, N. J. 08109

ROCK ISLAND   see   ROB LEE MUSIC

ROCKET   see   MCA

ROLLIN' ROCK   6777 Hollywood Blvd., Hollywood, Cal. 90028

ROLLING STONES   see   ATLANTIC

ROME   1414 E. Broad St., Columbus, Ohio 43205

RONN   see   JEWEL

ROULETTE   17 W. 60th St., New York, N. Y. 10023

ROUND   see   UNITED ARTISTS

ROUNDER   186 Willow Ave., Somerville, Mass. 02143   Distributes:
   F & W, Physical

ROYAL RECORDS   397 S. Walter Ave., Newbury Park, Cal. 91320

RURAL RHYTHM   Box A, Arcadia, Cal. 91006

STN   3102 Francis St., Denison, Tex. 75020

SAMI   see   JGJ

SANSKRIT   7515 Wayzatu Blvd., Suite 232, Minneapolis, Minn.
   55343

SAVOY   see   ARISTA

SCEPTER   see   SPRINGBOARD

SEQUATCHIE   Star St., Box 432, Dunlap, Tenn. 37327

1750 ARCH RECORDS   1750 Arch St., Berkeley, Cal. 94709

SHANACHIE   1375 Crosby Ave., Bronx, N. Y. 10461

SHANNON   P. O.   Drawer 1,   Madison,   Tenn.   37115

SHEBA   see   RAY LAWRENCE

SHEEPWATER   Box 505,   Hailey,   Idaho 83330

SHEFFIELD LAB   P. O.   Box 5332,   Santa Barbara,   Cal.   93108

SHELBY SINGELTON CORPORATION   3106 Belmont Blvd. ,   Nashville,   Tenn.   37212   Distributes: Sun

SHELTER   see   MCA

SHIH SHIH WA AS   8120 Oakland Ave. S. ,   Bloomington Minn.   55420

SIGNATURE   see   RCA

SIRE   see   MCA

SIRENS   616 N.   Rush St. ,   Chicago,   Ill.   60611

SISTER SUN   345 Waltham St. ,   Lexington,   Mass.   02173

SKYLINE   see   ADELPHI

SKYLITE-SING   1008   17th Ave. S. ,   Nashville,   Tenn.   37212

SMASH   see   PHONOGRAM

SMITHSONIAN CLASSIC JAZZ   P. O.   Box 14196,   Washington,   D. C.
20044

SMITHSONIAN COLLECTION   P. O.   Box 1641,   Washington,   D. C.
20013

SOLID SOUL   see   MIR-A-DON

SOLO   see   RICO

SONYATONE   Box 567,   Santa Barbara,   Cal.   93102

SOUL   see   MOTOWN

SOUND CURRENT   823 North Fairfax Ave. ,   Los Angeles,   Cal.
90046

SOUTHLAND   see   JAZZOLOGY

SPANISH MUSIC CENTER   Belvedere Hotel,   319 W.   48th St. ,   New
York,   N. Y.   10036

SPARK Peer-Southern Prods. ,   1740 Broadway,   New York,   N. Y.
10019

SPECIALTY   8300 Santa Monica Blvd., Hollywood, Cal. 90069

SPINDIZZY   see   COLUMBIA

SPITBALL   Box 680, Gratigny, Miami, Fla. 33168

SPIVEY   65 Grand Ave., Brooklyn, N.Y. 11205

SPRING   see   POLYDOR

SPRINGBOARD   947 U.S. Highway 1, Rahway, N.J. 07065 Distributes: Catalyst, Mistletoe, Morningstar, Musicore, Sceptre,
   Trip, Viva

STACY-LEE   425 Park St., Hackensack, N.J. 07601 Distributes:
   Banana

STANYAN   8440 Santa Monica Blvd., Hollywood, Cal. 90069

STARDAY KING   see   GUSTO

STARR   Rt. 1, Radcliffe, Ohio 45670

STASH   Box 1009, Mattituck, N.Y. 11952

STEAM   see   EMANEM

STINGER PRODUCTIONS   Box 66, Dayton View Sta., Dayton, Ohio
   45406

STONEWAY   2817 Laura Koppe, Houston, Tex. 77016

STRATA EAST   156 Fifth Ave., Suite 612, New York, N.Y. 10010

STUDIO 1   Taxewell, Va. 24651

SUB MAUREEN   P.O. Box 147, Hyannisport, Mass. 02647

SUM OF US   1105 Grover Lane, Norman, Okla. 73069

SUN   see   SHELBY SINGLETON CORPORATION

SUNBEAM   13821 Calvert St., Van Nuys, Cal. 91401

SUNNY MT.   P.O. Box 14592, Gainesville, Fla. 32604

SUPER   Box 92, Wilmette, Ill. 60091

SURVIVAL   P.O. Box 1171, New York, N.Y. 10080

SUSSEX   6255 Sunset Blvd., Suite 1902, Hollywood, Cal. 90028

SWALLOW   see   FLAT TOWN

SWALLOW TAIL   Box 843, Ithaca, N.Y. 14850   Distributes: Front
  Hall

SYMPOSIUM   204 Fifth Ave. S.E. , Minneapolis, Minn. 55414

TH   10124 N.W. 80th Ave. , Hialeah Gardens, Fla. 33016

TIG   1100 Ralph Ct. , Hobbs, N.Mex. 88240

TK   495 S.E. 10th Court, Hialeah, Fla. 33010

T-NECK   see   COLUMBIA

TAKE HOME TUNES   P.O. Box 496, Georgetown, Conn. 06829

TAKOMA   P.O. Box 5369, Santa Monica, Cal. 90405   Distributes:
  Briar, Devi, Thistle

TAMLA   see   MOTOWN

TAZ-JAZ   1112 Mount Lowe Dr. , Altadena, Cal. 91001

TENNVALE   P.O. Box 1624, Huntsville, Ala. 35807

TESTAMENT   see   COMBINED MKTG.

THISTLE   see   TAKOMA

360 RECORDS   269 W. 72nd St. , New York, N.Y. 10023

THRESHOLD   see   LONDON

TITANIC   43 Rice St. , Cambridge, Mass. 02140

TOM CAT   450 N. Roxbury Dr. , Beverly Hills, Cal. 90210

TORCHE   P.O. Box 96, El Cevrito, Cal. 94530

TORO   7027 Twin Hills Ave. , Dallas, Tex. 75231

TOUCHE   P.O. Box 96, El Cerrito, Cal. 94530

TOWA   Box 161E, Rt. 1, Beckley, W.Va. 25801

TRADEWINDS   Box 8294, Honolulu, Hawaii 96815

TRADITIONAL   P.O. Box 8, Cosby, Tenn. 37722

TREEHOUSE   4413 South River, Independence, Mo. 64055   Distributes: Rising Star

TRI-AD   16666 S.W. Roosevelt Dr. , Lake Oswego, Ore. 97034

TRIBE   see   BLACK FIRE

TRIP   see   SPRINGBOARD

TRI-STATE   Rt. 1, Box 15, Hope Mills, N. C.   28348

TRIX   Drawer AB, Rosendall, N. Y.   12472

TRUTONE   428 Briarwood Lane, Northvale, N. J.   07647

TULIP   Box 3155, San Rafael, Cal.   94902

TUMBLEWEED   1368 Gilpin St. , Denver, Col.   80218

TUNE   2211 Woodward Ave. , Muscle Shoals, Ala.   35660

TURNAROUND   6470 8th Ave. , Grandville, Mich.   49418

20th CENTURY   8255 Sunset Blvd. , Los Angeles, Cal.   90046

UK   see   PHONOGRAM

UNI   see   MCA

UNION GROVE   see   FIDDLER'S GROVE

UNIT CORE   P. O. Box 3041, New York, N. Y.   10001

UNITED ARTISTS   6920 Sunset Blvd. , Hollywood, Cal.   90028   Distributes: Blue Note, Brown Bag, Douglas, Grateful Dead, Poppy, Round

VANGUARD   71 W. 23rd St. , New York, N. Y.   10010

VAYA   see   FANIA

VERTIGO   see   PHONOGRAM

VERVE   see   POLYDOR

VETCO   5828 Vine St. , Cincinnati, Ohio   45216

VIRGIN   see   COLUMBIA

VISTA   350 S. Buena Vista St. , Burbank, Cal.   91521

VIVA   see   SPRINGBOARD

VOKES   Box 12, New Kensington, Pa.   15068

VOX   211 E. 43rd St. , New York, N. Y.   10017

VOYAGER   424 35th Ave. , Seattle, Wash.   98122

WANGO 4802 Harford Rd., Baltimore, Md. 21214

WARNER BROTHERS 3300 Warner Blvd., Burbank, Cal. 91505
   Distributes: Bearsville, Bizarre, Capricorn, Dis-Creet, Raccoon,
   Reprise

WARPED RECORDS 8924 S. Austin, Oak Lawn, Ill. 60453

WARREN COUNTY P. O. Box 433, Indianola, Iowa 50125

WATT Watt Works, 6 W. 95th St., New York, N. Y. 10025

WES FARRELL 9200 Sunset Blvd., Suite 620, Los Angeles, Cal.
   90069

WESTWOOD 541 Fulmer Ave., Akron, Ohio 44312

WHID-ISLE Box 615, Clinton, Wash. 98236

WINDFALL 1790 Broadway, New York, N. Y. 10019

WINKLE c/o Bob Emberton, 1301 Lee St., Carthage, Tex. 75633

WISHBONE 4014 Kingman Blvd., Des Moines, Iowa 50311

WOODEN NICKEL 6521 Homewood Ave., Los Angeles, Cal. 90028

WORD 4800 W. Waco Dr., Waco, Tex. 76703 Distributes: Canaan, Lights, Myrrh, Paragon

WORLD JAZZ see AUDIOFIDELITY

XANADU 3242 Irwin Ave., Kingsbridge, N. Y. 10463

YAZOO 245 Waverly Pl., New York, N. Y. 10014

ZAP see REBEL

ZEBRA BREATH 320 Ohio River Blvd., Sewickly, Pa. 15143

ZENO P. O. Box 1273, Littleton, Col. 80120

ZIM P. O. Box 158, Jericho, L. I., N. Y. 11753

England (Britain)

A & M see CBS

A RECORDS Flat 4, 14 Blakesley, Ealing, London W5

ABBEY Abbey St., Eynsham, Oxford

ACE OF CLUBS see DECCA

ACTION see B & C

AD-RHYTHM 14a The Broadwalk, Pinner Rd., North Harrow, Middlesex

APPLE see EMI

ARGO 115 Fulham Rd., London SW3

ARISTA 49 Upper Brook St., London W1Y 2BT

ATLANTIC 17 Berners St., London W1

B & C TROJAN 326 Kensal Rd., London W10 Distributes: Action, Charisma, Mooncrest

BASF see DECCA

BBC RECORDS see POLYDOR

BALMALCOM HOUSE Kingskettle, Fife, Scotland KY7 7JT

BALLAD 16 Cradley Park Rd., Dudley

BARCLAY see RCA

BELL 49 Upper Brook St., London W1Y 2BT

BELTONA see DECCA

BIG BEAR see TRANSATLANTIC

BIG BEN 52 Shaftesbury Ave., London W1V 7DE

BLACK LION see TRANSATLANTIC

BRADLEYS 12 Bruton St., Mayfair, London

BROWN LABEL 30 Madden Ave., Chatham, Kent

CBS 17/18 Soho Square, London W1V 6HE Distributes: A & M, Blue Horizon, Embassy, 7-60,000 series, York

CAMDEN see PICKWICK INTERNATIONAL

CAPITOL see EMI

CARNIVAL see POLYDOR

CAROLINE 2-4 Vernon Yard, 119 Portobello Rd., London W11

CHAPTER ONE see DECCA

CHARISMA see B & C

CHECKER see PHONOGRAM

CHELSEA see RCA

CHESS see PHONOGRAM

CHRYSALIS 388/396 Oxford St., London W1N 9HE

CLADDAGH c/o CRD, Lyon Way, Rockware Ave., Greenford, Middlesex UB6 OBN

COLUMBIA see EMI

COLUMBIA STUDIO 2 see EMI

CONTOUR see PICKWICK INTERNATIONAL

CORAL see DECCA

CUBE RECORDS Essex House, 19-20 Poland St., London W1V 3DD
   Distributes: Hi Fly

DJM 71 New Oxford St., London WC1

DANDELION see WEA

DAWN see PYE

DECCA 9 Albert Embankment, London SE1 7SW Distributes: Ace of Clubs, BASF, Beltona, Chapter One, Coral, Deram, Eclipse, Emerald, Gem, Gull, London, Rex, Teldec, Telefunken, Threshold, Uni

DERAM see DECCA

DOUBLE-UP see EMI

DOVETAIL 10 Seaford Ave., New Malden, Surrey

EMI 20 Manchester Square, London W1A 1ES Distributes: Apple, Capitol, Columbia, Columbia Studio 2, Double-Up, Elektra, HMV, Harvest, Hi Fly, Invictus, MCA, One-Up, Parlophone, Probe, Purple, Rak, Regal Starline, Regal Zonophone, Rhino, Stateside, Talisman, Vine, Wave, Waverley

ECLIPSE see DECCA

ELEKTRA see EMI

EMBASSY see CBS

EMBER Suite 4, Carlton Tower Place, Sloane St., London SW1

EMERALD c/o Vogue Records, 113-115 Fulham Rd., London SW3

ENGLISH FOLK, DANCE, AND SONG SOCIETY 2 Regent's Park
Rd., London NW1 7AY

ENTERPRISE 1367 High Rd., Whetstone, London N20

FLYRIGHT 21 Wickham Ave., Bexhill-on-Sea, Sussex

FONTANA see PHONOGRAM

FOUNTAIN see RETRIEVAL RECORDINGS

GTO 17 Barlow Pl., Broton St., London W1X 7AE

GALLIARD c/o Stainer & Bell Ltd., 82 High Rd., London N2 9PW

GEM see DECCA

GOLDEN GUINEA see PYE

GOLDEN HOUR see PYE

GROSVENOR 16 Grosvenor Rd., Handsworth Wood, Birmingham
B20 3NP

GULL see DECCA

HMV see EMI

HALCYON see VINTAGE JAZZ MUSIC SOCIETY

HALLMARK see PICKWICK INTERNATIONAL

HARVEST see EMI

HY FLY see EMI

IMPACT see TOPIC

INCUS 87 Third Cross Rd., Twickenham, Middlesex

INVICTA c/o Sydney Thompson, 513 Uxbridge Rd., Hatch End,
Middlesex

INVICTUS see EMI

ISLAND 8-11 Basing St., London W11

JOY see PRESIDENT

LEADER see TRANSATLANTIC

LIBERTY see UNITED ARTISTS

LONDON see DECCA

MCA see EMI

MFP see MUSIC FOR PLEASURE

MGM see POLYDOR

MARBLE ARCH see PICKWICK INTERNATIONAL

MATCHBOX see SAYDISC MATCHBOX

MERCURY see PHONOGRAM

METRO see POLYDOR

MIDDLE EARTH see PYE

MOONCREST see B & C

MOSAIC c/o Graham Collier Music, 51 Nevern Sq., London SW5
  9PF

MUSIC FOR PLEASURE 8 Blyth Rd., Hayes, Middlesex Distributes:
  Classics for Pleasure, Sounds Superb

NEPENTHA see PHONOGRAM

OGUN 4 Chequers Parade, Eltham, London SE9

ONE-UP see EMI

OUTLET 63-67 Smithfield Square, Belfast BT1 1JD, Northern Ireland

PAMA see PYE

PAN see SAGA

PARLOPHONE see EMI

PEARL Pavillon Records, 48 High Street, Pembury, Tunbridge
  Wells, Kent

PENNY FARTHING see PYE

PHILIPS see PHONOGRAM

PHONOGRAM   Stanhope House, Stanhope Place, London W2 2HH
    Distributes: Checker, Chess, Fontana, Mercury, Nepentha,
    Philips, SSS International, Vertigo

PICKWICK INTERNATIONAL   The Hyde Ind. Estate, The Hyde,
    London NW9 6JU Distributes: Camden, Contour, Hallmark,
    Marble Arch, Sun

POLYDOR   17-19 Stratford Place, London W1N OB1 Distributes:
    BBC Records, Carnival, MGM, Metro, Select, Track, Verve

PRESIDENT RECORDS   Kassner House, 1 Westbourne Gardens,
    Porchester Rd., London W2 5NR Distributes: Joy, Rhapsody

PROBE   see EMI

PURPLE   see EMI

PYE   17 Great Cumberland Place, London W1H 8AA Distributes:
    A & M, Dawn, Golden Guinea, Golden Hour, Middle Earth,
    Pama, Penny Farthing, Sonet, Spark, Specialty, Spiral, Stax,
    Vanguard

QUALITON   c/o Selecta, 125/127 Lee High Rd., Lewisham, London
    SE13 5NX

R & O   48 Smithfield Square, Belfast BT1 1JO, Northern Ireland

RAK   see EMI

RCA   50-52 Curzon St., London W1Y 8EU Distributes: Barclay,
    Chelsea, RCA International

RCA INTERNATIONAL   see RCA

RAFT   see WEA

READERS' DIGEST   7-10 Old Bailey, London EC99 1AA

RED LIGHTNIN'   35 Cantley Gardens, Gants Hill, Ilford, Essex

REDIFFUSION   9 Dean St., London W1

REGAL STARLINE   see EMI

REGAL ZONOPHONE   see EMI

REPRISE   see WEA

RETRIEVAL RECORDINGS   48 Eversley Ave., Barnehurst, Kent
    DA7 6RB Distributes: Fountain

REVELATION   287 Camden High St., London NW1 7BX

REX   see   DECCA

RHAPSODY   see   PRESIDENT

RHINO   see   EMI

RISTIC   c/o John R. T. Davies, 53 Britwell Rd. , Burnham, Bucks

S. C. A. M.   P. O. Box 202, Leith D. O. , Edinburgh EH6 5RD

SRT   17 Royal Terrace, Glasgow

SSS INTERNATIONAL   see   PHONOGRAM

SAGA   326 Kensal Rd. , London W10   Distributes: Pan

SAYDISC MATCHBOX   Saydisc Specialized Recordings, The Barton,
   Inglestone Common, Badminton, Gloucestershire, GL9 1BX

SELECT   see   POLYDOR

77 RECORDS   Dobells Jazz Record Shop, 77 Charing Cross Rd. ,
   London WC2   Distributes: Swift

SONET   see   PYE

SOUNDS SUPERB   see   MUSIC FOR PLEASURE

SOUTHERN SOUND   Chris Wellard Records, 4 Chequers Parade,
   Off Passey Place, London SE9

SPARK   see   PYE

SPECIALTY   see   PYE

SPIRAL   see   PYE

SPOTLITE   Tony Williams, 300 Brocklesmead, Harlow, Essex

STAGFOLK   Shackleford Social Centre, Nr. Godalming, Surrey

STARLINE   see   EMI

STATESIDE   see   EMI

STAX   see   PYE

STEM   11 Mount Ephraim Rd. , London SW16 1NQ

STRING   33 Brunswick Gardens, London W8 4AW

SUN   see   PICKWICK INTERNATIONAL

SUNSET   see   UNITED ARTISTS

SWEET FOLK ALL   74 Shrewsbury Lane, Shooters Hill, London
    SE 18

SWIFT   see   77 RECORDS

TBB   3 The Quillett, Neston, Wirral, Cheshire

TALISMAN   see   EMI

TAMALA MOTOWN   6 Lygon Pl. , Belgravia, London 5W1

TANGENT   176a Holland Rd. , London W14

TANGERINE   570 Kingsland Rd. , London EC8

TELDEC   see   DECCA

TELEFUNKEN   see   DECCA

THERAPY   21 Pinewood Court, Broad St. , Sale

THRESHOLD   see   DECCA

TOPIC   27 Nassington Rd. , London NW3 2TX   Distributes: Impact

TRACK   see   POLYDOR

TRAILER   see   TRANSATLANTIC

TRANSATLANTIC   86 Marylebone High St. , London W1M 4AY   Dis-
    tributes: Big Bear, Black Lion, Leader, Trailer, Village Thing,
    Xtra

TROJAN   see   B & C TROJAN

TURTLE   33-37 Wardour St. , London W1

UNI   see   DECCA

UNITED ARTISTS   37-41 Mortimer St. , London W1   Distributes:
    Liberty, Sunset

VJM   see   VINTAGE JAZZ MUSIC SOCIETY

VANGUARD   see   PYE

VERTIGO   see   PHONOGRAM

VERVE   see   POLYDOR

VILLAGE THING   see   TRANSATLANTIC

VINE see EMI

VINTAGE JAZZ MUSIC SOCIETY 12 Slough Lane, Kingsbury, London NW 9 Distributes: Halcyon, VJM

VIRTUOSI RECORDINGS 18 Chancer Cres., Donnington, Newbury, Beaks, RG13

WEA 54 Greek St., London W1 Distributes: Atlantic, Dandelion, Elektra, Raft, Reprise, Warner Brothers

WARNER BROTHERS see WEA

WAVE see EMI

WAVERLEY see EMI

WESTWOOD Camp Farm, Montgomery, Mid-Wales SY15 6LU

WORLD RECORD CLUB Box 11, Parkbridge House, Richmond, Surrey

XTRA see TRANSATLANTIC

YORK see CBS

ZONOPHONE see EMI

Canada

A & M 939 Warden Ave., Scarborough, Ont. M1L 4CS Distributes: Casino, Haida, Penny Farthing, Mushroom

AQUARIUS see LONDON

ARPEGGIO see RCA

ATTIC see LONDON

AXE see GRT

BANFF see LONDON

BARN SWALLOW 120 Clare St., Winnipeg, Man.

BIG WHEEL 3933 30th Ave. S. E., Calgary, Alta. T2B 2C7

BIRCHMOUNT see QUALITY

BOOT see LONDON

BROADLAND see QUALITY

CBC   see   RADIO CANADA INTERNATIONAL TRANSCRIPTION

CBS   see   COLUMBIA

CANADIAN TALENT LIBRARY   2 St. Clair Ave., W., Toronto, Ont.

CAPITOL   3109 American Dr., Mississauga, Ont.   L4V 1B2

CAPRICE   see   LONDON

CASINO   see   A & M

CELEBRATION   see   QUALITY

CODA   Box 87, Sta. J, Toronto, Ont.   Distributes: Dogwood, Sackville

COLUMBIA   1121 Leslie St., Don Mills, Ont.   M3E 2J9   Distributes: CBS, Harmony, True North

CORNER STORE   see   QUALITY

CYNDA   see   LONDON

DAFFODIL   see   GRT

DISQUES ZODIAQUE   see   TRANS WORLD

DOGWOOD   see   CODA

DOMINION   Canadian Music Sales, 44 Advance Rd., Toronto, Ont.

FRANCO DISQUE   see   TRANS-CANADA

FUNKEBEC   see   LONDON

GRT   3816 Victoria Park Ave., Willowdale, Ont.   M2H 3H7   Distributes: Axe, Daffodil, Smile

GOLDFISH   see   LONDON

HAIDA   see   A & M

HARMONY   see   COLUMBIA

IXTLAN   271 Davisville Ave., Toronto M4S 1H1

JS   see   JAZZ STUDIES

JAZZ STUDIES   186 Old Orchard Rd., Burlington, Ont.   L7T 2G1

KANATA   see   QUALITY

LIKEABLE   Box 2123, Winnipeg, Man.

LONDON   1630 Midland Ave. , Scarborough, Ont. M1P 3C2   Distributes: Aquarius, Attic, Banff, Boot, Caprice, Cynda, Funkebec, Goldfish, Rodeo, Spark

MCA   2450 Victoria Park Ave. , Willowdale, Ont. M2J 4A2

MWC   see   QUALITY

MARCHE   see   TRANS WORLD

MUSHROOM   see   A & M

NIMBUS 9   see   RCA

OLD ROAD   5207 Cavendish Blvd. , Montreal

PENNY FARTHING   see   A & M

POLYDOR   6000 Cote de Liesse, Montreal, Que. H4T 1E3

QUALITY   380 Birchmount Rd. , Scarborough, Ont. M1K 1M7   Distributes: Birchmount, Broadland, Celebration, Corner Store, Kanata, MWC

RCA   101 Duncan Mills Rd. , Suite 300, Don Mills, Ont. M3B 1Z3   Distributes: Arpeggio, Nimbus 9

RADIO CANADA INTERNATIONAL TRANSCRIPTION C. B. C.   International Service, Box 6000, Montreal, Quebec   Distributes: CBC

RODEO   see   LONDON

RUMOUR   Box 173, Stratford, Ont.

SPPS   see   TRANS-CANADA

SACKVILLE   see   CODA

SMILE   see   GRT

SPARK   see   LONDON

SPRINGWATER   56 Clinton St. , Guelph, Ont. N1H 5G5

TRANS-CANADA   300 Baig Blvd. , Moncton, N. B.   Distributes: Franco Disque, SPPS

TRANS WORLD   1230 Monte de Liesse Rd. , Montreal, Que.   Distributes: Marche, Disques Zodiaque

TRUE NORTH   see   COLUMBIA

UNITED ARTISTS   6 Lansing Sq., Suite 208, Willowdale, Ont. M2J
    1T5

WEA   1810 Birchmount Rd., Scarborough, Ont. M1P 2S1

WOODSHED   R.R. 1, Emsdale, Ont. P0A 1J0

SPECIALTY RECORD STORES

The following record stores handle specialized orders for rare or difficult to acquire material (mainly in the fields of jazz, blues, folk, country, and ethnic). With many labels, record stores are the only source of distribution. Superior service for the smaller, independent labels makes the following stores highly recommended. Write for catalogues. While these stores are not mainly library suppliers, they may offer discounts.

UNITED STATES

County Sales
Box 191
Floyd, Va.   24091

Rare Record Distributing Co.
417 East Broadway
P. O. Box 10518
Glendale, Cal.   91205

Roundup Record Sales
P. O. Box 474
Somerville, Mass.   02144

Down Home Music
10341 San Pablo Ave.
El Cerrito, Cal.   94530

CANADA

Coda Jazz and Blues Record
   Centre
P. O. Box 87
Toronto, Ontario
M4J 4X8

ENGLAND (handles Europe as well)

Dave Carey--The Swing Shop
18 Mitcham Lane
Streatham, London SW16

Collet's Record Centre
180 Shaftesbury Ave.
London WC2H 8JS

Dobell's Record Shop
75 Charing Cross Road
London WC 2

Flyright Records
18 Endwell Rd.
Bexhill-on-Sea
East Sussex

Peter Russell Record Store
24 Market Avenue
Plymouth PL1 1PJ

ARTIST INDEX

An alphabetical index of artists and groups with variant names. Records with several artists are not analyzed (unless displayed prominently on the album titles), nor are individuals' names indexed from the groups they comprise.

Abadi, Marden 2876
Abba 1001
Abercrombie, John 2877, 4249
Abiodun, Admiral Dele 4580
Abrahamson, Ronney 1002
Abrams, Bob 2050
Abrams, Richard 3059
AC/DC 1, 2
Ace 3
Aces 4391
Ackerman, Will 2443
Acme Bluegrass Co. 2051
Acme Country Band 2052
Acuff, Roy 1621
Adam, Clift 1003
Adam, Margie 2444
Adams, Arthur 2878
Adams, Derroll 2445, 2446
Adams, George 2879, 2880
Adams, Linda 2447
Adams, Paul 2447
Adams, Pepper 2881
Adams, Trevor 1622
Adderley, Cannonball 2882-4
Adderley, Nat 2885
Ade, Sunny 4581
African Brothers Band 4582
Agrovators and Revolutionaires 4583
Agudo, Luis 2886
Airborne 4
Akendengue, Pierre 2887
Aketagawa, Shoji 2888
Akiyoshi, Toshiko 2889
Akiyoshi-Tabackin Big Band 2890, 2891

Akkerman, Jan 5
Alamo, Tony 5095
Alba 2448
Albany, Joe 2891, 2892
Alberto y Lost Trios Paranoias 6
Albion Country Band 2449
Albion Dance Band 2450, 2451
Albright, William 3030
Alcapone, Dennis 4584
Alcorn, Alvin 2893
Aldrich, Ronnie 1004-6
Alessi, Billy 1007, 1008
Alexander, Monty 2894, 2895
Alexander Brothers 2053
Ali, Rashied 2896
Alice Cooper 7-8
Alkatraz 9
Alke, Bjorn 2897
All-Star Brass 5096
Allard, Louis-Paul 5186
Allard, Michel 1009
Allen, Henry 2898-9
Allen, Rex, Jr. 1623-5
Allison, Mose 2900
Allman, Gregg 10
Allman Brothers Band 11
Allred, Bill 2901-2
Allspice 4585
Allmeida, Laurindo 1010-11
Alpha Band 12-13
Alsop, Peter 2452
Alton, Roy 4586
Altschul, Barry 2903-4, 3024, 3182
Amalgam 2905

Mouzon, Alphonse 3185, 3880
Moxy 592
Moyes, Fred 5250
Mtume 3881
Muckram Wakes 2729
Mud 593-5
Muddy Bottom Boys 2305
Muddy Waters 4513-4
Muhammad, Idris 4910
Mulcahy, Mick 2730
Muldaur, Geoff 596
Muldaur, Maria 597
Mull, Martin 5251
Müller, Werner 1424-5
Mulligan, Gerry 3247, 3882
Mumps 1426
Munde, Alan 2112
Munich Machine 1427
Muribus, George 3883-4
Muro, Don 3885
Murphy, Dudley 2306
Murphy, Elliott 598
Murphy, Michael 1873
Murphy, Noel 2731
Murphy, Rose 2732
Murphy, Turk 3886-7
Murphy, Walter 4911
Murray, Anne 1428
Murray, Bruce 1429
Murray, David 3888-9
Murvin, Junior 4912
Muscle Shoals Horns 1430
Muscles 4515
Muse, Lewis "Rabbit" Anderson
  4516
Musgrave, David 2307
Music Improvisation Co. 3890

Nakamura, Terou 3891
Namyslowski, Zbigniew 3892
Nana 3893-4
Napoleon, Phil 3875
Nascimento, Milton 4913
Nash, Graham 211-2
Nash, Johnny 4914
Nashville Bar Association 1874
Nasty Pop 599
National Jazz Ensemble 3896
Natural Life 3897
Naughton, Bobby 3898
Navarro, Fats 3899-3902
Nazareth, 600-1

Near, Holly 1431
Necessary, Frank 2247, 2308
Neil, Al 3903
Nektar 602
Nelson, Jim 1875
Nelson, Louis 3904
Nelson, Rick 603-4
Nelson, Willie 1876-80
Nesmith, Michael 1881-2
New Black Eagle Jazz Band
  3905-7
New Central Connection Un-
  limited 605
New City Grass 2309
New Commander Cody Band 606
New Dalta Ahkri 3908
New England Conservatory Coun-
  try 1883
New Excelsior Talking Machine
  1432
New Grass Revival 2310-1
New Legion Rock Spectacular
  607
New Leviathan Oriental Foxtrot
  Orchestra 3909
New Mississippi Sheiks 4517
New Orleans Rascals 3910
New Riders of the Purple Sage
  608-9
New South 2312
New York Mary 3911
Newbeats 4915
Newborn, Phineas Jr. 3912
Newbury, Mickey 1884
Newman, David 3913
Newman, Jimmy C. 1885
Newman, Randy 610
Newton, James 3914
Newton-John, Olivia 1433-4
Nichols, Herbie 3916-7
Nichols, Red 3918-9
Nicks, Stevie 120
Nicra 3920
NiDhomnail, Triona 2733
Nielsen, Chris 1886
Niemen 3921
Niewood, Gerry 3922
Nighthawks 3923-4
Nightingale, Maxine 4916
Nigrini, Ron 1435
Nilsson, Harry 611-2
90 Degrees Inclusive 4917
Nistico, Sal 3925-6